P9-EFJ-362

Infancy

Infancy

Its Place in Human Development

Jerome Kagan
Richard B. Kearsley
Philip R. Zelazo

With the assistance of
Cheryl Minton

Harvard University Press
Cambridge, Massachusetts, and London, England

Printed in the United States of America
Second printing 1979

Library of Congress Cataloging in Publication Data

Kagan, Jerome.
Infancy.

Bibliography: p.
Includes index.
1. Day care centers—United States. 2. Infant psychology. I. Kearsley, Richard B., joint author. II. Zelazo, Philip R., joint author. III. Title.
HV854.K3 362.7'1 77-26970
ISBN 0-674-45260-7

Preface

The idea for the research summarized in this book began in late 1968 when popular and scientific debate was coalescing around the twin issues of the importance of early experience and the wisdom of expanding day care facilities for infants and young children. Many child psychologists and pediatricians were apprehensive about the possibility of large numbers of young children enrolled in day care centers because they feared that group care experience for infants would dilute the intensity of the child's attachment to the mother and perhaps retard cognitive development. These worries stemmed from historical presuppositions, extant theory, and preliminary empirical data on the effects of institutionalization on early development. Since it seemed likely then that Congress might appropriate and the president might approve the release of funds for the establishment of day care centers—possibilities that were, of course, not realized—it seemed useful to initiate a study that would provide some initial information on this issue.

Because a field experiment of this magnitude is much too large for any single investigator, it was fortunate that chance had placed the authors in the same community, with similar motivation, and that public and private funding sources were willing to support the work so generously. Our initial plan to work exclusively with black children in the Roxbury area of Boston had to be abandoned when political pressures forced us to shift location to the South End of Boston. Thanks to the friendship of the Chinese-American community in Boston we were able to complete the study in close accord with our original plans. The officials of the Chinese Christian Church were helpful in persuading local community leaders of the value of the research and of the potential benefit to the community of a day care center that would remain as a neighborhood day care center after the investigation was completed. Since the neighborhood in which the day care center was located had a significant proportion of Chinese families, we felt it appropriate to enroll about one-half Chinese and one-half Caucasian infants in the research program. Although this decision was essentially politically motivated, the opportunity to compare the growth of Chinese and Caucasian children provided theoretically provocative information.

The question we probed cannot be answered by any one investigation. Fortunately, several other studies of day care were being implemented at the same time and, as we shall see in chapter 3, the results of most of these studies are consonant with our conclusions. The questions that surround the many influences on early development are complex, and this book makes only a small contribution to the generalizations that the future owes us.

We faced a major problem in deciding how to present the results of our investigation. In order to arrive at some tentative conclusions about the influences of group care outside the home, we gathered a large corpus of data on matched groups of infants, one group attending a day care center and the other cared for at home. The empirical information is also relevant to some very specific concerns of developmental psychologists, especially the growth functions for the response dispositions of infants and the intraindividual stability of those dispositions. Because the day care issue has a wider audience than the other two themes, we have prepared a major text and an appendix. The text presents the theoretical foundations of the work and a concise summary of the effects of group care on development. The extended appendix, which is more technical and intended for a professional audience, has the empirical detail that the interested scientist demands. The reader who wishes to consult the evidence for the summary statements made in chapter 5 can find it in the companion appendix.

We had slightly different responsibilities during this long project. Although Kagan, Kearsley, and Zelazo jointly designed and monitored the work, Kearsley was responsible for the daily supervision of the day care center and Zelazo and Kagan for supervising the evaluation of the infants. Minton and Kagan were responsible for the analysis of the data. Because heavy responsibilities fell upon Kearsley and Zelazo at the completion of the data-gathering phase of the project, Kagan volunteered to prepare the first complete draft of the book, and he assumes responsibility for this particular organization of ideas. However, all the authors are in essential agreement with the major conclusions that are summarized in chapter 6. Whenever the sex of an individual is not specified, we have followed the convention of using masculine pronouns; we apologize to those who dislike this practice.

There are many individuals we wish to thank for their intelligence, loyalty, and plain hard work during the course of the project. This book could not have been completed without them. The caretaking staff at the day care center included Jean Soo Hoo, Alma McKinnon, Marion Moccia, Connie Arce, Louisa Lok, Dorothy Hahn, Ada Molina, Ada Jimenez, Kim Wong, Ida

Gee, Adrienne Gurevitz, Hanna Chu, Nun Chang, Judy Gillespie, James Kelly, and Marie Noons. In addition, Dorothy Wong, Sandra Lin, and Esther Tan helped us in community coordination.

The staff responsible for the research evaluations included Sheila Brachfeld, William Browne, Teresa Chu, Marcie Crary, Jean Erdman, Rebecca Hartman, Katherine Haspel, Mary Hueners, Carol Newman, and Thomas Witt.

Doris Simpson and Carole Lawton deserve a special measure of thanks for typing the numerous drafts and redrafts of the text.

We are grateful to many who helped with data analysis, initial pretesting, and the necessary activities associated with an extensive research project. This group includes Lisa Braverman, Peter Brinkley, Leslie Brody, Alex Dill, Fred Dodd, Henriette Kates, Howard Levin, Michael Massing, Michael Moore, Daniel Naiman, Barbara Nash, Michael Novey, James Poppell, Hope Reisman, Judy Rosencrantz, Lauren Schaefer, Charles M. Super, Mark Szpak, and Pamela Zeller.

We are especially grateful to Dr. Dorothy Worth and Dr. Alfred Frechette, former director of the Division of Family Health Services and Commissioner of the Massachusetts Department of Public Health; their support was of inestimable value during the early phases of the work. In addition, the Reverend Peter Shih and the board of directors of the Chinese Christian Church were helpful throughout the investigation.

Finally, we thank Michael Cole, Frances D. Horowitz, Charles Richman, and Robert B. McCall for extensive comments on the manuscript. We have gained much from their critical reviews.

This research was made possible by grants from the National Institute of Child Health and Human Development, Office of Child Development, the Spencer Foundation, and the Carnegie Corporation of New York. Jerome Kagan was a Belding Scholar of the Foundation for Child Development during the period when the first full draft was prepared.

Contents

Tables

Figures

Infancy

1 The Enigma of Development

> In history there are no inner laws, nothing which even remotely resembles automatism, nothing which gives us the right to predict. The record of the past is a cultural becoming which shall not lend itself to easy reductions . . . We make judgment on no part of the past unless we have in mind the picture of the perfect state, the divine city where man was as he ought to have been.
>
> B. C. Brundage, *Two Earths, Two Heavens*

The eras of an intellectual discipline are delineated by sets of central questions, each of which is yoked to a preferred method of inquiry. Some questions are answered, if only temporarily; many are discarded because they were improperly framed; most are reworded to accommodate new information. Physicists have explained, at least for now, why eclipses occur, do not worry about the "aether" and attempt to determine the number of basic particles rather than define an atom.

Psychology, too, has answered, discarded, and rephrased questions during its short history. We now have some insight into the nature of color vision, do not ask about the essence of will, and probe the conditions that monitor the performance of a coherent set of actions rather than seek the intrinsic meaning of reinforcement. Developmental psychology, with a much shorter history, has clarified some puzzles that provoked quiet brooding among sixteenth-century scholars. Infants apparently perceive the primary hues and are afraid of events they do not understand. We have stopped looking for the bewitching spirits that make infants ill or cranky and have begun to substitute statements about the enhancement of competences across problem domains for principles of intelligence.

The incentive for writing this book was to communicate the results of a recent experiment on the effects of group care outside the home on the young child's psychological development. A proper appreciation of our findings requires prior discussion of why that question was posed and presentation of a rationale for the strategies selected to answer it. When scientists invest an unusual amount of effort in an attempt to bribe nature to yield one of her secrets, they must persuade themselves that the question is worth asking. Public and private institutions are willing to support research on the relation of food additives to cancer, smoking to health, industrial pollutants to atmospheric ozone, or maternal drug abuse to the newborn's integrity because a sufficient number of informed citizens suspect that these theoretically possible relations might be probable. A century from now some or all of these questions will appear silly to historians of science who will wonder, as we do now about Franz Gall's suggestion that character can be diagnosed from bumps on the head, why we bothered with the issue at all. Thus this book tries to be more than a research report. In an attempt to provide a rationale for the investigation, it confronts the ideological foundations of modern developmental psychology.

The impetus for our research came from three related presuppositions that are part of modern psychological theory. The first is that the experiences of the infant exert a profound influence on its contemporaneous development. Since a day care center seems, on the surface, to be different from the typical home setting with respect to the quality and duration of the children's interactions with surrogate caretakers and with other children, it had been assumed that infants would develop differently in the two environments.

The second, more serious, assumption is that experiences during the first year extend far into the future and alter, in some mysterious way, the structures and processes that will emerge in the 3-, 4-, and 5-year-old. Such a view assumes considerable continuity in development. There are, of course, many examples of continuity in biological growth. Imperfect division of the first few cells of the fertilized ovum can produce cells with forty-seven chromosomes, a condition that will lead to anomalous morphological and functional attributes much later in embryogenesis. Administration of male sex hormones to a female hamster during the first five postnatal days alters behavior with a male when adult status is reached. Despite many hidden connections in growth, however, we cannot assume that every quality in the present has a link to the remote past. It is possible that only a small and very select set of psychological events contributes to the child's future profile.

The mother-infant relation is at the center of the third presupposition. For the last three centuries most commentators on development have been certain that nature intended each infant to be close to its biological mother. Very few animal species violate that maxim, a fact implying that nonadherence to that norm is potentially perilous. Roussseau's rhetoric has a modern ring: "When mothers deign to nurse their own children, then will be a reform in morals; natural feeling will revive in every heart; there will be no lack of citizens for the state; this first step by itself will restore mutual affection . . . when women become good mothers, men will be good husbands and fathers" (Rousseau 1911, pp. 13-14). Because infants in full-time day care centers are separated from their mothers for so many days during the year, it was reasonable to expect that a day care experience outside the home would not be conducive to future psychological health.

These three presuppositions—the influence of early experience, continuity in development, and the centrality of the mother-infant relation—were combined into one of the major contemporary propositions about human development. In its most general and optimistic form it stated that an infant required an emotionally close, nurturant relation with a single caretaker, preferably the biological mother, in order to become a secure, motivated, and competent adolescent and adult. John Bowlby, who used the word *attachment* to name this emotional bond between infant and mother, had François Mauriac introduce the central chapter in his influential book; Mauriac stated, "We are moulded and remoulded by those who have loved us; and though the love may pass, we are nevertheless their work, for good or ill" (Bowlby 1969).

In a companion volume on separation Bowlby wrote, "as we found that there is a strong case for believing that gnawing uncertainty about the accessibility and responsiveness of attachment figures is a principal condition for the development of an unstable and anxious personality so is there a strong case for believing that an unthinking confidence in the unfailing accessibility and support of attachment figures is the bedrock on which stable and self-reliant personality is built" (Bowlby 1973, p. 322).

With the prospect of group day care for young children increasing as the number of married women in the labor force increases, it seemed proper to test the validity of this popular hypothesis. To determine if that popular belief has some measure of correctness, we compared the development of a group of children who attended a specially run day care center over the first two and one-half years of their lives with a similar group who remained at home. But in reflecting on the scientific work during and after its completion we have been forced to consider issues of broad theoretical concern. Hence before presenting the results of our research, we feel it useful to provide some historical and theoretical perspective. We are convinced that the scientific data will be better appreciated if they are reflected in a larger mural, not unlike the wisdom of devoting a few months to reading about the history of Greece before visiting the Acropolis.

There are several themes to consider. What exactly is the nature of early psychological development? Is it likely that experiences before the first birthday could alter the psychological profile of a 3-year-old or a 13-year-old? Clarification of these and other issues requires an analysis of the meaning of development, continuity, and the concept of stage, for both Sigmund Freud and Jean Piaget parse the stream of development into qualitatively different phases. Since theorists wear different lenses as they look at the growing child, it is necessary to attend to cultural differences in the conceptualization of the aims of development. If Americans see independence and commitment as representative of maturity, and Buddhists see interdependence and detachment from desire as *telos,* then either one or both are wrong, or we must conclude that it is not possible to discover the psychological goals of growth independent of a social setting. Finally, the idea that variation in the intensity of love mothers feel for their infants can affect the future well-being of the children invites a critique. It is possible that this notion became a central element in the consciousness of parents only during the last few hundred years.

The meaning of development

The concept of development is cast in sharper relief if it is compared with other forms of change. Change, which entails alteration in structure or process, comes in three varieties, depending on the permanence of the alteration and whether or not an ultimate purpose is imposed. One class of change, perhaps the most common, is a temporary fluctuation in state. A half-dozen times a day a hungry 3-month-old's heart rate rises as he kicks and cries. We ordinarily do not assume that the twenty minutes of increased physiological and motor reactivity over the course of a day produce any permanent alteration in the child's psychological structures.

In a second class of change, a structure is destroyed or a normal process moved to permanent deviance. The loss of the ability to retrieve recent memories, common in senility, is due, we suppose, to structural changes in the central nervous system.

The third meaning of change is the one reserved for development. The alteration appears to be orderly; the emergent form or process lasts for a reasonable time; usually the new state is judged to be more desirable than the one that is vanishing. It is healthier, better organized, more complex, competent, efficient—or any other evaluative term one chooses to apply. The chemist says that crystals of salt develop from ions in solution, but notes that the solid salt dissolves when placed in solution, because decomposition is not a primary characteristic of development. Development does not always have a positive connotation. On occasion we say that a tumor or psychosis *develops,* because we presume structures change from simple to complex. Evaluating a change as an instance of development is, therefore, a value judgment that is not inherent in the observation. There is an awesome change between the cooing, creeping 6-month-old and the 3-year-old who talks and walks. We say the child has developed, not only because profound changes in the central nervous system permitted the new behavior to appear, but also because we are sure that walking and speaking are better than creeping and babbling. The loss of memory in old age is less likely to be called development, even though it, too, may be the result of structural changes in the central nervous system. Recent interest in the study of aging has led a few to view the entire life span as a developmental sequence.

What we choose to label development, then, often reflects our judgment of the complexity, utility, and efficiency of an emerging phenomenon. That judgment is never free from our values. The recognition that one's behavior has violated a standard, which typically appears between two and five years of age, is characterized by unhappiness and occasionally by nightmares and inhibitions that do not facilitate adjustment. But since the capacity for that recognition accelerates the adoption and practice of the community's values, there is no quarrel over treating it as a developmental advance.

During the first two months of life the powerful role of movement and contour on infant attentiveness is gradually subdued by the child's attraction to discrepant events. By seven weeks of age a major change occurs in the child's pattern of attentiveness to visual events (Ruff and Turkewitz 1975). The child now scans the internal elements of a bounded figure rather than tracking the outer contour, and his distribution of attention is less influenced by the purely physical variables of size, number of discrete elements, and amount of contour. Pattern and the discrepancy between past and present become more critical. We treat this change as development because we assume the 2-month-old more actively relates what he knows to his current experience. In order for him to be attentive to events different from his past experience, we must attribute acquired cognitive structures to him, for recognition of a discrepancy could not occur without some knowledge, and knowledge is desirable. The change, however, has a negative implication, for the child becomes increasingly vulnerable to distress if he cannot assimilate the unusual. Although the changes of the first two months have both positive and negative implications, because acquisition of cognitive structures increases adaptation, it is given priority over the accompanying distress and the change is classified as developmental. Improved cognitive functioning and better adaptation to social demands are the criteria used to decide that certain categories of change are also instances of psychological development.

Development connotes orderly, organized change toward a hypothetical ideal. The assumption that each child is growing toward a better, happier, more efficient form is a friendly idea to most of us, even though it is neither empirically nor philosophically obvious. It is not clear that the 20-year-old's capacity for depression is a welcome competence that the 4-year-old lacks, or that the 15-year-old's capacity for homicide is to be preferred to the innocuous play of the 5-year-old.

Considering development as orderly change that moves toward a valued end state, theorists differ in the goals they regard as desirable, just as philosophers vary in the goals they assume man should seek, be they purity, merit, competence, detachment, serenity, or sensual pleasure. Theories of development contain profound presuppositions about a *telos* and the hypothetical mechanisms that make change orderly and coherent.

Flexibility, control, self-consciousness, strength, coordination, task competence, freedom of choice, and speed of cognitive processing all appear to increase with age. But depression, chronic anxiety, guilt, ambivalence, insomnia, vacillation, and hatred also become more common. Although the

West has awarded development a positive connotation, that decision is not universal. Eastern philosophers view the newborn as an infinitely pure and wise entity whose perceptions become fogged through early experience. As a result the adult years should be devoted to regaining the original clarity of understanding lost during the intervening period.

Even though physical scientists have warned us that a rational analysis of nature does not permit strong inferences about purpose, the possibility of a labyrinth without a center, a speeding car without a destination, or a life of action without a special goal is so disheartening that we try to detect purpose in the occasions of experience. Darwin guessed that the primary purpose was survival of the individual to reproductive maturity. Some modern biologists have sharpened the emphasis on reproduction and assumed that nature's secret intention for each of us was to project the maximum number of gametes into the next generation. Fecundity is the invitation behind nature's winking eye. But if fecundity were the central goal, why not, as C. H. Waddington suggests, create organisms that consist only of large bags full of gametes and be done with it (Waddington 1975)? Adaptation of a species to an ecological niche is one reasonable purpose, for the production of many offspring means risking that food supplies may be outrun or members of the group forced to leave safe regions and wander off to places where predators are waiting to strike.

It is likely that contemporary Western scientists, living in a human society that is intensely competitive, individualistic, and friendly to the view that maximal accumulation of status, power, and wealth defines adaptation, have projected that mental attitude onto nature. Fitness in animals—which is analogous to adaptation in human beings—is defined as the reproductive success of the individual relative to others. This assumption was not a commanding induction from data, but a presupposition that found some affirming evidence, and it is difficult to disprove. In the case of both human beings and animals, the organism is supposed to maximize an intensively narcissistic mission and accumulate either goods or offspring, both of which can be counted so that the scientist can quantify degree of fitness and separate the more from the less well adapted.

But François Jacob has implied that there is not one purpose that guides human psychological functioning, but many: "Since Darwin, biologists have progressively elaborated a reasonable, although still incomplete, picture of the mechanism that operates in the evolution of the living world; namely, natural selection. For many it has been tempting to invoke a similar mechanism of selection to describe any possible evolution, whether cosmological, chemical, cultural, ideological, or social. But this seems condemned to fail from the outset. The rules of the game differ at each level. New principles have, therefore, to be worked out at each level" (Jacob 1977, p. 1163).

Our intention is not to quarrel with the modern biological assumptions, but to ask about possible criteria for evaluating psychological development. We suggest that understanding is one of the distant lights toward which the child moves. The parade of milestones of the opening years can be understood as originating in attempts to predict or understand the world. A blind 8-month-old explores her father's face as if she were trying to create a representation of that unusual topography. The 12-month-old looks around with puzzled expression if she can't find a toy she saw her mother hide in a basket. A 3-year-old cautiously offers a toy to an unfamiliar peer in the hope that the peer's reaction to the overture will identify him as friend or foe. The victory that Jean Piaget has called formal operational thought is characterized by profound intellectual advances that permit the adolescent to detect cacophony in beliefs so he can tune them into a more harmonious pattern. Cognitive structures, like germ cells, are sent forward to assimilate, master, and comprehend new situations. The psychological structure, which might be regarded as the unit of selection, is monitored, altered, or eliminated depending on whether it accomplishes its primary mission of understanding the unexpected and maintaining uncertainty within reasonable bounds.

What we want to know

What do we want to know about human development? It is a question we rarely raise because we tacitly assume, without much reflection, that we know. It is like asking a man who is running for a bus on a lovely spring day, "Wait, why are you going downtown?" Each scientific discipline has a special set of puzzles it would like to solve; developmental psychologists generally wish to understand four classes of phenomena.

First, we want to explain normative, ontogenetic changes in behavior and competence that appear to be universal. There is consensus that a theory that acknowledges the interaction of maturation and environment is necessary to account for these phenomena of growth. We want to understand why separation anxiety does not occur until the last third of the first year, just prior to language, why the ability to project a psychological state onto another person occurs during the third year of life, just prior to guilt.

Since we shall be using the term *maturation* frequently, it is useful to define it. *Psychological maturation* refers to those competences and associated performances that emerge as a result of normal growth of the central nervous system in any reasonably natural environment. We acknowledge that one can arrange conditions to retard, alter, or even destroy normal maturational sequences. It is more difficult, if not impossible, to create a maturational competence through environmental intervention if the organism is not prepared. Maturational competences require certain environmental conditions if they are to be actualized, and differences in experience are often associated with the time of emergence of the competence. Gilbert Gottlieb notes, "the time or age of appearance (or some other quantitative feature) of neuroanatomy, neurophysiology, or behavior such as size, threshold, amount, latency is regulated by function. In the absence of experience, the behavior (or neural feature) in question might ultimately develop, but it will appear later than it would in the presence of appropriate experience'' (Gottlieb 1976, p. 225.)

Second, we wish to explain variations in behavior among individuals in a specific context during any developmental stage. Some infants will not reach for a toy they watched being covered by a cloth until twelve months (reaching for the object is called the object concept or object permanence response); others display this response at seven months. Some cry intensely when their mother leaves them; others do not even fret. Some 8-year-olds can recall the order of twelve pictures; others cannot perform that feat until they are adolescents.

Next, we want to explain intraindividual variations in behavior and competence in different contexts during the same developmental era. A child is likely to smile at a mask of a human face at five months of age, but not at a car rolling down a ramp. At thirty months the probability of smiling in response to these two events is completely reversed. A 1-year-old is likely to cry if his mother leaves him with a stranger at a laboratory, but less likely to cry if that event occurs at home. Explaining variation in behavior across situations requires a theory of contexts. We are far from this goal.

Finally, we wish to explain extreme deviance, phenomena like schizophrenia, autism, and suicide, which, like freak waves on the ocean's surface, are difficult to predict because they may not be on a continuum with normative processes.

The first class of events, the universal changes, is the focus of interest for stage theories. The other three belong to the domain normally called *personality,* a term that has lost much of its original meaning and now floats relatively free of its source. Study of personality, which burgeoned with the introduction and growth of psychoanalytic theory, was originally intended to refer to a small set of dimensions of difference in affect, motivation, and behavior that were influenced by experiences during the psychosexual stages, as well as by anxiety, defense mechanisms, and Oedipal conflict. Personality was not supposed to refer to any individual variation like tempo of walking, spatial ability, or a preference for permissive sexual norms. Although psychoanalytic theory has lost a great deal of its original power, the interest in human variability has not. The word *personality* has remained popular but, severed from its origins, has wandered aimlessly, picking up strange friends until it has become synonymous with the study of almost any variation. That is a problem, for reliable variation among children and adults has many causes. We must distinguish among variation within one person in different times and places, variation among persons in the same time and place, and variation among persons from different societies.

These three classes of variation have different origins. We often confuse the first two because we measure variation among individuals but want to make predictions about a single person. A husband's yelling at his spouse is best predicted by the behavior of the wife and by the husband's mood. Variation in frequency and intensity of anger outbursts over a year among all New Yorkers is best predicted by temperature, time of day, and social class membership—a totally different set of variables. If we wish to understand variation in one person's behavior we should first examine the contexts he enters. But variation in the behavior of a group of children or adults in the same situation must result, in part, from past experience. Variation between individuals living in different cultures will be due, in part, to belief systems and social and economic structures. These sources of variation are, of course, complementary. The Whitings, for example, have found that variation in nurturant, dominant, or dependent behavior among children from six quite different cultures was due partly to contextual constraints and partly to the psychological consequences of modernization (Whiting and Whiting 1975). One observes many more instances of nurturant behavior among children in societies where 9-year-olds are regularly assigned the task of caring for infants than in societies, like our own, where children are not typically in the presence of many younger children nor assigned responsibilities for child care. That fact does not mean that American 9-year-olds are fundamentally less nurturant than rural Mexican or Philippine youngsters, but rather that they have less opportunity to express such behavior.

The goals of development in Western society

Each society holds deep, unquestioned assumptions about the nature of man and the goals of development. These presuppositions have the same epistemological status as Euclid's axiomatic definitions of points and straight lines or Newton's postulation of an aether. The axioms that announce man's essential qualities and the future states toward which he is growing have changed over the fifty centuries of essays on his nature, as have the axioms of the physical world. Let us see if we can discern the assumptions that are so central in contemporary Western society they never seem to require a defense.

Autonomy versus sociability Growth is believed to be characterized by an increasing desire and ability to pursue personal goals with minimal restriction from the actions or the expectations of others and by the capacity to cope alone with the problems of reality. Caricatures of this ideal are everywhere. The solitary problem-solving adult—scientist, inventor, athlete, or cowboy—represents its distillations. The ideal adult is presumably free of restriction, instrumentally competent, and respected by peers whose help he does not need. The developmental history of these qualities assumes a progression from the undifferentiated, dependent state of infancy to the differentiated independence and instrumental capability of the adult. There is, however, a complementary assumption to provide some balance: human beings are presumed to be social animals who naturally prefer to be with people rather than alone, to walk with a companion in the forest, to talk rather than keep silent. The sociability axiom is not viewed as inconsistent with the assumption of autonomy, even though every social interaction contains an implicit set of rules and therefore entails a slight loss of freedom. But its constraint is gentle and so vulnerable to rupture that the inconsistency is rarely noted. The individual moves easily in and out of psychological contact with others and is always prepared to sever the relation if the social contract bites too deep into his freedom of choice and action. The presumed need for social interdependence places a brake on autonomy, preventing members of society from flying off into private spaces where they are unrestrained by the obligations inherent in a social contract.

Sensual excitement versus serenity Whereas the first pair of complementary axioms is concerned primarily with each actor's relations to others, the second pair of complementary axioms has to do with private experience and pits affective sensuality against placid serenity. Man is supposed to be motivated to maximize sensory pleasure and to minimize pain. It is obvious that this directive is not always followed—adults voluntarily go to work rather than sleep late, care for crying children rather than abandon them, and sit by sick relatives rather than ignore them. Therefore, the original eighteenth-century axiom has been transformed from sensory pleasure to psychological benefit. Man's first preoccupation is to act in ways that bring psychological pleasure, with sex, food, and warmth at the core, and money, power, status, and fame at the periphery. The rush toward private sensual delight must be restrained, or man will either burn himself out or be in continual rage at frustration of his desires. Hence, it is assumed that man also needs the ability to endure distress, to accept, with placidity and serenity, the vicissitudes of everyday life.

Potent action versus passive contemplation A third pair of axioms places action and contemplation in opposition. The Western moral imperative is to be materially constructive, to make a noticeable effect on the world. The work axiom prevents the self from investing all affect in its own autonomy and sensuality. The balance is achieved by the assumption that man must invest emotion in something outside the self—be it job, children, or a hobby. But action without planning is dangerous and each individual must pause occasionally for thoughtful reflection.

Erik Erikson captured the essence of the Western ideal of autonomy and potency in an essay in which he listed the premises that were more disguised in his earlier writings. He wrote, "To be grown up, in any language and vision, has a particular quality of standing tall, so proudly and yet so precariously that there is a universal need to attest to and to protest that one knows where one stands and that one has some status in the center of a vision of a new, or, at any rate, forever, renewed, human type'' (Erikson 1976, p. 18)—a modern statement of Rousseau's warning, ''All wickedness comes from weakness.''

Although most cultures recognize both poles of these three dimensions, they differ on which side of the center they prefer. The West chooses autonomy, sensuality, and action; the East interdependence, serenity, and contemplation. The ideal in classic Japan was to become part of another group, to be receptive to the ideas of others, to attain an inner calm, and, especially, to attain the state of *amaeru* in which one depends on and presumes another's benevolence (Caudill 1973).

In Islam, the ideal (*halim*) is self-restraint, endurance of distress, faith, and the surrender of autonomy to God; assertiveness and power (*jahil*) are negatively valued. In Islam, the tension is not between autonomy and social interdependence but between confidence and humility. Since fate has predestined each life, no person has a true capacity for autonomous choice. Autonomy cannot be a basic developmental goal because it is not sufficiently uncertain.

The West's preference for distinctive individual accomplishments that separate each agent from the group is yoked to a concern with early experience. In the West the central developmental assumption is that social experiences during the opening years of life determine the degree to which the adult will be able to balance the three pairs of vectors. This view has been held by most commentators on development during the last 200 years. The implicit premise is that parental reactions to the child's distress and burgeoning abilities determine his final position on the basic dimensions. Parental indifference will move him away from people; too much protection will make him too dependent. Excessive restriction will retard autonomy; too little restriction will be inimical to the development of work habits.

THE DESCRIPTION OF INFANTS

A conception of what we want children to become inevitably influences the categories we use to describe them, and the evaluative attributes we assign to infants are occasionally the opposite of the valued traits we wish the adult to attain. The infant and young child are used as a projective screen, not unlike the way middle-class observers use the lower class to define what is undesirable. The West values autonomy; the self is supposed to resist becoming completely dependent upon another and to grow toward individuation. Erik Erikson writes of the gradual attainment of an ego identity, Margaret Mahler of a firm body boundary, Roy Schafer of a sense of separation of self from others. This preoccupation with separateness belies some uncertainty over reaching adulthood with the secure confidence that one can be both alone and yet productive and happy. In the middle of the nineteenth century, Ralph Waldo Emerson called this quality self-reliance: "Trust thyself, every heart vibrates to that iron string . . . Whoso would be a man must be a nonconformist . . . Nothing is at last sacred but the integrity of our mind" (Emerson 1891, pp. 36-37).

Because they see development as progression toward these related ideals, theorists have assumed that the infant has minimally differentiated psychological functions—that the infant is a being without autonomy. Some speak of the infant as having no "body boundary" and being incapable of differentiating self from others. Some emphasize the dependence of the infant on adults, implying a chronic vulnerability to distress should the target of attachment depart. The undisguised implication is that the dissolution of self in others and an anxious, addictive dependence are undesirable qualities the infant must and will outgrow unless he is improperly socialized. It is probably not a coincidence that those Americans who opposed the abolition of slavery in the latter part of the eighteenth century described the Negro as lazy, dependent, and without a sense of self (Jordan 1968).

These evaluative descriptions of the young child are not universal. The Japanese, who prize intimate interdependence in adults, view the infant as too autonomous. Parents tempt the infant into a more dependent role. Japanese mothers rush to soothe the infant when he cries, respond quietly to his babbling, and typically sleep with the infant during the evening. The aim of these actions is to encourage the social intimacy and dependence that are requisites for adult life (Caudill and Weinstein 1969).

Lack of body boundary and inability to separate self from others are not the only qualities we assign to the young child. A society with diverse values requires that its citizens be tolerant of the perspective of others and capable of taking the point of view of another. Those who cannot are immature. Following Piaget, the young child is described as egocentric and unable to assume the role of another, even though many mothers have watched their 2-year-olds place a toy cup and saucer in the correct orientation in front of a teddy bear.

Historical shifts in ascribed traits can reveal secular changes in the local ego ideal. During the 1930s, when control of all aggression was the civilized goal to grow toward, Melanie Klein wrote of the unrestrained primitive aggression of the infant. She explained the nursing infant's clamping on the nipple as an expression of that instinctual aggression. Since the Second World War, nonviolent forms of aggression have lost some of their negative value, and that trait has been dropped from the infant's vita.

When a reasonable conformity to benevolent authority was the ideal, young children were described as willful. As the roll of events began to taint all moral imperatives given by elders, regardless of their status, some felt it necessary to promote a more personalized conscience to a higher position. Children who conformed to the requests and commands of benevolent adults out of fear of punishment or reprisal were reclassified as immature (Kohlberg 1966). When control of sexual impulse was the European ideal at the turn of the century, Freud described the young child as an uncharted libidinous surface. Now that access to sexual passions has become a new criterion for maturity, few care about the infant's sexuality and the oral-anal-phallic trivium has the musty smell of a newly uncovered crypt.

Finally, seventeenth-century Europeans, who were concerned with retaining the esteem of their peers and avoiding the shame that follows violation of group standards, projected a preoccupation with group acceptance onto the young child. Advisors to parents who were concerned with the task of socialization emphasized the child's need for praise and suggested that parents should capitalize on the child's natural fear of humiliation. Three hundred years later the Western adult is more preoccupied with finding some person or activity that will at least contain, but perhaps subdue, an anxiety that breeds on the absence of meaning in activity and of trust in human encounter. Correspondingly, modern theorists project onto the infant and young child, not shame, but anxiety over loss of a loving and caretaking adult.

The selection of descriptors for the young child is one instance of the more general problem of categorization. The parsing of human experience has been the subject of philosophical essays for centuries, and the variety of classification systems reflects the profound presuppositions of the classifier. Nature presents us with an infinite number of events, each of which shares some qualities with another. That experience seems sufficient to lead humans to group the events that share common dimensions and to name them.

A central legend of the Mayan Indians who live in the villages that border Lake Atitlán in northwest Guatemala concerns the final battle between the great Indian warrior Tecun Uman, who was on foot, and the Spaniard Pedro Alvarado, who was on horseback. After hours of battle, Tecun Uman inflicted upon his opponent what he thought was a fatal wound. Because he had never seen a man on horseback, he thought the horse and rider an organic entity and so turned away, believing himself victorious. Alvarado dismounted from his fallen horse and killed Tecun Uman, winning the Guatemalan territory for the Spaniards.

Although the risks we run in misclassifying phenomena are not as serious as those taken by Tecun Uman, scientists are always vulnerable to misdirection if they do not categorize natural phenomena in a way that is faithful to nature. A potentially serious error in the study of infants is the use of comparative categories whose meaning is derived from a contrasting descriptor for adulthood. In the physical sciences, categories are usually invented a posteriori to name a new phenomenon. A new particle name is invented each time a physicist discovers a unique and reliable energy function in an accelerator. Or, as in the case of the *quark,* a new name may point to a potential, as yet undiscovered, phenomenon that might mediate events believed to be meaningfully related. In both cases, reliable phenomena lead; the categories follow.

Unfortunately that script is followed less frequently in the social sciences, where newly discovered reliable relations are less common and the categories treated as theoretical terms are too often everyday words borrowed from the language of the larger society, like *egocentric, retarded,* or *fearful.*

Since each event has more than one dimension, it can participate in more than one category, or set of shared dimensions. Theoretically, an event can participate in as many categories as it has dimensions. Consider, as a simple example, the natural event we call "a cow." The dimensions of that event include, on the one hand, leather and meat, but, on the other, the fact that a cow carries its young internally and nurses its infant. The first set of attributes leads one to classify cows with trout, lobster, and truffles because all are marketable commodities. The second set of dimensions leads one to classify cows with weasels, wolves, and gazelles under the superordinate category of mammals. The category selected depends on the purpose of the classifier.

Consider an event more closely related to the theme of this book: the 1-year-old child runs crying to his mother upon seeing a stranger. Presented with that event, we can focus on the "crying" and classify it as an instance of an emotion, or focus on the "running to the mother" and classify it as motivational. We believe it is not useful to debate whether the child runs to the parent because he is "afraid" or because "he wants his mother's solace." Each classification is correct; the one we select depends on our purpose.

Psychological events have as their major dimensions:

1. a response or sequence of responses
2. a change in feeling state
3. cognitive representation of a goal
4. an immediate incentive
5. an historical or genetic component
6. a physiological component
7. a context (social as well as nonsocial)
8. ease of alteration . . . and perhaps many more

An observer can selectively emphasize any one or more of the foregoing dimensions in his classification, depending upon the use he wishes to make of the classification.

Some of the uses (or purposes) of a classification of an event include:

1. describing (the child cried)

2. explaining by relating the event to inferred states in the present (the child is anxious; the child wants his mother)

3. explaining by relating the event to the product of past experience

(the child has become attached to his caretaker)

4. including the classification as part of a larger logical or theoretical system (the child is in Stage IV object permanence)

5. maximizing communication with others (the child is afraid)

6. contrasting with a future developmental state (the child is immature)

7. generating an aesthetic feeling in another (the child is psychically vulnerable)

8. relating an event normally classified in the language of one discipline to the language of another discipline (the child's reticular formation is physiologically aroused).

Each of these classifications would potentially be legitimate if an observer were to see a 12-month-old child crying at departure of the mother. The one chosen would depend on the purposes of the observer and the quality he regards as distinctive.

Usually the observer uses one of two frames in selecting categorical terms. Either he notes which attributes are distinctive from a set of norms he brings to the phenomenon and he chooses terms that implicitly announce a contrast with those norms, or he relies on functional relations inherent in the phenomenon of interest and selects terms that serve as constructs to unite the covarying phenomena. We are suggesting that until now psychologists have employed the first frame more often than the second. Descriptive categories like *undifferentiated, oral, egocentric, narcissistic,* or even *sensorimotor* connote qualities whose meaning is dependent upon a comparison of infant with adult. Babies seem to spend a lot of time feeding and mouthing objects; therefore it is tempting to conclude that oral satisfactions have a special place during the opening years of life. But if European adults at the turn of the century had devoted a large portion of their day to feeding, Freud probably would not have chosen that classification. We believe that we are more likely to attain insight into the psychology of the infant if we attend to reliable relations between empirical phenomena and use them as the basis for categorization. As we shall see in chapter 2, that strategy leads us to classify early infancy as a time when retrieval memory is fragile. At the least we must try to overcome the urge to cast the infant in our shadow. We must be sensitive to the difference between constructs that describe the infant's behavior and those that evaluate him relative to adults.

We ask too much from the study of the young child. We are not satisfied by knowing how he "works" as a living and complex entity. We use him, on occasion, as the elite use the peasant, to define ourselves. That need is a distorting mirror that prevents us from a clearer perception of this object of interest. Let us not mimic the queen in Snow White who wants assurance of her beauty, but approach the human infant with the detachment needed to understand him.

The concerns of developmental psychologists

Individual variation American psychologists wear two sets of lenses as they watch the occasions of experience that describe development. One transmits variation among children—some talk a lot, others little; some strike, others are victims. The other transmits similarities. Most children speak between one and three years, show stranger anxiety between seven and fifteen months, and shame between three and five years. The variation in timing and intensity of these developments appears blurred in comparison with the vividness of the commonality. The preoccupation with difference, which has become a fetish in the United States, is due partly to adult uncertainty about differences in power, dominance, and status. Only some can attain status, wealth, and power in a community where, theoretically, all are supposed to. Each quality is a primary node of uncertainty, and all are sensitized to minor, often trivial, differences among children because society will amplify those tiny differences in talent among 3-year-olds into impossible gulfs among adults. The most frequent qualifiers for neutral nouns among Americans include *big, great, hard,* and *strong*—adjectives of potency. The words *beautiful, lovable,* and *reliable* are far less frequent in the speech of Americans but appear in the top ten adjectives among speakers of Bengali, Cantonese, and Japanese (Osgood, May, and Miron 1975).

Americans are excited by and addicted to finding differences in talent, but relatively indifferent to the remarkable regularities in development. We note how varied 1-year-olds are in their disposition to smile, to vocalize, or to protest separation from their mothers. But if we retreat a few steps and examine the growth function for these behaviors we note remarkable similarity. The tendency to vocalize at novel visual events increases linearly from three through nine months of age. The tendency to smile at an unfamiliar female decreases linearly across the same period. The disposition to cry at maternal departure displays an inverted U function—infrequent below 8 or after 24 months and most frequent in between—with the sharpest increase between nine and thirteen months. Although there is some variation in the intensity of these reactions or the slope of these functions, the uniformity is impressive.

The meaning of continuity Although uncovering regularities in the psychology of the young child satisfies a deep desire for understanding and for beauty, the pragmatic streak deep in many American psychologists has nurtured the hope that, as a dividend, we would gain a purchase on the future. Some developmental psychologists might lose interest in the young child if they believed that the phenomena they were analyzing lasted less than a few months or years. Thus an important basis for intense interest in early development is faith in a strong version of continuity from very early childhood to adolescence and beyond.

The concept of continuity bears a complex relation to those of identity and constancy and to contrasting, but complementary, constructions of a world that is continually changing while retaining frozen moments. Is the six-inch yellow pencil lying motionless on the desk the same pencil at 10:05 AM that it was 10:00 AM? That may seem to be a silly question, but as Bertrand Russell has noted, such questions often veil profound enigmas. If we believe that the pencil is a collection of electrons, neutrons, hadrons, and quarks that are interacting with each other and the surround, then its properties at 10:05 cannot be the same as those that existed five minutes earlier. That conclusion usually provokes irritation and the confident rebuttal that despite the presumed invisible changes at the particle level, the pencil, for all practical purposes, has not changed across the five-minute interval. It is still yellow, still capable of making marks on paper, and still six inches long. It has retained its identity because its qualities have displayed continuity over time. Both statements are true because the meaning of identity and, by implication, continuity, depends on the perspective assumed. When we move from pencils to living systems, the utility of a relativistic stance is more obvious. And when we add psychological qualities to our sphere of consideration the importance of perspective is overwhelming.

Assumptions about constancy and change depend on the level of analysis and, therefore, the language of description. The collection of proteins we call chromosomes numbers forty-six in all nongerm cells. That number is constant from cell to cell, from generation to generation. The category *forty-six* imposes a continuity on a set of events which, at a microscopic level, are dynamic and mutagenic.

A biologist or psychologist acknowledges that although the organism never stops changing, the rate of change in a quality often varies. When he observes that rate slow to some critical value, he is prepared to apply the word *stability*. Body weight displays a rapid rate of change during the first fifteen years of life, after which it slows. It is at the point of slowing that we say a person's weight has attained some degree of constancy. When the variation in a quality over a reasonable time interval is small relative to its average value, we are inclined to award constancy to that quality. But the size of the ratio we will treat as diagnostic of constancy varies with the characteristic. For stature or for time to press a button in response to a signal we demand that the ratio be very small; for IQ we accept a much larger ratio. A variation of three IQ points over a one-year interval for a person with an IQ of 100 is regarded as error; we say that the person's IQ has remained constant. A 3-percent variation in adult height over a year would be cause for alarm. Each domain carries unstated understandings regarding the ratio of variation to average value that is indicative of constancy.

Let us now turn to popular psychological variables whose metrics are occasionally interval scales, but more often ranks based on test scores and frequencies of overt behaviors. How do psychologists decide that a particular quality is constant? An ipsative analysis is one that only considers variation in a particular individual's qualities over time. The more common, normative procedure is to evaluate the individual's variation relative to some larger referent cohort, or peer group. Compare these two strategies in arriving at a judgment of constancy for the number of unrelated words a particular child can recall. A verbal recall task is administered to a child every month from three through fifteen years of age. We wish to decide at what point, if any, the child's recall score attains some constancy. That decision depends, in part, on how we organize the data. If we examine the data month by month we note a slowly rising curve and are likely to assume constancy early. But if we group the data by years we will note a sharply rising curve that does not reach a plateau until about eight years, with the ratio of variation to the mean approaching one to seven. Suppose we perform the same study with nineteen additional children and find among them no year-to-year variation in their performance after age eight. All nineteen always remember seven words. We would now regard the performance of our original subject as less constant and might retract the original assignment of stability to his memory performance. Decisions regarding the constancy of a quality often differ, depending on whether the analysis is ipsative or normative. A person can come to display less change in some quality, relative to his past behavior, and yet be more variable over the same time period than members of a cohort with whom he is being compared.

Psychologists typically base judgments of constancy on normative rather than ipsative evidence. The decision is based on the subject's maintenance of his rank order on some quality, not on his behavior in relation to himself. Child psychologists often quantify the number of seconds of vocalization an infant displays when presented with a set of visual stimuli. If a child's absolute vocalization times varied dramatically from occasion to occasion, but he retained the same rank order, the psychologist would conclude that vocalization was a stable quality for this child, despite the fact that an ipsative analysis revealed a high ratio of variation to the mean. Chinese infants are far less likely than Caucasians to vocalize in response to visual and auditory events from seven through twenty-nine months of age, although vocalization increases greatly for both groups over this interval. The stability correlations for vocalization among Chinese children are moderately high during this period, despite the sizable intraindividual variability over time.

A more common practice in studies of long-term stability of human traits is to correlate two sets of ranks on two different variables. In this case an ipsative analysis is not possible, for the child cannot be compared with himself with respect to rate of change for a particular behavior. For example, a group of infants are ranked on mean length of utterance at eighteen months and on IQ score at five years. The metric for and meaning of length of utterance have nothing in common with the metric and meaning for IQ. But if the children retain their relative rank orders over time, we are tempted to say that some hypothetical quality has remained stable. Some call that quality "intelligence."

Developmental theorists make predictions about the future form of some early behavior that they assume undergoes a lawful transformation. The theorist hypothesizes that a certain early disposition makes a child more or less vulnerable to the establishment of a future structure or behavior. Although the theoretical prediction implies an ipsative analysis, the empirical implementation is almost always normative. For example, a popular hypothesis in psychological theory states that a child who displays signs of anxiety following maternal separation at one year of age will be dependent on his mother at age five. In order to verify this prediction one must follow a group of children longitudinally and demonstrate that those who displayed more distress than their peers at one displayed more dependency than their peers at five. If this result emerges, the investigator concludes that a child's insecurity or fearfulness is stable. But that statement could not be made without a referent group, for all infants show some distress following some maternal departures, and all 5-year-olds show some dependency. Moreover, a change in the comparison group at age five might alter the decision about stability. A child might be high in the rank order for both separation distress at one year and dependency at age five, relative to one referent group, but if the referent group at age five changed, he might have a markedly different position, and the decision about stability might be altered. Consider a real, rather than a hypothetical, example. At both twenty and twenty-nine months of age Chinese children are more inhibited and wary with an unfamiliar peer than are Caucasians. As a result, the correlation between signs of fearfulness at twenty and twenty-nine months for the pooled group of Caucasians and Chinese is moderately high, and one is tempted to conclude that the trait of apprehension is stable over the nine-month period. But if the correlations are run separately for Caucasians and Chinese, there is no stability of inhibition within either group.

A poor black child in a Boston school whose reading scores over a two-year period are both at the thirtieth percentile on a standardized reading test would be regarded as having a stable reading score. But if that child were moved to a rural Kenyan school, he would be likely to be reading in the seventieth percentile, despite no real change in his reading ability.

The meaning of stability or continuity of a psychological quality, when based on normative correlational analysis, is to be differentiated from the logical meaning of identity or the constancy of a quality based on an ipsative analysis. The confusion in the uses of these two terms has made the study of psychological stability ambiguous and vulnerable to justified criticism. When statements about psychological stability are based only on sets of rank orders, we must always add a statement about the qualities of the referent group with whom the subject is being compared. It is useful therefore to distinguish among 1) variation in the rate of change of a particular quality within an individual, 2) relative variation in the rate of change of a particular quality within a referent group, 3) maintenance of a relative rank on a variable whose metric remains constant, and 4) maintenance of relative rank on variables with different metrics. Most psychological research on stability falls into one of the last two classes. We shall consider this issue again in chapter 5 in a discussion of the constancy of attentiveness.

Near and far explanations of human development

The satisfying quality of an explanation largely depends on the degree to which the "space" between the presumed original event and subsequent phenomena is filled with mediating propositions. It is unsatisfying to explain the appearance of April's apple blossoms by citing the seed from which the tree grew or to attribute October's falling leaves to gravity, for each explains both too much and too little. These causes do not provide the intermediate, effective facilitators of the phenomena. This issue is of special relevance when we attempt to interpret adolescent or adult behavior as a function of the events of early childhood.

The psychological structures produced by the childhood experiences remain dynamic, undergoing consolidation and transformation. Some may even become free of the original experiences that produced them. The beliefs, motives, or behavioral dispositions of adolescence are often such an extreme transformation of earlier events that an explanation of the present in terms of the original experiences is woefully incomplete. It is not completely satisfying to explain Mahatma Gandhi's asceticism as a likely outcome of his childhood experiences. The older the child, the less powerful are explanatory propositions that rely heavily on early experience and the more we require contemporary descriptions to pave the path to the remote past.

Each developmental journey contains many points of choice where the individual can move in any one of several directions. After each choice the probability of some final outcome is changed a wee bit. A perinatal trauma alters the probability of future academic success by some small amount. Nurturance by the mother, arrival of a sibling, presence of authoritarian qualities in the father, and degree of success in the first grade make up successive event complexes, each of which moves the child toward certain beliefs and actions and away from others and changes the final probability of his attaining some future state.

The evolutionary tree may be an appropriate metaphor for psychological development. We do not explain man by pointing to protozoa, even though the existence of protozoa is a remotely past event that made the existence of man a little more likely—we point to the entire evolutionary sequence. Similarly, we can not explain a 10-year-old's phobia by listing his early childhood experiences. The symptom can only be understood as a coherence of many past events, for the present is a severe limitation of all the possibilities that existed in the past. An explanation of a profile of behavior at any moment resides in a set of conditional probabilities associated with alternative itineraries over the course of development. The number of choices between origin and final outcome is a critical factor in determining the relation of infancy to later behavior and might be likened to the mutation rate in a species—the higher the mutation rate, the less stable a particular structure over time. If the child grows up in an environment where many new pressures demand psychological choices, there is likely to be less predictability over time than if fewer choices are available.

Waddington (1975) has noted that biological development is characterized by a series of branching points and, depending on the direction specific groups of cells take at each junction, alternative paths of development occur. So too with psychological development. A child born in a certain nation, region, city, class, or ethnic group has a large but limited number of alternative life routes. What varies among children of different cultures or subgroups is the fan of itineraries likely to be followed. It might be possible, based on statistical inferences from empirical data, to make statements about the number and nature of the envelope of paths, but impossible to predict a priori the particular path that will be taken, for we cannot know ahead of time what branching points will occur in each child's journey. The first child born to a pair of well-educated parents who are professionals is likely to have a professional vocation, but it is impossible to predict his specific role. The arrival of a sibling, success in school, relation to peers, values of the referent group—each of these events is a hill in Waddington's epigenetic landscape, a bump in the road that forces the child to select a new direction. Once a direction is taken toward a particular goal, the child resists being detracted from that path. This phenomenon bears a resemblance to Waddington's notion of canalization in embryological development. Once a tissue develops a competence, to become muscle, it is difficult to deter it from its appointment. Once a child decides that he wants to be the best in his class, he resists efforts to move that goal down in the hierarchy. Alternatively, once a child decides he is incompetent in mathematics, it is difficult, though not impossible to dissuade him from that belief. However, since all children prefer to be free of uncertainty, rather than burdened with it, and competent rather than without talent, there is a force that nudges all children toward similar, more adaptive paths.

The meaning of stage

The discussion thus far has depicted development as an envelope of processes changing at different rates over time. When the rate for a particular dimension slows we are tempted to call it stable. Psychologists also assume that individual processes are not growing independently. Sets of functions are yoked together. Moreover, not all the functions are present at birth, and some join the developmental parade on a regular schedule. These two premises require the invention of a special construct, *stage.* Although there is not complete agreement on the definition of this term (Wohlwill 1973), the concept is usually applied to covariation in the rate of growth of sets of related psychological dimensions that form an invariant sequence. "The usefulness of the stage concept remains an open question today and its potential promise unfulfilled" (Wohlwill 1973, p. 236). Nonetheless its popularity invites further discussion.

A major issue associated with the stage concept is the abruptness of the transition. Does a smile or the first word appear suddenly or gradually? Resolution of this issue is, of course, a matter of perspective. Certainly many external events appear suddenly; the controversy concerns the abruptness of the hidden processes. A wave breaking on a shore is a separate, bounded phenomenon. But an engineer measuring changes in hydrostatic pressure 100 yards out from the beach would note a more gradual, less discontinuous phenomenon. Although the 4-month-old infant's smile in response to her mother's face seems to appear without any preparation, its display is dependent on the gradual establishment of a schema for a human face which has been growing imperceptibly from the first week of life. Stages in psychological growth are typically inferred from constellations of public events.

There are two meanings to the word *stage*—one descriptive and the other theoretical. The descriptive meaning is easy to understand. Psychologists assume that there is a correlation among the child's characteristics during particular periods in his development. Similarly, in embryology one distinguishes between the stage of the embryo and the stage of the fetus. During the former the organs—brain, stomach, liver—are differentiated and not yet fully formed. When all organs have appeared in their initial form, the period of the embryo is terminated, and the period of the fetus, characterized by growth and enlargement of the organs rather than differentiation of new ones, begins. At a descriptive level, that separation into two stages seems reasonable and has the appearance of being helpful. But the distinction does not explain anything about growth.

Most psychologists are not satisfied with a descriptive concept of stage and want a more powerful theoretical one, which implies that there are, first, regular relationships among the structures and actions of one era and, second, a necessary relation between the structures of one stage and those of a succeeding one. When Piaget says the period from six to eleven years of age defines the concrete operational stage, he means that there is a necessary relation between the ability to conserve mass and to multiply classes—two competences characteristic of this stage. Similarly, there is a necessary relation between the ability to exhaust systematically all logical solutions and the conviction that one cannot solve a problem—competences characteristic of the formal operational stage attained during adolescence. The depression that accompanies a life crisis one cannot handle requires the formal operational competence to believe that one has exhausted all possible solutions.

Although a correlation between two abilities can imply a common and necessary underlying structure, it need not. The 8-month-old has recently acquired both the ability to display fear of a stranger and the ability to sit up. There is no good reason to assume that there is a relation between these two competences; the close temporal emergence of certain abilities during particular periods of growth can reflect a common source, but need not.

The second and stronger implication of the stage notion is that the competences gained during one stage are necessary for and are incorporated into the later one. The ability to detect an event as discrepant emerges during the opening months of life and controls the child's selective distribution of attention to objects and people in his life space. About six months later a new competence emerges. The child can now retrieve representations of past experience and generate predictions; hence the infant shows object permanence and distress both to strangers and to separation from his caretaker. Obviously if the child cannot detect a discrepancy, he will not be prompted to use the new competence. The prior ability is necessary for the display of the later one. But there is no good reason to assume that the ability to detect discrepancy is part of the competence involved in the ability to retrieve a schema, compare it with the present, and generate relations between them. The child must be able to support and coordinate his head and arms if he is to walk without falling down. In that sense, the earlier masteries are required for the later one. But the mechanisms that permit control of head and arms are not the central ones involved in walking. This view is in accord with the biologist's description of embryological development. The simple cell zygote gradually changes to a blastula and then develops a longitudinal axis, as if from a silk hat. The longitudinal axis was, of course, a potential in the genome, but it is in no way derivative of a structure in the zygote except that the prior state had to exist.

The distinguished neuroembryologist Viktor Hamburger comments on the discontinuity in motility patterns of embryo and newborn fetus. The motility patterns of the embryo have no parallel in postnatal behavior and the "integrated activities, such as walking or pecking of food which are performed with reasonable perfection soon after hatching or birth by all precocious animals have no antecedents in prenatal motility" (Hamburger 1975, p. 176).

Neither does the evolution of a morphological structure or process form a continuous stagelike series from simple to more complex. George Simpson notes, "Some such sequence as dogfish-frog-cat-man is frequently taught as evolutionary (i.e. historical). In fact, the anatomical differences among these organisms are in large part ecologically and behaviorally determined, are divergent and not sequential, and do not in any useful sense form a historical series" (Simpson 1958, p. 11).

The ability to speak increasingly complex sentences, to anticipate loss of nurturance, to experience shame or guilt, to operate on several bits of information simultaneously, to assume a hypothetical set, and to examine the logic of a set of properties are inserted into the ongoing growth process at regular times. The degree to which each process is derived from former competences is not clear. In some cases earlier abilities may be necessary for later ones, but the later ones add a qualitatively different dimension that is not in a strict sense an outgrowth of the earlier.

Further, it is not obvious that merely because one response system appears before another, it must. For example, most 3-year-olds experience fear of parental punishment if they violate a standard on lying, whereas many 8-year-olds feel guilt following the same violation. It may be possible for the older child to possess a capacity for guilt even though he never experienced any fear of parental punishment. Perhaps all that is necessary for guilt is recognition of whether the act was wrong or right and realization that one had a choice with respect to committing the wrong act.

Recently, some psychologists and psycholinguists have suggested that there are prerequisites for language in the actions of the preverbal infant. One group defines *prerequisite* as "a development that must occur before a second development, dependent in some way on the first, can take place" (Bates et al. 1977, p. 249). Investigators committed to this view follow infants from before the first birthday until the emergence of language, trying to detect the connection between the attainment of object permanence or particular gestures and the first words. They argue, for example, that the 6-month-old's pointing to a bottle is analogous to, or necessary for, the verbal demand, "milk," which appears about one year later. It is difficult to affirm or refute that position. Since there is, at present, no firm empirical basis for the hypothesis, we interpret the attractiveness of this idea as reflecting a strong desire to believe in a necessary link between the present competence and the distant past.* As Roger Brown has noted, "arguments about the origin of language were not so much arguments about prehistory as they were arguments about the essential nature of man" (Brown 1973, p. 63).

In order to pose more clearly the problem raised by an epigenetic view, we can examine the child's behavior following the departure of the caretaker to whom the child has developed an attachment. The typical reaction of a 1-year-old is inhibition and perhaps crying, because of the development of cognitive processes that permit the child to ask a question he cannot answer. At four the same event typically elicits no obvious reaction. However, if the

*The preference for positing continuous processes rather than discrete entities is also seen in the resistance of many nineteenth-century physiologists to the idea that neurons were independent units. They believed that nerve cells were connected to each other by protoplasmic bridges. Since these scientists had already accepted the discreteness of other cell types in the body, it appears that Western scientists are fundamentally friendly to the assumption of continuity unless evidence proves otherwise.

4-year-old thought that the departure meant permanent loss, he might become upset. There is no reason to believe in a relation between these two phenomena separated by three years even though one always follows the other. By age forty the possibility of a permanent parental loss might provoke no anxiety. Each stage is characterized by salient events that may have no analogue at later or earlier stages.

Incentives, too, are unique to eras of development. Chastisement by a parent, rejection by a peer, or failure at a task have maximal incentive value at different stages of development. During each stage the person is vulnerable to particular intrusions during certain phases of growth. Once the stage is over, the event loses some or all of its significance.

An interesting analysis was performed by Robert McCall on infant test data from the Berkeley longitudinal sample. The data consisted of early forms of the Bayley scale administered monthly from 1 to 15 months of age, every three months until 30 months, and semiannually until 5 years. Initially McCall performed a principle component analysis on the data and correlated the principle component scores across age.

The data revealed major discontinuities at 3, 8, 13, and 20 months. That is, the intraindividual cross-age correlations for the scores that indexed the major factors dropped at these points. The correlation from 3 to 4, 5, 6, or 7 months was high, but the correlation from 3 to 8 months was low. Similarly, the correlations for scores across the 8 and 13 month points were low. Correlations were higher between adjacent ages that were within developmental eras, that is, between 3 and 7 months or 8 and 12 months.

A similar result occurred in our longitudinal analysis of attentiveness, vocalization, and smiling in response to visual and auditory events in a group of children seen at 4, 8, 13, and 27 months (see Kagan 1971). There was very little intraindividual stability from 4 months to 8, 13, or 27 months, or from 8 to 27 months, but moderate relations between 8 and 13 months and 13 and 27 months, which is in accord with McCall's findings.

These two sets of data, using different populations and dependent measures, imply that major psychological changes occur around 8 months of age and again after the first birthday. It is probably not a coincidence that the nodes of change occur at these times. As we shall see in chapter 2, retrieval memory expands at 8 months, and language and symbolism appear after the first birthday. The introduction of these competences changes the bases of psychological functioning. Children who are precocious in entering the prior stage when schemata for absent objects can be retrieved are not necessarily early in entering the later stage of symbolism and language. The junctures in development are like transitions in a journey where both speed and mode of travel change during different phases. One drives a car to the airport, flies to Athens, sails to Heraklion.

There are invariances of order due to the operation of genetically controlled mechanisms, but there need not be closely dependent relations between all the structures of successive stages. This suggestion implies that when certain new competences are added to the pattern of existing abilities a new structure is created and earlier ones may vanish. Once the young child realizes the class to which the dog next door belongs, he may never again be able to react to any dog as if it were outside of any category. When the trellis cells of the embryo's nervous system have fulfilled their function of guiding migrating neurons to their destination, they vanish. The cells were like scaffolding for a building, and are needed no more. It may be useful therefore to question the strict connectivity of competences and the strong form of the epigenetic view. As there are discontinuities in phylogeny—man's language ability is not an obvious derivative of baboon's signaling behavior—or in the growth of a plant from seed to bud to blossom, so too there may be more discontinuities in psychological development than we have wanted to acknowledge. The state of being a caterpillar always occurs before butterflyhood, but it is difficult to discern the competences that the adult butterfly inherited from the hairy larva. In declaring a faith in strong psychological continuity from stage to stage we may have been committing the ancient error of *post hoc ergo propter hoc*.

It is not obvious, therefore, that the assumption of a thick cord of connection between stages, a contingent relation between earlier and later structures, is always useful. This idea is attractive to the Western mind, which likes the notion of unitary, deep structures that explain phenotypically diverse performances. Both Plato and Aristotle posited a hidden continuum behind the discreteness of the external world. Aristotle applied that bold idea to living forms and assumed a hierarchy of classes of animals and plants that were part of a seamless surface—an idea that centuries later came to be known as the "Great Chain of Being."

"In all the visible, corporeal world we see no chasms or gaps. All quite down from us the descent is by easy steps in a continued series that in each remove differ very little one from the other . . . We have reason to think that it is suitable to the magnificent harmony of the universe, and the great design and infinite goodness of the architect, that the species of creature should also, by gentle degrees, ascend upwards from us toward his infinite perfection, as we see they gradually descend from us downwards" (Locke 1898, p. 293). If connectedness is part of nature's grand scheme for life, then it is reasonable to guess that it is applicable to psychological ontogeny. Moreover, it is less pleasing to consider that each of the successive classes of behavior that mark growth rests on its own bottom. Modern theories, like ancient ones, satisfy our deep longing for a hidden unity that weaves experience into a seamless fabric. We do not like to see anything wasted or thrown away—perhaps that is why the principle of conservation of energy is so aesthetically pleasing. The possibility that the intensity, variety, and excitement of the first years of life, together with the extreme parenting effort those years require, could be discarded like wrapping paper that is no longer needed is a little too threatening to our Puritan spirit.

The preference for an unbroken relation between infancy and later childhood can also be traced to Plato's assumption in the *Timaeus* that all events have prior causes. It can be traced as well to the arguments proposed by medieval philosophers to affirm the existence of God. Contemporary arguments for the origins of adult personality in infant experience bear a strong resemblance to Thomas Aquinas's defense of the idea of God. Aquinas accepted the Greek premise that all dynamic events had a prior cause. He believed that if one traced all movements back to the original incentive, one would arrive at the original unmoved mover, which for Aquinas was God. Psychologists who believe that adult behavior is a partial derivative of early experience apparently assume that adult dispositions must have a connection to earlier ones, the earlier ones to still earlier ones, and in this regress one arrives at the nursery convinced that one sees in a newborn's thrashing or lethargy the origins of antisocial behavior.

There is also strong phenomenological support for faith in connectedness. We reflect on our past and have the illusion of a unity. The illusion is based partly on our need to seek coherence in our own lives and partly on a pressure to see rationality and causality in our decisions. It is distressing to believe that the actions and experiences of the fifth year are not participants in our experiences at age thirty-five.

A fourth reason for emphasizing continuity between stages in development may derive from the notion that preparing the child for the future is like helping him "save for a rainy day." Application of that maxim to psychological development leads to the deduction that if children are treated optimally during the early years of life, the healthy beliefs and behaviors established during that first period will be adequate protection against later traumas. This idea may be true, but there is no commanding proof of its correctness. Over ninety percent of America's children stay with their families most or all of their childhood and adolescence. When 16-year-old children from different families differ in adjustment there is a tendency to assume that these differences are due to early experience rather than to what occurred later or what is occurring at the moment. Consider two 16-year-old boys from the same neighborhood, one an excellent student, the other a delinquent and high school dropout. It is useful to perform a mental experiment to point out the force and the potential fragility of the belief that the differences are due to experiences of the boys' first half decade. Imagine an alert, social, and happy 3-year-old, a child who appears secure, curious, creative, and spontaneous. Now imagine that child being transferred to a toxic home environment, in which she is beaten without reason and exposed daily to violence, cynicism, and self-derogation. When we return ten years later it is likely that we would see a 13-year-old that resembled the siblings in her foster family. In fact, the intuition is that we would be unable to see many of the strengths that were established during the first three years. Now perform the opposite experiment; remove a 3-year-old from a toxic environment and transfer her to a benevolent home. Intuition suggests that this child would be markedly different from the siblings and peers who remained in the more destructive context. This mental exercise suggests that the structures created by the first three years of experience will only be stable if the early environment is maintained.

A final and more recent source of the prejudice for continuity is contained in the developmental theory Freud proposed, which was amplified by the first generation of his disciples. Freud argued that the experiences of the infant could create psychic structures whose sphere of influence might extend far into the future. Although he disavowed Otto Rank's theory of birth trauma, he did propose that the occasions of anxiety during infancy were likely to sensitize the older child. In *The Problem of Anxiety* (Freud 1936) he argued, by analogy, that the anxiety of the older child and adult was related to the distress experienced by the infant when he was separated from his mother or when he failed to be gratified. The implication was that if the infant were protected from these unsettling experiences, the basis for later distress would be muted. Freud conceptualized this idea as follows: "anxiety proves to be a product of the psychic helplessness of the infant which is the obvious counterpart of its biological helplessness" (1936, p. 77).

In his next paragraphs Freud suggested that there was a continuum between separation from the mother and the anxieties of the future. He even likened the loss of the mother to the loss of the penis: "castration anxiety which makes its appearance in the phallic phase is separation anxiety also, and is similarly conditioned. The danger here is separation from the genital" (1936, p. 78).

Although Freud avoided stating an explicit connection between the anxieties of the infant and those of the adult, he edged close enough so that those who followed could be bolder. Erikson suggested that the infant who has trust in the availability of his caretaker gains a psychological advantage that is not easily destroyed, stating, "Mothers create a sense of trust in their children by that kind of administration which in its quality combines sensitive care of the baby's individual needs and a firm sense of personal trustworthiness within the trusted framework of their culture's lifestyle. This forms the basis in the child for a sense of identity which will later combine a sense of being 'alright,' of being oneself, and of becoming what other people trust one will become" (Erikson 1963, p. 249).

With the intervening years the idea that the infant's continued contact with and access to the mother can protect him from future distress has become both more explicit and more firmly held. Many contemporary theorists hold that the balance between the anxiety provoked by absence of caretaker and the sense of trust established by her presence generates structures or potentialities in the infant that must affect future functioning. One component of that future functioning is the child's sense of worth.

The child's perception of his value

One of the long-lasting structures that is supposed to be shaped during infancy and early childhood is a sense of emotional security—an idea closely related to the notions of trust, attachment, and love, and one of primary concern to mothers who are considering day care for their children. Many parents and psychologists assume that if the infant is loved he will forever be protected from the slings and arrows of misfortune. If the young child is not loved, he will be continually vulnerable to the slightest disruption or frustration. Recall Rousseau's prescription that mother's milk will cure society's ills.

Why has this assumption been so strongly held by Western theorists and parents during the last 300 years? It was far less prevalent during the medieval period and is not part of the folk theory of many non-Western societies. One basis for this premise stems from the universal need to believe in a force that can protect the child from future threat. Some cultures assume that fate or benevolent, transcendental forces wield that power; others assert that it is either inherited or a function of growing up in a healthy and harmonious community. Our own society, wedded to instrumentalism and the power of family experience, places its faith in a properly orchestrated set of parental actions that are supposed to insure the child's future or place it at risk. Indeed, the originality in Freud's theorizing is in the suggestion that parental practices with the young child can affect his adult profile of sexual experiences and behavior, for the popular assumption at the turn of the century was that sexual perversions were a product of either heredity or degenerate social conditions.

Faith in the protective quality of proper parental behavior is an instance of a more general Western belief that catastrophe can be averted by taking the appropriate prophylactic action, whether it be baptism or breast-feeding. We would like to believe in a recipe of caretaking practices that can be applied to the young child to inoculate him against future misery and failure. During most of this century many American psychologists have assumed that there was a set of specific parental behaviors that always signified love or rejection, for there was an enormous degree of commonality among investigators in definitions of these concepts. Harsh physical punishment and absence of social play and of physical affection were typically regarded as signs of rejection, and it would be almost impossible for an American psychologist to rank a mother high in both aloofness and a loving attitude. Yet Alfred Baldwin has reported that in the rural areas of northern Norway, where farms are many miles apart, one sees maternal behavior that an American observer would regard as rejecting in an American mother. The rural

Norwegian mother sees her 4-year-old sitting in a doorway, blocking the passage to the next room. She does not ask him to move, but bends down, picks him up, and silently moves him away before she passes to the next room. Although a middle-class observer might view this lack of communication as indifference and hence a sign of dislike, most mothers in this Arctic outpost behave this way and the children do not behave the way rejected youngsters should by our theoretical propositions.

During the early seventeenth-century European and Colonial parents were advised to beat their children in order to tame their inherently evil character, and otherwise respectable and well-educated parents inflicted severe punishment upon their dependents, punishments that would be classified as extreme abuse today. Samuel Byrd of Virginia, for example, made a dependent of his drink a "pint of piss" because he wet his bed (Plumb 1975). Then, as well as in the present century, many children of upper-class English families were rarely at home with their parents. After birth they were sent to a wet nurse in a nearby village until weaning, perhaps at two years of age. They then returned home for a period before being sent away to boarding school. Sir Robert Walpole, born in 1676, rarely spent more than a few weeks in his home each year between six and twenty-two years of age. Since this pattern was common, it is unlikely that parents thought they were being cruel or that their children felt they were unloved. Indeed it was not until 1623 that England passed a law against mothers killing their illegitimate children (Hanawalt 1977), and one historian has noted that "women who killed in childbirth were sometimes regarded as responsible and sometimes not" (Hurnard 1969, p. 169).

In his autobiography John Stuart Mill describes his father as aloof, stern, and lacking in affection: "the element which was chiefly deficient in his moral relation to his children was that of tenderness." But Mill, unlike most modern adults, did not treat this combination of qualities as reflecting hostility. Rather he assumed his father had repressed his tender feelings, and he added that he felt no sense of resentment toward the father, "I was always loyally devoted to him . . . I hesitate to pronounce whether I was more a loser or gainer by his severity" (Mill 1944, pp. 36-37).

Evaluation of a parent as hostile or accepting cannot be answered by knowing the parent's behavior, for neither love nor rejection is a fixed quality of behavior. Like pleasure, pain, or beauty it is in the mind of the beholder. Parental love is a belief held by the child, not a set of actions by a parent.

The view that a child's perception of parental love is like an immunization assumes a prominence in contemporary society that it may not have had in earlier periods or may not have in other contemporary societies. Many American children are uncertain about whether they are valued by their family, and parents are eager to communicate to their children that they love them. Unhappiness, failure, and psychopathology in adolescence and adulthood are often attributed to the absence of parental love during infancy and early childhood. Prior to the midseventeenth century it was far less common to find Europeans referring to the importance of the love relation between parent and child when they discussed the conditions that promoted optimal development. The child needed proper nutrition, physical protection, a good education, faith in God, and parents who were consistently firm in their discipline.

An elite and wealthy Florentine, Leon Battista Alberti, wrote an essay on the rearing of children in the middle of the fifteenth century which contrasts sharply with modern beliefs (Alberti 1971). Although Alberti acknowledged that parents exert a significant influence on the training of character and believed that early experience contributes to the formation of adult personality, he did not regard a mother's love as a major element in that process. Alberti suggested that it was the duty of the father, not the mother, to train the son to strive for honor and fame, and to develop the ability to determine one's destiny through competence and power—a combination of qualities that constituted *virtù.* Attainment of those sacred attributes was accomplished through parental vigilance, identification with the child's victories, and provision of appropriate examples. When Alberti listed the qualities most important to a happy family he failed to mention love: "The intellect, prudence, and knowledge of the old [people] together with their diligence are what maintain the family in a happy and flourishing state, and adorn it with praise, glory and splendor" (Alberti 1971, p. 46).

Alberti seemed indifferent to the mother's sentiments, confessing that he was not sure whether a mother or wet nurse was better for an infant, for a woman's influence on the young child was mediated primarily through the quality of milk she provided, not through her attitudes or practices. "We must therefore see to it that a child's nourishment at that age is as good as possible. We must see to it that the nurse is happy, clean, without passions or tumultuous spirits and that she leads a good life and is not immoral or intemperate in anything" (1971, p. 59).

There is no indication in the essay that Alberti ever considered the possibility that adult failure might result from insufficient parental affection during the early years of life.

In all of Thomas More's *Utopia,* written one century and a half later during the second decade of the sixteenth century, there is less than a page devoted to parental treatment of young children and no mention of the psychological relation between parents and children. More was not worried about foster care for an infant whose mother could not nurse "since the child who is thus fostered looks on his nurse as his natural mother" (More 1964, p. 80). And children older than five years were supposed to serve adults in the dining hall or if "they are not old and strong enough stand by—and that in absolute silence." Since More was describing an ideal human community, the failure to dwell on the love relation between parent and child implies that this idea was not salient in the consciousness of some sixteenth-century men of letters.

The Dutch minister John Robinson, writing in the early seventeenth century, also felt that a child needed parental severity more than affection. Consequently fathers were better for children than mothers, "for forming virtue and good manners by their greater wisdom and authority and ofttimes also by correcting the fruits of their mother's indulgence by their severity" (J. Robinson, in Greven 1973, p. 11). Robinson acknowledged that parents naturally are affectionate toward their children, but rather than celebrate that spontaneous emotion, he urged parents to suppress it. "There is running in the breasts of most parents a strong stream of parental affection toward some one or other of their children . . . either for its beauty or wit . . . or some other fancied good in it, which is always dangerous and oft harmful." He advised that if parents cannot gain control of their affections, "it is wisdom to conceal them from young children" (in Greven 1973).

But by the end of the seventeenth century, explicit recognition of the significance of the love relation between parent and child had emerged. Locke advised parents to love their children: "He that would have his son have a respect for him and his orders must himself have a great reverence for his son" (1898). Rousseau warned that if parents—and he meant both mothers and fathers—did not establish affectionate ties with their children, vice was inevitable. Anticipating Bowlby's emphasis on the infant's attachment to a single caretaker Rousseau advised against the mother having a wet nurse or substitute caretaker. But if that decision had been made, then "the foster child should have no other guardian, just as he should have no teacher but his tutor . . . A child who passes through many hands in turn can never be well brought up" (Rousseau 1911, p. 24). And by the middle of the nineteenth century, the modern view that a mother's love was not only sensed by her infant but essential to his future welfare was being articulated by essayists. Horace Bushnell, a Congregational minister in Hartford, Connecticut, advised,

> If the child is handled fretfully, scolded, jerked, or simply laid aside unaffectionately, in no warmth of motherly gentleness, it feels the sting of just that which is felt towards it; and so it is angered by anger, irritated by irritation, fretted by fretfulness; having thus impressed just that kind of impatience or ill-nature which is felt towards it, and growing faithfully into the bad mold offered, as by a fixed law. There is great importance, in this manner, even in the handling of infancy. If it is unchristian, it will beget unchristian states, or impressions. If it is gentle, even patient and loving, it prepares a mood and temper like its own. There is scarcely room to doubt that all most crabbed, hateful, resentful, passionate, ill-natured characters; all most even, lovely, firm and true, are prepared, in a great degree, by the handling of the nursery. [Quoted in Greven 1973, p. 166]

There are probably many reasons for the constructive significance that was beginning to be ascribed to early parental affection during the seventeenth and eighteenth centuries. As more mothers were freed of necessary toil they may have become receptive to a new set of responsibilities. It is reasonable to assume that they would choose child-rearing as a primary activity in which to invest effort and affect. Moreover, since the urban child of the bourgeoisie had lost his economic value, one might expect parents to begin to view the child as an object of sentiment, and even pleasure. Further, one might speculate that the growth of Protestantism was accompanied by a subtle substitution of parental love of child for God's love as the family replaced the medieval concept of the Mother Church.

Each of these factors has both intuitive appeal and some fragile empirical support. Perhaps a more fundamental reason for the increasing emphasis on the necessity of a love relation between parents and children was the emerging self-consciousness surrounding the child's independence, individualism, and personal desires. The concept of the child was being differentiated as an entity separate from the family. Stone notes that during the Middle Ages the newborn child was often given the same first name as a dead elder sibling. But this practice died out by the late eighteenth century, suggesting that the child's name had become a personal quality that could no longer be transferred from one child to another (Stone, unpublished, 1976).

As the seventeenth century came to a close, Locke's writings reflected the growing sentiment against the assumption that man was naturally disposed to be subservient to divine and royal authority, and for the view that all are born free. That change in premise happened to be accompanied by an increased permissiveness toward the older child's independence from the family, and, concomitantly, an emergent concern with the importance of parental love. Now, for the first time, "it was increasingly common to hear that parents were obliged to love them and to prepare for the day when they would go out into the world as free and equal adults" (Burrows and Wallace 1972, p. 260). In "Some Thoughts Concerning Education," Locke (1794) advised parents to rely less on restriction and punishment and to exploit the child's capacity for shame and fear of parental displeasure as means of training character. Love withdrawal was to be used as a strategy of socialization.

Thus, as unquestioned acquiescence to God and family lost their moral force to individualism and the development of an autonomous ego, parental love assumed a position of prominence. Is this correlation causal, the joint product of more fundamental factors, or an accident? We favor the second of these positions and shall try to support that view.

The rise of an urban middle class during the late sixteenth and early seventeenth centuries was probably accompanied by the realization that children were less obvious economic advantages. Youth were not needed to help with agricultural work or to care for infants and very young children.

The middle-class father, feeling economically more secure than the sixteenth-century rural parent, was probably less concerned about becoming economically dependent on his grown sons when he was too old to work. It is likely, then, that the child's role gradually changed from an object of utility to one of sentiment—from water jug to silver vase. Although the child could not contribute to the family's economic position, he could enhance the family's status by mastering academic skills and attaining prestige and positions of status in the larger community. Now more parents would begin to identify with their children because of the latter's potential accomplishments. This change in the child's function in the family could have produced an enhancement of the attitude we call parental love.

A second basis for an increased consciousness regarding affectionate relations between parent and child rests on the assumption that seventeenth-century parents began to recognize that an aloof, authoritarian attitude, which seemed to be effective in producing obedience and conformity in children, was not conducive to autonomous achievement. The latter profile requires a different set of parental attitudes. Fear of authority is a potent incentive for inhibition, but it is far less effective as a goad for continued striving toward goals that require the invention of ideas and actions. The desire to maintain the positive regard of parents is a more appropriate incentive for such striving. It is possible that the seventeenth-century middle-class family rediscovered that principle of human functioning, or at least became more conscious of it, as the stereotype of the ideal child changed from passive conformity to active, autonomous mastery.

The economic and social changes that led to new parental attitudes may have also created new nodes of uncertainty in children. The preadolescent in a fifteenth-century farming village had an opportunity each day to realize that he was an object of value, since his work made a material contribution to the family's welfare. His virtue was evident in the results of his work. The 13-year-old son of a middle-class official in eighteenth-century London did not have that advantage. His sense of virtue was not based on the products of his labor, but on his psychological qualities. He could not point to a plowed field or a full woodpile as a sign of his utility. As a result, this child may have been more uncertain about his value, more dependent on parental communications assuring him of his worthiness and preoccupied with parental attitudes toward him.

We are suggesting that there is theoretical substance to the correlation between the emphasis on the child's independence and autonomous achievement (along with the decreasing concern with conformity and the child's economic contribution to the family) and the awarding of formative power to attitudes of parental affection. The correlation reflects, in part, the growth of a folk theory implying that confidence, independence, and the drive for accomplishment require a belief in one's value and potency and a reluctance to lose parental love. We do not know whether the folk theory is valid empirically or merely believed to be correct by the community.

As hinted earlier, parental love may have become viewed as a psychological nutrient because a celebration of individualism implies that any protective amulet must be possessed by the individual; it cannot be a force whose potency depends on a shared function with others. Since urbanization and industrialization made it likely that many adults would be distant from family and early friendships, the protective shield was of little value if it required proximity to family. Although modernization made strength, health, and endurance less necessary for successful survival, uncertainty still remained a potential enemy. Loss of a loved one, temptation, and rejection were always possibilities in tomorrow's sunrise, regardless of one's position or wealth. Anxiety gradually became the adversary against which one needed protection. Benjamin Franklin wrote that uneasiness was the basic human motive, and nineteenth- and twentieth-century theorists from Sigmund Freud, Alfred Adler, and Otto Rank through John Bowlby, Mary Ainsworth, Rollo May, and Haim Ginott amplified that theme. The assumption is intuitively appealing, for our most unpleasant moments seem to occur when we are uncertain about how another will treat us, how our actions and products will be received, how to decide what to believe, and how to deal with possible danger. The popular belief is that early parental love, which leads to the private conviction that one is valued, can protect child and adult from that state of distress.

Is it likely that there is a special set of treatments that,by itself, would lead any child to believe he was or was not valued? Adolescents who have been locked in a room for two to three years excuse their mothers' actions by confessing that, because they were such difficult children, their mothers were correct to restrict them. Many persons who had nurturant and devoted parents during the early years feel unloved as young adults. The belief that one is not valued does not lie in a particular set of parental actions, but in the child's construction of those actions.

In our society, characterized by dramatic variability in child-rearing practices, children have the opportunity to compare their treatment with those prescribed by the culture and those they see displayed by other parents. These comparisons provide important information that helps the child decide whether his treatment is better or worse than others and, by implication, whether he is or is not valued. The child comes to discover what privileges, actions, and treatments reflect parental concern and affection. He compares his receipt of these symbolic prizes with the lot of others in his referent group, usually siblings and age mates in his subculture. That information allows him to decide if he is loved. Rather than view this belief as relative and resilient, parents and psychologists have made it a material entity—a beauty mark that the child carries with him for the rest of his life.

What evidence has sustained the belief? The major empirical evidence comes from study of pathology. Western psychologists defined parental love in materialistic terms. The basic ingredients were physical affection, sacrifice of the self's interests for that of the child, consistency of care, and enjoyment of interaction with the child. All of these are reasonable definitions of parental affection. Some scientists then argued that children who did not have this set of experiences during early childhood were more likely to display dispositions in adulthood that they called psychotic, asocial, or neurotic. The syllogism was as follows.

> Premise 1: If the child is loved, the adult will be psychologically healthy. Premise 2: This adult is not psychologically healthy. Conclusion: Therefore this adult was not loved as a child. This conclusion is valid, even though the truth value of the original premise may be questioned.

Consider the alternative, invalid syllogism, which has a retrospective first premise.

> Premise 1: If this adult is psychologically healthy, he was loved as a child. Premise 2: This adult is not psychologically healthy. Conclusion: Therefore this adult was not loved as a child.

Many parents and psychologists have made the mistake of assuming that since the first argument is logically sound, the second must be also. The invalid second argument is one reason for the belief in the ''power of parental love.'' There is no persuasive evidence, however, to show that most unhappy adults were unloved as children. We look at distressed adults and assume they were not loved, forgetting that many factors could have intervened between an early childhood full of love and an unhappy adulthood.

Many have assumed that the belief in ''one's value'' remains stable from early childhood through adolescence and adulthood. Of the millions of children who do not receive adequate amounts of early affection, only a small proportion develop pathology, and of the group with adult pathology, a large proportion may have been loved during early childhood. At the moment, we do not know if there is a strong relation between early child treatment and later adult pathology, even though there may be a strong relation between the older adolescent's belief that he is not valued and the frequency of his bouts of distress. The error comes from assuming that the adult's belief in his value is a derivative of a specific set of early parental treatments.

It is useful to view a person's belief in his value as dynamic and continually subject to change depending on life context. If the adolescent or adult finds himself in an environment where his ''traits'' are valued, whereas in prior contexts they were not, the belief is subject to modification. By contrast, if he feels valued in one situation and finds himself in a context where all around him do not prize his extrinsic and intrinsic qualities, his prior belief may be subject to modification. One of us spent two days with an adolescent girl who had been locked in a room, strapped to her bed from twenty months of age until she was thirteen years old. After a few years with a foster family she did not behave like a girl who believed she was rejected by humanity. She approached strangers, initiated physical contact, and seemed to expect kindness, not hostility, from adults. Her extreme isolation did not permit her to compare her treatment with others. She had no information to allow her to conclude that she was not valued. A subject cannot tell how large or distant an object is if he is looking at it through a box that prevents him from making any comparisons. Judgments of value, like size and distance, require an anchor.

It is not easy to ascertain whether lack of parental affection in childhood does indeed make a serious contribution to future psychic illness, but the reasons are not strictly empirical. When we ask, "Does temperature contribute to the probability of snowfall?" we only need gather easily obtained objective data to answer the query. But in the case of the contribution of parental love or rejection, we are in difficulty because we are asking, "Does a mental state in the child contribute to a future mental state in the adult?" The first interpretation of the question is private and concerned only with the adult's belief about the validity of the functional relation. If the adult believes that a set of experiences influences the future state, he will act as if it were so. The second interpretation of the question is empirical and asks if there is an objective relation between the child's perception of favor or disfavor and adult sequellae. That version of the question has not been answered satisfactorily because parental rejection is not a set of actions by parents, but a belief by the child. The only way to exit from this frustrating position is to determine if there is any observable relation in a culture between the actions and communications of parents and the child's belief that he is or is not favored. There are no data that have demonstrated unequivocally the relation between specific parental actions and the child's belief, even in our culture. Working-class American parents punish and restrict the child much more than middle-class parents, yet there is no evidence indicating a class difference in perception of parental favor. Kipsigis mothers have older siblings care for their young children, while Israeli mothers on kibbutzim use metaplot (surrogate caretakers). There is no evidence indicating that Kipsigis- or kibbutz-reared children feel less in parental favor than others. We are tempted to suggest that each child constructs a theory of the actions that imply parental favor and disfavor. The content of the theory is based on local conditions and will not necessarily generalize to other communities in any detail.

What seems unique in modern Western society is the popularity of the thought that one might not be valued by one's family. Historical events may have been responsible for introducing this idea as a major node of apprehension, and therefore of illness, just as social changes have been responsible for new anxieties over nuclear waste, racial violence, and municipal defaults. Mayan villagers worry about not having enough food, about slanderous gossip, and about the actions of gods. A society can create a new source of distress by introducing a new belief. Many modern mothers share Rousseau's conviction that a mother should not give her infant to a substitute caretaker. In violating that natural obligation she believes she is not only placing her child's development at risk but she is also increasing the likelihood that another socially disruptive adult will join the community. It is reasonable, therefore, that American parents worry about the consequences of day care during their children's early years.

Forces in development: the mechanisms of change

The enigma that continues to resist solution is the bases for the appearance of a new psychological competence—the presumed foundation for a stage—and the reasons for the many transitions in profile that characterize growth. Jean Piaget, Sigmund Freud, Jerome Bruner, Lawrence Kohlberg, Robert Fantz, Roger Brown, Robert McCall, Michael Lewis, and many others have described parts of the ontogenetic parade, but the essential mechanisms of change remain disguised. It is likely that they will include the maturation of structures and processes in the central nervous system that permit new psychological competences to appear, encounters with information that are dissonant or inconsistent with existing knowledge, and, finally, environmental demands for new instrumental actions and ideas.

The maturation of new competences We assume that growth in specific areas of the central nervous system permits a new psychological ability to emerge (Gottlieb 1976). Some of the best examples are the amplification of memory and the ability to stand, toward the end of the first year; and the ability to understand and speak language, during the second year. It is possible that the adolescent's ability to manipulate symbolic propositions in a network, the seminal skill of formal operations, is also dependent on prior biological changes in specific brain systems, as the appearance of the embryo's first heart beat waits upon tissue growth. Although statements that describe the beat of the heart cannot be reduced to propositions describing the tissues, the former function—which is emergent—cannot occur until the morphological changes have been completed. Because we have so few clues to the correlation between site of maturation and emerging psychological process, most scientists, including Piaget, have simply assumed a correlation and concentrated on describing in psychological language the emergent properties.

The consequences of encounter with information Perhaps the most common incentive for psychological change is encounter with an event that shares relations with the child's knowledge. Such encounters often lead to the creation of a new structure, the process Piaget calls accommodation. The child with a schema for a regular human face sees a facial mask with the eyes rearranged, recognizes a relation between the event and his schema for the face, and assimilates the distorted face to his schema. He now knows of the possibility of a disarranged face and will assimilate a distorted mask more quickly in the future, even though his schema for the regular face may not have changed at all. What has been altered is the potential to assimilate a new class of events to a schema more rapidly. This sensitization process resembles the effect of an inoculation of antigen on the capacity of an antibody to recognize a protein. A second, more profound meaning of accommodation is structural alterations in knowledge. Suppose that after his first birthday a child sees only distorted faces. Soon the schema for a normal face would be altered and the rearranged facial elements would be part of a new schema. The child's recognition of his sex role category provides another example of accommodation. From the time a child appreciates that he or she is a boy or girl he or she will try to maximize the self's profile to the cultural prototype for his or her own sex. Although the cognitive competence necessary to hold that belief is probably present by the end of the second year, the belief can emerge very late in some child-rearing contexts. Recognition of one's class or ethnic role, of the capacity for reproductive fertility at adolescence, or of loss of vitality in late middle age are other beliefs that mediate important transitions when they crystallize. The birth of a sibling forces the 3-year-old to realize he is not the center of parental concern. He must accommodate himself to that fact, and new beliefs are created in him. Helen Koch and others who have worked on the psychological correlates of ordinal position believe that the birth of a new sibling is most threatening to the older child when he is between two and five years of age. Perhaps one reason is that the knowledge generated by the arrival of the baby is most difficult for the child to understand at that time and demands a reorganization of his existing beliefs.

The cognitive processes that permit changes in belief remain mysterious. Most theorists simply state that the mind changes following encounter with new or discrepant information. The emergence and elaboration of the child's first spoken utterances provide an example of this process and a place to search for mechanism. We believe the child continually employs inference to establish new structures, where inference has its old-fashioned meaning —an event that the child understands only partially provokes him to generate hypotheses the aim of which is to gain more complete understanding. If such a guided guess is followed by a feeling of cognitive harmony—regardless of its external validity—the inference is treated as a valid belief until disconfirmed.

Consider a simple example. A 2-year-old child is shown a toy cup, car, and cat and names the correct item following three successive requests from an interrogator. Now the interrogator asks the critical question. She replaces the three toys with two new, but equally familiar, objects and one odd-shaped piece of wood which is maximally unfamiliar. The examiner waits a few seconds to permit the child to consider the toys and then says in a matter-of-fact tone, "Give me the zoob." The child, in an equally matter-of-fact manner, hands the odd-shaped piece of wood to the adult. The speed and confidence with which the 2-year-old responds implies that she regards the question as reasonable; and she assumes that the unfamiliar object must be the correct referent for the unfamiliar word.

A 21-month-old girl had her picture taken in our laboratory; while a floodlight was directed at her she complained about the heat. Two weeks later, in a different room, she was shown the picture of herself. Almost at once she exclaimed, "Hot, hot," announcing her inference that the picture she was viewing was the one taken two weeks earlier. We checked with the parents and discovered that in the intervening fourteen days she had seen at home pictures of herself taken by her parents but had not said, "Hot, hot." Apparently, she inferred that the color slide in front of her was the one taken with the floodlight.

We suggest that this mechanism mediates learning not only new semantic forms but also a great many concepts, beliefs, and rules. A 6-year-old child disobeys and her mother yells at her. The father, who is tired from a long commute home, is annoyed by the noisy interruption and sharply rebukes the mother for disturbing his quiet reading of the newspaper. A marital argument ensues. The parental squabbling is an unexpected puzzle for the child and in an attempt to explain its occurrence, she infers that the reason for the fight was her initial disobedience, not the father's low tolerance for frustration.

Membership in a role category, be it age, sex, ethnic group, or class, is also accompanied by the inference that the classification of self is appropriate. An 18-year-old American male has been taught that a strongly felt desire for a romantic and sexual relation with a female is one of the critical attributes of his gender. If he does not experience that motivation, he has a puzzle to solve. Our society provides him with a classification that is presumed to explain the absence of the expected inner experience. He infers that he must be a homosexual, an inference that resolves the uncertainty surrounding the inconsistency between his original sex role assignment and his lack of motivation, and one that leads usually to a new set of behaviors.

As we indicated earlier, the child's belief that he is valued or disliked is a guess based on many pieces of information that have been woven into a coherent theme. Because our society, unlike small, isolated, subsistence farming villages, permits the child and adolescent many alternatives for action and judges the child by the consequences of his choices, the most critical beliefs held by a child are those that summarize his attributes—assets as well as liabilities—and his expectations of attaining culturally desired goals. These structures are profoundly complex inferences—summaries taken from an enormously large number of separate and usually inconsistent experiences. When we say a person's fate lies in his character we imply that it is difficult to alter these deep suppositions that took so long to create.

Therapeutic intervention, be it weekly psychotherapy, daily tutoring in arithmetic, or a change of foster homes, is an attempt to provide the child with information that will be inconsistent with an existing belief deemed to be maladaptive. The hope is that the child will use the new information to generate a new inference that is likely to facilitate constructive action. In a compelling essay on the bases for change following therapeutic intervention, Albert Bandura has written: "Change is achieved by different methods derived from a common cognitive mechanism. The apparent divergence of theory and practice can be reconciled by postulating that cognitive processes mediate change but that cognitive events are induced and altered most readily by experience of mastery arising from effective performance" (Bandura 1977, p. 191).

The resistance to placing inference in such a central psychological position has been due, in part, to the historical commitment to an isomorphism between experience and resulting cognitive structures, a belief that was remarkably strong in the nineteenth century. In an attempt to limit the possible psychological outcomes of an event, theorists assumed that there was a very specific and knowable relation between a particular event—be it a loud noise or a spanking—and a consequent effect on brain or mind. Indeed, the central presupposition in Piagetian theory is that the structures of modern logic are demanded by the everyday experiences children have with objects and people. There is reason, however, to doubt the strictness of the correlation and to affirm that empirical information is necessary but insufficient. For example, consider the standard procedure used to assess conservation of number in the young child. A 5-year-old is shown four objects lined up in one-to-one correspondence and affirms that the two rows have the same number of objects. If, as in the standard Piagetian procedure, the adult examiner moves the objects in one row closer together so they occupy less space, the 5-year-old child says that the new shorter row has fewer objects. But suppose the objects are moved in a different way. Specifically, the examiner says that there is a naughty teddy bear who continually messes up his toys; she then uses the teddy bear to create the same alteration in the perceptual appearance of the array. Now the 5-year-old insists that the two rows have the same number of objects (McGarrigle and Donaldson 1975). The child assumes that reduction in length of the row was only accidental with the teddy bear. Even in the restricted test situation we call conservation of number, the child is making inferences about the actions of the examiner.

Two tentative principles can guide a better understanding of development. The more fragile the knowledge base, the less predictable the inference. Thus young children hold many private and enigmatic beliefs that surprise us and are difficult for us to comprehend. The 5-year-old is gullible and easily persuaded to believe in the existence of an invisible string or a ghost because each imaginary entity can be a reasonable inference from a given experience.

A more important principle is that changes in structure require an incentive for a new inference, and variety in daily experience contains those incentives. We believe this is why the belief systems of most American children are less rigid than those held by most children in the large number of isolated settings that exist in the world. The more isolated children are less often provoked to examine existing ideas and to question the legitimacy of their beliefs.

External demands Finally, environmental demands for new behaviors and cognitive talents can also mediate transitions. A 7-year-old Kipsigis girl is asked to care for her baby sister; an American 7-year-old is required to read and write. An adolescent who must care for his unexpectedly widowed mother inhibits his existing dispositions toward dependency and learns how to balance the family budget. External demands force the invention of new beliefs and skills. New information gives the child more choice and a more leisurely context for emergence of a new idea.

Of the three bases for transition, the first is the most uniform because it is part of our inheritance. Transitions that follow encounter with new information and environmental demands are less orderly because we cannot easily control or predict them. Biological maturation of psychological competences forms the spine of development, guaranteeing that the 12-year-old will be able to remember an instruction with six different elements, while the 4-year-old will not. But biological development cannot guarantee that all 12-year-olds will believe they are either happier than their parents or confident that they will be able to deal with most problems. Variation in psychological growth is due not only to variation in rate of maturation of the central nervous system but also to the extraordinary variability in encounter with dissonant information and external demands. If two 15-year-old girls, one from a large city and one from a village in Guatemala, were set down in a hostile, unfamiliar environment—a hut on the Antarctic ice shelf—their differential adaptation would be more a function of prior exposure to new information and demands than to the maturational age of their central nervous systems. Prolonged isolation of primates does not impair basic cognitive competences, but does affect the ease with which the animal adjusts to unfamiliar situations. Perhaps that is why the Western youngster might have the advantage in our hypothetical relocation, for she has experienced a more varied and challenging environment.

The earth is ready to accept seed in April but someone must exploit that readiness. Environmental opportunities must be present to provoke use of a competence that has matured. One of the ongoing debates among psychologists concerns the reasons for differences in cognitive functioning among children from varied social classes, as well as variation within a particular class. A few psychologists assume that the central nervous system of some children is basically defective and that some competences simply are not present. Others believe the central nervous system is maturing more slowly in some children, and so the child is temporarily retarded. Still others argue that the environment has not demanded the competence; therefore, the child has not mapped it onto a performance.

The forces that act on the growing child bear a nice relation to those that influence the development of a queen bee. The genetic and environmental factors represented by biological constitution, nutrition, and temperature interact to determine which egg of the many will become queen. But once a queen emerges, she emits a chemical substance that prevents new queens from developing. A similar force exercises some control of the child's development. The mere presence of a more talented child affects a particular youngster's expectations and motivations. Later-born siblings in America are less likely than firstborns to attain exceptional school grades or achieve positions of eminence. The social context has a determining influence beyond the biological constitution and historical experiences of a particular child. Two 3-year-olds with equivalent biologies and past histories will develop differently if they are placed permanently in new social contexts where one is the most talented and the other only moderately so.

A child can develop a behavior profile of withdrawal or deference as an accommodation to a history of parental domination. But the same posture can arise, as if spontaneously, if the child is placed in a situation with several more dominant peers, regardless of the child's past disposition. Nine out of ten 18-month-olds will, regardless of their basic personality, exhibit a short period of inhibition when they discover an unfamiliar child in a room where they had been happily playing moments earlier. One reason prediction of developmental outcomes is difficult, even when we think we know the genetic predisposition of the child and the history of past experience, is that we cannot know the future contexts in which the child will be placed. That may be one reason the intraindividual stability coefficients for cognitive, motivational and behavioral qualities rarely rise above 0.5.

The psychological consequences of maturation of the central nervous system are not knowledge, but changes in process—better memory or the ability to coordinate information more quickly. As a result of the new process new cognitive structures are built. Once one is able to hold two ideas simultaneously and examine them together, one can detect their relation and create a new concept. Thus structural change often follows the introduction of a new function. But structural changes enhance existing processes, for enhanced articulation of an idea makes it easier to remember, to analyze, or to use it as symbol and metaphor. Hence the novelties that Piaget has said are the essences of a particular stage of development have at least two different origins, one in the maturing processes, the other in the developing cognitive structures.

The relation between biological maturation and psychological experience

Tension always surrounds discussions about separate biological and psychological determinants of growth, for there is still confusion over the meaning of the relation between these terms.

The lawful changes that occur over the life span are obviously under the direction of the rather strict script contained in the genome, which guarantees that we will crawl before we run and babble before we speak. All 2-year-olds carry a small number of potentialities that attract them to contour and curvilinearity and dispose them to stop playing when an unexpected event occurs. Ernst Mayr (1974) has called these *closed systems*. The *open systems* are created by the experiential events that control the variability and time of appearance of inherited competences as well as the intensity, frequency, and asymptotic level of functioning of these dispositions. The open systems delineate the profile of psychological characteristics that allow us to detect class, regional, ethnic, and national differences with greater ease than is good for us or for society. The complementary action of closed and open systems is a new way of phrasing the sentence that appears in every textbook on human behavior: "The interactions between biological and environmental forces determine the psychological growth of the organism." What in heaven's name does that fourteen-word sentence mean?

We cannot answer that question definitively and invent a crisp metaphor for the textbook phrase for several reasons. One reason stems from the historical debate between science and the church that began almost five centuries ago. The two institutions became accommodated to one another following a treaty that awarded material events to science and psychic ones to the church. Each was supposed to honor the intellectual sovereignty of the other. The major philosophical statements of the seventeenth and eighteenth centuries were attempts to keep the truce sturdy, as science became stronger and the church weaker. A second reason is less profound but of consequence. Analysis, which is the preferred mode of science, assumes a special form in psychology. Since psychological phenomena are so variable, social scientists were drawn to statistical techniques that assumed—as an unproven presupposition—that one could analyze a unitary phenomenon, say the child's height, achievement score in reading, or hallucination, into its separate biological and experiential causes and assign a weight to each. We resist Whitehead's metaphysics, which assumes that the raw materials of science are occasions of experience, each with a duration and an essential unity that is a synthesis of the individual components that comprise it.

"Any attempt to analyze it [the occasional experience] into component parts injures it in some way. But we cannot do anything with it unless we do analyze it. A first step toward analysis is to dissect the unity into an experiencing subject and an experienced object. The dividing line between these two is both arbitrary and artificial. It can be drawn through various positions and wherever it is drawn it is never anything more than a convenience" (Waddington 1975, p. 4).

A favorite model of explanation is the multiple regression equation with its partial coefficients that assume that some causes are more important than others. This model permeates our daily practices and our conceptualization of nature and prevents us from viewing an event as a product of a coherence of forces. Consider a Christmas snowfall created by the complementary interaction of humidity and temperature. It seems inappropriate to ask which factor is more critical, or to assign different beta weights to temperature and humidity. We seem to have less trouble acknowledging such complementary interactions when both forces act in a material mode than when the names for the forces originate in different linguistic domains —like biology and psychology. The power of biological analyses has persuaded us of the utility of treating discrete, material, neurological elements as primary and the less discrete psychological events as derivative of the former. But consider the case of a Taiwanese merchant who visits a shaman because of a chronic pain in his chest. The shaman tells the merchant he has angered an ancestor; if he makes restitution he will be relieved. The merchant leaves the shaman with less distress than when he arrived (Kleinman 1975).

Many Western psychiatrists and psychologists are likely to spend hours arguing whether the symptom was primarily due to psychological or to physiological factors. But suppose there is a synergy between the merchant's physiology and his psychology. Many Taiwanese with his physiology but fewer worries might not develop his somatic symptoms; many with his collection of uncertainties but not his physiology would not have the distress. An infant with damage of the brain stem following perinatal trauma who is raised in a familial environment where no psychological acceleration occurs will display some cognitive deficits at age six. With the same set of birth conditions a child growing up in an environment that provides many opportunities for cognitive development is less likely to display the intellectual deficit. A black child in an all-white classroom experiences a quality of psychological tension that he would not experience in a classroom of black children. Such examples illustrate a more general principle; namely, mutual interaction between an element and the larger field in which it exists creates a new entity. The new entity is not a part of either the element or the field, and the sentences that describe the transcendental—or emergent—entity cannot be completely replaced with sentences that describe the original element and field without losing some meaning. A hallucination is a part neither of the brain nor of the structures created by past history. Physics provides the best metaphor: An accelerating electric charge is placed in an electromagnetic field and they mutually influence each other. The charge is described in terms of velocity and energy, the field in terms of strength, and their interaction produces a third, quite different phenomenon, radiation, which is described in terms of frequency. The radiation is neither part of the field nor part of the charge; it is a product of the interaction of charge and field.

Psychological phenomena—the perception of red, the ability to recall five numbers, or smiling in response to a face—are analogous to radiation. They are the result of the mutual interaction of particular neural structures and processes in the larger field we call the central nervous system. The perception of red is no more a part of the cells of the retina, thalamus, or cortex than radiation is part of the field or electric charge that generated it. Biological forces contribute to and are necessary for psychological phenomena, but the characteristics of the latter are, like radiation, a product of the interaction. The most detailed knowledge of neural organization, including all the significant synapses in the embryo of a chicken, for example, at a given stage of embryogenesis, would not permit prediction of the actual movements of the embryo at that stage. All we can say is that the state of differentiation of the nervous system at a given stage limits the range of behavioral potentialities. The maturation of the nervous system sets serious constraints on the range of behaviors possible but cannot explain them.

Selecting a question

To return to a question posed at the outset: How does a scientist decide what is a significant question in which to invest effort? "It is an individual and subjective matter not amenable to rational analysis," is a popular but perhaps hasty reply. There are periods in the history of scientific disciplines when scholars lose direction and barbaric empiricism dominates inquiry. A discipline is most vulnerable to this mood when it is without a sturdy theoretical structure and is forced to use intuition or the pragmatic press of social need, which are usually noncomplementary, as a guide to investigation.

Psychology has been in this unfortunate state for almost a decade, ever since psychologists recognized that the accumulated evidence did not permit continued loyalty to either psychoanalytic or behavioral theory, both of which had provided direction to experimentation for close to one-half century. The primary mission of science is to provide evidence that allows the scientific community to decide whether an integrative hypothesis is more or less useful. Although psychology has not had many such significant hypotheses in recent years, the apparatus of science has not been dismantled and an inherent momentum has kept the machinery running. The consequences have been a literature that has become increasingly fragmented, a graduate student body that does not appreciate the difference between a significant question and a trivial one (although it does understand the difference between difficult and easy experiments), and an ennui among some practitioners of this science. Journalists and legislators may sense this impotence, for attacks on science are stronger and more confident in the social than in the natural sciences.

Although it is not possible to write algorithms for initiating research, informal criteria can be applied to evaluate the theoretical relevance of a particular question. At least three factors determine the importance of an empirical question at a particular time in the history of a discipline. We shall not comment on the morality of whether the problem should be investigated, only on the judgment of the potential importance of the work. We use the simple word *important* because it summarizes a primary incentive for the scientist—especially the active, young investigator, who wants to feel both creative and useful while gaining recognition from his elders. Important research is likely to bring both prizes.

Society's view—relevance Public and private institutions as well as citizens with power can and do determine the relative significance of a problem. If the public is concerned with an issue that can be clarified by information, the scientist will be tempted to categorize that question as important. This class of problem has acquired the adjective "relevant," and we are witness to a major accommodation to this source of pressure as private and federal funding sources give increasing priority to relevant research. The effect of teaching styles or a new curriculum on school achievement, the effect of a new drug or form of psychotherapy on remission of symptoms, the persuasiveness of birth control propaganda, and the effect of day care on child development are of this class. Because the promise of funds and a feeling of effectiveness are the potential dividends for relevant work, it is easy to tempt scientists to use the larger community's opinion as the sole basis for choice.

It is instructive to compare the current list of relevant topics with the list of twenty-five years ago, which would have included the etiology of school phobia, the determinants of morale in the armed forces, and the validity of projective tests of personality. It is not that these three problems are less complex or have been solved, but rather that each seems less urgent now. It has become less fashionable to study these questions, in part because the community focus has shifted to other claimants for its attention.

The scientist's view—unexplained order The scientist's criterion for importance is more likely to be the existence of an orderly natural phenomenon that is incompletely understood. The reason for ocean tides, falling objects, eclipses, and the cooling of hot bodies attracted seventeenth-century scholars because of the unexplained predictability of these events. Psychology has its share of unexplained regularities—the acquisition of language between one and five years, the seasonal migrations of birds and fish, the infant's fear of strangers and separation from parents, the effect of temporal lobe lesions on cognitive functioning, and changes in moral reasoning with age are only a few of the puzzles to be solved. Some of these questions meet the first criterion of relevance; most do not.

Often scientists assume there is a greater range of regularity than is warranted, because they have not sampled the events in question in a sufficiently broad set of contexts or among a sufficiently large variety of subjects. Early investigations using white rats found that a delay of greater than one second between the conditioned and the unconditioned stimuli regularly impaired the classic conditioning of a response, and it was believed that a universal principle had been discovered. However, the work of John Garcia and his colleagues reveals that rats can learn a conditioned avoidance response to toxic substances with temporal delays of hours (Garcia et al. 1966).

The detection of regularity need not be accompanied by an elegant explanatory hypothesis during the initial stages of inquiry. The initial discovery and early probing of alpha waves were not associated with complex explanatory statements; the explanations were generated long after the accumulation of data. Of course, serendipity favors the sophisticated mind, but a continued vigilance for disguised regularities that may cloak a universal relation may be the most neglected trait in young scientists. When chance and keenness of mind combine to lead to the discovery of another regular relation, the work is usually judged to be significant.

The ideal answer A third criterion for importance of a question is the most subjective, but perhaps the most influential in determining the potential importance of an empirical pursuit. Most scientists hold a conception, often poorly articulated, of the basic enigma they wish to understand. A set of interpretive statements with particular conceptual terms is linked to this conception. Usually scientists cannot work directly on the basic question because of inadequate methodology. The empiricist therefore selects a problem he believes to be closely related to the prototypic question, trusting that interpretation of the data generated by the derivative problem will inform the more seminal theme.

Consider a few examples. Some psychologists who wished to understand how children learn arithmetic might have chosen to study an animal's ability to learn a maze, trusting that the interpretive statements to be applied to the latter problem could be appropriately applied to the former. Drive, reinforcement, delay of reward, schedule of reinforcement, and distinctiveness of cues, which are the concepts that bear the burden of explanation in maze-learning, were applied for a period to the description and interpretation of the acquisition of academic skills. With the advantage of hindsight, we now realize that the application is questionable. But there are instances when the generalization is more reasonable. Many psychologists believe that lower-class children do not learn new ideas or perform well in school, even when they possess the necessary competence, because they have a low expectancy of success. They feel helpless to gain the goal they desire. Martin Seligman (1975) found that dogs who first experienced electric shocks they could not avoid, later failed to learn relevant information that would have made it possible to avoid shocks. Seligman used the term "learned helplessness" to explain his results. Until additional data lead us to question the utility of that concept, it seems more reasonable to generalize from Seligman's studies to the classroom than from maze-learning to the classroom.

The reasonableness of the relation between a particular study and the larger problem defines the significance of the work. The student is often demoralized after his first few investigations, for he tends to see the study as the isolated goal and loses sight of the relation between his interpretation of the data he is gathering and a more fundamental puzzle. The scientist can evaluate the potential significance of a specific investigation by analyzing the similarity between the form and content of the statements he expects to use on the data he is gathering and the form and content of the type of interpretive statements he would like to use to resolve the ultimate problem. If there is overlap between the sets of propositions, the problem is more likely to be significant.

Let us contrast two scientists, both of whom regard the potentiality for chronic depression as a significant problem but who hold different sets of idealized interpretive statements. One thinks in terms of uncertainty, dissonance, and violation of standards; the other in terms of hormonal and biochemical changes, perhaps involving adrenalin and dopamine. Each would and should pursue different experimentation. However, if the scientist who views depression as a function of guilt were to initiate a study of behavioral effects of punishment in rats, it is less likely he would gain significant information on the primary issue than if he were to study transgressions in children.

An empirical study that fills all three criteria—relevance, regularity, and consonance of current inquiry with the idealized problem—is likely to award the psychologist the greatest personal satisfaction. Although the primary question that provoked and funded the work reported in this book was the socially relevant issue of the effect of day care on early development, we designed our evaluations to provide information on some basic theoretical issues in early development. During the opening two years of life, attentiveness, vocalization, smiling, and fearfulness display regular growth functions, but we do not yet understand the relation among these dispositions nor the effect of varied experience or infant temperament on the profile of behavioral display.

A second theoretical issue is the predictive power of variation during the first year of life—the question of continuity throughout early development. We wished to gather information on this theme and devised procedures that would maximize the similarity in response classes across the period of study.

The procedures we chose were consonant with our prejudices that cognitive processes are central in development and that the maturation of new cognitive competences permits new affects and behavior patterns to appear. We suppose that the maturation of the central nervous system leads to major changes in the cognitive functioning of the infant and we wanted to describe part of that process. Finally, we are not friendly to the construct of a general intellectual ability or developmental quotient and favor instead a classification that fragments the competences of the young child into classes of processes-*cum*-contexts, a view promoted by J. P. Guilford (1959) for adolescents and adults.

These idealized conceptions led us to concentrate on assessment procedures that brought us as close as possible to the infant's perceptual and cognitive functioning rather than his maturing motor abilities. Our preference for postulating specific cognitive functions led us to minimize the amount of time we devoted to standard tests that yield developmental quotients (we did give some Bayley items); hence we did not administer the Stanford-Binet at the last assessment at twenty-nine months. The interpretive statements we wanted to impose on the data could not accept IQ as a main semantic term. The belief—call it illusion if you wish—that we were providing information on both socially relevant and theoretically significant questions permitted us to maintain a zeal throughout the investigation that is the essential reward of scientific work and to make play of what appeared to some to be hard work.

In other sciences or in other historical periods the foregoing discussion might seem such a statement of the obvious that one might charitably assume it was written by three senile academicians for an after-dinner speech to a chamber of commerce. But psychology seems to us to have lost its way. The loss of faith in both behavioral and psychoanalytic theory has left the discipline without a conceptual edifice to which fealty can be given and from which ideas for experiments can be easily drawn. This loss of guidance has been accompanied by a mistrust of ideas and an excessive reliance on significant statistics. If a positive correlation of + .30 between height of teacher and improvement in reading in a Montana second grade classroom, even though unexpected and probably not replicable, is given the same respect as a correlation of + .30 between the growth of linguistic competence during the first three years in siblings, we are in serious trouble. On occasion we behave as if numbers cannot lie. Psychologists should be more cognizant of the history of our sister sciences. Lord Kelvin, one of the most eminent scientists of the nineteenth century, made Darwin apprehensive because Kelvin's calculations indicated that the earth was not old enough to have undergone the long evolutionary changes Darwin's theory required. It turned out that Kelvin's numbers were incorrect. If every investigator reflected more seriously on the sensibleness of his data and the explanatory language applied to them, psychology might progress at a rate more commensurate with the profundity of its social responsibilities and the complexity of its themes.

2 The Infant

> Many writers on theory of knowledge held that from a single occurrence nothing is to be learnt. They think of all empirical knowledge as consisting of inductions from a number of more or less similar experiences. For my part, I think that such a view makes history impossible and memory unintelligible. I hold that, from any occurrence that a man notices, he can obtain knowledge . . .
>
> Bertrand Russell, *An Inquiry into Meaning and Truth*

Each generation of parents holds a set of beliefs regarding the essential nature of the infant, the human qualities valued by the local community, an informal theory that stipulates the experiences and supernatural interventions that can enhance or retard the child's acquisition of those qualities, and a subjective estimate of the likelihood that the child will eventually command the valued characteristics should the family make the necessary investment of emotional and material resources. Before the changes in attitudes that followed the Second World War, Japanese parents regarded the infant as untamed and autonomous (Caudill and Weinstein 1969). Because both child and adult must be able to enter into deeply dependent relations with others—called *amae* (Akita 1970)—the mother's task is to draw the baby into intimate dependency on her through quiet, conscientious nurturance. By contrast, the modern American mother projects dependence and helplessness on her infant. She realizes that relentless autonomy will be required of the adolescent, and so she promotes independence in her young child. Thus, while the distressed Japanese infant is attended with short delay, the American baby is often allowed to cry for a few minutes, presumably to prepare him for more serious future frustrations.

The Rajput mother of Northern India assumes a less active role than either the Japanese or American. Since the Rajput believe the future is controlled by supernatural powers, and since the occupational future of the child is relatively certain—the boy will be a farmer and the girl will be a farmer's wife—there is little motivation for them to intrude into the infant's life. So for most of the first two years the child is a passive observer of experience (Minturn and Hitchcock 1963).

Plato's suggestions to Athenian parents illustrate nicely the relation between the conception of the ideal and the local theory of development. Because fourth-century Greeks idealized the harmonious coordination of mind and body, Plato advised mothers to keep their infants in motion and to rock them to sleep rhythmically (Jaeger 1944). The early exposure to rhythm presumably sensitized the infant, making it easier for the adolescent to master difficult motor coordinations. The dynamic hypothesis that seems to underlie the advice is probably not much different from the one held by American parents. If one were to ask American parents what practices they should initiate with the infant so that the adolescent would appreciate music, the common reply would probably be, "Play good music to them." The assumption made by both Plato and the contemporary parent reduces to the following imperative: In order to promote an affinity and preparedness for a competence in later childhood, expose the infant to some reasonable representation of the relevant experience.

Plato's theory of the origin of adolescent sulkiness or aggression was also not much different from our own: A coddled baby becomes a sulky adolescent; a bullied baby becomes a misanthrope. Since there was no good support for either statement, then or now, the fact that advisers 2,400 years after Plato make the same assumptions he did says more about how the adult mind works than it does about the development of the child. It is easy, however, to surmise how adults might come to such conclusions. Parents who respond every time their babies cry tend to have more irritable babies, at least temporarily. The association between adult practice and infant attribute has been noted by many, but it cannot be assumed that the trait induced in infancy would persist indefinitely. Such a prejudice ignores the fact that with maturity the child becomes aware of the standards of his culture and begins to relinquish habits that his family dislikes. Because sulkiness is not generally admired, the child can relinquish the habit, just as he gives up his earlier dispositions to soil his clothes and spill his cereal. But because the best guess about the future is the present, if there is no other information, Plato's prophecy is reasonable (Jaeger 1944).

Freedom from fear was another central quality of the ego ideal, or *paideia*, of fourth-century Greece. Because adolescents were to suppress apprehension, Plato suggested exposing the baby to events that would help him conquer early fears, an ancient example of desensitization theory that is also applied by the Gusii of Kenya (LeVine 1963). Many nineteenth-century Europeans held the opposite belief. Dr. P. Chavasse, a pediatrician who wrote popular books of advice, warned parents that if adults told the young child frightening stories, he would become timid and "continue so for the remainder of his life" (Chavasse 1869, p. 169). The nineteenth-century Europeans' wary attitude toward fear was a specific instance of their more general concern with any source of excessive excitement in the child. Excessive use of mind could cause too much blood to flow to the brain, they thought, and produce an inflammation that might lead to insanity or idiocy. "How proud a mother is at having her precocious child; how little is she aware that precocity is frequently an indication of disease" (Chavasse 1869, p. 361).

Chavasse's conviction that fright was physically and psychologically dangerous has a parallel among many Mayan descendants living in northwest Guatemala, who believe that *susto*—best translated as fear—can produce serious illness. Indeed, they believe that if an adult is suddenly frightened, his heart can tear away from the thoracic cavity, rise to the throat, and choke him. They usually restrict the infant during most of the first year in order to prevent chance encounter with people or objects that might provoke fear.

Because reality continuously monitors parental apprehensions, local health conditions strongly influence the hierarchy of parental concerns. In the majority of the world's isolated subsistence farming communities, infancy is a period in which illness and death are common, and supernatural forces—the evil eye, divine powers, tainted caretakers—are believed to be causes of catastrophe. There is less concern than in modern countries with accelerating mental and motor development, for the major task of infancy is to survive it. Preoccupation with the infant's health was also characteristic of eighteenth- and nineteenth-century Europe, where most professional advice focused on the health of both mother and wet nurse, especially the quality of breast milk. The introduction of sterile water, pasteurized milk, vaccinations, and uniformly better medical care muted these worries and replaced them with concern over the child's psychological growth. Modern parents assume that most of the serious problems of infancy are psychological in nature and are mediated by the actions of caretakers. Americans therefore regard a rejecting attitude and failure to play with the infant with the same alarm as seventeenth-century English pediatricians regarded the quality of a diseased mother's milk or unclean nipples. Thus, the facts of everyday life monitor adult concern, whether its focus is physical health, psychological retardation, excessive fearfulness, or intellectual precocity. At the same time, the history of the culture influences both the local theory used to explain distress and the rituals to be initiated in order to prevent and alleviate symptoms and hasten the child's protected movement toward maturity.

A metaphor for infancy: the Darwinian heritage

Just as each society holds a local theory about the basic nature of the young child, investigators too hold presuppositions about the essence of infancy. They are often influenced by a dominant scientific paradigm with explicit implications for the human psyche and an implicit metaphor for infancy.

A good example from recent history is contained in the essays on the infant that followed the publication of Darwin's evolutionary theory. By positing a continuum in evolution, Charles Darwin reclassified the human species and its infants as members of the category "animal." Animal behavior was regarded as instinctive, inflexible, and therefore resistant to change, and so a paradox was created. How was it possible for man to be varied in custom and habit—so flexible and progressive—if he were such a close relative of creatures whose behavior appeared to be excessively stereotyped and rigid? One way to resolve the dilemma was to attribute importance to the period of infant helplessness in humans because it seemed more prolonged than that of other animals. Because most nineteenth-century scholars assumed that all qualities of living things had a purpose, it was reasonable to ask about the purpose of man's prolonged infancy. John Fiske, among others, argued that infancy was a period of maximal plasticity, the time when adults were to teach children skills and ideas they would carry with them throughout life.

In a lecture at Harvard in 1871, Fiske noted that man's power to control his environment and to enhance progress had to be due to his educability—a potential Fiske believed animals lacked. How then to explain why man was so educable? Using popular rules of inference, Fiske looked for other major differences between man and animal, and of the many candidates he could have selected—language, the opposable thumb, upright stature, an omnivorous diet, sexual activity throughout the year and not just during estrus—he selected the prolongation of infancy. By the logic of his argument, nature had to have an intended purpose for the incompetence and dependence of the initial three years of human life. Since the most likely purpose is to educate the child, he asserted, it must be the case that the child is maximally malleable or susceptible to training during that early period. That conclusion was congruent with a deep belief in continuity of character from infancy to later childhood; it served to keep parents self-conscious about their actions with their babies; and it was an argument for building good schools. It also provided an experiential explanation for individual differences in adult success, which was attractive to a democratic and egalitarian society (Fiske 1883).

Many writers have stated as casually as they would remark about the weather that the obvious purpose of the long period of infant helplessness is to render the infant susceptible to experience and to the parents' molding of his character. At the turn of the century, Millicent Washburn Shinn had anticipated Hebb's hypothesis (1949) that with phylogeny the period of early learning was extended in the service of producing a more complex organism. Shinn wrote, "Nothing is so helpless as the human baby and that helplessness is our glory for it means that the activities of the race have become too many, too complex, too infrequently repeated to become fixed in the nervous structure before birth; hence the long period after birth before the child comes to full human powers. It is a maxim of biology that while an organism is thus immature and plastic it may learn, it may change, it may rise to higher development and thus to infancy we owe the rank of the human race" (Shinn 1900, p. 33).

The infant's helplessness was a gift to our species, a sign of the child's preparedness to be tutored and an invitation to parents to begin to shape the plastic creature nature awarded them. There are of course no sound empirical or theoretical reasons for assuming a relation between the prolonged period of instrumental incompetence in the human species and a receptivity to environmental intrusions that is greater than the receptivity of infants of other species. Animal behavior is extremely vulnerable to experience. Monkeys placed in black boxes for six months emerge with bizarre habits, whereas human infants growing up in a variety of environmental contexts display the same developmental milestones in the same sequence. But Fiske's principles seemed intuitively correct and effectively resolved the paradox created by Darwinian theory.

Accepting Darwin's notion that man is on a biological continuum with animals Ernst Haeckel coined a catchy phrase—ontogeny recapitulates phylogeny. This principle provided a guide to observers of the infant. The child revealed what we inherited from our primate progenitors; watching the baby in the protective quiet of the sunlit nursery was a way to observe the wild panorama of evolution. The facial frown, piercing cry, and energetic flailing of the infant's arms were directly traceable to our untamed ape ancestors. Early scientific investigations of the infant were also influenced by a much older idea, promoted by Jeremy Bentham, that the purposes of a child's actions are to maximize pleasure and to avoid pain.

Reports published near the turn of the century consisted of naturalistic impressions of both sequences of motor behavior and patterns of vocalization, crying, smiling, and laughing that presumably reflected states of fear, anger, and pleasure. The affects of loneliness, sadness, and pride were generally ignored, for it was fear and anger that announced man's kinship with animals. Moreover, while the nineteenth-century metaphor for the infant was incompetence, the metaphor for the 3-year-old was selfishness. In a book popular during the last fifteen years of the century, the author suggested that the child naturally developed egoism, narcissism, and individualism: "If we wish to understand the meaning of the actions of little children and to direct their wills in a useful and progressive manner, we must bear in mind that all their tendencies, whatever they may be, begin and end with egoism" (Perez 1888, p. 290).

Perez ignored the 3-year-old who kissed his mother, played with his baby sibling, or offered restitution to a child he had just struck—behaviors that did not seem egoistic. He advised that egoism must be tamed through moral training by parents. Central to this training was insistence on obedience and an encouragement of the reflective judgment necessary to control passion, aggression, and narcissism. The assumption that the will of the young child had to be tamed was popular with many nineteenth-century parents who probably would not have quarrelled with the statement that "the right of the parent is to command, the duty of the child is to obey. Authority belongs to the one, submission to the other . . . In infancy the control of the parent is absolute, that is, it is exercised without any due respect to the wishes of the child'' (McLaughlin 1975, p. 22). And at least one upper-class parent, the Reverend Francis Wayland, was not reluctant to starve his 15-month-old son into obedience when the infant refused a piece of bread proffered by a generous father (McLaughlin 1975).

By contrast, American parents now regard spontaneity and autonomy, rather than control and obedience, as the central traits to promote and would regard the behavior of the Reverend Wayland, the fourth president of Brown University, as an instance of child abuse. The twentieth century encourages the emotional expressiveness the nineteenth century wanted to curb because parents believe that free access to affect and autonomous posture toward others will be adaptive when today's infants become tomorrow's young adults.

The initial studies

The joint influence of the evolutionary doctrine, which claimed for the infant a maturational sequence of fixed action patterns, and the assumption of malleability to tutoring, which laid emphasis on learning, led to two movements in the early study of the infant. One group, led by Mary Shirley, Henry Halverson, Arnold Gesell, Orvis Irwin, Wayne Dennis, Myrtle McGraw, Karl Pratt, and Nancy Bayley, studied the maturation of the young infant's locomotor and instrumental competences. This group dominated American child psychology during the early decades of the twentieth century. The second group, led by John Watson, was less active empirically (it was not until the 1950s that rigorous studies of infant conditioning and learning were initiated) but had strong theoretical force.

Then a significant event occurred that had little to do with infancy and that, in the opinion of some, was probably unfortunate. Binet's original intelligence test, invented during the first decade of the twentieth century, was standardized as the Stanford-Binet test, and psychologists began to promote the idea, latent in the society, that infants inherited differing amounts of an entity called intelligence. That seemingly innocuous premise, not present in Binet's original conception, motivated developmental psychologists to study this hypothetical quality during the first years of life. As a result, scales of infant intelligence were developed. Nancy Bayley in Berkeley, California, and Arnold Gesell in New Haven, Connecticut, were among the leaders of this movement, and their scales of development, along with those of Psyche Cattell and Charlotte Buhler, became popular. Bayley did most of her important work between 1933 and 1945, Gesell between 1922 and 1946. While Bayley did not make any strong theoretical statements about the meaning of the developmental quotient, Gesell did, and his writing articulated a controversy that had been partially veiled—the degree to which maturation or learning controlled development. Gesell assumed that the developmental quotient reflected the child's differential rate of growth at the moment of testing. There was no constraint on that statement. The quotient did not refer to a specific domain of development but rather to the whole child—in anticipation of Spearman's *g*. Although Gesell acknowledged that the concept of constancy of development rate seemed naive and unsophisticated, he argued that, considering the state of methodology, it was serviceable. Pragmatic considerations took priority over good sense.

It is not surprising that much interest was generated by the new infant intelligence tests. The historical events that produced an industrialized technology helped to make intellectual skills the sine qua non for psychological survival and one's vocation the most critical component of the definition of self—more central than family, clan, ethnicity, religion, or place of residence.

"What do you do?" is one of the first questions one asks of another on an airplane or at a party, and the brief answer—a word or two—places the respondent in a category that defines his status, power, economic potential, and intelligence in a way that almost parallels the potent symbolism of caste in India. A large proportion of modern parents want their children to be white-collar professionals and recognize that an education of good quality is the most important prerequisite to attaining that goal. The quality of an education, in turn, necessitates acquiring the skills and values that permit good academic performance during the first twelve years of school. If that goal is attained, entrance into a good college and professional school will be easier. The intellectual competence of a child is, therefore, a more salient source of uncertainty for the average American parent than the child's health, character, physical prowess, or virtue. Contemporary scientists study the effect of prematurity, prenatal stress, perinatal trauma, or early malnutrition on intellectual functioning, rarely on motivation, temperament, or physical endurance. Advice to mothers emphasizes rituals and the purchase of toys that are supposed to promote precocious growth of cognitive skills, rather than interventions that might affect cooperativeness, honesty, vitality, or empathy. Since the Enlightenment, and in an accelerated fashion since the Industrial Revolution, we have needed an increasing number of technically trained adults. When a society needs to fill a role, it awards to those who can assume the role all the secular prizes it commands and invents instruments to monitor the degree to which its youth are acquring the critical role-defining qualities. These assessments are done regularly, so that everyone knows who is likely to make steady progress toward the goal and who might drop along the way. It is not surprising that during the early decades of this century tests of infant intelligence were developed, whereas tests of infant empathy, strength, sociability, or irritability were not. These last qualities did not seem to bear any relation to the final goal; the others did.

The influence of Freudian theory

Although study of the development of mental and motor competence dominated child psychology during the first three decades of the century, beneath the surface lay an uneasiness that was based in part on the political philosophy of the two major Protestant nations in the Western community. America and England wanted to believe in the eventual attainment of an egalitarian society where, if conditions of early life were optimal, all citizens potentially could attain dignity and participate effectively in the society. Indeed, almost two centuries earlier, just before the American Revolution, journalists, ministers, and statesmen wrote impassioned essays stressing how important early family treatment and proper education of the child were to prevent crime and safeguard democracy. Despotism could be eliminated if all children were well nurtured and properly educated, a conviction not unlike Plato's assumption that if one knew what was good, immorality was impossible. From America's birth until the present a majority has believed that the correct pattern of experiences at home and school would guarantee a harmonious society. This view, which was in accord with the doctrine of infant malleability, invited each generation of parents to project onto the infant their political hopes for the future. Every infant was a fresh canvas, and the community was ready to receive a psychological theory that would make social experience the major steward of growth. When psychoanalytic theory was introduced to the United States during the 1920s and 1930s, the academy therefore gave it a warm reception. Until that time the infant had been seen as a socially isolated organism impelled by inevitable maturational forces. Psychoanalytic theory placed the child in a social matrix in which the parents' actions became a central determinant of the child's development and a phenomenon to study in its own right. It is possible that one reason psychoanalytic theory was more popular in the United States than in continental Europe was that America wanted to believe in the infant's susceptibility to adult influence. American parents were ready to celebrate a theory of development that made family primary and treated infancy as the optimal time to mold the child, as Shinn and Fiske had insisted several decades earlier.

Freud also implied that the family had a prophylactic force. Although Freud was as concerned with the creation of healthy, mature adults as he was with the avoidance of psychological distress, those who promoted Freudian theory in the 1940s and 1950s subtly shifted the emphasis to the latter issue. The infant was considered vulnerable to trauma and anxiety, so caretakers were advised to be thoughtful about their behavior if they were to avert deviant emotional growth and the accompanying susceptibility to the disquiet and defensive maneuvers that became known as neurotic disorder. The promotion of independence and instrumental skills in an incompetent organism was subordinated, temporarily, to the prevention of emotional distress and psychic impotence. The former attitude puts parents on the offensive; the latter on the defensive.

The Freudian era peaked in America from 1940 to 1960 under the intellectual leadership of Anna Freud, Margaret Ribble, Ernst Kris, Katherine Wolf, René Spitz, Sibylle Escalona, Phyllis Greenacre, Melanie Klein, John Bowlby, and a host of others who complicated the existing metaphor for infancy. Vulnerability to anxiety was added to the quality of malleability. The glowing optimism contained in Shinn's description of the child suddenly seemed ingenuous. Rearing a baby was a serious and difficult mission with many shoals to avoid. Each child was a potential phobic, obsessive, depressive, or, in the extreme, schizophrenic, and parents were warned against the potential danger of practices they had regarded as innocuous. The prevention of psychological pathology had replaced earlier worry over physical disease. And in both periods mothers had the responsibility for taking all necessary precautions, for in addition to a belief in the infant's vulnerability to experience, the West also had an implacable faith in adult effectiveness. Parents can prevent future pathology if they act properly, it was thought.

Psychoanalytic theory led to reformulations of old phenomena in social terms. The fears of infancy, which had been seen as maturationally inevitable, were renamed as separation anxiety and stranger anxiety. The new adjectives implied social causation. One of the most significant constructions wrought by psychoanalytic theory was the introduction of ideas of maternal acceptance and rejection. Parents have always been ready to accept the notion that they should care for their children, for they have always realized that attention to the child's physical needs was necessary for his survival. Parental concerns focused on protecting the child from illness, providing food and opportunities for instrumental mastery, and tutoring the child in good habits. But it was less common for parents to brood about whether their child sensed that he was loved. Theorists whose scaffold was psychoanalytic theory, such as Erik Erikson, Melanie Klein, John Bowlby, and Mary Ainsworth, suggested that the child required psychic security and freedom from anxiety; they considered an affectionate maternal attitude toward the infant the single most significant factor determining whether the infant attained those precious states.

The original psychoanalytic variables of interest—duration of nursing, severity of weaning, and age of toilet training—are no longer of interest today. By the late 1940s (see Orlansky 1949; Caldwell 1964) the research record was not in accord with prediction. Some concluded that the theory was incorrect; others that it was difficult to investigate psychoanalytic propositions. Whatever the reason, the failure to confirm the theory led to a restlessness and receptivity to a new paradigm, which was being written by Piaget and is reflected today in the cognitive focus of modern research on the infant and young child.

Quantification of parental practices surrounding feeding, weaning, and toilet training was replaced by observations of parental talking, playing, and encouragement of cognitive development. Despite the change in content, the centrality of adult-infant interaction was retained, so that recent research results point to the importance of the mutual and reciprocal relation between infant and parent. Thus, psychoanalytic theory deserves extraordinary credit for pointing the empiricist's nose toward social experience as a monitor of development.

The modern period

The extraordinary scientific interest in human infants during the last ten years owes its vitality to many independent forces, each with its own special questions and presuppositions about the young child. The uniformly reliable relations among social class, reproductive risk, and difficulty in mastering academic skills have led many clinicians to the view that 3 to 10 percent of American newborns suffer from some degree of impairment of central nervous system functioning caused by either prenatal or perinatal trauma or infection. These injuries, though difficult to diagnose, are assumed to contribute to later cognitive deficiency. Since early detection of impairment, perhaps during the first year, could lead to early rehabilitation of damaged children, many investigators are trying to develop such diagnostic instruments.

The current interest in developmental psycholinguistics, stimulated by Noam Chomsky's bold assertions of the innateness of speech mechanisms and Roger Brown's careful observations and graceful integrative summaries, has led to elegant studies of speech perception in the young infant and the suggestion that the baby processes consonants with a discreteness that implies the presence of special neural structures for this purpose.

Perhaps the two sturdiest supports for the zealous study of the young child come from ethology and the attempt to integrate classic behaviorism and psychoanalytic theory into a modern statement of the importance of the role of social experience in development. Both are concerned with the effective stimulus event that engages the infant's attention and subsequently either releases species specific responses or serves as a conditioned cue for modification of an existing behavior. It was inevitable that the West's subscription to mechanical causality between events, in preference to coherence among events, when combined with the methodological principles of stimulus-response psychology, would lead psychologists to inquire about the essential stimulus conditions that released the universal responses of sustained attention, babbling, smiling, and crying. In addition, those who were curious about the cognitive functioning of the infant were searching for objective ways to probe the infant's mind. The experiments of Robert Fantz published in the mid-1950s provided a methodology that met the needs of both groups. He found that with remarkably simple methods one can infer the characteristics of events that engage prolonged attention from infants, and he raised the possibility that one could infer something about mental processes from these objective data. In the twenty years since those first experiments, our knowledge of perceptual dynamics in the infant has gone from almost total ignorance to a few tentative principles.

Perception and cognition in infancy

The infant enters the world prepared to attend to changes in physical stimulation in all modalities. We have learned the most about the visual modality because it is the easiest to study; the child announces his attentional investment in an event by orienting his eyes toward it. If the newborn is placed in a comfortable supine position below a white frame containing a single black vertical stripe, his eyes hover near the border between black and white, crossing it repeatedly. His attention is captured by the locus of maximal change (Haith 1966). Change also produces temporary inhibition, for 3- to 5-day-old infants will stop their repetitive sucking on a blind nipple if there is sudden movement of a light source.

Experiments designed to determine the events most likely to engage attention often follow a similar procedure. The infant is exposed repeatedly to a particular event—say five to fifteen trials—until his attention wanes. The gradual decrease in attention is called habituation. Following habituation the infant is exposed to a different stimulus. If he displays an increase in attention, called dishabituation, we assume he detected the element or elements that were altered in the second event. Studies using this procedure have revealed that contrast, movement, and change in light flux are powerful determinants of both initial orientation and sustained attention in the infant. Newborns are extremely sensitive to changes in the amount of contour in a pattern. After being exposed repeatedly to either a two-by-two- or a twelve-by-twelve-square checkerboard, they gradually look less at the repeated event. But they show increased attention if shown the other checkerboard pattern (Friedman, Bruno, and Vietze 1974).

In the auditory mode, rate of change in sound energy predicts whether interest, reflected in cardiac deceleration and eye-opening, or defensive avoidance, reflected in cardiac acceleration and eye-closing, will occur (Kearsley 1973).

These effects are likely to be mediated by basic processes in the central nervous system. The brain responds to the repeated presentation of a brief visual stimulus with a characteristic wave form called the visual evoked potential. The time interval from the exposure of the visual stimulus to the first two peak voltages in this wave form decreases regularly during the first year (Connors 1973). B. Z. Karmel and his colleagues have demonstrated in young infants a curvilinear relation—an inverted U—between the density of contour in a visual figure, on the one hand, and both fixation time and amplitude of the visual evoked potential, on the other. After six weeks of age, prolonged attention and maximal amplitudes of the peak in the wave form typically occur in response to stimuli with greater contour density. Karmel suggests that contour-dependent neural activity is the basis for the amount of visual attention (Karmel and Maisel 1975). The number of discrete elements also influences attention, even when amount of contour is controlled. A figure with twenty squares, each one-eighth inch on a side, with a total of ten inches of contour is looked at longer than a figure with four squares, each five-eighths inch on a side, and therefore with the same total amount of contour (Fantz and Fagan 1975).

The young infant is also attracted to curvature. A newborn will study an unframed curved pattern more than a linear one, and by eight weeks of age will attend longer to a bull's-eye than to a checkerboard, and more to curved than to linear patterns, even if the stimuli are internal to a frame. Infants look longer at concentric than nonconcentric patterns and, when pattern is controlled, look longer at patterns composed of arcs than those composed of straight lines (Ruff and Birch 1974). In a related study, 10-month-old infants became more excited and paid more attention when a dishabituating curved segment followed familiarization to a straight line segment than when the events were reversed (Hopkins 1974). The preference for curvature and concentricity is less likely to be a generalization from the eyes of the face than a reflection of basic neural mechanisms, because even the newborn prefers curved to straight line segments (Fantz and Miranda 1975). It is possible that activation of hypercomplex cells by stimuli that deviate from straight line contours mediate the sustained fixation. These data imply that the first schemata will favor circular forms that contain contour and movement. The eyes of the human face fit these criteria and 8-week-olds immediately seek out the eyes of a newly introduced face whereas younger infants scan the chin and hairline.

Infants also respond to differences in wavelength as though they perceive the categories of blue, green, yellow, and red exactly the way adults do (Bornstein 1975; Bornstein, Kessen, and Weiskopf 1975). Four-month-old infants look longer at the center hue of the color categories blue, green, yellow, and red than at the boundaries (for example, blue-green or red-yellow). Further, infants look longer at the center hues for red and blue than for green or yellow, matching adult ratings of the pleasantness of these colors (Bornstein 1975).

The very young infant seems prepared to orient to fundamental dimensions in the external world. Contour, movement, concentricity, curvilinearity, and color have a claim on his attention, especially when each represents an alteration in the immediate perceptual field. The infant does not have to learn where the information might be located; nature has awarded the newborn a small set of clues to help him discover the hidden prizes.

The reaction to information

One of the most important competences of the central nervous system is the ability to detect the similarity between an event and a mentally stored representation of past experience, and to form a new schema or to alter an old one in a way that reflects the relation between the contemporary perception and the older knowledge. That process requires that the event engage a relevant schema, the first form of recognition memory. Infants as young as ten weeks of age, and perhaps younger, have the capacity for such recognition. In one experiment (Super 1972) 10-week-old and 4-month-old infants were exposed for several minutes to a standard stimulus (an orange sphere that moved vertically in front of a black wooden backboard). The sphere was pulled up and down by a wire connected to a motor behind the backboard. As the ball reached the top of the backboard, lights flashed on for approximately one second. The full cycle of the ball lasted eleven seconds during which the ball was visible for about seven. Each subject was exposed to this vertical parade until the infant had looked at the event for a minimum of three minutes. Experimental subjects were returned to the laboratory either one day or two weeks later to view the same event, while controls of the same age saw the stimulus for the first time. Infants who had been exposed to the stimulus a day earlier showed more behavioral interest initially, but became bored more quickly than those who were seeing it for the first time; those who returned two weeks later gave less obvious evidence of recognition memory. It appears that 10-week-olds can recognize aspects of a brief and unusual experience after a twenty-four-hour delay.

What determines the similarity between an event and the schema for that event? Let us for the moment restrict the discussion to visual events like faces, bottles, and mobiles. Of the two traditional approaches to this problem, the more popular has been to analyze the event into its independent analytic dimensions and to assume that the number of physical dimensions in which two events differ is a rough index of their degree of psychological difference. In the simplest use of this principle, checkerboards of 4, 16, 64, or 144 squares are shown to infants. If each black or white square is considered a "dimension" (or "element"), the 144-unit checkerboard is regarded as differing more from the 4-unit design than it is from the 16-unit pattern. (Occasionally, the word *complexity* is used to describe this dimension. But since complexity, in most cases, is synonymous with the number of squares, and that dimension is less ambiguous in meaning and no less explanatory than the descriptive term complexity, it is preferred.) Psychologists have also compared the infant's reactions to polygons of differing numbers of angles—5, 10, 20—where each angle is regarded as a unit. The greater the difference in the number of angles between any two forms, the larger presumed difference between the whole figures. But in both checkerboards and polygons the amount of contour has also varied and Karmel and Maisel

(1975) have shown that among infants 6 to 20 weeks of age, attentiveness, as well as the amplitude of the second peak voltage in the evoked potential, is a curvilinear function of the square root of the density of contour in the pattern. Thus, amount of contour is one dimension infants, at least those under 4 months, use to evaluate the similarity of two events.

The importance of pattern

But the world rarely presents infants or children with events that differ in only one dimension—like number of squares or centimeters of contour. Most events differ on many dimensions at once. Consider as an event a stationary red sphere. An analytic approach assumes that the sphere is composed of at least two dimensions—its form and color. A blue sphere or a red block presumably differ in only one dimension from the red sphere, whereas the blue cube would differ in two dimensions. Hence the blue cube differs more from the red sphere than from the other two.

There is an empirical advantage in regarding an event as composed of independent dimensions, but we must determine the construction rules that permit synthesis of the whole event from the simple dimensions. Psycholinguists assume sentences are synthesized by syntactic rules from sets of morphemes. There is a lesson to be taken from the rich work on psycholinguistics. The longer the unit is a part of psychological structure, the more coherent it becomes. For example, the sentence "The dog likes chicken" may initially be amenable to treatment as a composite of four discrete words for a 3-year-old, but it certainly is not for an adolescent. A 30-year-old should treat a sentence changing three of the four words—"The canine prefers poultry" as more similar to the original than the sentence "The cat likes chicken," where only one word has been changed. A theory of perception and discrepancy must therefore accommodate dynamic changes in knowledge over time. It is this idea that lies behind the second, less popular, approach of viewing knowledge of events as continually emerging, coherent wholes, rather than an unstable composite of unitary dimensions. A star is a coherent unit as different from a circle as it is from a triangle. This view makes it more difficult to initiate empirical research, for it does not offer an easy means of analysis and demands a language for pattern. Unfortunately, there is little guidance available to those who are friendly to that view. The infant probably attends to both the whole and the individual dimensions, with the pattern always clamoring for primacy. The infant is capable of representing both individual dimensions and whole patterns, for 5-month-old infants detect changes in the spatial arrangement of a set of three distinct geometric forms, as well as changes in orientation of the background frame (Wiener and Kagan 1976). A major challenge to theory and investigation is discovering the primary dimensions for classes of patterns since a given dimension (for example, size or color) is probably not of equal salience for all classes of events.

If we restrict ourselves to visual events, relevant dimensions might include:

Linearity of dimensions within a pattern
Curvature of dimensions within a pattern
Symmetry of the pattern
Redundancy of the individual dimensions
Color of the dimensions or pattern
Contour density
Verticality of the whole pattern
Horizontality of the whole pattern
Circularity-concentricity of the pattern

In addition, we must take into account the relation among dimensions in a particular pattern, for example, the relative size or spatial placement of a dimension. Consider a black outline circle enclosing two dark, symmetrical circles arranged horizontally (see table 2.1 for the stimuli). This particular stimulus appears to be the minimal event a 4-month-old will react to with a smile, implying that it is the critical pattern for a face. The standard figure can be analyzed into at least six dimensions: 1) the relation of elements to the circular frame, 2) horizontal placement of the internal elements, 3) symmetrical placement of the elements, 4) the shape of the elements, 5) size of the elements, and 6) the number of elements. In order to investigate the differential salience of these dimensions in an experiment that used these stimuli each dimension was manipulated separately. The technique was to habituate 10-month-old infants to a pair of identical standard stimuli (the circular frame with the two horizontally placed circles), and then to expose different groups of infants to the twelve different transformations illustrated in table 2.1. The twelve independent experimental groups with sixteen infants in each group were exposed to changes in symmetry of the elements, orientation of the elements, shape of the elements, relative size of the elements, number of elements, and relation of elements to the frame, while a control group continued to see the same standard event. In this procedure, the infant first viewed a horizontal placement of a pair of the standard stimuli while coders quantified the duration of his looking at each of these identical events. This experience was followed by the replacement of one of the standards (right and left position were counterbalanced) with one of the events illustrated in table 2.1. The salience of the transformation was indexed by the difference in percent time the infant spent looking at the discrepant event minus the percent time the infant spent looking at that location on the previous trial when the standard event was present.

Several related measures of salience were examined—the proportion of infants who showed increased attention to the transformation, the median increase in attention, and the proportion of each group who showed a positive change in attention of 20 percent or more. This percentage was chosen as a criterion because the distribution of change scores showed an obvious

TABLE 2.1. DISHABITUATION OF ATTENTION TO VARIOUS TRANSFORMATIONS ON STANDARD CIRCULAR FIGURE REPRESENTING A FACE (PERCENT FIXATION TIME TO THE TRANSFORMATION MINUS PERCENT FIXATION TIME TO THE STANDARD FIGURE IN THAT LOCATION ON THE PREVIOUS TRIAL).[a]

EXPERIMENTAL GROUP[b]	INDEX OF CHANGE			
	MEDIAN INCREASE IN FIXATION (%)	PERCENTAGE OF GROUP WITH INCREASE IN FIXATION	PERCENTAGE OF GROUP WITH INCREASE IN FIXATION $\geq 20\%$	AVERAGE RANK ON ALL THREE MEASURES
1. Larger size	21	88	63	1.0
2. Vertical pattern	20	81	50	2.0
3. Smaller size	10	69	25	4.2
4. Oblique pattern	5	56	31	6.0
5. Relation to frame	10	69	19	5.5
6. Larger number	5	75	19	6.0
7. Smaller number	6	50	19	8.0
8. Shape variation 1	3	63	19	8.2
9. Relation to frame	4	69	6	9.0
10. Shape variation 2	3	56	19	9.8
11. Shape variation 3	-3	44	25	10.0
12. Asymmetry	-2	50	19	10.3
13. Control	0	44	6	12.0

[a] For 208 10-month-old infants in 13 experimental groups; each group of 16 infants was shown a different stimulus. F overall = 2.03, $p < 0.05$.

[b] Groups 1 and 2 are significantly different from each of groups 7-13 by t test for mean increase in fixation.

break at this value. As table 2.1 reveals, on all three measures the transformation that contained the larger circular elements and the one with the vertical rearrangement of the circles elicited the greatest increases in attention for most children, whereas those transformations that altered the shape of the internal elements elicited far less attention. Even though the "face" with three circles had more total contour and more elements (and therefore was more complex), it was less potent than the event that altered size and norizontal placement, suggesting a special sensitivity to spatial pattern and relative size.

The infant's sensitivity to changes in size has also been documented in a study of successive discrimination. Ten-month-olds were initially habituated on a single schematic human figure composed of one-inch orange squares and dishabituated on transformations of that figure in which the total area of the figure was increased by only 7 percent. The transformation was created by adding one square element to that part of the figure that represented the head, arm, or leg of the schematic figure. The infants showed an obvious and significant recovery of attention to these relatively subtle changes in size (Linn, Hans, and Kagan, unpublished, 1976).

We are not suggesting that size and spatial arrangement of internal elements will always be more salient than shape or number. Rather, we believe that the salience of a discrepancy is a function of the relation of the event to the child's schemata. It is likely that the more finely articulated the schema, the more sensitive the child will be to alterations in spatial pattern and relative size of internal dimensions, as opposed to their shape. The 10-month-old has a finely articulated schema for a human face, and we suppose that the standard stimulus we used in table 2.1 engaged that schema and thus yielded the pattern of results.

The mind is always working on its knowledge, trying to create represen tations that permit the most efficient recognition of the forms that are func tionally equivalent for the child. The mind rushes toward organization and pattern whenever possible; it moves toward a prototype.

However, had the standard event been minimally related to any schema, say an irregular outline with a pair of trapezoids placed in the lower third of the figure, the order of salience might have been different. Number and shape of elements might have produced the greatest recovery of attention. These data imply that it may not be possible to discover absolute principles that predict the salience of a particular dimension across all events. The principles must be stated in terms of the relation of event to schema. This generalization also seems to apply to recognition memory in older children. Transformations of organized scenes are not uniformly detected more easily than the same transformation in a less well organized scene. Detection depends on the nature of the scene and the class of transformation (Newcombe 1976).

Discrepancy and salience of dimensions

Discrepant events that differ from schemata in both dimensions and pattern alert the child and eventually lead to changes in knowledge. Discrepant events share either salient dimensions or salient aspects of pattern with the acquired schema. For the 2-month-old a representation of a human face must have a pair of eyes if it is to be regarded as discrepant from the normal face, for facelike stimuli without eyes are not awarded much attention. But by age one the schema has changed and a face without eyes is treated as if it were a transformation on a human face. Similarly, the horizontal arrangement of eyes is a central dimension of the face, for 4-month-olds typically show the greatest increase in attention when that attribute is altered. But a few weeks later the nose and mouth have become salient. With experience, additional dimensions become integrated into this schema and a new pattern is consolidated. Increasing differentiation of an event and consolidation into a new pattern proceed simultaneously, as Heinz Werner (1948) suggested years ago.

The salience of a dimension is a function of physical as well as informational parameters. The informational value of an event is correlated in part with the degree to which it helps to distinguish it from other events, and in part with environmental consequences. The eyes are physically salient because of their contour and concentricity. But they also have informational salience, since variations on the eyes (closed, open, or narrowed) provide important information to the child regarding the state and probable behavior of another person. The ears are less salient physically and contain far less information.

Dimensions that are invariant across transformations in the child's experience become candidates for salience. For a Bushman child who has seen only brown-skinned faces, a white face is a salient discrepancy. Obviously, salient dimensions will change as new invariances are discovered. A pattern that is transformed on many dimensions simultaneously may not sustain attention as long as one that transforms only one dimension. When one follows several presentations of a two-inch orange cube with a small yellow cylinder—changing size, shape, and color—the infant shows initial alerting, but less sustained attention than if the small orange cube is simply replaced with a smaller cube. Similarly, if one changes a red sphere into a red cylinder, there is more sustained attention than if the red sphere is transformed into a green, irregularly shaped polygon in which both form and color arc altered (Hopkins et al. 1976). In the auditory mode, a musical event that changed only rhythm or melody elicited greater attention than an event that changed both (Kinney and Kagan 1976). Events that have a narrow band of regular variation in their dimensions but retain a basic pattern are likely to become articulated schemata. New events belong to three broad classes, excluding replications of the same event. There will be variations on nonsalient physical dimensions, which are treated as minimally discrepant; variations on salient physical or high-information dimensions that comprise the class of moderately discrepant events; and finally, replacement of both salient and nonsalient dimensions, best regarded as novel events.

One question of importance is whether there are any absolute dimensions that will always be salient for a specific event or whether the salient dimensions are always dependent on, or relative to, the discrimination being made between or among events. For example, does the child always recognize the event "dog" by the same set of central dimensions, or do the dimensions change depending upon whether the child is differentiating a dog from a cat? An extreme interpretation of Eleanor Gibson's discussion of perceptual development (1969) implies that the salient dimensions are always relative for Gibson is primarily concerned with the dimensions used to discriminate one event from another. If we are only differentiating an event from some other event, then the salient dimensions will always be relative to the specific discrimination to be made. But we are not always making a discrimination between events. A face is recognized by the relation of eyes, nose, mouth, and facial outline. That pattern is used to recognize a face regardless of what event we may wish to differentiate it from. Gibson might reply that if the world only contained creatures with bilateral eyes and a centrally placed nose and mouth, the human face might have a different set of salient dimensions, and that therefore there is no absolute set of dimensions for the face. But even in such a world, it is likely the eyes would still be a physically salient aspect of the schema. Mushrooms have a highly similar but distinctive physical pattern that is easy to recognize, and it takes considerable training for a person to learn the signs that distinguish edible from poisonous mushrooms. It is likely that certain physical dimensions will be primary in the schema of some events even though the child may use different dimensions to differentiate among similar classes of events. Thus, there are two quite different phenomena—the physically salient dimensions that initially dominate the schema and dimensions used to discriminate among similar events. The child is not always trying to determine the difference between two events. Recognition of event A is not synonymous with the observation "that is A and not B." The first is an identity operation, the second involves negation; these are two quite different logical operations.

Relation of attention to discrepant experience A controversy exists over whether the relation of attention to discrepant events is linear or curvilinear. Before summarizing the evidence on this controversy it is necessary to distinguish between the child's initial orientation to any change in physical parameters—intensity, frequency, rhythmicity, wavelength, contour, number of elements—and sustained attention following the initial three to five seconds of orientation (Cohen, Gelber, and Lazar 1971). As for the former, it appears that the more the stimulus differs from the infant's expectations, the more likely he will be to show an initial orientation to it. The basic demonstration of this fact goes back to Fantz's original studies, which show that after familiarization with a visual event the infant will look longer at a changed stimulus than at a familiarized one. The effect is so reliable it deserves to be a principle—the principle of change—and it appears to be operative during the opening days of life.

It is also important to distinguish between the two classes of change. The first involves changes in the events that are likely to be correlated with a change in pattern of discharge of the central nervous system because they involve changes in spatial or temporal distributions of physical aspects of the stimulus. Amount of contour, orientation of dimensions, curvature, number and size of elements, hue, and movement belong to this class. The second class of change we might call informational, for its members do not necessarily involve alterations in the above dimensions.

The major controversy over both kinds of change, physical and informational, centers on whether the relation between the amount of change and sustained attention after initial orientation is linear or curvilinear. McCall and his colleagues have summarized the attempts to determine the nature of this relation (McCall, Kennedy, and Appelbaum 1977; McCall and McGhee 1976). They found that when the experimental manipulations involve the addition of elements or dimensions, the effect is usually linear, as long as the density of contour is not too small or too large. When the manipulations involve rearrangements of dimensions into a new pattern, the resulting function tends to be curvilinear. The researchers concluded, "There are at least seventeen separate samples of infants that displayed the inverted U-discrepancy function. Seventeen exemplars of one specific quadratic curve would appear to make the discrepancy hypothesis plausible and worthy of further examination" (McCall and McGhee 1976, p. 13).

In one elegantly designed experiment (McCall, Kennedy, and Applebaum 1977), 10-week-old infants were exposed to color slides of the stimuli shown in figure 2.1 (arrows at twelve, one, two, and three o'clock orientations). The child was familiarized with one of the stimuli until he reached a criterion of habituation of attention, and then was presented a new stimulus for a single trial. Independent groups of infants were familiarized and dishabituated on different combinations of the four stimuli. The physical qualities of the objects were important, independent of the discrepancy effect, for the vertical and horizontal placements (stimuli A and D) were looked at longer than the two oblique stimuli. Figure 2.2 shows the expected inverted U-shaped discrepancy function for attention after the variance attributed to the physical properties of the familiar and new stimuli were removed.

A second study with similar design, logic, and sample used two-by-two, four-by-four, eight-by-eight, and sixteen-by-sixteen-square checkerboard patterns. As expected, the checkerboard pattern with the greatest number of

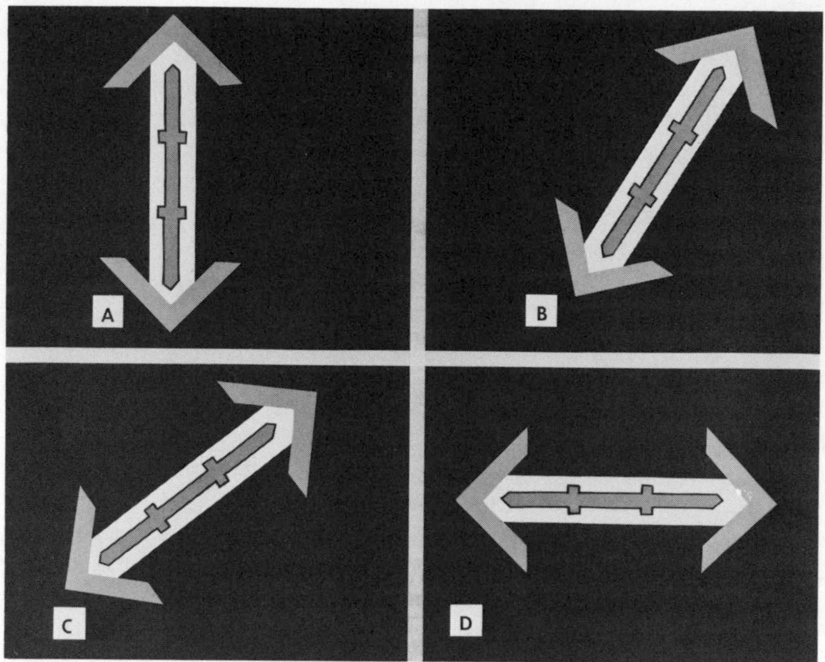

Fig. 2.1 *Stimuli used in McCall, Kennedy, and Appelbaum study* (1977).

elements and most contour recruited at least four times as much attention as any other stimulus. But when the effects of the specific stimulus were removed, the inverted function emerged, although it was more emphatic when the discrepancy represented a shift toward a stimulus with more contour rather than one with less (see figure 2.3).

Earlier studies are in accord with this hypothesis. Super et al. (1972) allowed 4-month-olds to see a three-dimensional mobile consisting of three elements arranged horizontally. Independent groups were given mobiles to take home that differed in the amount of change from the original (see figure 2.4). Three weeks later all the children returned to see the original form. The largest increase in fixation time from the first to the second session occurred for the group exposed at home to the asymmetric rearrangement, not the stimulus that was most discrepant from the standard.

The curvilinear relation also holds for older infants. As part of an extensive longitudinal study, 27-month-olds were shown a three-dimensional human form, two transformations that rearranged the human form, and a free form that resembled no meaningful object. The last was most different from the original. The two rearrangements of the human form produced longer fixations than either the regular or the free form.

We interpret the pattern of attention to the twelve different transfor-

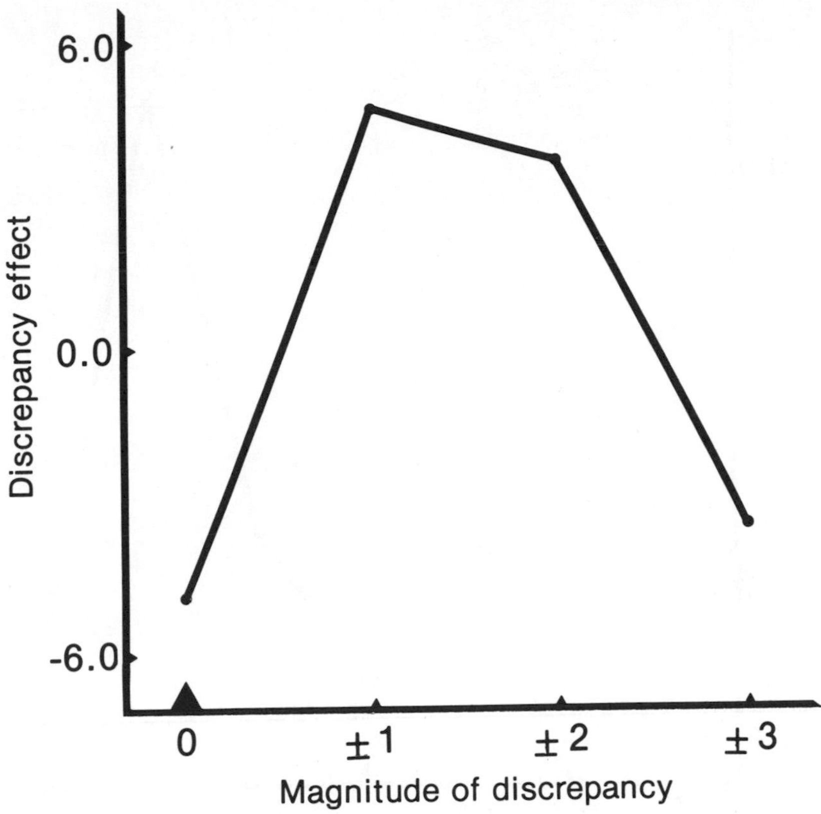

Fig. 2.2 *Relation of effect of discrepancy on attention as a function of magnitude of discrepancy for stimuli in figure 2.1 (after McCall, Kennedy, and Appelbaum 1977).*

mations of the schematic face in table 2.1 as an instance of the curvilinear function. The stimuli that only changed the shape of the internal elements provoked short attention from the 10-month-olds, presumably because they were too easily assimilated to the schema of a face since the basic dimension of a pair of horizontally placed elements in a circular frame was retained. The stimuli that were very serious distortions of a face (one or three internal elements or the circular elements placed outside the frame) did not provoke prolonged attention; the presumed reason is they could not be assimilated to the 10-month-old's schema for a face. The four stimuli that altered the size and horizontal arrangement of the internal elements were "moderate" discrepancies and attracted the most attention.

Additional support for the curvilinear relation comes from two recent studies (Kinney and Kagan 1976; Hopkins et al. 1976). In the first, 7½-month-old infants were exposed to a music or speech episode. The dishabituating event for the musical episode was a French horn playing a six-

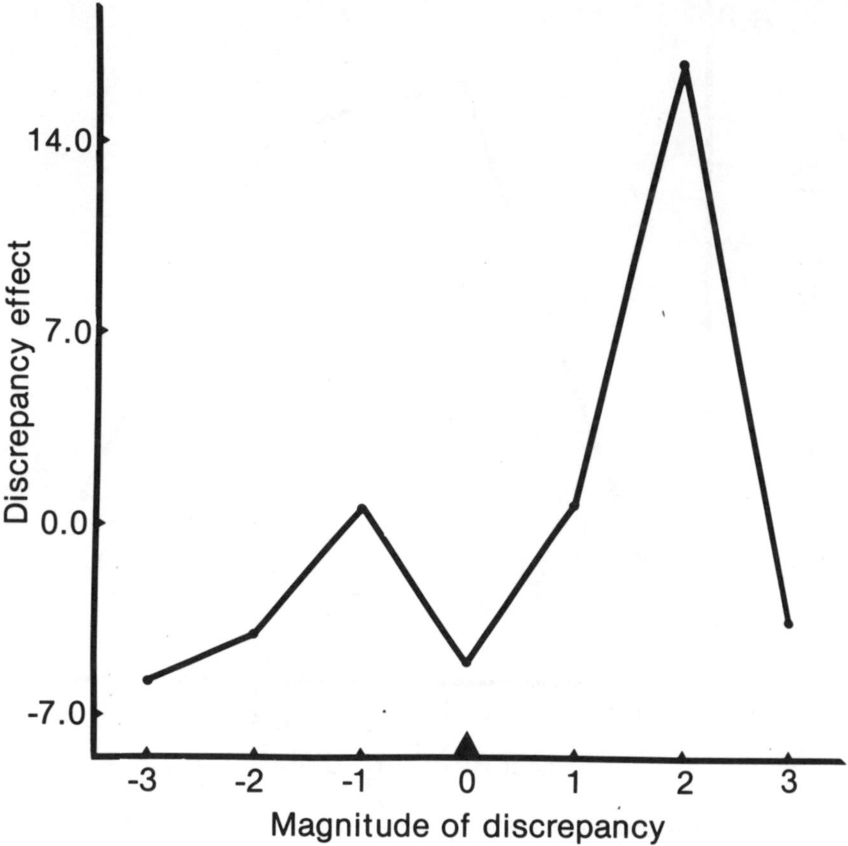

Fig. 2.3 *Relation of effect of discrepancy on attention as a function of magnitude of discrepancy for checkerboard stimuli (after McCall, Kennedy, and Appelbaum 1977).*

note melody. Three other musical patterns differed from this event by one, two, or three dimensions. The one-step difference involved only a change in melody; the two-step difference a change in both melody and rhythm; the three-step difference involved melody, rhythm, and timbre (a guitar).

The verbal stimuli in the same study involved the same paradigm. The dishabituating event was a series of nonsense syllables spoken in a particular rhythmic pattern. The one-step change altered only the rhythm; the two-step altered rhythm and the two internal syllables; and the three-step change altered rhythm and all four syllables.

After eight exposures to one of the standards, the child heard the dishabituating stimulus for five trials. Children showed the largest cardiac decelerations to the two-step, moderate change rather than to the greatest change. Moreover, orientation to the source of the sound, an index of atten-

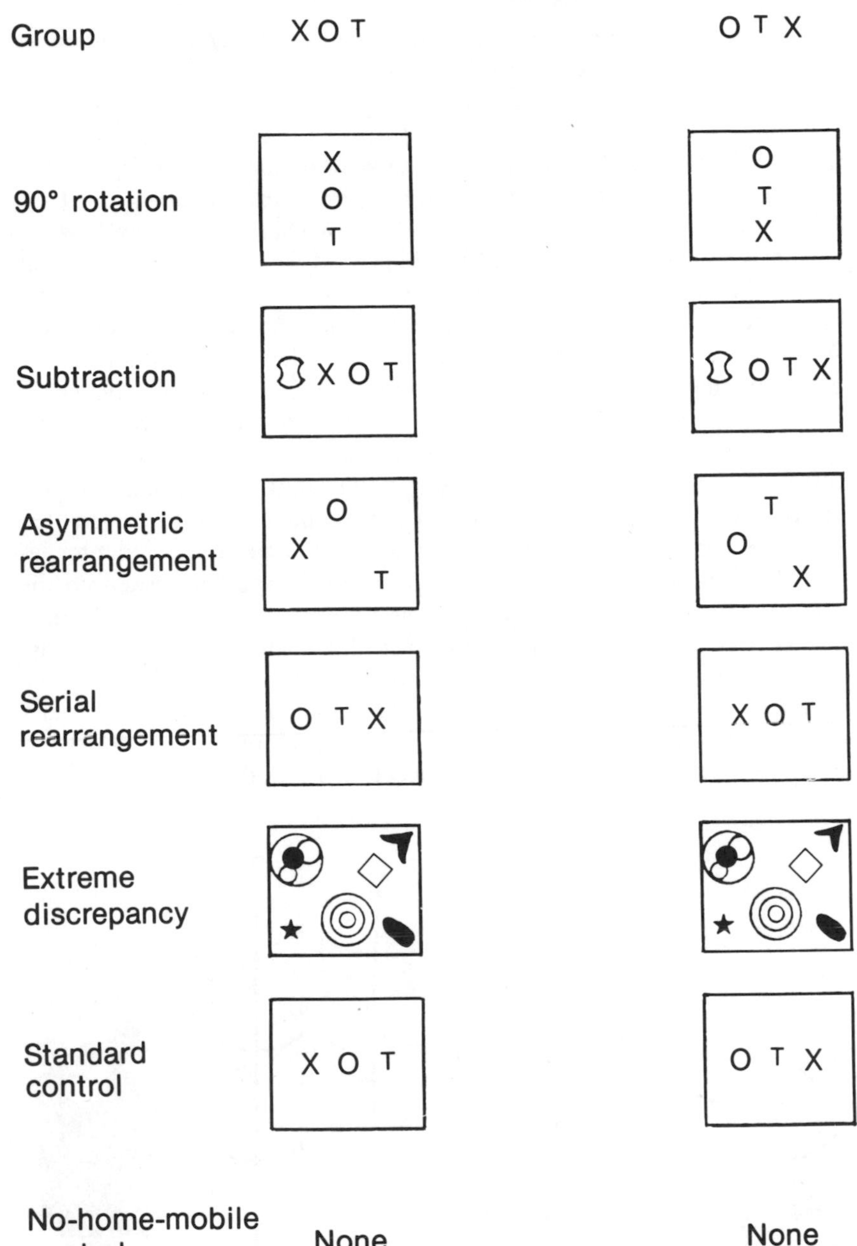

Fig. 2.4 *Stimuli used in the Super et al. study* (1972).

tion, was greater to the one- and two-step changes than to the largest change.

In the second study, 7½-month-old infants were habituated to either stimulus A or D in figure 2.5. Children exposed to A were dishabituated on B, C, D, or E; those familiarized on D were dishabituated on A, B, C, or E. Stimulus E was the novel or most discrepant object for all children. For infants habituated on A, stimuli C and D were moderately discrepant. For those familiarized on D, stimuli A and B were moderately discrepant. Each child sat on his mother's lap in front of a viewing chamber with a yellow bar in front of the infant. Each time the child pressed the bar the viewing box lit up and the child was allowed to view one of the objects for only two and one-half seconds so that assimilation of the event would be prolonged over trials. When each child had been habituated to a particular standard stimulus, the dishabituating stimulus was shown for three minutes. (Controls experienced no change.) The degree of recovery was computed by comparing the responding and attention during the last two minutes of habituation with the first two minutes of exposure to the discrepant event. The greatest recovery of operant responding, looking, and vocalizing occurred to the object that was three steps removed from the habituated stimulus—the cylinder for infants familiarized on the sphere; the sphere for infants habituated on the cylinder (see figure 2.6). The form that differed most from the original elicited less recovery than the moderately discrepant objects. Minute-by-minute analysis revealed the importance of distinguishing between the initial reaction to any change and sustained attention and excitement over a discrepancy. During the first minute of change, the novel form elicited as much recovery as the three-step change. That is, during the first minute

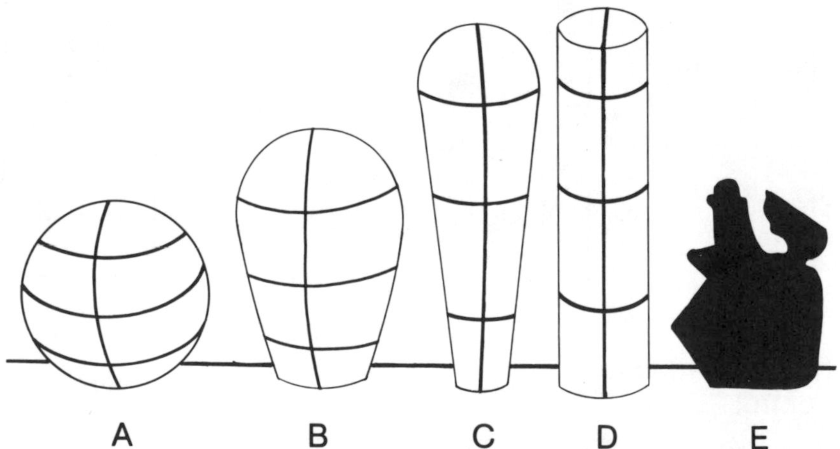

Fig. 2.5 *Stimuli used in the Hopkins et al. study (1976).*

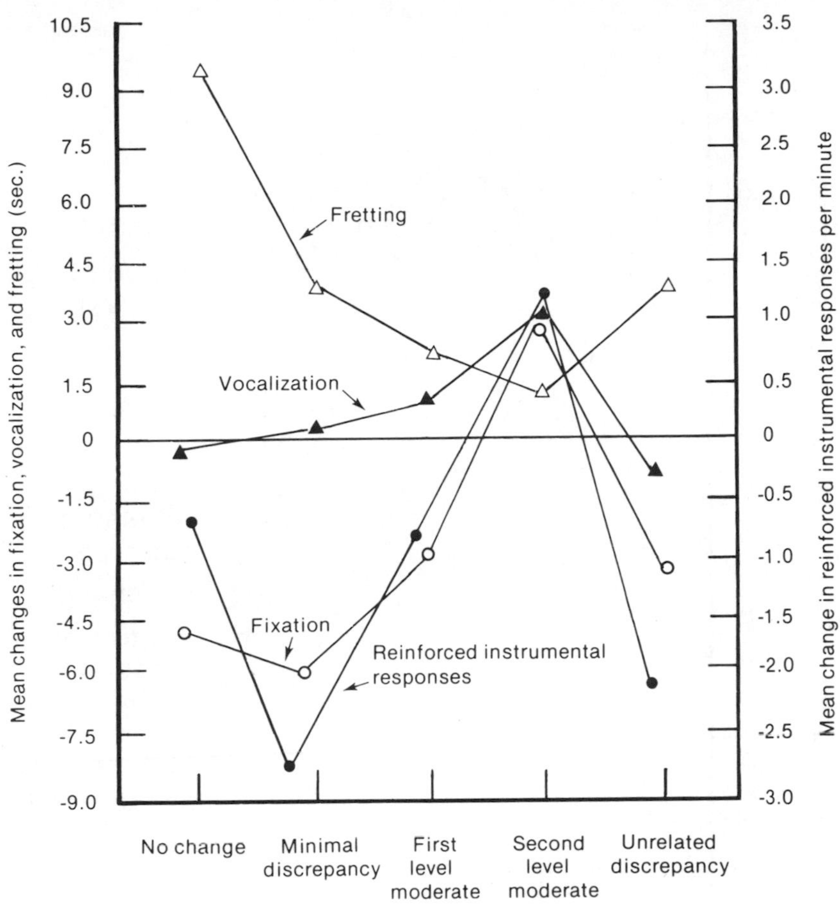

Fig. 2.6 *Changes in responsivity from the last two minutes of the standard to the first two minutes of the transformation.*

there was a linear relation between degree of discrepancy and recovery; but during the second and third minutes of the transformation, the novel form lost its power to hold attention while the discrepant events continued to produce attention and responding (see figure 2.7). Vocalization, which can be a reflection of excitement, was a much more frequent response to the moderately discrepant than to the novel event among girls, but not among boys.

The curvilinear relation is not limited to looking or listening. Fagen and Rovee (1975) trained 3-month-olds to kick in order to release a mobile composed of different numbers of elements—two, six, or ten objects. Infants who were shifted after training from a six-element to a two-element mobile showed a greater recovery of kicking than those transferred from a ten-ele-

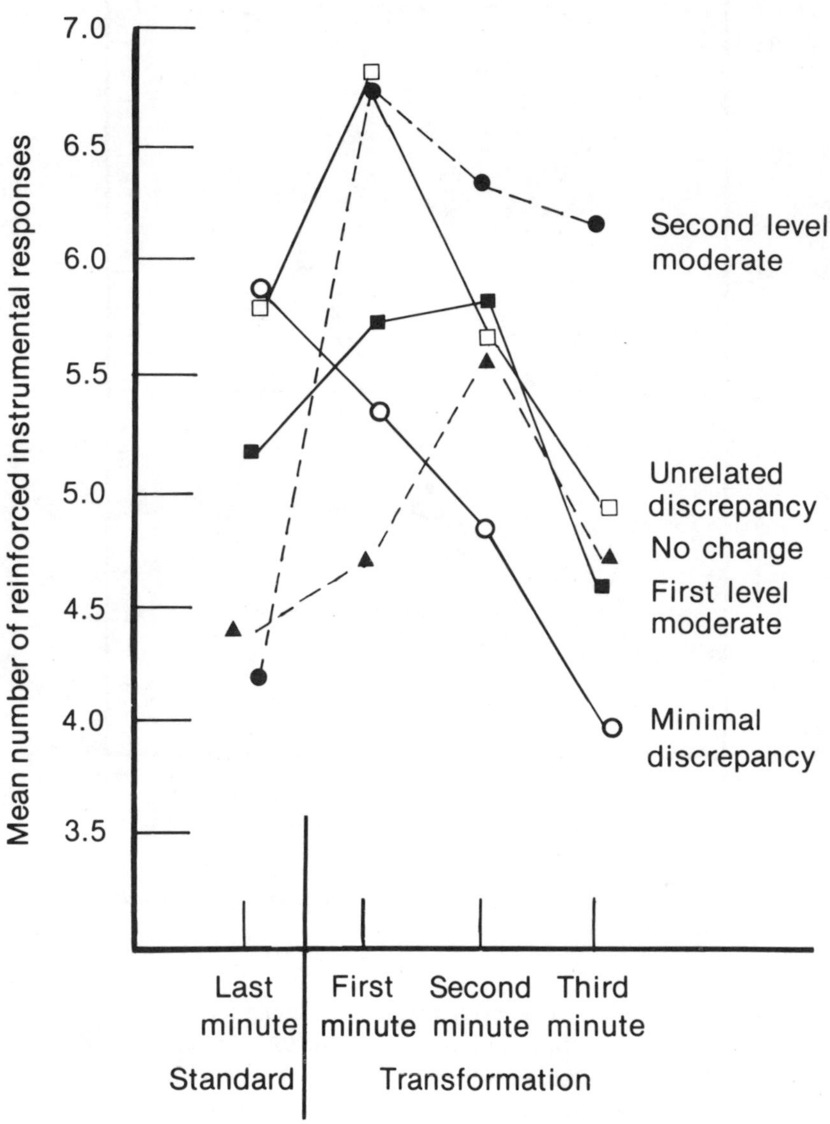

Fig. 2.7 *Mean number of reinforced instrumental responses during the last minute of the standard and the first three minutes of the transformation for each group.*

ment to two-element mobile. As with instrumental responding used in the study by Hopkins et al., a moderate change provoked more excitement than a larger change.

The total corpus of data suggests a curvilinear function for the relation of discrepancy to attention and excitement. The child is alerted by any change in information or stimulus energy and presumably tries to assimilate the event to an existing schema. We assume that an event that does not engage any schema is ignored after the initial orientation; an event that shares some dimensions with the original schema holds the infant longer because he attempts to assimilate that event to his knowledge. The linear relation between attention and discrepancy reported in some experiments may be due to the fact that the investigator did not differentiate between the initial orientation and prolonged attention or that the most extreme discrepancies shared a large number of dimensions with the habituated standard, or that the manipulation involved the addition of dimensions. If the events have only one or two dimensions, like checkerboards, the relation is more often linear because the basic form of the event remains the same. When the new event shares no dimension with the original, the infant does not try to assimilate it to the schema for the original event and attends to it for shorter periods of time.

The child is most likely to acquire new structures or change old ones after he has been exposed to an event that is related to his knowledge—a conclusion reminiscent of the notion of the "pacer" event suggested by J.M. Hunt over fifteen years ago (Hunt 1961). The child is most likely to profit from experience that engages what he knows but is not immediately assimilable, events we might call surprises. During infancy the surprise is contained in the physical dimensions of the event. Later the surprise is contained in conceptual dimensions. The child who believes boys are brave is alerted by information implying they are cowardly. If he has no opinion as to whether boys like sculpting clay, he will not brood about that information. Conceptual dissonance is the later symbolic analogue of stimulus discrepancy. Since discrepant events provoke mental work, an environment that contains discrepancy—variations on the child's knowledge—should lead to more rapid growth of knowledge. Environmental variety, by which we mean events with moderate discrepancy, should affect the rate of development in the first year. Support for this view comes from studies comparing the psychological development of children reared in homes with those reared in barren institutions or, in more exotic cases, locations where cultural mores lead parents to restrict children and avoid interaction with them. These children are late in attaining the normal milestones of infancy, such as stranger anxiety, spontaneity, object permanence, and, as we shall see in a moment, the stage when infants actively compare present experience with retrieved schemata in order to interpret discrepant events.

The growth of retrieval processes and prediction

It seems necessary to posit a new set of developmental processes that typically emerge by eight or nine months of age and seem responsible for a variety of phenotypically different phenomena. Before suggesting a name for these hypothetical competences, we will consider some of the reactions that emerge during the last third of the first year. Although temporal covariation among manifestly different phenomena does not necessarily imply a common mechanism, the scientist's affection for parsimony invites an attempt to invent a unitary process.

Increased attentiveness Toward the end of the first year the infant frequently displays greater attention to a variety of discrepant events than he did when he was six or seven months old. If an interesting event is shown to infants from four through thirty-six months of age—in either a cross-sectional or longitudinal design—there is often, but not always, a U-shaped relation between age and fixation time, with a trough around seven to nine months. For example, if masks or drawings of human faces are shown to children four through thirty-six months, attention is prolonged at four months, is markedly lower at seven to eight months, but increases through the second and third years (Kagan 1972). This developmental function for attention to facial masks holds not only for North American children but also for rural Mexican (Finley, Kagan, and Layne 1972) and Guatemalan children as well (Sellers et al. 1972). The U-shaped function also holds for nonsocial visual events as well as attentiveness to speech.

Thomas Bower (1974) has reported a U-shaped function relating age to the likelihood of the child's reaching for an audible object in total darkness. There is a high probability of reaching in the dark at four months, which declines precipitously at six or seven months, only to increase again through eleven months. This function, obtained with sighted children, is not different from the one observed in blind infants (Fraiberg 1968).

Inhibition to a discrepant event Before seven or eight months of age, the infant typically reaches at once for a novel object that is presented after repeated presentation of a familiarized standard, whereas an 11-month-old shows a short, but obvious, delay before reaching for the novel object (Parry 1973; Schaffer, Greenwood, and Parry 1972). The capacity for generalized motor inhibition to an unexpected event is not new, for newborns will inhibit both limb movement and sucking at a sudden onset of visual or auditory stimulation, and 3-month-olds will inhibit an operantly trained kicking response to a mobile different from the one on which they have been trained (Fagen, Rovee, and Kaplan 1976). But these instances of motor inhibition in the young infant seem to be reflexive, automatic reactions to a discrepant event rather than the volitional inhibition of a goal-directed reaching response that characterizes the older infant.

It also appears that the infant who can crawl does not always show avoidance of the deep side of what looks to him like a cliff (a "visual cliff") until after seven months of age, even though he is capable of perceiving the difference between the deep and shallow sides (Campos et al., in press). One interpretation is that the infant older than seven months pauses to evaluate the discrepant quality of the relation between tactile and visual cues and avoids approaching the deep side.

Inhibition is also the dominant initial reaction of 1-year-olds to the introduction of an unfamiliar peer; the child stops playing, ceases to vocalize, and may even retreat from a familiar caretaker. Marler (1976) has noted that among many animal species, including primates and birds, the dominant reaction to an unfamiliar member of the same sex and species is attack, not inhibition. Human child and monkey seem to possess different classes of prepotent reactions to the same class of event. In this case, evolution acted on the response to encounter with the unfamiliar, rather than on the capacity for recognition. What is impressive about the 1-year-old's first reaction to an unfamiliar child, in contrast to the behavior of a young baboon, is the muting of strong emotion—the absence of excessive fear or attack. Perhaps nature intended this posture to facilitate social bonding and the communication of information between members from different human family groups.

Apprehension toward discrepant events

A related change that occurs at this time is a dramatic increase in the likelihood of facial wariness, inhibition of play, and, occasionally, crying, in response to an event whose major characteristic is that it is a discrepant transformation of a schema for an earlier or immediately past experience. Scarr and Salapatek (1970) exposed infants two to twenty-three months of age to six different discrepant (or novel) events—stranger approaching the child, a visual cliff, a jack-in-the-box, a moving mechanical dog, facial masks, and a loud noise. Infants younger than seven months rarely showed any behavioral signs of wariness toward any of these events. The peak display of wariness usually occurred between eleven and eighteen months for most of these episodes and then declined. Loud noise was least likely to evoke wariness. Similarly, infants under seven months showed no signs of apprehension (crying, hiding, or withdrawal) when the mother, who had surreptitiously put a spot of rouge on her child's nose, brought her child up to a pair of contiguous mirrors, one of which reflected a slightly distorted image of the child. However, these signs of apprehension emerged after seven months and peaked during the second year, when over half of the sample displayed some form of avoidance (Schulman and Kaplowitz 1977). Similarly, infants older than one year showed avoidance, crying, or turning away when presented a videotape sequence illustrating another child or himself, whereas 10-month-olds, who were as attentive as the older infants, did not display any sign of uncertainty or inhibition, but were most likely to smile or vocalize (Amsterdam and Greenberg 1977). Although 4-month-olds rarely cried when they experienced an expanding object approaching their faces, simulating the collision of the object with the child, a third of a group of 8-month-olds and over one-half of a group of 12-month-olds cried. What is more important is that the older infants did not cry on the first exposure to this unusual event but only after two or three experiences of collision. This suggests that the "fear" was not a reflexive response to the perception of an impending object but rather the product of a failure to assimilate an extremely unusual event (Cicchetti and Sroufe, in press).

The effect on the child of the appearance of a stranger has been investigated many times in the last twenty years and the consensus from these studies is in accord with the data summarized by Scarr and Salapatek. Inhibition, facial wariness, or overt distress is infrequent prior to seven months, grows dramatically between that time and the end of the first year, and then declines (Bronson 1972; Morgan and Ricciuti 1969; Schaffer 1966; Spitz 1950; Stevens 1971; Tennes and Lampl 1969; Décarie 1974; Emde, Gaensbauer, and Harmon 1976). In a recent study in our laboratory, the behavior of 5-, 10-, 12-, and 20-month-olds was observed following the appearance and approach of an unfamiliar female adult. Although some 5-month-olds inhibited play for a while, maximal inhibition of play occurred among the 10- and 12-month-olds.

In the longitudinal study that we will describe, the first episode of the session was one in which the adult female who was to be the primary examiner for the succeeding episodes sat opposite the infant, who was seated on the mother's lap. The examiner initiated social interaction with the child for a minute, talking, smiling, and interacting with the infant in a nonthreatening way. The occurrence of fretting increased with age, with the largest increase between nine and one-half and thirteen and one-half months; smiling showed a linear decrease with age. The fact that fretting in response to the unfamiliar adult, presumably because of fear, shows its greatest increase at the age when attention and search begin to increase implies the emergence of a new cognitive process. However, this process does not seem to be closely yoked to the behaviors indicative of Piaget's stages of causality or the object concept (Décarie 1974).

It is interesting that the growth function for separation distress, the tendency to cry and show serious inhibition of play following departure of the primary caretaker, is similar among children being raised in the United States, barrios in urban Guatemala, subsistence-farming Indian villages in the Guatemalan highlands, Israeli kibbutzim, !Kung San bands in the

Kalahari Desert (Kagan 1976), and among infants diagnosed as suffering from "failure to thrive" (Jameson and Gordon 1977). Separation distress tends to emerge at about eight months, rises to a peak at thirteen to fifteen months, and then begins to decline (Kagan 1976). Moreover, in blind children the developmental course of distress in response to unfamiliar adults as well as to maternal separation is not much different from the function noted for those with sight. Selma Fraiberg gathered detailed longitudinal observations on ten blind infants observed bimonthly in their homes (Fraiberg 1975; Adelson and Fraiberg 1974). Not only did smiling in response to the voice of mother or other familiar person occur at about the same age for blind as for sighted children (three months), but apprehension and distress at being held by an unfamiliar adult emerged between seven and fifteen months, the same time when sighted children cry on encountering a stranger. Prior to seven months the blind child does not protest when picked up by an unfamiliar person, but after that age he becomes increasingly likely to cry or resist that action. The apprehension toward the stranger is immediately preceded by the emergence of manual exploration of the faces of familiar persons—a response that first appears between five and eight months. This act is akin to the active comparison and vacillation a sighted child shows when presented with a novel toy and a familiar toy. Both responses seem to reflect active comparison of present experience with a stored schema. The sighted child looks back and forth between the new and the old objects; the blind child explores his parent's cheeks, eyes, and nose as if he were comparing the information his fingers were extracting with the knowledge he possessed.

Separation protest, which grows most rapidly between nine and fifteen months in the sighted child, is only a few months delayed in blind children, emerging between ten and nineteen months, with a median age of eleven months, close to the median age for sighted infants. It is remarkable, considering the fact that the child cannot see that the parent is gone, that the blind child displays this milestone at about the same age as a normal sighted child. The incentive event for the blind child's display of separation distress is the sudden absence of the mother's voice or the absence of the sounds that accompany her bodily movements. Fraiberg describes the case of Karen, who showed her first sign of separation distress at about eleven months.

> Mother remarked that she can't leave Karen with anyone anymore, which has not been the case until very recently. Karen cries and is unhappy even with her grandmother whom she has known since birth. Added to Karen's behavior today is her need to always be in contact with mother . . . observers report at 11 months 13 days, "Karen let herself down to the floor and started to creep to the box which was about 2 feet away from her. She was somewhat hesitant or cautious but she was curious. At this moment mother got up to go to Debby (the younger baby sister) to give her the pacifier because she was fussing. Karen immediately started to whimper, reversed direction, and went

> back to cling to the mother's chair, and when mother sat down again reached to touch mother's arm. Mother then reached down and touched Karen's hair." [Fraiberg 1975, p. 330]

Karen stopped protesting at maternal absence by the end of the second year, the same age when separation protest begins to vanish in sighted children. Even though blind infants are deprived of a major source of information, the mind makes its normal appointments. There are two important implications in this result. First, it implies the flexibility of the central nervous system; the capacity to use auditory information to generate schema and maintain cognitive development when vision is not available. Many scientists have argued recently that each species possesses a built-in preparedness to certain stimulus modalities. Rats are prepared to learn an avoidance habit to taste as a conditioned stimulus but not to visual cues, but birds show the opposite response profile. Man is primarily a visual animal, and parental departure is primarily a visual rather than an auditory event. Yet the human child can, if necessary, efficiently use the subtle auditory information to detect absence of the mother. This substitutability of modalities announces the extraordinary versatility of the human central nervous system.

The second implication of the data on blind children is that statements declaring that sensory deprivation retards cognitive development may be overstating the case. Although the blind child is deprived of a major avenue of information, development of some major cognitive milestones of the first year is not delayed in a significant way. There is no simple linear relation between amount or quantity of information and rate of cognitive development. Rather, the child needs a certain amount of variety and discrepancy; it appears that for psychological competences to mature, variety can come from any modality. Dynamic biological forces that change during the opening years of life are relentless in seeking to make the appointments nature arranged for them.

The growth of memory

We believe that the temporal concordance of increased attentiveness, inhibition, wariness, and distress in response to discrepant events, is due to the emergence of several related cognitive competences. These include the child's ability to retrieve a schema related to his present experience despite minimal incentive cues in the immediate field and his ability to retain that schema in memory while he compares the retrieved structure with the present event in an attempt to resolve the discrepancy or inconsistency. The occurrence of wariness toward unfamiliar events may be the result of the child's failure to resolve the inconsistency between the discrepant event and his schemata, despite an attempt to do so. Support for these hypotheses comes from two similar studies of this age period. The first was a short-term longitudinal investigation of eight healthy middle-class Caucasian American children who were observed monthly in both home and laboratory from six to thirteen months of age. Most of the procedures administered to the children were designed to assess the growth of a memorial competence, and the work was supervised by Nathan Fox (Fox, Kagan and Weiskopf, unpublished, 1976).

The longitudinal study: procedures administered monthly at home

Vacillation In this procedure, the child was allowed to play with an attractive toy for thirty seconds. After familiarization the toy was gently removed; the examiner distracted the infant by talking to him for another thirty seconds, and then simultaneously presented the familiar toy and a second, new toy, alternating the side on which the toy was presented. On each monthly visit, the child was administered six trials with six different pairs of familiar and novel toys. Different toys were used on each of the visits. The major dependent variable was occurrence and duration of vacillation, the length of time the infant looked back and forth between the novel and familiar toy. Vacillation was defined as the horizontal movement of eyes or head between the two toys; we believe this movement reflects a cognitive comparison of the two objects. If the infant did not vacillate, that is, if he only looked at one toy or did not look at either during the thirty-second observation period, he was scored as not having displayed vacillation.

Object permanence and variations The children were administered a series of tasks, all requiring them to find an object they had watched the examiner hide. The procedures varied the amount of interference and the delay between the hiding and allowing the child to reach for the object.

1. Simple object permanence with cloth and screen. The object permanence tasks used both cloth and screen for hiding. The objects were small toys or a set of keys. Before each procedure the infant was shown the object and allowed to manipulate it and the cloth or screen for a few minutes before testing began. The following four tasks were designed to investigate the critical phase in the development of object permanence (called Stage 4 object permanence).

a. Cloth over object. The examiner showed the infant a small toy or set of keys. He then placed the object on the floor in front of the infant and covered it with a cloth. During each hiding the mother was asked to hold her infant's hands, releasing them after the cloth was placed over the object. The child's response was recorded.

b. Object under cloth. In this procedure the cloth was first placed on the floor in front of the infant. The infant was shown the object and allowed to manipulate it. The examiner then took the object from the infant and placed it underneath the cloth.

c. Object behind screen. A screen of cardboard (eight by ten inches, on a wooden base) was placed in front of the infant on the floor. While the mother held her infant's hands, the examiner moved the object over the center of the screen and then placed it behind the screen out of the infant's view.

d. Screen in front of object. The object was placed on the floor in front of the child. A screen was then placed in front of the object, between the infant and the toy.

2. Object permanence: "A not B" with two delays. Two identical cloths were placed several inches apart, one to the left and one to the right of the infant's midline. The toy hidden was a key or small number of keys on a thin metal chain, and the cloth with the key under it lay flat.

The child was allowed to play with the keys for a few seconds. The keys were then hidden under one of the cloths (hereafter called A). During the first three presentations the infant was allowed to pull the cloth immediately and to manipulate the object. After three consecutive successful retrievals at location A, the mother was asked to hold her infant's hands. While she did so, the examiner caught the infant's attention and hid the key under the cloth on the opposite side (hereafter called B). An observer then timed either a three- or seven-second delay beginning with the moment the object completely disappeared. After the appropriate delay, the observer signaled the mother to release the infant's hands. If the infant responded correctly (that is, searched at location B), the infant was allowed to play with the object for a few seconds. If the infant made an error (that is, searched at location A and did not correct himself within ten seconds), the examiner showed the key to the infant and allowed him to play with it for a few seconds. If the infant corrected himself within ten seconds, he was allowed to play with the object. If the infant did not search at all after the delay period, the examiner uncovered the object and handed it to him.

Following the first hiding at location B, the toy was hidden either two or three additional times at position B. During these trials there was no delay; the infant could search for the toy immediately. If the infant had not searched at all or had made the error and not corrected himself in the first hiding, the object was hidden three times. If the infant had not made an error in the first hiding or had made an error but corrected himself within the ten seconds allowed, the object was hidden twice at location B. After the B hidings, the object was hidden on the opposite side (location A) with the second of the two delay conditions. Two orders of the delay condition were employed; half of the subjects received the three-second delay first, followed by the seven-second delay; the other half received the seven-second delay first.

3. Object permanence: two cloths, absent object. This procedure was identical to that employed in the "A not B" task except that there was only a three-second delay and when the examiner hid the object at location B, he

kept it in his hand, shielding it from the infant's view. If and when the child searched correctly at location B, no object was present.

4. Object permanence: "A not B" procedure with substituted object. This procedure was identical to that in the "A not B" tasks. However, this time the examiner hid at location B an object different from the one the child had seen initially. If and when the child searched correctly at location B, he found an object different from the one he had watched the examiner hide.

5. Object permanence: screened hiding. Two identical cylindrical forms were placed in front of the infant. A small object was hidden under one of the cylinders, and the examiner then placed a screen between the infant and the cylinders for three seconds. The examiner then removed the screen, the mother released her infant's hands, and the infant's response was recorded.

Laboratory procedures

1. Attention to photographs of faces with delays. After mother and infant had become acclimated to a laboratory room, the lights were dimmed and a rear projection screen of glass was placed on the stage. The screen had a piece of cardboard taped over it with two open squares (four and one-half by six inches) with centers ten inches apart. Two Kodak Carousel projectors were used to project two slides simultaneously through the two openings. An observer timed the stimulus presentation; activation of the projector automatically marked the onset and offset of a stimulus presentation on a polygraph.

The infant saw the following sequence of stimuli: two identical photographs of smiling female faces, one in each aperture, for thirty seconds (called A faces). After an interval of thirty seconds, during which a homogeneous dark green light appeared in the squares, the infant saw one of the original photographs in one aperture and a different smiling female face (called face B) in the other. The position of the novel face varied across children and months. The faces were Ekta-chrome slides of smiling, adult, Caucasian females. No attempt was made to control for amount or distribution of hair, facial color, or contour. However, the size of all faces was identical for all stimuli, and each month a different pair of photographs was used.

The infant's fixation time and direction of gaze was coded by an observer from a small aperture beneath the screen. The observer recording fixation did not know which square either the novel or the familiar photograph appeared in. After the thirty-second presentation of the second set of photographs, there was a fifteen-second interval during which the room lights were turned on and the sequence of other tasks continued. At the end of the sequence of other tasks, which typically lasted twenty minutes, the lights were again dimmed and the screen placed on the stage. The infant was again presented with two photographs, in one aperture photograph B (the one shown twenty minutes earlier), in the other an entirely new face (photograph C). The photographs were presented for thirty seconds, while the direction of gaze of the infant was recorded. The square in which the novel face was presented varied across children and months. In order to properly counterbalance the presentation of photographs, twenty-four different photographs were used (eight trios of faces).

2. Attention to masks. A clay mask of an adult male face mounted on a wooden frame was presented on the stage. Each presentation of the mask lasted for twenty seconds with an interval of ten seconds between stimuli. The mask was presented repeatedly until the child became habituated to it. The criterion for habituation was defined as that trial when the total fixation to each of the last two trials was 50 percent less than total fixation time on each of the preceding two trials and less than the total fixation of the first trial. Two observers in the testing room behind the curtain coded the infant's fixation to the stimulus and his vocalization and fretting. The technician in the adjoining room, which contained a polygraph, calculated fixation time on each trial and indicated through headphones when the infant had met the criterion for habituation. Following the last habituation trial, a mask of a human male face with scrambled features—the transformation—was presented for two twenty-second trials with an interstimulus interval of ten seconds. If the infant began to cry, the trial sequence was halted until he became calm.

3. Separation distress. At ten and twelve months of age children in an unfamiliar playroom were observed following the departure of their mothers. When the child was playing happily, the mother rose and left the room. Observers coded the occurrence of fretting and crying.

Results

The results indicated remarkable behavioral similarity among the eight children in the age at which they met the criterion for each of these tasks. Table 2.2 presents the age at which each of the eight children "passed the tests" and the median age for all eight. All children displayed vacillation on four of six trials by seven months. One month later, all the children had passed the simple object permanence tasks on all four variations; in another month they showed successful performance on the "A not B" problem with a three-second delay. By ten months all solved the "A not B" problem with a seven-second delay. Moreover, soon after the children could solve the "A not B" problem with a seven-second delay they went to search at location A when they did not find an object at location B and cried at maternal departure. By eleven months most were mature enough to go to location A when they found a substitute object at location B. About one month later they looked longer at photograph C than they did at photograph B following a twenty-minute delay interval, looked longer at the scrambled mask

Table 2.2 Age at which each subject met criterion for solution of task in longitudinal study of Cambridge children.

Criterion	Age of subjects A-H (to nearest half month)								Mean age
	A	B	C	D	E	F	G	H	
Vacillation between old and new	6	7	7	7	6	6	6	7	6.5
Stage IV object permanence	7	8	8	8	7	8	7	7	7.5
A not B, 3-sec. delay	8	8	8	9	9	9	8	8	8.4
A not B, 7-sec. delay	8	9	9	10	9	10	9	9	9.1
Absent object	9	9	10	10	10	11	9	10	9.8
Substituted object	10	11	11	11	11	12	10	10	10.8
Screened hiding	11	12	12	12	11	12	12	11	11.6
Face photos: fixation for B>A, 30-sec. delay	9	9	9	9	9	9	9	9	9.0
Face photos: fixation for C>B, 20-min. delay	12	12	12	12	12	12	12	12	12.0
Masks: fixation for transformation greater than standard	12	12	12	12	12	12	12	12	12.0
Crying at maternal departure	10	10	10	10	10	10	10	10	10.0

than at the first presentation of the regular mask, and could remember the location of the toy even when the hiding place was screened for three seconds.

We suggest that a key to understanding these changes between six and thirteen months is an increase in the infant's ability to retrieve schemata from memory despite interference, to hold those structures on the stage of short-term memory, and to compare those retrieved structures with present events. The child of eight months, unlike the 4- or 5-month-old, is able to retrieve (not just recognize) a schema for an event that occurred more than a few seconds earlier when there is minimal perceptual support in the immediate field. The 8-month-old solves the object permanence problem because he can generate a representation of the absent object. However, if a screen is placed between him and the object, the schema is not articulated enough to survive. By thirteen months that distraction is irrelevant. The suggestion that a memory capacity is central to the object permanence victory is supported by the data on length of delay in the "A not B" paradigm. If the delay between hiding the object at location B and allowing the child to reach for it was seven seconds, 7- and 8-month-olds typically went to location A; if the delay was three seconds, these children did not make the error and went correctly to location B. But no 10-month-old made the error under either three- or seven-second delays, a result suggesting the growth of increased recall capacity between eight and ten months of age.

Further, we noted that it is not until twelve months that the child looked longer at photograph C than at B, following a twenty-minute delay after the last exposure to photograph B. And it was not until twelve months of age that the child would look longer at the transformation of the mask than he did at the first, unexpected presentation. Both of these phenomena imply that the child is retrieving the schema for an original event that occurred more than a few seconds ago and comparing it with his present experience. It appears that this capacity does not become reliable until the end of the first year.

The occurrence of separation distress in all eight children at ten months of age, in the middle of this growth process, is viewed as suggesting that a memory competence is contributing to the separation phenomenon. We shall argue in more detail later that in order to become distressed following departure, the child must retrieve the schema of the mother's presence after she has exited and compare that with his present experience. For those children who cry following maternal departure, that response typically occurs within twenty seconds of maternal exit. For those children who cry before the mother leaves the room—while she is getting up and walking toward the door—it is necessary to posit a different competence, namely, the capacity to predict a future event.

Before presenting a more general discussion, we will present the results of a recently completed similar cross-cultural study we conducted with Indian children growing up in one of two subsistence-farming villages on Lake Atitlán in the highlands of northwest Guatemala (Kagan et al. 1977). One of the villages, San Pedro la Laguna, has a population of about 5,000 and is a modernizing town. The other village, San Marcos la Laguna, has a population a little under 1,000, and although located only a few kilometers away, its inhabitants are poorer, more illiterate, and have more disease. They live in small thatched bamboo huts and are physically and psychologically more isolated than the people of San Pedro.

The Guatemalan study

The sample included eighty-seven infants five to twenty-one months of age who were tested in their homes with their mothers present. The examiner was an Indian woman who lived on the lake. The coder was a Caucasian woman who lived in each of the villages during the course of data gathering but whose permanent home was Guatemala City. In San Marcos all infants between five and twenty-one months of age who were healthy enough to be tested were administered the procedures. The age of the infants was verified in the municipal registration book that records all births. In the larger village of San Pedro, infants were chosen from a representative census of the village, with an attempt to balance the sample for sex of child and social class of family. The sample was composed of forty-five San Pedro infants (twenty-two boys and twenty-three girls) and forty-two San Marcos infants (twenty-three boys and nineteen girls).

Before collecting any data, the examiner and the coder visited the home of each subject on one or two occasions to become familiar to the household and to reduce the possibility that the child would be unusually apprehensive or inhibited during the procedures. When the two women felt that the child had overcome initial apprehension to them, the testing began. The procedures described below were administered over five to six separate sessions, for testing was terminated if the child became irritable or tired. We believe these data were gathered under optimal conditions.

1. Vacillation. The infant was allowed to play with a particular toy for twenty seconds, after which the examiner gently took the toy from the child, hid it for five seconds, and then presented the child simultaneously with two toys, the one he had just played with and a new one. The major variables were the number of times the child looked back and forth between the two toys (vacillation) and, if the child played, how long he played with each toy. Each child was given five different vacillation trials with five different pairs of toys. The five pairs of toys were the same for all children; however, order of presentation was controlled so that not all children were presented with the same pair of toys on the first trial.

2. Inhibition to novelty. The child was shown the identical toy for six repeated trials, each lasting about eight seconds, with an interval of about

three seconds between trials. On the seventh trial the infant was shown a single novel toy. Latency in the time to reach for the toy was coded on each trial; the behavior of interest was the tendency to inhibit reaching for the novel toy on the critical seventh trial. The procedure was repeated three times with three different pairs of toys. Although the pairs were the same for all children, the order of presentation of the pairs was varied so that not all children were presented with the same order of toy pairs.

The primary dependent variable was the difference in latency to reach for the novel toy minus the latency to reach for the familiar toy on the last standard trial. The criterion for inhibition was an increase in latency equal to or greater than one second.

3. Object permanence. All children were administered three object permanence problems in which toys were hidden under one or two cloths: (a) the standard object permanence problem, in which a toy is hidden under one cloth, (b) the two-cloth traverse problem, in which the examiner first places the toy under one cloth, and then moves it across an open space to a second cloth while the child is watching; and (c) the standard "A not B" procedure, in which the child is first allowed to find the toy twice under cloth A, but on the third trial watches the examiner hide the toy under cloth B. The delay between hiding the object at location B and permitting the child to reach for it was less than three seconds. In all three procedures the child was allowed to play with the toy for about thirty seconds before the examiner gently took it from him. These three procedures were not administered consecutively but interspersed throughout the session, in some cases, when the child was tired, the procedures were administered on different days.

4. Separation distress. The tendency to cry and show inhibition of play at maternal departure was assessed on the last testing session, typically the fifth or sixth time the child had been seen by the two women. The child was first allowed to play with an interesting set of toys for fifteen minutes. When the child was playing happily, both the mother (or some other primary caretaker) and the examiner left the room, leaving the infant alone with the coder, who had visited the home on at least five earlier occasions, and so was not totally unfamiliar to the child. The main variables quantified during the two minutes of caretaker's absence were amount of time playing, fretting, or crying.

5. Play. In addition to the fifteen-minute play session prior to the separation procedure on the last session, the child was also observed playing for a similar fifteen-minute interval in an earlier session. The ten toys were culturally appropriate and selected to invite "pretend" play in which the child used the toys symbolically. The children tended to play over 90 percent of the time in both play sessions. The variables of interest were total amount of time playing, as well as the amount of time the child engaged in simple,

relational, and symbolic-pretend play. Simple play was defined as the manipulation of one toy at a time. Relational play was coded when the child related two toys together. Symbolic-pretend play was coded when the child showed evidence of using the toy as if it were a real object in his environment. Typical instances of symbolic play included feeding a doll, treating a toy truck as if it were a vehicle, and combing a doll's hair or the child's own hair with a toy comb.

Results

Vacillation The earliest display of vacillation occurred at five months in San Pedro and seven months in San Marcos, and during these early ages more San Pedro infants showed vacillation. When the criterion for "success" was vacillation on two or more of the five trials, at least 50 percent of each group met the criterion by eight months of age. By eleven to twelve months all children were displaying vacillation on at least two of the five trials, and by one year all children were vacillating on at least four of the five trials, a few months later than the eight Cambridge, Massachusetts, children, to whom the same procedures were administered (see table 2.3).

When we examined the proportion of trials on which the child played more with the novel toys than with the familiar toys, we found that San Marcos children passed the median criterion by seven to eight months, San Pedro children by eleven to twelve months. By seventeen months all children played more with the new toy than with the old. We also examined the data for those occasions when the number of vacillations between the two toys was three or more (that is, when the child had to look at one toy at least twice and the other toy at least once). San Pedro children reached the median criterion by five to six months, the San Marcos children several months later, at eleven to twelve months.

Inhibition to novelty The first appearance of inhibition occurred at 5 to 6 months of age in San Pedro. The 5- and 6-month-old San Marcos infants were motorically too passive to respond in this situation. When inhibition on two of the three trials was the criterion, 50 percent of the San Marcos and San Pedro children met that criterion by nine to ten months. (A similar procedure administered to infants in Glasgow, Scotland, revealed that inhibition to novelty emerged at nine months [Schaffer, Greenwood, and Parry 1972]). Thus, inhibition to novelty tended to occur a little later than vacillation, and on both procedures the first appearance of the "response" occurred a month or two earlier in San Pedro than in San Marcos (table 2.4).

This procedure was one of the few that revealed a curvilinear function with age. The 5- and 6-month-olds, as well as the children over fifteen months, were less likely to show inhibition than the children from seven to

TABLE 2.3. DIFFERENCES IN VACILLATION BEHAVIOR AMONG CHILDREN IN TWO GUATEMALAN VILLAGES.

AGE (MOS.)	PERCENTAGE VACILLATING ON 1 OR MORE OF 5 TRIALS	PERCENTAGE VACILLATING ON 2 OR MORE OF 5 TRIALS	MEAN NUMBER OF VACILLATION TRIALS
SAN MARCOS CHILDREN (n = 42)			
5-6	0	0	0
7-8	83	50	1.5
9-10	83	67	1.8
11-12	100	100	3.8
13-14	100	100	4.6
15-16	100	100	4.3
17-21	100	100	4.4
SAN PEDRO CHILDREN (n = 45)			
5-6	83	67	2.5
7-8	83	67	1.7
9-10	50	50	2.0
11-12	100	100	3.7
13-14	100	100	4.0
15-16	100	100	4.0
17-21	100	100	4.0

fourteen months of age. The younger children were too immature to display the response; the older children inhibited their responses less often because they assimilated the novelty quickly and were bored with the procedure.

Object permanence The San Pedro children were slightly precocious compared with those from San Marcos, for at least half of them solved the simple object permanence and traverse problem at seven to eight months of age and the "A not B" problem by nine to ten months of age. The San Marcos children reached the median criterion for all three procedures at eleven to twelve months. All the San Pedro children were solving all three problems by eleven to twelve months, whereas this ability did not occur in San Marcos children until seventeen to twenty-one months of age (see table 2.5).

TABLE 2.4. DIFFERENCES IN INHIBITION TO NOVELTY AMONG CHILDREN IN TWO GUATEMALAN VILLAGES.

AGE (MOS.)	PERCENTAGE WITH INHIBITION ≥1 SEC. TO NOVEL EVENT, ≥ 1 TRIAL	PERCENTAGE WITH INHIBITION TO NOVEL EVENT ON 2 OF 3 TRIALS	MEAN NUMBER OF INHIBITION TRIALS
SAN MARCOS CHILDREN (n = 42)			
5-6	0	0	0
7-8	67	16	0.8
9-10	67	67	1.8
11-12	71	14	0.8
13-14	40	20	0.6
15-16	33	16	0.5
17-21	63	25	0.9
SAN PEDRO CHILDREN (n = 45)			
5-6	50	16	0.7
7-8	50	33	0.8
9-10	100	50	1.8
11-12	80	20	1.0
13-14	100	33	1.3
15-16	67	33	1.0
17-21	55	22	0.8

Separation distress By nine to ten months of age at least half of the San Marcos and San Pedro infants showed an inhibition of play of at least sixty seconds following maternal departure. This is the age when object permanence and inhibition of response to novelty are emerging in most infants. All three problems required the infant to remember an event that happened several seconds earlier. No 5- to 6-month-old child in either village was distressed, but all 9- to 10-month-olds in San Marcos cried to the departure, and at least 50 percent of the San Pedro children did. As can be seen from table 2.6, the growth function for the San Pedro infant resembles that found with North American infants tested in Cambridge, with separation distress first appearing around seven to eight months, peaking at twelve to fifteen months, and then beginning to decline. By contrast, the San Marcos func-

TABLE 2.5. DIFFERENCES IN ATTAINMENT OF OBJECT PERMANENCE AMONG CHILDREN IN TWO GUATEMALAN VILLAGES.

AGE (MOS.)	PERCENTAGE SOLVING OBJECT PERMANENCE PROBLEM	PERCENTAGE SOLVING TRAVERSE PROBLEM	PERCENTAGE SOLVING "A NOT B" PROBLEM
SAN MARCOS CHILDREN (n = 42)			
5-6	0	0	0
7-8	0	0	0
9-10	33	0	0
11-12	86	86	71
13-14	100	75	75
15-16	100	100	67
17-21	100	100	100
SAN PEDRO CHILDREN (n = 45)			
5-6	0	0	0
7-8	50	50	33
9-10	67	67	67
11-12	100	100	100
13-14	100	100	100
15-16	100	100	100
17-21	100	100	100

tion is bimodal, with a peak at nine to ten months, decreased distress at eleven to fourteen months, followed by an increase in upset. This was the only procedure in which the growth functions for the San Marcos and San Pedro infants were different, and more San Marcos children showed the critical reaction earlier. We believe this is because the San Marcos children have far less variety of experience than those in San Pedro, so that the separation event was a more discrepant experience for them and led to more irritability prior to one year of age. It was generally the case that the San Marcos children were more likely to cry in response to most of the unfamiliar testing procedures.

Play Relational play, in either or both of the play sessions, appeared in the children of both villages by seven to eight months of age, the same age it

TABLE 2.6. DIFFERENCES IN SEPARATION DISTRESS AMONG CHILDREN IN TWO GUATEMALAN VILLAGES.

AGE (MOS.)	PERCENTAGE FRETTING OR CRYING IN RESPONSE TO MATERNAL SEPARATION	PERCENTAGE SHOWING $\geq$ 60 SEC. INHIBITION OF PLAY FOLLOWING MATERNAL DEPARTURE
SAN MARCOS CHILDREN (n = 42)		
5-6	0	0
7-8	33	33
9-10	100	60
11-12	57	57
13-14	0	40
15-16	83	83
17-21	50	63
SAN PEDRO CHILDREN (n = 45)		
5-6	0	0
7-8	16	16
9-10	50	67
11-12	33	50
13-14	60	80
15-16	33	67
17-21	63	75

was first seen in North American children. Symbolic-pretend play first emerged at twelve months in San Pedro and thirteen months in San Marcos. By thirteen to fourteen months, one-half of the children were showing symbolic-pretend play, even though the absolute amount of time in which this response occurred was small, typically thirty seconds, or less, of the fifteen-minute period. San Pedro children played symbolically about thirty seconds, San Marcos children about fifteen seconds (see table 2.7).

In sum, children in both villages displayed a similar sequence of development and one that resembled the function for the Cambridge children. Vacillation was the first response to appear, followed by the almost simultaneous emergence of inhibition to novelty, object permanence, and separa-

TABLE 2.7. DIFFERENCES IN OCCURRENCE OF PRETEND PLAY AMONG CHILDREN IN TWO GUATEMALAN VILLAGES.

AGE (MOS.)	PERCENTAGE OF SAN MARCOS CHILDREN SHOWING ≥1 ACTS OF PRETEND PLAY	PERCENTAGE OF SAN PEDRO CHILDREN SHOWING ≥1 ACTS OF PRETEND PLAY
5-6	0	0
7-8	0	0
9-10	0	0
11-12	0	16
13-14	60	67
15-16	100	83
17-21	100	78

tion distress at nine to ten months. These behaviors were followed by symbolic-pretend play soon after the first birthday (see table 2.8). Although the Cambridge children tended to be a few months advanced over the more isolated Indian infants in emergence of object permanence and vacillation, perhaps because of the greater variety in their environment and their better health, the sequence of milestones was remarkably similar in both cultures. The results of both studies imply that growth of memory ability may be one of the central processes of the last half of the first year of life. It is not unimportant to note that longitudinal observations of one infant girl with Down's Syndrome revealed that vacillation, object permanence, the "A not B" error, and stranger and separation apprehension all appeared between seven and nine months of age (Goodrich, unpublished, 1977).

The centrality of memory during early development, with special reference to the object permanence procedure, is also supported by data from the animal laboratory (Rosenblum and Alpert 1974). Although adult monkeys can solve the object permanence problem (called the delayed response test by comparative psychologists) after a delay of hours, and adult chimpanzees after an overnight delay, 2-month-old rhesus macaques cannot perform reliably following only a five-second delay after 900 trials. Five-month-old macaque infants are a little better at this task, for they achieve 90 percent correct performance with five-second delays; but they cannot tolerate a delay as long as forty seconds. "The infant monkey is not capable of performing efficiently in longer delays until 8 or 9 months of age while 5 months appears to be a minimal age for attaining good performance with shorter delays," reported Robert Zimmerman and Charles Torrey (1965). Amplification of retrieval memory capacity, which is only a little advanced in monkey over human, seems to be critical for solving the object permanence problem.

TABLE 2.8. SEQUENCE OF DEVELOPMENTAL MILESTONES ATTAINED BY CHILDREN IN TWO GUATEMALAN VILLAGES.

	YOUNGEST AGE WHEN ANY CHILD FIRST MET CRITERION		AGE WHEN 50% OF AGE COHORT (MOS.) MET CRITERION	
RESPONSE	SAN PEDRO	SAN MARCOS	SAN PEDRO	SAN MARCOS
Vacillation: 2 of 5 trials	5	7	5-6	7-8
Vacillation: number of glances >3	5	9	5-6	9-10
Inhibition at novelty: 2 of 3 trials	6	8	9-10	9-10
Object permanence (Stage IV)	7	9	7-8	11-12
Object permanence: traverse	7	11	7-8	11-12
Object permanence: "A not B" (3-sec. delay)	7	11	9-10	11-12
Separation anxiety: crying	7	7	9-10	9-10
Separation anxiety: inhibition of play	7	7	9-10	9-10
Pretend play	12	13	13-14	13-14

W. S. Millar (1974) has invented a clever procedure that supports the hypothesis of a change in memory competence toward the end of the first year. Each infant, six or nine months old, was seated in front of an aluminum canister manipulandum. If the child hit the canister in front of him he was rewarded with sounds and changes in light in front of him. For some, a very distinctive green plastic ring circumscribed the area where the reward would appear. For others, the ring was absent and so the source of the reward was not visible. The 9-month-olds banged the canister even when the green ring was not present. The 6-month-olds increased their rate of striking the canister only if the green ring was present. These data imply that 9-month-olds activated schemata representing the reward that might be delivered if they exhibited proper behavior, while the 6-month-olds were too immature to activate—or remember—that idea and required a reminder in the form of the green ring in order to be motivated to hit the canister. "Six month olds, in contrast to 9 month old infants, are incapable of making the spontaneous use of centrally held information and relating it to ongoing activities," wrote Millar in 1974 (p. 515). H. R. Schaffer (1974) has also suggested that the new cognitive competence that emerges at this age is the ability to activate from memory schemata for *absent* objects and to use them to evaluate a situation: "Initially, each stimulus is treated in isolation; and although the memory store may be checked for representations of that same stimulus, it is not compared with different stimuli or their representations. In time, however, the infant becomes capable of relating stimuli to one another . . . As a result the strange stimulus can be considered simultaneously with the familiar standard, even though the latter is centrally stored and must therefore be retrieved" (Schaffer 1974, p. 22).

We believe that the stage that theorists call "short-term memory" collapses after most experiences, especially if the events are poorly articulated, in infants under seven months of age. Furthermore, the structures created in the past cannot be retrieved easily from long-term memory in the absence of relevant incentive events, even though the infant younger than six months displays recognition memory for some events after a two-week delay (Fagan 1973). But we believe that by nine to twelve months of age changes in the central nervous system permit the child to recall schemata without the benefit of relevant cues and to allow the stage of short-term memory to remain intact for a longer period of time. Hence the child is able to act on the basis of the information he has remembered.

Leslie Brody trained 8- and 12-month-olds in our laboratory to touch the one of two stimuli that had been lit and varied the delay between the offset of the lighted stimulus and the time when the child was allowed to make the operant touching response. For half the subjects a transparent screen separated the child from the stimulus during the delays (0, 3, 6, or 9 seconds). For the other half, the separating screen was opaque. Some of the 1-year-olds were able to remember which stimulus had been lit, even at the longest delay and when the screen was opaque. The 8-month-olds were generally unable to remember the location of the positive stimulus at 3-, 6- or 9-second delays when the screen was opaque, or at 9-second delays when the screen was clear.

In a similar study that had a longitudinal design, ten infants were seen monthly from 8 to 12 months of age. The infant's task on each visit to the laboratory was to retrieve a toy he had watched being hidden under one of two identical cloths. Delay (1, 3, or 7 seconds) and interference (no screen, a transparent screen, or an opaque screen) were varied, and all infants were tested under all conditions. The infants were administered increasingly more difficult items as they passed the easier tests. There was a steady improvement in the performance of all children during the 4-month period of study. At 8 months no infant was able to retrieve the object at a 1-second delay when an opaque screen was lowered during the brief interval, while four 8-month-olds could solve the problem with a 7-second delay if no screen was introduced. By 12 months of age all infants were able to retrieve the toy when the opaque screen was present for 1 or 3 seconds, and seven of the ten infants could solve the problem when the opaque screen was lowered for as long as 7 seconds (Szpak, unpublished, 1977). As in the earlier study, the ability to retrieve a representation of a brief, novel event after a 7- to 10-second delay during which an interfering and distracting event occurred increases linearly during the last third of the first year.

On the surface there appears to be a paradox. When 6-month-olds are shown a pair of faces, one of which they saw two weeks earlier, they look longer at the new face (Fagan 1973). But after only a nine-second delay, 6-month-olds do not seem able to recall which of two lights was lit. However, the paradox may be more apparent than real. In the latter situation, the child must retrieve a past event that was brief and unfamiliar and, what may be most important, *issue an instrumental response based on the retained information.* It is possible that an important element of the maturational advance at eight months is the ability to coordinate retrieved information with an instrumental action. Schaffer et al. have suggested that it is necessary to posit two quite different processes to explain the inhibition and wariness that emerge at around 9 months of age: "a perceptual learning process (concerned with the perceptual acquisition and storing of experience) and a response selection process (responsible for the choice of a motor response deemed suitable in the light of stored experience)" (Schaffer, Greenwood, and Parry 1972, p. 174). This supposition implies that the emergent competence at nine months involves the activation of alternative structures following recognition of a discrepant event.

The child's new capacity to retrieve structures for events not in the immediate field can help to explain some of the phenomena listed earlier. Let us apply this idea to the inverted U function for attention to transformations of familiarized events. The 4-month-old is highly attentive to a moderately discrepant event because he maintains attention until he assimilates the event to a relevant schema. As indicated earlier, the infant devotes less attention to events that are very similar to schemata he holds, or to those that are unrelated to his schemata, than to moderately discrepant events. As he grows older his reservoir of schemata is amplified and his ability to assimilate event to schema becomes more efficient. Therefore the 7-month-old *looks less* than the 4-month-old at a particular discrepancy. But that principle predicts that a 12-month-old should study the same event even less than a 7-month-old. Instead, he does quite the opposite; he is more attentive. One possible explanation for the increase in attention is that he detects new aspects of the stimulus that the 7-month-old misses. If the event is complex, like a face, that is not an unreasonable suggestion. But the U-shaped function relating attention and age holds for stimuli as simple as a design constructed of a few lines. We can also eliminate increased familiarity, for this phenomenon holds for events that are relatively unfamiliar to the child. But we can account for the increased attention at one year if we assume that the older infant is able to retrieve a representation of a repeated experience, hold it in memory, and try to relate it to the discrepant event in his perceptual field. If the event is a mask, he retrieves his representation of a regular face and tries to generate the relation between his knowledge of the normal face and the mask in front of him. As long as the trace of the past event remains articulated and the infant continues to relate it to his present experience in the service of understanding, he remains attentive.

An alternative explanation of the U-shaped function for attention does not focus on the increased attention at one year, but rather on the decreased attentiveness at seven months. Suppose that the masks or the block frighten the 7-month-old and he turns away from them. When he has subdued his fear several months later, he shows prolonged attention for the same reason he did at four months. The problem with this interpretation is that the 7-month-old reveals no signs of fear toward these events. He does not show facial wariness, freeze, bury his head in his mother's lap, nor cry, and he does not show the patterns of autonomic reactivity characteristic of states of fear. Rather, he seems bored!

The appearance of motor inhibition in reaching for the discrepant object implies that the child pauses while generating structures representative of the earlier event. During the period when that mental work is occurring the child remains inhibited.

This theoretical position implies that successful retrieval of a toy in stages 4 and 5 of the object concept sequence may be due, in large measure, to the enhanced ability to retrieve structures for past events, rather than emergence of the belief in the permanence of objects. Piaget, in *The Construction of Reality in the Child* (1954), offers possible interpretations for the 8-month-old's tendency to search at location A (after successful retrievals at A) rather than go to B, where he saw the toy being covered: "Three interpretations seem possible to us according to whether one attributes these strange behavior patterns to difficulties of memory or of spatial localization or to the incomplete formation of the object concept'' (p. 60). He dismisses the possibility that memory failure could be the major or only cause of the behavior because the infant seems to be so attentive to the placing of the object: ''The child is watching the object with the greatest fixity as it disappears in B yet immediately afterward he turns to A; it would therefore be unrealistic to admit that he forgets the displacements out of mere absent-mindedness'' (p. 64). Apparently Piaget equates the child's attentiveness to an event in the perceptual field with the capacity to retrieve and to hold a representation of that event on the stage of memory for seconds after the event has terminated. But these are quite different processes. Piaget hints that the second interpretation is more likely when he suggests that the infant does not assimilate the displacement of objects and localize them from the point of view of action. But he acknowledges that this mechanism alone also fails to account for the phenomenon.

Piaget then turns to his favored interpretation: For the infant the object does not remain the same from location to location because the object is not separate from its place. There is no such entity as a rattle, only a ''rattle in a hand,'' or a ''rattle under a cup,'' or ''a rattle on a table.'' The child's error in the ''A not B'' situation is due to the fact that, ''the object is not yet sufficiently individualized to be dissociated from the global behavior related to position A'' (p. 63).

But Piaget is reluctant to place all the explanatory power in this last mechanism and so declares simply, without detailed argument, that all three interpretations constitute a single explanation: ''Such then are the three possible explanations for the phenomenon: defect of memory, defect of spatial localization, or defect of objectification. But far from trying to choose among them, we shall on the contrary try to show that these three explanations, seemingly different, in reality constitute only a single explanation seen from three distinct points of view. It is only if one retained one of the three explanations to the exclusion of the two others that it would be disputable. But if all three are accepted, they are complementary'' (pp. 63-64).

Thus, although Piaget clearly wants to make memory a secondary phenomenon, he is reluctant to dismiss it completely. There are problems with Piaget's supposition that the knowledge of the toy's location under a cloth is contained in the action and spatial context in which it is first retrieved. First, how is it possible for the 8-month-old to retrieve the toy on its first hiding before he has ever reached for it? Moreover, why does the infant fail if the delay between the hiding and the opportunity to reach is too long, say ten seconds, whereas he does not fail if the delay is short? Finally, when a 9-month-old makes the ''A not B'' error, Piaget explains the search at location A, rather than at B where the toy is hidden, by claiming that the concept of the toy includes its location and that knowledge is contained in the prior motor actions toward location A. If this were true, the error should occur less often if the child were not permitted to have several successful motor retrievals at location A, but merely watched an adult examiner place the object at A. However, the probability of error among 9-month-olds is the same whether the child watches the toy being covered at location A or actually retrieves it at A prior to the reaching trial at location B (Evans 1973). In addition, recent data imply that the number of successful retrievals at location A is not consistently related to the probability of the "A not B" error (Gratch 1976; Butterworth 1977), and the child does not make the error if the delay between the hiding at location B and opportunity to reach is minimal (less than one second) (Harris 1973).

These data provide a challenge to Piaget's interpretation of stages 4 and 5 of the object concept, as well as to his view that the major source of knowledge during the first year is contained in sensory-motor schemes. Gerald Gratch has acknowledged the possible role of memory: "The A-B phenomenon is a real developmental event . . . study of how infants keep track of objects in space must be an integral part of any investigation of the development of object awareness" (1976). But Gratch is still not ready to deny Piaget's original position that the child's actions lead to the creation of his belief in the permanence of objects. He is not convinced that the object permanence victory is primarily the result of an emerging memory competence. Thomas Bower (1974), too, dismisses the role of memory in object permanence because 5-month-olds can recognize some past events. But Bower fails to appreciate the difference between recognition and retrieval, the importance of the degree of familiarity of the information originally witnessed and later recalled, and the additional burden of coordinating an action with a retrieved schema, all of which are essential components of the object permanence problem.

How different are these two views? At one level it must be true that a 12-month-old believes in the permanence of the hidden object. The child would not search for the toy if he did not believe it was there. Whereas Piaget simply posits the emergence of the cognitive structure called the object concept, we suggest that the structure—that is, the belief in the permanence of the object—can only occur after the memory ability has matured. The new structure is dependent upon the prior development of the new competence. There are similar examples in development. The child cannot acquire a representation of the human face (a structure) until he is competent to scan inside the boundary of a figure, somewhere between five and seven weeks of age. The smile of recognition at a human face indicates, therefore, both that the child is capable of internal scanning and the fact that he has acquired a schema of a face.

Thus one can view the 8-month-old's reaching for a covered rattle as reflecting either an enhancement in memory capacity or the initial development of the concept of the permanent object—or both. Each is a valid statement. The description one prefers to denote this era of development depends on one's theoretical purposes.

The emphasis on the process of memory, rather than on the structure called the object concept, in interpreting the child's behavior between eight and twelve months is in accord with other work on cognitive development in older children. The improvement in recognition and recall memory after six years of age may be due to activation of processes involving organization, rehearsal, and retrieval rather than new knowledge structures. The ability to answer correctly the question, "There are seven red wooden beads and four yellow wooden beads; are there more red beads or wooden beads?" depends in part, on the ability to hold the entire question in short-term memory and examine it mentally without the information vanishing. It may not necessarily be due to the presence of a new structure that represents the nesting of hierarchically organized classes. The same point has been made for conservation. It is not clear whether the older child's increased skill at retrieval occurs because of the memory stage remaining intact for a longer period of time, more rapid manipulation of the information, or better mental organization of the information. In the case of the 8-month-old, however, the first explanation is more likely to be correct; the information remains accessible for a longer time. It is less clear that this is the best explanation for the change in children's behavior with class inclusion problems at six and seven years of age. The hypothesis that toward the end of the first year the infant becomes capable of retrieving past information and applying that knowledge to the present will explain object permanence, increased vacillation, inhibition, and increased fixation time. But it will not explain, without additional assumptions, the apprehension, inhibition, and crying following separation from the caretaker.

Separation distress

A major phenomenon that emerges toward the end of the first year of life has acquired the name *separation anxiety* because the child becomes upset when he is separated from his primary caretaker(s). That label is misleading since the child is less likely to cry when he crawls or walks away from his caretaker or is taken away than when the caretaker leaves him. Indeed, H. L. Rheingold and C. O. Eckerman (1970) have shown that if a 1-year-old child crawls or walks from his mother into an empty room, so that he has no visual access to her, he shows minimal signs of distress. But if his mother should leave him, the probability that he will fret is much greater. However, if the father or another familiar adult remains with the child when the mother leaves, he is unlikely to become distressed (Kotelchuck 1972). It is only when a parent leaves the infant with an unfamiliar person or alone in an unfamiliar setting that he is likely to show apprehension. Furthermore, if the mother's departure occurs in a familiar context, like the living room of the child's home, the child is less likely to become distressed than if the separation occurs in an unfamiliar setting (Ross et al. 1975). If the mother departs through an atypical exit in the home (a closet), the child shows more apprehension than if she leaves by a more typical one, like the front door (Littenberg, Tulkin, and Kagan 1971). It seems that a primary incentive for the distress is the discrepant quality of the event. This hypothesis is in accord with the fact that infant rhesus raised from birth with either the natural mother or a terry cloth surrogate displayed equivalent levels of distress immediately following removal of the "mother," for her absence was a discrepant experience for both groups (Meyer et al. 1975).

There are two different aspects to the separation phenomenon. The first is the growth function for separation distress; the second concerns individual differences in intensity of distress during the period of its display. We are primarily concerned with the first aspect. As we have indicated, investigations of separation distress reveal that the probability of signs of distress to maternal departure—crying or inhibition of play—is low prior to eight months of age, rises rapidly from nine to eighteen months, and then begins to decline. In the first of a series of studies, middle-class American children from six to twenty-one months were observed in a situation with the mother, the father, and a strange woman. During successive three-minute periods one adult left or one adult entered so that the child was either with his mother, his father, the stranger, or pairs of these people, but never alone. He only became apprehensive, as signaled by crying and inhibition of play, when he was alone with the stranger, and he did not show crying or inhibition of play until he was nine months old. Beginning at nine months, and with increasing probability until eighteen months, the child would stop playing, protest, and cry if either mother or father left him alone with the stranger. But by 21 months these signs of distress began to wane (Kotelchuck 1972).

As we have indicated earlier, this growth function appears in children from lower-class families in Antigua, Guatemala (Lester et al. 1974), from Indian families living in isolated villages on Lake Atitlán in the Guatemalan highlands, as well as in infants being raised in a children's home on an Israeli kibbutz (Fox, in press) and among !Kung San infants living in isolated bands in the Kalahari Desert—settings which vary greatly in the amount of time the child spends in contact and interaction with his mother. Although the age of peak distress varied a little across these cultural settings, the growth function was the same (see figure 2.8). Even infants diagnosed as suffering from "failure-to-thrive," for whom some physicians posit a disturbance in affective relations with the mother, show serious inhibition of play and even some mild protest when their mothers leave them with a stranger during the second year of life (Jameson and Gordon 1977). Although most children show decreasing separation distress after their second birthday (Feldman and Ingham 1975; Maccoby and Feldman 1972), some

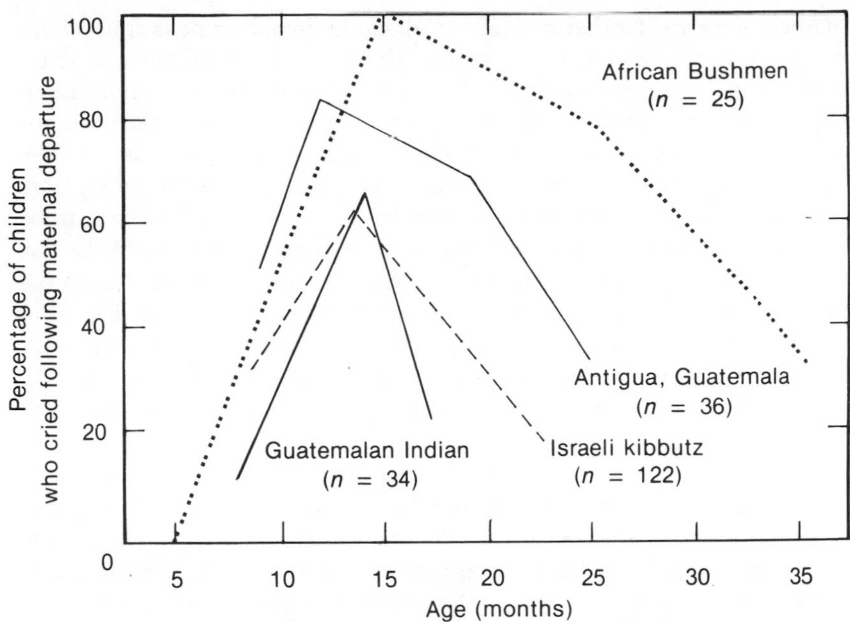

Fig. 2.8 *Percentage of children in four different settings who cried following maternal departure.*

will protest separation into the third year (Serafica and Cicchetti 1976). As we shall see in chapter 5, whether reared in day care centers or home, children showed the same growth function for distress at maternal departure across the period from three and one-half months through twenty-nine months, displaying peak distress from thirteen to twenty months.

An explanation of the consistency of this corpus of data must account for three facts: the inverted U-shaped function for separation distress in samples differing in frequency and duration of separation, the greater distress in unfamiliar than familiar settings, and the lack of relation between amount of prior mother-child interaction and the growth function for separation distress.

The traditional interpretation will not bear the burden of the facts. During a brief period in the 1940s and 1950s some psychologists regarded separation distress as a conditioned emotional reaction. The conditioned stimulus was absence of the mother when the child was experiencing extreme pain. The child associated the pain—the unconditioned stimulus—with the conditioned stimulus of "mother absence." Therefore when he saw the mother leave he had an anticipatory fear reaction. That interpretation, despite its initial reasonableness, does not explain why the developmental function for departure of the father is the same as it is for departure of the mother. Since the mother normally tends to the infant in need, one would not expect the father's departure to elicit the same amount of distress. Moreover, the age function for separation distress holds not only for children raised in a nuclear family with just one attentive caretaker but also for institutionalized children who have many caretakers (see Stevens 1971). The most telling critique of the traditional, conditioning position comes from the absence of differences in separation distress for pairs of children, those attending a day care center daily and those reared at home. Since the day care child more often experiences distressful situations while away from the mother, one would expect differential occurrence of separation distress in the two groups. The day care child has had ample opportunity to extinguish the "bond" between perception of maternal absence and painful distress. A conditioning interpretation would not predict equivalent growth functions for this behavior.

Another interpretation of separation distress that has been popular is the ethologically based theory of John Bowlby, as amplified by Mary Ainsworth (Ainsworth and Bell 1970; Ainsworth and Wittig 1969; Bowlby 1969). Although Ainsworth has suggested recently that separation anxiety is unlikely to be a sensitive index of the attachment of child to caretaker, the older version of this interpretation held that a bond of attachment develops between infant and mother as a function of the infant's display of certain behaviors toward the caretaker and the caretaker's response. In time the mutual interaction between infant and caretaker creates a bond so strong that it is to be regarded as an "attachment." It was suggested that this attachment emerges at about eight months, in part because that is the age when separation anxiety appears. The crying following maternal departure is presumed to reflect the child's anxiety over the possibility that the attachment bond is being broken and to be his attempt to regain proximity to the object of attachment. It is assumed that if the child were not attached to the person leaving, the departure would be nonthreatening and the child would not cry. The theory implies that the child would display no distress at the exit of a person with whom he has no strong emotional relationship. The prediction is generally true, despite the fact that a few 1-year-olds will cry when an unfamiliar person who has been in the house for a few hours departs, leaving the child with his parents. Since it is unlikely that the child has developed an "attachment" during such a short period, this irregularity is a little troublesome. On occasion a child will also cry when the mother reenters a room where the child is playing (Kagan 1974).

The major problem with the attachment explanation of the growth function for separation anxiety is the difficulty it has accounting for behavioral differences among children whose mothers differ in availability. If the distress reflects the child's recognition of the danger inherent in the mother's absence, one might predict that the more intense the mother-child relationship, the greater the separation distress. But that is not what empirical data reveal. Ainsworth and her colleagues, who have done the most careful and intensive study of separation fear, have reported that less sensitive and less responsive mothers have infants who cry the most in response to separation. They took this datum to mean that there were two kinds of attachments to the mother—secure and insecure ones. A reliably loving mother who always responds to her child's distress will, it is presumed, produce a child who is confident about the mother's availability. Therefore the child will not be threatened when she leaves. The child with no consistent caretaker has no attachment and therefore a caretaker's departure is not a threat. Only the child with an inconsistently reliable caretaker feels threatened and, therefore, cries when the caretaker leaves. Ainsworth assumed the relation between crying at separation and degree of attachment to be curvilinear. Minimally attached and maximally attached infants will be less threatened by maternal departure and hence will cry less than moderately attached children (Stayton and Ainsworth 1973).

The attachment interpretation of separation distress introduces the idea of "the child's confidence in his mother's whereabouts and accessibility." But the early Ainsworth hypothesis cannot explain why children reared in different environments mentioned earlier, extremes on an "availability of mother" dimension, show similar developmental functions for separation distress. Surely a child who is taken from his home to a day care center five days a week should be a little less certain of his mother's accessibility than one who is with the mother most of the day. Furthermore, such an interpretation will not fit data gathered by Stevens (1971) in an institution in Athens where infants experience regular changes in caretakers and, therefore, should be most likely to be insecure. Although most of these Greek infants have a favorite caretaker to whom they are "attached," they are maximally uncertain of her availability since they are never sure when she will be there to care for them. Nonetheless, the incidence of separation distress during the first two years in this group is not significantly different from that displayed by children in their own families. Separation distress rises between seven and twelve months, and sixteen of the twenty-four children (about 66 percent) showed separation protest prior to fifteen months of age—a rate of incidence comparable to that found for children reared in nuclear families.

Although the growth function for separation distress is not easily explained by attachment theory, it is possible, even likely, that individual differences in intensity or frequency of distress during the period eight to twenty-four months can be explained by quality of prior contact with caretakers.

A new interpretation of separation distress

We believe the growth function for separation distress, as well as the other phenomena of this era of development, require as a necessary, but not sufficient, condition the enhancement of the child's ability to retrieve schemata of prior events and to hold them on the stage of awareness for a longer period of time—what might be called *improved memory capacity*. Following departure of the mother, the ten-month-old child generates from memory the schema of her former presence in the room and holds that schema in memory while comparing it with the present. If the child cannot resolve the inconsistency inherent in the comparison, he becomes uncertain and may cry. But that hypothetical sequence is not completely satisfactory for several reasons. First, the 1-year-old occasionally cries when his caretaker is merely walking toward the exit, before she has left the room. Second, the child does not cry or become upset in similar situations when he compares past and present and cannot resolve the discrepancies they contain. For example, the 1-year-old becomes puzzled, but usually does not cry, when he fails to find a toy under a cover after having watched an adult place it there several seconds earlier. And the 1-year-old compares past with present all through the day in myriad contexts, yet distress is not a common event during most of the child's waking hours.

Therefore, additional processes must be postulated if we are to explain the reliable separation findings. A likely possibility is that the enhanced ability to retrieve and hold a schema of past experience is correlated with the ability to generate anticipations of the future—representations of possible events. There are two quite different mechanisms by which a predictive capacity might result in uncertainty. The first, which we favor, is based on the assumption that the 8- to 9-month-old has a new capacity best described as the "disposition to attempt to predict future events and to generate responses to deal with discrepant situations." The child begins, for the first time, to try to cope instrumentally with unfamiliar experience, not just assimilate it. If the child cannot generate a prediction or instrumental response, he is vulnerable to uncertainty and distress. If he can generate the prediction he may laugh, for laughter *in anticipation of a novel event* increases significantly after eight months of age (Sroufe and Waters 1976).

A second possibility is that the 8- to 12-month-old's ability to predict leads him to anticipate pain or danger as he watches his mother leave or reflects on her departure. The child's distress is not due to his failure to predict, but rather to the successful prediction of a threatening event. This view, which might be regarded as a conditioned fear response, has been a popular explanation for many years. Although it seems intuitively reasonable, we must ask why it is that infants all over the world, even those who are with their mothers for most of the day, suddenly expect an unpleasant event to occur when they are separated from their mothers between eight and thirteen months of age. The distress appears to be independent of the frequency with which they have experienced past unpleasantness when their mother was absent. We are tempted to reject the explanation because children whose mothers leave them often, for example, children in a day care center, do not show separation distress earlier or with more intensity than those who have their mothers with them continually. Hence, we favor, at least until more evidence accumulates, the view presented in the preceeding paragraph, that the 1-year-old tries to generate cognitive and behavioral reactions to events that alert him. A dynamic event (a jack-in-the-box or the mother going to the door) is more likely to elicit apprehension than a static event (finding an unexpected object under a cloth), for it is more apt to provoke questions like "What am I to do?" or "What will happen to me?" Inability to answer those implicit questions produces uncertainty. During or after maternal departure the child tries to generate a cognitive structure to explain the mother's absence or a behavior to alter the situation. If he cannot do either he is vulnerable to uncertainty. If, in addition, the child does not have some behavior, even a noninstrumental one, to exhibit when he experiences the uncertainty, he becomes especially vulnerable to distress and, perhaps, will cry (see Meili 1955). The child's need to have an action routine to initiate in a potentially uncertain situation is also seen in his reaction to an unfamiliar adult. If the stranger initiates interaction with a 1-year-old, and therefore provides an incentive for a counter-reaction from the child, the infant is less likely to cry or stay close to the mother than if the stranger sits passively (Ross and Goldman 1977).

McCall (in press) has come to a similar conclusion but uses slightly different language. McCall believes that when the infant can separate his actions from the objects and consequences that result from his behavior—an ability that has been called the separation of means from ends—he is vulnerable to uncertainty as to how to respond. Now, but not earlier, the infant is able to generate actions to deal with challenges; if he is uncertain as to what to do to retain or regain the departed parent or to deal with a discrepant event he becomes apprehensive and may cry.

> The theoretical argument can be summarized as follows. At approximately 8 months of age, the child's cognitive development first permits the separation of means from ends. Whereas previously the infant's response and its consequences were unitary, now their separation introduces an element of response uncertainty—either, "will this response have a desired consequence?" and/or "which of several responses shall I make?" Fear will only be displayed when the stimulus condition provokes such response uncertainty—that is, when stimuli (i.e., the stranger) prompt the infant to action and when the infant has sufficient experience with such stimuli to attempt to generalize several previously learned response patterns to such new stimuli. [McCall, in press, p. 72]

Distress is more likely to be the child's response to separation than to many other surprises in his daily life because the schema for the mother is well articulated and her presence is highly salient. The 1-year-old child will also cry to a jack-in-the-box or an electrically wired box that moves unpredictably; the discrepant event need not be the presence of an unfamiliar person or maternal departure. But the event must engage a salient or well-articulated schema. Distress does not occur to most discrepant experiences in the laboratory or in the child's daily encounters because the events are relatively unfamiliar. The minute or two of familiarization in the laboratory is not sufficient to create a firm schema, so that when a transformation occurs, the schema for the old event is evanescent, the inconsistency is muted, and less uncertainty is generated. If the event is salient and the schema well articulated, the difference between present and past remains clear. The importance of an event's salience is revealed in some observations in the object permanence situation. Six-month-olds who failed to reach for a hidden object under the typical administration reached for a toy that had first been made salient. In one procedure the object was a button which, when pushed, produced a distinctive reinforcement. After many experiences of pushing this button the 6-month-olds reached for it when it was hidden under a cloth. Apprehension occurs more often in response to separation than to other discrepant events in 8- to 12-month-olds because for them the schema of the mother and her former presence is salient.

We are left with one final puzzle with several possible solutions. Why does the presence of either a familiar person or familiar setting reduce dramatically the occurrence of uncertainty and crying in response to maternal departure, as it also does for encounters with strangers (Skarin 1977)? And why does the presence of the mother, especially if she is close by, reduce the likelihood of fear toward many other discrepant events?

The first possibility is that there is a continuum of uncertainty within which each child has a threshold that, when crossed, leads to inhibition and crying. The familiarity of setting or person acts to buffer the uncertainty and to keep it below the critical threshold. The child detects the mother's absence in the home and tries to understand it, but he does not become uncertain enough to display inhibition of play or crying.

A second possibility is that the context is an essential part of the child's conceptualization of any figural event, and the infant implicitly classifies all contexts into familiar and unfamiliar ones. A dynamic figural event that is discrepant in an unfamiliar context may not be so in a familiar one. However, this is unlikely since the child sometimes reacts with inhibition and fear to a discrepancy while he is sitting on his mother's lap.

A third possibility is that the presence of a familiar person or setting provides the child with opportunities for responses when uncertainty is generated. Recognition of the opportunity to behave buffers uncertainty. Distress does not occur when the mother leaves the child with the father because his presence provides the child with a potential target for a set of behaviors. That knowledge appears to keep uncertainty under control. This last interpretation is profoundly cognitive. We are suggesting that the infant does not have to move toward the father; *he only has to know that the parent is present.* The blind 1-year-old does not have to see the mother to be protected against distress; the child must only know that she is in the room. Knowledgc of the availability of a familiar caretaker is sufficient to hold anxiety at bay, a principle that is also true of adults.

In sum, the protest to separation during the latter part of the first year requires the postulation of the following hypothetical sequence of four processes.

1. The ability to retrieve from memory schemata of past salient events with minimal incentive cues and to hold those representations on the stage of short-term memory so that comparison of past and present is possible. The essential maturing competence appears to be the enhanced ability to hold the retrieved schema and current perception in awareness for a longer period of time.

2. The attempt to predict possible future events and to generate instrumental reactions to deal with discrepant experience.

3. The inability to resolve the inconsistency between past and present, to predict future possibilities, or to generate a coping reaction produces uncertainty.

4. The occurrence of distress and crying due to lack of opportunity to issue a behavior in reaction to the state of uncertainty.

It is probably not a coincidence that the growth function for separation distress resembles closely the child's increasing tendency to relate external information to himself. In an experiment mentioned earlier, mothers of children nine to twenty-four months old unobtrusively rubbed a little rouge on the child's nose, then placed the child before a mirror. The probability that the child would touch his nose was very low for 9-month-olds but increased linearly through the second year, paralleling the growth curve for separation protest (Lewis and Brooks 1975). We suggest that the older children were relating the discrepant information in the mirror to their schema of the self. In attempting to resolve the uncertainty resulting from that cognitive process, they touched their noses. Following maternal departure the child also tries to relate the event to possible consequences for himself. In the case of the red nose, the 20-month-old answers the question about the discrepancy and does not become upset; in the case of departure, he cannot answer the question and becomes apprehensive.

This cognitive interpretation of separation protest implies that early onset of separation anxiety should be characteristic of cognitively precocious children who enter the new stage of functioning a little early, say at eight to nine months of age. There is some support for that prediction. In one study of 10-month-old girls, middle-class, in contrast to working-class, mothers spent more time in face-to-face contact with their daughters, spoke to them more often, entered into more reciprocal vocalization, and more often encouraged walking. That greater variety of experience apparently facilitated rate of cognitive development, for the middle-class children vacillated more when presented with an old and a new toy—they looked back and forth about 2.2 times, in contrast to 1.4 times for the working-class children. When these girls were placed in the separation situation (the mother left the child alone in an unfamiliar room) more middle- than working-class children cried within ten seconds following maternal departure (Tulkin 1970).

In an earlier study (Kagan 1971), 160 Caucasian firstborn children were observed at four, eight, thirteen, and twenty-seven months. At all four ages, the children saw a set of masks. Fear of these facial masks was infrequent but occurred primarily at eight months, in accord with the norms for stranger anxiety. Thirty-nine percent of the upper-middle-class children but only 17 percent of the working-class children cried when shown the masks. We interpret this to mean that the upper-middle-class children had entered the new cognitive stage earlier. These children were also observed in a standard separation situation at eight months. After a play session the mother left the child alone in an unfamiliar room with the toys he had been handling earlier. Only 28 percent of the working-class children cried, in contrast to 66 percent of the upper-middle-class children. Therefore, at eight months, when separation protest is just about to appear, middle-class children are more likely than working-class children to display the distress. We suggest that the middle-class children were cognitively more mature and were actively relating the experience of departure to their prior knowledge. Cognitively precocious children should also arrive sooner at the stage when they can resolve the discrepancy contained in the separation, so that during the second year, protest should be less common among cognitively advanced children. Weinraub and Lewis (1975, 1976) have reported in unpublished work that 2-year-olds with high scores on the Bayley Scale of Infant Development, and on vocabulary tests, were least likely to show apprehension (as measured by disruption of play) following maternal departure in a laboratory situation. Thus cognitive factors predict age of onset of separation distress before the first birthday and the age of its disappearance before the third birthday.

The alleviation of fear The fear following brief separation recedes after two years of age, when the child is able to resolve the event or issue instrumental reactions. The child knows where the mother is or knows that she will return. His experiences have allowed him to generate a structure that resolves, mediates, or interprets the inconsistency. That representation can be regarded as a primitive kind of operation, for it accounts for the discrepant transformation. In macaque monkeys, fear in response to an unfamiliar member of the species, as evidenced by avoidance of an unfamiliar adult female monkey in a compartment, emerges at four months and vanishes by twelve months. In human infants the analogous fear is first seen around seven months and is over by fifteen months. The fear of strangers lasts about eight months in both species.

The child will always be vulnerable to new uncertainties, such as the dark or lightning, that temporarily cannot be resolved. Although the content of the fears of childhood change, the mechanisms may remain similar. We are not suggesting that all of the fears of childhood involve the processes we invoked to explain separation distress. We suggest only that some fears may result from the child's unsuccessful attempt to resolve the inconsistency between two schemata or to generate a future possibility in a situation in which he has no opportunity to cope after failing to understand a discrepancy.

Fear of the dark typically does not appear until three years of age because the 2-year-old child probably does not try to generate possibilities when night falls. He requires knowledge to know that ghosts and wild animals are possibilities when the lights go out. Once he has that knowledge, he automatically activates it and if he cannot satisfactorily deal with the structure imagined he becomes uncertain. The child's level of cognitive maturity will determine when he is able to generate possibilities; experience determines what those possibilities might be and how he might cope with them. Specific knowledge determines the content of the fear and when it will decline. At puberty, youth generate possibilities about the use of their sexuality. Some will remain apprehensive for a long time if they do not have experiences that provide therapeutic knowledge. Other sources of uncertainty will be local to a culture or subculture. The fact that most fears of preschool children are of unusual objects like snakes or lions or imaginary ones like ghosts implies that when the child has fragile knowledge he is especially vulnerable to fear. He knows about the actions of cars and water, knows how to cope with them, and can predict their future states. As a result they elicit less uncertainty than jungle animals.

Theories of disquiet and cure The 4-year-old child experiences psychic distress because he has a fever, feels guilty over a lie, or anticipates parental punishment. But at this early age he has no theory of etiology for his disquiet. He responds to distress almost reflexively by approaching a primary caretaker who has been a source of support in the past. But by six years of age, or a little earlier, he will have a hypothesis about the cause of his distress—school failure, peer or parental rejection, illness, parental coercion or punishment. His choice of coping actions will be correlated with his diagnosis. If he believes his distress is due to school pressures, he will either work harder or withdraw effort. If parental displeasure is singled out as the cause, he will either try to please his parents or become hostile toward them. Whether the child adopts a coping or a phobic strategy will be a function of his expectancy of gaining the goal (he believes coping will alleviate the distress) and of the actual constraints inherent in the immediate environment (his family may not permit him to withdraw effort from school). There are class differences in both theories of disquiet and preferred coping responses.

Middle-class children are more likely to decide that potential school failure and parental disfavor are the bases for uncertainty because the environment has made these goals salient. More lower-class children are likely to believe that poverty and street violence are the bases for their disquiet. The family and the proximal social groups teach the child what bogeymen to worry about and suggest different sets of alleviating procedures. The child who has an authoritarian father and who worries about being reprimanded and coerced is likely to decide that the gaining of power is curative. The child with indifferent parents decides that the gaining of an accepting relation is therapeutic. Some of the major uncertainties across societies include health, money, parental favor, peer acceptance, status, power, physical harm, coercion, task failure, competence, spirits, ghosts, gods, attractiveness, sexual ability, punishment, shame, guilt, and humiliation for failing to behave in accord with sex, age, and moral standards. The differential salience of these states will be determined by culture, historical period, and of course, experience in the family.

A CLARIFICATION

Although we have stressed the importance of enhancement in memory processes during the last half of the first year, all the behavioral changes of this period cannot be fully explained by that hypothesis alone. Moreover, we fear there is some ambiguity surrounding the statement that it is not until eight months that the child can retrieve a schema for a past event.

Since the 3-month-old, and perhaps the newborn, will dishabituate to an event that is a transformation of a habituated standard (even after a twenty-four-hour delay), it is necessary to acknowledge that the 3-month old can retrieve, under some conditions, a representation of a prior event. (John Watson (in press) calls this process reactive memory, in contrast to regenerative memory, which involves retrieval with minimal cues in the field.) The infant could not recognize an event (E') as different from a historically prior event (E) unless he retrieved some aspect of the latter. One-month-old infants who had heard about 700 repetitions of an originally unfamiliar word over a two-week period began to behave as if they recognized the word even after a forty-two-hour interval during which they did not hear the stimulus (Ungerer, Brody, and Zelazo 1977). These data imply that the very young infant can retrieve a schema for a past event, but establishment of the schema is often slow and the retrieval competence is vulnerable to long delays. We suggest that the major differences between the cognitive functioning of the 10-month-old and 3-month-old are that the older infant can establish a schema more quickly, can retrieve a representation of the prior event E with minimal stimulus incentives in the immediate field after a longer temporal delay between E and E', and can hold the representations of E and E' in short-term memory for a longer period of time. As a result, the older child shows both more prolonged attention to E' and more vulnerability to uncertainty because his ability to remember both E and E' for a longer time permits him a longer period to work at resolving the discrepancy between the two events. If the child cannot do so, he becomes vulnerable to distress. These hypothetical competences can account for the increased attention to discrepant events after eight months of age, the inhibition in the face of novelty, and the increase in distress to unexpected experiences. However, as we have indicated earlier, these competences alone are insufficient to explain separation distress. We believe it is helpful to posit an additional disposition in the child to activate structures that resolve the inconsistency and to generate possible actions toward a discrepant experience. The 10-month-old cries as his mother gets up to leave because he reacts to that event with an attempt to cope with her imminent departure. If he fails to generate coping reactions, he becomes vulnerable to uncertainty (Meili 1955; Bronson 1972). We emphasize the new disposition because we have found that behavioral performances typically follow acquisition of relevant cognitive structures by several months. The overt naming of events *follows* the creation of cognitive representations of those events. Imitation of a parent drinking coffee does not occur until after the first year, although it is likely that the 10-month-old infant holds a cognitive schema for that experience. Behavioral vacillation between old and new toys first occurred at six to seven months in the Cambridge children we tested, several months after the infant could detect a discrepant experience.

In sum, it appears that two complementary abilities that emerge around eight months of age can help to explain the phenomena of this period: the increased ability to hold past and current experience in active memory and the disposition to generate cognitive structures that attempt to relate past and present or to deal with the unexpected. The enhancement of memory permits the child more time to work at the puzzles inherent in unexpected events; but if he fails, it places him in a position of uncertainty. We believe that these new functions are the direct consequence of maturational changes in the central nervous system, involving perhaps the ascendance of forebrain mechanisms. It may not be a coincidence that the proportion of quiet sleep—with no rapid eye movements—which is relatively constant from three to nine months, shows a major increase at nine to ten months, the age when memory is enhanced (Emde and Walker 1976), and that the occurrence of sleep spindles in the EEG (twelve to fourteen Hertz and prominent in the precentral area) during Stage 2 sleep shows a large decrease during the last half of the first year (Tanguay et al. 1975). Since many physiologists believe that the neural control of sleep shifts from brain stem to forebrain mechanisms during the first year (McGinty 1971), it is reasonable to suggest that the diverse behavioral changes that suddenly and rather uniformly appear toward the end of the first year are released by structural or biochemical events that are essential components of ontogenesis.

Apparently Freud was approaching a similar insight toward the end of his career. In a prophetic paragraph he questioned the formative power he had assigned earlier to variation in infant experience with the caretaker and suggested that maturational forces would guarantee that all infants would display some common developmental profile. Freud wrote, "the phylogenetic foundation has so much the upper hand over personal accidental experience that it makes no difference whether a child has really sucked at the breast or has been brought up on the bottle and never enjoyed the tenderness of a mother's care. In both cases the child's development takes the same path" (Freud 1964, p. 188).

The second year: symbolism and metaphor

As early as the first birthday some children will treat an object as if it were representative of something other than it is. A child treats a stick like a telephone or handles moist sand as if it were a mass of flour. Even in the isolated village of San Marcos, where toys are uncommon, the majority of 15-month-olds will apply a small toy comb to a doll's head or "feed" sand to a puppet. Among North American children this new addition to the child's repertoire of behavior usually appears between eleven and thirteen months. In a recent study, the play of sixty-four infants between 9½ and 15½ months of age was coded for instances of "symbolic" play. Typical examples included stirring a toy spoon in a cup, babbling into a toy telephone, or hitting a ball with a toy bat. Few 9½-month-old children displayed this class of behavior, but by 13 months an average of six such actions occurred in a fifteen-minute play period (Zelazo and Kearsley 1976).

This competence appears to be accompanied, or perhaps immediately preceded, by the ability to treat physically different exemplars of people, animals, food, or furniture as if each belonged to a particular category. Ross (1977) presented 12-, 18-, and 24-month-olds with ten different toys belonging to one of the four categories named above. On the eleventh trial the child was shown two toys, a novel instance of the old category and a physically similar member of a new category. All the children, including the 1-year-olds, showed a distinct and significant tendency to play more with the toy that belonged to the new class, a fact suggesting that the 1-year-old who pretends to feed a doll is probably treating the toy as if it were a member of a conceptual category.

Although these actions resemble those witnessed in other people and are appropriate to the objects manipulated, before the child is 2 years old she will be able to impose a transformation on an object and treat a doll as a salt shaker or a piece of paper as a blanket. Now the child is not merely implementing an action witnessed in the past on an object that is a replica of the real, but she is subordinating the qualities of the object to her ideas. Since the idea originated in the child rather than being released by the object's qualities, the play can be called symbolic. The object's attributes were subordinated to the mental representation in a process that, strictly speaking, is neither assimilation nor accommodation, for the 2-year-old who "shakes salt from a doll's head" assimilated the doll to her schema of a person (not a salt shaker), and ignored rather than accommodated to the primary qualities of the doll.

The appearance of these behaviors requires us to assume that by the second birthday the child is able to generate representations that are transformations—not copies—of events experienced in the past. In less than twenty-four months, nature has transformed the newborn, whose cognitive functions were dominated by the physical nature of reality, to a toddler, who uses reality to serve his fantasy.

A particularly lovely example occurred in a verbally precocious 26-month-old girl who was playing with a set of toys that included two small dolls (about two inches long) a small bed (about four inches long) and a large bed (about one foot long). After she placed one of the small dolls on the small bed, she scanned the rest of the toys, noting aloud that she needed another bed. She looked directly at the large bed, touched it, but did not pick it up. After almost two minutes of quiet and careful study of all the available toys she finally selected a small wooden sink, about four inches long, placed the second small doll in it and placed this arrangement next to the other small bed which already had a doll. Apparently satisfied, she declared, "Now Mummy and Daddy are sleeping." How can we explain the clear rejection of the large bed, an appropriate object, in favor of the sink, which she knew was not a bed? It seems reasonable to suggest that she had generated an aesthetic standard regarding the appropriate sizes of the two beds—both had to be small. In order to meet that standard, she distorted reality a bit and used an object which obviously belonged to the wrong functional category because one of its dimensions was consonant with her conception of what was appropriate. She used those aspects of reality that served her fantasy and rejected those that did not—an action that reveals the inherent ambiguity in phrases like *accommodation* or *reality testing*.

The capacity for symbolic play and fantasy is followed by the first display of a primitive form of metaphor in which the child treats a salient dimension of one event as representative of a quite different event. Some 2-year-olds and almost all 3-year-olds will treat a pair of wooden blocks of different sizes as representative of a parent-child dyad because they have extracted size as a relevant discriminating dimension for the categories adult and child. In one experiment children were shown two blocks of different sizes and the examiner said, "I have a daddy and a baby; which one is the daddy (or baby)?" The 2-year-olds scanned the two forms and pointed to the larger one if the request was for the adult and to the smaller if the examiner had asked for the baby. A few children under two years of age consistently selected the larger of the two pieces of wood as the "daddy" and the smaller one as the "baby," across different size pairs regardless of the absolute size of each form, indicating the capacity for understanding a relative dimension. One verbally precocious 22-month-old was even able to rationalize her response. When asked why she selected the larger object to represent the parent, she replied, "It's bigger."

The child becomes capable of more complex metaphors at a later age when an inference about an absent quality is required—when he goes beyond the given information. A child recognizes that the major dimensions of day, in contrast to night, are light and warmth. He also knows that fires are characterized by light and warmth. As a result, he may treat redness as symbolic of day. For if warmth is a quality of both day and fire and the fire is red, the mind is willing to assume that redness is a quality of day. The basis for the conclusion is the rule that if two events share some qualities they probably share more.

Events that share salient qualities are treated as symbolic relatives. The disposition to award to event A a quality belonging to event B merely because A and B objectively share a few other attributes also occurs when the child identifies with a role model. The child knows that he and his parent share gender and last name, as well as other characteristics. He goes beyond that objective information and concludes, incorrectly, that he also shares the competence (or incompetence) of the parent. This disposition, which can be seen as early as age three, seems to be fundamental to cognitive functioning, even though it is an obvious violation of Aristotelian logic. The syllogism the child is using seems to be:

> If this boy is John Smith, then he has red hair. If this is John Smith's father, he has red hair and is competent. Therefore, competence is a quality of the boy John Smith.

The illogicality of that conclusion is more obvious in the following:

> If this is a man, it breathes oxygen and has two legs. If this is a bird, it breathes oxygen, has two legs, and flies. Therefore flying is a symbolic quality of man.

Child and adult only use the special logic of metaphor when the shared dimensions are salient. Since oxygen consumption and two-leggedness are not salient characteristics of man, flying is not a metaphorical human quality. When cultures agree on salient dimensions of events they should agree on metaphors. Males are almost always larger than females, and large size tends to be universally symbolic of maleness. But cultures do not agree on the salient dimensions of corn, cows or trees, so for these objects metaphorical substitutions will differ across cultures. North Americans treat a large wavy line as metaphorical for happiness and a less active line as representative of sadness. Among the Kipsigis of western Kenya, where sadness is viewed as a major emotion, the metaphor is reversed. North Americans treat a rock from an open hearth as a dangerous and potent object; the Mayans regard it as the quintessential symbol of womanhood. The Western Apache hold a metaphorical relation between dogs and children because both are always hungry, and between ravens and widows because both beg for food (Basso 1976). Cultural differences in the salient, identifying dimensions of events and concepts necessarily lead to differences in the permitted substitutions.

From schema to action

How do we get from knowledge to action—from schema or category to behavioral implementation? The impenetrability of that problem—not unlike the impenetrability of the puzzle of how DNA produces protein, how a pattern on the retina leads to the perception of a tree, or how energy is derived from the atom—continues to numb us. The mind must possess representations of motor acts. We ask a child to put his hand on his head and open his mouth and he obeys our instructions. The child watches another throw a football and may copy that action after one nonparticipating observation. There must be an executive process which is able to translate the schematic representation of an act into a motor sequence, the way DNA codes messenger RNA and messenger RNA monitors the construction of amino acids.

A process must exist that represents the actions of others and can separate the action from the agent—to divide an event into two parts, as an enzyme splits a larger molecule. A 2-year-old picks up a telephone for the first time and imitates the position, posture, and vocal attitude of his parent. It is not necessary for the child to practice the action or initially display it in crude form. The first display of an observed act is often faithful to the original event, not a trial-and-error affair. Since the mind holds many representations of motor acts, why do we see only some of them? What determines when or whether they will be implemented? This question is a natural bridge to the process that has been called imitation, but that simple label effectively disguises the complexity of the phenomenon.

Imitation The time when apprehension and uncertainty to maternal separation and unfamiliar children are growing most rapidly is also the time when reliable imitation of the acts of another emerges. The child initiates an act he observed and does not simply react to the behavior of another. Let us be clear about the phenomena we are discussing. An 18-month-old watches his mother dial the telephone. A few minutes or hours later he goes to the telephone and repeats that action. The motor response is in the child's motor repertoire, for it involves only picking an object up and holding it to the face. The young child did not have to learn any new motor coordination; the act was potentially present in the repertoire. The origin of the act was simply viewing the model perform it. Or the adult can directly invite the child to imitate an action. The adult taps her finger several times on the table and the child, smiling, reproduces that action either at once or a half hour later. We have seen some 21-month-old children reproduce an unusual action that was demonstrated by a model a month earlier. When a 20-month-old child came to the laboratory, she saw a model put a wooden ball on a small slab of white wood and say, "This doll is very tired; we must put him to bed. Night, night, dolly." When the child entered the same room one month later and encountered the same set of objects (about twenty objects), she immediately put the wooden ball on the slab of wood and said, "Night, night."

The reproduction of a witnessed act usually does not emerge until the end of the first year of life or the beginning of the second and increases in a linear fashion through the second year. Some investigators have claimed to have seen imitation in 2-to-3-month-olds. But even their enthusiasm acknowledges the fragility and ambiguity that surrounds the infant's action. One is never quite sure that the infant stuck out his tongue as a selective response to the observer's similar action. One reason we doubt that the 2-month-old is capable of selected imitation comes from a recent study in our laboratory in which we compared the probability of a 6- or 10-week-old infant sticking out his tongue to an adult repetitively sticking out her tongue close to the baby's mouth, an adult approaching the baby's mouth with a black pen that moved back and forth at the same rate as the tongue, or an adult presenting a ball close to the mouth. Both the moving tongue and moving pen, but not the ball, were equally potent releasers of the child's tongue protrusions. Thus it appears that at this very early age there are special sets of events that are capable of releasing particular responses like tongue protrusion, but since it decreases with age it is likely that at two months this response is reflexive in nature and not an attempt by the child to match a specific behavior to one recently witnessed (Jacobson 1977). But by the time he is eighteen months old, there is no doubt that the child is matching his behavior to another's action.

What competences must we award to the 18-month-old to explain imitative performance, which emerges prior to or contemporary with the appearance of spoken language? Both phenomena require the disposition to extract a faithful representation of the behavior of another as well as the ability to retrieve and implement specific responses. Since we know, as mentioned earlier, that the 12-month-old can create and retrieve a representation of an event, what has to be explained is why the child implements this knowledge in action. Those who regard the behavioral event as axiomatic must explain why the implementation is typically delayed until the first birthday.

We start with one important fact. First, when the child imitates a motor act—that is, when he issues an action that duplicates one he has witnessed—he generally, but not always, duplicates the action as a unit, suggesting that he has the ability to perform the act and is not imitating in order to learn the action. Second, the action is primary; the objects used in the behavior are secondary, at least during the second year. We have observed the behavior of 15-month-old children in a standard test situation after a model placed one of several dolls on one of the two toy beds. It was not uncommon for some children to use a toy doll and bed other than the ones used by the model, while preserving the essential action of placing a doll on a bed. But the child might not have implemented that action, even though it was in his repertoire, unless the model had acted first. We must therefore ask two questions: What is the function of the model, and what determines what actions and whom the child will duplicate?

It seems to us that during the second year, and perhaps the third, the model serves primarily as an incentive or organizer for the action, the way a mother duck serves as an incentive for her infant ducklings to follow or the way a bright red disk releases the pecking response in a hungry pigeon.

One function of the model is to move an action that was, at one moment, low in the hierarchy of probable responses to a higher position. But observations of children fourteen to twenty months old suggest a second, more complex function. Consider a child who has played for fifteen minutes with a set of toys and failed to display any "pretend" acts. He has put blocks into a pail, banged some toys together, or brought all the objects to his mother. After fifteen minutes, a familiar woman who has been in the room invites the child to watch her play. The model applies a toy nursing bottle to an animal and explains that the animal is hungry; she places a doll on a small toy bed and notes that the doll is tired and applies a cloth to a doll's face, explaining that it is dirty. The model then returns to her seat on a couch near the mother. It is not uncommon for children not only to imitate one or two of the actions just modeled but also to display some behaviors which have no obvious relation to those that were displayed. The child will pick up a toy telephone and pretend to talk to another person, or pour imaginary liquid into a cup and drink it. Although these responses were not modeled, they, too, belong to a class we might name "acts displayed by others." We have even seen a child who has just watched an adult display a novel action (the model placed four small animals under a cloth) first display an act she saw the adult model express a month earlier and then, moments later, place the four animals under the cloth. The model's behavior seems to function as an incentive to cue a class of behavior stored in the child's mind, the class we have just named "acts displayed by others." This interpretation implies, albeit speculatively, that the young child, like the adult, approaches situations with a dominant psychological frame. By frame, we mean a state that resembles a set, point of view, or *Aufgabe*. We are friendly to Marvin Minsky's definition: "A frame is a data structure for representing a stereotyped situation—like being in a certain kind of living room or going to a child's birthday party. Attached to this structure are several kinds of information. Some of this information is about how to use the frame. Some is about what one can expect to happen next. Some is about what to do if these expectations are not confirmed." (Minsky 1974).

A particular 15-month-old confronted with a set of toys may use as a generator of action a frame that contains the prepotent responses he normally uses with toys—carrying them to others, putting them in a pail, rolling them on the floor, hitting two of them together. The model's act of feeding the doll has the same function as a cue does in studies of recall memory with adults. The model's act reminds the child of another source of actions he can initiate with the toys; namely, those behaviors the child has seen others display. The child is now under the influence of a new frame that becomes an additional source of behavior.

Although this hypothesis attributes considerable cognitive complexity to the 18-month-old, it does not violate existing information on his capacity and seems necessary to account for the behaviors described.

We still have not explained why a child duplicates an action he has witnessed moments or days earlier, and why children do not imitate every act they have observed. How can we explain the selectivity of the act chosen for public display? These phenomena require postulating at least four quite different mechanisms for imitation.

The simplest, and perhaps earliest, determinant is the desire to prolong the excitement produced by the reactions of others to the child's actions. The mother vocalizes and infant babbles back. The mother repeats her action and the child responds. This dialogue continues, if the mother is willing, until the child has become habituated to the variety and excitement.

A similar mechanism is involved when the child performs an action he observed that produces consequences that are discrepant or interesting. He once saw his father play the piano and so he bangs the keys, generating sounds that delight him.

But perhaps the most important determinant of the act imitated is the desire to match behavior to a previously acquired schema for that act. The child possesses or creates a schematic prototype for a response he has witnessed, but he experiences some uncertainty over his ability to behave consonant with the prototype. It is that state that provokes the child to issue the act. The child duplicates an act he has seen as a reaction to uncertainty surrounding that response because it is in the process of being mastered. A model picking up a telephone serves as an incentive for a 15-month-old because of his uncertainty over his ability to perform the response, but not for a 9- or 48-month-old, both of whom possess the ability to pick up the toy. The 9-month-old has no expectation of being able to carry out the act; the 4-year-old is certain he can implement it. Since children have seen their parents pick up telephones many times, the uncertainty lies less with the assimilation of the perceptual experience than with the execution of the act. We suggest that *acts over which the 1- to 2-year-old child experiences some un-*

certainty with respect to overt display are most likely to be imitated. That notion requires the child to possess a schema for the act and a representation of his competence to perform that act, as well as the ability to relate those two representations. He must actively coordinate two schemata, one for the act and one for his competence. The ability to compare two representations was also necessary to explain separation protest at age one, for we suggested that separation distress would not occur unless the child compared his knowledge with current experience. In imitation he must compare a representation of his ability to perform an act with a representation of the act he has observed. This argument implies that if the child has too much uncertainty about his ability to perform a witnessed act, he may show signs of distress. And we have observed many children twenty to twenty-three months of age show a marked increase in inhibition, protest, clinging to the mother, and even crying, after they watched a familiar woman display three complex acts (with very familiar toys) that may have been too difficult for the child to assimilate or retrieve with fidelity. After several monthly exposures to these same three acts the children's protest and inhibition subsided: the children gleefully initiated the acts, or fragments of them, immediately after the model had completed her demonstration.

Finally, the child may imitate a model in order to gain mastery of the role of another. The fact that a person rather than a machine displayed the act contributes to the likelihood of imitation. We are forced, therefore, to assume that the young child perceives a psychological relation to the model, specifically, that he holds a representation of himself or herself in the position of the model. This assumption requires a representation of the self as an object similar to the model. This is a new competence, for the 6-month-old seems to treat other children as "objects that move" without recognizing their human qualities. The 6-month-old hits another child as if he were a ball or fingers another child's hair as if it were a furry blanket. But by eighteen months the child hugs another as he has been hugged, offers him a toy as he has been offered toys, and speaks to the other as he has been spoken to. By the second year he awards another human being a quality he recognizes as belonging to him. Michael Lewis and Jeanne Brooks have shown that during the second year, but not earlier, the child is likely to touch his nose if he sees a red spot on it as he looks in a mirror, whereas he only stared at that reflection at twelve months. By eighteen months he will label a picture of himself as "baby"; by age two he will apply his name to that picture and will look longer at an illustration of himself than of another child (Lewis, personal communication). Thus after the ability to represent and retrieve a schema of a past action and after one's potential ability to display it, a third competence to be developed is possession of a representation of self as an object that shares similarity with another human being. The child possesses the cognitive category "human" by one year (Ross 1977), and less than a year later has included the self in that category. Just as a child who has uncertainty over implementing an act will imitate it, so the child who has uncertainty over playing the role of another will also imitate the person who represents that role. We have seen 2-year-olds who are perfectly coordinated crawl clumsily on the floor while saying, "Look at me, I'm a baby," suggesting that the crawling was an attempt to play the role of infant. Uncertainty over display of an action or over assuming the role of another are twin incentives for imitative acts.

Kurt Fischer and his students have provided a particularly elegant demonstration of this principle (Watson and Fischer 1977). Infants fourteen to twenty-four months of age watched an adult demonstrate three actions using herself, a doll, or a wooden block as the agent of action. The three actions were eating from a cup, lying on a pillow, and washing hands, arms, and face with a cloth. After completing the modeled demonstrations, the adult left the room and the child was allowed to play with the toys the model had used. Over three-quarters of the infants and all the 2-year-olds displayed some pretend play during the spontaneous play session. There was a linear increase with age in the child's tendency to use the block as the agent of action, indicating the maturation of a more symbolic attitude. But the important result, as far as this discussion is concerned, was the relative decline with age in the occurrence of imitative acts in which the child was the agent of action, in contrast to an increase in the more symbolic imitations. These two growth functions suggest that as the action becomes easier to implement, it loses its incentive quality. The authors of the experiment wrote, "the child imitated pretend behaviors at or near his highest cognitive capacity and ignored those that he had long mastered" (Watson and Fischer 1977, p. 835).

By age three to four, the child will imitate another in order to increase his similarity to a model. Now the act is clearly secondary, for almost any act that distinguishes the model will do. The girl wants to wear a hair scarf or to bake a pie because she wishes to increase her similarity to her mother.

This discussion makes response uncertainty central to a great deal of behavior that has been called imitation. An alternative view is that if the experience of witnessing a model perform an act is moderately discrepant, it will alert the child. The alerting is sufficient to provoke the imitation. This interpretation assumes that the mechanism that bridges attention and action is the excitement generated by a discrepant event. The postulation of such a mechanism is reasonable, for many have shown that all that is necessary for a pigeon to peck at a disk is to generate excitement related to food by making a pigeon hungry and showing it some grain and to provide a disk. The bird is prepared by nature to peck if it is aroused and a disk is available. If the event of a person performing a certain act were moderately discrepant, it would excite the child, and if the act were in the child's repertoire, as pecking is for a pigeon, the response would occur. The problem with this interpretation is that "imitation" can occur minutes, hours or months after the model's behavior, long after the excitement generated by the model's action has waned. Therefore, as one catalyst for imitation we emphasize the child's uncertainty surrounding his ability to display the response. Of course, all this imitative behavior occurs before the child realizes that the action of the model might lead to a goal that satisfies a motive, a mechanism that does not emerge until the third or fourth years.

The dynamic discussed here bears a resemblance to one of the major forces behind behavior in adolescents and adults: the desire and disposition to initiate tasks that are challenging, just because they are challenging. The older child and adolescent, like programmed missiles, seek out contexts where there is some uncertainty over mastery. The adolescent wants to test his competence and seeks out actions that he both values and is a little unsure of implementing. The student who is more confident of his ability in science is likely to major in physics, mathematics, or biochemistry; the one who is slightly less confident is more likely to select the social sciences. As a person is the best ''releaser'' for imitation in a 1-year-old, the social value of a task is the releaser for the adolescent and adult. But the trigger for both seems to be uncertainty of performance.

Each of the bases for imitation is appropriate to speech. The 2-year-old will gleefully play word games with his parents in a lively exchange of babbling and speech and will try out new words just for the fun of it. The 2-year-old will, while alone with a doll, scold the inanimate object for not eating properly and will say words or phrases he has heard that are just a little in advance of his own linguistic ability. In the latter case, the child may use language to resolve uncertainty. The word or phrase selected for expression represents a structure that is in the process of being mastered. The child sees a cat in a context that is discrepant (for example, on top of a car), is alerted by the discrepancy, and utters the word ''cat.'' The speaking of the word in that context may be analogous to imitating an act whose mastery is uncertain. The naming is not necessarily intended to communicate anything. It is the child's response to the state created by a sequence that began with detection of the discrepant event, and was followed first by a temporary state of uncertainty and then by assimilation of the experience.

During the early stages of language acquisition, from the first to the third birthday, the child frequently expresses one and two word utterances that do not appear to be in the service of communicating information or announcing a state of need. Rather, these bursts of language seem to be epiphenomenal to the resolution of a state of uncertainty created by encounter with an unexpected or discrepant event that the child is in the process of mastering verbally. The event creates a temporary state of uncertainty, and the verbal labeling that follows assimilation of the event in a 2-year-old is analogous to the smile that follows assimilation of a face in a 4-month-old.

Recall that Ross (1977) showed 12-, 18-, and 24-month-olds ten physically different objects, each representing a particular category (for example, ten different animals or ten different edible foods), then presented a pair of physically similar objects. One of the pair was a physically novel instance of the category the child had previously seen, and the other was a member of a new category. The children who were mature enough to speak typically labeled the member of the new category—not the old one—a finding that suggests that the alerted state produced by the unexpected object from the new category elicited a verbal label in the service of resolving the uncertainty, as if producing the word helped the child to master the event. Ross also found that the 2-year-olds more often spontaneously named those parts or functions of the toys for which they had a verbal label. If the stimulus was a doughnut-shaped object, the child named the whole object and called it a ball. If the object was a dog, she might label a part, like the tail or legs; if the object was a bed, she might label its function and say "sleep"; if an apple, she might say, "bite." The syntactic class of the word was less important than the semantic association of the object with some word or phrase that happened to be in her repertoire.

Following a detailed analysis of extensive data from two young children, Patricia Greenfield and Joshua Smith (1976) suggested that during the one-to-two-word stage the child's language is monitored in part by the uncertainty surrounding the event being named. If a child saw his mother putting on her sock, he was likely to say "sock," not "Mummy's sock," because, we suggest, it was obvious to both mother and child that the sock belonged to the mother. But if he saw a pair of stockings on a bed and the mother approaching, he would be more likely to say, "Mummy's sock" because, as Greenfield and Smith implied, there was some uncertainty about the relation between the stocking and the mother in the second context.

The act of speaking the word may not necessarily function to resolve uncertainty. Rather, the state of excitement generated by understanding a situation that was initially uncertain may provoke the utterance, as laughter follows the punch line of a joke.

The child's uncertainty over the degree to which he has mastered a particular word is also a major determinant of which words the 1- to 2-year-old will imitate. Evidence comes from an experiment in which the speech of six children (sixteen to twenty-five months of age) was recorded in the home and coded for the occurrence of speech that was a repetition, in part or whole, of a preceding utterance by an adult. The children "imitated only words and structures in speech that they heard which they appeared to be in the process of learning. They tended not to imitate words and structures that they themselves either used spontaneously and so presumably knew, or did not use spontaneously at all and so presumably did not know" (Bloom, Hood, and Lightbown 1974, p. 416).

In a similar study the spontaneous conversations of two 2-year-old boys and their babysitter were recorded for a six-month period and analyzed for the time course of speech forms that were imitative of another person. Imitative utterances did not seem to be communicative in function and often involved new and unusual words. But the important finding in this context was that, initially, the child uttered a form after the model had uttered it. This phase was followed by a period during which the child uttered the word in both imitative and spontaneous contexts and finally a period when the word was not imitated any more, presumably because it had been mastered (Moerk 1977).

These observations imply that the child is continually and unconsciously monitoring the degree of uncertainty present in a situation; the language forms he selects are reactions to that uncertainty and may even be attempts to eliminate it. Uncertainty may not be the only, or even the major, determinant of expressive speech, but it does appear that early language, like sustained attentiveness, smiling, crying, and imitation, are natural sequellae to the young child's continuous unraveling of puzzles. The child is alerted by an event that he did not expect or one that is discrepant from his knowledge. He attempts to understand it. If it is an event for which he has a name, he may label it. If it is a complex action for which he has no appropriate phrase, he may duplicate it, especially if he has a little uncertainty over his ability to implement the behavior. On the penultimate page of Roger Brown's summary of early language acquisition he suggests that "children work out rules for the speech they hear, passing from levels of lesser to greater complexity simply because the human species is programmed at a certain period in its life to operate in this fashion on linguistic input" (Brown 1973, p. 412).

Each phase of development is marked by some universal nodes of uncertainty that are gradually resolved, as well as local, idiosyncratic sources of uncertainty that are a product of variation in knowledge reservoirs. As we shall see in chapter 5, the period between eight to thirteen months is marked by uncertainty over a variety of events because of the child's new ability to retrieve the representation of a prior experience. As a result, he is vulnerable to the distress that follows his inability to accomplish the resolution. By two years, when the resolution comes more quickly, the event has lost its power to provoke an uncertain state. By four years of age, the child has acquired standards of proper and improper action and is mature enough to reflect on alternative actions. He now becomes vulnerable to the uncertainty generated by having to select one action over another, as well as the uncertainty that follows behavioral violation of a standard. The adolescent is vulnerable to the uncertainty that follows recognition of a lack of coherence among beliefs, in addition to the incentives that characterized the earlier developmental stages.

But during the opening two years, when there are no propositions for standards or beliefs, the major sources of uncertainty are experiences that engage perceptual schemata that are not immediately assimilable or action schemes that are in the process of being perfected. These events provoke a brief period during which the system is organized to subdue the unexpected intruder. Victory is often announced by language, action, and laughter; defeat by inhibition and irritability.

It seems necessary, therefore, to distinguish between those actions that are directed at attaining a specific external goal and those acts that are released when the child has some confidence, but still moderate uncertainty, over the successful implementation of a response. That combination seems to propel the knowledge into action. This dynamic seems necessary to explain the changing parade of behaviors that mark the opening years of life. A 1-year-old child faced with a set of toys—balls, blocks, cloths, dolls, and animals—will spend some time banging and throwing and some time displaying pretend acts. But after eighteen to twenty months, the same child faced with the same toys will suddenly show one or two instances of spontaneous categorization. The child will put all the wooden balls in one part of the carpet and all the small animals in another location. Why did these behaviors appear? They are neither imitative of any event witnessed nor instrumental in the usual sense of that word. It seems necessary to assume that as the child becomes capable of detecting similar dimensions among events he will, during the period when this competence is maturing, implement that knowledge in action, as if Plato's "to know the good is to do the good" were guiding the child's behavior. It does not seem fruitful to ask why the child categorized all the wooden balls or what motive impelled that action. The proper question seems to be, "What conditions occasioned the behavior?" In this case, the conditions were the emergence of a new competence that was not yet mastered. The growth of an ability over which there is some response uncertainty seems to define the critical conditions of performance. That hypothesis seems to explain a great many instances of imitation and language behavior. It also may be operative when one set of competences replaces another—the time of transition between stages. Although in many cases the performances of the more mature stage are instrumentally more effective and permit the gaining of new goals or the attaining of old goals more efficiently, such advantages are not always obvious. The capacity for simple metaphor, which usually appears by the third year, leads the child to express this new talent in language. A girl notes her dresses are closely packed in a closet and comments, "Look, all my dresses are friends." It is unlikely that that sentence was issued to acquire any external prize or to reduce dissonance. Rather, the sentence was constructed and displayed just because it was possible to do so. And after a few weeks or months, when that expression no longer has any aura of uncertainty, one may never hear it again. Robert White (1959) edged very close to this idea in his important essay on competence, but he placed this phenomenon in a motivational framework because it was extremely difficult for an American psychologist in the 1950s—even a creative one like Robert White—to avoid viewing most behaviors as goal-seeking or as conditioned reactions to drive or motive states. The notion of autochthonous perceptual processes was tolerable; but the possibility that an action, which spent effort and energy, occurred just because it could occur contradicted two basic presuppositions of the psychology of that time, the notions that, save for reflexes, responses had both a purpose and a history.

The view being developed here does not deny that large corpora of behavior fulfill those two traditional criteria. However, careful observations of young children require acknowledgment of the fact that some important classes of behavior dominate the stage of performance for awhile just because the organism is somewhat capable of their display—a condition reminiscent of Jean-Paul Sartre's recognition in his later years that he wrote simply because he was capable of writing (Sartre 1964).

Before the second birthday, children can compare events to schemata, generate predictions of the future, and impose acquired schemata on actions.The next victory is the comparison of two schemata or categories. By age four, children regularly relate representations of past or future actions, feelings, or cognitive structures to each other and to an evaluative standard. By seven years, or even a little earlier, they are able to relate a cognitive structure to a coherent or hierarchically organized network of structures; the child can explain why a transformed piece of clay has the same amount of substance as it did before its shape was altered. By adolescence children can examine sets of related propostions for internal consistency and coherence.

There are two lines of progress in this parade of growth. The first is from passive recognition of past experience, characteristic of the opening weeks of life, to active retrieval and implementation of knowledge and action, which emerge toward the end of the first year. The second is from the active relating of present events to structures, which emerges at eight or nine months, to the relating of structure to structure, structure to larger network, and finally the relating of propositions within a network, a competence which appears at adolescence. This sequence is likely to be monitored by maturation. But experience affects the richness, variety, and articulation of the structures in the cognitive repertoire, and the rate at which operative processes are established, and provides incentives that invite the child to use emerging competences as quickly as they mature.

This paradigm may have implications for emotional development. In the adolescent and adult the phenomena psychologists call emotional are the product of the person's relating a feeling pattern to a conceptual network. That process probably does not appear until three years of age, and prior to that time emotional events are the product of relating event to schema.

During the first year, discrepant events are either assimilated or not assimilated, and the feelings that parents are prone to label joy, contentment, and fear are generated. During the preschool years, when children can relate thoughts, actions, and feelings to standards, they become vulnerable to shame, anxiety, guilt, and disgust. Several years later they can relate events and feelings to larger networks, and new affects become possible. Children can refer the actions of another to a network that permits them to judge the intention of the other and thus become vulnerable to that special form of hostility that follows the decision that the other's intention was purposeful. The child is now capable of depression following task failure, for he relates a performance not only to a personal standard but to the performance of others. He becomes vulnerable to the affect we call "inferiority feelings" when he can seriate the self's qualities in relation to the qualities of others. The adolescent is able to examine the coherence of beliefs and becomes capable of experiencing special emotions if he detects inconsistency. We have no consensual names for these last emotional states because the affect names that are currently popular in psychology, many of which have been popular for centuries, are based on an epistemology that emphasizes either quality of feelings or class of action, rather than the cognitive process of comparing events, structures, and actions. We use the word *guilt* to name the affect that follows the telling of a lie (which a 6-year-old can experience), as well as the affect that follows recognition that one holds inconsistent attitudes toward a loved one, which a 6-year-old cannot generate. Similarly, we use the word *depressed* to name both the feeling of a 5-year-old child who loses a parent and of an adolescent who knows he has exhausted all possible ways to cope with a failed romance.

Classification schemes for affects, symbols, concepts, or propositions proceed from the presuppositions of the classifier and what use he plans to make of the classification. Linnaeus categorized animals by similarity in morphology rather than habitat because he was interested in speciation and believed that similarity in anatomy was a more faithful index of species than similarity in locale. What is our intention in classifying cognitive structures? What problems are we trying to solve? If our purpose is to parse development into stages and to explain age changes in intellectual efficiency, we should probably classify structures by their complexity, abstraction, and logical quality; this has been Piaget's strategy. But if our aim is to demonstrate the universality of cognitive evaluations, we should classify by content, as Osgood has done. If we want to classify structures to permit computer simulation of thought we should probably focus on the formal quality of propositions. If our purpose is to rank children on ease of learning to read and do mathematics, we should focus on acquired knowledge, especially vocabulary. Each purpose is served best by a particular classification scheme.

When compared with our knowledge of two decades ago, our present understanding of infancy is rich in new insights. But there are still more questions than answers. Having examined the bases for the strategies we chose in our empirical study of the effect of group care on early development, let us now turn to a review of research on that problem.

3 Early Experience and Infant Development

> Mothers have as powerful an influence over the welfare of future generations as all other earthly causes combined.
>
> *On the Education of Children,* 1814

When psychology separated from philosophy toward the end of the last century, it took as one of its problems the latter's concern with the contents of the conscious mind. The mind was a vessel of small pebbles, some of which fell under the glare of awareness. By training people to focus the beam of awareness and to describe what they saw, one hoped to gain information on the quality of the contents. Although psychologists soon abandoned that form of the question contemporary psychology has returned to a restatement of a similar theme: how does the mind transduce experience and what does it do with that information?

Although the modern question is concerned with processes rather than contents, many psychologists remain loyal to mental structures and assume that they ordinarily display continuity over time. One basis for the supposition of continuity is the materialistic prejudice that all psychological experience is ultimately transformed into a set of chemical molecules (Bennett et al. 1964; Crick 1966). Since some classes of experience are correlated with material changes in the brain, it is tempting to suppose that there is a material correlate of every psychological structure. If so, the metaphor for mind becomes reels of tape in a tape recorder. The structures derived from experience will, unless tampered with, remain unaltered and potentially available for retrieval. Their permanent availability implies their power to influence the future.

The belief that early experience has a profound and lasting effect on the child, wedded to the traditional attitude that the home is the best place to rear an infant, has produced reasonable caution about the possibly harmful effects of care outside the home, especially during the early, formative years. Such was the consensual opinion when we initiated our study of the effects of group care on the infant. Since the attitude is still popular, it may be useful to examine its bases in more detail.

Faith in the primacy of early experience

The fundamental premise behind our research was that experience exerts a primary force on the young child's development and the earlier the experience the more profound its influences. The bases for this assumption lie everywhere, in our history as well as our contemporary literature. Two hundred years ago clergy and statesmen regularly affirmed the critical importance of the early years. They urged mothers to stay home with their infants and young children and to treat them tenderly, while political leaders worked for the establishment of public schools to insure that the child was exposed as early as possible to responsible models who would guarantee proper development of his character.

It is important to note that the potency of early experience was never restricted to one or two aspects of development; it was assumed to influence intellective, emotional, and social development. John Bowlby and Mary Ainsworth have warned of the danger of insecure attachments to the mother during infancy as a result of frequent separations from that primary caretaker, suggesting that such experiences might have a detrimental influence on the young adult's ability to relate to others. Indeed, some pediatricians are even convinced that the experiences of the first postnatal hour cast their shadow on later childhood. "There is a sensitive period in the first minutes and hours of life during which it is necessary that the mother and father have close contact with their neonate for later development to be optimal," wrote Marshall Klaus and John Kennell (1976, p. 14). Victor Denenberg (1964), Seymour Levine and others have shown that slight physiological stresses can affect the capacity for emotion and fearfulness in adult animals, as well as in the offspring of the next generation. And many writers suggested that lack of stimulation, which is better conceptualized as lack of experiential variety, retarded intellectual and motor development permanently.

Although there was some empirical support for these claims, the degree of conviction with which the more general belief in the permanent effects of early experience was held often exceeded the trustworthiness of the available information. Indeed, the original investigations were initiated in order to affirm rather than to refute the original premise. Both investigators and a receptive audience were sensitized to the slightest support for the presupposition, and resistant to refutations unless the evidence was so dramatic that it could not be ignored. Why is the presupposition that early experience exerts a profound influence on the future so firm? There are at least five relatively independent bases for it.

THE DESIRE FOR EGALITARIANISM

John Locke's metaphor of the *tabula rasa* summarized with poetic power the desire of many seventeenth-century intellectuals to make experience, especially early experience, primary in the shaping of man's mind.

On the surface, Locke's metaphor was used as a weapon against Spinoza, Leibniz, and the continental rationalists who preferred to attribute to the mind innate ideas that were not the product of encounters with life. Although the debate between Locke and the continental rationalists seemed to be a philosophical disagreement over the likelihood of innate ideas and the differential beauty of mathematical versus empirical truths, there was a hidden agenda, as there are in most ideological controversies. In this case two more profound issues fueled the debate. One was the continuing attempt by the liberal intellectual class to weaken the secular power and dogmatism of organized Christianity. An attack on innate ideas was equivalent to an attack on religion. In addition to the desire to weaken the Church's hold on the citizenry, there was a commitment to egalitarianism. The Church held as a basic tenet that some were born superior to others because they were born in wedlock to Christian parents, so that from the beginning their minds were stocked with superior ideas and sentiments. Moreover, the Church claimed nothing the non-Christian could do would make it possible for him to attain spiritual equality. To Locke and others the doctrine of innate ideas was an obstacle to the attainment of political equality. The only way to insure that society would attain this ideal was to subscribe to an epistemology wherein all infants are equally skilled or unskilled at birth and to place experience in the role of unbiased tutor to all. Under these conditions the society could, if it wanted, arrange for the experiences of all of its children to be equivalent and by that action guarantee that their minds would be equally pure and alert. For Locke believed that men were by nature "all free, equal and independent," a statement that reflects the close relation between his politics and his epistemology. America professes to believe in Locke's idealized conception even more than does his native England. Citizens who desired an egalitarian society would be attracted to a psychological theory that insisted that experience is the primary determinant of psychological differences among human beings. Since 3-year-olds differ so from one another, both between and within homes, those friendly to Locke's view would be driven to the conclusion that early experience must be the cause of that variation.

The influence of the Protestant ethic

A second historical force behind the primacy of early experience comes from the Protestant maxim that one must prepare for the future. The accumulated tally of good deeds influences one's state of virtue. As in the Hindu view of karma, the good deeds constitute a tote board that announces each person's present moral posture. If a person's next life is determined by the virtue displayed in the present, then the future is, to some degree, knowable through careful attention to each day's actions and experience. The child is more likely to attain salvation if the environment encourages and supports its virtuous behavior. It is the parents' responsibility to provide the proper environment, the earlier the better. The hope that the future could be a little more certain if one managed the present properly became a creed for parents and social scientists. Just as each person prepared for salvation through good deeds in the present, parents prepared their children for psychological salvation through proper nurturing when they were young.

Samuel H. Smith wrote in 1796, "Were man able to trace every effect to its cause he would probably find that the virtue or the vice of an individual, the happiness or misery of a family, the glory or the infamy of a nation have had their sources in the cradle over which the prejudices of a nurse or mother have presided. The years of infancy are those in which the chains of virtue or of vice are generally forged . . . in proportion to the length of time any idea occupies the mind does it acquire strength and produce conviction" (Smith in Rudolph 1965, pp. 192-193). Noah Webster wrote, "Youth is the time to form both the head and the heart. The understanding is indeed ever enlarging but the seeds of knowledge should be planted in the mind while it is young and susceptible and if the mind is not kept untainted in youth, there is little probability that the moral character of the man will be unblemished . . . it is more difficult to eradicate bad habits than it is to impress new ideas" (Webster, in Rudolph 1965, p. 41).

The writings of America's intellectuals in the eighteenth and nineteenth centuries, influenced strongly by Protestants with an egalitarian ideal, urged mothers to care for their young children, implying that such care was not unlike gathering wood in August to prepare for December's frigid winds. Political and religious philosophy supported the view that early experience not only had a palpable impact on the early behavior of the young child but that, in addition, the effect was long-lasting and not easily undone.

Our language of description

It is probably important that our language reflects a bias favoring continuity in individual qualities. The adjectives we use to describe children rarely refer to the age of actor or the context of action. Like the names of colors or the shapes of forms, they imply a stability over time and location. We apply adjectives like *passive, irritable, intelligent, dependent,* or *labile* to infants, children, and adults, as if the meaning of these terms were not altered by growth. This is not characteristic of all languages. In Japanese, for example, different terms are used to describe superior mental abilities in infant and adult. When the same word is used to denote an abstract quality in child and adult, despite differences in the behavioral expression of the quality, the mind is tempted to assume a psychological connection between the two stages. Thus our language of description invites an assumption of permanence, rather than change, in abilities, motives, and temperamental characteristics.

Our rank order society

A fourth reason for maintaining a strong belief in the sustaining power of early experience is an inevitable consequence of entrenched social practices in our society, particularly the tendency to rank children on valued traits both in and out of school. This practice sensitizes every parent of a preschool child to the fact that rankings will be made as early as the end of the kindergarten year. Those evaluations will influence the quality of the education the child will receive through elementary and high school, the probability of gaining entrance into a good college and, it is assumed, the child's future vocational success, happiness, wealth, and dignity. Very few societies practice this severe grading of children with such efficiency and zeal. In most other communities in the contemporary world, as throughout history, a child is assigned responsibilities when he seems ready, not at a particular age. Furthermore, children are usually given assignments they can master, like working in the field, carrying water, or caring for younger children. Parents in subsistence-farming communities in Africa and Latin America do not award status to children in accord with their ability to carry water or care for infants. Status in the community is usually attained later in adulthood by continuing hard work, loyalty, and accumulation or inheritance of land and livestock, not by one's relative competence on motor, language, or social skills when one is six years old.

We do quite the opposite. The industrialized West needs less than half of its youth to assume positions of responsibility for others or to master technical skills, each of which is tied to the rewards of status, wealth, and dignity. Our commitment to a meritocratic system forces us to select candidates from the best trained. But training is cumulative, and the best colleges will select the best trained adolescents. Moreover, the well trained have an effect on the less well trained; the presence of the former persuades the latter that they cannot attain the same level of competence. They draw this conclusion early, perhaps by age ten or eleven, and once it is drawn, their motivations can become relatively fixed and their place in the rank order stable.

Most parents either know this sequence or sense it. From the perspective of parent and child, the aim is to be ahead early in the race. The goal is to be as high in the rank order as possible when the race begins, usually by five or six years of age. Most people believe, validly we think, that a 6-year-old who is relatively high in the rank order on reading skill, IQ, or control of aggression is more likely to remain high than to plummet. Hence they are sure that the child who gets off to a good start in the development of culturally valued attributes is likely, other things equal, to remain ahead. Americans see a life span as a long race course with most runners of roughly equivalent ability, speed, and endurance at the beginning of the competition. But some begin the race a few days before the others. Once the late starters begin to run they make good progress, but most never catch up to the few who started a little earlier. That view, which is partially compatible with the facts, would lead parents who want their children to gain positions of status, challenge, dignity, and wealth to assume that the differences at age five, which are so obvious, are the result of what happened before that time. Hence they want to guarantee that their children will have the best possible set of early experiences. This is a compelling argument! Infants of similar temperament and background do differ on a variety of psychological attributes by age three or earlier and it is likely that those differences are partly a function of family experiences.

THE PHYSIOLOGICAL SUBSTRATE OF PSYCHOLOGICAL EXPERIENCE: THE MIND AS TAPE RECORDER

Nineteenth-century psychological science made a contribution to the doctrine of infant determinism. Psychology was born in laboratories like those of Hermann von Helmholtz and Edward Titchener where the first questions psychologists asked of nature were related to Locke's first source of knowledge—the ideas derived from sensation. The remarkable contemporary discoveries of neurophysiology and neurobiology, derivatives of the early nineteenth-century work of Helmholtz, Georg Müller and others, have reinforced the view that it is possible to translate psychological experience into sentences with purely physiological content. This reductionistic attitude to psychological variables has extraordinary consequences for the layman's attitude toward the sequellae of experience. An introspective view of psychological experience is characterized by transience and change. One feels hunger now but did not moments ago; one is thinking of a sandy beach now, but of one's work a minute earlier. More important, each person experiences shifts in opinions and gains new facts each day. In the growing child the impression of change is even more dramatic. The progression from crawling to walking, from babbling to speech, from unawareness of responsibility to guilt occurs over a period of only a few years. But descriptions of the brain, especially prior to the 1960s, were less dynamic. Most of an adult's neurons are present at birth, and every neuron has the same set of forty-six chromosomes. Many of the connections between receptor cells, ganglia, and cortical areas are presumably fixed at birth or soon after. Given the recent claims that experience affects the weight of the brain and that early stimulation can add dendritic spines to cells or alter the sensitivity of the visual cortex to vertical or horizontal lines, one is tempted to view the central nervous system as very similar to Locke's tablet—a soft surface that accepts material marks that are difficult to erase.

There is a potential paradox lurking in a psychological characterization of human functioning marked by change, but an older biological view that implies permanence. (Only recently have neurobiologists emphasized the enormous plasticity of central nervous system structures.) The majority of educated citizens has been friendly to the older, more static biological conception for two reasons. First, neurophysiology is a more elegant science than psychology. Its facts are more replicable and its methods more objective than those of the social sciences. Since certainty is the primary criterion the modern West uses in evaluating knowledge, the traditional neurobiological view of experience has been attractive. Second, most prefer a materialistic conception of psychological concepts. Neurons are physical entities that can be seen under the microscope and one can produce material changes in the nerve cells of an organism by controlling its experience. For example, mice reared in darkness possess far fewer thornlike projections on the dendrites of neurons in the cortex (called dendritic spines) than mice reared in light (Valverde and Ruiz-Marcos 1970).

Since most American scientists, as well as other educated laymen, are receptive to the notion that psychological experience is translated into material changes in the neuron—like a mark on a tablet—it is easier to assume that the marks are fixed rather than transient. Messages written on blackboards are not altered spontaneously. They can be erased or more information can be added. (The latter possibility has always seemed more reasonable than the first.) But since no two experiences are identical, there is the temptation to reject the possibility of original marks being modified after their initial registration; a conclusion that is strengthened each time we haphazardly retrieve a very old memory.

The belief that experience produces a permanent change in the central nervous system, with the corollary that the brain directs thought and behavior (rather than vice versa), leads to the conclusion that early experience must be important, since the first structures will direct the later ones. If development is like the building of a house, where the form and quality of the foundation determine the integrity of the subsequent frame, then first experiences should have an overwhelming priority. The iron filings on the fresh tape will be permanently altered and if no one erases the message it will be preserved with fidelity for an indefinite period of time.

But suppose we consider the mind as more like a painter and her canvas than a tape recorder. We stumble on an artist who has completed a scene containing only a tree and a bush. When we return one year later, the painter has been working continually, the tree and bush have become part of a thick forest scene and neither form is recoverable. Although the newborn infant begins life as a cell, the protoplasm in the original zygote has been totally transformed—it is gone. A material basis for psychological structures does not demand the corollary of indefinite stability of initial elements.

Evidence for plasticity and reversibility Recent studies of recovery of function following early damage to parts of the central nervous system, although still controversial, at least imply a capacity for resilience. In an elegant study R. D. Lund and his colleagues removed a single eye from either newborn or mature rats and studied the distribution of nerve growth from the remaining eye to the superior colliculus or dorsal lateral geniculate body, two "way stations" between the retina and visual cortex. In the one-eyed newborn they found growth over the entire area of the colliculus. But if the eye was removed ten days after birth, the new growth did not occur (Lund, Cunningham, and Lund 1973). In most rodents mating behavior is highly dependent on the sense of smell; hence if the lateral olfactory tract is cut in adult hamsters, mating activity is eliminated. But if the same operation is performed on the newborn hamster, adult mating behavior is spared (Devor 1975).

Moreover, some animals seem to be capable of almost complete recovery of some behavioral functions following severe traumatic injury to the central nervous system. For example, if bilateral lesions of somatosensory cortex are created in newborn and adult cats, the operated adults are unable to solve tactile discrimination tasks while the operated newborns, when tested as adults, are quite competent (Benjamin and Thompson 1959). After an extensive survey of the relevant literature on recovery of function following changes in the central nervous system Donald Stein concluded, "I think that the real issue of functional recovery after infant lesions lies somewhere between the extreme claim on the one hand, that all recovery is a myth, and the claim on the other hand, that there is a total lack of specificity and therefore complete plasticity in the developing brain" (1976).

Recent reports on the malleability of animal behavior are in accord with Stein's reasonable conclusion. One of the most famous reports in the animal literature describes the phenomenon of imprinting. As described by Niko Tinbergen and Konrad Lorenz, imprinting refers to the precocial bird's tendency to follow the first salient, usually moving, object it encounters. As a result the bird's natural tendency to follow its biological mother can be altered and it can be made to follow a man or a moving sphere. Even this habit, which was believed to be fixed, can be reversed (Hess 1972; Hoffman and DePaulo 1977), as can a monkey's attachment from a member of its own species to a spayed female dog (Mason and Kenney 1974). And Harry Harlow and his colleagues have been able to rehabilitate, in less than six months, withdrawn and hyperactive macaques who spent their first half year in complete isolation because the infant monkeys who were their therapists would not let the isolates alone. After days of tugging and biting they forced the patients out of their shell (Suomi and Harlow 1972). Equally dramatic rehabilitation occurred in cebus monkeys who were restricted to solitary cages from two to six months of age and then given daily group experience for the next six months. The stereotypy and inhibition produced by the isolation had vanished after the six months of rehabilitation (Elias and Samonds 1977).

Evidence from human studies It is more difficult to find equally commanding demonstrations of dramatic changes in human development. But individual strands of evidence, each too weak to bear the burden of proof alone, can be woven into a fabric with some persuasive power. After the Second World War, the International Social Service arranged for middle-class American families to adopt homeless children, most of them from Greece and Korea, who had lived uncertain lives during the war. When the children arrived in the United States their ages ranged from about five months to ten years. Thirty-eight of these children were followed by a team led by Samuel Waldfogel of the Judge Baker Guidance Center in Boston. About eight of the thirty-eight children were judged initially to display severe signs of anxiety. The initial problems in the new adoptive homes were overeating, sleep disturbance, nightmares, and excessive clinging to the new parents. One 22-month-old girl screamed at the sight of a bed, soiled, and showed a strong fear of men for over a month. But over the years these symptoms vanished. The vast majority of the children made good school progress and there was no case of learning disability among them. The authors wrote,

> The thing that is most impressive is that with only a few exceptions they do not seem to be suffering either from frozen affect or the indiscriminate friendliness that Bowlby describes. As far as can be determined their relationships to their adoptive families are genuinely affectionate. To be sure, one is justified in drawing only preliminary conclusions from these observations. It is conceivable that the damage inflicted by the early deprivation has left a permanent mark which will only make its full influence felt later on. The possibility also remains that later developmental crises or subsequent loss may reactivate the initial trauma, and undermine the integration which has been achieved. Nevertheless, the degree of recovery observed in most cases could not have been predicted from the writings of those who have studied the effects of separation most carefully. The present results—tentative as they are—indicate that for the child suffering extreme loss, the chances for recovery are far better than had previously been expected. [Rathbun, DiVirgilio, and Waldfogel 1958, pp. 413-414]

In a similar study 229 Korean girls who had been adopted by middle-class American families when they were between two and three years of age were followed for at least six years. The children were divided into three groups, based on their degree of malnutrition at the time of admission—below the third percentile for height and weight, between the third and twenty-fourth percentile, and the twenty-fifth percentile and above. At the follow-up, a minimum of six years after admission to the American foster homes, all were in elementary school. All the children surpassed the expected mean height and weight of Korean children. The average IQ of the three groups was 102, 106, and 112, respectively, and although the severely malnourished group had a slightly lower IQ than the best nourished, the mean of the former group was equal to that of the average American child. And the average IQ of the severely malnourished children was forty points higher than that reported for similar Korean samples returned to their original home environments. School achievement scores were adequate, and all three groups were performing at a level equal to or better than the average American child (Winick, Meyer, and Harris 1975). This degree of recovery of intellectual skills and physical health does not occur among malnourished children who are returned to their poor environments after a period of rehabilitation. Malnutrition and disruption of normal family experiences during the first two years of life only predict later impaired cognitive development if the child remains in the same destructive environment. Development can be affected benevolently if the child is exposed to new experiences or contexts that sculpt the skills required for successful adjustment (Richardson 1976).

There seems to be a synergism between early physiological and psychological trauma and an environment that does not support adaptive dispositions. Eight-month-old middle-class infants who are developmentally retarded on Bayley's scale are not intellectually different at age seven from middle-class children who were not so diagnosed. But retarded 8-month-olds growing up in lower-class homes remain intellectually retarded during the preschool and school years. Many institutionalized infants who display a passive, quiet, and withdrawn appearance at one year because they have been restricted to barren cribs can be rehabilitated, indicating that the infant possesses extraordinary potential to respond to a new environment during the early years of life (Dennis 1973; Flint 1966). Investigators who expect the apathy and passivity produced by institutionalization to be resistant to amelioration are usually surprised by how quickly therapeutic intervention restores the child's vitality. In one study a small group of frightened, passive, quiet 2- to 4-year-old children, who had been raised in an overcrowded institution with too few caretakers, was allowed to participate regularly in play sessions with adults and a few other children in the institution. In less than eighteen months the veil of indifference lifted and the affective vitality so characteristic of 4-year-olds emerged. The investigator was not prepared for such easy progress and wrote,

> We had not anticipated that the older children, who had suffered deprivation for periods of 2½ to 4 years would show swift response to treatment. That they did so amazed us. These inarticulate, underdeveloped youngsters who had formed no relationships in their lives, who were aimless and without a capacity to concentrate on anything, had resembled a pack of animals more than a group of human beings

> . . . As we worked with the children it became apparent that their inadequacy was not the result of damage but rather was due to a dearth of normal experiences without which the development of human qualities is impossible . . . After a year of treatment many of these older children were showing a trusting dependency toward staff and volunteers and in view of their degree of self reliance in play and routines, seemed to be developing feelings of self trust. [Flint 1966, pp. 138-139]

Children who had been adopted from a Lebanese institution for foundlings before their second birthday (with developmental quotients that hovered near 50) and placed in good foster homes eventually attained average IQ scores of approximately 100, in contrast to those who remained in the institution whose test scores continued to reflect profound mental retardation (Dennis 1973). The investigator wrote, "it appears that experiential deprivation which occurs before the age of two does not have lasting intellectual consequences if followed by normal everyday cognitive experience" (Dennis 1973).

Recently psychologists have been following the development of a girl named Genie who, at thirteen and one half years of age, was removed from a home where she had been immobilized, isolated from contact with others, and physically beaten for most of the first thirteen years of her life. When discovered she was malnourished, unable to stand erect, and without language, "a primitive and unsocialized victim of unprecedented deprivation and social isolation" (Curtiss et al. 1975, p. 146). After only four years in a normal environment she developed some language, learned many social skills, was able to take a bus to school, and expressed some of the basic human affects. Moreover, on some of the performance scales of the Wechsler Intelligence Scale for Children she obtained scale scores as high as eight or nine. Although she is still markedly different from an average California 18-year-old, Genie has grown remarkably, and in a relatively short period of time (Curtiss et al. 1975).

The mind has some of the properties of an elastic surface, easily deformed by a shearing force, but often able to rebound when that force is removed. After summarizing studies that reported rather optimistic outcomes for children with psychological symptoms who were placed in supportive homes, Kadushin argued for "recognition that children have varying capacities to deal with potentially traumatic conditions and that these strengths enable them, when provided with a healthier environment, to surmount the damaging influences of earlier developmental insults" (Kadushin 1970, p. 199).

At the end of a report describing the ease with which ducklings can be made to substitute one imprinting target for another, Howard Hoffman and Peter DePaulo arrived at a similar conclusion: "in the domain of social attachments nature is so designed as to make the notion of immediate irreversible environmental effects a concept of extremely narrow application—if it has any application at all . . . The popular conception of imprinting has been to justify the notion that failure to be exposed to all sorts of environmental stimuli at an appropriate time dooms an organism to be permanently disadvantaged. Our work would seem to indicate that this is not the case. Nature can in fact repair some of the unfortunate vagaries of environmental experience. Apparently it does so through the continually expanding and adjusting effects of learning" (Hoffman and DePaulo 1977, pp. 65-66).

As long as we conceptualize the contents of the mind as a pattern of iron filings we will be tempted to regard psychological structures as hardened steel rather than warm wax. Since existing data are so fragile, it is not possible to decide the issue of malleability solely on empirical grounds. But is it logically possible that any set of structures or behaviors in a 2-year-old might not be capable of alteration by application of proper experience at the proper time?

Studies of normal children reveal that behavior and cognitive structures normally undergo dramatic alteration with development. There is hardly a psychological structure in the 10-year-old that is not a replacement or transformation of one that was present in the 2-year-old. The 2-year-old who is terrified of dogs or the dark usually discards the phobia in a year or two. The 2-year-old is not yet capable of guilt, taking the perspective of another, or formal operational thought, but each will emerge with development. Most normally reared American children change from an idealistic view of their parents during early childhood to one in which both resentment and realism emerge during adolescence. Imperfections in parents that went unnoticed at age five become the central dimensions of the older adolescent's conception of his family. Since these attitudes are resilient, why assume that a 2-year-old's excessive fear of or hostility toward an adult cannot also be changed under the guidance of proper experience? Since the structures that represent the 2-year-old's schema of his mother or concept of an animal change with development, it is reasonable to assume that some of the structures produced by trauma during infancy can also be altered. We are led to suggest, therefore, that if a psychological structure established in early childhood is to be maintained for a long period of time, and some are, it must be supported by the current environment.

Evidence favoring this conclusion can be found in the results of several longitudinal investigations of children from working-class and middle-class American families, most of whom grew up in relatively normal homes. After reflecting upon their extensive corpora of data, most of the investigators felt that variation in psychological qualities observed during the first two or three years of life was not predictive of variation in culturally salient and age-appropriate characteristics five, ten, or twenty years later. For example, Jean Macfarlane, Lucile Allen, and Marjorie Honzik analyzed the reports of mothers of forty-one children who were part of the larger Berkeley Guidance

Study sample in order to investigate the stability of behavior problems in normal children from twenty-one months to fourteen years of age. The authors concluded, "Our findings show that, although there is a tendency for problems to be present for varying lengths of time, change rather than persistence is of the greater significance. Not only are changes occurring all the time in these behaviors, but there are certain epochs in the child's life when the problem patterns tend to be disrupted. A year after the 'epoch' the old pattern may be resumed, but not with the same intensity that was present before" (1954, p. 174). The same authors continued, "Predictive significance as measured by interage correlations reveals several facts of interest. One is how nonpersistent for a long age span most problems are" (1954, p. 219).

Macfarlane and colleagues also evaluated a group of 30-year-old participants in the Berkeley Guidance Study who had been followed from birth through eighteen years. They concluded that prediction of differences in adjustment among the adults was difficult because "The preschool period does not have such irreversible effect as current theory assumes. Personality development and maturing continue to occur after adulthood is reached" (Jones, Macfarlane, and Eichorn 1959).

A similar long-term study of seventy-one children who had grown up in southwestern Ohio from 1929 to 1957 revealed little relation between variation in fearfulness, activity, dependency, tantrums, aggression, and shyness during the first three years of life and variation in a variety of culturally salient behaviors during adolescence and early adulthood. However, differences in intellectual achievement, sex-typed behavior, and social spontaneity displayed during later childhood (from six to ten years) did predict theoretically related responses during early adulthood (Kagan and Moss 1962).

There is little support for the view that the behavior of the 1- or 2-year-old provides a clear preview of the adult behavioral profile. But that demand may be too severe; perhaps the actions of a 1-year-old provide a clue to qualities to be seen only a few years later. However, here, too, the existing information is frustrating to those who believe that the combination of forces that created a particular envelope of dispositions in a 1-year-old must continue to be potent; differences among infants in activity, irritability, and affectivity do not predict profiles during later childhood.

For example, Nancy Bayley (1964) found little evidence for consistency in selected individual qualities from infancy to later childhood. Observers made ratings of personality variables in infancy (ten to thirty-six months), early childhood (two and one-half to eight years), and late childhood (nine to twelve years). There was only moderate stability within each of the three age periods and minimal stability across longer intervals. "A study of children's behavior over time, when one compares specific variables, presents a confusing array of changing patterns," Bayley wrote (1964, p. 93).

The New York Longitudinal Study (Thomas et al. 1960; Thomas et al.

1963; Thomas and Chess 1972; Birch et al. 1962; Chess, 1967) was designed to study the stability of temperamental dimensions in 136 middle-class children living in New York City. The data consisted primarily of parental descriptions of the child's responsivity gathered during interviews conducted at three-month intervals from the child's birth through age eighteen months, at half-yearly intervals until five years of age, and annually after the child was five years old. Ratings of the child's behavior based on the interview data led to the creation of nine categories of infant temperament. The children tended to retain their relative position on some temperamental patterns over the first two years of life. However, when these children were evaluated at age five the earlier stability had vanished.

It has been observed that "Behavioural ratings in the first six months of life are of no predictive value in relation to the child's temperamental characteristics as shown during his school years . . . it seems unlikely from the currently available findings that any strong relation will be found between ratings in early infancy and measures of temperament in later childhood" (Rutter 1970, pp. 53-54).

Indeed, when the children they studied were six to twelve years of age, Alexander Thomas and Stella Chess (1972) concluded, after a thorough evaluation, that the children who were coping successfully with the demands of the middle school years were not characterized by any particular temperamental pattern displayed during infancy.

A more objective and analytic study reported minimal predictive relation between dimensions of newborn reactivity and behavior during the preschool years. Variation among newborns in tactile sensitivity, motor reactivity, sucking behavior, or respiratory rate was not related to a selected set of behaviors two and one-half years later. The authors of that study wrote, "It appears that the newborn behavioral repertoire is not a rich source of clues to the nature of later behavior" (Bell, Weller, and Waldrop 1971, p. 131).

After finding relatively unimpressive intraindividual stability of scores on the Brazelton Newborn Scale over infants' first four days of life, Frances D. Horowitz asked rhetorically why psychologists were so interested in the stability of an infant's qualities, writing that "The only reason for expecting long term prediction from neonatal assessment is believing or placing one's bets on hypothesizing that the influence of environmental factors on developmental outcome is likely to be minimal or so uniform as to function as a constant. If one views development as an interactive or transactive process and if one cannot now specify the values of the environmental factors involved in this process, prediction is not only not possible, it is not a valid criterion for judging the utility of neonatal assessment" (Horowitz 1977).

Finally, one of us has recently completed a study of 10-year-olds who are firstborn, Caucasian, from working-class and middle-class families living in the Boston area, and who had been evaluated extensively four times during the first three years of life. In the original study the infant's attentiveness, vocal excitability, activity level, irritability, and disposition to smile were assessed at four, eight, thirteen, and twenty-seven months of age. Variation in these behaviors prior to one year did not predict theoretically reasonable qualities at twenty-seven months of age. "We have been continually impressed at the changes in attentiveness, affect, and activity that occur in individual children. One hyperkinetic, restless, and inattentive infant boy was placid and quiet at 27 months. Another boy who rocked his entire body and sucked his forearm throughout the three 8 month episodes—and had worried the staff—did not appear atypical at 27 months" (Kagan 1971, p. 176).

Although there was suggestive stability of variation in attentiveness from thirteen to twenty-seven months, attentiveness at both ages was positively related to the educational level of the family and, by inference, to different experiences at home. This situation provided us with an opportunity to evaluate the assumption, stated earlier, that a particular quality in a young child is not likely to persist unless the environment continues to support it. We recently evaluated sixty-eight of the children who had been members of the original longitudinal sample.

Unlike most follow-up studies, which are inductive and administer a varied array of procedures, this assessment was relatively specific. We wished to determine if variation in attentiveness, affectivity, activity, and irritability would predict intelligence test scores, reading ability, and reflection-impulsivity at ten years of age.

The most relevant finding in this context was that the educational level of the family was the best predictor of both IQ and reading skill (the correlations averaged about 0.5 to 0.6). Although individual differences in attentiveness at thirteen and twenty-seven months correlated with both IQ and reading scores, when the contribution of parent education was statistically controlled the predictive relations became minimal. Thus we suspect the relation between infant attentiveness and later reading score or IQ is due to the fact that middle-class infants and children are exposed daily to experiences different from those of children from working-class families, and these differences, over time, produce the different test scores. We suggest that if a highly attentive upper-middle-class 2-year-old were to have been transferred to a working-class home he might not have become a highly skilled reader and if a minimally attentive young child from a working-class home had been transferred to a professional family he would have both attained a higher IQ and become a more skilled reader. When we compared children from the same social class who contrasted in both reading ability and IQ, we did not find major behavioral differences between them as infants.

There was evidence that perhaps some temperamental qualities do predispose an infant to develop in a particular way. The infants who frequently displayed the smile of assimilation in response to discrepant events were more likely to be reflective than impulsive at age ten.

The data from this study do not provide much basis for enthusiasm among those who contend that the experiences of the first two years create structures and action profiles which are relatively fixed and which will persist, no matter what environmental circumstances follow (Lapidus, Kagan, and Moore, unpublished 1977). It is true that the existing corpus of data does *not* permit one to conclude that the experiences of infancy are of no consequence for later childhood. But it does imply that if the structures created by those early encounters are not supported by the child's current environment one should be prepared to see dramatic changes.

All of this information is relatively recent and has not yet penetrated public consciousness. There is resistance to its implications because the reasons for maintaining faith in the primacy of early encounters are intuitively attractive. A particular recipe of interactions is still seen as an elixir young children need to obtain society's highly valued prizes. From Locke to Freud there has been consensus that early experience set permanent directions, because everyone hoped that parents could control the future and prevent anomalous development in their children. As the range and the mystery of variation in adult status increased from the eighteenth century to the present the danger of being "left out" made parents seek some explanation for that variation. The suggestion that early experience was the primary force was partially satisfying because it resolved uncertainty, provided rituals that reduced parental anxiety, made material encounters between the child and his environment the bases for negative outcomes and, above all, was rational.

Experience and early development—a selected review

Before considering some concrete illustrations of the effect of early experience on development we must consider two problems. The first is that most observers conceptualize the young child to be passive to the influence of the caretaker, rather than recognize the reciprocal nature of the parent-child relation. Second, since there was no sophisticated theory to guide past research, the scientist was forced to treat every action of the parent toward the child as significant as any other action, and the variables coded were discrete, fragmentary, and isolated from meaningful, long-lasting sequences. Psychologists coded the relative frequency of actions like praising, kissing, touching, talking, and smiling. This is not an unreasonable position to assume when theory is fragile, but it is unlikely to reveal coherences that may be discovered when theory guides observation.

A far more serious problem arises with respect to which dependent variables are studied. Rather than assume that the experiences have differential influence on specific systems and search for particular functional relations between adult input and developing infant profiles, many investigators selected as criteria holistic, evaluative concepts like IQ or developmental quotient. That decision is easy to understand. Many child psychologists are tacit pragmatists. They know the child's developmental quotient at three years is predictive of the older child's intellectual abilities—the correlations ranging from about 0.2 to 0.4. Hence discovering which elements in the environment seemed to influence early developmental quotients had practical significance. Discovering the relation between a mother's actions and the young child's tendency to vocalize in response to a familiar adult or to withdraw from a stranger was less appealing because most investigators believe, probably correctly, that those dependent variables in the 1-year-old do not predict anything of pragmatic importance.

Intelligence test scores gathered at age three predict IQ and school performance a decade later (Honzik, Macfarlane and Allen 1948). That fact is usually interpreted as indicating that a quality of the child is stable and independent of the continuing environment in which the child is growing. What is ignored is the fact that the education and occupation of the child's parents are also correlated with the child's intelligence quotient at both age three and age thirteen, and at about the same magnitude, namely, 0.4 to 0.6. A choice of interpretations can be imposed on that pattern of correlations. The popular one is that the child possesses a quality called intelligence that influences scores on developmental scales and is actualized by experiences in the family during the first three years of life. The quality remains stable; hence developmental quotients at age three predict IQs at age ten. But what might that entity be? The data are literally ranks of scores on tests that ask quite different questions. The test at three years assesses the child's vocabulary and invites him to build a block construction and copy a circle. The IQ test at age thirteen asks about general information, assesses arithmetic skills, evaluates short-term memory for numbers, and asks the child to define a set of words. Even though many of the questions are different, many psychologists believe that an entity called "potential for intellectual growth" is stable, and they use height as an analogy. Even though a child's height changes with age, stature at three predicts stature at six. Since a child's potential for physical growth is a genetically determined characteristic, it is reasonable to assume that intelligence, like height, is an essence that cannot be lost.

An alternative interpretation takes seriously the fact that educational level of family is correlated with the scores at both age three and age thirteen and assumes that the practices of well-educated parents are such as to produce a high developmental quotient at each age. All children eventually master the items on the test at age three. Those who have experienced the proper environments master them a little earlier than others and hence have a higher developmental quotient. Similarly, well-educated parents will behave in ways toward their children that will lead them to attain higher scores on the later test items a little earlier. Hence the positive correlation between the quotients at three and thirteen may not be due to the continuity of any essence called intelligence, but rather reflect the continuing effect of experiences associated with being reared in a well-educated family. Consider an analogy to the fecundity of two neighboring nations in two periods, say twenty years apart. Nation A practices birth control while nation B does not. Since the birth rate of nation B is higher than that of A at both points, one is tempted to conclude that nation B has a basically higher reproductive potential than A, when in fact the reason for the stability is the presence of a third factor; namely, failure to practice birth control.

The infant's attachment to its caretaker is another holistic quality that investigators tried to quantify in evaluating the effect of early experience. Although the term attachment was originally promoted by John Bowlby, the image of Harlow's monkeys clinging tightly to their terry cloth surrogate mothers illustrates the intended connotation of the construct—emotional security. The young infant, who becomes distressed regularly, requires a familiar object to whom he can orient, and with whom he can interact, for these responses alleviate distress. Few would quarrel with that statement. It is obvious that by the time the infant is six months of age, or even earlier, some people are better able to alleviate an infant's distress than others. It is no surprise that these special people are the ones with whom the child has had frequent contact. They are the targets of the child's attachment. There are at least two reasons why familiar people would be better at alleviating distress than unfamiliar ones. The popular interpretation is that an emotional bond has become established between the child and the target of attachment as a result of many hours of interaction, satisfying as well as unsatisfying. The act of approaching the mother, rather than a neighbor, when one is upset reflects a profound difference in depth of relation to each of those adults.

An alternative view of attachment is that infants do not ordinarily approach unfamiliar people or objects, especially in unfamiliar surroundings. If two people are both familiar but unequally so, the child typically chooses the more familiar. Although the child's choice is consistent over occasions, the psychological basis for the choice need not reflect a profound difference in the emotional relation between the child and the two classes of adults.

Empirical data support the first view, promoted by Bowlby, that attachment refers to a profound affective relation between child and caretaker that is not based solely on the frequency of interaction between child and caretaker. Eighteen-month-old kibbutz-reared children who spend twenty of twenty-four hours in an infant house with a metapelet are less distressed when with their mother and an unfamiliar woman than when with the metapelet and an unfamiliar woman. Surely the caretaker was as familiar as the mother, and had talked with, praised, and nurtured the child more often than the mother. Yet the child was less anxious with the biological parent.

A second relevant fact comes from the study to be summarized in this book. At twenty months of age each child was in a room with the mother, the primary day care teacher (or a friend if the child was reared at home), and an unfamiliar woman for forty-five minutes. After fifteen and thirty minutes the adults changed chairs spontaneously, an event that alerted the child. Both day care and home-reared children were more disposed, by a factor of seven, to approach their mother than the day care teacher or familiar friend. Despite the fact that the primary caretaker at the day care center had been familiar to the child for seventeen months, the child behaved toward her as though she were a visiting aunt.

Domestic research has focused on these two abstract qualities of the infant—his growing intellect and his attachment to caretakers. Psychologists have asked how smart and how secure the child is because both intelligence and security are believed to be the sine qua non for successful adjustment in our society and because it was believed that these qualities were stable over time.

The effects of infant experience A select number of studies of the early years represented in this section deal with only two issues—the relation between social class and early cognitive development and the effects of form of rearing other than the nuclear family. The literature on the effect of early care on the child's development, especially the interaction between care and social class, is so remarkably consistent in its message (considering the difficulties associated with this kind of inquiry and the variety of samples and procedures used) that one is tempted to regard the findings as true. The consensus is that the social class of the child's family correlates consistently with his level of cognitive development as early as one to two years of age. The magnitude of these correlations is low at age two (usually about 0.2) but increases with age to about 0.5 or 0.6 during late childhood (Deutsch 1973; Werner 1969; Kagan 1971). This effect was as strong in America fifty years ago (Stroud 1928) as it is today, and occurs throughout contemporary Europe, as it did in the Europe of the past (Decroly and Degard 1910). The relation between class and cognitive development also holds in rural, subsistence-farming villages in Guatemala (Klein, Irwin, Engle, Yarbrough 1977).

The summary mentioned in chapter 2 of a longitudinal investigation of 180 firstborn Caucasian infants studied from four to twenty-seven months of age (Kagan 1971), showed that at twenty-seven months the middle-class children had larger vocabularies and performed better on a specially prepared embedded figures test than those from working-class families. One major variable of interest was the child's changing pattern of attention to visual and auditory events. At the earliest age (four months) there was no relation between the child's attentiveness to discrepant visual events and his social class background. By eight months a slight positive relation had emerged and by one year the infants of better-educated parents were significantly more attentive than those from families who had less than a high school education (the correlation was about 0.4). That result was interpreted to mean that the middle-class children had entered the new phase of amplified memory capacity a little earlier than the children of working-class families, and it was supposed that advantage was because of the greater variety and challenge they received at home. There is still justification for that interpretation.

Among boys, the higher social class of the child's family the greater the increase in attention from eight to thirteen months. Among girls there was a relation between class and increases in attention between thirteen and twenty months. The relation between class and attention at eight, thirteen, and twenty-seven months was generally greater for girls than for boys. That finding was not unique. Howard Moss (1967) had also reported a stronger relation for girls than for boys between amount of face-to-face contact between mother and infant and duration of attention to schematic faces shown to the 3-month-old child in a laboratory ($r = 0.61$ for girls and 0.00 for boys). In Kagan's 1971 study over five hours of observations in the homes of each of ninety of these children at twenty-seven months of age had indicated there were social class differences in the behavior toward daughters that did not occur for sons. Specifically, upper-middle-class mothers chided their daughters more than their sons for task incompetence and were more concerned with competence than were lower-class mothers.

A subsequent study (Tulkin 1970) also gathered extensive home observations on 10-month-old girls from both lower- and middle-class families within the same geographical area. Tulkin found significant class differences in verbal interaction and play. Upper-middle-class mothers had more face to face contact with their children and vocalized more to their daughters. They also encouraged and rewarded their daughters more for individual mastery. These experiences should have led to precocious development of the cognitive structures that mediate attention at thirteen and twenty-seven months.

When the girls were observed in the laboratory, the middle-class girls were more likely to vacillate between new and old objects and were more attentive to taped samples of speech. Most important, the middle-class infants seemed to be more thoughtful when confronted with a problem. In the problem situation the infants were exposed to a tape recording of the voice, either the mother or a stranger, while the mother sat to one side of the child and the stranger on the other side. Each middle-class child looked at her mother following the termination of her speech and at the stranger following the termination of the stranger's voice—as if the child were inquiring as to the source of the voices. The children of the working-class did not show that differential behavior, the difference implying that more of the upper-middle-class 10-month-old girls had entered the stage of actively comparing schema and experience. Since the upper-middle-class girls had been exposed to greater variety of experience at home, it is reasonable to suggest that their history may have been one determinant of their precocity.

A significant study of the relation between home experience and development, by Burton White and his colleagues, adopted a strategy that had a degree of boldness most investigators shun (White and Watts 1973). On the basis of tests and evaluations of a group of children three to five years of age, White and Jean Watts invented a list of psychological characteristics they called *competence.* Competent children had the ability to engage and maintain the attention of adults in socially acceptable ways; use adults as resources; to express affection and hostility to adults and peers; lead, follow and compete with peers; and imitate adult rules. The competent children showed linguistic skill, pride in mastery, and sensitivity to discrepancy and inconsistency. They were able to anticipate consequences; deal with abstractions, letters, and numbers; take the perspective of another; make interesting associations; plan and carry out multistage activities; and focus attention on two events at once.

The investigators then classified a group of fourteen 1-year-olds and seventeen 2-year-olds as competent or incompetent based on the classification of their older siblings. It should come as no surprise that twenty-one of the twenty-two competent children came from professional and white-collar families; only one came from a working-class family. On the other hand, six of the nine incompetent children came from blue-collar families and only three from white-collar homes. Not one of the incompetent children was being reared by a family of professionals. The investigators followed the development of the group of 1- and 2-year-olds for almost a year, observing them at home and testing them. The competent children were more proficient at language and on many cognitive tasks. Mothers of the more competent children were more verbally interactive with their offspring, stimulated their intellectual development more and encouraged mastery more than the mothers of the less competent. If we assume that the infants were not significantly different at birth, the data imply that experience in the home does indeed influence the child in expected ways. Since the skills measured by White and Watts are the cognitive talents that will be the basis of the child's eventual rank among his peers in school, these data reinforce the belief that early experience gives the child an early advantage that can be measured as early as two years of age. Although we cannot specify the mechanisms that produced the advanced cognitive development, the data imply that the family has an enormous power to mold the child. As suggested before, this is one reason parents are apprehensive over giving up that power; they fear that the child's future intellectual potential may be seriously harmed.

One mechanism that might explain the ubiquitous class differences is variety of experience and opportunity to practice maturing competences. If one could demonstrate that variety is related to cognitive development within a lower-working class population faith in this idea would be strengthened. In one study that supports the hypothesis, the Bayley Scales of Mental Development were administered to seventy-seven 6-month-olds and the

Stanford-Binet IQ test when each infant was three years old. At the earlier age, each child was observed in the home in order to assess the quality of stimulation, especially the emotional and verbal responsivity of the mother, the mother's involvement with the child, the availability of appropriate play materials, and the organization of the physical environment.

The children were classified into three groups on the basis of both the six- and thirty-six month scores. The ten children whose IQ scores at three years were at least twenty-one points higher than their developmental quotients at six months were called "increasers." The seventeen children whose IQs at age three were at least twenty-one points lower than their scores at six months were "decreasers." The remaining fifty children were called "nonchangers." The families were generally working- and middle-class, and about two-thirds black and one-third white. As expected, the children with increasing developmental scores had mothers who were more involved with them and provided appropriate play materials. Since the sample varied in both class and ethnicity, it is possible that the familial variables coded were not the effective ones, but rather that other experiences, covarying with class and race, were more salient (Bradley and Caldwell 1976). In a second, more persuasive study (Yarrow, Rubenstein and Pedersen 1975), investigators worked with forty-one 6-month-old black, lower-middle-class infants. The study was limited to one-half year of home observations and assessments. There was a moderate correlation (about 0.4) between the children's developmental quotients on the Bayley scale and the amount of kinesthetic stimulation they experienced at home. The authors created an index of "variability of stimulus input" which predicted each subject's Bayley Developmental Quotient and amount of vocalization, goal-directed activity, and object permanence. Multiple correlations were computed, with kinesthetic stimulation, variety of experience, and maternal vocalization used as predictors. The multiple R, with an overall index of cognitive development as the criterion, averaged between 0.6 to 0.7. Variety of experience seemed to facilitate rate of cognitive growth during infancy. An interesting finding was that the relation between mother's behavior and child's cognitive development was more lawful and stable for girls than for boys. This is analogous to the finding of the longitudinal study discussed earlier that social class of mother predicted vocalization and language for girls but not for boys (Kagan 1971). The replication of that result on a totally different sample suggests an important generalization. Kagan had speculated then that the greater variability in temperament among infant boys may have attenuated the lawful relation between family experience and cognitive development. Yarrow and his colleagues noted that the day-to-day stability of behavior was less for boys than for girls, and that the split half reliability of the Bayley Developmental Scores was lower for boys than for girls (0.77 versus 0.94).

There seems to be consensus that differences in class are consistently associated with differences in aspects of cognitive development. The most popular interpretation of this association is that middle-class parents provide a greater variety of experience and more consistent stimulation of language development. Both factors accelerate the infant's cognitive development by a few months with respect to the standard milestones seen during the first two years.

The effect of form of care A question of more recent interest pertains to the effect on the child's growth of arrangements of rearing, other than the nuclear family. Nonfamily arrangements include day care experience and residential group care in institutions. Although this literature is more tentative than studies of the effects of social class the initial impression of most investigators is that daily group care—if it is of good quality—does not seem to have much of an effect, either facilitating or debilitating, on the development of most children. The one exception to that conclusion seems to hold for children from poorly educated and less privileged families. If such children attend well-run centers they perform a little better on the standard tests of development during the first year of life than do children from similar backgrounds reared only at home. However, the group context must be a good one.

One of the earliest studies of the value of group care found that 3- to 5-year-olds from poor families gained twenty points on the Merrill-Palmer test of development, compared with five points for controls reared at home, after only six months of group care (Barrett and Koch 1930).

Most of the recent investigations find no major differences in cognitive, social, or emotional development between children in day care centers and those reared at home. A comparison of Swedish infants twelve to eighteen months of age cared for in their own homes, other homes, or day care centers revealed no consistent differences among the three groups on a standard assessment of cognitive development (the Griffiths Scale) or in response to separation from the caretaker, despite some differences in the form of adult interaction in the different settings (Cochran 1977).

Bettye Caldwell and her colleagues enrolled a small group of children in a day care center attached to Syracuse University. The children, five to twenty-two months of age, came from black and white working-class and middle-class families. They remained in group care for two to five years. When the subjects were of preschool age, a control group of children who had been reared at home and who were matched with the day care group on sex, race, and age was collected, and both groups were enrolled in a new center. All the children were observed and rated between three and four and three-quarters years of age. There were no differences between the two groups with respect to sociability with peers, cognitive functioning, or attitudes toward the teacher. The ratings suggested that the children who had been in day care for the longer period were less cooperative with adults, slightly more aggressive and more active (Schwarz, Strickland, and Krolick 1974; Caldwell et al. 1970). An earlier report on this sample (Caldwell et al. 1970) had reported no differences between the two groups in degree of attachment of infant to mother as assessed from interview data.

J. Ronald Lally (1974) has been studying a group of low-income families enrolled in a program providing advice and support to parents as well as day care for their children. From six to fifteen months of age the children attended a special center half-days; from 24 to 60 months they participated in a full-day program. The Stanford-Binet and other tests were administered at three and four years of age to this experimental sample as well as to two control groups, one matched on parental education, and one from better-educated families.

The experimental subjects had higher IQs than the lower-class controls at both ages (although the difference was smaller at age four than at three). However, the middle-class children obtained the highest scores. The difference between the average IQ (138) of the 4-year-old middle-class controls and the average (110) of the experimental subjects was much larger than the difference between the scores of the day care subjects and lower-class controls (102). Hence social class was a more important determinant of IQ than method of rearing, a result in accord with other studies. It should be noted that the lower-class experimental subjects did have slightly higher IQs than the lower-class controls.

One of the most extensive assessments of the effects of day care—either group care or care in a home other than the child's own—on the behavior of preschool children was summarized by Marcia Lippman and Barbara Grote (1974). The sample was relatively large and predominantly Caucasian. The main analysis compared sixty-six triplets of children matched on sex, race, and number of parents in the home and amount of mother's education. One group attended a group day care center for at least nine months prior to assessment and for an average of two years; members of the second group were cared for in homes other than their own (family day care) for about the same length of time; and a third group was reared at home by the natural parent. A large battery of tests administered to the children assessed variables like curiosity, relation to parents, sex-typing, achievement, control of impulse, and cooperation. There were minimal differences among the three groups on most of the measures. Children in day care were not different from home controls in cooperativeness, preference to be with parents in time of stress, recall memory, or sex-typing. One of the few differences that emerged implied that day care children were slightly more realistic than home controls in estimating their abilities; the home controls tended to over-estimate their cognitive skills. But the main thrust of the results is contained in the study's concluding section: "Although no claim can be made to have obtained valid measures of all the aspects of development, the overwhelming similarity of the 4 year olds in the three settings on most task measures and by our subjective evaluation, would suggest that we need to reevaluate some of our unbased clichés about the influence of day care on development'' (Lippman and Grote 1974, p. 290).

Karen Vroegh (1976) came to the same conclusion after comparing 114 children twelve to thirty-six months of age who either attended a day care center or were cared for in a home other than their own for most of the day. Ratings of the children's behavior by either day care teachers or the women who cared for the children in their homes revealed no important differences in behavior between the two groups. Vroegh concluded,

> For the most part, the data presented here do not indicate that there are negative effects on typical infants enrolled in typical day care experiences in our country. When the length of time in day care at the time of testing is controlled, it appears that there are generally no differences in the social-emotional development, cognitive development, or physical development between children who have been in day care 9 months or less and children who have been in day care one year to 18 months.
>
> Because the conclusions of this study were based on data from children who were in day care situations typical of the care many children experience while their parents work, it appears that there is more solid ground for stating that day care does not appear to harm infant development. [Vroegh 1976]

Reuven Kohen-Raz (1968) compared the Bayley scores of Israeli infants being raised on kibbutzim, in middle-class homes, or in institutions in Israel. There were no differences in developmental scores between the children reared on kibbutzim and those at home, but the institutionalized children obtained lower scores than the other groups. (See also Kostizewski 1973). Hence, it was not group care itself but the type of group care that was the critical variable.

Roberta Collard (1971) found that institutionalized infants, eight and one-half to thirteen months of age, explored less with toys than lower-middle-class or middle-class children being reared at home. Jane Raph and her colleagues (Raph et al. 1968) compared three groups of children—one group who had attended a nursery and kindergarten for about three years, a second group who attended only kindergarten for a year, and a third with no group care experience. Observations revealed no differences in sociability, quality, or style of interaction with peers or teachers among the different groups. Extended experience with other children in a group care setting does not necessarily influence subsequent patterns of sociability with peers, a finding implying no simple relation between frequency of encounter with peers and specific behavioral consequences.

One of the few reports that implied that day care is potentially harmful (Blehar 1974) contained a sufficient number of soft spots to warrant a cautious attitude toward the author's conclusions. Mary Blehar compared ten

30-month-old children who had been in day care for four months with ten 30-month-olds reared at home; she also compared ten 39-month-olds who had been in day care for about four months with ten children reared at home. Her assessment followed Ainsworth's "strange person" situation, which is designed to assess the child's reaction when his mother departs, leaving him with an unfamiliar adult in an unfamiliar setting. The older children in day care were more likely to cry and search for their mothers than were the home controls, but this difference was not significant among the younger children. The study is marred by small sample size, and by its brevity—the children were only in day care for four to five months before being assessed. It is also marred because the samples were not matched on ordinal position: 80 percent of the day care children were firstborns but only 60 percent of the home controls. Since firstborns may be more likely than laterborns to cry in a separation situation, it is possible that the differences Blehar reported are confounded with differences in ordinal position. The findings of the Blehar study contrast with those of another study, in which observations of children five to thirty months of age during their first month of attendance at a day care center revealed rapid adjustment to the new setting, with major decreases in crying and increases in play (McCutcheon and Calhoun 1976). Other recent studies similar to Blehar's in design have not replicated her data nor substantiated her conclusions (Doyle in press; Hock 1976; Brookhart and Hock 1976).

Ellen Hock (1976) performed a longitudinal study comparing seventy-four infants whose mothers were not working and therefore were home most of the day, with eighty-three infants whose mothers worked during part or all of their first year of life. The two groups of infants behaved similarly toward their mothers at one year of age in the Ainsworth experimental situation and showed no differences in apprehension toward maternal departure. Among the children of working mothers, those who were cared for at home were not different from those who were cared for in another location while the mother was working. The child's temperament seemed to be a better predictor of his apprehension in the "strange person" situation than his amount of contact with his mother.

In a related study by the same research team, Joyce Brookhart and Ellen Hock (1976) observed 10- to 12-month-olds in the Ainsworth separation situation in both home and laboratory, comparing the behavior of eighteen middle-class infants reared at home with fifteen who were attending a day care center for most of the day. Although most children showed a greater increase in apprehension after maternal departure in the laboratory than at home, there was no difference in the behavior of the home and day care groups. The authors wrote, "The findings offer no support to the notion that the day care experience adversely affects the infant's relationship with his mother" (Brookhart and Hock 1976).

Anna-Beth Doyle compared 12 children of ages six to thirty months in day care with twelve matched controls who had been reared at home. One of the assessment situations was Ainsworth's strange person situation. The day care children did not cry or seek proximity to the mother any more frequently than the home controls, thus contradicting Blehar's suggestion that day care can produce emotional insecurity in the child. Indeed, very few of the children in either group showed avoidance of the mother upon reunion. Doyle suggested that perhaps one reason for the difference between her finding and Blehar's is the fact that the ratio of child to staff was 4 to 1 in Doyle's day care group but 6 or 8 to 1 in Blehar's.

In a later unpublished paper Doyle (1975) compared three groups of eleven children—groups attending day care, reared at home, or being cared for outside the home by a mother surrogate such as a grandmother or babysitter. The average time the first group had spent in the day care setting was about four and one-half months. The children ranged in age from about six to twenty-five months at the beginning of the study, with an average age of about eighteen months. There were no significant differences among the three groups in Cattell IQ scores, language development, or behavior in the Ainsworth separation situation. This result is inconsistent with Blehar's hypothesis that children in group care are more insecure than children in home care when separated from their mothers because their attachment to the mother is diluted (Doyle 1975).

More counterevidence to Blehar's hypothesis comes from a longitudinal evaluation of infants in a day care setting from four to twelve months of age that revealed that the young infants showed essentially no distress at being left with their surrogate caretakers. At twelve months, the age when separation protest is most likely to appear in most children, some moderate distress did appear, however (Ricciuti 1974).

Extensive naturalistic observations of middle-class children aged seventeen to twenty months in day care and home settings have revealed that the home-reared children cried more often in the home setting than did the children observed in the day care setting. Moreover, the infants in day care did not seek more tactile contact with their caretakers than did home-reared children and did not show any obvious adverse effects of the daily separation from the parent (Rubenstein and Howes 1976). The absence of any obvious difference between day care and home-reared infants is also seen in a comparison of 6-month-old infants cared for at home by the mother or a surrogate caretaker. Despite some differences in the caretaking practices of the mothers and caretakers, the infants in both groups were remarkably similar on a variety of indexes of development (Rubenstein, Pedersen, and Yarrow 1977). The authors wrote, "These data highlight the relative invulnerability of infants to daily separation from mother in the first six months of life" (p. 530).

A study of older children (Winett et al. 1977) evaluated the cognitive performance of children three to five and one-half years of age who had spent nine months or longer either in a day care center ($n = 45$), with a babysitter ($n = 15$), at home ($n = 43$), or with a mix of babysitter care and day care ($n = 31$). The third group came from families of higher social class than the other three, which were matched in class background. The children were administered tests of language development and a special preschool cognitive battery. There were no important differences among the three types of rearing groups that came from similar social class backgrounds. However, the children from the better-educated families in the "mixed group" attained higher scores on all tests. Again the experiences associated with social class, rather than the form of supplementary rearing, seem to have the greatest influence on cognitive development.

Halbert Robinson and Nancy Robinson (1971) compared sixteen children enrolled in group care during infancy or at age two with sixteen children who were matched on sex, race, and social class but who had not been in group care. All the children were tested between two and one-half and four and one-half years of age with Bayley and Stanford-Binet tests. At age four there were no important differences between the group care and home control middle-class children. But the black day care children, most of whom came from economically deprived families, attained higher scores than the black children being reared at home in lower social class families. It was concluded that children ordinarily reared in environments where the language skills and strategies tapped by the IQ tests are not encouraged seem to be affected by the practices of the middle-class group care environment.

This finding was nicely substantiated in a cross-cultural study by P. Herbert Leiderman and Gloria F. Leiderman (1974). The subjects were sixty-seven Kikuyu infants from eastern Kenya, many of whom were cared for by older sisters, friends, or relatives for a large part of the day. Following observation at their homes the children were classified as being in predominantly monomatric, predominantly polymatric, or in mixed homes on the basis of the percentage of time the mother was the principal caretaker. In the monomatric class the mother is principal caretaker more than 75 percent of the time; for the polymatric group the mother is principal caretaker less than half the time. The families were divided into social class levels based on amount of land, livestock, and source of income. The children were tested on the Bayley Infant Scale of Development at two intervals. The important result, and the one we shall refer to later, is that the lowest Bayley developmental quotients (DQs) occurred among children reared monomatrically in the poorer homes. The average DQ of these children was 84 on the mental and 89 on the motor scale, while the other groups achieved scores close to or over 100. There were no differences in DQ associated with either monomatric or polymatric rearing for children from the wealthier families. The Leidermans suggested that the infants in poorer homes who were being raised primarily by their mothers did not experience as much variety as those reared in poorer homes by several caretakers. Observations of the home settings revealed that polymatrically reared infants from poorer families experienced more frequent social interaction (21 percent) than those reared monomatrically (8 percent) because there were more caretakers with whom they could interact. As in the Raph study, if the child is from an environment where response opportunity and variety are usually restricted, it appears that the extra variety that comes from multiple caretakers tends to facilitate cognitive development. Hence, the relationship between variety of experience and cognitive development is not continuous but behaves like a threshold function. The Liedermans' finding is confirmed by our own that the working-class Chinese-American infants, who may have encountered the least variety of experience, were the only ones to show some select cognitive gains as a function of attendance at the day care center.

In Kohen-Raz's comparison of Israeli children (1968) mentioned earlier in this chapter, most infants from the kibbutz and home groups had better-educated parents (all had completed high school and most had university degrees) than the institutionalized children. Five different women tested the children on Bayley scales, and the data were grouped into four age categories: one to four months, five to seven months, eight to twelve months, and fifteen to twenty-seven months. Although the mental scores of the kibbutz children were higher than American norms, we are primarily interested in the intergroup comparisons among the three Israeli samples. There were no consistent differences between the children being reared on the kibbutzim and those in private homes. At six months the kibbutzim-reared children had a higher score than the home-reared, but at no other age was this true. By contrast, the institutionalized children had lower scores from three through twenty-seven months. Similarly, on the motor scale there was no kibbutz versus home difference and the institutionalized children again obtained lower scores prior to fifteen months. After fifteen months their scores were not significantly inferior to kibbutzim- or home-reared children. As is true of our study, despite the apparent differences in experience between an infant house and a nuclear family (different amounts of contact with mother and with other children), the rate of attainment of the basic milestones of infancy and early childhood does not seem to be influenced by that variation in environment. It is the environment of the institution that seems to be disadvantageous. Although Kohen-Raz did not collect observations in the three settings it is reasonable to suggest that variety of experience and opportunity to practice maturing competences are the critical events that were absent in the institution but present in both the kibbutz and the nuclear family settings.

Structural designations like day care, infant house, or institution are crude ways to summarize a set of modal experiences that are the critical determinants of growth. If a setting designated as ''day care'' has high infant to caretaker ratios, minimal supervision of staff, and no planned curriculum its atmosphere approaches that of an institution. The children attending such a center should not develop in accord with normative expectations. Mary Peaslee (1976) studied twenty-five 2-year-olds who had been attending four different unlicensed day care centers in Polk County, Florida, since they were two months old, comparing them with twenty-five home-reared children matched for sex, class, and ethnicity. Slightly more than half the children were black and 80 percent were from middle-class homes. The 2-year-olds in day care obtained significantly lower scores on the Bayley mental scale, tests of language development, and tests of color matching and discrimination. The black females in day care obtained consistently poorer scores than all other subgroups while the white home-reared males tended to perform the best. On most tests the white males in day care were not significantly different from the black females reared at home, a result that suggests interaction between ethnicity and form of care. However, the day care centers sampled in this study had ratios of sixteen to twenty-four infants to one adult and were primarily custodial. Hence, the conditions in the centers approached those typical of inadequately staffed institutions.

One of the best studies in this area (Tizard et al. 1972) involved children living in different long-term residential nurseries in England, most of whom (about 70 percent) had been enrolled as infants. Observations of the children and the settings, as well as test scores gathered when the children were between two and five years old, revealed that the language comprehension scores of children in the group settings were not significantly different from the norms for home-reared English children. Most important the children in nurseries that were well organized, and where staff stimulated the children linguistically attained better language comprehension scores than children in nurseries where staff engaged in much less verbal interaction with the children. This is one of the few instances in which one finds covariation between an outcome variable and a relevant environmental experience in a group setting. In this case the more the staff used language with the children and encouraged their language comprehension, the better the children's language comprehension scores. It must be noted that spontaneous expression of language did not covary with the general quality of the nursery.

The difference associated with adequately versus poorly staffed nurseries also holds for benevolent versus less benevolent adoptive homes. Leila Beckwith (1971) studied a group of twenty-four children placed in adoptive homes between five and ten days of age. The children were observed and administered the Cattell and Gesell tests twice during their first year of life. The greater the variety of experience in the home, the higher the Cattell Developmental Quotient. Children who were observed to experience minimal verbal and physical interaction and to be restricted in their opportunity to practice maturing competences attained the lowest scores.

The power of a therapeutic institution to enhance cognitive development is nicely demonstrated in a study of 132 children who were admitted into a therapeutic milieu when they were between two and eight years of age. Those whose initial IQ was under eighty who remained in the institution at least one year gained over twenty points on the Stanford-Binet. Regardless of initial IQ level the twenty-three children who stayed more than fourteen months in the institution gained an average of fifteen IQ points (Gavrin and Sachs 1963).

The young child's tendency to grow toward health is seen in a study of twenty-four children admitted to day care at three and one-half months and given the Bayley test at six, twelve, and sixteen months and the Stanford-Binet at twenty-four and thirty-six months (Ramey et al. 1973). Most of the children who scored lower on developmental quotient at six months gained in score and approached normative values. Those with high scores at six months remained high throughout the end of the first year. As shown also in the report by Lee Willerman et al. (1970), these results suggest that retardation in infancy may be predictive of later retardation only if the child remains in an initial environment that does not encourage cognitive growth. Transfer to a nonfamilial environment that is conducive to growth seems to facilitate intellectual development.

Although, as indicated earlier, the empirical basis for the conclusion is still weak, the better controlled studies imply that among young children from reasonably supportive families, group care programs that provide experiential variety and are administered by an involved staff do not seem to affect the child's cognitive or social development in an obvious way. The presence of multiple caretakers or other children and their potential for providing different patterns of encounter do not appear to be of significant import for the cognitive and social criteria assessed in these studies. Either these criteria are too crude to detect real differences among the groups or the wrong variables are being assessed, *or,* indeed, there are only minimal or even trivial differences between children who have experienced good group care and those reared at home.

After an independent review of the literature on infant day care Henry Ricciuti came to the same conclusions:

> On the basis of the research data available thus far, there appears to be no evidence to support the view that extended day care experience beginning in the first two years of life has a disruptive influence on the affectional relationships between infant and mother. In fact, there are some data suggesting that under favorable circumstances such experience may make it somewhat easier for children to adapt comfortably to unfamiliar social situations requiring a willingness to tolerate some distancing from mother . . . there appears to be little or no persuasive empirical research evidence thus far indicating that infant day care experience is likely to have unfavorable developmental

consequences. This is a valid generalization whether one considers the child's intellectual development, affectional relationships between child and mother, or subsequent peer relationships and responsiveness to adult socialization influences. [Ricciuti 1976, pp. 34-35 and p. 40]

If it is difficult to demonstrate dramatic effects of varied forms of rearing on contemporary behavior, it seems unlikely that differences in early forms of rearing will affect future psychological functioning. We are not the first to look skeptically at the hypothesis that specific experiences during infancy have profound effects on the cognitive, social, and motivational profile of later childhood. Over twenty-five years ago, Harold Orlansky reviewed much of what was known about the relation between infant experience and later personality functioning (with a 149-item bibliography). He concluded, "This paper reviews some of the empirical data bearing on the theory that various features of infant care determine adult personality. Our conclusion has been largely negative and we have been led to substitute a theory which emphasizes instead the importance of constitutional factors and of the total cultural situation" (Orlansky 1949, p. 42).

Fifteen years later, Bettye Caldwell (1964) and Leon Yarrow (1964) took similar assignments. Caldwell reviewed the recent work on the effect of infant care on the child's development, and Yarrow studied reports on the effects of separation of the child from parents. Each was forced to conclude that the existing data did not provide much support for the view that certain experiences in infancy constrain the child's future in a fixed way. Caldwell suggested that parental attitude was more important than specific parental behaviors and that social class differences are always demonstrable, while correlations between specific practices and outcomes in the child are more difficult to find. Yarrow's summary statement was similar in tone: "On the whole the data do not differentiate clearly between the effects of the separation experience *per se* and the reinforcing conditions following separation . . . With regard to the separation experience itself, the potentially traumatic effects of the event can be reduced. For the young infant, the strangeness and the unpredictability of the environment associated with varied changes may be as significant as the loss of the mother figure" (Yarrow 1964, pp. 127-129).

The belief that experiences during the early years have a profound influence on later development is too strongly held by many Americans to be cast aside solely on the basis of existing evidence. What is needed is a different theory of early development. Most American parents are devoted to their infants and want them to be happy and successful. They realize this prize is not easily won and are uncertain and anxious about the child's future. The uncertainty is tempered if the parents believe in the efficacy of a set of actions they can initiate with the child. The ritual actions they will choose will derive in part from their personal theory of development and in part on the views promoted by the society. The contemporary culture paints a relatively clear stereotype of the typical unsuccessful adolescent. He comes from a poor family with many children and a harassed or neglectful mother who is unable or unwilling to give her infant consistent and devoted attention. Observation of that life sequence, which has some validity, becomes transformed into a rather strict cause-and-effect principle; a mother's devoted and attentive care to her young infant is critical for his future psychological health. In addition, since many parents find it easy and enjoyable to play with their young children, it is reasonable that many would conclude that those early interactions would provide prophylaxis against future psychological trauma.

Let us be clear about the implications of this discussion. We are not suggesting that parents should stop caring, interacting, or enjoying their young children. They should continue to do all those things. The evidence suggests, however, that reasonable variation in infant care by mothers or surrogate caretakers may not be associated with differences in future psychological functioning. It is suggested, moreover, that during the preschool and early school years the child's perception of his value in the eyes of his family takes precedence over the experiences of infancy. The child of school age detects the contrast between his qualities and resources and those of his peers; that recognition can lead him to judge himself as privileged or disenfranchised. These postinfancy events, we suggest, have a more formative influence on future profiles than many of the encounters of the first year or two. This restatement of the earlier conclusions by Caldwell and Orlansky implies that attendance at a day care center should not, in itself, affect the child's development in a serious way as long as the parents hold a positive attitude toward their children and the surrogate caretakers are nurturant, attentive and conscientious.

Parental concerns about day care

Many American mothers remain honestly concerned about the effects of group day care on their children. Their disquiet is maintained by five nodes of uncertainty. They worry that day care centers might dilute the emotional attachment of infant to mother; retard the young child's cognitive development; fail to train the child to control his anger, aggression, or passivity effectively; or affect the child through the potentially polluting influence of other children. Finally, the middle-class mother conceives of herself as the effective socializing agent and worries about transferring this role to others.

The attachment of infant to mother It is generally believed that effective socialization and maintenance of the child's emotional security depend on the continued nourishing of a strong, affective bond between infant and mother or primary caretaker. If the relation is broken regularly for long periods during the day, the child's attachment to his caretaker is presumably weakened and the two goals become more difficult to attain. The popular theory of socialization assumes that the child must be dependent on and have a strong emotional relation to the parent. If he is not, the mother will not be able to use their relationship to persuade the child of the importance of adopting parental standards. Dilution of the child's attachment to the mother raises the specter of a disobedient, aggressive, academically retarded child who will spurn the values his parents cherish.

The significance attributed to the attachment of infant to mother derives, in part, from psychoanalytic theory and partly from the highly publicized reports of Harry Harlow's animal experiments. A key essay, from the perspective of developmental psychology, was written by René Spitz during the 1940's. Spitz had visited some poor orphanages in South America where infants, who were not regularly attended by the adult staff, were extremely apathetic and displayed high rates of morbidity. Spitz concluded that the lack of attachment to a specific adult caretaker was the reason for their anomalous development. He ignored the lack of variety in their life space, their lack of opportunity to practice maturing competences, and their poor physical health.

Malnourished Guatemalan Indian infants living in isolated villages display a similar apathy and high rate of morbidity and mortality; 40 percent of the children die during the first two years. But since these infants are rarely out of their mothers' sight and are nursed on demand, their inattention and illness seem due to poor nutrition, frequent infection, and lack of experiential variety rather than lack of attachment. A close attachment to the mother did not protect these infants from passivity and temporary cognitive and motor retardation. By contrast, kibbutz-reared 2-year-olds, who spend most of their hours in an infant house away from their mothers, are alert, lively, and very healthy. Spitz appears to have arrived at his interpretation a little too hastily.

Psychologists have been selective in the evidence they use to support the claim that the infant-mother relation should be broken as little as possible during the first year of life. They have pointed to the poorer school performance and more frequent asocial behavior of lower-class children whose mothers are forced to work in order to support the family. But they have ignored the smaller number of mothers who are professionals who leave their young infants with responsible surrogate caretakers in the home, because there was no evidence to indicate that the development of this group was anomalous. Many developmental psychologists greeted John Bowlby's long essays on attachment with applause and initiated studies relating separation anxiety, as an index of intensity of attachment, to the salience of the mother's presence in the infant's life. Since separation protest does not appear until the last half of the first year, because maturational factors control cognitive functioning, it was concluded that it took about eight months for an attachment to develop. The few studies that found middle-class children showing separation protest earlier than working-class children were interpreted as indicating that middle-class infants had a closer attachment to their mothers. This finding served to strengthen the original premise, for many believed that middle-class women were better mothers. And middle-class children were, of course, superior at culturally valued skills. Thus the evidence and assumptions seemed to form a coherent whole.

This theory of the infant years is not shared by parents in many parts of the world, nor was it the view of parents of earlier eras, as pointed out in chapter 1. Many middle-class mothers in eighteenth- and early nineteenth-century France sent their young infants to live with wet nurses in a poor part of the city or an outlying village for a year or more. If these mothers had thought this experience was psychologically debilitating presumably they would not have made that decision. Unfortunately, the health conditions in the homes of many of the wet nurses were less than satisfactory and by the late nineteenth century, when the high rates of morbidity and mortality were publicized, the practice of boarding infants with wet nurses declined in popularity. But its abandonment reflected a concern over physical illness, not over anomalous psychological development.

The supposition that infants and mothers must remain together during a child's infancy is strong in current American thought. Despite the intuitive appeal of this idea, there is no firm empirical evidence indicating that daily separation from the mother seriously dilutes the infant's attachment to the parent nor any firm evidence that a close, unbroken relation protects the child from later psychic trauma. However, given the combination of ambiguous evidence, the culture's affection for the centrality of the child-mother bond, and the dominant psychological theory of the century, it should not be surprising that most mothers would worry about sending their infants to a day care center. Although their apprehension may be legitimate, it gains its validity from intuition, not sound evidence.

Retardation of cognitive development A second node of anxiety is the belief that the infant requires special interactions with the parent if intellectual development is to proceed optimally. The factual basis for this supposition is a bit sturdier, as shown earlier in this chapter. Infants in environments that contain minimal variety are a little late in passing the major milestones of development, when compared with those reared in environments with a great deal of variety and opportunity for practicing emerging competences. Since adequate intellectual development is essential for success in modern America, parents may well wonder if surrogate care could provide the experiences required for normal development. Indeed, Robert Zajonc (1974) has suggested that with each child added to a family the amount of interaction each child in the family receives is diluted by some fixed amount and his intellectual potential impaired.

American parents regard their children's intelligence as if it were a primary psychological organ. This prejudice is reminiscent of Plato's conviction that a person possessing correct knowledge cannot help but make morally proper choices. It is also reflected in the writings of the decade following the Revolutionary War when Robert Coram, Noah Webster, and others wrote that education was the best prophylaxis against despotism. If a person knew the law he would obey it. Salvation, too, was dependent on proper tutoring for no one could appreciate the principles of Christianity without proper education. Thus the ignorant were likely to be full of vice and susceptible to the devil's temptations. A half-century ago we regarded mentally retarded people as moral defectives, for a weak intellect made a child vulnerable to impulsive and morally devious actions. In the years after the Civil War it was assumed that vice and corruptibility were a product of ignorance and that education and knowledge could alleviate these stains. The twin attitudes that vice is established early and education can uproot it is seen in Noah Webster's "On the Education of Youth in America" where he wrote:

> The only practical method to reform mankind is to begin with children, to banish, if possible, from their company every low bred drunken immoral character . . . Virtue and vice will not grow together in a great degree, but they will grow where they are planted and when one has taken root it is not easily supplanted by the other. The great art of correcting mankind therefore consists in prepossessing the mind with good principles. For this reason society requires that the education of youth should be watched with the most scrupulous attention. Education in a great measure forms the moral characters of men and morals are the basis of government. [In Rudolph 1965, p. 67]

Robert Coram, editor of the *Delaware Gazette*, affirmed Webster's views when he wrote,

> Information is fatal to despotism . . . In a republican government . . . every class of people should know and love the laws. This knowledge should be diffused by means of schools and newspapers and attachment to the laws may be formed by early impressions upon the mind. [In Rudolph, 1965]

For Coram, as for Plato, to know what is true is synonymous with being moral. Knowledge is the key to morality, and preparedness for acquiring knowledge requires intelligence. We want our politicians, judges, doctors, lawyers, and teachers to be intelligent. David Halberstam captures this American bias in *The Best and the Brightest.* Robert McNamara, McGeorge Bundy, Walter Rostow, and others who surrounded John F. Kennedy in the early 1960s were chosen because they were intelligent, rational, and dispassionate, not because they knew how to manage a defense department or run an antiguerilla war in Vietnam. We harbor the belief that an intelligent person can analyze any complex situation into logically rational categories. And if those categories can be stated in mathematical form, decisions can be made without the interference of sentimental prejudice. Persons who can perform this mental activity well are assumed to have a special biological quality that can be applied, like a wizard's baton, to all troublesome situations. They are good shamans who deserve our respect, reverence, and awe. We reject the Greek view that emotion should moderate a penetrating rationality. The less colored by affect, the firmer and more reliable the intellectual conclusion. To be smart is to possess a basic biological characteristic that cannot be lost easily.

Americans emphasize rational intelligence over other human attributes, in part, because they recognize that a person's opinions and philosophy are culturally determined. We have been taught to be tolerant of other people's beliefs because they are presumed to be largely the product of their idiosyncratic experiences. But intelligence is supposed to be made of different stuff. Despite the longing of many Americans to have variation in all psychological qualities the consequence of experience, most Americans, even some libertarians, believe that mental ability is influenced, at least in part, by biology. We are helped in this prejudice by the fact that some diseases associated with mental deficiency are known to be biological in origin. Level of intellectual talent is seen as a profound reflection of each person's essence. Intelligence is seen as a psychological manifestation of a physical entity, the way beauty depends on the arrangement of eyes, nose, and mouth on the frame of the face. Intelligence may be the only human trait that the contemporary West regards in absolute terms, in contrast to the more relativistic attitudes our society takes toward individual variations in feelings, beliefs, and values. This attitude toward the nature of intelligence conflicts with the equally strong desire to prove that John Locke was right and to arrange environments so that all individuals can be competent.

Moreover, morality and character seem to be products of our will; we have the sense that we can be honest and kind if we choose. But insight, an elegant metaphor, or a creative invention seem beyond volition or simple persistence of effort, despite Edison's epigram about the ratio of perspiration to inspiration. This belief is based on the faith that forces beyond our control are contributing to mental ability. And a society that respects rational, material explanations so highly finds it reasonable to suppose that the special force is a biological one emanating from heredity.

If we believe we can affect change in a personal quality, we are likely to award formative power to the environment. If we have the sense that motivation is insufficient, we are more prepared to award influence either to external forces, like social prejudice, or to biological factors like heredity. Most societies award a special potency to qualities that cannot simply be willed, like the ability to trance or being born with a caul. Moreover, rare qualities are more exciting than common ones. A leaf seems less beautiful than a flower; a robin not as lovely as a heron, not because of symmetry of form but, we suggest, because the second instance is less common. (Of course, some rarities are devalued, mental retardation, schizophrenia are among them, but that is because they violate basic assumptions about proper behavior.) Human qualities that are infrequent and seem beyond our sphere of personal influence have a special power either to awe or frighten us. We are tempted, quite naturally, to attribute their occurrence to lawful, legitimate forces we cannot control. Since we do not want to believe that the attainment of power and status, which we have come to eroticize, is arbitrary, we satisfy our twin desires to be democratic and egalitarian while retaining orderly procedures for the transfer of power from one generation to the next by using intelligence as a basis for awarding access to positions of status. Since status is correlated with virtue in the West, the intelligent are likely to be regarded as morally pure.

The assumptions we make about intelligence are not universal. In Confucian China, for example, men strove to achieve morality, not power, and the source of morality was believed to be not knowledge but external circumstances. Unlike our belief that men are born with unequal intelligence, the Taoist and Confucianist believed that all men were born with equal merit and equal potential to be *jen*, the ideal person. The reason the West stressed intelligence and the East ethics is not at all clear. Economy, social structure, heterogeneity of values, and contact with other groups are probably all influential.

American parents worry more about their children's intellect than about their physical appearance, vigor, health—or even their happiness. The amount of shame or pride shown by an American middle-class mother over a body blemish or a happy disposition is small when compared to the emotion felt when a parent suspects her child is intellectually behind or a genius. We have placed a special stigmata on any impairment of intellect because access to power in the West requires education and education requires intelligence. Most Americans have little sympathy for the interpretation of intelligence, offered by one of the leaders in the field of Artificial Intelligence: "My own view is that this is more of an aesthetic question, or one of sense of dignity, than a technical matter. To me intelligence seems to denote little more than the complex of performances which we happen to respect but do not understand" (Minsky 1961).

Since most American parents believe that the experiences of the early years of life are the catalysts that act on the biological substrate the child brings into the world, it is natural that they should want to guarantee the child the very best set of early encounters. It is true that if day care were not as stimulating and accelerating of cognitive development as home-rearing, the child's future might be seriously harmed.

Teaching the child control of impulse Since anger, tantrums, aggression, dependence, and passivity are viewed as dispositions that the young child acquires easily but gives up with reluctance, it is commonly thought that learning to control these behaviors must begin during the early years. The mother who sees her task as teaching the child to inhibit these reactions believes this task requires continued supervision so that psychological or physical punishment or corrective encouragement can be applied whenever the forbidden behavior occurs, and she plans to use her emotional relation to the child to insure that he eventually tames those villains. She is not sure that the hired caretaker will be as conscientious as she in punishing the unpredictable acts at the right time, and she fears the child will not be as willing to curb his impulses for the caretaker as he will be for her. Such parents fear that group care runs the risk of sending the child down the road to ruin.

There are some ancedotal bases for this prejudice. Group care environments in the United States are noisier and wilder places than most living rooms. There is more pushing and snatching of toys in a day care center with twenty 2- and 3-year olds than in an apartment with two children. Many day care workers, trained in a philosophy of permissiveness toward aggression and emotional spontaneity, are reluctant to punish every misdemeanor. Staff also tend to protect the helpless and passive child and not to make special efforts to demand autonomy and independence from one who is excessively shy or clinging. The day care teacher in modern America, unlike his counterpart in the People's Republic of China, is generally tolerant of a wide range of behavior in young children and is not unduly concerned with bringing all the children under her care to some ideal criterion. The parent with an articulated ideal and coherent philosophy of child-rearing might be anxious about such a loose attitude toward socialization and, as a result, might view the day care environment as dangerously indifferent.

The polluting effect of peers Many parents believe the child is vulnerable to the influence of other children, for each child is a potential model for one's own to copy. If other parents are not as conscientious as oneself in the training of good habits, one's child may be tempted to adopt the unwanted qualities he sees in his peers. Socialization is difficult enough without the extra burden of worrying about other children undoing the caretaker's efforts at home. The fear that children, especially those from less advantaged classes and ethnic groups, have polluting power, is not new. In the nineteenth century, Jacob Abbott warned mothers to keep their sons and daughters away from other children, especially lower-class children, because they might learn bad habits from them: "Keep children as much as possible by themselves—away from evil influences—separate—alone. Keep them from bad company, is very common advice. We may go much farther, and almost say, keep them from company, good or bad . . . all history and experience shows . . . that the mutual influence of man upon man is an influence of deterioration and corruption . . . It seems as if human nature can be safe only in the state of segregation; in a mass it runs at once to corruption and ruin'' (Abbott 1836, p. 297). Some of the strong emotion that surrounds desegregation and busing reflects the worry that incorrectly socialized children will infect the good ones with bad ideas and provide incentives for undesirable behavior.

The mother as the responsible agent A final reason for resistance to day care, at least by the middle-class mother, comes from her conception of herself as the effective agent in monitoring the growth of her child. She is afraid that entrusting the child's experiences to the unmonitored behavior of hired workers might bring harmful results.

A basic controversy over the selection of constructs to describe or explain individual development concerns where to place responsibility for action, affect, and thought. Each society and each individual walk a tightrope between assigning responsibility to self or to outside forces. Although the Greeks awarded the gods the power to control major catastrophes they retained some islands of sovereignty for man to influence. And even the gods were not in complete control, for fate placed some constraints on their potency. Psychological theories assign different proportions of variance to the executive processes of self versus the lawful or stochastic events in the space outside the sphere of conscious volition. Psychoanalytic theory divided the territory into id and ego. The former was beyond control, while part of ego was free to affect the future. The person was not responsible for the consequences of acts and emotions that were derivatives of the unconscious, only those initiated by the conscious ego.

Behaviorism, especially in the extreme form suggested by B.F. Skinner, has aroused much emotion because some think it implies that each of us is tied to our surroundings by iron chains that pull at us in ways that we cannot control. Genetic theories of psychopathology or intelligence are threatening to many citizens because they relegate to an unseen biological force the processes we wish to believe are free. It is probably not a coincidence that biologically based theories which promote a more fatalistic view typically blossom following periods of social unrest. John Pelzel (personal communication) has suggested that following the fall of the Han civilization in ancient China the normally rational and controlled Chinese drifted toward the magical qualities of Taoism. Such a drift also occurred soon after our Civil War, and has emerged again several decades after the socially destructive events that began with the rise of the Third Reich and ended with Vietnam, Watergate, and civil and racial strife. Such a dense onslaught of attacks on the culture's values cannot help but persuade many individuals that they are not in control of their lives and that forces which they cannot influence are determining their daily experience. That mood, which has become increasingly common in the West, has produced books like *Chance and Necessity* and *Helplessness,* and movies like *The Tall Blond Man with One Black Shoe,* a film which made chance the director of a set of experiences that a young musician believed were a function of his own talents. As social conditions stabilize, strategies for coping realistically with threats have a chance of becoming organized and the self is likely to take back what it gave away under duress.

Each person makes a judgment about the degree to which he is in control of the major events in his life, based in large measure but not totally on his personal construction of reality. If major consequences that affect one's daily life are beyond one's control—like court-ordered busing, earthquakes, pollution of air and water, influenza epidemics, rampant vandalism, irresponsibility in government—then one has no choice but to award power to impersonal forces outside the self's tiny sphere of activity. As a result, each person feels less potent. The less powerful and less wealthy in most societies are more likely to ascribe power to outside forces than those who are more privileged. The Middle Eastern belief in possession by spirits is typically restricted to the lower classes and occurs far less often among those with wealth and prestige. Children from less affluent and less well-educated families are more likely to attribute their failure in school to biological incompetence, the prejudice of the teacher, or unfair tests than to lack of motivation and persistence. Orville Brim and his colleagues (1969) found that the belief that intelligence is inherited, rather than responsive to effort, is much more firmly held by lower-class than by middle-class adolescents.

The middle-class mother still sees herself as in control of her child's development, and she is reluctant to let that responsibility slip into the hands of others. Moreover, she believes that a mother who surrenders primary responsibility for her child's socialization is violating a basic moral imperative. Hence she anticipates feelings of guilt or shame, as well as possible criticism from neighbors, friends, and relatives, for failing to honor the first duty of a parent. Commitment to this image of the maternal role may be the most important source of resistance to group care for the young child.

Each of these issues has produced legitimate apprehension over group care for infants. Indeed, these themes are so intimately woven into the fabric of the culture's belief system that one of the authors of this book, firmly convinced of the legitimacy of each of these concerns, spoke out strongly against day care for infants only a few short years ago. His argument merely echoed the sermons of the Congregational minister Horace Bushnell who wrote, over a century ago,

> it will readily occur to you that irreparable damage may be and must often be done by the self indulgence of those parents who place their children mostly in the charge of nurses and attendants for just those

years of their life, in which the greatest and most absolute effects are to be wrought in their character . . . Many parents do not even take pains to know anything about the tempers, the truthfulness, the character generally of the nurses to whom their children are thus confidingly trusted . . . They give over to these faithless and often cruelly false hirelings of the nursery, to be always with them, under their power, associated with their persons, handled by their roughness, and imprinted day and night by the coarse, bad sentiments of their voices and faces, these helpless, hapless beings whom they call their children, and think they are really making much of, in the instituting of a nursery for them and their keeping . . . Now is the time when her little one most needs to see her face and hear her voice and feel her gentle hand. Now is the time when her child's eternity pleads most entreatingly for the benefit of her motherly charge and presence. What mother would not be dismayed by the thought of having her family grow up into the sentiments of her nurse and come forward into life as being in the succession to her character! And yet how often is this most exactly what she has provided for. [In Greven 1973, pp. 173-174]

4 The Setting and Procedures

> Pure empiricism is believed by no one, and if we are to retain beliefs that we all regard as valid we must allow principles of inference which are neither demonstrative nor derivable from experience.
>
> Bertrand Russell, *An Inquiry into Meaning and Truth*

During the late 1960s, this nation became aware of the large number of mothers who were working or who wanted to work and of their frustration at being unable to find reliable sources of day care for their young children. Magazines and newspapers asserted that the United States needed more day care centers, and certain senators and congressmen began to prepare legislation to fund the establishment of centers for infants as well as preschool-age children. Although many parents and psychologists were not unduly restive about the psychological consequences of surrogate care for 4- and 5-year-olds, they did worry about its effects on infants. The assumptions elaborated in chapters 1 and 3 led most to believe that it would probably be harmful to separate the baby from its mother, for the conscientious mother was thought to be the infant's best source of consistent physical care, emotional security, and cognitive challenge. Middle-class infants were simply better off at home. The stereotype of the lower-class family being promoted by both professional and popular articles, however, led some citizens to suspect that surrogate care might be therapeutic for the less-advantaged child because the stability and predictability of daily life in the center might make him emotionally more secure and cognitively advanced than his counterpart reared at home. This suspicion did not appeal to persons who disliked the notion of a society whose privileged children had access to their own mothers while children of the poor had only substitutes.

The prediction that the government was about to fund thousands of day care centers despite the uncertainty of the consequences led some psychologists to plan scientific studies of this socially important issue. Given the prejudices we have listed, the ideal investigation would have randomly assigned children of the different economic and social classes to day care centers of different quality and monitored their progress. Ethical considerations made such a design impossible. Scientists cannot randomly select families and force them to send their children to day care centers of different quality; nor can we purposefully create conditions we believe harmful to infants and ask parents to submit their infants to these conditions for the sake of science.

Two strategies are feasible. The first is to let nature perform the experiment. One looks for day care centers that vary in quality and then studies the infants in these settings. The most obvious defect of this strategy is that the quality of care a family chooses typically varies with the social class of the family, and it is almost impossible to separate the effects of the day care environment from the effect of the class of the family, which is correlated with the child's health, home conditions, and mother's practices. The second strategy, which we chose, is to establish a day care center with a program the investigators can control and monitor, try to persuade both working-class and middle-class families to enroll their children in the center, locate families of comparable social class who plan to rear their children at home, and compare the development of the two groups. Such a design is constrained because it permits evaluation only of the possible consequences of good quality care and can say nothing about the consequences of undesirable day care centers. The reader should remember as he studies the results of this investigation that we are evaluating how children grow under surrogate care conditions that are, according to current theoretical views, similar to home rearing.

A second, perhaps less important, constraint was that we were unable to observe the day care children in their home settings. We knew what kinds of experiences each infant had at the center and would have liked to evaluate home experiences, but many of the parents, especially the Chinese, were reluctant to have us enter their homes for the amount of time we needed to obtain a representative picture of those environments. Finally, fiscal constraints made it necessary to terminate the study when the children were twenty-nine months old. Some readers may object that the psychological effects of attendance at a day care center are most likely to be observed at four and five years of age and that twenty-seven months of surrogate care is not sufficient to have an important influence. There is no rational way to reply to that objection.

Two important advantages accrued from the design we chose. First, the families were representative of working-class and middle-class groups—this was not a study of the infants of professors, lawyers, and doctors. Second, because the center was located in a working-class neighborhood (in Boston) and employed as caretakers women who lived in the community, most of whom had no college training and no formal instruction in child psychology, the caretakers were representative of those most likely to be employed as caretakers if day care were to be expanded in the United States.

The sample

The subjects were Chinese and Caucasian children from both working- and middle-class families in the Boston area. The original design called for three matched groups of children. One group of thirty-three infants attended a day care center we created and administered. They were enrolled one at a time over the course of a year until we had filled our sample size; at enrollment the infants were no younger than three and one-half months and no older than five and one half months, and they participated in the program until twenty-nine months of age. The home control group consisted of sixty-seven infants, thirty-two of whom were matched with those in day care in age, sex, ethnicity, and social class but living at home during this two and one-half year period. A third group was planned to comprise infants in other forms of group care outside the home, either in a day care center or custodial care for part of the period from three and one half through twenty-nine months of age—a mixed care group. However, it was not possible to find a large sample of children attending another day care center who were also closely matched in class and ethnicity with the experimental group; we were only able to find sixteen such infants. The mixed care infants were not included in the analyses that compared the effects of day care and home-rearing. They were only included when we combined the groups to analyze the effects of ethnicity, sex, or social class. Table 4-1 lists the size of each group by type of care, ethnicity, class, and sex.

Ideally, each group should have retained its status for the duration of the study. Unfortunately, three children left our experimental day care center after twenty months, and three from the large home control group began to attend an outside day care center; hence they were not included in the analyses of the data collected when the children reached twenty-nine months of age.

The criteria for accepting children into the nursery were dictated by the research design. Children were either first or second-born; the products of full-term, normal pregnancies, without serious neurologic, physiologic, or genetic disorders; and between three and one half and five and one half months of age. Each infant had had a normal physical examination by a pediatrician both at birth and just before being enrolled in the day care program. Enrollment of experimental subjects in the day care group required geographic proximity, but there were no restrictions regarding economic and ethnic factors. Although the majority of infants did not live in an economically affluent section of Boston, they were not from economically deprived families. The families were intact, supportive of their children, and, except for one or two instances, appeared to provide an environment adequate to sustain normal physical and psychological development.

Since a segment of the black community did not want black children evalu-

TABLE 4.1. DISTRIBUTION OF CHILDREN IN EACH OF THE GROUPS BY FORM OF REARING, SEX, ETHNICITY, AND SOCIAL CLASS (n = 116).

	DAY CARE		HOME CONTROL		MIXED	
ETHNICITY AND SOCIAL CLASS	M	F	M	F	M	F
Chinese						
Working class	4	5	9	6	0	0
Middle class	3	4	6	9	5	2
Caucasian						
Working class	5	2	5	14	1	0
Middle class	5	5	6	12	5	3

ated we elected to enroll a limited number of black infants, but not to include them in the research study. Seven black infants were enrolled; they received all the same care and services provided to the other children participating in the experiment, but they were not involved in any aspect of the research program.

Before a child was enrolled, both his parents were given an opportunity to visit the center, to talk at length with the project director, and to watch a demonstration of the testing procedures. Although the parents were advised that we wanted them to continue in the program until their children were twenty-nine to thirty months of age, they understood that they could withdraw their children at any time. Fewer than 6 percent of the total number of children enrolled in the project in day care and home control groups were withdrawn prior to termination of the study. As just noted, several parents withdrew their children because they were moving away; we asked the parents of two subjects to withdraw their children from the program because of infrequent or haphazard attendance.

The experimental day care center

The Tremont Street Infant Center occupied 7,000 square feet of space on the ground floor of a large, low-income urban housing project situated in the South End of Boston. During the period of the study approximately 40 percent of the project's residents were Chinese, 40 percent black, and 20 percent Caucasian. The majority of the families in the immediate area were working-class; some were unemployed welfare recipients. Because one criterion for enrollment was that the infant's family live within fifteen minutes of the center by automobile, the majority of enrollees lived in the immediate vicinity and reflected the ethnic variety of the local community.

Approximately 60 percent of the 7,000 feet was used as the area for care of the children; 25 percent was used for a research laboratory; and 15 percent for offices and support facilities like the kitchen, lavatories, and space for storage.

The nursery had child-sized toilets and sinks, as well as sinks with adjacent diapering tables in the nursery proper. In a laundry room with washer and dryer clothes soiled during the day could be laundered, and parents were asked to provide a change of clothes to be kept at the nursery. A small kitchen equipped with a commercial dishwasher, a stove, refrigerator, and food storage areas completed the support facilities. The laboratory area was sufficiently separate from the nursery area so that infants scheduled for testing could enter the laboratory without passing through the day care section of the facility.

The primary nursery area was a large, open, carpeted room measuring approximately forty by seventy feet. The space was divided so that as the first group of infants became toddlers (thirteen through thirty months) they were physically separated from the younger infants (three and one-half to thirteen months) who had entered the program later. The reason for partitioning the space was to provide environments where each of the two age groups could engage in exploratory behavior in an atmosphere that did not constrain them yet protected them from physical harm. Separation into two age groups was accomplished by means of a series of elevated modular carpeted platforms within which the infants were free to move while being protected from the overenthusiastic intrusion of the older toddlers. One end of the large room consisted of floor-to-ceiling windows overlooking the inner courtyard of the housing project. Separate areas for infants and toddlers were designated for sleeping at either end of the large room. At the toddler end there was access to a room used primarily for activities like sandbox, water play, and finger painting. There, a movable hinged storage compartment about three feet high was the boundary between infant and toddler areas. The toddlers could look into the area where the infants were playing but could not enter unless one of the teachers made access possible. The playroom also had an elevated "treehouse" equipped with toys. It had a tentlike roof and sides of nylon net to prevent the toddlers from falling out or dropping objects into the infant area. The treehouse also provided a post for individual staff members to observe the nursery without disurbing the activity of the children.

Staff

One of the investigators (R.B.K.), a pediatrician, had responsibility for the operation of the day care component of the program. The daily operation of the nursery was under the management of a nonteaching director, who, in addition to coordinating the program's activities, was concerned with maintaining the facility, ordering supplies, and recruiting a cadre of substitute teachers whenever one of the regular teachers was ill or on vacation.

The day care center accepted infants at 8:00 AM and anticipated that parents would be able to pick up their children not later than 5:00 PM. For one or two mothers who had to be at work before 8:00 AM, an exception was made, as were a few for the 5:00 PM closing time. Initially, we had planned to have present full-time personnel especially trained by us the entire day. When it became apparent that the late afternoon was not particularly productive for the children, for they were often tired or sleepy, we altered the pattern so that the full-time trained staff arrived early in the morning with two or three staying late in the afternoon in a supervisory capacity. These supervisors were aided in the late afternoon by a number of high school students who served more to babysit than to implement the curriculum of the program.

The teacher-to-child ratio was maintained at one to three for infants and one to five for toddlers. Each child stayed with a single caretaker throughout the first thirteen to fifteen months in the infant section and with a second teacher the remainder of his time in the program. Most children moved from the infant to the toddler section somewhere between the ages of thirteen and fifteen months when they were walking with coordination, were moderately self-sufficient, and could feed themselves fairly well. The qualifications for a position as a day care teacher included having raised children, enjoying infants, and being responsive to criticism, able to articulate suggestions, and appreciative of the need to implement the curriculum. We were less concerned with the potential teacher's prior formal education than with her capacity to care for infants and toddlers in a sensitive, warm, responsive fashion while establishing a relation of trust and accountability with the parents. Most of the teachers selected had completed high school but had little college training. We were fortunate in having minimal change in personnel over the course of the study; during the five years that the center was in operation only two of the nursery staff left. The stability of staff was due, in part, to a reasonably generous starting salary and our continued emphasis on the importance of the staff's role in the center.

Although each teacher shared in the care of other infants, her primary duty was responsibility for one set of infants, with whose parents she was expected to establish a close personal relationship. She was to exchange with the parents of each child information about the child's behavior every day. This was not possible for certain children who were transported to and from the nursery in our van; the teachers attempted to maintain telephone contact with the families of those children at least two or three times a week.

At the height of the program there were fifteen infants under the care of five teachers assisted by two teachers' aides and twenty-five toddlers cared for by five teachers and two aides. Although the aides were usually younger women, one was a grandmother. Each aide's responsibility was to help with feeding and diaper changing and to look after one or two babies whenever a teacher was engaging a single child in a more intimate interaction.

To ensure close relationships with the families the pattern of teacher selection reflected the pattern of enrollment. Approximately half of the day care teachers were bilingual in Chinese, 30 percent bilingual in Spanish, and 1 bilingual in French; the remainder spoke only English. We decided that the language between adults should be English. Two Chinese families requested that the teacher use the home language when speaking to the child; all others wanted their children spoken to in English.

Curriculum training

Upon entering the program each teacher had a period of training during which the program was explained and a curriculum manual that had been written by us was amplified and demonstrated. The curriculum rested on a small number of assumptions. We assumed that during the first year of life the infant's cognitive and social development are enhanced by one-to-one interactions with a caretaker involving moderate transformations of the familiar—surprises. This assumption was based on the results of many studies showing that the infant becomes emotionally excited by and attentive to events that are moderate discrepancies from his schemata. We assumed, further, that these encounters with the discrepant tempt the child to accommodate the new event so that new cognitive structures are created and his natural tendency to be alerted by and to attempt to understand the familiar is being encouraged and amplified. Since the infant typically smiles and laughs during these successful bouts with the unfamiliar the adult caretaker, who is the source of the uncertainty, should be viewed by the infant as a source of pleasure and information. Considerable one-to-one vocal and verbal interaction between infant and caretaker was encouraged because of the importance modern American society places on vocally expressive behavior in infants and the early display of language. Finally, we acted on the assumption that the opportunity to explore a safe environment with many toys would enhance motor development and facilitate the child's sense of effectiveness in dealing with the world of objects.

These simple assumptions about exposure to variety through the actions of the caretaker, vocal and verbal interaction, and freedom to explore and play with a variety of objects were the keystone of the curriculum at the center. Daily each caretaker conscientiously initiated several one-to-one interactions with each of the infants in her care when the infants were alert, well fed, and relatively happy. During interaction periods, which lasted as long as the infant remained attentive and interested—a few minutes to twenty minutes—the caretaker would present surprises to the child. Typically an infant would experience between one and two hours of this interaction each day. When the children were awake they played on the carpeted floor of the center, where they found a wide variety of toys for manipulation and study. In good weather the older infants were taken to neighboring parks or areas in downtown Boston for outings of one to two hours.

During the second year of life the child becomes able to supply his own surprises, so for toddlers the emphasis of the curriculum was shifted to stimulation of language, a symbolic approach to materials, and mastery of motor and cognitive competences. In the one-to-one interaction periods the caretaker read to the child; thumbed through a picture book, naming the object illustrated; or encouraged games and activities that treated objects as symbols. Moreover, the play environment provided the child with objects that permitted him to exploit his new cognitive capacities and motor skills. Group singing and games were frequent and, as during the first year, outings to parks and outside play during good weather.

In sum, the curriculum had a middle-class American bias; it encouraged cognitive development, one-to-one affective interactions between adult caretaker and child, and successful mastery of experience.

Since teachers had interpreted the curriculum manual as a directive to engage the child continually in cognitively stimulating activity, they tended at first to be intrusive and to interrupt the child's activity in order to engage him in interaction. With time, the teaching staff as well as those responsible for supervising daily curriculum activities became aware of the importance of observing the child first to decide whether or not he was actively absorbed in something before initiating interaction with him.

The teachers also came to appreciate that if an infant was neither tired nor hungry, his fussing was often evidence of boredom. Attempts at soothing him had less effect than providing him with a stimulating activity, however simple. Talking or singing to the child, or giving him a brightly colored string of beads to gaze at or giving him a toy to manipulate often stopped the fussing and led to an episode of sustained interaction.

Much time was spent not only during the teachers' initial training, but also at the monthly staff meetings (when the nursery was closed), discussing the teacher-child relation. Their levels of expectations with regard to the children's behavior was a recurring topic. The effect of these discussions was most noticeable in their treatment of the toddlers' eating habits. At lunchtime the toddlers commonly sat, five or six to a table, at three or four tables eating their meal. Because the teachers believed that toddlers were mature enough to feed themselves, the toddlers did so, although with varying degrees of success.

The teachers sometimes found it necessary to chastise toddlers for consistently shoving or striking other children. They discovered that the most effective mode of punishment was to place the misbehaving child in a chair in the middle of the playroom for five minutes. The child would fuss or cry when placed in the "naughty chair," while his peers would stand around shaking their heads and admonishing the miscreant. This was a somewhat ludicrous situation, but effective in imparting to the child the information that he had done something that was unacceptable in the nursery setting. The effectiveness of this approach became apparent as the program progressed, for parents would comment that the child behaved differently in the day care setting than he did at home, particularly with regard to the niceties of social behavior.

The stability of the caretaking staff and the assignment of a child to a particular teacher led to an attachment between nursery teacher and child. Each child developed a hierarchy of preference as to which caretaker he would seek out when he was distressed or when he wanted to share an experience. The child's primary caretaker was sought first. If she was not available, one of the other adults was approached, usually the child's secondary teacher.

The children expressed little distress when brought to the center each morning. The teacher would greet the parent—typically the mother—and child in the waiting room, help undress the child, exchange news of the day, and inquire about the child's well being. The parent would then leave, and the child would enter the nursery and become involved in the day's routine. Neither was any obvious joy expressed by the child when he saw his day care teacher in the morning, nor any particular distress in seeing the parent depart. However, at the end of the day there was obvious elation at reunion when the child saw the parent standing in the doorway of the nursery. Those who could walk or crawl would go to the parents, and the younger ones would also indicate recognition of their parents and their desire to join them.

The personalities of the teacher and child became an issue when several of the teachers, especially in the infant section, reported that they could not establish the kind of relationship with particular babies that they felt was necessary. The reasons were varied and at times inexplicable. We were sufficiently well staffed so that it was possible to switch infants from one caretaker to another during the first month or two of their involvement in the program in order to accommodate personality factors.

Age of entry appeared to be an important variable with regard to the infant's adjustment to the day care setting. In the usual pattern, the mother spent a portion of the first day with the child, a smaller portion the second day, and thereafter, if the child seemed to have adjusted to the nursery, she left shortly following her arrival in the morning. It was our experience that the 3½-month-olds' adjustment was accomplished more quickly and with less obvious distress than the 5½-month-olds'. A few 5½-month-olds required five or six days of maternal attendance before becoming content to have the mother leave the first thing in the morning.

Another variable that appeared to influence the children's adjustment was regularity of attendance. Mondays were usually characterized by more irritability and a more disruptive atmosphere within the nursery than Tuesdays or Wednesdays. Even the short interruption of routine occasioned by the weekend seemed to exert a negative influence on the children's adjustment on Monday morning. Children who were absent for a week or two because of illness or vacation often went through an episode of readjustment upon returning to the nursery. However, there were large individual differences in the degree of adjustment.

Parental involvement

Because the Tremont Street Infant Center was experimental, the issues of curriculum content, admission criteria, staff selection, and parental participation within the nursery were determined in large measure by the constraints of the program's experimental design. The parents did not lack opportunities to express their opinions about various aspects of the program; and especially because the nursery served a community with a culturally diverse population, the staff was sensitive to the need for establishing and maintaining communication not just between parents and administration, but also among the parents themselves. The final responsibility for policy decisions belonged to the principal investigators, however. The pressing need for infant day care within the community, combined with the staff's willingness to accommodate individual requests whenever possible, resulted in our experiencing few serious conflicts during the five years of the nursery's operation.

Parents were encouraged to make their concerns known to the teachers caring for their respective infants. Their relations with the primary teacher helped parents understand the dynamics of the nursery; it also allowed us to modify the program to more closely approximate particular cultural or social expectations held by the parents. The teachers' bilingualism enhanced understanding and the air of informality that contributed to the program's acceptance by the parents and the community at large. False impressions, misunderstandings, and the sense of uneasiness that often surround such research undertakings were dealt with much more effectively by teacher and parent than they could have been by research staff and leaders of community organizations.

At a series of "parent nights" both research and nursery personnel discussed the program's progress and answered parents' questions. During these meetings, at the close of a nursery day, substitute teachers cared for the infants, leaving parents and staff free to interact. The meetings were particularly useful early in the project; they were held every other month during the first year and every three months subsequently. Attendance was high for the first five or six meetings and then began to drop off as parents' concern lessened and their better understanding of the nursery program allayed their initial fears. Some of their apprehension concerned issues that had not initially appeared to us to be important. One was the introduction of the multilevel platforms to subdivide the nursery, on which the Chinese parents, in particular, feared the children might injure themselves. Once the parents saw the platforms and climbed on them they were assured of their safety. Food was another issue of concern to the Chinese parents. Some foods are considered "hot," others "cold," a designation having little or no relationship to the temperature of the food ("hot" foods include grapes, pineapple, and eggplant; "cold" foods include pork, watercress, and lettuce). Under certain conditions one variety is considered more appropriate than the other —for example, a feverish child should not be fed "cold" food. To accommodate such concerns we distributed menus a week in advance so that parents could indicate any items they did not want served to their children. Although a few parents restricted their children's diet and provided their food, the majority of parents permitted their children to eat what the rest of the group ate.

The issue of control and punishment of aggressive behavior always required a great deal of discussion. We had decided not to use physical punishment or complete isolation as a means of controlling or extinguishing unwanted behavior. We decided to rely more on the strength of the social bond between the child and his teacher and the mild embarrassment of the "naughty chair." Many parents wanted us to use physical punishment if their children misbehaved. Many of the Chinese parents, who demand a high level of compliance, were apprehensive that the apparent lack of control within the nursery might be deleterious to their children's socialization and influence the children's behavior at home. It appears that the child is capable of behaving differently in two settings. We learned that the Chinese subjects were as controlled and quiet as their siblings at home and in the neighboring community, but at the day care center their behavior was more active and was like that of their non-Chinese peers. Many of the Caucasian parents, particularly middle-class, permissive ones, commented on how much better behaved their children were in the nursery than at home. The child appears to be capable not only of forming multiple social attachments during his first two and one-half years of life but also of responding to different social expectations.

Although the issue of toilet training occupied many hours of discussion, it was resolved largely by the children themselves. We had decided to make potty chairs available in the toddler section in addition to the regular toilets in the separate bathroom. Watching others who had become toilet trained at home or in the nursery make use of the more public facilities effectively trained children who were curious. Some parents insisted that their children begin to be trained at one year of age and implemented that timetable at home, but we did not attempt to train children that young in the center. On the other hand, some parents did not want any toilet training of their children. Nonetheless, the majority of the children had been toilet trained prior to their departure from the program at thirty months.

Assigning new babies to particular teachers or changing assignments became an issue in several instances because of parental preference for or dislike of particular teachers. Whenever obvious differences in personality, culture, or philosophy of child-rearing made an assignment untenable, we acceded to parental preferences. Parental dissatisfaction was surprisingly low, considering the broad spectrum of cultural and social backgrounds of staff and families.

Health care

Health care within a nursery for infants and toddlers is of obvious importance. Since the director of the center was a pediatrician, it would have been possible to diagnose and treat unwell children on the spot and resolve most problems related to the children's physical well being. However, we decided that the center would not function as a primary source of health care for the community, not because such a resource was not needed or would not have been utilized, but because it was beyond the scope of the research project. Moreover, we reasoned since the day care center was an integral part of a health care unit, it would only fractionate the family's ongoing medical care if it were to take on the responsibility for the health needs of just one member of the family, the child. When a child became ill during the course of the day or was considered ill by the teacher when he arrived, or when his parent had a question about a child's physical state, he was examined. If immediate treatment was necessary it was initiated by the director. Follow-up care was always delegated to one of the available health care resources of the community. Parents were encouraged to seek continuing medical care at a nearby community health clinic, the outpatient department of any of the several teaching hospitals in the city, or from private physicians.

We had decided we would permit the children to continue attendance when they had colds or upper respiratory illnesses if they were not febrile. If they were receiving medication, we would administer it during the day. We would not attempt to isolate them from the rest of the group, since by the time a child has been diagnosed as having a cold or upper respiratory infection he has already exposed his peers to his illness. We experienced no major outbreaks of diarrhea or impetigo, but two or three outbreaks of viral conjunctivitis—a highly contagious disorder—spread throughout the nursery. Each time over 40 percent of the children were either coming down with this disorder or being treated for it we closed the nursery for three or four days or a long weekend. When there was a great deal of viral infection within the community, we had it in the nursery.

Although we did not attempt to document this phenomenon, the clinical experience of the director suggested that the incidence of minor illness among this population of day care infants was comparable to that found among second-born and third-born infants reared in the home and exposed to the illnesses of older siblings. The criterion for deciding whether a child should be allowed to continue in the nursery when he was afebrile yet suffering the side effects of such an illness was whether he could actively participate in the nursery routine. If he was fussy or cranky, we felt it was better for him to be at home than within the nursery for we were not equipped to cater to the special needs of an ill child. One or two exceptions were made when this would have meant an undue hardship for a child's family, or causing the mother to lose her job.

For children of the age span represented in our nursery, one of the leading causes of morbidity and mortality is accidents at home. Our staff was trained to anticipate and prevent accidents; many hazardous situations typical of homes were avoided in the nursery. The careful consideration given to providing a safe play environment and a vigilant staff proved valuable. The day care facility functioned for five years without one major accident.

General observations

Relations among children Six of the 40 babies who enrolled in the day care program established and maintained a continuing close tie with another. Four boys and two girls formed these special friendships noted toward the end of the children's first year, usually with another infant of the same age and sex being cared for by the same teacher. The associations remained stable through the toddler phase. Although these children took part in group activities and were not actively excluded by the other children, a member of a pair usually sought out his friend when left to himself.

A third child's attempting to join any of the pairs of children playing usually resulted in some form of friction. Introduction of an extra child did not seem to be a problem with larger groups of playing children, particularly those supervised by an adult.

Toddlers were often observed engaged in long episodes of solitary play or moving from one activity to another. Observing these children moving from the sandbox to a reading group or to a singing group reminded one of an adult strolling among the booths of an enclosed shopping arcade. The physical pattern of the nursery permitted this freedom of movement and allowed the child to exercise maturing capacities.

Teacher-child relations The staff of mature women, experienced, at ease in the care of infants, and confident in their own abilities, proved conscientious, comfortable in their day-to-day relationships with parents, and responsive to their role as active participants in a research oriented program, a role in which they took pride and pleasure. The comfort and safety of the center and such support facilities as safe transportation and well-prepared meals contributed to an atmosphere within which young children could receive sensitive care by a competent staff.

The gradualness of expansion of the nursery population as the first subjects matured and moved to the toddler section meant that at no time were there large numbers of "new infants" entrusted to the care of an inexperienced staff. The small number and closeness of ages of the children cared for by an individual teacher, frequent verbal and physical exchanges of affection between teacher and child, minimal turnover among the staff or the children, and relationship of trust established between teachers and parents provided an "institutionalized" form of the extended family. The depth of this trust was shown by Chinese-speaking parents' allowing a child to spend weekends with her English-speaking day care teacher.

The language of the nursery being English and some teachers being bilingual in Chinese (and others in Spanish and French), we discovered that the Chinese-speaking toddlers addressed the English-speaking teachers in English and all of the Chinese-speaking teachers in Chinese, with the exception of one Chinese teacher who only spoke English. None of the Chinese children adopted any of the Spanish words spoken by some children; English-speaking children adopted no Chinese words and few of the Spanish words they heard. Even though they could speak only a few English words, many of the Chinese toddlers were fluent in Chinese by the time they left the nursery. Despite their spending much of their waking time in a predominantly English-language environment, the language of the home appears to have exerted an overriding influence on their productive speech.

Visitors

We had assured parents that their children would not be cared for in a fishbowl. Visitors were not allowed within the nursery during the day; if they were interested in the physical setup, they were invited to come either before the children's arrival or after they had left for the day. On those few occasions when we violated this practice, it was apparent that the introduction of a strange person into the nursery caused significant disruption among both infants and nursery staff.

Criteria for assessment

The selection of dimensions to be assessed and the establishment of standards for scoring reflected contemporary American values. Analysis is the primary approach in the physical sciences. The goal is to find the most elementary units that, in concert, are transformed into surface events. Since living systems evolve over much longer time periods, there is as much interest in predicting the future form of a contemporary process as there is in analyzing the fragments that compose the evanescent present. The varied purposive directions organisms may take assume a special significance in developmental psychology, for the child psychologist must choose for study a small set of potentialities from the many that might be actualized. The choice reveals a personal conception of what is ideal.

Students of human development find it almost impossible to avoid taking sides with respect to criteria, and the history of psychology is littered with their choices—sensory acuity, tapping speed, libido, low anxiety, formal operational thinking, grades in school, IQ, and income are just a few. We can divide the criteria into two major classes—those that appear in all or almost all humans as a result of growing up in any normal environment and those that are culturally specific. The latter can be further subdivided into those that are orthogonal to "adaptation" and those that either facilitate or obstruct it. That rather bold statement requires a definition of adaptation. We could choose number of children, wealth, amount of leisure time, longevity, power, ability to defend oneself when attacked, or a dozen more. Clearly, a judgment must be made that must be defended, in part, on intuitive grounds, not solely on the basis of empirical fact. Those judgments reflect the deepest theoretical commitments of the scholar who makes them.

To select human qualities to evaluate we need first a prototype, a conception of ideal development so that we can quantify deviance from the ideal or the rate at which a child is approaching it. Every psychologist, biologist, and historian describes his domain with a prototype in mind. People, species, and nations are compared on the analytic dimensions that comprise the prototype. When American psychologists describe a child, they usually use sentences that include terms like *autonomy, dependency, intelligence, sociability, anxiety, aggression,* and *dominance* because those attributes are related to our ego ideal. They rarely talk about the child's endurance, running speed, singing ability, body form, love of nature, or gentleness because those qualities are believed to be less relevant to future adaptation.

The community's perception of the requirements for adaptation is one source of the hierarchy of valued qualities attached to each role. The second source, which is less pragmatic, has deep roots in a local conception of beauty and sacredness whose history is not easily traced. In our own society, intelligence, alertness, sociability, fearfulness, and a secure relation to the mother are infant qualities of the first type. Cuddliness, vigor, and symmetry of facial features belong to the second, more transcendental set. Parents are more interested in the effects of day care on the first group of traits, for they alter the child's chances of later adjustment. This is one reason we evaluated attentiveness, cognitive competences, social behavior, and attachment to the mother, but did not try to measure physical strength, rate of physical growth, response to music, or hunger and sleep cycles.

A second set of valued characteristics, in addition to intellectual competence, includes adeptness in social situations and the ability to make and maintain friendships with ease, while not being excessively sensitive to occasional rejection or temporary loneliness. The attributes that enable each person to maintain a delicate balance between excessive dependence and aloof isolation we will call the "interpersonal cluster." Self-confidence, the expectation that one can deal with challenge and stress, and the perception that one is valued and loved might be called the "self-esteem cluster."

For each of these clusters an informal theory summarizes the experiences of childhood that presumably facilitate the acquisition of these qualities. Many parents believe that talking to infants, exposing children to books, interesting toys, and challenging problems and, of course, good teachers and schools, constitute catalysts for the competence cluster. We can assess how well or fast a particular child is progressing toward academic competence at any time by administering tests of language and reading proficiency, ability and willingness to concentrate, and talent in solving conceptual problems. The whole procedure takes less than an hour.

Many parents believe that interpersonal skills are acquired through interaction with other children. These experiences presumably persuade the child that social interaction is pleasant, and teach him how to resist domination and to initiate and maintain friendly relations.

Parents are least clear about how to help the child gain self-esteem. Most agree that an emotionally close mother-infant relation is mandatory. Over a quarter century ago Anna Freud and Dorothy Burlingham wrote a book summarizing their observations of English children separated from their families during the Second World War and raised in residential nurseries. Their conclusions about the significance of the mother-child relationship are still regarded as valid by most American parents. They wrote,

> An infant in a residential nursery may acquire the rough and ready methods of social adaptation which are induced by the atmosphere of the toddler's room . . . they may acquire conventions and behavior patterns . . . and an imitation of its elders, but neither of these processes, though adding to the growth of the child's personality, will lead to the embodiment of moral values. Identification . . . takes place under one condition only: as the result and residue of emotional attachment to people who are the real and living personifications of the demands which every civilized society upholds for the restriction and transformation of primitive instinctive tendencies. Where love objects of this kind are missing the infant is deprived of an all important opportunity to identify with these demands . . . Success or failure in education in the residential nursery will therefore depend on the strength of the child's attachments to them. If these relationships are deep and lasting the residential child will take the usual course of development and become an independent, moral and social being. If the grownups in the nursery remain remote and impersonal figures or, if as happens in some nurseries, they change so often that no permanent attachment is effected at all, institutional education will fail in this important respect. Children will then show defects in their character development, their adaptation to society may remain on a superficial

level and their future be exposed to the danger of all kinds of dissocial development. [Burlingham and Freud 1944, pp. 125-126]

The present inquiry into the effect of early group care accommodated the catechism of the community. But suppose this investigation had been initiated in the same city 150 years earlier. Adults with power and dignity in the Boston of 1825 were pious Christians who valued obedience to older authority, inhibition of aggression, sexual modesty, and reverence of God. Parents believed they could insure socialization of these attributes if they insisted on obedience within the family, punished all signs of aggression and sexuality, and insulated their child from other children, especially those from less religious and economically less secure homes who might lead their child from virtue. It is likely we would have created test situations that assessed the child's ability to resist influence from peers, rather than his tendency to initiate contact with them. And we would have celebrated the child's dependence on his mother rather than his independence.

This relativism in choice of criteria is especially relevant to the current project because half of our families were Chinese, some of whom held traditional Chinese values. One of these values is that children should be quiet, not talkative. The battery we devised, reflecting the biases of middle-class American society, assessed the infant's tendency to vocalize and the 2½-year-old's talkativeness and richness of vocabulary. Had we constructed the battery from the perspective of our traditional Chinese parents we might have created an assessment situation in which a child sat opposite an adult, and hidden observers coded how long the child remained quiet before speaking—the longer the delay the more mature the child. Such a decision would have puzzled most American psychologists and administrators of grant awarding agencies. Since "remaining quiet" is regarded as maladaptive in our society, we did not create such an assessment situation, but not because talkativeness in 2-year-olds is universally more mature or desirable, but because it is inappropriate to the larger society in which these children will have to function. Other variables assessed, such as, for example, attentiveness and sensitivity to discrepancy, are likely to be universally adaptive and to display a growth pattern over the first three years that may be representative of children in all locales.

Assessment procedures

The gulf between the names of the qualities psychologists wish to assess in young children and the specific behavioral variables finally coded is not unlike that between one's fantasy of an ideal Caribbean cruise and the experience of living twelve days in a small cabin on a sixty-year-old boat during the rainy season. Psychologists usually know what constructs they wish to quantify but typically do not have methods sensitive enough to evaluate the attributes that define the concept. We were interested in five major characteristics that met three criteria—they reflected important aspects of growth during the first three years of life, they were expected to be vulnerable to variations in rearing environments, and they were capable of quantification.

Attentiveness The first characteristic was attentiveness to unexpected visual and auditory events as well as sensitivity to discrepant transformations on familiarized events. Since the child learns a great deal about the world by attending to moderate transformations on his knowledge, by quantifying each infant's pattern of attentiveness we hoped to determine major variations among children in this basic human function. Additionally, duration of attentiveness to discrepant events often shows a U-shaped growth function over the period from three to twenty-nine months of age. If this is indeed a normative function, we hoped to determine which children were showing precocious and which retarded development. We presented the infant six different classes of visual events and two auditory events and coded the infant's attentiveness to a series of repeated trials as well as transformations on the stimuli that were presented repeatedly. Since heart rate has been used by many psychologists as a supplementary measure in studies of attentiveness, we recorded the child's continuous heart rate during these stimulus episodes.

Excitability A second characteristic of interest, related to both temperament and experience, was affective excitability to stimulus events. Vocalization and smiling are two of the most obvious indexes of affective arousal that accompany attentiveness; motor activity and fretfulness are signs of affective states that usually reflect lack of attention. Some children regularly babble when they are excited by an event they are studying or have assimilated. We assumed that the frequency of vocalization was a function of several factors; including basic temperament and history of one-to-one vocal interactions with adults. The latter assumption is based on studies that show that infants with parents who talk with them a great deal are more vocal in response to visual and auditory events than those whose parents are more quiet. Since vocalization to discrepant events might reflect the amount of prior verbal interaction with adults and since such interaction often predicts later language development, it seemed useful to quantify this characteristic. Smiling in response to discrepant events is another variable that indexes assimilation as well as temperamental qualities. Individual differences in smiling might index the degree to which the infant comprehended our procedures, and, therefore, could serve as a partial diagnosis of level of cognitive maturity. Motor activity and fretting in a situation in which the child is being presented with interesting events are two variables correlated with lack of interest and with the ease with which boredom is engendered. We were interested in the growth functions for all four variables in order to gain basic information on their normal ontogeny.

Reactivity to others A third domain of interest was the child's reactivity to unfamiliar children and adults. Excessive inhibition in a social situation is regarded by most American parents as undesirable; some believe that experience with a variety of adults and children promotes a more spontaneous posture with others. Since such interaction, especially with peers, is more frequent in a day care center, most people would predict that the day care experience would promote less shyness with unfamiliar adults and children than rearing only at home. We created formal situations in which the child interacted with the adult examiner, one unfamiliar child, and finally a group of unfamiliar peers in an unfamiliar day care center. We quantified indexes of spontaneity like time spent playing and social overtures to another child.

Attachment The child's emotional bond to the parent was an obvious focus of concern. Many parents and psychologists suspect that taking an infant each day to a day care center would weaken the intensity of the child's attachment to the parent when compared with the attachment of a child at home with the mother all day. We measured the child's attachment to the mother in two different situations. In the first we observed and coded the child's behavior when he was in a room with toys and his mother, a familiar woman (the caretaker from the day care center or a friend of the family) and an unfamiliar adult woman. We noted to whom the child went for comfort and relief of distress when he was bored, tired, or apprehensive. A second procedure involved the popular separation situation. Although we have argued that separation protest is not a sensitive index of the child's attachment to the mother, when the research was being planned in 1969, we and other psychologists believed that separation anxiety reflected degree of attachment. It seemed useful to compare day care and home control children on this behavioral reaction.

Later cognitive functioning Although language, perceptual analysis, and memory are not the only cognitive processes that are developing during the opening two and one half years of life, they are important and relatively easy to evaluate in 2-year-olds. We created procedures to assess the child's vocabulary, ability to solve test problems involving embedded figures, and memory for location of familiar objects. We also administered selected items from the Bayley Developmental Scale in order to evaluate the relation between the child's performance on a standardized test and performance on the procedures for which there are no national norms.

Testing

Each child was assessed by a research staff who were not involved in any aspect of caretaking and whose offices were in Cambridge, Massachusetts, several miles from the day care center. Infants were assessed at 3½, 5½, 7½, 9½, 11½, 13½, 20, and 29 months of age. The assessments from 3½ to 13½ months occurred in the special laboratory at the day care center that was separate from the area where care was administered (figure 4.1); the assessments at 20 and 29 months occurred in our laboratories on the Harvard University campus.

Although the focus of interest was a comparison of children in day care with those reared totally at home, we were also curious to learn more about the relations among psychological qualities during infancy and especially about the stability of those qualities within individual children. To satisfy

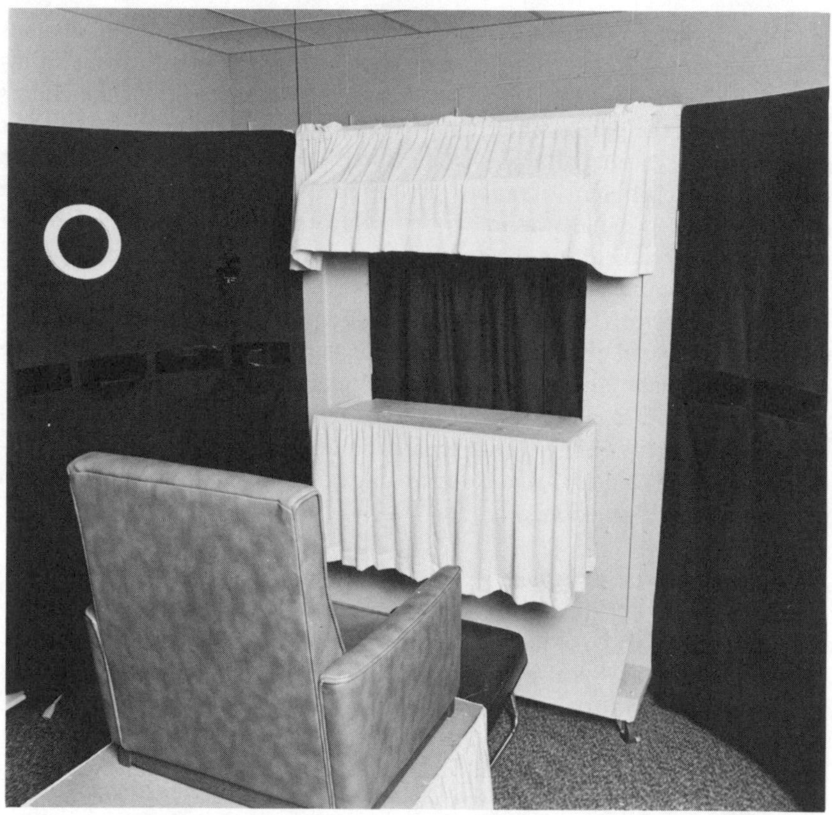

Fig. 4.1 *Setting for laboratory assessments.*

this curiosity we chose procedures that yielded phenotypically similar behaviors over the period from 3 ½ to 29 months of age.

The lists that follow briefly describe the test situations and the psychological variables that were coded. The procedures are listed in the order in which they were administered during a particular session. The social interaction episode was designed to assess reactivity to an unfamiliar adult; the block, masks, light, car, auditory, and slide episodes assess attentiveness and affect; the attachment and separation episodes assess the child's relation to his mother; the free play episodes at 13, 20, and 29 months were designed to assess mode of interaction with an unfamiliar peer; and the Bayley scale, vocabulary, concept formation index, embedded figures test, and memory for locations procedures were designed to assess aspects of cognitive development, especially in the older child.

Battery at 3½ and 5½ months

EPISODE	VARIABLES CODED
1. *Social interaction with an adult:* Female examiner interacts with the child for 2 min. at the beginning of the test session. For the first minute the examiner, seated across from the child who is sitting on the mother's lap, tries to stimulate the child to vocalize and smile. For the second minute the examiner's behavior is more constrained: she talks to the baby for 15 sec., smiles for 15 sec., touches the child for 15 sec., and moves her face toward the child's for 15 sec.	Whether or not child fixates examiner Whether or not child vocalizes Whether or not child smiles Whether or not child frets
2. *Block:* Child is shown a 2-in. wooden block 8 times, then a discrepancy (1 ½-in. wooden block) 5 times, then the original standard 3 times. During each trial the examiner's hand lifts the block out of a blue box, moves it in front of the child several times, and replaces the block in the box. Each trial lasts 10.5 sec.; inter-	Duration of each fixation of stimulus Duration of each vocalization Duration of fretting Duration of each smile Duration of leaning toward or pointing to the stimulus Duration of arm waving Duration of twisting of body Continuous heart rate

stimulus interval is 4.5 sec. (See figure 4.2.)

3. *Auditory 1:* Child hears 12 repetitions of a particular meaningful phrase 4.5 sec. in duration,	Duration of each fixation of the speaker baffle Duration of searching movements,

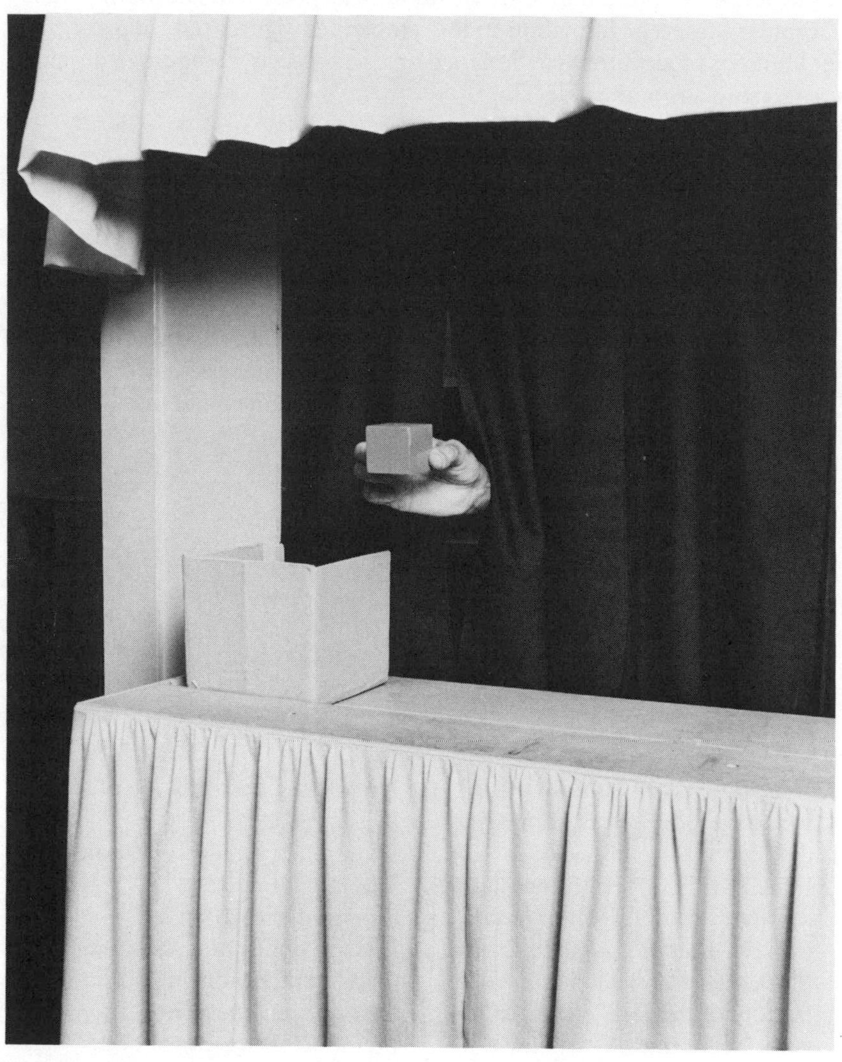

Fig. 4.2 *Presentation of block stimulus.*

followed by 5 repetitions of a nonsense phrase, followed by 3 repetitions of the original standard. The interstimulus interval is 5 sec. The meaningful phrase is "Drink the good milk." The nonsense phrase is "Plice la delf klim." English-speaking children are spoken to in English; the Chinese children in Chinese dialect. The speaker baffle is located to the left and above the child's head.	defined by the appearance of alert posture, motor quieting, and eyes moving in short saccades Duration of vocalization Duration of each smile Duration of fretting or crying Duration of leaning toward or pointing to the speaker baffle Duration of arm waving Duration of twisting of body Continuous heart rate
4. *Masks:* Child is shown a series of 4 different human masks (regular, scrambled, no eyes, and blank) in a fixed order twice each for 20 sec. (see figure 4.3.)	Same as block episode
5. *Light:* Child is shown 10 repetitions of an 11-sec. sequence in which the examiner's hand moves an orange rod in a circular arc until it contacts a bank of 3 light bulbs that light upon contact. This is followed by 5 repetitions of a discrepant transformation in which the examiner's hand touches the orange rod but the rod does not move and the lights go on 4 sec. later, which is followed by 3 repetitions of the original standard. The trial lasts 11 sec. with 5-sec. interstimulus intervals (See figure 4.4.).	Same as block episode
6. *Auditory 2:* Same as Auditory 1 except the child hears a different meaningful phrase 4 sec. in duration for the initial 12 repetitions. The discrepant transformation involves 5 repetitions of another meaningful phrase. The interstimulus interval is 3½ sec. The	Same as auditory 1

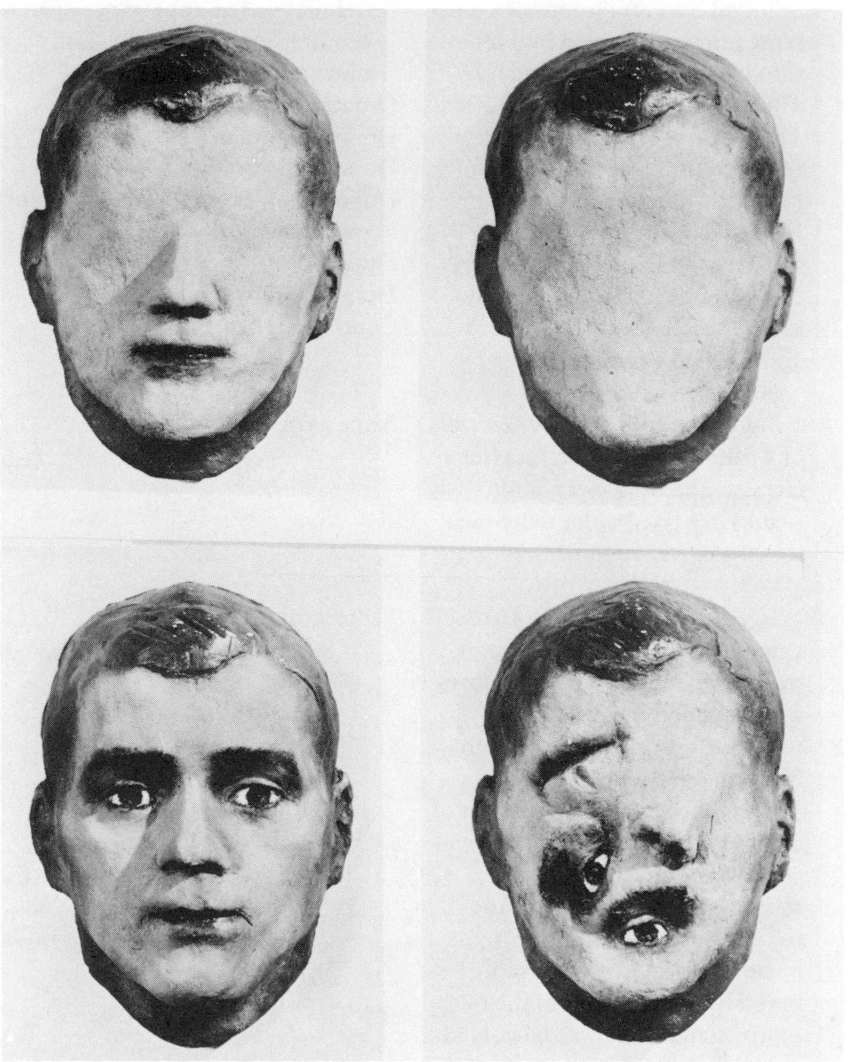

Fig. 4.3 *Stimuli used in masks episode.*

first meaningful phrase is, "Give me a big smile." The second is, "Throw me the red ball."	
7. *Separation:* Mother leaves child alone while child is happily playing with toys for a maximum of 2 min.	Occurrence of fretting or crying Latency to the first fret or cry

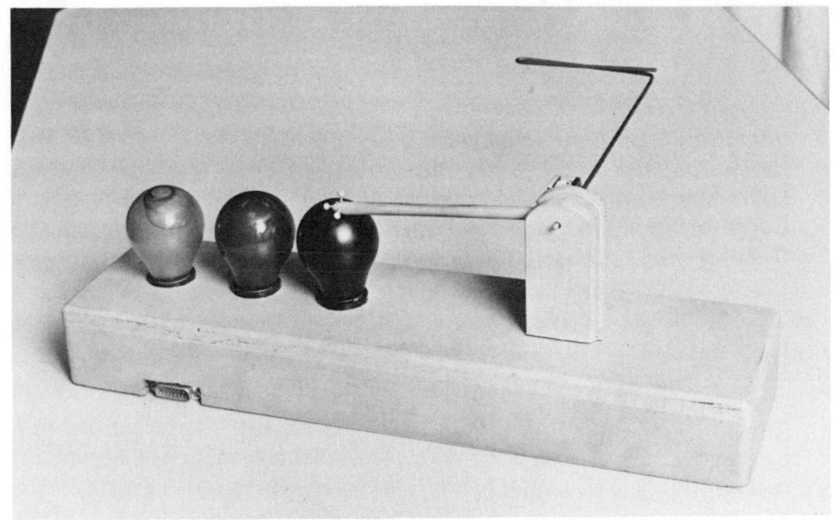

Fig. 4.4 *Apparatus used in light episode.*

8. *Social interaction:* Same as initial social interaction.	Same as first social interaction

Battery at 7½ months

EPISODE	VARIABLES CODED
1. *Social interaction**	*
2. *Block**	*
3. *Auditory 1**	*
4. *Light**	*
5. *Separation**	*
6. *Bayley Developmental Scale:* Child is administered selected items from the Bayley Developmental Scale in the standard way. (See table 4.2 for specific items.)	Child's passing or failing of each item
7. *Social interaction**	

*Same as at 3½ and 5½ months.

TABLE 4.2. BAYLEY DEVELOPMENTAL SCALE ITEMS ADMINISTERED AT 7½ MONTHS OF AGE.[a]

Mental scale item

79 Vocalizes 4 different syllables during session.
89 Responds with appropriate motor act to verbal request such as "Bye, bye," or "Where is the light?"
75 Definitely looks for spoon that has fallen over side of table.
86 Uncovers toy that has been covered by a tissue.

Motor scale item

32 Picks up cube, with complete opposition of thumb and finger.
30 Scoops up pellet on table.
35 Shows partial finger prehension of pellet.
41 Shows fine prehension of pellet—picks up pellet with thumb and forefinger.
28 Rolls from back to stomach.
33 Shows prewalking progression on the floor—child crawls or creeps from prone position.
27 Sits alone for 30 sec. or more.
29 Sits alone steadily without support, with back straight.
31 Sits alone with good coordination while playing.
36 Grasps examiner's fingers and pulls self to standing position.
34 Makes early stepping movements with underarm support.
40 Steps with support of examiner's hands.
42 Walks with slight support.
37 Raises self to sitting position.
38 Uses furniture to stand up unaided.
43 Sits down intentionally.
45 Stands alone for few seconds.

[a] Listed in usual sequence of administration.

Battery at 9½ months

EPISODE	VARIABLES CODED
1. *Social interaction**	*
2. *Block:* Same as at 3½ and 5½ months except initial repetition of the standard is reduced to 6 trials and the number of discrepant transformation trials is reduced to 3.	*

3. *Auditory 1:* Same as at 3 ½ and 5 ½ months except initial repetition of the standard is reduced to 8 trials.	*
4. *Masks**	*
5. *Light:* Same as at 3 ½ and 5 ½ months, except initial repetition of the standard is reduced to 8 trials.	*
6. *Auditory 3:* Child hears 8 repetitions of a meaningful phrase 5 sec. in duration, followed by 5 repetitions of the same words arranged in an ungrammatical order, followed by 3 repetitions of the original standard. The interstimulus interval is 3.5 sec. The meaningful phrase is "Hello, baby. How are you today?" The transformation is "Are today. How baby you hello?"	Same as auditory 1*
7. *Car:* Child sees a small wooden car stand on top of ramp, roll down an incline, and strike a styrofoam form, which falls on contact for 8 trials. In the discrepant event, repeated for 5 trials, the car strikes the form but the form does not fall; followed by 3 repetitions of the original standard. Car stands on top of ramp for 5 sec. then rolls down ramp in 6-sec. trial, followed by 7-sec. interstimulus interval. (See figure 4.5.)	Same as block and light episodes plus one extra variable: anticipatory fixation of the styrofoam form during the early phases of the trial before the car has struck the object.
8. *Slides:* Child sees a set of 5 chromatic slides projected on a screen. In each set an object or a	Same as block and light episodes

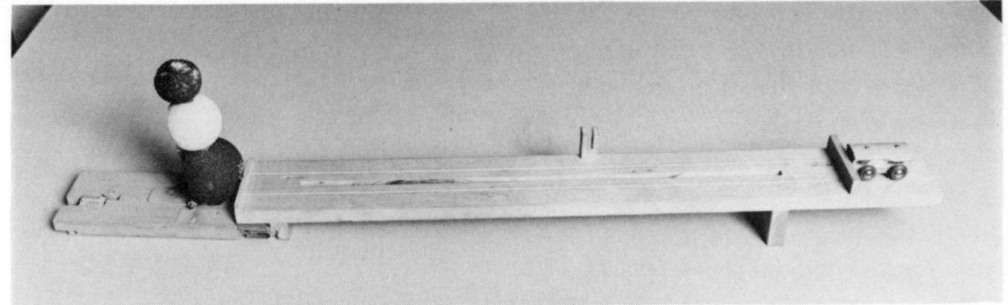

Fig. 4.5 *Apparatus used in car episode.*

background gradually becomes transformed into a second object or background. The items are

a. woman—bottle
b. rabbit with one background —rabbit with different background
c. cat—dog
d. baby—panda
e. girl—pail

Each slide is shown 6 sec. with no interstimulus interval; presentation of 5 slides lasts 30 sec.

9. *Separation**	*
10. *Social interaction**	*

*Same as for 3½ and 5½.

Battery at 11½ months

EPISODE	VARIABLES CODED
1. *Social interaction**	*
2. *Block†*	*
3. *Auditory 1†*	*
4. *Light†*	*

5. *Auditory 3*†	†Same as at 9½ months
6. *Car* †	†
7. *Slides* †	†
8. *Separation**	*
9. *Social interaction**	*

---

*Same as at 3½ and 5½ months.
†Same as at 9½ months.

Battery at 13½ months

EPISODE	VARIABLES CODED
1. *Social interaction**	*
2. *Solitary free play:* Child plays in a room with his mother and a set of age-appropriate toys for 15 min.	Duration of each attentional involvement with a toy Duration of proximity to mother (within 12 in.) Duration of looking at mother Duration of each smile Duration of vocalization Duration of fretting or crying
3. *Free play with an unfamiliar peer:* An unfamiliar peer of same age, sex, and ethnicity as the subject and the peer's mother are introduced into the room with a new set of toys, and the subject is allowed to play for 25 min.	Duration of each attentional involvement with a toy Duration of proximity to unfamiliar woman Duration of proximity to own mother (within 12 in.) Duration of touching unfamiliar peer Duration of fretting Duration of vocalization Duration of social interaction child initiates with unfamiliar peer Duration child stays when peer initiates interaction

	Child withdraws when peer initiates an interaction Duration of looking at unfamiliar peer Duration of looking at unfamiliar mother Duration of looking at own mother
4. *Light 2:* Same as light episode at 9½ months for the initial 8 repetitions, followed by a different discrepant transformation in which the rod moves across the circular arc without a hand being visible. The rod touches the lights. When it returns to its initial starting point, the lights go on, and after 4 sec., the examiner's hand appears near the lights and lights go off. Trial is 13 sec. long; interstimulus interval is 5-sec.	*
5. *Auditory 3*†	†
6. *Masks:* Same as at 3½ and 5½ months except each mask is only shown once.	*
7. *Car*†	†
8. *Bayley scale:* Selected items on the Bayley scale administered in standard form. (See table 4.3.)	
9. *Separation**	*
10. *Social interaction**	*

*Same as at 3½ and 5½ months.
†Same as at 9½ and 11½ months.

Table 4.3. Bayley Developmental Scale items administered at 13½ months of age.[a]

Mental scale item	
104	Pats whistle doll in imitation of examiner.
105	Dangles ring by string in imitation of examiner.
102	Uncovers box to retrieve toy on request.
107	Puts beads in hole in box in imitation of examiner on request.
115	Closes round box in imitation of examiner on request.
109	Places pellet in and removes pellet from bottle on request.
111	Builds tower of 2 cubes in imitation of examiner.
95	Imitates scribbling of examiner.
98	Holds crayon adaptively.
112	Shows spontaneous scribbling with crayon.
125	Imitates definite crayon stroke.
106	Imitates words like "mama," "daddy," "baby."
117	Shows object when asked.
113	Says 2 words during session.
Motor scale item	
47	Stands up from prone position on back on request.
45	Stands alone for few seconds.
46	Walks alone 3 steps without support.
49	Walks sideways watching a pull toy.
50	Walks backwards watching pull toy.

[a] Listed in usual sequence of administration.

Battery at 20 months

Episode	Variables coded
Session I.	
1. *Attachment:* Child is observed for 45 min. in a room containing his mother, an unfamiliar woman, and his primary caretaker from day care center if child is day care subject or a familiar friend of his family if he is a control.	Duration of proximity to each of the three adults Duration of touching each of three adults Duration of looking at each of three adults Number of times child brings toy to each of three adults Number of times child smiles at each of three adults Duration of vocalization Duration of fretting or crying

2. *Light 3:* Same as at 13½ months except 6 standard and 3 transformation trials are given.	*
3. *Auditory 3:* Same as at 13½ months except 6 standard and 3 transformation trials are given.	†
4. *Car:* Same as at 13½ months except 6 standards and 3 transformation trials are given.	†
5. *Discrepant Chromatic Slides:* Child sees a series of 14 chromatic slides one at a time each illuminated for 14½ sec. with no interstimulus interval. In this series 5 of the slides depict discrepant events. The slides are a. Boy and girl b. Man in chair c. Man in dress (discrepant) d. Man and woman e. Cat f. Oversized cat with girl (discrepant) g. Woman setting table h. Woman holding head in hand (discrepant) i. Man in car j. Man with four arms (discrepant) k. Boy l. Girl m. Girl sleeping in tub (discrepant) n. Man in bed	Same as block episode*
6. *Vocabulary recognition:* Child is shown 15 sets of pictures of three objects and asked to point to the object (italicized) that the examiner names. a. *fork* spoon knife	Number of words correctly recognized

b. banana *apple* orange
c. chair sofa *table*
d. *carrot* lettuce tomato
e. shirt skirt *pants*
f. horse *chicken* cow
g. scissors *pot* shoes
h. *tree* cup flower
i. girl standing *girl sitting* policeman standing
j. *toothbrush* row boat duck
k. sink refrigerator *stove*
l. hat *comb* watch
m. moon necklace *star*
n. *clock* baby bottle bookcase
o. *pig* dog cat

SESSION II

1. *Solitary free play:* Child is in room with his mother playing with a set of age-appropriate toys for 21 min.	Duration of attentional involvement with each toy Duration of time child relates 2 or more toys Duration of looking at mother Duration of proximity to mother Duration of each smile Duration of vocalization Duration of fretting or crying
2. *Peer play:* An unfamiliar peer of the same age, sex, and ethnicity as the child enters the room with the peer's mother and a new set of toys is brought in. The subject's behavior is observed for an additional 21 min.	Duration of involvement with each toy Duration of relating 2 or more toys Number of times child initiates aggressive play with peer Number of times child initiates cooperative play with peer Number of times child stays when he is approached by same peer Number of times child withdraws when he is approached by unfamiliar peer Number of times child resists coercion or aggression by unfamiliar peer Duration of proximity to mother

Duration of looking at peer
Duration of looking at mother
Duration of vocalization
Duration of fretting or crying

3. *Bayley scale:* Selected age-appropriate items are administered. (See table 4.4.) — Passing or failing of each item

4. *Separation**

*Same as at 3½ and 5½ months.
†Same as at 9½ and 11½ months.

Battery at 29 months

SESSION I

1. *Maternal description of child's attributes:* The mother is given 16 cards each listing a different attribute typical of 2½-year-olds. She studies each card while the examiner reads them. The mother is asked to rank those behaviors most characteristic of her child by sorting the cards initially into four piles. She is then asked to sort within each pile, thus providing a ranking of the 16 attributes from most to least characteristic of her child. The items are:
   a. Talkative, talks a lot, both alone and with other people
   b. Often will not do as I say
   c. Plays for a long time alone
   d. Dislikes the dark
   e. Wants own way a lot and protests when he or she does not get it
   f. Laughs a lot, tends to smile and laugh easily
   g. Sleeps deeply without interruption
   h. Is patient, does not demand to get his or her way at once
   i. Shy with strange adults
   j. Fights with playmates
   k. Fusses or cries when I leave home
   l. Is very active motorically, likes to run around a lot, enjoys muscular activity
   m. Timid or shy in new places
   n. Cautious before acting; thinks before he or she acts
   o. Plays easily with playmates
   p. Stays with me a lot, does not want to be away from me

TABLE 4.4. BAYLEY DEVELOPMENTAL SCALE ITEMS ADMINISTERED AT 20 MONTHS OF AGE.[a]

Language scale item	
126	Shows comprehension of verbal requests. On request, puts doll in chair, gives doll a drink, wipes doll's nose.
128	Identifies 3 parts of doll.
127	Uses words to make wants known.
36	Says sentence of 2 words.
130	Names 1 picture on request.
132	Names or points to 3 pictures on request.
139	Names or points to 5 pictures on request.
141	Names 3 pictures.
148	Names or points to 7 pictures.
149	Names 5 pictures.
124	Names 1 object.
138	Names 2 objects.
146	Names 3 objects.
Nonlanguage scale item	
119	Builds tower of 3 cubes in imitation of examiner.
143	Builds tower of 6 cubes in imitation.
129	Places 2 round and 2 square blocks correctly in form board.
142	Places any 6 blocks correctly in blue form board.
155	Completes blue form board in 150 sec.
125	Draws definite stroke in any direction in imitation of examiner.
147	Differentiates direction of strokes in imitation.
135	Changes from drawing straight line to scribbling in imitation.
157	Attempts to fold paper in imitation of examiner.
120	Places round block in pink form board.
137	Places all 3 blocks in pink form board.
151	Places all 3 blocks in upside-down block.
154	Makes exact copy or puts 3 blocks in row and pushes them in imitation of examiner's model of a train.

[a] Listed in usual sequence of administration.

EPISODE	VARIABLES CODED
2. *Solitary free play:* Child plays in room with mother and a set of age-appropriate toys for 21 min. as at 20 months.	Duration of each attentional involvement with a toy Relational play, child relates 2 or more toys while playing (pouring imaginary tea into a cup, for example)

	Duration of looking at mother Duration of proximity to mother Duration of smiling Duration of talking Duration of fretting
3. *Free play with an unfamiliar peer:* An unfamiliar peer of the same age, sex, and ethnicity and the peer's mother are introduced into the room with a new set of toys, and the subject is allowed to play for 28 min.	Duration of each attentional involvement with a toy Imitation (within 15 sec.) of an act performed by the peer Duration of talking Duration of fretting Duration of looking at mother Duration of looking at peer Number of initiations of aggression to the peer Number of initiations of cooperative play with the peer Number of times child remains in place when approached by the peer Child withdraws when approached by the peer Child resists coercion or dominance by the peer

4. *Concept Formation Index:* We modified the Concept Familiarity Index developed by Dr. Francis Palmer of the State University of New York at Stony Brook to assess the child's understanding of 31 concepts. The child is seated opposite the tester at a small table and is asked to play a game. For example, the tester presents two small toy dogs and asks the child to "put the dogs *in* the box." Two boxes are available, one is "bottom up," the other open and empty. The child's response is recorded by a coder in the observational room. The concepts are *in, big, littlest of 3, out of, little, biggest of 3, up, white, moving, not moving, black, down, on, under, around, in front of, behind, over, close, open, more, full, long, plate on cloth, hard, empty, soft, short, cloth on plate, top, bottom.*

EPISODE	VARIABLES CODED
5. *Separation:* Same as at 3½ and 5½ months.	Same as at 3½ and 5½ months.

Session II (minimum of 7 days after Session I)

Episode	Variables coded:
1. *Visit to unfamiliar day care center:* The child, mother, and a female observer visit an unfamiliar day care center near our laboratory. Mother, child, and observer enter a room in the day care center with 10 to 15 children of approximately the same age who, along with their teacher, continue their activities. After the mother is seated, the observer codes the subject's behavior for 30 min. If the child appears comfortable, the mother encourages the child to join the other children. The mother is instructed to remain in her seat throughout the session while the coder follows the subject. Eight variables were coded on a prepared form in 10-sec. blocks for 3 10-min. epochs. Each 10-minute epoch was followed by a 2-min. rest period until 30 min. of coding were completed.	Duration of proximity to mother Duration of fretting Duration of looking at another child or group of children Duration of reciprocal play with another child involving cooperative interaction Duration of cooperative play initiated with another child Initiation of an aggressive act directed toward another child Child remains in place when approached by another child Child withdraws when approached by another child Duration of playing with objects or toys

2. *Embedded Figures Task:* Upon returning from the unfamiliar day care center the child is seated at a table opposite the examiner and administered an embedded figures task (see figure 4.6). For the nine practice items the child is to find a picture that is identical with a model, where the foils are similar to the model in form. The child is shown a standard picture, a bird for example, and asked to point to the bird in the illustration that was exactly like the bird on the standard card. The standard always remains present above the illustration. For the critical test items the standard to be located is embedded in a series of distracting lines. There were nine critical test items, three involving a cat, three a car, and three a flower. The examiner records the latency to the child's first response, from the moment search begins until the child offers a solution hypothesis and whether the child's response was correct or incorrect. If incorrect, the child was asked again to find the standard.

Fig. 4.6 *Sample item from Embedded Figures Test.*

3. *Memory for locations:* The task requires the child to recall the location of a familiar object after it is hidden under one of five distinctive containers. For example, the experimenter may hide a toy shoe under a brightly colored pyramidal container. A barrier is placed in front of the containers for 5 sec., the barrier is removed, and the child asked to find the shoe. The number of containers and number of objects hidden are increased from one object under one container to a maximum of 5 containers and 5 objects. During the first 5 training trials only 1 object was hidden under 1, 2, 3, 4, or 5 containers. For the 4 critical test trials, 2, 3, 4, or 5 objects were hidden under the 5 containers. The child is asked to find 1 of the objects. If successful, he is also asked to find a second object. (See figure 4.7.)

4. *Laboratory battery:* After a recess the child is brought to a different testing room and administered 4 of the episodes used on previous test sessions.

EPISODE	VARIABLES CODED
a. *Light:* Same as at 13½ months.	Same as at 13½ months
b. *Auditory 3:* Same as at 13½ months.	Same as at 13½ months
c. *Car:* Same as at 13½ months.	Same as at 13½ months
d. *Slides:* Same as at 20 months.	Same as at 20 months

5. *Interview with Mother:* The last item in the battery is a 30- to 40-min. interview with the mother. Information is gathered on the number of other adults who routinely care for or relate to the subject, past illnesses, mother's opinion about selected aspects of her child's intellectual, social and personality development, amount of time the father was available, and extent of father's involvement in caretaking.

Fig. 4.7 *Stimuli used in memory for locations test.*

Data analysis

Interobserver reliability was assessed for each of the major behavioral variables on a small sample of children at all ages from three and one half to twenty-nine months. We computed the correlation between the scores of two independent coders for a particular child and then averaged the correlations for all the children. The data used in the analyses were for duration of occurrence of the variable in question. When one observer coded a particular variable the duration of occurrence coded by the other observer comprised the second value. Table 4.5 contains the mean and median reliabilities for the variables and sample sizes used in the reliability analysis. When the

TABLE 4.5. INTEROBSERVER RELIABILITIES FOR MAJOR BEHAVIORAL VARIABLES.

VARIABLE	MEAN COEFFICIENT OF RELIABILITY	MEDIAN COEFFICIENT OF RELIABILITY	SAMPLE SIZE
Laboratory episodes			
First fixation	0.82	0.86	33
Total fixation	.89	.93	36
Vocalization	.81	.89	37
Fretting	.87	.93	12
Smiling	.66	.79	14
Activity: lean	.79	.97	19
Activity: wave	.77	.80	44
Activity: twist	.89	.96	15
Activity: search	.89	.94	10
Activity: anticipatory fix	.77	.79	10
Play and attachment episodes			
Length of epoch of play	.95	.97	23
Relational play	.81	.88	16
Proximity to an adult	.86	.99	23
Looking at another person	.89	.94	41
Vocalization	.91	.93	18
Fretting	.89	.96	10
Touching an adult	.78	.99	3

sample sizes are small, it is because that variable did not occur frequently in the sample of children selected for the evaluation of interobserver agreement.

All of the laboratory data, both behavioral and heart rate, were recorded on polygraph charts, and all of the play and attachment data on Esterline-Angus chart paper. Data from the remaining procedures were recorded on specially prepared forms. During the data reduction phase we continually checked on the reliability of the process by assigning a corpus of data already coded by one person to an independent analyst. Over 90 percent of the raw data were checked by at least two people before being punched on cards for computer analyses.

The tachometer records of each child's heart rate were analyzed for absolute heart rate, change in heart rate following onset of the stimulus event, and heart rate range during the trial. The details of this analysis are summarized in chapter 5. Since heart rate is seriously affected by state, especially motoricity and irritability, heart rate was only reduced when the child was attentive. Fixation time had to be 80 percent of total exposure time, and fretting and crying had to be minimal. These rather strict criteria meant that heart rate was not coded on all trials. As with the behavioral data, all reductions of the heart rate data were checked by one other coder. The final corpus of data was placed on tape for computer analyses.

We performed two related analyses of the effects of group care. The first was the comparison of the matched pairs in which each child who attended our day care center was matched on age, sex, ethnicity, and education of both parents with a home control. A second analysis involved all the children in the experimental day care center and all the children in the home control sample, some of whom were not perfect matches. Using this larger home-reared group allowed us to ask about the effects of ethnicity, class, and sex, as well as form of rearing. Maximal sample sizes for the matched pairs analysis was thirty-two pairs—one less than the size of the day care group. The number was a little smaller at some ages. When all the children were included—day care, home control, and mixed groups in order to inquire into the effects of ethnicity or sex—the sample size was 116. Table 4.1 lists the sizes of each group by care, ethnicity, class and sex, and Table 4.6 summarizes the procedures administered at each age.

The total corpus of data is relevant to four separate issues. The first, of course, is the question of differences between the day care and home-reared children; the second involves the differences in profile between the two ethnic or social class groups; the chapter that follows deals primarily with these questions. The study was also designed specifically to inform two theoretical themes that dominate study of the human infant. One has to do with the growth functions for attentiveness, vocalization, excitability, and social play, and the other with the intraindividual stability of these attributes across the first two and one-half years of life.

TABLE 4.6. EPISODES ADMINISTERED TO THE CHILDREN AT EACH AGE.

PROCEDURE	AGE (MOS.)							
	3½	5½	7½	9½	11½	13½	20	29
Social interaction	x	x	x	x	x	x		
Block	x	x	x	x	x			
Auditory 1: meaning to nonsense	x	x	x	x	x			
Masks	x	x		x		x		
Light	x	x	x	x	x	x	x	x
Auditory 2: meaning to meaning	x	x						
Separation	x	x	x	x	x	x	x	x
Bayley items			x			x	x	
Auditory 3: word order				x	x	x	x	x
Car				x	x	x	x	x
Slides: five sequences				x	x			
Free play: solo and peer						x	x	x
Attachment							x	
Discrepant slides							x	x
Vocabulary							x	
Concept index								x
Visit to unfamiliar day care center								x
Embedded Figures Test								x
Memory for locations								x

5 The Effect of Group Care and the Influence of Ethnicity

> So my answer to the question "How do you know? What is the source or the basis of your assertion? What observations have led you to it?" would be: I do not know: my assertion was merely a guess. Never mind the source or the sources . . . But if you are interested in the problem which I tried to solve by my tentative assertion, you may help me by criticizing it as severely as you can; and if you can design some experimental test which you think might refute my assertion, I shall gladly, and to the best of my powers, help you to refute it.
>
> Karl Popper, *Conjectures and Refutations*

The form of presentation in this chapter is relatively straightforward. We shall consider first the growth functions for the attentiveness, vocalization, smiling, activity, and irritability responses to the visual and auditory episodes that were administered from three and one-half to twenty-nine months. We expected each of the above variables to display regular developmental functions, anticipating that there would be a U-shaped function for duration of attention for visual and auditory episodes, but a more linear function for frequency of vocalization and smiling. The obvious advantage of a longitudinal design is that it permits the investigator to compare independent groups with respect to their developmental functions for a particular response rather than to rely on group differences at one point in time.

This section is followed by a discussion of the cognitive battery and the measures of attachment, separation distress, and social play administered at the older ages. We performed two related analyses in order to assess the effect of participation in the day care program. In the more stringent test, we compared pairs of children who were matched on sex, ethnicity, and social class. One member of the pair attended the day care center; the other was reared totally at home. The second analysis, which involved all the children in the sample, was typically an analysis of variance with care and ethnicity as independent factors. Since the day care and home-reared infants were so similar in psychological profile, while the Chinese and Caucasian children differed, we shall dwell as much on the latter findings as on the former.

Patterns of response to visual and auditory events

Although attentiveness and affectivity to the visual and auditory episodes displayed obvious growth functions across the period three and one-half through twenty-nine months, there were no consistent effects of form of care on either level of reactivity or shape of the growth function that related age to responsiveness. This conclusion held for the matched pairs of day care subjects and their home controls as well as the total group. Of the three independent variables—care, ethnicity, and social class—form of care was clearly the least important. No test episode produced consistent differences between day care and home control children at two or more ages, nor were the few correlations between care and ethnicity noted in one episode typically present in another. (See figures 5.1-5.3.) The developmental functions for attentiveness, vocalization, smiling, activity, and irritability seemed to be affected more by maturational forces and the specific characteristics of the stimulus event than by the experiences associated with home or day care environments.

The occurrence of smiling provides a particularly nice example of the importance of the stimulus event; each of the episodes produced a different growth function. The human stimulus, the female adult in the social interaction procedure, provoked a great deal of smiling among infants during the early part of their first year (about 80 percent of the 3-month-olds smiled at her), but smiling decreased with age (only 40 percent of the 13-month-olds

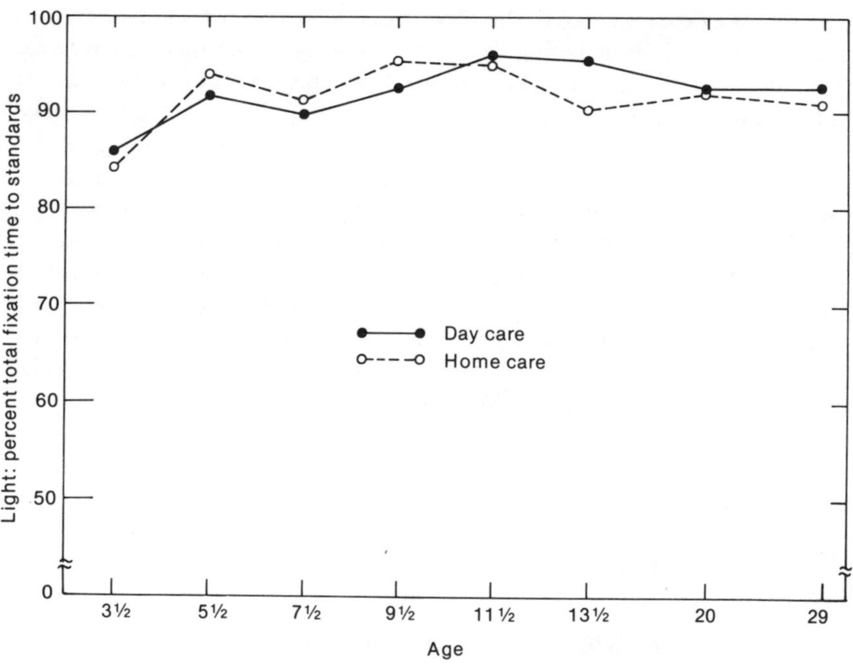

Fig. 5.1 *Growth functions for percent total fixation time to the light episode, for day care subjects and home controls.*

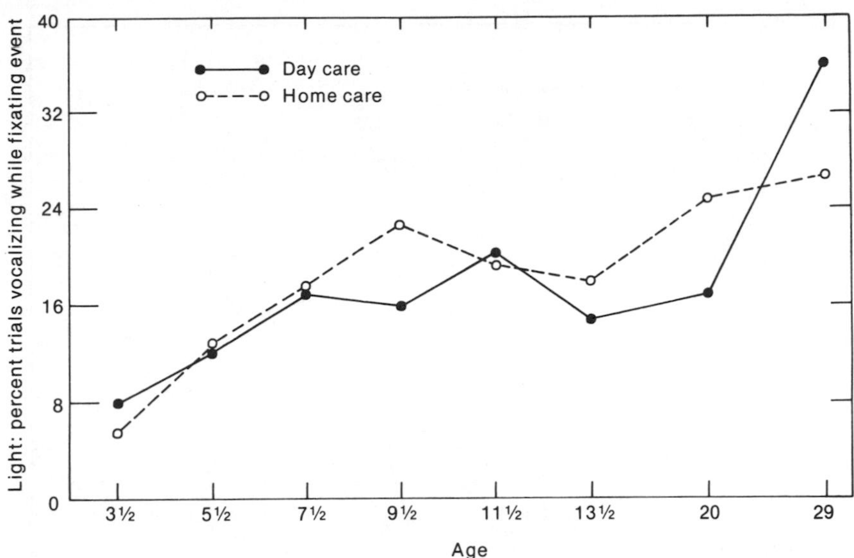

Fig. 5.2 *Growth functions for percentage of trials of light episode during which the child vocalized, for day care subjects and home controls.*

smiled). Smiling in response to the nonsocial block, light, and car episodes displayed the opposite function. Smiling was generally infrequent during the first year of life (less than 20 percent smiled) but increased substantially with age so that over half of the children smiled in response to the light and the car at twenty and twenty-nine months; this fact implies an increased capacity to assimilate the discrepant experience contained in those episodes. The growth function for smiling in response to the nonsocial visual events parallels the growth of fear to the less comprehensible discrepant events (for example, a jack-in-the-box or maternal departure). The parallel is in accord with the theoretical suggestion discussed earlier that toward the end of his first year, the infant can retrieve complex schemata from memory with greater ease than before and is able to compare them with present experience and thus is more likely either to assimilate discrepant events quickly or to be left in a state of uncertainty as a result of failure of assimilation. Since the light and car were dynamic events occurring for six to ten seconds each, it was probably difficult for the child under one year of age to establish a well-articulated schema for them. The older infant's enhanced competences for retrieval and comparison may have facilitated his establishing a schema for these events and eventually assimilating them. The very low rate of smiling in response to the auditory episode, even at twenty-months, is a result most likely of the fact that even the 2-year-old's schemata for language were not sufficiently firm to permit the child to relate the information to a pre-existing structure.

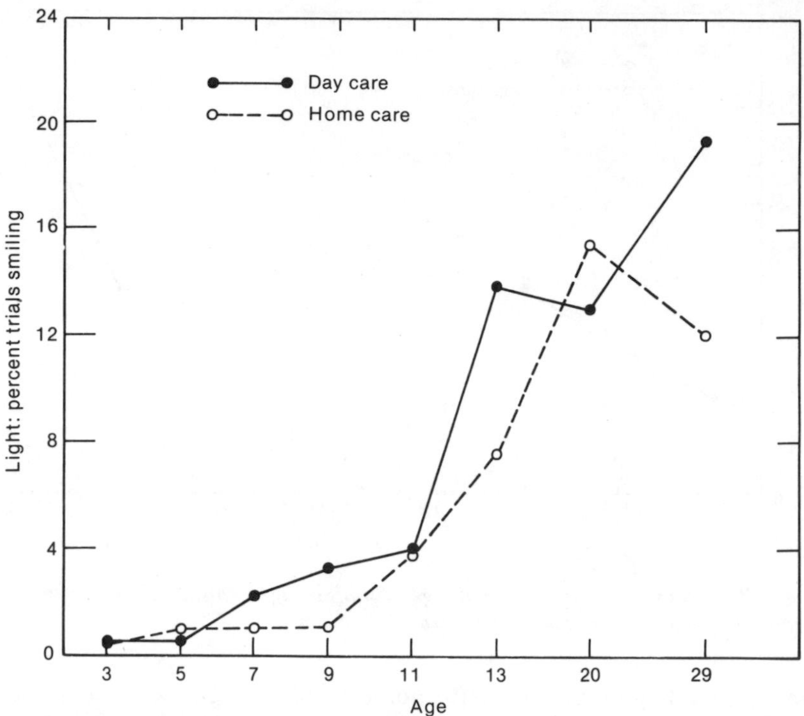

Fig. 5.3 *Growth functions for smiling in light episode for day care subjects and home controls (percentage of trials during which the child smiled).*

The growth functions for vocalization, which was more frequent than smiling, were more similar across episodes. On most episodes, 50 to 75 percent of the children vocalized at least once; by twenty-nine months of age they vocalized in about 30 percent of the trials. Vocalization increased with age for most episodes, with the exception of masks and social interaction. It is more probable that the unfamiliar examiner and masks elicited uncertainty and subsequent inhibition of vocalization than that these events were so easy to assimilate that no excitement was generated. Vocalization increased from three through nine months of age and again from thirteen through twenty-nine months. The existence of a plateau from nine to thirteen months implies a period of inhibition corresponding to the emergence of wariness toward a variety of discrepant events.

Irritability and restless twisting generally showed inverted U-shaped functions with peak irritability and restlessness from nine to thirteen months, followed by a sharp decline at twenty-nine months. Smiling displayed a complementary relation to twisting and fretting. When the latter two responses were increasing, smiling remained low, but as twisting and fretting declined, smiling increased. If we assume that smiling reflects assimilation of an event, it appears that prior to assimilation there is a period of tension and irritability. As the child matures and becomes better able to assimilate the event, motoricity and irritability decline. But despite the extraordinary variability in the level of and developmental pattern for these responses, day care and home-reared infants were remarkably similar in their reactivity to each of the episodes.

Empirical support for the emergence of a new phase of cognitive functioning at around eight months of age, which was discussed in chapter 2, was revealed in the selected occurrence of U-shaped growth functions for attentiveness—fixation time for the visual episodes and search in response to the auditory episodes. Both day care and home-reared infants displayed these functions, in response to the last transformation and three return trials of the light, and to all three phases of the auditory episode. (See figures 5.4 and 5.5.)

Examination of fixation times in the block episode over the period from three to eleven months of age revealed that 67 percent of the children showed a U-shaped curvilinear function to the standard, transformation, and return trials or to more than one of these phases. The modal age for the trough in attention to the block was seven months; seventy percent of the infants whose data displayed the U-shaped function showed their shortest fixation times at seven and one-half months. The U-shaped function occurred most often to the return trials.

In the light episode the theoretically expected curvilinear function (with a trough at seven months) occurred to the last transformation trial, and the three return trials (see figure 5.4); evaluation of the curvilinear function was accomplished by computing the *F* values for the quadratic component of a repeated measures analysis of variance. The *F* value was statistically significant for the three return trials of the light ($F = 3.89, p < 0.05$).

Inspection of each child's fixation times revealed that 76 percent of the children showed a trough to the standard, transformation, and return trials or to two or three of these phases and the modal age was seven months. Over 90 percent of the children who showed a trough displayed it at seven or nine months. About 80 percent showed a trough to the three return trials or to both the return and transformation trials and 6 percent showed a curvilinear function to all three phases of the episode—standard, transformation and return trials.

The growth function for search to the auditory episode, defined as the simultaneous occurrence of motor inhibition, saccadic movements of the eyes, and a posture implying alert attentiveness, was also U-shaped for all three phases of the episode (see figure 5.5), with an unambiguous trough at seven and one-half months. The statistical test for curvilinearity revealed a significant quadratic component for each of the three phases of the episode. ($F = 4.11, p < 0.05$ for the standards; $F = 4.69, p < 0.05$ for the

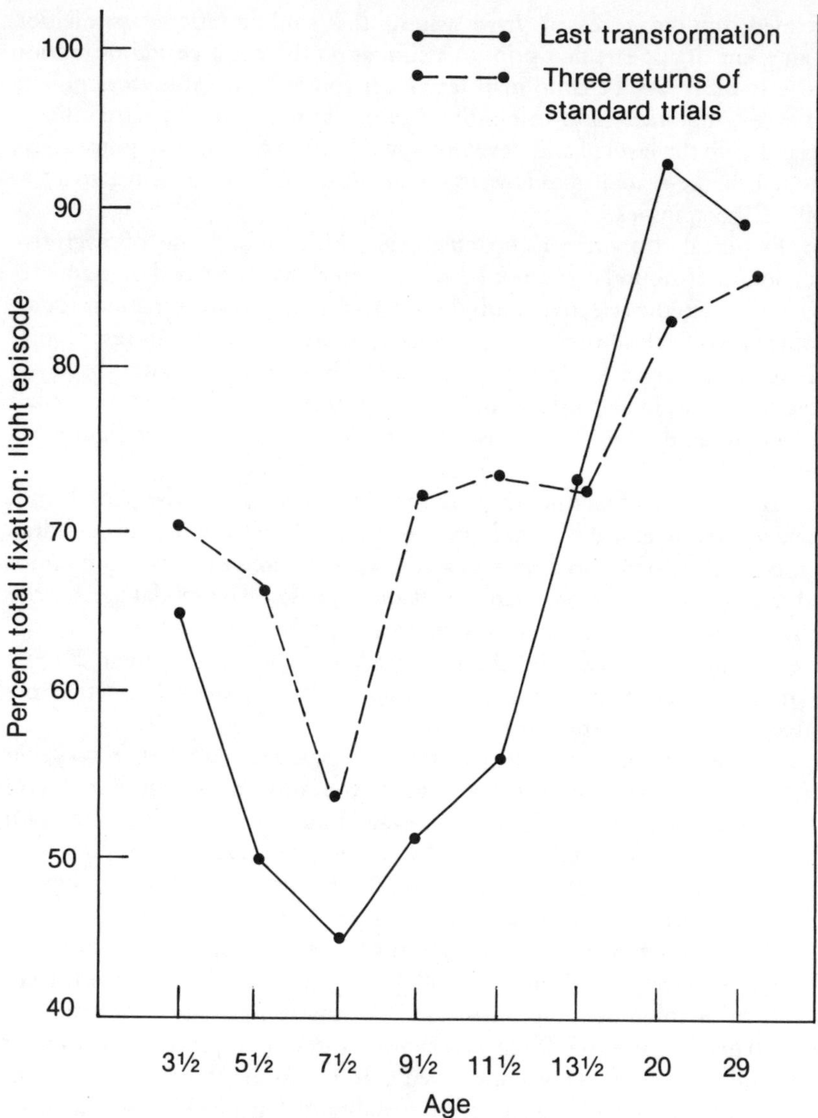

Fig. 5.4 *Percent total fixation time to the light episode for the last transformation and the returns of standard.*

Fig. 5.5 (*opposite*) ***Percent total search in the auditory episode for the three phases of the episode.***

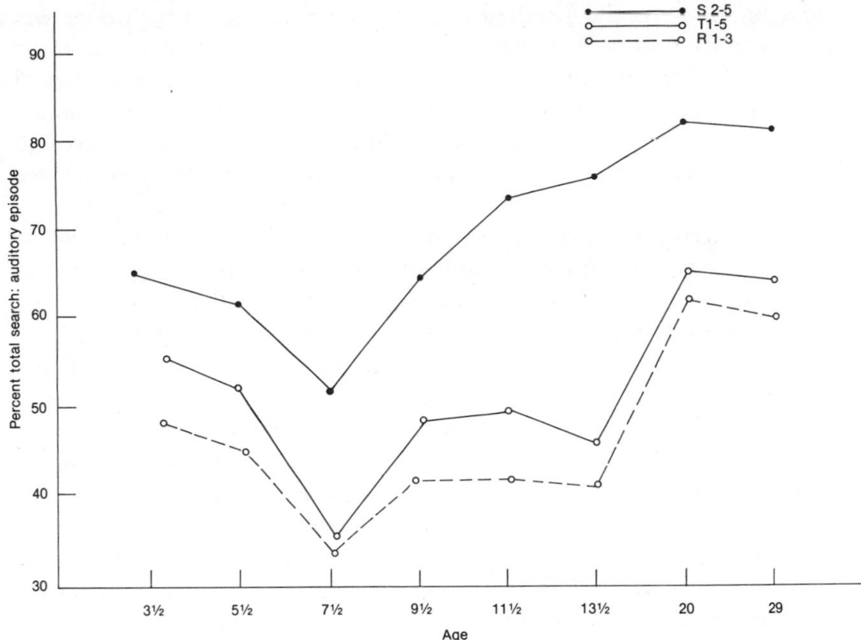

transformations; $F = 5.74$, $p < 0.01$ for the returns).*

The increase in search behavior for the transformation and return trials at twenty and twenty-nine months implies that the older children treated the word order transformation as a more serious discrepancy than the 13-month-olds. We suggest that the younger children treated the transformation as an acoustic discrepancy, whereas the older children treated it as a linguistic discrepancy. Perhaps the 5-month-olds assimilated the event to their schema for the qualities of a human voice, whereas the 20-month-olds tried to relate the words in the distorted communication to their representation of the meaning of the grammatically correct phrase presented during the standard. From thirteen to twenty months of age is the period when spoken language appeared in almost all of the children. The fact that search behavior in response to speech began to rise at nine months, at least four or five months before the subjects spoke any words, is in accord with the popular hypothesis that the child's cognitive appreciation of language precedes his verbal expression.

Examination of the individual records revealed that 78 percent of the children showed a U-shaped function for search to standard, transformation,

*In chapter 5 all references to auditory episode for the period 13-29 months are to the Auditory 3 stimuli. References to Auditory 2 for the period 3-11 months are to Auditory 2 for 3 and 5 months and to Auditory 3 for 9 and 11 months.

and return or two or three of these phases. The modal age for the trough was seven months, and the curvilinear function was most likely to occur to the standards and transformations. Of the infants who showed the U-shaped function, 65 percent displayed the trough in attentiveness at seven months. The middle-class Caucasian girls, the children who would be advanced in language at 3 years of age, were most likely to display the trough to all three phases of the episode.

The curvilinear growth function for search behavior in response to speech is remarkably similar to that found in the study of the development of a sample of Indian children living in two isolated villages in northwest Guatemala, which was described in chapter 2 (Kagan et al., unpublished). In that study an auditory episode was administered to eighty-seven infants between five and twenty-seven months of age. Each child heard a recording of an Indian dialect phrase best translated as "Come here, I'll pick you up" repeated for twelve trials followed by five repetitions of a meaningless phrase and then three repetitions of the original standard. The occurrence of search behavior (which was coded only once per stimulus trial) followed a U-shaped function for infants in both villages with a trough at seven to eight months.

The entire corpus of data we have dealt with thus far is in accord with the earlier suggestion that new cognitive competences appear in most infants as they enter the last few months of their first year. It appears that these new processes, which seem to mature at the same time in both day care and home-reared infants, exerted a more important influence on the infants' reactivity to our episodes than did the experiences associated with form of rearing.

Ethnicity had the most consistent influence across episodes and age, even though the Chinese and the Caucasian children did not differ on all episodes. The Caucasian infants were generally more vocal and smiled more than the Chinese, especially during the first year. Although the 3½-month-old Chinese children smiled at the female examiner during the opening minutes of the session as often as the Caucasians—80 percent of the infants smiled at this early age—the older Caucasian infants smiled more frequently than the Chinese. The later difference in smiling is likely to reflect the acquired tendency to display social smiling to an initially unfamiliar adult. We suggest that the home experiences of the Caucasian children, which apparently were not altered by the day care environment, disposed them to smile at an actively interacting adult. Generalizations about ethnic differences in smiling must be restricted according to the age of the child and the information to which he is responding. Since large ethnic differences in smiling occurred after seven months, not earlier, we favor an interpretation that emphasizes the role of family experience, although we cannot rule out biological factors.

Caucasians were also more vocal on most of the episodes, with the exception of the initial interaction with the examiner, but this difference did not appear until the end of their first year of life. As with smiling, ethnic differences in frequency of vocalization during the last part of the first year may be a product of differences either in the infant's inherent temperament or in experiences at home. Because the ethnic differences in vocalization occurred primarily to the nonsocial episodes (light and block), it is unlikely that this effect is due to direct conditioning of vocalization. Caucasian children had not been rewarded at home for vocalizing to a light or block episode. However, the Caucasian infants' stronger disposition to vocalize may be the result of dynamic interactions with parents in which vocalization was generated by gamelike encounters so that they acquired a tendency to vocalize when aroused by interesting events. We are unsure about the role of temperament as a mediator of this difference in vocalization for two reasons: first, because it did not occur until after five months of age and was absent at some ages, and second, because data on rural, isolated Guatemalan infants support the experiential interpretation. The block, light, car, and auditory episodes were administered to a group of isolated children living in eastern Guatemalan subsistence farming villages. Although there were minimal differences in frequency of smiling between the Guatemalan infants and the North American day care or home-reared children, there were extraordinary differences in vocalization—the Guatemalan infants were extremely quiet. Observation of the Guatemalan infants in their homes revealed a frequency of verbal interaction between mother and child that was far less than has been observed in North American families.

The ethnic differences in smiling and vocalization seem to have little to do with level of cognitive functioning. There were no ethnic differences in level of attentiveness or form of the growth function for fixation time. There is no indication that the cognitive development of Chinese and Caucasian children proceeds at a different rate, only that Caucasians are a little more excitable and less inhibited (Bronson 1972). This effect was also noted in social situations.

Statements about ethnic differences in a particular response or growth function must always specify the stimulus situation to which the child is responding. There was no growth function for smiling in general, only for smiling to a particular episode. The ethnic differences in smiling or vocalization were specific to certain episodes at certain ages. The infants' profile of reactivity did not reveal a general factor that might be called "developmental level of competence." Rather, there seemed to be many single threads that changed their qualities with development, implying that it may not be theoretically useful to ascribe to an infant a unified cognitive competence that can be assumed to generalize across tasks at all ages.

Infants differ, of course, in the age at which a specific competence or function emerges, peaks, or declines. But these differences seem trivial in comparison with the more impressive variation that is the product of maturational forces operating on the information available in any reasonably normal environment.

Primatologists also study the emergence, growth, and decline of different behavioral systems in the developing animal. Mouthing among very young macaques, for example, is replaced by rough-and-tumble play after a few months. Primatologists do not assign developmental quotients to infant monkeys based on how adroitly each young monkey mouths another, expecting the score to predict the quality of later rough-and-tumble play, because they realize that each of these response systems has an inevitable but only temporary place in ontogeny.

Some developmental psychologists may have erred in committing themselves to the theoretical usefulness of a single index of level of development and treating phenotypically different and often unrelated behaviors as potential reflections of that evaluative construct. The infant seems to possess a set of differentiated response systems whose organization is adjusted following external encounters in a way that is in accord with the child's maturational stage. We suspect that the principles that describe these changes must include a detailed statement of context and that ranking children on a single index of ability distorts nature in a serious way.

Stability of behavior across age

In chapter 1 we suggested that most parents and social scientists in our society favor the idea that the young child's psychological qualities are biased toward stability unless environmental changes force new profiles upon the child. But the available evidence summarized in chapter 3, although meager, does not favor that assumption. This study furnishes information relevant to that question because the dramatic differences among infants under one year in level of attentiveness and tendency to vocalize, smile, or display restless activity were not predictive of variation in similar qualities during the second and third years. For example, infants who were highly attentive or very vocal during the first 9 months were not extremely attentive or vocal 12 months later. (See tables 5.1 and 5.2.)

When the stability of each response was examined by episode, the pattern of cross-age correlations for each episode tended to reveal two generalizations. First, there was intraindividual stability over one or two ages but rarely long-term stability from 5, 7, or 9 months to 20 or 29 months. Typically, attention at 5 months was correlated with attentiveness at 7 months; 7 with 9 and 11; and 9 with 11, 13, and occasionally 20 months, or 13 with 20 and 20 with 29 months. The response remained stable for periods of less than 10 months; there were very few instances in which attentiveness at 3 or 5 months predicted attentiveness after the first birthday. In general, the period between 7 and 11 months was the best time to predict future atten-

TABLE 5.1. CROSS-AGE STABILITY FOR AVERAGE TOTAL FIXATION TIME (ALL TRIALS, ALL CHILDREN).

	AGE (MOS.)[a]						
AGE (MOS.)	5	7	9	11	13	20	29
3	.04	.12	.13	.13	.07	−.09	−.01
5		*.36*	*.42*	.19	*.29*	*.34*	.02
7			*.36*	*.37*	.14	*.32*	.23
9				*.47*	*.38*	*.38*	.22
11					*.27*	*.42*	.20
13						*.41*	.15
20							*.31*

[a] Coefficients in italics are significant at $p < 0.05$ or better.

TABLE 5.2. STABILITY OF VOCALIZATION ACROSS AGE FOR ALL SUBJECTS.[a]

AGE (MOS.)	3	5	7	9	11	13	20	29
3		0.11	0.08	0.28[b]	0.17	0.13	0.03	0.25
5			.12	.32[c]	.07	.05	−.09	.11
7				.26[b]	.23[b]	.05	.14	.01
9					.53[d]	.32[c]	.33[c]	.41[c]
11						.28[b]	.16	.28[b]
13							.26[b]	.25
20								.22
3	. . .	.24	.17	.30	.30	.28	.24	.36
5	−.04	. . .	.18	.58[d]	.16	.07	−.04	.03
7	−.05	.01	. . .	.25	.11	−.02	.14	−.01
9	.22	.01	.16	. . .	.57[d]	.37[b]	.05	.50[c]
11	.02	−.05	.22	.42[c]	. . .	.39[b]	.00	.44[b]
13	.04	.01	−.04	.20	.14	. . .	−.03	.62[d]
20	−.11	−.23	.02	.37[b]	.13	.30	. . .	.46[b]
29	.07	.29	−.06	.29	.04	−.02	−.07	. . .

[a] Chinese to right and above diagonal; Caucasians to the left and below.

[b] $p < 0.05$.

[c] $p < 0.01$.

[d] $p < 0.001$.

tiveness, while attentiveness at 3 or 5 months was minimally related to behavior at a future date. In a final analysis we pooled the data across episodes. We standardized each child's total fixation time for those episodes that were positively intercorrelated at each age and computed an average *z* score for the percent total fixation to all trials for the pooled episodes at each age. At 3 and 5 months the average *z* score was based on attentiveness to block, light, and mask; at 7 months to block and light; at 9 and 11 months to block, light, and car; and at 13, 20, and 29 months to light and car.

Attentiveness at 3 months did not predict attentiveness at any future age and attentiveness prior to 20 months was unrelated to fixation times at 29 months. Significant, although modest, correlations held for the period 5 to 20 months (*r* ranged from 0.27 to 0.42) (see table 5.1).

These standardized indexes of attentiveness revealed no consistently significant difference between day care and home-reared groups or between Chinese and Caucasian children. Attentiveness was monitored, we believe, by a profound interaction among the nature of the event, the child's understanding of the stimulus, and temperamental factors. The generally modest stability correlations from 5 months on imply that individual differences in attentiveness to these discrepant events during the opening months of life do not provide a sensitive preview of attentiveness at age 2 or 3. This conclusion is affirmed by similar data from an earlier longitudinal study (Kagan 1971) and from recent tests on a group of 10-year-olds who had participated as infants in that earlier study. We found no important relation between variation in attentiveness to visual episodes during the first year and intelligence scale scores, reading ability, memory for sentences, or reflection-impulsivity at 10 years of age. The dramatic variation in attentiveness among young infants may have little future consequence.

The stability of differences in vocalization varied by ethnic group. There was minimal stability among the Caucasian infants, and moderate among the Chinese. Because each child's level of vocalization tended to be similar across different episodes at a given age, we created a summary variable for each child: the mean proportion of trials a child vocalized for all of the visual and auditory episodes at a given age (social interaction was omitted). The intercorrelations among the scores at each of the eight ages were computed for Chinese and Caucasian children separately as well as for the combined group (see table 5.2).

Although there was little cross-age stability among the Caucasians, among the Chinese there was moderate stability from 9 months on. Vocalization at 9 months predicted behavior at 11, 13, and 29 months; vocalization at 11 months predicted behavior at 13 and 29; vocalization at 13 and 20 predicted behavior at 29 months. The apparently greater stability of vocalization among the Chinese may be due to the continuity of a tendency to vocalize or to be completely quiet, rather than continuity of a level of response, since many more Chinese than Caucasians failed to vocalize at all.

Smiling was so infrequent prior to 9 months that it was impossible to assess either its generality from episode to episode or its stability. Even after 9 months, cross-episode generality was low. In order to compute stability of the response from age to age, we averaged the child's smiling across all episodes at a particular age, excepting social interaction. The resulting coefficients revealed no cross-age stability for any pair of ages (the highest phi coefficient was + .21). There does not seem to be a stable individual disposition to smile, at least in response to these episodes, that subdues the power of the specific task and the child's developmental stage.

Fretfulness showed short-term stability over periods as long as a year, but not longer. Fretting at 9 months correlated with irritability at 11 and 20 months, but not at 13 or 29 months. Fretting at 3, 5, or 7 months was not predictive of later irritability. The disposition to display restless twisting showed short-term stability for periods of 2 to 9 months but not longer.

With the exception of vocalization among the Chinese infants, cross-episode generality and cross-age stability were not robust. Variation among infants younger than 9 months in attention, vocalization, smiling, and motor activity had minimal power to predict phenotypically similar behaviors during the second and third years of life. The evidence does not support the notion that there exist individual dispositions for attentiveness, affectivity, or activity that are stable from the middle of the first year through 29 months of age. As we have indicated, the nature of the task and the child's developmental stage exert a greater influence on infant behavior than inherent, individual dispositions.

Ethnic differences in cardiac lability

The changing levels of heart rate during periods of rest or attentiveness are influenced both by sympathetic and parasympathetic stimulation as well as by forces intrinsic to the structure of the heart. When a child or adult attends to a visual or auditory event his heart rate seems to pass through three successive phases (Porges 1974). During the first two seconds the reaction appears to be mediated by the vagus nerve and corresponds to what physiologists call the orienting reflex. A secondary response occurs within two to six seconds after stimulus onset. The amount and direction of change in heart rate are functions of the intensity and informational value of the stimulus event. If the stimulus is intense, unexpected, or causes a startle the heart rate typically rises; if the event is of interest, anticipated, and not too intense the heart decelerates. The secondary response is followed by a sustained tonic response, which seems to be under more voluntary control. During this third phase, sustained attention to an event is often, but not always, accompanied by a decrease in the variability of heart rate and a greater coupling of cardiac and respiratory rate (Porges, in press). It may be that the individual differences in variability of heart rate apparent in newborns are due to differences in sustained attention or to differences in the balance between sympathetic-excitatory and parasympathetic-inhibitory influences on the heart.

We coded the variability of each child's heart rate during each stimulus presentation in our tests because our informal observations of the infants had suggested marked variation in this attribute and infants who had seemed to us to be behaviorally more inhibited had tended to have less variable heart rates (see figure 5.6 for examples of high and low variable heart rates). One obvious index of variability is *heart rate range*. It is defined as the difference between the highest and lowest heart rate on those trials when the child was highly attentive and not irritable. Trials when fixation time was less than 80 percent or when more than one second of fretting occurred were omitted from consideration; thus the child's absolute heart rate levels are not near the upper limit of the child's cardiac range.

To our surprise, the Caucasian infants displayed larger heart rate ranges on most trials of all episodes at almost every age, although there were no social class or rearing differences in heart rate variability. This consistent difference between Chinese and Caucasian infants was not solely a function of larger or more frequent cardiac decelerations or accelerations among the Caucasians. In a separate analysis, we compared the heart rate ranges of the two groups for those trials in which neither an acceleration nor deceleration occurred; that is, when the child showed no obvious change in heart rate on the stimulus trial compared with the three seconds prior to the onset of that trial. The Chinese continued to show smaller average heart range values than Caucasians at most ages and in most episodes. Even when we eliminated all trials on which a vocalization, smile, or motor action occurred as well as all trials on which a deceleration or acceleration occurred, the Chinese

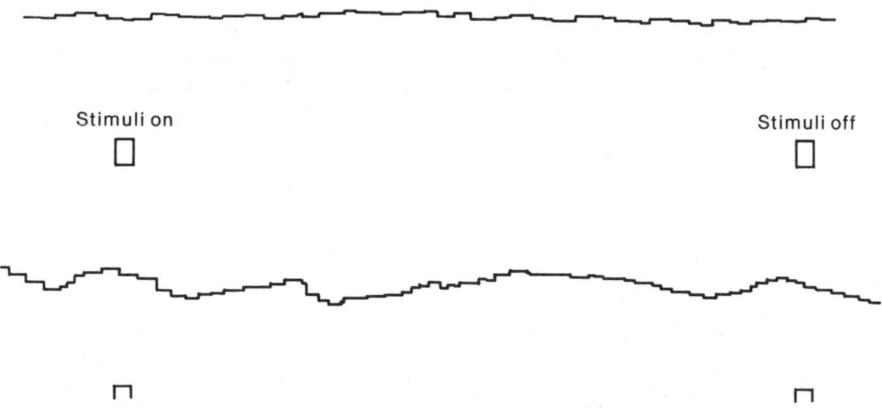

Fig. 5.6 *Samples of low and high variable heart rates.*

continued to have smaller heart rate range values. Finally we correlated, for Chinese and Caucasians separately, the mean of each child's two lowest ranges (for all episodes at a particular age) with the proportion of trials on which the child vocalized, smiled, waved, fretted, twisted, as well as the percent of fixation time. There was no consistent relation between attentiveness, fretting, vocalization, or motoricity and the magnitude of the child's two lowest heart rate ranges.

In order to determine if the Chinese children also had more restricted heart rate range under conditions when they were not attending to any event, we computed the range values for the 5 seconds prior to the beginning of each episode—a time when the child was seated on his mother's lap but his attention was not directed at any particular event. For a random sample of ten Chinese and ten Caucasian infants, the range values were again smaller for the Chinese than for the Caucasians at 5, 9, 11, and 13 months of age. Hence the ethnic difference is not restricted to those times when the child is maximally attentive.

The stability of heart rate range Because the Chinese children had less variable heart rates at every age, and no other variable yielded such a consistent ethnic difference, we evaluated the long-range stability of cardiac lability. The two variables chosen for analysis were the mean of the two lowest ranges during each episode and a derived variable, the average of the mean of the two lowest ranges across all episodes at a particular age. The correlation between these two variables was remarkably high, typically 0.70 to 0.85. The correlations were computed separately for the two ethnic groups since a positive relation for the entire sample might reflect a difference between the groups rather than the rank order stability of the children within each ethnic group. The data revealed remarkable stability for the Chinese and moderate stability for the Caucasians (see table 5.3). Among the Chinese, the range at 3 and 5 months predicted the range during the first year, and from 7 months on the range was stable at all ages. For example, the values at 7 months correlated with the two lowest ranges at every succeeding age (for example, + .80 at 9 months; + .52 at 29 months). Among the Caucasians, stability was present but less consistent. Not only was heart rate more stable for the Chinese, but its stability was more impressive for Chinese than for Caucasians. Moreover, the magnitude of these stability correlations, as well as the duration of the stability, exceeded that found for any other behavioral variable quantified in this investigation.

The persistence of the lower heart rate ranges for the Chinese infants was revealed in an analysis in which we divided the distribution of the mean of the two lowest ranges at each age (across all episodes) at the median and determined which children were consistently above or below the median on 6, 7, or all of the 8 ages at which the laboratory episodes were administered. All of the 11 infants whose range values were consistently low were Chinese.

TABLE 5.3. CROSS-AGE STABILITY FOR THE MEAN OF THE TWO LOWEST RANGES, EPISODES POOLED (CHINESE AND CAUCASIAN SEPARATELY AND CHINESE AND CAUCASIAN POOLED).[a]

CHINESE AND CAUCASIAN SEPARATELY								
AGE (MOS.)	3	5	7	9	11	13	20	29
3	. . .	.31	.53[b]	.61[d]	.57[c]	.77[d]	.05	.39
5	.16	. . .	.44[b]	.53[c]	.53[c]	.30	.37	.39
7	.32	.07	. . .	.80[d]	.73[d]	.61[d]	.46[b]	.52[b]
9	−.10	.21	.01	. . .	.74[d]	.56[d]	.49[c]	.43[b]
11	.31	.32	.53[c]	.25	. . .	.75[d]	.59[d]	.61[c]
13	−.26	.01	−.11	.59[d]	.32	. . .	.50[c]	.54[c]
20	.25	.11	.65[d]	−.13	.58[c]	−.29	. . .	.54[c]
29	−.25	.10	.17	.52[b]	.37	.34	.33	. . .

ALL SUBJECTS—CHINESE AND CAUCASIANS POOLED								
AGE (MOS.)	3	5	7	9	11	13	20	29
3	. . .	.27	.44[c]	.26	.43[c]	.21	.21	.15
5		. . .	.30[b]	.42[d]	.48[d]	.19	.28[b]	.29
7			. . .	.49[d]	.63[d]	.31[b]	.55[d]	.41[c]
9				. . .	.51[d]	.58[d]	.30[b]	.47[c]
11					. . .	.52[d]	.58[d]	.52[d]
13						. . .	.21	.47[c]
20							. . .	.48[c]
20								

[a] Chinese to the right and above the diagonal; Caucasians to the left and below.
[b] $p < 0.05$.
[c] $p < 0.01$.
[d] $p < 0.001$.

Eight of the 11 children whose values were consistently high were Caucasian ($p < 0.05$ by exact test).

Stability of heart rate range has been found in other samples. More than 10 years ago we had collected data on heart rate reactivity to two auditory episodes (resembling the ones administered here) on a group of firstborn Caucasian infants seen at 8 and 13 months of age who were part of the longitudinal sample described by Kagan (1971). To compare it with the findings reported above, we reanalyzed the heart rate data for cardiac range for 27 boys and 27 girls who had good data at both 8 and 13 months. The stability correlation for the mean of the two lowest ranges was + .44 ($p <$ 0.01), which is comparable to the coefficient obtained with this sample.

We also compared heart rate data we had gathered during two visual episodes and one auditory episode for the 8 middle-class Cambridge children described in chapter 2 whom we followed from 6 to 13 months of age. These children had been administered the same visual and auditory episodes each month. Heart rate range was remarkably stable for the 7-months interval; the average stability correlation from age 6 to 13 months was + .78.

Although longitudinal data gathered by Lewis and his colleagues on 15 to 17 infants seen at 2, 4, 12, 24, 36, and 56 weeks of age revealed less impressive intraindividual stability of heart rate range, it should be noted that these data were gathered during a 15-minute rest period rather than during periods of attentiveness to visual or auditory events (Lewis et al. 1970). Nonetheless, despite the small sample size, variability at 4 weeks was moderately correlated with variability at 24 weeks ($r =$ + .43); and variability at 36 weeks correlated with variability at 56 weeks ($r =$ + .38).

The various sources of evidence indicate that heart rate range may be one of the most stable individual attributes of infants during the first two years of life.

As will be seen, the Chinese children showed more inhibition in unfamiliar social situations and more distress at separation from the mother than did Caucasians. Since it was the Chinese children who had less variable heart rates, it is possible that children with a disposition to be inhibited in uncertain situations might also be more vigilant in our laboratory situation. This is a reasonable possibility as studies of children and adults imply that an attentively vigilant attitude toward unexpected events is associated with the stabilization of heart rate. A piece of evidence from an earlier longitudinal study conducted at the Fels Research Institute is in partial accord with this speculation (Kagan and Moss 1962). In a special session in that study the heart rate variability of thirty young adult males, who were Caucasian and primarily middle class, was assessed during a ten-minute rest period. For each subject the trough-to-peak differences in each cardiac cycle during the ten minutes were measured, and the third quartile value was selected as the index of cardiac variability, which John and Beatrice Lacey have called cardiac arrhythmia. Fourteen of the men had been rated on behavioral passivity on the basis of observational data gathered during their first three years of life. The index of passivity emphasized behavioral inhibition to uncertain and challenging situations: "The six boys [of the 14] who were below the median on early passivity were all above the median on degree of heart rate arrhythmia in adulthood. Of the eight most passive boys, six were below the median on cardiac variability in adulthood ($p < 0.05$). Thus passivity in childhood was associated with a minimal degree of spontaneous cardiac arrhythmia in adulthood'' (Kagan and Moss 1962, p. 81). These data hint at a relation between a temperamental disposition favoring inhibition in uncertain contexts and a more stable cardiac rhythm. A stable temperamental disposition may be lurking beneath the surface of those provocative findings and we plan to probe this intriguing relation more deeply in the future.

Cognitive functioning from thirteen to twenty-nine months

Although form of rearing seems to have had little influence on the pattern or level of attentiveness or affectivity to moderately interesting visual and auditory events, these events tapped but a limited aspect of the infants' psychological functioning. We shall now consider the assessments of more complex cognitive competences administered during the children's second and third years—memory for locations, embedded figures, conceptual vocabulary, and scores on the Bayley developmental scales.

Memory for locations (*twenty-nine months*) No child failed to understand the requirements of the task and all passed the preliminary practice items. Most children were successful when one or two items were hidden but had difficulty when three or more items were hidden under one of the five receptacles. Only 20 percent of the children were able to retrieve the first object requested when asked to find one of five different toys hidden under five different receptacles. Because this result was not different from chance expectation, it may be that the five-item problem was too difficult for these children. There was no difference in performance between the day care and home-reared children nor between the different ethnic or class groups (see table 5.4). Since willingness and a capacity to remain quietly attentive

TABLE 5.4. PERCENTAGE OF CHILDREN PASSING EACH OF THE TEST ITEMS ($n = 77$).

GROUP	1 HIDDEN OBJECT	2 HIDDEN OBJECTS	3 HIDDEN OBJECTS	4 HIDDEN OBJECTS	5 HIDDEN OBJECTS
Day care					
Chinese	92	57	29	50	14
Caucasian	78	89	33	44	11
Home control					
Chinese	85	71	29	42	13
Caucasian	80	73	27	37	30
Percentage of all children	83	71	29	42	20

throughout the episode are probably the most important competences required for solution of this problem, it appears that the sources of variability for this characteristic lie within the child's temperament and experiences at home.

On the final trial, when the position of the receptacle was changed without the child's knowledge, 35 percent of the children went to the position where they had seen the object hidden, and 23 percent went to the specific receptacle under which it had been placed. The remaining children made some other response. Neither class, care, nor ethnicity was related to the dispositions to choose location or receptacle.

A small independent sample of twenty-nine middle-class children had been administered this procedure at home; eighteen of them were twenty-seven to twenty-nine months of age and eleven were thirty through thirty-six months of age. The performance of the younger children was comparable to that of the current sample, for 80 percent solved the easiest item and 28 percent solved the most difficult. Among the older children, 55 percent solved the most difficult item, a result implying that only a few additional months of maturity facilitates a child's ability to solve the five-item problem.

Embedded Figures Test (29 months) There was no effect of care, ethnicity, or class on the time required to find the item or on accuracy of performance. Day care children had a mean of 7.5 out of 9 correct on their first solution hypothesis; home controls had a mean of 7.3 correct. Most children were competent at this task.

Recognition vocabulary (20 months) Day care and home-reared children performed equivalently on the fifteen-item recognition vocabulary test; the average child recognized about half of the items. Caucasian children performed significantly better than the Chinese on three items—*chicken*, *tree,* and *pig*—perhaps because they had heard these words more often at home.

Concept formation index (29 months) Form of rearing had no significant effect on the level of mastery of thirty-one basic semantic concepts. Children from middle-class families, whether from the day care or home control groups, attained higher scores than those from working-class families, a result unlike that of the vocabulary recognition test but consistent with the findings of other investigators.

When scores on the concept formation index and recognition vocabulary tests were pooled and standardized, there was still no significant difference between the scores of home and day care children. However, we should note that the children with the two highest scores (greater than 1.5 standard deviations above the mean) were both home-reared middle-class Caucasians.

But since the lowest scores were obtained by home-reared, working-class Chinese children, no consistent effect of home-rearing held across both ethnic groups.

The scores of the matched pairs of day care and home control children being equivalent (means of 15.9 and 16.4, respectively), it appears that day care neither enhanced nor retarded acquisition of semantic concepts that are part of the vocabulary of most 4-year-olds. The belief held by some that children attending day care centers are likely to be retarded in the growth of vocabulary was not supported by these data.

The Bayley scales Each child was administered selected items from the Bayley Developmental Schedule at seven and one-half, thirteen and one-half, and twenty months. Only in these procedures did form of rearing appear to have a clear effect on an aspect of cognitive functioning. The day care children obtained higher scores on the nonlanguage items administered at twenty months. This result is not unreasonable because day care teachers had spent much time with the infants, encouraging them to imitate acts they had first demonstrated. The many form boards present in the play area of the center had provided the children with the opportunity to practice the skills assessed on this particular subscale of the Bayley at twenty months of age.

Although neither ethnicity nor social class was consistently correlated with the Bayley scale scores, the working-class Chinese children living at home had the lowest performance at all ages (see table 5.5). This is the only evidence in the study indicating that the experiences encountered by children in our day care center might have facilitated the development of some aspects of cognitive functioning. On most procedures, the day care and home control groups were remarkably similar.

Attachment to the mother

Because, as indicated in chapter 3, many parents and psychologists have feared that regular attendance at a day care center during the opening years of life might dilute the intensity of the infant's attachment to the mother, we attempted to assess this construct. Admittedly, any single evaluation procedure might be insufficiently sensitive to the subtlety of this process. If reasonable indexes of attachment do not reveal a difference between day care and home-reared children, one cannot conclude that there are none, but only that differences in attachment are at least not grossly obvious. We used two quite different procedures to evaluate the child's attachment to the mother—observation of the child's behavior with the mother and other adults at twenty months of age and observations of the child's tendency to protest maternal departure from three and one half through twenty-nine months of age.

TABLE 5.5. RANK ORDER OF THE EIGHT GROUPS BASED ON PERFORMANCE ON SELECTED BAYLEY DEVELOPMENTAL SCALE ITEMS AT 7½, 13½, AND 20 MONTHS (LOW RANK EQUALS GOOD PERFORMANCE).[a]

	Day care				Home control			
	Chinese		Caucasian		Chinese		Caucasian	
Bayley items	Class 2	Class 1	Class 2	Class 1	Class 2	Class 1	Class 2	Class 1
7½ mos.								
Mental	4	2.5	5	6.5	8	6.5	2.5	1
Motor	6	7	3	2	8	4	5	1
13½ mos.								
Mental	2.5	4	5.5	2.5	8	1	5.5	7
Motor	4.5	8	4.5	1	7	6	2	3
20 mos.								
Language	7	6	4	1	8	5	2	3
Nonlanguage	5	1	4	2.5	7	2.5	8	6
Average rank	4.8	4.8	4.3	2.6	7.7	4.1	4.1	3.5

[a] Class 2 is working class; a child is classed as a member of class 1, middle class, if one or both parents had some college education.

Attachment session (20 months) The attachment procedure, the first of the episodes administered at twenty months, occurred in a large room decorated like a living room. The four actors were the child, the child's mother, an unfamiliar woman, and, for the day care children, the familiar primary caretaker from the center, while for the home controls it was a female friend with whom the child had had previous contact. The child was given only a few toys because we wished to promote mild boredom in order to see to whom the child went for comfort, if and when he became satiated with the toys. In order to create mild apprehension in the child, each of the three adults suddenly stood up and took different seats after fifteen and thirty minutes of the forty-five-minute session. This event, apparently unprovoked from the child's point of view, alerted most of the children. We noted to whom the child oriented after the adults changed their location and whether the child changed his proximity to any of the adults.

The question of interest was whether the day care experience had altered the child's tendency to seek his mother when he became bored or apprehensive. As we shall see, the day care and home control children did not differ in occurrence of separation protest. But seeking the mother when mildly uncertain may be a more reasonable index of the child's attachment to the mother than separation distress, since the latter is influenced by the child's level of cognitive development. The major variables quantified were proximity to, looking at, touching, or vocalizing to each of the adults, as well as irritability.

The profile of behavior for most of the children was remarkably similar —they spent much more time near the mother than near the familiar woman (a ratio of 7 to 1) and rarely played near the unfamiliar stranger (see table 5.6). Although Caucasian day care subjects and Caucasian home controls behaved similarly throughout the session the Chinese children in day care spent more time near their mother and less time near the familiar woman (especially during the early part of the session) than did those raised at home. These data imply some initial uncertainty on the part of the Chinese children in day care, a suggestion that gains force from the observation that the Chinese children were more likely to be looking at the unfamiliar woman, also Chinese, when they were near their mothers or sitting on their mothers' laps.

When the adults rotated their locations twice during the session, we coded each child's behavior for the thirty seconds prior to the adult's move and compared it with his behavior during the thirty seconds after the move. Since some children were near their mothers at the time of the movement, a simple change score might have given a distorted picture of the effect of the intervention, so we constructed a five-point scale that reflected the child's tendency to approach the mother at the time of the adults' movement. The scale scores were as follows: 1 point—child is not proximal to mother either before or after the move; 2 points—child is not proximal to mother before

TABLE 5.6. PROXIMITY TO MOTHER, FAMILIAR ADULT, AND STRANGE ADULT FOR ATTACHMENT SESSION AT 20 MONTHS OF AGE (MEAN VALUE IN SECONDS FOR EACH 15-MINUTE PERIOD).[a]

		CHINESE		CAUCASIAN	
PERSON PROXIMAL TO	PERIOD	DAY CARE	HOME	DAY CARE	HOME
Mother	1	127.6	84.3	57.9	53.1
	2	116.8	86.3	54.0	69.3
	3	105.2	84.3	74.1	57.7
Familiar adult	1	4.2	13.6	10.2	16.7
	2	4.4	11.9	9.1	17.6
	3	4.1	25.1	13.6	24.3
Stranger	1	0.4	0.4	0.5	2.1
	2	0.6	1.1	1.3	1.8
	3	0.1	0.3	0.3	2.1

[a] Significant effects for proximity: duration of proximity to mother—ethnicity $F = 9.61$, 1/64, $p < 0.01$; duration of proximity to stranger—ethnicity $F = 4.24$, 1/64, $p < 0.05$; ethnicity x person $F = 7.93$, 2/128, $p < 0.001$.

the move and is proximal to mother for ten seconds or less after the move; 3 points—child is not proximal to mother before the move and is proximal to mother for more than ten seconds after move; 4 points—child is proximal to mother before the move and is proximal to mother for twenty seconds or less after the move; 5 points—child is proximal to mother before the move and proximal to mother for more than 20 seconds after the move. The higher the child's score, the greater his tendency to be proximal to his mother after the move. There was no difference between the behavior of day care and home-reared children for either or both rotations. At the time of the first movement, the Chinese children were more likely than the Caucasians to be near their mothers during the thirty seconds prior to the rotation and to remain near her for the next half minute. The Caucasians were more likely to be playing away from their mother at the time of movement and less likely to approach her after the movement.

The most important finding is the overwhelming preference all children showed for their mothers when they were bored, tired, or distressed. Day care subjects and home controls, both Chinese and Caucasian, selected their mothers as the primary target seven times more often than the other familiar adults. A remarkably similar finding has been reported by Dale Farran and Craig Ramey (1977) for lower-class black infants of a similar age. If approaching the mother when bored or uncertain is regarded as one index of attachment of child to mother, it appears that the day care children were no more nor less strongly attached to their mothers than the home controls.

Some investigators (Blehar 1974) have implied that day care children are less secure and more prone to apprehension in mildly uncertain situations than home-reared children. There was a slight tendency for this prediction to be verified by the data for the Chinese but certainly not for the Caucasian children.

Separation protest A second measure many investigators have regarded as indicative of the child's attachment to the mother is the degree of protest displayed in response to the mother's departure in an unfamiliar context. The procedure we used for children from three and one-half to twenty-nine months of age was identical on all sessions. Toward the end of each assessment session when the child was playing happily in a room, the mother said, "Good-bye," and left the child alone in the room. We noted the occurrence and duration of fretting or crying for a 2-minute period. Figure 5.7 shows the percentages of children in day care and the home-reared groups who fretted or cried following maternal departure. The growth function resembles that found for many other samples of children. Fretting or crying was low prior to 9 months, rose to a peak at 13 months, when 86 per-

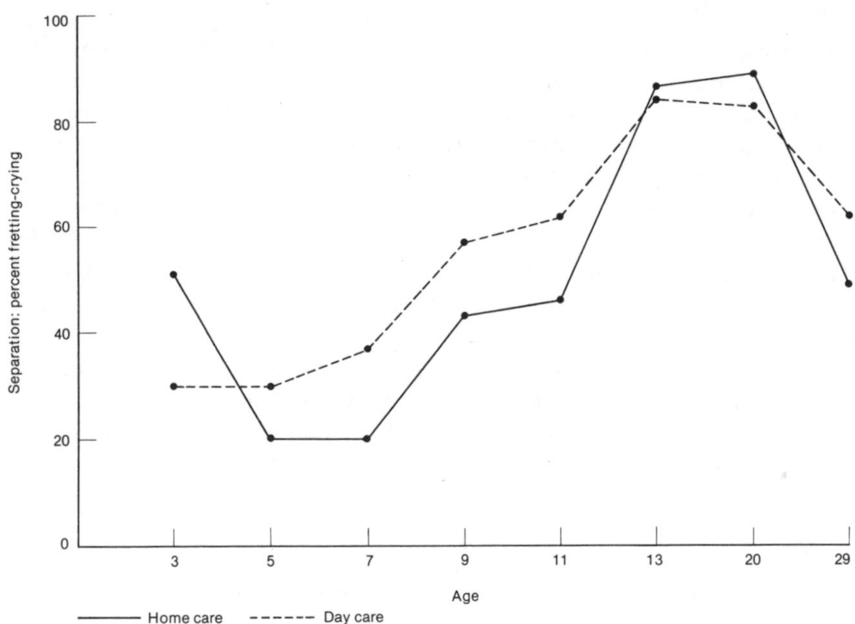

Fig. 5.7 *Percentages of day care and home control children displaying fretting or crying at departure of the mother.*

cent of the children protested, and then declined. The latency to crying showed a sharp decline at 9 months and displayed its lowest values at 13 and 20 months. The likelihood of the child's approaching the mother upon her return to the room was greatest at 20 months (it should be noted that all children were mobile by 11 months of age).

Of the total of 87 children observed in the separation protest situation, 59 participated in this episode on all of 6 occasions from 5½ through 20 months. Every one of the 59 cried on at least one of the 6 occasions; most cried on 2 or 3 occasions. The distribution of protest for the 59 was normal, with a mean, median, and mode of three protests. Since cross-sectional studies of separation protest typically report between 40 and 75 percent of a sample displaying protest at any one age, some investigators have suggested that this phenomenon is not a universal developmental event. The current data imply that the protest may be a regular milestone for all children.

Since the period from 9 to 13 months was the time of greatest protest, we examined the behavior for the 3 episodes at 9, 11, and 13 months for the 83 children who had participated at all three ages. Crying on all 3 occasions was the most frequent pattern (31 percent of the group cried all three times), and 13 months was the age when crying was most likely to occur.

Thus separation protest displayed a regular growth function for the majority of children. As we indicated in chapter 2, we believe this is due to the maturation of new cognitive processes, for the developmental course for separation distress has been replicated on independent samples of infants in the United States (Kotelchuck 1972), infants from lower-class families in Antigua, Guatemala (Lester et al. 1974), Indian infants residing in rural Guatemalan villages (Kagan 1976); children being reared in infant houses on Israeli kibbutzim (Fox 1977); and !Kung San children growing up in the Kalahari desert in Botswana (Kagan 1976). In all of these studies, the mother left the child with an unfamiliar adult. In two of the studies the child was left, on a different occasion, with a familiar adult; the child rarely cried following maternal departure if the adult who remained was familiar (the father for the American samples, and the metapelet in the kibbutz study). The child cried and showed serious inhibition of play only when left with an unfamiliar adult. In the studies in all of these cultures, age was related to separation protest by an inverted U function, similar to the one noted for both the Chinese and the Caucasian day care subjects and home controls in the present study. It appears that the occurrence of separation distress is monitored by the child's level of cognitive development. Although it is probable that the time of emergence and growth function for separation distress are mainly related to maturing cognitive competences, it is possible that during the 12-month period when separation distress is most likely to occur, the intensity of protest will covary with the quality of the mother-child interaction and perhaps with temperamental factors. Evidence for that possibility comes from the kibbutz study; firstborns were significantly more distressed by the separation than later-borns, even though the growth function was the same for both groups.

If protest to separation is primarily a regular maturational event that occurs during the period from 9 to 29 months of age and lasts only a short time until it is resolved, we should not expect long-term stability of this disposition, but rather short-term continuity for successive ages. The data affirm that expectation.

In order to assess cross-age stability of protest in response to maternal departure, we computed a matrix of phi coefficients across the 8 ages for the Caucasian and Chinese children separately because the Chinese were more distressed than the Caucasians. We also computed the matrix for the pooled group. Stability occurred only over short intervals (see table 5.7). Among the Chinese, there was a significant predictive relation from 7 to 9 months and from 11 or 13 to 20 months. Among Caucasians, comparable predictability was present from 11 to 20 months and from 13 to 29 months. The tendency to protest separation seems to be influenced primarily by the child's stage of development, although there is an individual difference variable operating over the short range because some children are likely to protest on more occasions than others. As we shall see, this individual disposition was primarily associated with ethnicity, and minimally related to social class or to day care experience.

Although neither the large sample nor the matched pairs analyses revealed any differences between the day care subjects and home controls in

TABLE 5.7. CROSS-AGE STABILITY OF DISTRESS TO SEPARATION (PHI COEFFICIENTS).[a]

AGE (MOS.)	3	5	7	9	11	13	20	29
3	. . .	.16	.21	.20	.05	.04	.30	.16
5	.20	. . .	.00	.21	.06	.14	.03	.22
7	.36	.00	. . .	.32[b]	.07	.18	.24	.20
9	.06	.02	.17	. . .	.28	.03	.05	.32
11	.03	.17	.04	.31	. . .	.28	.37[b]	.16
13	.06	.08	.04	.07	.16	. . .	.56[c]	.16
20	.00	.01	.06	.16	.47[c]	.15	. . .	.30
29	.37	.33	.29	.14	.39	.49[b]	.24	. . .

[a] Chinese to the right and above the diagonal; Caucasians to the left and below.

[b] $p < 0.05$.

[c] $p < 0.01$.

pattern of protest, the Chinese children protested earlier and more often than the Caucasians (see figure 5.8). Of the 59 children tested 6 times from 5 to 20 months, almost 25 percent of the Chinese protested on 5 or all 6 of the sessions, while only 6 percent of the Caucasians protested as often. Moreover, the Chinese showed separation protest at an earlier age than the Caucasians; the age when more than 50 percent of the children fretted was two months earlier among the Chinese (9 months) than among the Caucasians. Finally, the session had to be terminated earlier for Chinese than for Caucasian children at every age from 9 through 29 months (the difference was significant at 13, 20, and 29 months), because of their greater distress.

Occurrence of separation anxiety during the period of its maximal display, from 9 to 29 months, was independent of most of our other variables, including behavior during the attachment session. There was no relation between seeking proximity to mother during the attachment session at 20 months and the number or intensity of separation protests. Even though more Chinese showed apprehension in both contexts, those who showed the most wariness in one situation did not necessarily behave fearfully in the other. Children who showed separation protest a little earlier than others (at 9 months) were more likely to remain close to their mothers during the solo play session at 13 months (but not at 20 or 29 months). Children who

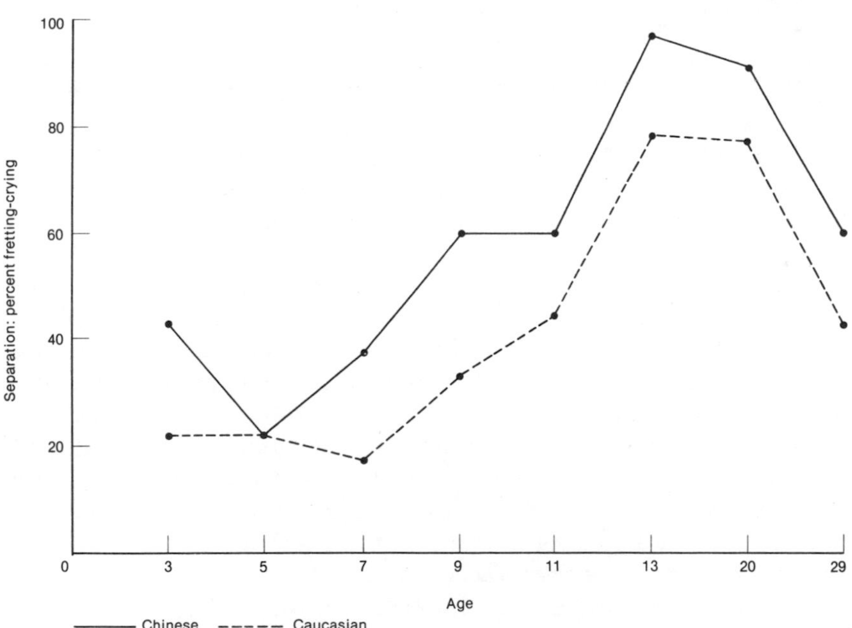

Fig. 5.8 *Percentages of Chinese and Caucasian children displaying fretting or crying at departure of mother at different ages.*

showed separation protest late, at 29 months, were likely to remain near their mothers during the solo play and peer-interaction sessions at 13 and 29 months. We conclude that there is a small proportion of children who are more vulnerable to apprehension in some unfamiliar situations. But this individual contribution to the likelihood of protest seems more closely related to ethnicity than to form of care. Although it is likely that home experiences of the Chinese made them more vulnerable to this particular distress, it is not clear specifically which experiences are vital. The complete absence of any difference between day care and home control children within each ethnic group indicates that daily separation from the mother over a two-year period is not relevant to this phenomenon.

Social behavior

The final domain to be assessed was social behavior with an unfamiliar child. Intuition suggests that a child in a day care setting with many other children should develop different attitudes and dispositions toward age mates than the child reared at home, and, perhaps, be less inhibited and more interactive when he encounters an unfamiliar peer. The focus of the three play sessions was behavior with and apprehension toward an unfamiliar peer of the same age, sex, and ethnicity as the subject. We were concerned with both possible differences between the two rearing groups and developmental changes in the quality of the child's behavior. The assumption that there might be a regular course of development for initial apprehension with another child would be affirmed readily if the several potential indexes of uncertainty were to display similar growth functions. Under these conditions we would be able to decide which groups of children were more and which less apprehensive and at what age the apprehension was maximal. The data did not permit an easy answer to these questions.

Growth functions across age There is good reason to assume that when a child is made uncertain by an unfamiliar or unexpected event he is likely to inhibit both active play with objects and vocalization and to seek proximity to a familiar person. For example, following maternal departure when in an unfamiliar room, the vast majority of 1- to 2-year-old children show a dramatic decrease in time spent playing with toys compared with their behavior when the mother was present (Kotelchuck 1972). Subhuman primates also show inhibition of play to a discrepant event: "At the first sight of alarm if a predator threatens or when fighting breaks out in the troop, play is one of the first activities to cease. Tension and fighting are almost wholly antithetical to play . . . if something new and strange appears, play ceases . . . Play normally occurs in an atmosphere of familiarity, emotional reassurance and lack of tension or danger" (Dolhinow and Bishop 1970, p. 165).

We assumed that changes in play, vocalization, and proximity to the mother would be sensitive indexes of the young child's level of uncertainty to the peer, at least when the child was one to two and one-half years of age. The growth functions for these variables, as well as for fretting and smiling, during the initial solo session when the child was with his mother indicated that the children became less apprehensive over the period from thirteen to twenty-nine months. When the child was playing and only his mother was in the room, proximity to the mother and fretting decreased linearly over age, while vocalization, playing, and smiling increased. There was a greater decrease in these behavioral signs of uncertainty between twenty and twenty-nine months than between thirteen and twenty months. This pattern is in accord with the growth function for separation protest and the increase in vocalization and smiling in response to the car and light episodes. The uncertainty generated by the unfamiliarity of a playroom or a laboratory episode appears to decrease significantly after twenty months of age.

The similar growth functions for proximity to mother, vocalization, and play during the solo sessions led us to hope that these variables would behave similarly following the introduction of the unfamiliar peer and permit statements about the developmental course of peer apprehension. Unfortunately, the changes in these variables were not identical.

The majority of the children showed inhibition of either play or vocalization or both, as well as increased proximity to the mother following the introduction of the other child. Over 80 percent of the children played and talked less when the peer was present than during the solo session when the child was alone with his mother. This was true at all three ages, although most children tended to show the greatest inhibition of play and the most staring at the unfamiliar child at either thirteen or twenty months rather than at twenty-nine months, a trend that suggests that apprehension was waning at the oldest age. We suspect that the unfamiliar child and not the mother was the primary incentive for the child's inhibition. Joseph Jacobson (1977) has confirmed this suspicion by comparing the behavior of pairs of children who knew each other with the behavior of pairs who were unfamiliar to each other; all children were observed three times in a longitudinal study, when they were ten, twelve, and fourteen and one-half months old in the same room we used for our 20-month-olds' and 29-month-olds' play sessions. Jacobson found that the child displayed much less play, more staring at the other child, and more time proximal to the mother when the other child was a stranger than when he was familiar. Additionally, Martha Zaslow (1977) found that kibbutz- and family-reared Israeli children, when placed in a situation similar to the one we used, looked more at the unfamiliar peer than at the peer's mother.

Because more children in our study showed their greatest inhibition of play at twenty months (43 percent of the group) than at thirteen or twenty-nine months (33 and 24 percent) there appears to be an inverted U-shaped function for apprehension to an unfamiliar child. The growth function for the third quartile value for duration of attentional involvement in play provided the most convincing support for the curvilinear growth function. In this analysis, the temporal durations of each child's attentional involvements with toys were cast into a frequency distribution, and the third quartile was selected as an index of sustained play. All four subgroups (form of care versus ethnicity) showed their greatest decrease in the third quartile value at twenty months. The older child was expected to be more capable than the younger of longer investments of attention, but in fact the 20-month-olds had the greatest difficulty sustaining long periods of attention in play, so that the effect of uncertainty created by the unfamiliar peer was maximal at twenty months. Moreover, average time spent playing (playing time divided by the number of discrete epochs of play) also showed the greatest decrease from the solo to the peer session at twenty months of age.

Because the source of the child's apprehension is the presence of the unfamiliar peer, the growth function for duration of staring at the peer provides a clue as to the probable time of maximal uncertainty. The children reared at home stared at the peer maximally at twenty months; the day care children at thirteen months; and no group showed maximal staring at twenty-nine months (see figure 5.9).

A very sensitive index of apprehension is duration of staring at the peer while remaining in close proximity to the mother. Children reared at home showed the largest values at 20 months, day care children at thirteen months; the thirteen-month-old day care group's values were almost identical to the 20-month-old home controls' values. We assume that the child stares at the peer in an attempt to resolve questions like, "What will he do?" "What should I do with him?" If these questions go unanswered the child becomes uncertain, stops playing, and may approach the mother. These data suggest that for the day care subjects, especially the Caucasians, the maximal uncertainty to the peer occurs a little earlier than for the children reared at home. When with the peer, the majority of the day care children played the least with the toys when they were thirteen months old; for home controls minimal play was at twenty months of age. The day care children stared longest at the peer at thirteen months, the home controls at twenty months. The day care experience seems to have accelerated by a few months the normal growth function for apprehension toward an unfamiliar child, causing it to emerge and vanish a little earlier, especially among the Caucasian children.

The matched pairs analysis revealed remarkably similar behavior for most of the variables. Both day care and home-reared groups showed inhibition of play and vocalization as well as increased proximity to the mother following the introduction of the other child. Both groups showed increased fretting and staring at the peer, and the magnitude of change in behavior from the solo to the peer session was similar for both groups. However, as indicated earlier, at twenty months the home control children were more

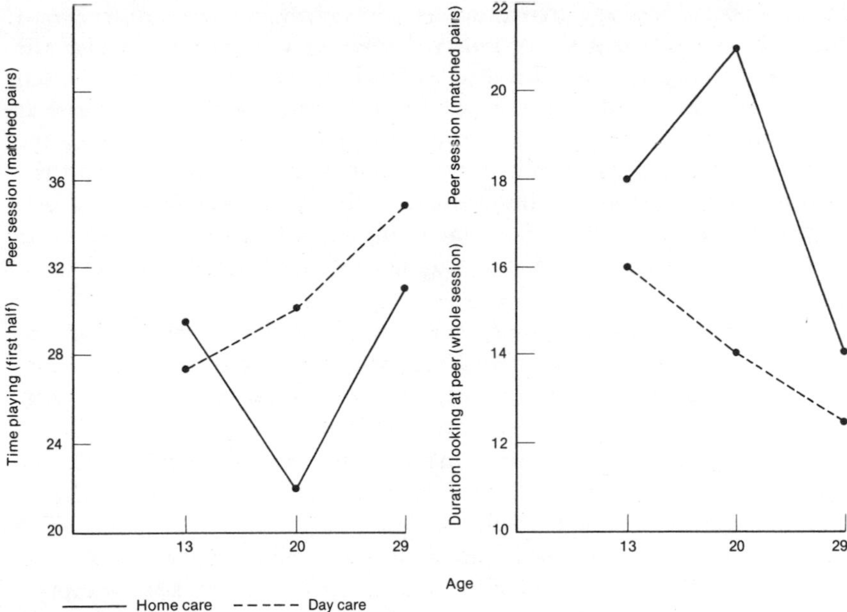

Fig. 5.9 *Absolute time spent playing (per minute) with the peer and duration of looking at peer (in seconds per minute), for matched pairs of day care subjects and home controls.*

uncertain than those in day care, for they stared longer at the unfamiliar peer, especially while proximal to their mothers, and played less than their counterparts in day care. However, by twenty-nine months, these differences in apprehension had vanished, the home controls had become more interactive, and the differences between the groups became minimal.

Although the day care experience tended to make children a little less inhibited, it did not make them more likely to initiate social interaction with the other child. Such behavior was rare for all children. Daily experience with other children during the second year does not seem to lead to more social forms of play after the child has passed the age when initial inhibition is no longer common. At the end of the first year and during the middle of the second year, when apprehension toward an unfamiliar child is most likely to occur, prior experience with other children tends to buffer the inhibition a little. But when all children have matured to a point where initial apprehension is waning, the day care experience does not seem to be highly relevant.

Although the Chinese and the Caucasian groups had similar inverted U-shaped growth functions for inhibition toward the peer, the Chinese were more inhibited than the Caucasians at all ages, especially at twenty months. The Chinese children stayed closer to their mothers, played and vocalized less, and were more irritable. The Chinese children made fewer initiations, either cooperative or aggressive, and were less likely to engage in reciprocal play. The day care experience buffered some of this uncertainty, for the Chinese youngsters in day care were less proximal to the mother and played and vocalized more during the peer session than the Chinese reared at home. But the day care experience had less of a therapeutic effect among the Caucasians. Ethnicity generally had a greater effect on inhibition with the peer than form of rearing. This fact implies that home experiences and perhaps temperamental qualities are more important than contact with other children in a group care setting in shaping the child's initial reaction to an unfamiliar child.

The inverted U-growth function for inhibition in the presence of an unfamiliar child has been replicated in a cross-sectional study of ninety-six Israeli infants tested at fourteen, twenty, and twenty-nine months of age (Zaslow 1977). Half the subjects lived in nuclear family households in Jerusalem, the other half in infant houses on kibbutzim, visiting the parental home only for a few hours in the late afternoon and early evening. The children were observed in solo and peer play sessions in a procedure that was as similar as possible to the one used in this study. Each child's behavior was coded first while he played in an unfamiliar setting where his mother was reading a magazine or book, and then when an unfamiliar peer and his mother were introduced into the room.

Both kibbutz and family-reared Israeli children showed their greatest inhibition of play at age twenty months, as in the current study. However, group rearing exerted an effect; the kibbutz reared 29-month-olds showed minimal evidence of inhibition, whereas the family-reared 29-month-olds were still showing apprehension, although less than at twenty months. Observations of the children in the more natural setting of the infant house revealed that more complex social interaction, including reciprocal play, showed a dramatic rise between twenty and twenty-nine months of age, as if the waning of the inhibition permitted the release of complex social patterns of behavior. (See figure 5.10.)

Although imitation of a peer, reciprocal play, and offering or seizing of toys displayed different growth functions, the functions were similar whether the setting was the infant house with familiar children or the experimental playroom where the children were strangers. This finding implies that when the child is mature enough to resolve the uncertainty generated by the presence of another child, he will begin to enter into reciprocal interactions and inhibit responses like offering of a toy, which is a strategy for gaining information about the other child (Zaslow 1977).

Other investigators' observations lend support to the idea that some initial apprehension toward other children is an inevitable component of a child's development during the second year of life and inhibits complex forms of interaction. Naturalistic observations of groups of middle-class 18-month-olds who were attending a day care center or were being reared

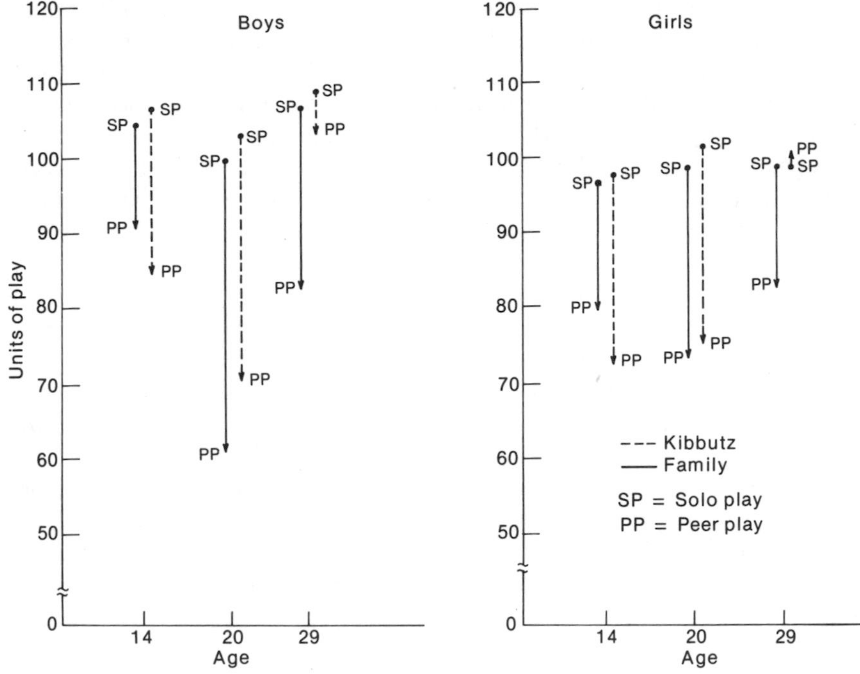

Fig. 5.10 *Change in play from solo to peer session for kibbutz-reared and nonkibbutz-reared children (from Zaslow 1977).*

totally at home revealed no major differences in the quality of peer interaction (Rubenstein and Howes 1977).

One of the authors of this book (J.K.) is currently studying pairs of same sex, same age children who play together each month throughout the second year of life in a controlled laboratory setting with their mothers present. Many of the children under two years of age show apprehension and inhibition with the peer, even though they have been with that child in the same setting on three or four prior occasions. The apprehension is not due to the fact that the child has forgotten the other child, for mothers tell us that their children assert on the trip to the laboratory that they are going to see a particular child. They even describe to the mother the procedures they will encounter. Nonetheless, many 18-, 19-, and 20-month-old children show obvious and prolonged apprehension with each other.

The inhibition also appears with a videotaped image (Amsterdam and Greenberg 1977). Infants fifteen and twenty months old showed avoidance, crying, or turning away when shown a videotaped sequence illustrating another child or themselves. By contrast, 10-month-olds, who were as attentive as the older infants, smiled and vocalized and did not show signs of inhibition or apprehension.

It appears that the age of onset of wariness toward another child can be predicted by the developmental level of the child's play a few months earlier, as shown by Jacobson (1977), suggesting that the apprehension is being monitored, in part, by the maturation of cognitive functions. Jacobson observed a sample of twenty-three children in three different situations longitudinally at ten, twelve, and fourteen and one-half months. In one procedure, the quality of the child's play with toys was observed while he was in a room with his mother. In the other two procedures, the child played with a familiar or an unfamiliar child of the same age and sex. There was very little evidence of apprehension with the unfamiliar peer at ten months of age; the infants neither moved toward their mothers nor showed inhibition of play while the other child was present. Subsequently, some children showed high levels of inhibition at twelve months; others not until fourteen months. However, earlier or later appearance of apprehension and inhibition in the presence of the other child was related to maturity of the child's play at ten months. At this age most of the play with toys was of two types—either mouthing or banging of a single toy or relational play, a more advanced response in which the child relates two toys that typically are associated in the child's experience. For example, the child hits a cup and saucer together or touches a spoon to a cup. It has been demonstrated that the relational behavior generally replaces the simpler type between nine and thirteen months of age. The 10-month-old children who showed higher levels of the more mature play were more likely to display high levels of apprehension to the unfamiliar peer at twelve months. The 10-month-olds whose play was less mature did not show high levels of apprehension until fourteen and one-half months of age. If we assume that the amount of relational play at 10 months reflects the rate at which certain aspects of cognitive functioning are maturing and also that the emergence of apprehension toward a peer is due to the emergence of the functions of prediction and evaluation discussed in chapter 2, then it is not unreasonable to find, as Jacobson did, that the maturity of play at ten months predicted time of onset of uncertainty in the presence of a peer.

Jacobson's data, together with the data of the present study, imply that both developmental stage and prior experience with peers influence degree of initial apprehension with other children. The maturation of cognitive competences determines the basic developmental function for peer apprehension and guarantees it will begin at or soon after the first year, peak during the second year, and decline during the third year. It appears difficult, but perhaps possible, for experience to prevent nature from keeping that schedule. However, extensive experience with peers can affect the age of emergence and decline of the apprehension and perhaps its intensity during the period of its display.

Stability across the three play sessions Although the child's developmental stage and the nature of the situation controlled most of the variation in the solo and peer situations, it is still possible that some children might have a stable disposition to be inhibited or relatively free over and above the obvious effects of age and the presence of the other child. In order to investigate the possibility, we computed the cross-age correlations for the three major indexes of inhibition—time spent in playing, in vocalizing, and in proximity to the mother—for the solo and peer sessions separately and for the two ethnic groups. Since the Chinese were more inhibited than the Caucasians, higher interage correlations for the pooled sample could reflect the stability of the Chinese-Caucasian difference in degree of inhibition.

In general, cross-age stabilities for proximity to the mother or time playing were not robust. There was no cross-age stability either for proximity to mother or for play when behavior during the session with the peer was the predictor, and minimal stability when behavior during the solo session was the predictor. The absence of continuity across the sixteen month period of the testing implies that dynamic changes occur in the behavioral indexes of uncertainty and affirms the conclusion drawn from the results of the visual and auditory episodes. Developmental age and context exerted the most profound effects on the behaviors we quantified. Individual differences noted at one age or in one context might be stable for a few months, but as the interval lengthened, stability vanished. The selective stability across the period thirteen to twenty or from twenty to twenty-nine months implies that the episodes reflected some aspect of the child's disposition but one that was continually subject to change.

This conclusion is affirmed by a short-term longitudinal study of identical twins and same-sex fraternal twins whose degree of uncertainty and inhibition in a playroom situation and during administration of the Bayley Infant Behavior Record were assessed five times from nine to thirty months of age (Matheny and Dolan 1975). Intraindividual stability coefficients across the twenty-one-month interval were low, but the profiles of change in "adaptability" to the two situations were more similar for the identical than for the fraternal twins, implying that temperamental factors were influencing the children's behavior. The authors concluded,

> The low-level correlations for adaptability over ages within the same settings, however, indicate that developmental change also contributes to the lack of continuity . . . Between 9 and 30 months, the child's repertoire of possible responses expands enormously. This period of study includes marked advances in locomotion, speech, and cognitive abilities in general; it comprises increased wariness of strangers, strengthened affective bonds toward primary caretakers, and the autonomy-asserting behaviors often attributed to the "terrible two's." It is not surprising, therefore, that age-to-age correlations for any given personality dimension tend to be low . . . The within-pair analyses, however, indicate that there is a genetic influence upon these changes. Either across settings or across ages, the identical twin pairs were found to change more in concert than the fraternal twin pairs. Thus, while

> the measures of adaptability are subject to change across settings or across time, the changes do not appear to be capricious. Rather, the changes that occur seem to be partially regulated by genetic influences. [Matheny and Dolan 1975, pp. 1109-1110]

In our study initial apprehension to an unfamiliar peer displayed a curvilinear function over the period from thirteen to twenty-nine months of age, especially for home-reared children. The effect of care, which was not dramatic, was associated with an earlier peaking of uncertainty for the day care subjects than for the home controls. The ethnic differences in intensity of inhibition, both for day care and home control children, suggested that the Chinese were more vulnerable to uncertainty in this context. It is not clear whether the effect was mediated totally by home experience or whether temperamental factors influenced it. As in the laboratory episodes, the influence of ethnicity was more pervasive than the influence of social class or group care.

Visit to an unfamiliar day care center

Each child was taken to an unfamiliar day care center with his mother and one female observer for a thirty-minute observational period during the second of the two observation sessions when the child was twenty-nine months old. The observer coded the child's proximity to his mother, play with objects, staring at and play with other children, and fretting. Every ten seconds the coder recorded which of the behavioral variables had occurred; the child could attain a maximal score of six for each variable for each minute of observation. There was very little fretting or play with other children; the other three variables occurred with reasonable frequency. The data may reflect the child's initial apprehension in this unfamiliar setting.

Proximity to the mother and staring at another child decreased dramatically over the thirty-minute observational period, a result implying a substantial decline in apprehension. Play with toys, however, did not display an obvious change over time. Although for the day care and home control children values were similar for proximity to the mother and staring at the peer, the day care children played with the available toys a little more often than did the home controls, which suggests they may have been slightly less apprehensive in this situation. There were no differences related to rearing with respect to the initiation of a social overture to another child. Among the home controls, 60 percent made at least one social overture in comparison to 50 percent of the day care group. Thus prior experience in a day care center did not make it more likely that the child would be more social in another group care context.

As in the other peer play episodes, the Chinese were more inhibited than the Caucasians. They stayed closer to their mothers for a longer time, played less, and were less likely to initiate overtures to other children. The home-reared Chinese had the lowest play scores and the highest proximity scores of any group. As with some of the cognitive measures, the day care experience seemed to alleviate the strong apprehension and inhibition characteristic of the home-reared Chinese. Since the Caucasians were generally less fearful, the day care experience had a minimal effect on them. (See tables 5.8-5.10.)

Only fifty-five of the ninety-one children made any social overture toward another child, and form of rearing had no effect on this variable. However, the Chinese children were less likely to initiate social contact than the Caucasians (chi square = 8.76, df = 1, $p < 0.01$); only 43 percent of the Chinese made at least one social initiation, compared with 76 percent of the Caucasians. The largest difference between the day care subjects and home controls occurred among the working class children of both ethnic groups, with the day care children of working-class origin being less inhibited than the home controls from the same social class. Among the middle-class children, the day care versus home control difference was considerably smaller.

The effect of the day care experience, although not extreme, was in the expected direction. One might anticipate that the day care children would

TABLE 5.8. AVERAGE SCORES FOR PROXIMITY TO MOTHER ACROSS 10-MINUTE TIME BLOCKS AND FOR TOTAL PERIOD.[a]

	TIME BLOCKS (MIN.)			
GROUP	1-10	11-20	21-30	TOTAL PERIOD
Chinese				
Day care	3.7 units/ min.	3.0	2.5	3.1
Home control	3.8	3.7	3.5	3.7
Caucasian				
Day care	3.4	2.1	2.5	2.7
Home control	1.8	1.5	1.3	1.6
All day care subjects	3.6	2.6	2.5	
All home controls	2.8	2.6	2.4	
All Chinese infants[b]	3.7	3.3	2.9	
All Caucasian infants	2.6	1.9	1.9	

[a] Each value represents rate, the number of 10-second units per minute during which the behavior occurred.
[b] Ethnicity $F = 5.99$, 1/59, $p < 0.05$.

TABLE 5.9. AVERAGE SCORES FOR PLAY WITH OBJECT ACROSS 10-MINUTE TIME BLOCKS AND FOR TOTAL PERIOD.[a]

GROUP	TIME BLOCKS (MIN.) 1-10	11-20	21-30	TOTAL PERIOD
Chinese				
Day care	3.5 units/min.	3.9	3.3	3.6
Home control	1.8	2.4	1.9	2.1
Caucasian				
Day care	4.5	4.2	4.1	4.2
Home control	3.7	3.8	3.5	3.6
All day care subjects[b]	4.1	4.1	3.7	
All home controls	2.8	3.1	2.7	
All Chinese infants[c]	2.7	3.1	2.6	
All Caucasian infants	4.1	4.0	3.8	

[a] Each value represents rate, the number of 10-second units per minute during which the behavior occurred.
[b] Care $F = 5.25, 1/59, p < 0.05$.
[c] Ethnicity $F = 6.29, 1/59, p < 0.05$.

be a little less inhibited in this novel setting and hence would play a bit more. But the similarities between the two rearing groups were more obvious than the differences. As with most of the other variables, it appears that rearing experiences in the home and temperament exerted a more profound effect on each child's behavior than the experience of 100 weeks in group care.

The mother's description of the child

It will be recalled that when the children were twenty-nine months old their mothers ranked a set of sixteen qualities from most to least characteristic of their child. Mothers of the children in day care did not generate rankings markedly different from those reported by the mothers who reared their children totally at home. The matched pairs were given similar rankings, with two exceptions; the home control mothers felt their children were less patient and shyer with adults than did the mothers of children in day care. This result is theoretically reasonable since the day care children are exposed to a variety of adults during the day. It is important to note that the mothers of day care children did not regard their offspring as more disobedient or more aggressive than did the home control parents. Since the parental judgments are consonant with our independent observations, it seems reasonable

TABLE 5.10. AVERAGE SCORES FOR LOOKING AT PEER ACROSS 10-MINUTE TIME BLOCKS AND FOR TOTAL PERIOD.[a]

GROUP	TIME BLOCKS (MIN.)			TOTAL PERIOD
	1-10	11-20	21-30	
Chinese				
Day care	3.3 units/min.	2.6	2.0	2.6
Home control	3.7	2.9	2.9	3.1
Caucasian				
Day care	3.4	2.6	2.3	2.8
Home control	4.2	3.5	3.3	3.7
All day care subjects[b]	3.3	2.6	2.1	
All home controls	4.0	3.2	3.1	
All Chinese infants	3.5	2.8	2.4	
All Caucasian infants	3.8	3.1	2.8	

[a] Each value represents rate, the number of 10-second units per minute during which the behavior occurred.

[b] Care $F = 5.21$, 1/59, $p < 0.05$.

to conclude that the day care experience did not seriously alter the socialization of those character traits parents care so much about.

There were hints of an ethnic difference. More Caucasian mothers reported that "talkativeness," "laughing," and "activity" were characteristic of their children than did Chinese mothers, who tended to report that "staying close to the mother" was more characteristic of their children. The mothers' reports are in accord with our other observations in the laboratory indicating that the Chinese children were more fearful and less affective than the Caucasians. The ethnic differences in attributes awarded differential rank were also consonant with this conclusion, for Chinese mothers regarded "fear of the dark" as more salient and "disobedience" as less salient that did Caucasian parents. (See table 5.11 and 5.12.)

In a second analysis, we examined ethnic difference in the distribution of the traits placed in the top or bottom three ranks—the most and least characteristic qualities of the child. Caucasians were more likely than Chinese to place talkativeness, laughing, and activity among the traits given high salience. More Caucasians than Chinese mothers gave the lowest ranks to dislike of the dark, patience, fighting, and fussing when mother leaves.

In order to determine if there was a relation between the rankings and the individual data, we correlated each child's rank for talkativeness, playing alone, dislike of the dark, shyness, and staying close to mother with the-

TABLE 5.11. MEAN RANK ASSIGNED TO 16 TRAITS FOR ALL SUBJECTS AND FOR THE TWO ETHNIC GROUPS (LOW SCORE REPRESENTS MATERNAL JUDGMENT THAT THE TRAIT IS HIGHLY CHARACTERISTIC OF HER CHILD).

TRAIT	ALL SUBJECTS	CHINESE	CAUCASIAN	p[a] VALUE	RANK
Talkative	6.7	8.7	4.7	<0.001	4
Often disobeys	9.8	11.1	8.4	<.01	13
Plays alone	7.8	8.9	6.6	<.05	6
Dislikes dark	9.1	7.6	10.7	<.05	9
Wants own way	7.6	7.7	7.4	. . .	5
Laughs easily	5.0	6.5	3.4	<.001	2
Sleeps easily	8.8	9.5	8.1	. . .	8
Patient	11.9	11.7	12.1	. . .	16
Shy with adults	9.4	8.5	10.3	. . .	10
Fights with peers	10.0	7.8	12.2	<.001	14
Fusses when mother leaves	9.7	8.4	11.1	<.05	12
Active	4.7	5.9	3.5	<.05	1
Timid	9.3	9.1	9.4	. . .	10
Cautious	10.8	11.8	9.7	<.05	15
Plays with peers	6.3	6.3	6.3	. . .	3
Stays close to mother	8.3	5.5	11.1	<.001	7

[a] Significance of difference between ethnic groups.

oretically related variables derived from the other episodes administered at thirteen, twenty, and twenty-nine months. The children whose mothers said they were shy with adults and timid in new places vocalized less during the peer play sessions at all three ages and showed greater inhibition of play with the unfamiliar peer at thirteen and twenty months. Moreover, the rankings of shyness and timidity were apparently specific to those qualities, for the rankings of the behavior labeled "fusses when mother leaves" and "stays close to mother" were correlated with proximity to mother during the peer play session at all three ages, whereas the rankings of shyness and timidity were not. The children who were characterized as "fussing when mother leaves" also showed high proximity to mother during the attachment session and the greatest inhibition of play at twenty months. It is interesting that rankings for fear of the dark did not correlate with proximity to mother or play. Indeed, the children who were presumably afraid of the dark showed less inhibition of play in the presence of the unfamiliar peer at thirteen and twenty-nine months, a result indicating that the mothers were not ordering their children on a general dimension of fearfulness. (See table 5.13.)

TABLE 5.12. PERCENTAGE OF PARENTS WHO PLACED TRAIT IN THE TOP OR BOTTOM 3 RANKS, BY ETHNIC GROUP.[a]

TRAIT	TOP 3 RANKS			BOTTOM 3 RANKS			CHI SQUARE	P
	ALL SUBJECTS	CH	CA	ALL SUBJECTS	CH	CA		
Talkative	38%	17%	56%	4%	5%	4%	15.2	<0.001
Often disobeys	7	2	11	16	26	8	7.9	<0.05
Plays alone	20	12	27	14	17	12		
Dislikes dark	21	33	11	34	21	44	8.7	<0.05
Wants own way	14	24	6	7	12	4	9.5	<0.01
Laughs easily	49	31	64	4	9	0	12.5	<0.01
Sleeps easily	14	7	19	14	17	11		
Patient	1	2	0	31	34	29		
Shy with adults	12	17	8	19	12	25		
Fights with peers	10	22	0	30	19	38	14.2	< .001
Fusses when mother leaves	13	24	4	29	24	33	8.4	< .05
Active	46	29	60	6	12	2	10.6	<0.01
Timid in new place	10	12	8	28	21	33		
Cautious	2	2	2	35	50	23	7.2	<0.05
Plays with peers	24	22	25	2	2	2		
Stays close to mother	23	44	6	24	12	33	20.2	<0.01

[a] Ch = Chinese; Ca = Caucasian.

TABLE 5.13. CORRELATIONS BETWEEN SELECTED VARIABLES AND MOTHERS' RANKINGS (RANK OF 1 = HIGHEST SALIENCE).

VARIABLE, BY AGE (MOS.)	DISLIKES DARK	SHY WITH ADULTS	FUSSES WHEN MOTHER LEAVES	TIMID IN NEW PLACES	STAYS CLOSE TO MOTHER
Peer play session					
Vocalization					
13 mos.	–.33[a]	.31[a]	.09	.12	.33[a]
20	.06	.22	.04	.32[a]	.06
29	–.19	.38[b]	–.05	.36[a]	.11
Amount of time playing					
13	–.26	.18	.18	.23	.52[c]
20	–.01	.36[a]	.40[b]	.39[b]	.49[b]
29	–.26	.02	.00	.17	–.09
Change in play from solo session					
13	.44[b]	–.31[a]	–.18	–.30[a]	–.15
20	.06	–.33[a]	–.34[a]	–.28	–.42[b]
29	.23	–.06	.01	–.20	–.06
Proximity to mother					
13	.05	.00	–.40[b]	–.14	–.50[c]
20	.10	–.17	–.42[b]	–.24	–.39[b]
29	.00	–.11	–.32[a]	–.22	–.28
Attachment session					
Proximity to mother at 20 mos.	–.06	–.19	–.41[b]	–.01	–.41[b]
Traits					
Dislikes dark	. . .	–.31[a]	.19	–.22	.11
Shy with adults	–.31	. . .	.10	.50[b]	.13
Fusses when mother leaves	.19	.10	. . .	.03	.61[c]
Timid in new places	–.22	.50[b]	.02	. . .	.05
Stays close to mother	.11	.14	.61[c]	.05	. . .

[a] $p < 0.05$.
[b] $p < 0.01$.
[c] $p < 0.001$.

These data imply that the mothers' rankings have some external validity. Since their descriptions were in accord with our objective assessments, we are a little more certain of our conclusion that day care and social class had a minimal effect on the children's behavior, while ethnicity was moderately associated with apprehension and affectivity.

Summary

Given the absence of consistently large differences across a variety of assessment procedures, it seems fair to conclude that the day care and home-reared children developed similarly with respect to cognitive, social, and affective qualities during the first three years of life. Although there was extraordinary variability among the children attending the center as well as among those reared at home, most of that variability could not be attributed to the effects of form of care. In the final chapter, we shall consider some explanations for the lack of difference between the groups reared differently and for the provocative differences between the Chinese and Caucasian children.

6 Synthesis and Implications

> We can, through the removal of false factual beliefs, render certain moral beliefs inapplicable. But we cannot in the same way ever decisively justify their application.
>
> A. C. Danto, *Mysticism and Morality*

The complete corpus of data does not offer much support for the view that quality group care outside the home has an important effect on the young child's development. Growth patterns for attentiveness and reactivity to discrepant events were primarily influenced by maturational forces and the nature of the event. Although there was variability in quality of response, it was more closely associated with ethnicity than with form of care. It is surprising that 3,500 hours of regular contact with other young children had little influence on degree of apprehension, responsiveness, or the disposition to be aggressive or cooperative with an unfamiliar child. Although there was considerable variability in social behavior it was not under the primary influence of form of rearing. Attachment to the mother and rate of cognitive development, the two critical concerns of American parents, did not appear to be altered by the day care experience. The children in group care treated the mother as if she were the primary agent of nurturance, and no mother indicated, in either her formal rankings or informal conversations, that her child had become either estranged or indifferent to her psychological pressures for socialization. The assessments of language, memory, and perceptual analysis failed to reveal any obvious advantages or disadvantages to the day care experience. Although this research has limitations, notably the absence of a comparison group exposed to less-than-adequate day care, moderate sample size, and no observations at home, it is, at the moment, one of the best scientific studies on this issue. Our answer to the central question that provoked the investigation is that a child's attendance at a day care center staffed by conscientious and nurturant adults during the first two and one-half years of life does not seem to produce a psychological profile very much different from the one created by rearing totally in the home. This conclusion is based on our formal assessments as well as informal observations of the children over the 2½ year period.

These data do not add credibility to several popular expectations about early group care. Although it is reasonable to assume that daily encounter with other children during their first two years might speed up the maturation of the social interaction sequences usually seen in 3- and 4-year-olds, our data did not provide commanding support for that prediction. The 20- and 29-month-olds were simply not very sociable, and cooperative and aggressive play occurred infrequently. There were as many shy children in day care as there were among those reared totally at home. On one occasion we satisfied our curiosity about a particular girl who was inordinately shy with a strange peer in the twenty-month assessment by bringing an unfamiliar peer to the day care center; the girl retreated at once to her day care teacher, even though she was in her own territory.

Some investigators have suggested that caretaking by several adults other than the mother weakens or dilutes the infant's emotional bond to the mother and promotes an insecurity which makes children more prone to seek their mother when frightened or bored. Each day care subject in our study had two primary caretakers in addition to the mother—one caretaker from three and one-half to thirteen months and a second caretaker from thirteen to twenty-nine months. In addition, all received some care from other adults at the center. Nonetheless, day care subjects and home controls were equally likely to choose the mother as the target for solace and attentive nurturance when they were bored, tired, or afraid, and all the children preferred the mother to any other adult by a factor of 7. And the day care children were neither more nor less apprehensive than the home reared infants in uncertain situations.

The growth function for separation distress was remarkably similar for both rearing groups. Separation protest emerged at seven to nine months, peaked during the middle of the second year, and then declined in most children. This result, which has been replicated on many independent samples, implies that the growth function for separation protest is due primarily to the maturation of cognitive competences in any reasonably varied environment. Intensity of protest as well as age of first display and eventual decline of protest are probably monitored by specific experiences with caretakers and by temperamental factors. But the developmental course of the protest during the period six to thirty-six months is a function of maturing cognitive functions. These data are in accord with recent studies that report no important behavioral differences in the Ainsworth "strange person" situation between children of working mothers who have mother-surrogate caretakers and those being raised primarily by their biological mothers (Brookhart and Hock 1976).

Day care, when responsibly and conscientiously implemented, does not seem to have hidden psychological dangers. Since this generalization flies in the face of much popular belief, it is wise to maintain a skeptical attitude toward it. One valid objection may be that our methods of assessment were not sufficiently sensitive. It is always possible that a given set of procedures yields an insufficiently sensitive index of a given construct; the history of psychology is littered with such errors. For example many investigators who had found no social class differences on the Bayley scale under one year concluded that class had no effect on cognitive development during the first year of life. But when different methods were employed—such as time of fixation to discrepant events or vocalization in response to samples of speech —class differences emerged; the Bayley scale had just not been sensitive enough to detect them (Kagan 1971). Of course, it is logically impossible to assert that the day care and home control children are not psychologically different. Those who believe that good quality group care makes a positive difference have a responsibility to invent more sensitive ways of demonstrating the validity of their hypothesis. We will be among the first to accept that finding if their data so indicate.

But suppose that our methods were sensitive and that any differences in cognitive, social, and affective development between the day care subjects and home controls were trivial or transient. How is it possible that day care produced such insignificant effects, considering that the day care children spent as much time in the center as they did at home? One possible interpretation assumes that the child's psychological experiences at home have a priority because they are more salient and more affectively charged than those at the center. Let us consider some speculative bases for the differential salience of caretaking experiences at home and at the center. The biological mother being the primary caretaker at home for most of the children, the question becomes: Why does the mother's psychological impact on her child seem to be greater than that of the female caretakers in the day care environment? Part of the answer may be that the greater unpredictability of the mother causes her to become a more salient object in the infant's construction of reality.

Each of the caretakers in our center was keenly aware of the psychological diversity among the subjects as well as the differences in values between each mother and herself. As a result, each caretaker was unlikely to hold rigid standards for each child regarding talkativeness, cooperativeness, cleanliness, aggression, quality of play, or the age when particular developmental milestones should be reached. She was likely to be more relaxed than the mothers about these issues because she identified less profoundly with the children in her care. It was neither a source of deep pleasure if one of her children was slightly precocious in learning to drink from a cup nor a source of anxiety if a motorically retarded child spilled his milk every day. This tolerant attitude toward diversity in growth patterns led the caretaker to give each child considerable license to behave in accord with his temperamental disposition and relative level of maturity. With the exception of occasional bursts of aggression or prolonged crying, the caretaker did not intervene or impose constraints when the child seemed occupied and happy. Consequently, the child did not have serious uncertainties about the caretaker's actions when he was exploring his environment.

By contrast, the typical mother is more profoundly identified with and emotionally involved with her young child than is the surrogate caretaker. She subscribes to a set of standards and vigilantly watches her child for deviations from those standards. A mother who believes that any defiance of her requests is a sign of future rebelliousness, may quickly and firmly react to defiance with disapproval or punishment. Most mothers hold standards for cleanliness, potentially dangerous acts, aggression, talkativeness, and time of walking, talking, and other developmental milestones. The mother continually monitors deviations between her child's developing profile and her idealized standards; when the deviations become too large she intrudes into the child's life space and attempts to shape his behavior so that it is in closer conformity with her understanding of what is appropriate. Each intrusion—be it punishment, praise, affection, or command—punctuates the child's ongoing behavior and consciousness and creates a temporary node of uncertainty that alerts the child to the mother and to the action just issued. The next time that the child is in a similar context or entertains the possibility of initiating an action associated with prior intrusions, he generates a schema for the mother and the action and is uncertain of the consequences. Only when parental action toward a behavior is so consistent as to allow the child to establish a firm expectation about the parental response does the child's uncertainty subside. This speculation implies that the typical mother is a more distinctive source of uncertainty for the child than the other caretakers; the mother is less predictable—more difficult for her child to understand. In the language of classic psychoanalytic theory, the mother is more highly cathected than the caretaker. In the more modern language of information processing theory, the mother is a more salient event. Since the parent's behavior poses a more difficult problem for the child than that of the caretaker, the parent is a more affectively charged object. Of course, if a caretaker were to behave like our caricature of a mother (that is, if she were to hold fixed standards for the behavior of the child and were to intrude should the child deviate from the standards), the caretaker would also become highly salient and affectively charged. But in a typical American day care center—and certainly in our center—most caretakers do not behave in this manner.

This argument is supported by the results of five hours of naturalistic observations on fifteen middle-class infants seventeen to twenty months old attending a day care center and fifteen infants of the same class and age being reared at home (Rubenstein and Howes 1976). Directions, orders, reprimands, and prohibitions were given by the adult caretaker to the child four times more frequently in the home setting than in the day care center.

Crying—an index of uncertainty and frustration—was also more frequent at home than at the center.

Another reason for the mother's salience to the child is that the mother is more likely than others to be present when the child is experiencing extreme degrees of distress or joy. When the child in day care is very ill he usually stays home and is cared for by his parents. The emotional feelings surrounding the morning wakening and the evening preparations for bedtime are often highly charged periods; these events occur at home. Family interactions over the weekend are likely to possess a special emotional quality not experienced at the center. Finally there is likely to be more emotionally charged one-to-one interaction with the child, both pleasant and unpleasant, at home than at the center. At home the child is a more central focus of adult communication; at the center the child is one of many. From the child's perspective, the home is quite different from the center; his experiences within the family appear to have a special power that render the day care encounters less relevant.

It is interesting to note that a recent study of kibbutz-reared children who spent over 20 hours of each day in an infant house with a metapelet also revealed the salience of the mother over another caretaker (Fox 1977). The 12- to 15-month-old child was more likely to approach the mother than the metapelet when a female stranger was in the room with both caretakers, and was less apprehensive when with the mother and a stranger than when he was with the metapelet and the same stranger. It is the nature of the psychological interaction between child and caretaker that is important, not the amount of time each spends with the other. Perhaps that is why the American father, who typically spends little time with the child in the first two or three years of the child's life, is a salient figure who can buffer uncertainty and placate the infant.

This analysis of the relation of caretaker to infant has implications for the concept of attachment. Few would question the common observation that caretakers can be ordered with respect to their power to allay distress and the probability that they will be selected by the child when he is bored, frightened, hungry, or in pain. The persons at the top of that hierarchy are the primary targets of attachment. An early explanation of this fact, derived from classic learning theory, assumed that the hierarchy was a function of the history of successful and rewarding ministrations. That interpretation will not do. Since the caretakers in our study fed and diapered the babies as often as did their mothers, and the metaplot in the kibbutz ministered to their charges far more often than did the mothers, the sheer number of gratifying, nurturant interactions is not likely to be the primary determinant of attachment. It is likely that the psychological significance of any nurturant act depends on the prior salience of the nurturant figure.

We do not know if these speculations are valid. However, these data, as well as the results of the studies reviewed in chapter 3, do suggest that children from intact and psychologically supportive families who experience good surrogate care during infancy and early childhood resemble home-reared children from their own social and ethnic group to a greater degree than they do children of other ethnic and class backgrounds who are in the same extrafamilial environment. The effects of the home appear to have a salience that is not easily altered by a nurturant and cognitively challenging group care context.

It is obvious that these findings do not imply that *any* day care context would produce the same pattern of results. The data of our study are not to be regarded as providing scientific support either to those who believe that any form of extrafamilial care is innocuous or to those who doubt that such care can repair the psychological effects of a pathological home environment. When the surrogate care is conscientious and the home environment supportive, the young child's development appears to be under the stewardship of the home's influence.

Some policy implications

The existing data on group care are not complete enough to permit many firm statements about what characteristics of day care centers critically influence aspects of psychological development. No investigation has systematically varied ratios of caretaker to child, amount of space, number and quality of toys, or nature of curriculum and then estimated the effects of variation on these dimensions. Hence, recommendations must come from extensive experience with group care and wise guesses from available reports. Because recommendations are likely to be distorted by the prejudices of their authors, they are to be interpreted with caution. Consensus among experts is probably the best safeguard against invalid conclusions until better information is available.

The Federal government's role in regulating day care

We have shown that if the ratio of children to caretakers is not large, the staff is conscientious and well supervised, and there is some professional monitoring of the child's development, group care does not seem to have an important effect on the infant's development. Unfortunately, the characteristics of day care that can be monitored and regulated objectively by a governmental agency, like years of education of the staff members or number of toilet facilities in the day care center, are not likely to be of crucial importance. The attributes that are of importance among caretakers include a fondness for children, prior experience in raising children, some knowledge of child development, and a tolerance for the views of others. These qualities are not easily measured and therefore cannot be monitored effectively. Perhaps the best monitor of the quality of care is the family itself; the parents of a child in the center should be able to effect changes in the institution when they feel their child is developing anomalously. Government agencies could monitor day care centers by supporting inspection teams that would evaluate the children and staff at particular centers to determine if the development of the children was within normal limits. Although it is difficult to establish what a governmental agency's role should be in regulating the quality of care, the attributes that can and should be regulated include the following.

The ratio of staff to children During the infant's first three years of life, a caretaker should not be responsible for more than three infants. Our day care project found that responsibility for more than three infants placed a serious psychological burden on the individual caretaker. Moreover, in environments where the ratio is much greater, children suffer temporary retardation in cognitive and affective development. Children raised in institutional environments where one caretaker is responsible for many infants (often eight to twenty) typically are retarded in cognitive, affective, and social development (Peaslee 1976).

Space It is difficult to estimate the minimal amount of space each infant should have in a group care center. In addition to the space for sleeping, bathing, and toileting, it is estimated that an infant and toddler should have at least 100 square feet for play and for opportunities to exercise maturing motor and psychological competences. This does not mean that all centers with thirty infants must have 3,000 square feet, but rather that each child have adequate space to locomote, and that there should be some space around the child so that he or she can play alone without being continually intruded upon by other children. A center with thirty infants should probably have a minimum of 2,000 to 3,000 square feet of space. This is a guess based on experience and not a conclusion based on fact. One of us (J. K.) visited the People's Republic of China in 1973 and saw infant care centers with far less space than this; although the infants there seemed a little less attentive and less alert than American infants, 5-year-olds in the same housing complex were developmentally mature.

Age of admission It is probably unwise to admit an infant to the day care center before he is four weeks of age. During the opening month of life, the home environment may provide better protection against contagious infection, and it seems reasonable to assume that the mother would want to be with the very young infant during the early part of the postnatal adjustment. Even the People's Republic of China, which encourages early group care for infants, allows the mother two months with her newborn infant at home.

Some investigators have reported that from seven to eighteen months of age the child is especially vulnerable to being separated from the familiarity of the home. Since infants enter a new stage of cognitive functioning around seven to eight months of age, when they become vulnerable to fear following exposure to unfamiliar events or people, it is suggested that mothers who wish to enroll their infants in day care be encouraged to do so when the child is between one and seven months or older than fifteen to eighteen months of age.

Characteristics of personnel Although personnel of day care centers do not have to be college graduates or to have undergone extensive professional training, formal training is obviously of some value. But it is suggested that the caretaker's age, personality, and prior experience are more important than formal training. Women, especially those who have reared children, are probably best qualified for infant care, although younger or older women are also able to perform surrogate duties effectively and men are not inappropriate caretakers. It is also suggested that ethnic and social class membership of the staff should represent that of the parents who are using the center. Subcultures in the United States differ in their values, and some mothers feel reassured when some members of the staff represent their hopes and worries. Parental involvement in the center should be encouraged so that parents do not conclude that the responsibility for their child's development is out of their control. Parents must continue to believe that responsibility for the direction of their child's development is primarily theirs, not the staff's. Whether through regular meetings with staff, volunteer work at the center, or representation on the board of directors of the center, parents should be involved.

Risks There are three major risks associated with group day care for infants. The first concerns physical health. There is no question that colds and mild infections are more frequent in group care settings than they are in the home because of the constant contact with children who are temporarily ill. The child who is ill should be placed in a special room or area away from the rest of the children. In cases of epidemic, the center may have to be closed. It would be useful if a nurse or medical paraprofessional were available to care for mild illness and for routine mishaps. The center should have a reliable relation with a hospital or physician so that emergencies can be dealt with at once.

A second risk associated with day care is that the child who is temporarily quiet and withdrawn can become excessively isolated in a group care center where staff members are busy. The quiet, apathetic child who bothers no one can easily be forgotten.

A third risk concerns the course of cognitive development. Because language competence is one of the most important skills in our society, day care planners should encourage a one-to-one interaction between staff and the young child so that language development is enhanced. Day care environments for infants that restrict the child to cribs or playpens prevent the toddler from practicing maturing competences and retard the development of problem-solving skills (Peaslee 1976).

These dangers associated with day care of poor quality must not be minimized. The day care center in which the infant has reasonable attention from a conscientious caretaker, opportunity for active and playful interaction with an adult, stimulation of language, and opportunities for play seems to place the child at only minimal risk, however.

The Effect of Class and Ethnicity

Although social class did not prove to be a powerful variable in this study, its sphere of influence was not unexpected. The children of well-educated parents had better language skills and were more spontaneously verbal during the second year than those from less well-educated homes, as had been expected. Class was unrelated to attentiveness, attachment, social behavior, and cognitive talents other than linguistic ability.

The differences between Chinese and Caucasian children were the least equivocal and the most coherent. The Chinese children, both day care and home control, were less vocal, less active, less likely to smile to many, but not all, of the laboratory episodes, and were more apprehensive in the social and separation situations. The Chinese children were quieter, stayed closer to the mother, played less when they were with unfamiliar children or adults, and cried more often following maternal departure. Finally, the Chinese consistently showed more stable heart rates during the laboratory episodes. This cluster of qualities implies a disposition toward inhibition among Chinese children, a disposition that may have a partially biological basis. Daniel Freedman (1974) has reported that Chinese-American newborns are calmer, less labile, and are placated more easily than Caucasians:

> The European-American infants reached the peak of excitement sooner and had a greater tendency to move back and forth between states of contentment and upset. They showed more facial and bodily reddening probably as a consequence. The Chinese-American infants were scored on the calmer and steadier side of these items . . . The Chinese-American newborns tended to be less changeable, less perturbable, tended to habituate more readily and tended to calm themselves or to be consoled more readily when upset. In other areas (sensory development, central nervous system maturation, motor development, social responsivity) the two groups were essentially equal. [Freedman 1974, p. 150, p. 154]

Freedman also summarized observations made in the homes of upper-middle-class Chinese-American and Caucasian infants during the infants' first five months, revealing that the Chinese children were less labile, active, and irritable than Caucasians. More evidence comes from observations of Chinese and American preschool children in Chicago nursery schools; the Chinese-Americans were more emotionally controlled than the Caucasians (Green 1969). Gordon Bronson (1972) also noted less motor reactivity to novel events among infants of Asian ancestry than among Caucasian infants.

In our study, with the exception of heart rate range, we did not find significant differences between the two ethnic groups until the last half of the first year of life and the ethnic differences were more pronounced among children from the working class than from the middle class. We have good reason, therefore, to assume that familial experiences are contributing to the behavioral differences between the ethnic groups.

What are the possible bases for each of the four most consistent domains of difference—smiling and vocalization in response to the laboratory episodes, language skill at twenty-nine months, degree of inhibition and apprehension in the peer and attachment situations, and lability of heart rate?

Smiling and vocalization The Chinese children after seven months of age generally vocalized and smiled less than the Caucasians in response to the laboratory events. Since the 3-month-old Chinese smiled and vocalized as much as the Caucasians in the social interaction situation, the differences at one year of age cannot be the result of any fundamental or inherent resistance to affective display. We are left, therefore, with at least four other interpretations of the later differences.

The first is that the stimulus events we chose did not interest the Chinese, for smiling and babbling typically accompany involved information-processing. But since the Chinese were as attentive as the Caucasians, this hypothesis seems unlikely.

A second possibility is that the Chinese were less able to assimilate the events in the episodes; vocalization and smiling often occur as epiphenomena to assimilation. If the Chinese had greater difficulty comprehending these events, they would have been less reactive. This interpretation, which implies cognitive retardation in the Chinese child, is not attractive because there was no indication in the other data that the Chinese children were cognitively less prepared to assimilate these events.

A third possibility is that Chinese parents are less likely to play and interact with their infants in an affective manner and do not respond to the child's babbling and smiling with contingently reinforcing actions. Hence the child's disposition to babble and smile to interesting events is muted. This is essentially a conditioning interpretation. Although we did not gather home observations, our Chinese staff members, who know the community in which the children live, believe that consistent parental reward and stimulation of babbling and smiling in the infant is less common among Chinese than Caucasian families. This position is also supported by our observations in Guatemalan villages, where vocalizations in response to the laboratory episodes were seriously reduced, relative to the North Americans' responses, and where home observations indicated that the mothers and older siblings did not enter frequently into playful and verbal interactions with the infants. Thus the differences between ethnic groups in excitability could be the result of home experience.

Finally the Chinese may have been more apprehensive, for a state of uncertainty typically leads to inhibition of vocalization and smiling. The laboratory events were discrepant from the child's normal experience; that is one reason their attention to them was prolonged. If these events elicited greater uncertainty in Chinese than in Caucasian babies, we would have expected less babbling and smiling. At the moment we favor a complementary relation between these last two mechanisms—less reinforcement for affective display and a lower threshold for uncertainty toward discrepant experience among the Chinese children.

Language skill The Chinese attained lower scores on the Concept Formation Index at twenty-nine months of age and the language items of the Bayley scale at twenty months, although there was no ethnic difference on the recognition vocabulary test. Some of the words and phrases on the Concept Formation Index are more complex in Chinese than in English, especially the words *over* and *around* on which the Chinese did less well than the Caucasians. (It will be recalled that the test was administered in a Chinese dialect to those infants whose parents spoke Chinese at home.) Moreover, Chinese parents may encourage language development less actively than Caucasian families. The positive correlation, among Chinese, between vocalization to the laboratory episodes, on the one hand, and the Concept Formation Index and the Bayley Language scores, on the other, suggests that home experience may be partially responsible for ethnic differences in both phenomena.

Social behavior At thirteen, twenty, and twenty-nine months, during the peer play and attachment sessions as well as the visit to the unfamiliar day care center, the Chinese stayed closer to their mothers and played and vocalized less than the Caucasians, a combination of behaviors that is diagnostic of wariness or apprehension. It is possible that these contexts were less familiar to the Chinese than to the Caucasians—if we had only studied home-reared children that possibility would have been reasonable—but the greater wariness also occurred among the day care children, who had been exposed to many other children and numerous adults. On a few occasions we had observed children when an unfamiliar child or adult entered the day care center; more of the Chinese had shown apprehension and had sought their caretakers. The testing rooms where the play sessions occurred were as unfamiliar to the Caucasians as they were to the Chinese. During the attachment sessions, when the child was with two very familiar adults, the Chinese children continued to display more inhibition than the Caucasians. For these reasons we do not believe the differences in social behavior between the two ethnic groups are due to the fact that the social situations were more unusual for the Chinese, and we return to the hypothesis we used to explain the difference in reactivity to the laboratory events. The Chinese may have a lower threshold for uncertainty or apprehension in mildly uncertain situations—an idea with at least four possible meanings.

One meaning of lower threshold is psychological. The Chinese may attempt to generate more predictions or persist longer in attempts to assimilate the discrepant event, yet fail to comprehend it. As a result, they become more uncertain. However, there is no other information in the battery of assessments to support that notion. There is no indication that the Chinese children were either more or less prepared cognitively to generate predictions than the Caucasians.

A second explanation of a lower threshold for uncertainty among the Chinese is that they may differ from the Caucasians in the activation of mechanisms that counter initial inhibition. Any tendency to action is likely to subvert behavioral inhibition, and Caucasian children, as we have seen, are motorically more active than the Chinese.

A third possibility is that the Chinese and Caucasians do not differ in level of uncertainty, but that the behavioral inhibition is more easily released by a given level of uncertainty in Chinese than in Caucasian children. This interpretation will not explain the more frequent movement toward the mother nor the more frequent separation protest displayed by Chinese children; neither response is the product of an inhibition on action.

A fourth speculation is that the Chinese experience greater arousal of those physiological systems normally activated following recognition of an unfamiliar event. One index of such fearfulness is cardiac acceleration, but the Chinese did not consistently show more frequent or larger accelerations than the Caucasians. A related argument is that the physiological feedback that accompanies apprehension and inhibition is not more intense but persists longer in the Chinese children. Whereas nine out of ten children initially showed some decrease in play and some increase in proximity to the mother following the introduction of the unfamiliar peer, the major difference between the Chinese and Caucasian children is that the latter seemed to overcome their inhibitions more quickly. The Chinese continued to hover near the mother. Let us assume that inhibition of play and vocalization, as well as reluctance to leave the mother, are mediated by a certain level and quality of internal feedback from those physiological systems activated by the perception of the unfamiliar. If it is true that this physiological feedback persists longer in the Chinese than the Caucasians, their behavioral inhibition should persist for a longer period of time. The more stable heart rates of the Chinese children could be regarded as supportive of this idea, for under conditions of continued vigilance adults tend to maintain a steady heart rate with low variability for a long period of time.

Heart rate The early appearance of a more stable cardiac rate among the Chinese children studied implies differences between ethnic groups in the organization of those inhibitory central nervous system processes that mediate the steadiness of cardiac rate. An alternative implication is that the Chinese are temperamentally more prone to become vigilant in an unfamiliar context, so that their heart rates remain more stable. It is not possible, given the available data, to decide which alternative is more valid. However, both imply an inborn disposition that contributes to the wariness and inhibition displayed in the situations we presented in the laboratory. We do not claim that experience cannot alter this disposition, but only that the Chinese infant initially displays a behavior profile to his caretakers and to other children that is likely to elicit reactions that strengthen rather than transform the original disposition.

Intraindividual stability

The present data contribute to the debate surrounding the stability of psychological qualities during the opening years of life. In chapter 1 we distinguished between the ipsative and normative meanings of continuity. Although an ipsative analysis indicated that for infants from seven to eleven months of age fixation time was stable for attentiveness to laboratory episodes, most of the data did not lend themselves to a similar analysis, either because the variable was infrequent or the same variable was not measured over many assessments. The present discussion of stability, therefore, is based on the usual correlational analyses that reflect the degree to which children retain their relative rank on two distributions over time.

The evidence indicates even less stability over the first two and one-half years of life than we reported in an earlier longitudinal study (Kagan 1971). In the present investigation, attentiveness, vocalization, smiling, and heart rate reactivity during the first year were not very predictive of behavior at two and one-half years of age. Indeed, prior to seven months there was little continuity across periods as brief as two months. After seven months, attentiveness, smiling, and vocalization were typically stable across two- to nine-month periods, but it was rare for reactivity at seven or nine months to predict the same or a theoretically related disposition at twenty-nine months.

This lack of intraindividual stability also held for signs of apprehension to the unfamiliar peer. Inhibition at thirteen months was unrelated to inhibition at two and one-half years, although there was short-term stability across a seven to nine month interval. Similarly, the tendency to protest separation did not show long-term continuity—some infants showed protest on the early assessments; others began their protest later. The appearance of separation distress early in the first year of life did not predict distress during the second and third years. The average child protested on about three successive occasions, and fearfulness in these situations was unrelated to apprehension in other contexts (the unfamiliar peer or attachment situations). There was no evidence that a child carried a generalized behavioral trait of fearfulness across his first two and one-half years (see Matheny and Dolan 1975).

These conclusions are affirmed by the findings of others. When infants eight to twelve months old were visited at home on three separate occasions within a ten-day period by three different strangers in order to evaluate the stability of a fearful reaction to the unfamiliar person, only thirty percent of the infants who displayed apprehension on the first visit continued to display a negative reaction on the two subsequent visits (Solomon and Décarie 1976). Extensive data on fourteen children followed longitudinally during their first year of life failed to find much covariation between stranger distress and protest to separation; each variable had its own growth function and there was little evidence of intraindividual stability of a disposition toward fearfulness (Emde, Gaensbauer, and Harmon 1976).

These observations would not have been surprising to Freud, who realized that many childhood sources of anxiety vanish in time. In *Inhibition, Symptoms and Anxiety* he wrote,

> The phobias of very young children, fears of being alone or in the dark or with strangers—phobias which can almost be called normal—usually pass off later on; the child "grows out of them", as we say about some other disturbances of childhood. Animal phobias, which are of such frequent occurrence, undergo the same fate and many conversion hysterias of early years find no continuation in later life . . . Signs of childhood neuroses can be detected in all adult neurotics without exception; but by no means all children who show those signs become neurotic in later life. It must be, therefore, that certain determinants of anxiety are relinquished and certain danger-situations lose their significance as the individual becomes more mature. [Freud 1959, pp. 147-148]

Heart rate range provided the one exception to the fragile evidence for continuity. Among the Chinese, but less among the Caucasians, cardiac lability was remarkably stable from seven months on. The robustness of that stability was not reflected in behavior, however.

The absence of long-term intraindividual stability for infant temperamental dimensions like attentiveness, activity, and affectivity is in accord with the results of other longitudinal investigations that we summarized in chapter 3. The study by Kagan (1971), which assessed a large group of Caucasian, firstborn infants at four, eight, thirteen, and twenty-seven months for attentiveness, vocalization, smiling, and irritability in response to a variety of visual and auditory events, found little evidence that individual variation on these qualities in infants under one year predicted variation on similar characteristics at twenty-seven months of age or differences in IQ and reading ability at ten years of age.

In another extensive study of the stability of temperamental dimensions, known as the New York Study (Thomas et al. 1960; Thomas et al. 1963), interview and observational data on temperamental dimensions like passivity, adaptability, threshold of responsiveness, intensity of reaction, and mood were gathered continually during the period of infancy. Preliminary data from the New York Study seemed to indicate some threads of continuity, but later reports revealed no relation between ratings of these temperamental dimensions during the first year of life and a variety of behaviors at age five (Rutter et al. 1964; Rutter, Korn, and Birch 1963; Rutter 1970).

The available information indicates either that the obvious variation among infants during their first year is of no future consequence or that the threads of continuity are few in number and extremely subtle. It will be recalled that the infant's disposition to display the smile of assimilation to representations of faces was related to a reflective (in contrast to an impulsive) disposition on the Matching Familiar Figures Test at age ten (Lapidus, Kagan, and Moore 1977). Because the smile of assimilation during infancy appears to be more heritable than attentiveness, vocalization, or activity level (Kagan 1971), there is some rational basis for the belief that some component of the psychological variation among infants has a future. Although variation in the more obvious qualities of attentiveness, activity and irritability seems to have a short life, even persons most skeptical of the continuity assumption would acknowledge that available information is not yet sufficient to declare the case closed. The main effect of recent empirical reports has been to shift the burden of proof from those who argue against continuity from infancy forward to those who argue in favor of that idea.

Many of the psychological dimensions we assessed showed lawful growth functions—a time of emergence, a period of plateau, and a decline. The growth functions for these variables did not resemble those typically found for size of vocabulary or stature, which increase in a generally linear fashion with age and display moderate stability from after the first birthday to the second, third, and fourth years. Unlike recognition vocabulary, attentiveness, smiling, vocalization, play, motoricity, and proximity to mother are under the strong control of the context of evaluation. The number of words the child has mastered is independent of the setting of evaluation—he can be tested at home or in the laboratory. Attentiveness is never independent of a specific incentive situation, for each child has a potential to invest attention in events that are at optimal levels of discrepancy from his schemata. The suggestion that behavior depends on its context is at odds with the conviction of many mothers and clinicians that some children have great difficulty maintaining attention across many contexts. We have seen such children and verify that impression, but we failed to find evidence for such a quality in our study, perhaps because this attribute typically emerges later, during the third and fourth years, and because our sample did not contain many such extreme children. Perhaps a major reason for our failure to find stability of attentiveness is that during the child's first twenty-nine months his attention to episodes such as these is being monitored heavily by his stage of cognitive development. When the infant passes through the transitional period at seven to nine months and his short term memory is amplified, attentiveness increases. At thirteen months there is a brief period of heightened fearfulness, which also affects attention. The introduction of these new qualities resulting from the maturation of new psychological functions tends to mask individual differences in the potential for attentiveness to discrepant experience.

Verbal skills, however, displayed both coherence and short-term continuity. The 20-month vocabulary and Bayley mental scores were correlated with the concept formation index at twenty-nine months, and, among Chinese, the highly vocal infants were verbally more proficient. (In his earlier longitudinal study one of us [Kagan 1971] had also found a verbal cluster to be coherent and stable.) Indexes of linguistic competence show more coherence and continuity than do indexes of attentiveness or affective display because evaluations of language tap the possession of cognitive structures (how many words a child understands or uses), whereas evaluation of attentiveness or affect taps dynamic processes. The reaction to a repeated joke provides a fair analogy; a person's comprehension of the verbal message will be highly stable from one occasion to another, but his tendency to laugh at or even listen to the joke will not be stable since one hearing changes the interest value of the communication. We must distinguish between the cognitive structures that represent events, which are apt to be stable, and the dynamic processes that are activated in problem situations. The structure of the cells of the stomach wall maintain their form over a long period of time; the secretion of hydrochloric acid is less stable, for it depends on food arriving in the cavity. IQ scores are much more stable than personality variables, in part, because the former reflects acquired knowledge, whereas the latter is concerned with dispositions that are potentials for action. Moreover, when we assess stability of process we are usually inquiring about differences in the frequency with which a particular competence possessed by all persons is actualized. When we assess acquired knowledge like vocabulary, we are determining which children have and which do not have the structure. The latter cannot display the knowledge under any set of conditions.

One puzzle remains. Why is the long-term stability of the size of a child's vocabulary more stable than almost any dimension studied by psychologists? Not only are vocabulary scores highly stable from year to year but the vocabulary score on a standard intelligence test is highly correlated (about 0.8) with the total scale. The number of correct answers given by a 7-year-old on a ten-minute vocabulary test is a remarkably good predictor of his present and future school success. Why should size of vocabulary behave like stature in its power to predict a future state? One popular interpretation is that children differ in their basic ability to learn new verbal concepts so that 2-year-olds with a large vocabulary are simply more alert to language and more proficient at extracting meaning from speech. Since that ability is permanent, they will continue to learn new words at a faster rate than others and will always be ahead. This interpretation resembles the one used for the stability of stature, which says that some children possess a genome for "being tall" and hence grow faster than their peers. There are two problems with such an interpretation for vocabulary. The first is that social class always correlates with vocabulary, and it is not reasonable to assume that the genes for vocabulary acquisition are held predominantly by middle-class children. Moreover, an infant born to lower-class parents but adopted early by a middle-class family is likely to have a vocabulary as large as other middle-class children (M. Schiff, personal communication [1977]). That fact vitiates a strong genetic interpretation, but not a weak one, for there is considerable variability in linguistic knowledge among middle-class children. A more serious criticism of the genetic view is that vocabulary level is not highly correlated with ease of learning a new set of symbolic forms. Wayne Holtzman, Rogelio Diaz-Guerrero, and Jon D. Swartz (1975) found no relation between IQ and ease of learning a new set of paired associates; and isolated 10-year-old rural Guatemalans, who have very limited vocabularies, were able to learn the semantic meaning of a set of twenty logograms after four or five paired exposures to each symbol and an oral statement of its meaning (Kagan et al. 1977). It is difficult to imagine that a large number of children have inherited a special inability to learn the referential meaning of oral symbols but are able to learn the meaning of visual symbols.

A second popular interpretation of the stability of linguistic knowledge assumes that children are similar in their ability to learn new words but that those who live in a family environment that exposes them to new language forms will have the richer verbal corpus. Thus, since most children remain in the same family environment, those who have more words at age two will continue to learn new ones at a faster rate because the environmental source of their linguistic repertoire remains constant.The analogue here is to a marble in a track. If two identical marbles are placed on two infinitely long inclines, one waxed and the other not, the former will move ahead of the latter at once and at any point in the journey will be ahead of the marble in the nonwaxed channel because of the continuity in the quality of the track, not because of any inherent differences in the marbles. But children are not marbles. It is more likely that some combination of environmental opportunity and special cognitive aptitude is closer to the true state of affairs.

The correlation of language skills with social class, which appears in every study, suggests that exposure to a more diverse language environment and to encouragement of verbal activity promotes linguistic competence. Since those environmental conditions remain stable, so does the rank order for size of vocabulary. But we are receptive to the idea that some children, for reasons that are still obscure, acquire language at a faster rate than others. Whether this aptitude is due to a special interactive relation with parents or to qualities inherent in the child is not clear. If the aptitude exists, it is quite specific, for the verbally advanced children did not perform better on the memory or embedded figures tests.

It is of interest to note that a long-term study of malnutrition and cognitive development in moderately malnourished children from rural Guatemalan villages indicates that food supplementation to pregnant mothers and young children is more likely to facilitate a child's scores on tests of vocabulary knowledge and verbal information than his scores on tests of perceptual analysis, memory, or reasoning (Klein et al. 1977). This could mean that the families of higher status, whose children ordinarily had higher verbal proficiencies, were most likely to have taken advantage of the food supplementation, or it could indicate that rate of acquisition of vocabulary reflects the integrity of the central nervous system. Indeed, those favorable to this last idea might speculate that individual variation in health, genetic inheritance, or pre- and perinatal trauma is likely to be associated with differential functioning of the language area of the brain and, therefore, with rate of development of the child's language skills during the first half dozen years of life. If this admittedly bold speculation were affirmed, then the fact that vocabulary scores are the best predictors of total IQ and later academic progress would be more reasonable, and those who favor a strong genetic component in intellectual functioning would be on slightly firmer ground.

Some occasions of stability reported in the earlier longitudinal study (Kagan 1971) were not verified in the present study. We did not find stability of "tempo of play" from thirteen to twenty-nine months. In the earlier investigation there was moderate continuity of infants' dispositions to invest attention in play with toys, either for long or for short spans, from eight to twenty-seven months although there was no continuity from eight to thirteen or thirteen to twenty-seven months. In the present study we did not assess play at eight months; so it is not possible to ascertain if we would have replicated the earlier results. Although these findings cast a little doubt on the stability of tempo of play, we believe it should not be totally discarded, for we have recently found that children who displayed a slow tempo of play at twenty-seven months were more likely, at ten years of age, to show a period of contemplative inhibition to difficult embedded figures test items, whereas those whose tempo had been fast at twenty-seven months tended to offer solutions at once. It should be noted that this tendency was not related to performance on the Matching Familiar Figures Test and should not be regarded as synonymous with the reflection-impulsivity dimension. Reflection-impulsivity refers to the child's tendency to consider alternative hypotheses carefully in a situation of response uncertainty where the child knows what he must do to arrive at the right answer. His concern with failure is a critical determinant of whether he will be reflective or impulsive. In the difficult embedded figures test items we used, most children did not know how to proceed with the problem. Some paused to think; others acted. The former were slow-tempo 2-year-olds, the latter showed fast tempo in their play.

When the children left our program at twenty-nine months of age they varied enormously in their psychological qualities. One could not predict that variability from their behavior during the first year, but the differences in inhibition, apprehension, and spontaneous affect between Chinese and Caucasian children were noted from seven months on. The Chinese children, as a group, remained more inhibited than the Caucasians, as a group, over the period from twelve to twenty months. This fact implies that conditions in the homes of both the Chinese and the Caucasian families were more stable than the qualities of individual children, for within each ethnic group there was considerable individual change over time. The conditions of rearing in both Chinese and Caucasian homes appeared to impose specific behavioral profiles on children although each child remained receptive to some change.

Stages in the first two years

The most significant theoretical finding of this work was support for an important transition in psychological functioning between seven and nine months of age. In chapter 2 we listed the dispositions that appear at this time and postulated that a change in the ability to retrieve and compare schemata of past experience was central to these new phenomena. Our laboratory data have strengthened that view. The crucial evidence was the U-shaped function for fixation time and search displayed by the vast majority of both day care and home control children and replicated in the data for the more isolated Guatemalan infants. Typically, short-term stabilities in attentiveness or reactivity did not cross the seven-month age barrier. Attentiveness to the block or light event was moderately stable from five to seven months, but not from five to nine months. An ipsative analysis of constancy of fixation time indicated that important changes in attention were smallest from nine to eleven months, soon after the transition.

A key to understanding the transition is the discovery that between eight and twelve months of age infants become able to retrieve schemata for the locations of hidden objects with delays greater than one to three seconds. This amplification in memory capacity has profound implications, for now the child can compare the present with more than just the wispy remains of an event that happened moments ago. Once the infant can reach back in memory and extract a representation of the past it is only a minor victory to generate a representation of the future. That competence, which we believe emerges soon after the amplification of retrieval memory, may be critical to a psychological explanation of the growth of separation protest, apprehension to peers, and wariness to the laboratory episodes. Our data showed a temporary increase in restless motoricity and irritability at thirteen months, the age when separation anxiety and the anticipatory fixations to the car event were at a maximum. At this age the child attempts to relate an event to his schema and tries to make a prediction of the immediate future. If he is not successful, he may become fretful, even in response to what seems to an observer to be an innocuous event.

Because we believe that separation distress and peer apprehension are mediated by a similar mechanism, we must address the fact that the former occurs a little earlier than the latter. The state of apprehension requires both the ability to generate questions that cannot be answered and a well-articulated schema for the event that is related to the discrepant one that cannot be understood. The 9-month-old has a much better schema for his mother and her possible actions vis-à-vis the child than he does for another infant. Hence when his mother leaves him alone with a stranger or in an unfamiliar room, he has a rich history of experience he can draw on to evaluate the significance of that event. The typical 9-month-old reared at home does not have as good a representation of another infant as of his mother and hence is less likely to generate a question about the actions of the other child. The child in day care should have a better set of structures for other children's actions than the home-reared child; we found earlier signs of inhibition to the unfamiliar peer among the day care children.

This set of moderately coherent findings on the age at which an infant displays signs of the transition may be useful to the clinician seeking an index of the rate of psychological growth or to the psychologist as an additional milestone of early childhood development. We know there is a transition in scanning strategies at four to eight weeks and a transition in rate of habituation and recognition memory at twelve to sixteen weeks, and now it appears there is a transition in memory at eight to ten months. When all the markers have been put in place we should have a much clearer map of this marvelously exciting period.

Relevance for theory

Does this corpus of data alter our faith in any of the popular assumptions of developmental psychology and does it inform any of the basic puzzles? That is a useful question since one test of the significance of research is its relevance to a discipline's presuppositions.

The recognition of intraspecies variation and the possibility that some forms had become extinct were incompatible with the eighteenth-century view that the world had been created at one moment and nothing had changed since that time. The dissonance provoked by those facts forced many to ask again, "Why the variation?" and to expect an answer different from the one contained in the Bible. Once the question had been asked with a fresh perspective, the solution proposed by Charles Darwin, Alfred Wallace, and others became more likely.

Child psychologists are concerned with three questions: 1) How can we explain the psychological changes that accompany growth? 2) How can we explain variation among children at any one stage? 3.) How stable are the structures produced by early experience?

The popular answers to the first two puzzles, at least among American psychologists, have emphasized the role of experience. The child's opportunities for interaction—with objects and with people—were supposed to be the catalysts for psychological change. Psychology's initial resistance to Piaget was due, in part, to his insistence that experience alone was insufficient to account for behavioral development and that the maturation of competences that waited upon changes in the central nervous system had to be a part of the developmental equation. The current data support Piaget's view. The age functions for attention, vocalization, smiling, as well as separation distress and peer apprehension seem to reflect fundamental biological changes that permit the infant to process information in different ways at different ages. Although experience monitors the age of emergence or decline of a competence and the asymptotic level of proficiency, it cannot, except under extreme circumstances, stop the appearance of those functions that are part of our genome nor prevent the disappearance of those that have lost their value.

The results presented here may help solve the puzzle of variation among children of the same age while countering the occasionally glib assumption that individual differences in behavioral profile are predominantly the result of prior experience. The day care environment contained, for many of our subjects, a markedly different set of events from the ones at home, yet we could not detect any consistent consequences of the day care encounters, save the slight difference in initial interaction with other children. Moreover, the variation within sex, class, and ethnic groups was, in most cases, almost as great as the variation between them. We believe that the child's temperamental qualities, especially activity level, inhibition in contexts of change, and lability, exerted important influences on the behaviors we coded. These factors must be accommodated; a given experience should not be expected to have a uniform effect on all children. The explanatory power attributed to environmental events must be shared with the consequences of biological maturation and temperamental dispositions.

These data and studies cited here also provide counterevidence to the traditional assumption of the stability of variation in early behavior. With the exception of heart rate range, we found very little intraindividual stability from the first to the second and third years of life for attentiveness, excitability, or fearfulness. Change, not stability, seems to be the most prominent characteristic of the opening year of life. We suspect, but have not yet documented, that the late childhood and adolescent personality traits we are fond of—like self-confidence, intellectual ability, motivation, hostility—do not become firmly established until the child is six to ten years old, after attitudes toward self and others have become structured as a result of identification with parents, class, and ethnic groups, and following opportunities to arrive at conclusions regarding one's competences and liabilities relative to peers. Although one of us (J.K.) had a similar suspicion in 1962 (Kagan and Moss 1962), only now does it seem more obvious.

Comments on ethics and the application of scientific facts

Every community needs some assurance that it has protection against a small set of potential dangers. The alien group that might seize its property and restrict its freedom of decision and action is a potential enemy for all societies. Most communities have a cohort of men to call upon in order to reduce this uncertainty. A second danger, internal to the group, is the disquiet that grows when there is too great a disagreement on values among the legitimate members of the society. One protection against this threat is to impose a common set of standards on the community; Plato, Hobbes, and Mao Tse-tung argued forcefully for that strategy. Our own society, committed to egalitarianism, tolerance, and liberty, rejects that temptation. We believe that one way to combat that peril is to gather knowledge, hoping that when the community learns the facts their respect for reason will lead to a shared perspective and a resolution of quarrels. A third danger lies with the uncertainty of the future. Here, too, our society believes that facts are useful; by providing a preview of future perils, they give us time to prepare for or prevent them. Although facts are not without utility, they are not as effective as many believe as guides for action on issues that are primarily ethical.

It is useful to know whether day care of good quality has a psychological effect on infants. If it does not, as we have suggested here, that fact quiets those who believe it is harmful. If it does make a difference, those who claim it is innocuous would have to rethink their position. But neither outcome implies that we should increase or decrease the availability of day care. That is an ethical decision not contained in the facts.

We need a corrective to the popular belief that the results of scientific research are to be used not only to enhance understanding but also as the primary basis for deciding issues that are touched deeply by personal values. We would like to believe, with the Greeks, that reason reveals morality. The Greeks assumed that beyond the sensory world of diversity were enduring substances that comprised reality. Thales thought it was water; Anaximander treated it as a boundless entity; Heraclitus insisted it was fire; and Plato supposed it to be a set of geometric forms. But despite the variability in the form of the answer, they agreed that there was a small number of abstract, enduring substances that were the essential bases of natural experience. Since the motion of these entities gave rise to all natural phenomena, including man's thoughts and actions, in principle, man's values and beliefs could be derived from natural laws. Plato then added a critical assumption. The substances in motion were ideal forms with a natural disposition to move toward the good. Since man's thoughts were the product of the motion of these ideal forms, knowledge of what was good would inevitably lead to morally proper behavior. By attributing value to nature's elemental substances, Plato provided ethics with a foundation in natural law. Faith in the power of intellect to reveal proper conduct was subdued during Christianity's high period, when morality was given by God's word and faith in authority replaced reason as the procedure to discover virtue. But when post-Renaissance science emerged, it insisted again that the facts of nature were to be the basis for ethics.

Each historical era holds a few primary assumptions which have to be defended against the attacks that inevitably result from the roll of social events. And each period awards differential status and power to the particular intellectual weaponry selected to defend the presuppositions, whether logic, appeal to authority, phenomenology, or empirical fact. The quintessential enigma in fourteenth-century Europe was whether God existed. Thomas Aquinas defended God's existence by logical argument; he would have chosen a different strategy today. The two central uncertainties of modern society are whether there is a priority of significance that can be assigned to an organism's actions and whether there are any absolute moral truths? Because science, which has been given the responsibility of answering the first of those questions, depends on objective evidence, facts have become the most potent method of persuasion and the preferred basis for decisions. Although the significance of an action is quite different from its moral standing, some scientists have tried to reduce these two quite separate issues to one by tacitly assuming that significance is to be judged by adaptive value and by subtly promoting the idea that the morality of an action could be decided by its adaptive significance. Konrad Lorenz, for example, suggests that aggression is a significant act because it permits the animal to survive; he allows the uncritical reader to conclude that a behavior that is in such accord with nature cannot be totally immoral. Others award significance to sexual behavior since it leads to an increase in the population of a species.

The publication of E. O. Wilson's *Sociobiology* (1975) stimulated scholarly discussions aimed at determining what ethical principles, if any, could be deduced from present knowledge of the biological bases of behavior. Such inquiries are motivated, in part, by a desire to find some nonrelativistic basis for moral propositions. Since biology is a strong discipline it is hoped that information on man's inherited dispositions can provide a guide to an ethical code. Wilson wrote, "Scientists and humanists should consider together the possibility that the time has come for ethics to be removed temporarily from the hands of the philosophers and biologicized" (p. 562). But as a biologist he was wary of the responsibility he had just advocated, so a few pages later, he added, "It should also be clear that no single set of moral standards can be applied to all human populations . . . to impose a uniform code is therefore to create complex intractable moral dilemmas—those, of course, are the current condition of mankind" (p. 564). I. Eibl-Eibesfeldt had voiced a similar objection to the notion of relying on biological predispositions to rationalize man's actions when he wrote that there is "no doubt that ethologists do not intend to accept aggression as inevitable . . . there is no reason to accept behavioral dispositions as inevitable and uncontrollable" (1974, p. 53).

Roger Sperry, who has written forcefully and elegantly on this theme (1972, 1977), has tried to link a person's value decisions to his neurophysiology by making consciousness an emergent property of neural events that has the capacity to influence the very processes that sustain its existence. The assumption of a richly reciprocal relation between human decision and neural processes led Sperry to declare that, "Objective facts and subjective values become parts of the same universe of discourse . . . Human values are inherently properties of brain activity, and we invite logical confusion in trying to treat them as if they had independent existence artificially separated from the functioning brain" (1977, pp. 240-241). The criteria for final value decisions, when all the facts are in, is our guess as to nature's intention; Sperry continued, "what is good, right, or to be valued is defined very broadly to be that which accords with, sustains, and enhances the orderly design of evolving nature" (1977, p. 243). But even Sperry, who sees scientific fact as the very best guide to values, recognized, with Wilson, that science cannot deliver final absolute answers to moral dilemmas, only better informed ones, when he added, "The question is not whether science can provide final, complete or perfect answers but whether there is any alternative that does as well, by long term, future generation standards" (1977, p. 243).

Thus even those natural scientists who argue most forcefully for viewing man's behavior in an evolutionary or biological perspective do not go so far as to suggest that our moral evaluations of human behavior should accommodate only to what is known about man's biology or the actions of infrahuman species. They stop short of stating that what is true in nature should form the sole basis of what should be good for man. They recognize that truth is a quality that applies to propositions, not to events or people; *good* (or *bad*) is an adjective that applies to events, not sentences. There are neither good propositions nor true people.

The modern world forces many adults to be more competitive or aggressive than they wish to be, and they brood about the morality of those actions and related motives. When the biologist declares that competitiveness and aggression are natural responses (perhaps a true statement) his readers are prone to interpret that statement as meaning that such behavior is also morally proper. The press of everyday affairs demands certain behavioral accommodations, and we try as best we can to cover them with a veil of morality so that we can say that our actions are not only necessary but virtuous. Each adult needs guides for action in times of uncertainty, and it is reasonable that each looks to facts for that guidance. But we should not confuse such information with moral evaluation.

The procedures of science comprise one of the most powerful—some might say the most effective—ways to illuminate the nature of the world. The propositions that are constructed from the mysterious marriage of the concrete and the imagined are capable of bringing clarity, comprehension, and, on occasion, a feeling that combines delight, awe, wonder, and serenity into an emotion for which we have no name. Science is to be celebrated! But we still ask for more. Not satisfied with the gift of understanding we demand that the fruits of empirical effort also tell us what we ought to do when alternative actions require choice.

Knowledge and morality are, of course, not independent. There is a relation between what is and what ought to be; between an empirically based belief and an ethical one. Facts can eliminate incorrect bases for holding a moral conviction, and conditions in nature or society can lead to actions that become linked to moral imperatives. In a society with no married couples there can be no adultery; in a community with no centralized state there can be no treason.

Our moral concepts are not completely independent of our factual beliefs. Moral statements are seriously influenced by beliefs assumed to be true. Hence what ought to be true is not independent of what one believes to be true.

> Consider the ten commandments, for an obvious example. It is quite clear that they were issued to a group that believed in God and perhaps in other gods as well, so long as they were not ranked ahead of God himself. The first commandments would have no application were these beliefs absent. Or they would be empty and only trivially satisfied. The group quite obviously had a family structure, a marriage structure and some system of property relationships. An orphan does not fall within the scope of a commandment to honor his father and his mother. Without a (certain) form of marriage, adultery is logically impossible; adultery presupposes fornication, but the converse presupposition does not hold true. Theft entails, through the analysis of the concept, taking something, though the converse inference hardly holds, and there could be no theft without property, though physical preemption would remain. The commandments, too, presuppose certain traits of human psychology; covetousness, say. Were envy eradi-

> cated from moral psychology the tenth commandment would have no point, or, again, it would be trivially satisfied. Charity implies the existence of the poor as hope implies the absence of certitude: one cannot hope for what one knows will be the case. And so on. It is a fact that such morally charged terms as "honesty, thrift, chastity, courage, obedience" and the like require, if we are to explain their meaning, the elaboration of conditions that must be understood in purely factual terms. So at least part of the definition of any moral term will consist in factual ones . . . it is difficult to suppose the existence of any moral term that would be empty of factual content: morality is, after all, designed for men living in the world which inevitably presupposes certain facts or at least certain factual beliefs regarding the world and men. [Danto 1972, p. 10]

Some parents worry about whether placing their child in day care is morally defensible. Doubt over the morality of that action is most likely to occur when parents acknowledge the possibility that they might not care about their children. If they had no doubt there would be less anguish. Because modern parents are uncertain about the proper balance to be maintained between narcissism and devotion to their children, their decision to use substitute care has the potential to elicit guilt. In the Peoples' Republic of China or on Israeli kibbutzim, where extrafamilial care is common, the guilt may be less sharply felt.

If eighteenth-century Americans had not been so keen on basing ethics and legislation on natural phenomena, a great deal of conflict might have been avoided. During the century prior to the Civil War, many of the arguments for and against the morality of slavery hinged on whether the negro was of the same species as the white. If he was, he had to be awarded freedom; if he was not, slave owners were justified in denying him liberty. Empirical fact was used as the basis for deciding an essentially ethical issue. Why wasn't the eighteenth-century American more friendly to a different defense of ethics, either adherence to some absolute principle (like equality) or even the word of authority? Why did they and why do we regard empirical fact as the most potent defense of a moral proposition?

One reason is that empirical fact is supposedly objective. It resides in nature rather than opinion. It therefore seems impartial, and, by implication, just. Additionally, science, which is the coherent organization of fact, has gained the respect of the community through marvelously useful inventions that have permitted humanitarian advances, technical feats that magnify man's sense of potency, and the ability to predict a few brief moments in the future. As a result of these real victories, science and a rational approach to experience have acquired a secular power that makes it easy for citizens to expect that the knowledge generated by scientists is the best guide to morals.

Consider three ethical issues being debated in contemporary America—abortion, homosexuality, and racial segregation in educational institutions.

Proponents and opponents of all three themes are responsive to arguments of fact. Those concerned with abortion want scientists to tell them when life begins, as if that question had an empirical answer of the same order as, "At what time will the next solar eclipse occur?" Those who want more liberal legislation on homosexuality applaud when research shows that homosexuals have not inherited an anomalous disposition, and assume that the resolution voted by the members of the American Psychiatric Association that homosexuality was not a disease had scientific content. Opinions on segregation are influenced by published reports on the academic achievement of black children bused to integrated school settings. But such factual information is secondary to the quintessence of the ethical issue. The decision on abortion turns on whether a woman has the right to decide what to do with her body. The value conflict pits the mother's right to autonomy of personal choice against the fetus' right to life. These are transcendental themes which cannot be decided by an appeal to evidence. Since Western society currently holds individual freedom sacred, the Supreme Court's 1976 ruling sided with the mother.

Legislation on homosexuality also turns on whether adults are free to behave as they choose, and recent court rulings have used this premise in arriving at decisions. Attitudes toward busing to achieve racial integration in schools are also influenced by facts, for data on the academic achievement of children in integrated settings is always part of the argument. The moral dilemma involves the sacredness of each family's liberty set against the society's need to move more quickly toward an integrated community. The courts, being pragmatic, have waffled between the two positions, but consistent with their recent decisions on abortion and homosexuality, have leaned toward self-determination. There is, of course, little in natural law that affirms or refutes either ethical stance.

Western nations face a major decision regarding the primacy of individual freedom when it conflicts with the harmony of the larger community. Resolution of that dilemma should be made on the basis of a commitment to a particular set of values. We members of Western society cannot evade that responsibility by pretending that facts will make the proper choice obvious and save us the agony of having to choose between two of our most beloved ideals.

Although since the time of Galileo we have become accustomed to referring to the empirical sciences most matters of truth as well as of ethics, we have forgotten that the natural sciences confessed, at the beginning of this century, that their knowledge had no implications for morality, since nature had no values. Science, we were told, was "value free" and the citizenry would have to look elsewhere for ethical guidance. As the nineteenth century came to a close, many European intellectuals—scientists, philosophers, and novelists—were elaborating Immanuel Kant's distinction between knowledge and values and assenting to Sören Kierkegaard's plea that we recognize the unbridgeable chasm between what is known and what is good. Ethics was not to be found in reason, Kierkegaard claimed, but in each person's faith.

Despite the arguments of Kant, Kierkegaard, and others, the increasing power of science intimidated citizen and scholar, and in the years prior to World War I there was a need for an elegant philosophical statement that used the procedures of science, in this case logic, to justify the separation of fact and value. Allan Janik and Stephen Toulmin (1973) have suggested that Ludwig Wittgenstein's *Tractatus Logico-Philosophicus* was written, in part, to accomplish that mission. "Wittgenstein's radical separation of facts from values can be regarded as the terminus of a series of efforts to distinguish the sphere of natural science from the sphere of morality, which had begun with Kant, had been sharpened up by Schopenhauer, and had been made absolute by Kierkegaard" (p. 197). Wittgenstein's intention for the Tractatus was not only to write a critique of language but also to argue for the transcendent quality of ethics—to celebrate morality's permanent independence from objective knowledge. Trying to find a compromise between the physics of Hertz and Boltzmann and the ethics of Kierkegaard, Wittgenstein wrote, "it is impossible for there to be propositions of ethics . . . propositions express no theory that is higher—ethics is transcendental—ethics and aesthetics are one and the same" (1922). But the society was not receptive to such a declaration. It had been persuaded for over several centuries that the natural sciences could provide guides to moral imperatives. Since neither the Church nor philosophy was able to fill the void, (unfortunately, many twentieth-century philosophers lost interest in metaphysics and the problems of truth and morality and left the society more emotionally dependent on science than ever), the social sciences stepped forward to fill the breach. Psychology, sociology, and anthropology occupied the space abandoned by philosophy, the Church, and the physical sciences and implicitly promised to solve the problem of ethical guidance by gathering objective information on issues that were of concern to the community.

It is not clear that the social sciences can keep their promise. It is commonly believed, by scientists and nonscientists alike, that investigations of nonmodern cultures will reveal man's basic nature and that such knowledge will tell us how to adjust our ethics so that they are consonant with nature's wish rather than in opposition to it. It is unlikely that ethnographies can serve that function. Middle-class Americans allow their children to express anger and mild aggression because they believe it is in accord with nature. Many parents tell their children to defend themselves if coerced because they have been told that if anger is suppressed a child may develop psychosomatic symptoms or even depression, since empirical data have suggested that repression of anger and excessive control of aggression can lead to unhealthy somatic tension and psychic disquiet. But Jean Briggs (1970) challenged the universality of the principle. Among the Utku Eskimo of Hudson Bay, with whom Briggs spent twenty months, every display of anger in a child after age two is followed by a "silent treatment." Initially the child is upset, but after several years there are no more tantrums and little interpersonal aggression. However colitis, migraine headaches, and the other psychological symptoms that are presumed to result from suppressed anger are absent. Hence it is reasonable to ask: Is it basic to human nature to express anger or to suppress it? The answer seems to be "Neither." The consequences of suppression of anger are a function of the social context in which the child is adapting. In our own culture, where children can leave the home to play with friends and where the social norm is to defend oneself when attacked, it is adaptive to permit children some public display of hostility. But for a family living in an igloo nine months of the year, it is maladaptive to allow family members to live with anger for three-quarters of every year. Should they do so, it is highly likely that they would develop somatic symptoms.

Robert Edgerton (1971) evaluated personality traits like autonomy, independence, aggression, and sexuality in several African tribes, some of whom were pastoral and some agricultural. Within the same tribe, he found the pastoralists to be more likely to express anger and autonomy, while the agriculturalists were more likely to suppress interpersonal aggression. Edgerton argued that when two pastoralists developed mutual resentment they could separate and wander off with their property, while the settled agriculturalists could not. Both clusters of personality traits are natural, as are both modes of sustenance, and each economy carries with it a modal set of traits. Neither the agriculturalists nor the pastoralists are closer to human nature.

Comparative psychologists would like to make inferences about the essence of human nature from studies of animal behavior. Jane Goodall has commented that day care centers are not healthy for infants because nature intended mothers to be with their children during the first three years of life; Goodall bases her advice on the fact that chimpanzee mothers behave this way. But closely related species of macaque monkeys behave differently with their infants—the bonnet macaque relinquishes her infants to almost any other female in the living area, whereas the stubtail macaque ferociously protects her infant from the curious. Since there is so much variability of behavior among related species of our nearest subhuman kin, it is difficult to argue that the behavior of any one of them informs us of nature's intention for the human species.

Moreover, our selection of the behavior and species to study is often guided by current social preoccupations. The contemporary Western world requires competitiveness, a capacity for aggression and dominance, access to one's sexual passions, and an ability to be alone. Hence, scientists are tempted to investigate those qualities in animals rather than their opposites. There are many more studies of the effect of brain stimulation or ablation on aggression than on passive withdrawal. Yet one can probably alter passive behavior in a rhesus monkey as easily as aggression by destroying or stimulating parts of the brain. The comparative psychologist, who cannot help but be influenced by the unresolved issues in his society, may investigate mother-infant separation in primates because that topic is currently a node of uncertainty in the human community, not because it happens frequently among primates in natural contexts. Or he may investigate the influence of early social isolation on later development, because some scientists have claimed that educationally retarded children lack sufficient physical stimulation during the early years.

The plea for "relevant research" by congressmen and citizens is based on the assumption that such knowledge can guide ethical decisions about the building of day care centers, the education and socialization of children, and the treatment of delinquents. Science can suggest the mechanisms by which individuals decide whether an action or thought is good or bad and point to invalid bases for ethical positions; but it cannot supply the constructive basis for a moral proposition. Moral propositions imply that one action is better than another, and it is rarely the case that a particular action is good for all of the potential beneficiaries. The person at risk, his family, and the society in which the individual lives are three major social beneficiaries in our society; few acts are good for all three. Each moral decision carries with it an implied beneficiary; abstract moral principles rarely map across all situations. Classic Chinese society accepted this limitation on law; Western society resists it because of an affection for simplicity and abstract rules that subdue local perturbations.

The results of empirical research cannot be the sole guide for judging what is psychologically good for children or families. Regardless of the facts, each individual must make a value decision, for one cannot rely on evidence to rank the degree of benevolence associated with all possible outcomes for all possible targets. Hence, ethical decisions must be informed by a priori assumptions.

During the first three decades of this century a strong eugenics movement in the United States looked to the science of genetics as a basis for legislation on sterilization of immigrant populations (Ludmerer 1972). Supporters of this movement urged restriction of marriage and sterilization in order to reduce the occurrence of epilepsy, criminality, mental retardation, and insanity. Sixty years later, when the scientific bases for a genetic component to schizophrenia and certain forms of mental retardation were even stronger than they were in 1910, fewer Americans were receptive to the suggestion that individuals afflicted with these disorders be sterilized because our moral attitudes toward sterilization had become less permissive, not because science had shown the original idea to be faulty.

Facts are, of course, not irrelevant and at times are critically useful. As psychologists came to discover that most forms of criminality and alcoholism were not inherited, the position of the eugenicist became more difficult to defend. Prior to World War I eugenicists had spread the idea that there was a large increase in feeble-minded persons in the population and that these genetically tainted individuals were responsible for most forms of antisocial behavior (a fear reminiscent of the recent concern over lower scholastic aptitude test scores among contemporary high school graduates). This fallacious idea was weakened in 1919 when the results of intelligence tests on 1.7 million recruits were published. The IQ data indicated that 47 percent of American whites were feeble-minded. Since this proportion was so high it made the eugenicist's position appear foolish, an instance of knowledge making a moral position less tenable. Nonetheless many still held the old belief (Ludmerer 1972). Although scientific information had weakened the rational basis for the ethical view on sterilization, it did not, and, of course, could not, help Americans decide whether sterilization is a good or bad action to impose on any individual.

A final example of the necessity for a priori assumptions is more recent. Since World War II, federal and state legislators have been generous in support of educational functions and special instructional programs for children, especially those from poor families and those from ethnic minorities. Indeed, one of the rationales for such aid was that it would lead to greater economic equality in the nation. Christopher Jencks' controversial book *Inequality* (1972) challenged that premise. He used facts to argue that the decision to invest money in education in order to equalize income was ill founded. Although one could argue with some of the facts, even if they are valid, their utility lies in their power to refute those who want to base educational funding on a desire to reduce diversity in income. The facts do not imply that the community cannot decide, a priori, that it is still good to invest in education—for self-actualization, for appreciation of science and art, or for general enlightenment.

Where are the a priori assumptions necessary for ethical decisions to come from? If our ethics cannot originate in either facts or the opinions of a benevolent authority, where does the community find a basis for generating moral propositions? One source lies in consensual sentiment, which will change over time. Most Americans regard aggression, violence, dishonesty, and coercion as morally indefensible, and a referendum on each would reflect that deeply held belief. Indeed on each election day more and more moral issues are placed on the local ballot, indicating the community's receptivity to using public sentiment as a guide to ethical dilemmas. When the Supreme Court recognized how difficult it was to define pornography in an objective and logically consistent manner it declared that local attitudes should determine which books and movies violated sensibilities. The court legitimized the individual's private, emotional reaction as a participant in the creation and maintenance of values. It is extremely difficult to implement that strategy more broadly in our society because of the extraordinary diversity of opinion on critical issues and a deep resistance to having legally binding propositions rest, in any way, on nonrational grounds. That is one reason why science has been placed in the position of moral arbiter. Although science can help in this role by supplying factual evidence which disconfirms the invalid foundations of ethical premises, it cannot supply the basis for a moral proposition. Facts prune the tree of morality; they cannot be the seedbed.

It is a bit odd that this argument must be made in a book written and published in New England, for many of America's nineteenth-century philosophers, including Emerson, Peirce, and James, also rejected Locke's rationalist approach to ethics. Each held, with different degrees of conviction, that a person's feelings about an issue, even though unsupportable by logical argument or a coherent corpus of established fact, should be respected in matters of ethics. This attitude was present early in American history. James Wilson, a colonial philosopher of law, defended a phenomenological contribution to moral commitment: "If I am asked—why do you obey the will of God? I answer—because it is my duty so to do. If I am asked again—how do you know this to be your duty? I answer again—because I am told so by my moral sense of conscience. If I am asked a third time—how do you know that you ought to do that, of which your conscience enjoins the performance? I can only say, I feel that such is my duty. Here investigation must stop; reasoning can go no further" (in McCloskey 1967).

Jefferson held similar views, in part, because he wanted to insure that the farmer without access to training in logic, rhetoric, and science would still be able to construct a valid moral code. In a letter to a nephew he wrote,

> Moral philosophy. I think it lost time to attend lectures in this branch. He who made us would have been a pitiful bungler if he had made the rules of our moral conduct a matter of science. For one man of science there are thousands who are not. What would have become of them? Man was destined for society. His morality, therefore, was to be formed to this object. He was endowed with a sense of right and wrong nearly relative to this. This sense is as much a part of his nature as the sense of hearing, seeing, and feeling; it is the true foundation of morality . . . the moral sense or conscience is as much a part of man as his leg or arm. It is given to all human beings in a stronger or weaker degree, as force of members is given them in a greater or less degree . . . State a moral case to a ploughman and a professor. The former will decide it as well and often better than the latter because he has not been led astray by artificial rules. [In Boyd 1955]

Even though Jefferson's apparent anti-intellectualism was influenced by the desire to celebrate the common sense of the average citizen, such a prejudice does not necessarily indicate that the use of sentiment to help decide moral issues is either incorrect or, for that matter, dangerous. But as we have indicated, this view lost adherents in the years after the Civil War as science gained more respect and greater persuasive power. In the decade before the turn of the century W. K. Clifford wrote,

> Belief is desecrated when given to unproved and unquestioned statements for the solace and private pleasure of the believer . . . whoso would deserve well of his fellows in this matter will guard the purity of his belief with a very fanaticism of jealous care, lest at any time it should rest on an unworthy object and catch a stain which can never be wiped away . . . If a belief has been accepted on insufficient evidence the pleasure is a stolen one . . . it is sinful because it is stolen in defiance of our duty to mankind. That duty is to guard ourselves from such beliefs as from a pestilence which may shortly master our own body and then spread to the rest of the town . . . it is wrong always, everywhere, and for everyone to believe anything upon insufficient evidence. [In White 1972, pp. 188-189]

William James answered Clifford and insisted, with Jefferson, that a moral belief was not governed solely by scientific evidence: "A moral question is a question not of what sensibly exists but of what is good or would be good if it did exist. Science can tell us what exists, but to compare the worths both of what exists and what does not exist we consult not science, but what Pascal calls our heart" (1898, p. 2).

By taking this position, we are obviously not suggesting that evidence and logic should not participate in the resolution of ethical issues. The products of scientific research have contributed, occasionally in a major way, to changes in social practices that most citizens regard as ethical in nature. For example, evidence indicating that black children in segregated schools were not mastering basic skills at a normative level was part of the basis for the Supreme Court's 1954 ruling on school desegregation. More recently, research on the effects of maternal dietary, smoking, and drinking habits on the unborn child has produced evidence likely to alter both the attitudes and behaviors of pregnant women. We could name many more instances in which knowledge catalyzed alterations in beliefs or practices that fall within the sphere we classify as moral. But in all of these cases the evidence was maximally effective when a critical proportion of the community had already decided, before the evidence was available, what outcome was more virtuous, so that they were receptive to rational support for the new view or to factual bases for undermining the old one.

It is a tribute to man's respect and need for rationality that Darwin's thesis on the evolution of animal forms led many to question further their faith in creationism. But had they not been psychologically prepared to believe the data and argument Darwin organized, his evidence would have been ignored. Ernst Mayr (1977) has suggested that if Darwin himself had not begun to lose his Christian faith in the mid-1830s, he might not have had the illumination in September of 1838 that formed the essence of his theory.

Thus data, presupposition, and logic mix in a mysterious way to influence the values of a person or a community. As Morton White noted, "Sentiment is not enough, logic is not enough, and experience is not enough, if we wish to know and to know what to do. Each should be given its due by the intelligent man as he tests his stock of beliefs and actions" (1972, p. 310).

This research report on day care provides information that challenges some private and public opinions about the deleterious effects of good group care outside the family and provides a rough guide to the elements that comprise quality day care. But even if young children in day care are not hyperaggressive or minimally attached to their parents, it does not follow that day care is good for children. Parents differ in the goals they have for their infants and the pleasure they derive from raising them. These considerations are as relevant in determining a personal stance toward day care as the empirical facts.

Appendix
References
Index

Appendix

Additional, more detailed empirical information from our investigation is presented in this appendix that may be of more interest to the reader who has a professional interest in the infant *qua* infant than to the general reader. These data deal with the importance of the period from 8 to 12 months; the growth functions for attentiveness, excitability, and social play; the differential reactivity associated with ethnicity and class; and some of the basic theoretical issues presented in chapter 2.

PART 1: THE LABORATORY ASSESSMENTS

Because the infants' behaviors varied in a serious way to each of the episodes, the data are presented first by episode. Part 1 describes the growth functions by form of care, class, or ethnicity; considers the interrelations among the episodes as well as stabilities across age; and finally, summarizes the data on heart rate reactivity.

A word about the analytic procedures we applied to the laboratory data is in order. We first examined the distribution for each variable across the separate phases of each episode for the age, care, class, and ethnicity subgroups. The families were divided into two class groups on the basis of the educational attainment of the parents; in class 1 families one or both parents had some college background, while in class 2 families neither parent had any education beyond high school. We pooled the data for vocalization, smiling, fretting, and activity across all phases of the episode because, in most cases, there were no consistent relations of age, care, ethnicity, or class to the phase of the episode when the response occurred. It was not always possible to compute a repeated measures analysis of variance with all three major factors (form of care, class, and ethnicity) because of the restricted sample size. On many occasions one or two cells had too few subjects, and in a few cases, a cell was empty. In the analysis of variance, form of rearing was always a factor, usually complemented by ethnicity, since examination of the data indicated that ethnicity was more important than class. However, we always examined the means and standard deviations for the two class groups to determine whether class was interacting with ethnicity or care.

For those variables that were infrequent in occurrence, particularly vocalization, smiling, fretting, and activity, it was most appropriate to treat the data nonparametrically. Thus we usually determined what percentage of children showed the response at all, as well as the mean percentage of trials on which a particular response occurred. Finally, the repeated measures analysis across age eliminated the data for 3½-month-olds because of the smaller size of that sample. In order to maximize the sample size from 5½ months on, we did not include the earlier data in these age analyses.

As indicated in chapter 4, we performed two related analyses in order to assess the effect of group care. In the more stringent tests, we compared pairs of children matched on sex, ethnicity, and social class; one of each pair attended the day care center, while the other was reared totally at home. The second analysis was typically an analysis of variance that involved all the subjects in the day care center and all the controls reared at home.

Block episode

Fixation time The growth functions for both first and total fixation time revealed a linear increase with age in attention to the standards. The 3-month-olds were not only markedly less attentive than the older children, but, unlike the older infants, they were also less attentive to the first presentation than to the second and third, suggesting less initial alertness (see table A.1). If one ignores the 3-month-olds' data, four of the eight subgroups (care x class x ethnicity) displayed the theoretically expected U-shaped function on the first transformation and first return trial. Examination of each child's set of fixation times from 3 to 11 months revealed that the data for 67 percent of the children revealed a curvilinear function to the standard, transformation, or return trials or to more than one of these phases of the episode. Hence, the U-shaped function faithfully represents the behavior of the majority of infants. The modal age for the trough was 7 months (70 percent of the children whose data displayed a U-shaped function had their shortest fixation times at 7 months), and the U-shaped function occurred most often on the return trials. (See table A.2 for the distribution of the U-shaped function by age and phase of episode for those children whose data showed the curvilinear function.) For example, of the 32 children who had a U-shaped function on the return trials, 63 percent had a trough at 7 months, 34 percent at 9 months, and 3 percent at 5 months. Since fixation time for the returns was high at all ages (over 60 percent of total exposure time), the

TABLE A.1. PERCENTAGE OF TOTAL FIXATION TIME BY AGE AND TRIAL PHASE FOR EACH EPISODE (TIME FIXATION OF THE STIMULUS/TOTAL TIME STIMULUS EXPOSED).

	AGE (MOS.)							
EPISODE, TRIAL PHASE	3	5	7	9	11	13	20	29
Block								
S 2-5[a]	52.2%	81.1	83.6	88.2	86.6			
T 1-3	48.8	80.7	76.1	79.3	77.0			
R 1-3	45.0	72.1	66.9	73.2	72.1			
Light								
S 2-5	75.6	93.6	91.5	95.3	95.9	93.1	94.0	92.2
T 1-3	43.6	70.2	65.0	71.9	70.9	94.3	92.2	89.5
R 1-3[b]	66.2	68.6	54.5	73.5	72.8	72.4	82.4	85.4
Last T[c]	65.2	49.7	46.7	53.0	57.3	74.2	93.4	88.5
Car[d]								
S 2-5				98.7	98.6	98.2	98.5	98.2
T 1-3				92.5	87.3	86.7	91.0	92.5
R 1-3				89.2	88.4	84.3	82.8	87.5
Masks								
No eyes[e]	58.0	73.9		88.8		89.8		
Scrambled[f]	66.1	75.7		86.3		92.5		
Blank[g]	62.9	74.5		85.3		84.7		
Regular	77.8	79.2		87.3		84.9		
Auditory 1 (Search)								
S 2-5[h]	66.6	61.3	54.2	67.7	71.6	72.5	81.1	80.2
T 1-3[i]	59.3	55.7	36.5	54.0	56.0	46.3	65.3	69.3
R 1-3[j]	49.5	51.3	36.5	49.6	48.9	38.9	67.6	63.5

[a] F for age (5-11 mos.) = 2.91, 3/57, $p < 0.05$.

[b] F for age (5-11 mos.) = 7.32, 3/48, $p < 0.001$; (13-29 mos.) = 10.37, 2/51, $p < 0.001$.

[c] F for age (13-29 mos.) = 10.43, 2/51, $p < 0.001$.

[d] No significant effect of age.

[e] F for age (5-13 mos.) = 16.9, 3/58, $p < 0.001$.

[f] F for age (5-13 mos.) = 12.0, 3/58, $p < 0.001$.

[g] F for age (5-13 mos.) = 6.4, 3/58, $p < 0.003$.

[h] F for age (5-11 mos.) = 4.49, 3/56, $p < 0.01$.

[i] F for age (5-11 mos.) = 5.22, 3/55, $p < 0.01$; (13-29 mos.) = 7.12, 2/47, $p = 0.01$.

[j] F for age (13-29 mos.) = 12.17, 2/46, $p < 0.001$.

TABLE A.2. PERCENTAGE OF SUBJECTS WHOSE FIXATION TIME DATA FROM 3½ TO 11 MOS. DISPLAYED A TROUGH, BY AGE AND PHASE OF BLOCK EPISODE.

	AGE (MOS.)		
TRIAL	5	7	9
Standard (n = 17 Ss)	23%	48	29
Transformation (n = 26 Ss)	15	50	35
Return (n = 32 Ss)	3	63	34

trough at 7 months is not the result of irritability or lack of interest, but appears to reflect a psychological transition point.

We determined the percentage of children whose attention to the first two transformations or first two return trials increased compared with their attention to the immediately preceding two trials. When the criterion for dishabituation was an increase of at least 10 percent in fixation time, only 20 percent of the group met the criterion at 3, 5, and 7 months; it was lower at the two older ages. When any increase in attention was regarded as an index of dishabituation, about 50 percent showed dishabituation at the two younger ages, and about 35 to 45 percent at the older ages. The fewest children dishabituated to the transformation and return trials at 7 and 9 months.

Vocalization Vocalizations were typically brief in duration, lasting no more than a second. We computed both the percentage of children who vocalized on one or more trials, as well as the average percentage of trials in which a vocalization occurred while the child was studying the stimulus event (see table A.3). Both variables showed a linear increase with age. About 20 percent of the group vocalized at 3 months, and 70 percent at 11 months, with a plateau from 7 to 11 months of age. The growth function for mean proportion of trials on which a vocalization occurred was also linear, but it had a steeper slope because the older children who vocalized did so on several trials. During most visual episodes, in contrast to the two auditory episodes, vocalization was more common when the child was attending to the stimulus than it was during the interval between stimuli.

We determined what percentage of infants showed any increase in vocal response to the first two transformation and return trials compared with the immediately preceding two presentations (the last two standards or the last two transformations, respectively). The proportion increased with age, peaking at 25 percent for the transformations at 11 months of age and at 27 percent for the return trials at 9 months of age.

Smiling Smiling, which was infrequent, increased most between 5 and 7 months, the age when fixation time to the transformation was dropping (see table A.4), suggesting this is when assimilation of the event was likely. During the standard trials, smiling was most likely to occur in the middle of the series, usually in response to presentations 3 and 4.

Activity and fretting Twisting and waving increased linearly with age (see table A.5); the largest increase occurred between 5 and 7 months of age.

EFFECTS OF GROUP MEMBERSHIP

Fixation time There were no consistent effects of form of rearing, ethnicity, or social class either on duration of attention to standard, transformation, or return trials or on habituation or dishabituation functions. The class 2 3-month-olds from both ethnic groups had significantly shorter fixation times than class 1 infants for standards, transformations, and returns. But from 5 months on, the class effect was absent. Although the class 2 children were less alert at the youngest age, a few months later they were displaying a level of attentiveness comparable to that of class 1 children.

Vocalization and smiling Neither form of care nor class produced any consistent effect across age on vocalization or smiling. The Caucasian children were more vocal and smiled more than the Chinese at 9 and 11 months (see tables A.6 and A.7) but not at the two younger ages. Among the Chinese, the class 2 children in day care vocalized somewhat more than the class 2 children living at home. Among the Caucasians, that effect was reversed; class 2 home controls vocalized more than their class 2 counterparts in day care. The day care experience made the Chinese children from less well-educated families a little more vocal than they would have been had they been reared totally at home, but the interaction missed statistical significance.

Activity and irritability There were no care, class, or ethnicity effects for pointing, twisting, or waving. The class 1 children in day care, both Chinese and Caucasian, were the most irritable; the other groups were minimally fretful.

Comparison of variables The growth functions for attention, smiling, and vocalization were similar for most children and seem best understood as a function of maturing competences. The similarities between the rearing, class, and ethnic groups were far greater than the differences. The Caucasian children were more vocal than the Chinese at the two older ages. As we shall see, ethnicity was the most significant of our three variables, for Caucasians

TABLE A.3. VOCALIZATION IN EACH EPISODE, BY AGE: MEAN PERCENTAGE OF TRIALS WHEN VOCALIZATION OCCURRED AND MEAN PERCENTAGE OF SUBJECTS VOCALIZING GREATER THAN 0 FOR THE ENTIRE EPISODE.

	AGE (MOS.)							
	3	5	7	9	11	13	20	29
Block episode								
Mean % of trials[a]	3%	5	17	20	21			
Mean % of subjects[b]	20%	38	61	64	70			
Light episode								
Mean % of trials[c]	7	13	17	20	20	16	21	31
Mean % of subjects[d]	50	63	75	86	74	62	69	78
Car episode								
Mean % of trials[e]				11	17	20	24	35
Mean % of subjects[f]				58	57	69	80	82
Mask episode								
Mean % of subjects, by stimulus								
No eyes	16	20		29		24		
Scrambled	14	19		29		23		
Blank[g]	12	12		21		22		
Regular[g]	24	18		32		36		

Auditory 1								
Mean % of trials or intertrials								
Trials[h]	6	7	13	15	13	12	14	20
intertrials[i]	5	8	19	17	18	15	20	29
Mean % of subjects vocalizing								
During trials[j]	37	47	69	72	61	67	55	71
During intertrials[k]	39	47	73	72	70	70	64	76

[a] F (5-11 mos.) = 11.02, 3/57, $p < 0.001$.
[b] Cochran's Q, $p < 0.01$.
[c] F (13-29 mos.) = 6.26, 2/51, $p < 0.01$.
[d] Cochran's Q, $p < 0.01$.
[e] F (9-29 mos.) = 10.77, 4/39, $p < 0.001$.
[f] Cochran's Q, $p < 0.01$.
[g] Cochran's Q, $p < 0.05$.
[h] F (5-11 mos.) = 3.38, 3/56, $p < 0.05$; F (13-29 mos.) = 3.57, 2/48, $p < 0.05$.
[i] F (5-11 mos.) = 4.71, 3/56, $p < 0.01$; F (13-29 mos.) = 5.06, 2/48, $p < 0.01$.
[j] Cochran's Q, $p < 0.05$.
[k] Cochran's Q, $p < 0.01$.

TABLE A.4. PERCENTAGE OF SUBJECTS SMILING IN EACH EPISODE, BY AGE.

EPISODE	AGE (MOS.)							
	3	5	7	9	11	13	20	29
Block[a]	2%	9	22	22	23			
Light[b]	4	9	17	13	24	40	49	52
Car[b]				14	16	12	37	57
Mask								
No eyes[a]	2	3		10		11		
Scrambled[a]	4	1		8		8		
Blank	2	4		5		5		
Regular	12	9		5		6		
Auditory 1[b]	0	8	11	5	7	12	13	38

[a] Cochran's Q, $p < 0.05$.
[b] Cochran's Q, $p < 0.01$.

were more affective and active than the Chinese. It is possible that the familial environments of the Chinese children, especially those in class 2, inhibit vocal and motor excitement, while the home environments of class 1 Caucasians encourage vocalization and motor activity.

The matched pairs The matched pairs analysis revealed very little difference between the day care and home control children for attention, vocalization, smiling, or activity. There were only a few exceptions to that generalization. At the oldest age, the day care children were more likely to wave at the stimulus event; at the younger ages the day care children were more irritable than their counterparts reared at home. However, growth functions for vocalization, smiling, and attention were almost identical for the day care and home control pairs.

The light episode

Fixation time For the light episode as for the block, there was a linear increase in attention to the standards which plateaued at 9 months at about 90 percent of total exposure time and remained high through 29 months (see table A.1). The theoretically expected curvilinear function was present for the first three transformation trials, the last transformation trial, and the three return trials with a trough at 7 months (see figure 5.4). However, the quadratic test for curvilinearity was only significant for the three return trials.

Inspection of each child's fixation time data revealed that 76 percent of the children had a trough to the standard, transformation, or return trials or

Table A.5. Percentage of children displaying activity or fretting in each episode, by age and type of activity.

Episode	Age (mos.) 3	5	7	9	11	13	20	29
Block								
Leaning[b]	0%	11	22	31	63			
Waving	54	57	74	73	69			
Twisting[b]	10	10	23	31	37			
Fretting	23	17	18	18	27			
Light[a]								
Leaning	10	24	55	54	68	62	58	60
Waving	80	82	90	94	88	76	66	60
Twisting	18	37	56	75	67	42	32	19
Fretting	56	58	60	60	53	39	39	26
Car								
Leaning[b]				30	33	51	61	62
Waving				71	74	75	63	61
Twisting[b]				27	45	48	20	23
Fretting				32	34	32	27	30
Mask								
No eyes								
Leaning[c]	0	3		26		18		
Waving	28	32		36		24		
Twisting	0	5		6		20		
Fretting	8	12		9		9		
Scrambled								
Leaning[c]	0	1		30		22		
Waving[a]	32	35		43		35		
Twisting[a]	0	3		9		27		
Fretting	6	9		9		9		
Blank								
Leaning[c]	0	1		31		21		
Waving[a]	20	37		35		27		
Twisting[c]	0	6		15		32		
Fretting	10	9		8		14		
Regular								
Leaning	0	6		26		28		
Waving[b]	26	38		44		24		
Twisting	2	6		18		33		
Fretting[a]	16	10		17		21		
Auditory 1								
Waving[c]	70	80	80	85	71	81	67	59
Twisting[a]	8	25	41	49	52	58	27	33
Fretting[a]	29	26	35	39	30	43	22	17

[a] Cochran's Q, $p < 0.05$.
[b] Cochran's Q, $p < 0.01$.
[c] Cochran's Q, $p < 0.001$.

TABLE A.6. VOCALIZATION, BY AGE AND ETHNICITY, IN BLOCK EPISODE (%).

VARIABLE	AGE (MOS.)				
	3	5	7	9	11
Percentage of subjects vocalizing					
Chinese	25%	34	48	50	53
Caucasian	14	42	72	74	86
Mean percentage of trials when vocalizing occurred[a]					
Chinese	3	5	12	18	14
Caucasian	2	4	22	21	27

[a] F for age (5-11 months) = 11.02, 3/57, $p < 0.001$; F for ethnicity (5-11 months) = 5.16, 1/57, $p < 0.05$.

to two or three of these phases, and the modal age was 7 months. The data show that over 90 percent of the children who had a trough displayed it at 7 or 9 months; about 80 percent had a trough for the three return trials or for both the return and transformation trials; and 6 percent showed a curvilinear function for all three phases of the episode.

The dishabituation analysis revealed an inverted U-function, with most children showing increasing attention to the transformations at 13 months and to the returns at 11 months. When the criterion for dishabituation was restricted to an increase in attention of 10 percent or more of total exposure time, the percentage showing dishabituation dropped from 50 to 28 percent for the transformations and 81 to 66 percent for the returns.

TABLE A.7. PERCENTAGE OF SUBJECTS SMILING, BY AGE AND ETHNICITY, IN THE BLOCK EPISODE.

ETHNIC GROUP	AGE (MOS.)				
	3	5	7	9[a]	11[b]
Chinese	0%	3	20	9	11
Caucasian	4	14	23	32	33

[a] Ethnicity difference, chi square = 4.90, $p < 0.05$.
[b] Ethnicity difference, chi square = 4.21, $p < 0.05$.

Vocalization Vocalization in response to the light episode increased during the first year as it had to the block. The growth function for the percentage of children vocalizing was an inverted U, with a maximum of 86 percent of the infants vocalizing at 9 months of age. When the mean proportion of trials was the variable, the growth function was generally linear until 9 months; the largest increase occurred between 13 and 29 months—the time when language gains most in complexity and frequency (see table A.3).

Increased vocalization during the transformations also peaked at 9 months (32 percent of the children showed an increase in vocalization for the first two transformations); for the return trials, peak dishabituation occurred at 29 months, when 47 percent of the group showed increased vocalization.

Smiling Although smiling was infrequent during the first year (fewer than 25 percent smiled on any trial of the light episodes from 3 through 11 months), there was a large increase in smiling from 11 to 29 months, with 52 percent of the group smiling at the oldest age (see table A.4). Most of the smiling occurred on presentations 4 and 5 of the standards. The parallel functions for vocalization and smiling imply that during their second year of age, the children were better able to assimilate the light episode.

Activity and fretting The activity measures tended to follow an inverted U function with a peak at either 9 or 11 months of age (see table A.5). The higher levels of activity toward the end of the first year correspond to the age when attentiveness is increasing after the trough at 7 and 9 months. As attention increased at 20 and 29 months, activity as well as fretting decreased.

EFFECTS OF GROUP MEMBERSHIP

Since the transformation trials changed at the three older ages, we performed one analysis for the early period, from 3 through 11 months, and a separate analysis for the period from 13 through 29 months.

Fixation time Despite an initial difference in attentiveness favoring the class 1 infants at 3 months, as occurred for block, there was no difference between the classes in attention at the older ages. There were no differences in attentiveness at 3 months between the two ethnic groups nor between the day care and home control groups. The different rearing, class, and ethnic groups had very similar growth functions for fixation time, as well as for rates of habituation and dishabituation.

Vocalization The Caucasians were more vocal to the light and block episodes than the Chinese (see table A.8), especially at 11 months. The class 1 home control Caucasians, who would become the verbally most proficient 2-year-olds, were not highly vocal during the first year, suggesting that non-

TABLE A.8. VOCALIZATION, BY AGE AND ETHNICITY, IN THE LIGHT EPISODE (%).

	AGE (MOS.)							
VARIABLE	3	5	7	9	11	13	20	29
Mean percentage of trials when vocalization occurred[a-c]								
Chinese	4%	13	15	16	13	13	18	24
Caucasian	12	13	19	23	25	20	24	38
Mean percentage of subjects vocalizing[d,e]								
Chinese	44	60	63	83	58	53	61	67
Caucasian	56	65	85	88	88	70	76	89

[a] F for age (13-29 mos.) = 6.23, 2/51, $p < 0.01$.
[b] F for ethnicity (5-11 mos.) = 5.04, 1/58, $p < 0.05$.
[c] Ethnicity difference at 3½ mos $t = 2.34$, $p < 0.05$.
[d] Ethnicity difference at 7 mos., chi square = 4.2, $p < 0.05$.
[e] Ethnicity difference at 11 mos., chi square = 7.5, $p < 0.01$.

verbal vocalization to interesting episodes reflects general excitement and is not highly predictive of future linguistic competence.

During the first year, differences in vocalization were associated with ethnicity; afterward, differences were more a function of class. Class 1 children vocalized more than class 2 infants (see table A.9)—the difference was greatest at 20 and 29 months—and form of rearing only affected vocalization at 29 months, the age when vocalization was most frequent. Class 1 Caucasian children vocalized the most at 29 months (56 percent); class 2 Chinese and Caucasian children reared at home, the least (9 and 24 percent). The largest difference in vocalization between the matched groups occurred for the class 2 Chinese, indicating that day care experience had enhanced their vocalization. Indeed, the day care children in each subgroup were more vocal than the corresponding home controls from the same ethnic and class category, and the matched pairs analysis yielded a significant difference between day care and home control children.

Dishabituation of vocalization Form of care was uncorrelated with change in vocal response to the transformations or returns. At 13 and 20 months the Caucasians were more likely to become vocally excited during the return trials. And at all ages, more Caucasians than Chinese showed a change in vocalization, either an increase or decrease, at the transformed event. Apparently the Caucasian children are disposed either to be quiet or to become vocally excited in response to a discrepant event.

There was an important age effect with respect to the probability of quieting or increased vocal excitability at the transformations. More children displayed increased vocalization (rather than quieting) toward the transformations at 7, 9, and 11 months, but at 13, 20, and 29 months more children quieted. This pattern suggests a tendency toward inhibition of excitement toward a discrepant event after the first year of life. The pattern was not repeated for the first two return trials, where most of the children tended to become excited. It is possible that inhibition seemed more significant after the first year merely because more children were vocalizing. However, we can eliminate that interpretation, for the number of children vocalizing to the last two standards was equivalent at 7 and 13 months (36 percent vocalized at 7 months, and 38 percent at 13 months). Moreover, the fact that inhibition occurred on the transformations but not on the returns cannot be related to differing vocalization rates, because equal numbers of children responded vocally to the last two transformations and the last two standards at 13 months. Thus the inhibition in vocalization at 13, 20, and 29 months, which also occurred in the car episode, is not an artifact of increasing vocalization with age.

Smiling There was no difference in smiling between the two care or class groups but, as on the block episode, more Caucasians than Chinese

TABLE A.9. VOCALIZATION, BY AGE AND CLASS, IN THE LIGHT EPISODE (%).[a]

	AGE (MOS.)							
VARIABLE	3	5	7	9	11	13	20	29
Mean percentage of trials when vocalization occurred[b]								
Class 1	7%	16	15	19	18	19	27	39
Class 2	7	10	18	20	21	14	15	24
Mean percentage of subjects vocalizing								
Class 1	52	66	75	86	73	52	75	81
Class 2	48	59	75	86	76	73	61	72

[a] Class 1—one or both parents attended college; Class 2—neither parent had education beyond high school.
[b] F for class (13-29 mos.) = 4.98, 1/51, $p<0.05$.

smiled at each age. However, the difference was only significant at 7 months (see table A.10).

Activity and fretting There were no simple effects for care, ethnicity, or class during the first year. During the second year the Chinese children showed a decrease in twisting, while the Caucasian values remained high. Although there were no consistent effects of care or class on fretting, the three subgroups that fretted most often at 20 months were all Caucasian (class 1 day care and classes 1 and 2 home controls); there was a significant effect of ethnicity at 20 months.

Matched pairs The matched pairs analysis revealed no difference during the first 20 months. However, at 29 months of age, the day care children were more active, smiling, and vocal than their counterparts reared at home, a result suggesting that the day care environment facilitated display of motor and vocal excitability when processing interesting information. For the light episode, as for the block episode, there were neither consistent nor dramatic effects of care on attentiveness, with the exception of greater excitability among the day care children at 29 months. Ethnicity again proved to be the most powerful variable, for the Caucasians smiled a little more often and were more vocal, irritable, and active than the Chinese.

Car episode

Fixation time and anticipatory fixations Attention to the car episode remained relatively high at about 90 percent of exposure time from 9 through 29 months (see table A.1). However, the growth functions for the other variables suggest that the period from 9 to 13 months was characterized by more uncertainty than the period of the last two assessments, because the proportion of trials on which anticipatory fixation to the standard occurred was uniformly high (60 percent) at 9, 11, and 13 months, but dropped to 20 percent at 29 months. While the car rested at the top of the ramp prior to being released some children would quickly glance at the form resting at the bottom of the ramp, as if anticipating the sequence to follow. We interpret the anticipatory fixation as reflecting uncertainty about the sequence of the episode. The uncertainty prompts the child to check the target object before the car is released. After age 1 the child checks the target less often, probably because he is a little more certain as to what will happen. But he remains attentive.

It is probably not a coincidence that fretting and twisting were also high from 9 to 13 months, while smiling and vocalization, signs of assimilation, were low during this period and did not show their highest values until 20 and 29 months of age. There was a linear decrease in anticipatory fixations to the transformation and return trials from 9 through 29 months. Apparently,

TABLE A.10. SMILING, BY AGE AND ETHNICITY, IN THE LIGHT EPISODE (%).

VARIABLE	AGE (MOS.)							
	3	5	7	9	11	13	20	29
Mean percentage of trials when smiling occurred								
Chinese	0%	0	0	1	4	8	13	12
Caucasian	1	2	4	4	5	13	14	20
Mean percentage of subjects smiling								
Chinese	0	3	6	6	14	36	45	47
Caucasian	7	14	26	19	33	44	53	57

after the standard trials the child was able to predict what would happen and had less of a need to check the target.

Dishabituation Only about 22 percent of the children showed increased attention toward the transformations, with little change over age, in part because the event was so interesting that few children habituated during the presentation of the standards. More children showed dishabituation to the return trials—the most at 11 months (50 percent); the fewest at 20 months (23 percent).

Vocalization Vocalization increased linearly with age, peaking at 29 months, when 82 percent of the children vocalized at least once (see table A.3). The largest increases in vocalization during both the transformation and the return phases occurred at 20 and 29 months, with 36 percent of the children showing an increase in vocalization on the return trials at 29 months.

We examined the growth function for the children's tendencies to become excited or quiet on the first two transformations. Those tendencies were equal at 9 months of age but from 11 through 29 months the percentage of children quieting was greater than the percentage showing an increase in vocalization. The greatest difference between these opposed dispositions occurred at 11 and 13 months, the period when anticipatory fixations to car and separation distress were also maximal. More children quieted to the transformations than to the returns. This is not a function of differential vocalization over the course of the episode, for at 13 and 20 months the number of children vocalizing in response to the last two standards is the same as the number vocalizing to the last two transformations. We interpret the quieting in response to the transformations at 11 and 13 months as indicative of a disposition toward inhibition to discrepant events characteristic of the few months surrounding the first birthday (see table A.11).

TABLE A.11. PERCENTAGE OF SUBJECTS QUIETING OR INCREASING VOCALIZATION FROM LAST 2 STANDARD TRIALS TO FIRST 2 TRANSFORMATIONS OR FROM LAST 2 TRANSFORMATIONS TO FIRST 2 RETURNS IN THE CAR EPISODE.

VARIABLE	9	11	13	20	29
Transformations 1 and 2					
% quieting	16%	22	26	34	43
% increasing vocalization	15	10	7	24	25
Returns 1 and 2					
% quieting	20	23	20	30	30
% increasing vocalization	15	16	24	32	36

Smiling The growth function for smiling resembled that for vocalization with a major increase after 13 months when anticipatory fixations were decreasing. Peak smiling occurred at 29 months, with 57 percent of the children smiling at least once (see table A.4). Smiling dropped precipitously from the standards to the transformations, but rose again on the return presentations.

Activity and fretting Twisting increased from 9 to 13 months, when anticipatory fixations were high, and then declined for all phases of the episode. Fretting remained rather stable over age. Since most of the fretting at 1 year occurred during the standards, it is reasonable to suggest that some of the irritability was in the service of apprehension rather than boredom. (See table A.5).

EFFECTS OF GROUP MEMBERSHIP

There were no simple effects of care, ethnicity, or class on attentiveness or dishabituation to the car event. As with the two episodes above, patterns of attentiveness seemed to be under the stewardship of basic maturational forces and individual temperamental dimensions. The Chinese displayed more anticipatory fixation at 13 months, but this ethnic difference was absent at the other four ages. Class 1 children showed more anticipatory fixation than class 2 infants at 29 months, but not at any of the earlier ages.

There were no consistent care, ethnicity, or class differences for vocalization during the trials or between trials. Among the Chinese, day care children vocalized a little more than those at home, but this difference did not occur among the Caucasians. Indeed, among the Caucasian children, class 2 home controls vocalized a little more than class 2 children in day care. (The interaction was not significant.)

Although the car episode elicited the most interest and excitement, the ethnic differences in vocalization that occurred to the block and light episodes did not emerge for it. Because the car was not only the most interesting, but the last episode to be administered, the children were least inhibited, and ethnic differences were minimal. This result indicates the importance of specifying the context in generalizations about group differences in response dispositions. There were no simple ethnic or class differences in smiling in this episode. At 29 months there was a slight tendency for the Chinese to smile more than the Caucasians. Among the Chinese, day care children smiled more than those at home; among Caucasians the children at home smiled more than those in day care, yielding a significant interaction. The absence of the ethnic differences in smiling discovered on block and light affirms the importance of limiting generalizations based on one or two episodes. Children do not have dispositions; they have dispositions in particular contexts.

The ethnic difference in activity noted for light was present on the car episode but muted. The Caucasians waved more than the Chinese, especially at 11 and 29 months; at 20 months more Caucasians twisted than Chinese. There were no effects of care, class or ethnicity on fretting at any age (see table A.12).

Matched pairs The matched pairs analysis revealed remarkably similar behavior for the children in the two care groups. The day care children were more likely to point toward the stimulus at 20 and 29 months, but there were no differences in vocalization, attentiveness, smiling, or anticipatory fixation.

In sum, of the three episodes discussed thus far, responsivity to the car episode revealed the least consistent effects of care, class, or ethnicity. The significant ethnic difference noted for block and light on vocalization, smiling, and activity are dependent on those contexts.

Perhaps the most important result is the indication that toward the end of the first year the children became more uncertain, restless, and irritable. As this period of disquiet faded, smiling and vocalization increased, suggesting that the uncertainty present at the end of the first year was being resolved. The range of ages during which uncertainty and resolution occur varies with the specific event. Uncertainty toward strangers typically occurs from 7 to 13 months, to separation from a caretaker from 9 to 15 months, to

TABLE A.12. PERCENTAGE OF SUBJECTS WAVING AND TWISTING, BY AGE AND ETHNICITY, IN THE CAR EPISODE.

	AGE (MOS.)				
VARIABLE	9	11	13	20	29
Percentage waving[a]					
Chinese	75%	57	73	56	44
Caucasian	67	88	77	68	77
Percentage twisting[b]					
Chinese	35	39	49	6	17
Caucasian	19	50	48	32	31

[a]Ethnicity difference at 11 months, chi square = 7.6, $p < 0.01$; at 29 months, chi square = 5.1, $p < 0.05$.

[b]Ethnicity difference at 20 months, chi square = 6.0, $p < 0.05$.

the car episode from 11 to 13 months. But in all three cases, the uncertainty and inhibition appear toward the end of the first year.

Masks

Fixation time There was a linear increase in attentiveness with age rather than a U-shaped growth function. The major developmental change was a shift in maximal attentiveness from the regular mask at the early ages to the scrambled mask at 13 months. At 3 months the difference in total fixation time between the regular and scrambled faces favored the former; by 13 months the difference favored the scrambled mask (see table A.1).

We interpret this shift in preference to reflect a change in articulation of the schema for the regular face. At 3 months the infant has just created a schema for human faces. The regular mask is optimally discrepant from that structure; the disarranged face is too discrepant from that schema to maintain prolonged attention. As the schema for a normal face becomes better articulated, the regular mask is assimilated more quickly and the disarranged one is perceived as sharing dimensions with the schema for the normal face. This growth pattern provides a nice example of how changing cognitive structures mediated by experience monitor the profile of interest in external events. Differential control of attention does not rest with the stimulus *qua* stimulus but with the relation between schema and event.

Vocalization Vocalization while attending to the stimulus was more common than vocalization between trials, and there was more vocalizing at the two older than at the two younger ages (see table A.3).

Smiling The data for smiling affirm the earlier suggestion that the schema for a frequently occurring event changes continually. At 3 months, when the schema for the human face is just being established, smiling was much more frequent to the regular mask than to any of the other faces (see table A.4). The three discrepant masks did not share enough dimensions with the 3-month-old's schema for a normal face to permit assimilation. But by 9 and 13 months, smiling was most frequent to the face with no eyes and less frequent to the regular face. Between 5 and 9 months the schema for a face became better articulated, permitting the older infant to assimilate a pattern that lacked the features critical for the 3-month-old.

Activity and irritability Children at the two younger ages did not point at the masks, but at 9 and 13 months the regular mask elicited the most frequent display of this response. Neither waving nor twisting differed for any of the four stimuli (see table A.5). Although the incidence of fretting was low, the regular mask provoked a little more fretting at 9 and 13 months than the other masks.

Effects of Group Membership

There were minimal effects of care, ethnicity, or class on attentiveness to the masks. As in the block and light episodes, the 3-month-old class 1 children had significantly longer fixation times to the scrambled and regular faces than those from class 2, but there were no class differences at 5, 9, and 13 months. There were no consistent effects of care, ethnicity, or class on vocalization, smiling, activity, or fretting. The 13-month-old Caucasians were more vocal than the Chinese (chi square = 4.2; $p < .05$), but there were no ethnic differences in smiling.

Matched pairs analysis The matched pairs analysis revealed no significant differences between the care groups on any of the variables.

The masks provided the clearest indication of the importance of specifying the stimulus event in making generalizations about growth functions or group differences. Reactivity to the masks was only minimally correlated with care, class, or ethnicity, and each of the masks produced its own characteristic growth functions for attention, vocalization, and smiling.

Auditory 1

It will be recalled that for the first auditory episode the standard and return trials were the same meaningful phrase. From 3 to 11 months the transformation was a nonsense phrase; from 13 to 29 months the transformation was a change in the word order of the original standard.

Search Search, defined as the simultaneous occurrence of motor inhibition, saccadic movements of the eyes, and a posture implying alert attentiveness, habituated among the infants 7 months and older. As with the visual episodes, 3-month-olds were less alert initially. The older children showed maximal searching during presentation of the standard on trials 2 or 3; the 3-month-olds on trial 6.

The growth function for search was U-shaped for all three phases of the episode—standard, transformation, and return (see table A.1 and figure 5.5—with an unambiguous trough at 7 months and the largest increase occurring between 7 and 9 months. (The statistical test for curvilinearity revealed a significant quadratic component for each of the three phases of the episode). There was a slight decline in search to the transformation and return trials at 13 months, the age when the transformation changed from nonmeaningful speech to meaningful words in a nongrammatical sequence. Because this word order transformation contained meaningful words, it possibly was easier for the infants to assimilate; hence, the slight decrease in search. The major increase in search at 20 and 29 months implies that the older children were treating the word order transformation as a more serious discrepancy than they had at 13 months. We suggest that the younger children were treating the transformation as an acoustic discrepancy, whereas the older children were treating it as a linguistic transformation. The 5-month-olds were assimilating the event to their schema for the acoustic qualities of the human voice; the 20-month-olds were trying to relate the words in the distorted communication to their representation of the meaning and syntax of the grammatically correct phrase presented during the standard trials. During the period from 13 to 20 months spoken language appeared for almost all of the children. The fact that the increase in search began to rise at 9 months (at least 4 or 5 months before any spoken words appeared) is in accord with the popular hypothesis that the child's cognitive appreciation of language precedes overt speech expression.

The individual records of 78 percent of the children showed a U-shaped function for search on standard, transformation, or return or on two or three of these phrases. The modal age for the trough was 7 months, and the curvilinear function was most likely to occur to the standards and transformations. Sixty-five percent of the U-shaped functions had the trough at 7 months. The data for class 1 Caucasian girls—the children who would be most advanced in language at 3 years of age—were most likely to display the trough on all three phases of the episode. Since there were no sex differences in the percentage of children whose data had the curvilinear function for fixation time to the visual episodes, the presence of a difference between the sexes to the auditory event is of interest. One reason for the U-shaped function for search to the standard trials in the auditory episode, but not for fixation time to the standards on block or light, is the more obvious habituation of attention to the auditory than to the visual episodes.

Orientation to the speaker Since the speaker was located 90 degrees to the left of the direction of gaze of the child, it was an effort for the infant to orient to it. We believe that search reflects the child's attempt to assimilate the auditory event, while orientation to the speaker indexes the child's attempt to resolve uncertainty regarding the source of the sound. The children were far less likely to orient to the speaker (the mean was about 10 percent of the time) than they were to display search behavior (about 50 percent of the time), and there was less obvious habituation of orientation (see table A.13). The growth function for orientation to speaker was only suggestive of a U-shaped function from 3 through 11 months, with a trough at 7 months; but unlike search, there was a decline in orientation from 13 to 29 months. The difference between search and orientation at the oldest ages suggests that each is reflecting a different process. If orientation reflects the child's attempt to determine where the stimulus event is originating, it seems that the problem is solved quickly after 13 months.

Dishabituation No more than 50 percent of the group showed an increase in search to transformation or return trials at any age, and no clear

TABLE A.13. PERCENTAGE OF TIME CHILDREN SPENT ORIENTED TO THE SPEAKER, BY AGE AND PHASE OF AUDITORY 1 EPISODE.

	AGE (MOS.)							
PHASE OF EPISODE	3	5	7	9	11	13	20	29
S 2-5	12.2%	13.5	8.2	8.7	12.8	12.2	7.1	8.4
T 1-3	12.7	8.3	5.1	7.1	8.9	5.4	3.9	3.5
R 1-3	9.6	6.4	4.3	5.6	6.7	5.1	3.7	2.0

growth function emerged. There was a tendency for data to reflect increasing search on the returns, with a peak at 11 months, followed by a plateau. Dishabituation for orientation to the speaker was maximal at 11 and 13 months and declined at 20 and 29 months. The period around the first birthday marks a time of maximal uncertainty toward a variety of events, ranging from a discrepant language stimulus to separation; it is the time when the child is trying to relate an unfamiliar event to his knowledge but is unable to do so.

Vocalization For the auditory episode, unlike the block and light episodes, vocalization was more frequent between trials than during trials after 5 months of age. The typical reaction to the auditory event was a quiet state of attention during the stimulus, followed by babbling after termination. The mean proportion of trials on which vocalization occurred (following termination of the auditory event) was about the same as the mean for the visual events—about 20 to 25 percent. The percentage of children vocalizing rose from 39 percent at 3 months to 76 percent at 29 months, with a plateau from 7 to 29 months (see table A.3).

There was a complementary relation between the growth functions for vocalization and search. Search decreased from 3 to 7 months, while vocalization increased, a relation suggesting that as the child became capable of assimilating the event (hence, search decreased), excited vocalization appeared. When search increased at 9 and 11 months, vocalization upon termination stabilized.

Dishabituation of vocalization The number of children showing increased vocalization during the transformation or return trials increased with age to 9 months, declined at 11 and 13 months, and rose again at the two oldest ages. The dishabituation function for vocalization between trials revealed that a maximal number of children dishabituated at 29 months, in contrast to the maximal dishabituation of search at 11 to 13 months. This pattern is in accord with the hypothesis that excited vocalization, which reflects assimilation, should follow a period of uncertainty.

Smiling Smiling to the auditory episode was infrequent during the first year, even less frequent than to the block or light episodes (see table A.4). No child smiled at 3 months; 12 percent smiled at 13 months; and 38 percent at 29 months. It is not clear why smiling was less frequent to the auditory than to the visual episodes. Since some of the children must have been assimilating the speech stimuli during the second year, it is possible that the human infant may be preferentially programmed to smile in response to visual but not to auditory events.

Activity and irritability Because pointing was rare (there was no salient object in front of them to point to), we shall only consider waving and twisting. The growth function for the percentage of children waving was an inverted U with a peak of 85 percent at 9 months. (See table A.5). Data for twisting and fretting also suggested inverted U functions, with peaks at 13 months. The parallel growth functions for twisting and fretting can be interpreted in at least two ways. Some 1-year-old children may have become apprehensive to the speech stimulus after they had tried unsuccessfully to assimilate it. A second interpretation, which seems more likely, is that the children twisted and fretted because they became bored with the event. Peak fretting did not occur until trial 7 of the standards and rose linearly thereafter. Because only six trials were given at 20 and 29 months, it may be that the transformations occurred before the children had become bored, an explanation supported by the fact that fretting in response to the first three standards, before boredom would have set in, did not increase at 1 year and the maximum percentage of children fretting was only 5 percent.

EFFECTS OF GROUP MEMBERSHIP

Search Again, form of care was unrelated to attentiveness. The younger class 2 children (5, 7, and 9 months) searched more than class 1 infants to the standards and transformations, but this difference was not present at the older ages. If we assume that search prior to 1 year reflects the time it takes to assimilate the event to the schema for a human voice, these data imply that during the first 9 months, but not later, children of better-educated families perform the assimilation more quickly than those from less well-educated families (see table A.14). It is surprising that these differences vanish after the first year, when children of better-educated families are advanced in language development.

Ethnic differences occurred primarily at the older ages. Chinese children searched longer to the transformation trials from 9 to 20 months but not at the younger ages (see table A.15), a result implying that the older Caucasian children assimilated the speech more quickly than the Chinese.

There is an important difference to note between the class and ethnicity comparisons. The early class differences occurred to the standard, transfor-

TABLE A.14. PERCENTAGE OF TIME CHILDREN SPENT SEARCHING, BY AGE, CLASS, AND PHASE OF AUDITORY 1 EPISODE.

	Age (mos.)							
Phase of episode	3	5	7	9	11	13	20	29
S2-5[a]								
Class 1	69.0%	51.5	44.3	59.2	64.8	70.0	82.0	74.7
Class 2	64.3	71.3	64.1	76.2	78.3	75.1	80.1	85.6
T1-3[b]								
Class 1	65.7	44.9	30.6	51.5	53.9	49.7	64.8	61.5
Class 2	52.9	66.6	42.5	56.5	58.1	43.0	65.9	76.6
R 1-3								
Class 1	52.8	50.0	26.5	53.2	50.3	41.9	74.3	56.7
Class 2	46.4	52.5	46.5	45.9	47.4	35.9	60.1	69.5

[a] F for class (5-11 mos.) = 20.86, 1/56, $p < 0.001$; F for age (5-11 mos.) = 4.49, 3/56, $p < 0.01$.
[b] F for class (5-11 mos.) = 5.23, 1/55, $p < 0.05$; F for age (5-11 mos.) = 5.22, 3/55, $p < .01$.

TABLE A.15. PERCENTAGE OF TIME CHILDREN SPENT IN SEARCH AND ORIENTATION TOWARD SPEAKER, BY AGE, ETHNICITY, AND TRIAL PHASE OF AUDITORY 1 EPISODE.

VARIABLE, BY TRIAL PHASE AND ETHNIC GROUP	AGE (MOS.)							
	3	5	7	9	11	13	20	29
Search								
Standards 2-5[a]								
Chinese	69.0%	62.1	48.0	68.0	70.3	81.6	81.1	83.2
Caucasian	64.2	60.6	60.4	67.4	72.9	68.5	81.0	77.1
Transformations 1-3[b]								
Chinese	66.9	56.8	37.6	62.8	68.6	53.2	76.2	75.4
Caucasian	51.7	54.7	35.4	45.3	43.4	39.5	54.5	77.1
Returns 1-3[c]								
Chinese	50.1	52.0	34.4	62.3	57.1	52.1	74.0	68.2
Caucasian	49.1	50.6	38.6	36.8	40.6	25.7	61.3	58.0
Orientation to speaker								
Standards 2-5								
Chinese	15.6	12.9	7.2	8.9	14.5	13.5	8.3	10.9
Caucasian	8.7	14.1	9.2	8.6	11.1	10.9	5.9	6.0
Trials 1-3								
Chinese	14.4	6.2	5.6	7.9	12.2	7.5	7.4	4.3
Caucasian	11.2	10.4	4.5	6.3	5.6	3.2	.5	2.6

Returns 1-3								
Chinese	10.9	5.0	3.4	6.7	7.5	8.0	5.3	2.5
Caucasian	8.3	7.9	5.3	4.5	6.0	2.3	2.1	1.6

[a] F for age (5-11 mos.) = 4.49, 3/56, $p<0.01$.
[b] F for age (5-11 mos.) = 5.22, 3/55, $p<0.01$.
F for ethnicity (5-11 mos.) = 6.26, 1/55, $p<0.05$.
F for age (13-29 mos.) = 7.12, 2/47, $p<0.01$.
F for ethnicity (13-29 mos.) = 9.64, 1/47, $p<0.01$.
[c] F for age (13-29 mos.) = 12.17, 2/46, $p<0.001$.
F for ethnicity (13-29 mos.) = 11.34, 1/46, $p<0.01$.

mation, and return trials. The later ethnic differences held only for the transformations and returns; during the standards Chinese and Caucasian children showed equivalent search patterns. This pattern suggests that perhaps the older Caucasian children assimilated the transformations more quickly than the Chinese. As we shall see, the 29-month-old Caucasian children attained higher scores than the Chinese on the test of linguistic development.

Since significant class differences in search appeared only during the first year, group differences at one age should not automatically be regarded as permanent, and generalizations about group differences must include a statement that describes both age and context of assessment.

Orientation to the speaker There were no simple effects of care, class, or ethnicity for orientation to the speaker, although the Chinese had slightly higher scores than Caucasians after 11 months of age (see table A.15). During the era from 5 to 11 months the Chinese in day care looked longer than the home controls, while among Caucasians the effect was reversed, and home-reared children—especially those from class 1—oriented more toward the speaker than those in day care. We have no easy interpretation of that interaction.

Vocalization There was no effect of care on vocalization during the first seven assessments. Only at 29 months did the day care children become more vocal than the home controls. The Caucasians were more vocal than the Chinese at 9, 11, 20, and 29 months, which is in accord with the data for the visual episodes (table A.16). The effect of class, oddly enough, was opposite to that found for the visual episodes. Class 2 children vocalized *more* than those from class 1 at most ages, but the difference was only significant from 5 through 11 months, not during the second year (see table A.17).

Dishabituation More class 1 children showed increased search in response to the transformations from 9 through 13 months, but not at later ages, a result suggesting that class 1 children were linguistically advanced during this 4-month period. The class 2 children showed increased search to the transformation later, at 20 months. The most dramatic class difference occurred for dishabituation of vocalization (during the trial) to the transformation trials. Class 1 children tended to display an increase in vocalization to the transformation from 9 through 29 months, while the Class 2 children were more likely to quiet across this age span. There were no care differences, and ethnicity differences were minimal.

Smiling The day care children smiled significantly more than the home controls at 29 months (55 percent versus 27 percent), but not before. This result implies that more day care children assimilated the speech event,

Table A.16. Vocalization, by ethnicity and age: percentages of trials or intertrials during which vocalization occurred and percentage of subjects vocalizing, in Auditory 1 episode.

Trial phase and ethnic group	Age (mos.)							
	3	5	7	9	11	13	20	29
Vocalization during trials[a]								
% of trials								
Chinese	7%	6	4	11	10	12	8	14
Caucasian	5	8	3	19	17	12	20	27
% of subjects[b]								
Chinese	25	47	61	64	51	67	36	64
Caucasian	48	45	76	79	70	68	72	78
Vocalization between trials								
% of intertrials[c]								
Chinese	5	6	19	17	12	16	15	30
Caucasian	5	11	19	18	23	13	25	28
% of subjects								
Chinese	38	37	64	69	59	72	45	68
Caucasian	41	55	81	74	80	68	78	85

[a] F for age (5-11 mos.) = 3.38, 3/53, $p < 0.05$.
F for age (13-29 mos.) = 3.57, 2/48, $p < 0.05$.
F for ethnicity (13-29 mos.) = 8.64, 1/48, $p < 0.01$.
[b] Ethnicity difference at 20 mos., chi square = 7.6, $p < 0.01$.
[c] F for age (5-11 mos.) = 4.70, 3/56, $p < 0.01$.
F for age (13-29 mos.) = 5.06, 2/48, $p < 0.01$.

TABLE A.17. VOCALIZATION, BY CLASS AND AGE: PERCENTAGES OF TRIALS OR INTERTRIALS DURING WHICH VOCALIZATION OCCURRED AND PERCENTAGE OF SUBJECTS VOCALIZING, IN AUDITORY 1 EPISODE.

	Age (mos.)							
Trial phase and class	3	5	7	9	11	13	20	29
Vocalization during trials								
% of trials								
Class 1	8%	6	11	17	8	10	13	23
Class 2	3	9	15	14	18	13	14	18
% of subjects								
Class 1	46	39	62	77	52	66	55	79
Class 2	28	55	78	66	72	69	55	60
Vocalization between trials								
% of intertrials[a]								
Class 1	7	5	12	18	13	15	18	32
Class 2	3	11	25	17	22	14	22	27
% of subjects								
Class 1	46	41	67	74	71	66	68	82
Class 2	32	53	81	69	69	75	59	68

[a] F for class (5-11 mos.) = 7.10, 1/56, p = 0.01.

and is in accord with the fact that the 29-month-old day care children vocalized more than the home controls.

Activity There were no effects of care, ethnicity, or class on activity during the first year. Although all children showed a linear decrease in waving at the older ages, the Caucasians remained more active, as they did during the visual episodes. There was no simple effect of care, class, or ethnicity for twisting or fretting at any age.

Matched pairs There were no consistent differences between the matched pairs on any of the variables. The few exceptions can be noted quickly. At 7 months the home controls' data had a deeper trough for search behavior than did the data of those in day care, although the function was U-shaped for both, and day care children vocalized more than the home controls at 29 months. But for most variables the growth functions were similar for both rearing groups.

As with the visual episodes, there was no simple effect of care. Ethnicity and class differences were less striking than they were for the visual episodes. Caucasian children continued to be more vocal and motoric than the Chinese.

Auditory 2

The second auditory episode was administered at 3, 5, 9, and 11 months. The transformation for the two younger ages was a different meaningful phrase; at the two older ages the transformation was a change in the word order of the standard meaningful phrase.

Search and orientation Search was always less frequent to the second auditory episode than to the earlier one; exposure to an auditory episode 15 or 20 minutes earlier apparently reduced the child's uncertainty about the significance of the event. The U-shaped growth function noted for Auditory 1 occurred only to the standard trials, with the trough most frequent at 5 months.

Since this episode was not administered at 7 months, it is not possible to know whether search behavior would have been less frequent at 7 than at 5 months. Orientation also showed a U-shaped function. The trough occurred at 5 months to the standards, at 9 months to the transformations.

Increased search and orientation to the returns was most likely at 9 months, 4 months earlier than the peak value for Auditory 1. The sensitization provided by prior exposure to Auditory 1 seemed to shift the peak age of dishabituation, although it still occurred during the second half of the first year.

Vocalization As on Auditory 1, vocalization was more frequent between trials than during the trial, although less frequent to the Auditory 2, suggesting habituation of the excitement associated with the first episode. There was a linear increase in vocalization in both classes from 3 to 11 months with 80 percent of the children vocalizing at 11 months. As for dishabituation, whereas most children quieted to the transformation and return trials of Auditory 1 at 11 months, in Auditory 2, quieting occurred earlier, at 9 months.

Activity Twisting, fretting, and waving all increased during the first year as they did to Auditory 1. But when the children are cognitively mature and activate more complex structures in the service of assimilating the speech, restlessness declines. Fretting was low at 5 months; it was highest at 9 and 11 months, with 55 percent of the children showing fretting on at least one trial. We believe that boredom was the main reason for the irritability at the older ages since maximal fretting occurred toward the end of the presentation of the standards.

Effects of group membership There were no consistent class, care, or ethnicity effects for search for any phase of the episode. The class differences noted for Auditory 1 at 5, 7, and 9 months and the ethnicity differences at 9 and 11 did not occur on Auditory 2. The 3-month-old Chinese oriented to the speaker more often than the Caucasians (on standards 2-5) but no comparable difference occurred at the three older ages.

Similarly, there were no simple class, care, or ethnicity effects for vocalization, either during the trial or between trials. All groups showed the same linear increase in vocalization over age. The ethnicity effects noted in Auditory 1 did not appear on this second episode, a fact that affirms the wisdom of remaining cautious about group effects based on one context.

There were no consistent care, class, or ethnicity effects for activity or fretting. At 5 months the class 1 children showed more twisting and fretting, but this difference was absent at the other ages.

Matched pairs The matched pairs analysis revealed no significant differences between the two care groups for any variable, affirming the earlier conclusion that day care experience had little effect on responsivity to the auditory episodes.

A major difference between the first and second auditory episodes was the reduced responsivity to the latter, presumably the result of prior exposure to a similar event 15 minutes earlier. The expected U-shaped growth function emerged for search and orientation on both episodes. There were no effects of care on either episode, and the few ethnic or class differences that appeared on the first episode (for search and vocalization) did not occur on the second episode.

Social interaction

At the beginning and end of each assessment session from 3 to 13 months, the woman assigned to be the primary examiner for the infant for that day sat opposite the child (who was seated on the mother's lap) and, following a pre-established routine, talked, smiled, and touched the infant for 2 minutes while the child's smiling, fretting, vocalization, and fixation of the examiner were coded.

Attention to the examiner The children looked at the examiner a little over half the time; the growth function for the initial 2 minutes showed a linear decrease with age from 70 percent at 3 months to 50 percent at 13 months. However, attention to the examiner during the first minute at the end of the session followed a U-shaped function with a trough at 7 months.

Vocalization Vocalization and smiling decreased with age. This decrease in positive affect (in contrast to the increased smiling and vocalization on the other episodes) was accompanied by increasing irritability, implying apprehension. Since vocalization and smiling increased to the other nonsocial episodes but decreased in response to the female examiner who was trying to elicit these reactions, it is reasonable to conclude that the examiner elicited uncertainty in the older child. The high level of vocal response to the examiner at 3 and 5 months implies that the low levels of vocalization to block, light, and auditory episodes at 3 and 5 months are not due to any inherent inability to display this response, but rather to the fact that these nonsocial events did not excite the very young infant.

Smiling was more frequent in response to the female examiner than to any other event in the battery, including the regular mask, hence the optimal incentive for the smile at a human being at 5 months is not only the face but includes other aspects of the person.

Fretting showed a U-shaped growth function with a trough at 9 months and a sharp increase at 11 to 13 months, implying apprehension to the examiner toward the end of the first year. Even though each child was sitting on his mother's lap and, therefore, had a source of reassurance, 22 percent of the 13-month-olds fretted at least once during the initial 2 minutes of social interaction.

EFFECTS OF GROUP MEMBERSHIP

Separate analyses were performed for the 2 minutes of social interaction prior to the administration of any of the episodes and the 2 minutes after all the episodes had been completed. There were no consistent effects of care or class on attentiveness, vocalization, smiling, or fretting. However, older Caucasian children were more likely to vocalize during the final 2 minutes than were Chinese. Although this ethnic difference is in accord with the other episodes, it should be noted that it did not occur at 3, 5, or 13 months, only at 9 and 11 months.

Caucasian children also smiled more than the Chinese at every age from 5 to 13 months (see table A.18). But at 3 months, when smiling is most likely to reflect assimilation of the face, the Chinese and Caucasians smiled equally often. Over 80 percent of each ethnic group displayed the smile, a result suggesting that both groups had a well-articulated schema for the human face and were equally disposed to smile to that event. There was a decrease in smiling among the Chinese from 82 percent at 3 months to 29 percent at 13 months, but the Caucasian children continued to smile at a high level, decreasing from 80 percent at 3 months to only 60 percent at 13 months. Possibly after 5 months the smile serves not only as an index of recognitory assimilation but as an acquired social response as well. Since smiling at the examiner was high among the 3-month-old Chinese, the ethnic difference at the older ages is not due to any inherent resistance to smiling to a visual event. Rather, it is likely to be the partial result of social experiences that do not promote smiling at the later ages. The absence of a rearing effect implies different experiences in the homes of Caucasian and Chinese children.

There was a slight tendency for the younger Chinese to fret more than the Caucasians during the interaction at the end of the episode—a differ-

TABLE A.18. PERCENTAGE OF SUBJECTS SMILING, BY AGE, ETHNICITY, AND PHASE OF SOCIAL INTERACTION EPISODE.

	AGE (MOS.)					
PHASE OF EPISODE, ETHNIC GROUP	3	5	7	9	11	13
Beginning of episode[a]						
Chinese	82	69	61	46	34	29
Caucasian	80	83	71	83	66	60
End of episode[b]						
Chinese	82	59	42	49	46	42
Caucasian	87	83	74	83	72	63

[a] Ethnic difference 9 mos., chi square = 10.5, $p < .01$; 11 mos., chi square = 6.3, $p = .01$; 13 mos., chi square = 5.7, $p < .05$.

[b] Ethnic difference 5 mos., chi square = 4.2, $p < .05$; 7 mos., chi square = 6.3, $p = .01$; 9 mos., chi square = 9.0, $p < .01$; 11 mos., chi square = 4.5, $p < .05$.

ence opposite to the one noted for the light episode, where the Caucasian children were more irritable.

Matched pairs analysis There was only one difference associated with rearing. The 5-month-old day care children vocalized and smiled more than the home controls; this difference was absent at all other ages. As with the other episodes, care had a minimal effect on responsivity.

Slides at 9 and 11 months

At 9 and 11 months the children saw five sets of four related slides; each set began with depiction of a meaningful object which was transformed via slides 2 and 3 into a different meaningful object on the final slide. (See methods section in chapter 4 for description of stimuli.)

Attention was slightly greater at 11 than at 9 months; greater to the two discrepant slides in the middle of the series than to the meaningful objects at the beginning and end of each series; and greater to the slides illustrating human beings than those illustrating animals. Smiling and vocalization were generally more frequent at 11 months than at 9 months and most frequent in response to the human figures—baby, girl, and woman—at 9 months. At 11 months differences between stimuli in the amount of smiling and vocalization elicited were smaller. The depiction of the rabbit elicited as much smiling as the depictions of the baby and girl; the animal figures provoked as much vocalization as the human figures.

Effects of group membership

The child's behaviors to the first, middle two, and final stimuli were averaged across all five sets of slides, because the group data revealed an inverted U function for most variables. There were no care, class, or ethnicity effects for attention to any part of the series. At 9 months, the home controls were more vocal, especially in response to the woman, rabbit, and girl, but by 11 months the effect of care had vanished. There were only 3 instances (out of 10) in which the Caucasians were more vocal than the Chinese, and ethnic differences in vocalizations were less at 11 months than at 9 months because the Chinese showed increased vocalization across the 2-month period. The early difference was not maintained. The 9-month-old Caucasians also smiled more than the Chinese, but the ethnic difference was absent at 11 months. There were no consistent care, class, or ethnicity effects for activity or irritability.

Matched pairs There were no consistent rearing differences for attention, smiling, vocalization, or fretting, but the home control children showed more waving than those in day care.

Slides at 20 and 29 months

At the two older ages each child saw the same series of single slides, some discrepant and some realistic. Attention and vocalization were greater at 29 than at 20 months, and the age differences in attention were equivalent for the nondiscrepant and discrepant scenes.

Effects of Group membership

There were no care, class, or ethnicity effects for attention or for the difference in attention between the discrepant slides and the preceding nondiscrepant slides. Similarly, there were no significant effects of care, class, or ethnicity for vocalization, activity, or smiling, even though we found ethnic and class differences for these variables in other episodes.

Matched pairs analysis The matched pairs analysis revealed no important difference associated with care for any of the major variables, with one exception. The 29-month-old home controls smiled more than those in day care.

Summary of growth functions across episodes for the major variables

Fixation time

The three major visual and auditory episodes produced similar, but not identical, patterns of attention across age. Fixation, although high, generally increased to the visual standards across age. The U-shaped growth function for attention to the transformation was most obvious to the light episode and the first auditory episode, for which most subgroups had U-shaped functions with troughs at 7 months.

Smiling

The pattern of smiling in response to the various procedures reveals the importance of specifying both age and event, for each of the episodes produced different growth curves, and the effects of care, class, or ethnicity were dependent upon episode.

The most human incentive, the female adult in the social interaction procedure, provoked the most smiling during the first year. About 80 percent of the 3-month-old children smiled; about 40 percent of the 13-month-olds. Smiling was far less frequent to the masks—only 20 percent of the children smiled at least once to this event. Smiling was generally infrequent—less than 20 percent of the children smiled—to block, light, car, and auditory episodes during the first year. Because after the first year smiling increased substantially (more than half the children smiled to the light and the car at 20 and 29 months), we infer that their capacity to assimilate the discrepant experience contained in those episodes increased. The growth function for smiling to these nonsocial events parallels the growth of fear to less comprehensible discrepant events (for example, a jack-in-the-box) and to maternal departure. These parallels are in accord with the theoretical suggestion that toward the end of the first year the child is better able to retrieve schemata from memory and compare them with present experience, thus increasing the probability of either assimilating complex events or being left in a state of uncertainty as a result of failure to assimilate. The light and car were dynamic events occurring over a period of 6 to 10 seconds and it was probably difficult for the child under one year to establish a well-articulated schema for them. The enhanced retrieval and comparison competences available after one year may have facilitated the establishment of a schema for these events and eventually permitted their assimilation.

The lower rate of smiling to the auditory episode, even at 29 months, may be due either to a higher threshold for smiling in response to speech or to the fact that the 2-year-old's schemata for language were not firm and it was difficult for the child to relate the information to a pre-existing structure.

Vocalization

The growth functions for vocalization were more similar across episodes than they were for smiling. On most episodes, 50 to 75 percent of the children vocalized at least once, and by 29 months vocalization occurred on about 30 percent of the trials. Vocalization generally increased with age, except on the mask and social interaction episodes. Either the unfamiliar examiner and masks elicited uncertainty and subsequent inhibition of vocalization, or perhaps these events were easy to assimilate and therefore generated no excitement.

Comparison of response patterns Vocalization and smiling showed major increases at different ages. While smiling displayed a major increase from 13 to 29 months, vocalization increased in a major way from 3 through 9, and again from 13 to 29 months, with a plateau from 9 to 13 months. The pattern was especially clear for vocalization during the interval between trials of the auditory episode; there was a sharp rise in vocalization from 3 to 7 months, a plateau from 9 to 13, followed by a sharp increase at 20 and 29 months. This pattern is in accord with the suggestion that vocalization can reflect the excitement of assimilation and the processing of interesting information. The temporary plateau in vocalization at 11 and 13 months implies a brief period of inhibition corresponding to the emergence of wariness to a variety of events.

Fretting and twisting generally showed inverted U-shaped functions with peak irritability and restlessness from 9 to 13 months, followed by a sharp decline at 29 months, the age when separation distress was vanishing and anticipatory fixations were infrequent.

Finally, smiling had a complementary relation to twisting and fretting. While the latter responses were increasing, smiling remained low. As twisting and fretting declined, smiling increased. If we assume that smiling reflects assimilation of the event, it appears that prior to assimilation there is a considerable amount of restless twisting and irritability. As the child matures and becomes better able to assimilate the event, motoricity and irritability decline.

Generalizations A few generalizations stand out clearly from this detailed survey of the children's responses to the nine episodes over the 26-month period. First, the growth patterns for attentiveness, vocalization, smiling, activity, and irritability to specific episodes were generally similar for most children. The growth functions for each variable appear to be more affected by maturation in a context of common life experiences and the characteristics of the event than by the specific experiences associated with day care, class, or ethnicity. Vocalization increased over age to most episodes, social interaction being the exception, and the greatest increase in vocalization occurred after 9 months. Smiling was common to the social events at the early ages, and decreased over time, while smiling to the nonsocial events was infrequent initially and increased with age. Most children showed a period of uncertainty between 9 and 13 months, as reflected in anticipatory fixations to the car episode, increasing search behavior to auditory episodes, increasing attentiveness to the visual episodes, and vocal quieting to the transformation and return trials of the first auditory episode. This phase of development seems to be partially under maturational control.

The strongest evidence for the emergence of a new phase of cognitive functioning was seen in the U-shaped growth function for fixation time to the transformation and return trials of block and light episodes and search to the auditory episode, with a trough typically occurring at 7 or 9 months.

Growth patterns for responses and group differences were yoked to the nature of the episode. Smiling peaked at 7 months for the block, rose linearly for the light and the car, and decreased for interaction with the examiner and the regular mask.

The comparisons of care, ethnicity, and class were also specific to the event. Of the three independent variables—form of care, class, and ethnicity—care was clearly the least important. No episode revealed consistent differences between day care and home control children across two or more ages, and the interactions noted on one episode typically did not occur on another.

Although class effects were slightly stronger, they were not very sturdy. Class 1 children were more attentive at 3 months, but not at later ages, and they vocalized and smiled more at the light and car after the first year. On a few episodes the class 2 Chinese children in day care were more vocal and smiling than their class 2 counterparts reared at home, but this effect was never large.

Ethnicity produced the most consistent differences across episodes and ages, even though ethnicity differences did not occur in all episodes. The Caucasians were generally more vocal, and smiled more than the Chinese, especially during the first year. Caucasians smiled more during the social interaction sequence from 5 to 13 months. Since 3-month-old Chinese children smiled at the examiner as often as Caucasians (80 percent of the children smiled at that early age), the later differences cannot be due to difficulty in assimilation but rather, we believe, to the acquired tendency to display social smiling to an unfamiliar person. It was suggested that experiences in the Caucasian homes, which apparently are not altered by the day care environment, dispose the Caucasian child to continue to smile to an actively interacting adult.

More Caucasian than Chinese children smiled to the block episode at 9 and 11 months, but not earlier, and to the light episode at 7 and 11 months. But there were no ethnic differences to the car or auditory episodes. Thus generalizations about smiling must be restricted by age and informational context. Because the ethnic differences in smiling occurred after 7 months, and because 80 percent of the Chinese smiled at the examiner at the beginning of the day's procedures, we favor an interpretation that emphasizes the role of family experience, but cannot rule out biological factors. Caucasians were also more vocal in most episodes, except social interaction, but this difference did not appear until the end of the first and during the second year. The ethnic difference was significant to the block episode from 7 through 11 months, to light at 7, 11, and 29 months; to auditory at 11, 20, and 29 months; to masks at 9 and 13; and to the slide episodes from 9 through 29 months. Oddly enough, the social interaction episode, which produced an ethnic difference in smiling, did not reveal an ethnic difference in vocalization. Indeed, slightly more Chinese than Caucasians vocalized in response to the examiner during the first half-year.

Just as there was no growth function for smiling, only for smiling to a particular event, there was no general tendency for Caucasian infants to smile or to vocalize more than Chinese children, only a tendency to do so in specific episodes at specific ages.

Why did we discover so much context specificity in the first two years whereas many other studies find more generality across tasks? We believe that the explanation has to do with the age of the child, the tasks we used, and the responses we quantified. We sampled over varied contexts—visual and auditory, social and nonsocial—and coded the naturally occurring responses of infants to these events. Unlike knowledge of specific vocabulary, vocalization, smiling, and looking reflect the species-specific dispositions of infants to respond to situations that engage their schemata and attract their attention. Apparently these responses do not display much generality across episodes or within an episode across age during the first two years of life. This suggestion is in accord with other studies of infant growth. In an earlier study of Caucasian infants seen at 4, 8, 13, and 27 months, there was little predictive stability for similar variables from 4 or 8 to 27 months, no class effects until the end of the first year, and differing growth curves for different episodes. When R. B. McCall and his colleagues (McCall, Eichorn, and Hogarty 1977) examined the correlations between the principal components of the Bayley Scale scores during the first few years for the Berkeley longitudinal sample, they found apparent discontinuities in the pattern of intra-individual stabilities at 8, 13, and 20 months. Their data, as do ours, imply that it is not theoretically useful to ascribe to an infant a generalized competence that is presumed to cross tasks and to be relatively stable for several years.

Correlations within and across age

INTERCORRELATIONS AMONG FIXATION TIME, SEARCH, AND ORIENTATION TO SPEAKER

We intercorrelated the attentional variables for the visual and auditory episodes for all trials and for standards 2 through 5. Because the correlations for the standards revealed no information that was not contained in the correlations for all trials, and because the latter provided better evidence of stability than the former, we shall only summarize the data based on all trials.

There was not a consistently strong relation between search or orientation to the speaker on the auditory episodes and fixation to the visual episodes. On a few occasions significant cross-task correlations appeared, but they were infrequent and generally low (correlations averaged about 0.30). It appears that there is no common psychological process involved in these two response classes.

The auditory episodes Search and orientation were correlated at any one particular age, and there was cross-task generality for search and orientation across the two auditory episodes at the same age of testing (correlations ranged from 0.4 to 0.6). But the cross-age relations were weak. The best evidence of stability occurred when search behavior to Auditory I at 7 or 9 months was the predictor. Search at 7 predicted search at 9 and 11 months; and search at 9 months predicted search at 11 and 13 (r = 0.3), but not at 20 and 29 months. Search at 5 months was correlated with search at 7 months; search at 11 with search at 13 months. The U-shaped growth curve for search had a trough at 7 to 9 months, implying a transition period. Perhaps those children who passed through the transition to the more mature stage a little earlier than others (and had longer search values) continued to be precocious for a few months during the period of increased attention from 7 to 13 months. But after 13 months, when all children are in the more mature stage, the 9-month behavior loses its predictive power.

The cross-age correlations for orientation to the speaker were similar to those for search, although not exact duplicates, and indicated short-term stability. Orientation at 5 months was correlated with orientation at 7 and 9 months; orientation at 7 predicted behavior at 13 and 20 months; behavior at 9 predicted behavior at 11 and 13 months. There was no predictability from 13 or 20 months onward.

The visual episodes The interepisode correlations for fixation time at each age were positive but not high. The interepisode correlations were highest at 3, 9, and 11 months. Fixation of the examiner during the social interaction period was independent of attention to all other episodes, including the facial masks. There was no strong relation between attention to block and light at 5 and 7 months; from 9 to 29 months the interepisode correlations at a particular age ranged from about 0.25 to 0.40. The episode therefore exerted a more serious influence on attention than any disposition toward attentiveness inherent in the child. At 3 months there was a great deal of variation in general alertness, whereas at 5 and 7 months all infants were alert. At 9 and 11 months, presumably, some children had passed into the new stage of functioning, while others had not, but at 13 months all children should have been functioning at the new level. It is possible, therefore, that during transitional periods between stages of development, when attention is being mediated by different mechanisms, interepisode correlations will be higher than during periods when all children are at the same stage of cognitive development. As we shall see later, an analysis of variance across the periods indicates that variation in attentiveness was greatest from 9 to 11 months. When most children are at the same stage of functioning, the specific context seems to exert the major control on attention. It is noteworthy that this pattern of intercorrelations for fixation time is in complete accord with earlier data gathered on an independent longitudinal study across the period from 4 through 27 months (Kagan 1971).

Analysis of the pattern of cross-age correlations for the block, light, car, masks, and the first auditory episode reveals two generalizations. First, there was intraindividual stability over one or two ages but rarely long-term stability from 5, 7, or 9 months to 20 or 29 months. Typically, attention at 5 months was correlated with attention at 7 months, 7 with 9 and 11, 9 with 11, 13 and occasionally 20 months, 13 with 20, and 20 with 29 months (see table A.19). Intraindividual stability was limited to intervals of less than 10 months. There were very few instances in which attention at 3 or 5 months predicted attention after the first birthday, and only for the block episode did fixation time at 7 or 9 months predict fixation time at 29 months.

Second, the period between 7 and 11 months was the best time to pre-

TABLE A.19. SIGNIFICANT CORRELATIONS FOR STABILITY OF TOTAL FIXATION TIME AND SEARCH ACROSS EPISODES AND AGE (AUD. = AUDITORY EPISODE; Bl. = BLOCK EPISODE; Lt. = LIGHT EPISODE).

PREDICTOR: SEARCH IN AUDITORY 1 EPISODE

AT 3 MOS.	AT 5 MOS.	AT 7 MOS.	AT 9 MOS.	AT 11 MOS.
No significant correlations with search at later age	Bl. 5 mos. .26[a]	Aud. 9 mos. .25[a]	Aud. 11 mos. .33[b]	Aud. 13 mos. .23[a]
	Lt. 7 .40[b]	Aud. 11 .32[b]	Aud. 13 .31[b]	
	Lt. 11 .29[a]	Lt. 7 .30[b]	Bl. 9 .28[a]	
	Car 11 .35[b]	Lt. 9 .26[a]	Lt. 20 .26[a]	
	Aud. 7 .24[a]	Lt. 11 .32[b]		
		Car 11 .24[a]		

AT 13 MOS.	AT 20 MOS.	AT 29 MOS.
Car 11 mos. .25[a]	No significant correlations	No significant correlations
Lt. 13 .28[a]		

PREDICTOR: TOTAL FIXATION TIME IN BLOCK EPISODE

AT 3 MOS.	AT 5 MOS.	AT 7 MOS.	AT 9 MOS.	AT 11 MOS.
Lt. 3 mos. .43[b]	Aud. 5 mos. .26[a]	Bl. 9 mos. .42[b]	Aud. 13 mos. .24[a]	Lt. 11 mos. .33[b]
Mask 3 .50[c]	Bl. 7 .28[a]	Bl. 11 .31[a]	Bl. 11 .44[b]	Car 11 .32[b]
Mask 5 .28[a]	Lt. 7 .24[a]	Lt. 9 .23[a]	Lt. 9 .40[b]	Car 20 .26[a]
Bl. 7 .33[a]		Lt. 20 .39[b]	Lt. 13 .24[a]	
Bl. 9 .31[a]		Lt. 29 .31[a]	Lt. 20 .39[b]	
Aud. 20 .34[a]		Car 20 .29[a]	Lt. 29 .34[a]	
		Car 29 .30[a]	Car 29 .36[a]	
		Mask 9 .25[a]	Mask 9 .41[c]	

Predictor: Total fixation time in light episode				
At 3 mos.	At 5 mos.	At 7 mos.	At 9 mos.	At 11 mos.
Bl. 3 mos. .43[b]	Mask 5 mos. .26[a]	Aud. 7 mos. .30[b]	Bl. 9 mos. .40[b]	Bl. 11 mos. .33[b]
Mask 3 .41[b]	Mask 9 .31[b]	Lt. 9 .27[a]	Bl. 11 .31[b]	Car 11 .37[b]
Car 13 .34[a]	Bl. 9 .25[a]	Lt. 11 .35[b]	Lt. 11 .52[c]	Lt. 20 .38[b]
	Car 9 .23[a]	Car 11 .24[a]	Lt. 20 .36[b]	Aud. 20 .31[a]
			Car 9 .26[a]	Aud. 29 .36[a]
			Car 11 .26[a]	

At 13 mos.	At 20 mos.	At 29 mos.
Car 13 mos. .25[a]	Car 20 mos. .40[b]	Car 29 mos. .35[a]
Car 20 .32[a]	Lt. 29 .38[b]	
Aud. 13 .28[a]	Aud. 29 .31[a]	
Lt. 20 .38[b]		
Lt. 29 .29[a]		

Predictor: Total fixation time in car episode				
At 9 mos.	At 11 mos.	At 13 mos.	At 20 mos.	At 29 mos.
Lt. 9 mos. .26[a]	Bl. 11 mos. .31[b]	Lt. 13 mos. .25[a]	Lt. 20 mos. .40[b]	Lt. 29 mos. .35[a]
Mask 9 .30[b]	Lt. 11 .37[b]	Car 20 .29[a]		
Car 13 .43[b]	Aud. 13 .24[a]			
	Lt. 13 .27[a]			
	Lt. 20 .39[b]			
	Lt. 29 .40[b]			
	Car 13 .26[a]			

(cont.)

TABLE A.19 (cont.)

Predictor: Total fixation time in mask episode			
At 3 mos.	At 5 mos.	At 9 mos.	At 13 mos.
Bl. 3 mos. .50[c]	Lt. 5 mos. .26[a]	Bl. 9 mos. .41[c]	Aud. 29 mos. .45[b]
Lt. 3 .41[b]	Bl. 9 .30[b]	Bl. 11 .29[a]	
	Car 9 .30[b]	Lt. 20 .40[b]	
	Car 11 .29[a]	Car 9 .30[b]	
	Car 13 .24[a]	Mask 13 .43[c]	
	Mask 9 .25[a]		

[a] $p < 0.05$.
[b] $p < 0.01$.
[c] $p < 0.001$.

dict future attention, whereas attention at 3 or 5 months was minimally related to attention at a future date. The break in the pattern of continuity at 7 months corresponds to the age when the trough in growth function for attention appeared. This was the age for which we have posited a new stage of cognitive functioning, and by implication the age when the child's attention comes under the influence of a new set of neural and psychological mechanisms.

The data imply that during the period of transition into the new stage of cognitive functioning, individual variation in attentiveness is stable. After all the children have passed into the new stage, by 13 months, variation in attention becomes less predictive of the future. From 5 to 7 years most children are in transition into the stage of concrete operational thinking. It is likely that variation in the ability to conserve mass at age 5 will predict variation at age 7 in the tendency to successfully master the other groupings of the concrete operational stage. But by age 9, when all children are in the stage of concrete operations, the variation in quality of performance on grouping problems may be a poor predictor of variation in formal operational thinking at 13 years of age.

Constancy: An Ipsative Analysis

Some response variables, though not all, pass through transition periods when they come under the influence of new sets of forces. For these variables there will be poor intraindividual stability from the period before the age of transition to the period after it. By contrast, for those responses that remain under the influence of similar forces for long periods of time, like height or size of vocabulary, there will be less obvious discontinuity in the predictive coefficients.

The importance of the period from 7 to 11 months is also revealed in a quite different analysis of constancy. It will be recalled from our discussion of the meaning of continuity in chapter 1 that we suggested that an ipsative analysis of periods of constancy might reveal important information about the stages of growth. We suggested that, when the ratio of change in some response to absolute magnitude of that response approached a small value, one might infer constancy of that behavior for that interval. Since assessment of reactivity to the laboratory episodes provided an opportunity to evaluate that idea, we performed an analysis of total fixation time to the light and block episodes and search for Auditory I for standards 2 through 5 and the three return trials for those infants who had complete data for those episodes from 5 through 11 or 29 months. For each child we computed the ratio, for pairs of successive ages, of the difference in total fixation time between successive ages to the mean fixation time for that pair of ages. A low ratio indicated minimal change relative to the absolute amount of attentiveness; a ratio of zero indicated no change in relative attentiveness over that period.

Light episode Figure A.1 shows the ratio for the standards and returns for the light episode ($n = 48$ for standards 2-5; $n = 43$ for the 3 return trials). For the standards, the ratio was lowest from 9 to 11 months, the age when most children were entering the new stage of cognitive functioning, and when object permanence and separation anxiety emerged. For the returns, the lowest ratio was at 20 to 29 months. But the greatest decrease in the ratio for both standards and returns occurred between 7-9 and 9-11 months.

We also examined each child's six ratios to determine the age at which each infant showed his or her lowest ratio. Table A.20 shows the percentage of children who showed their lowest ratio at each pair of ages. In cases where more than one pair of ages had equal ratios, we chose the youngest age. The modal age for the standards was 9 to 11 months, and for the returns 20 to 29 months. These data imply that 9 to 11 months of age may be a critical interval when certain psychological processes stabilize. (It should be noted that this result is not an artifact of unusually low or high fixation times at this age. Fixations to the standards at 9 to 11 months were not significantly larger or smaller than fixations at earlier or later ages. Fixation time from 11 to 20

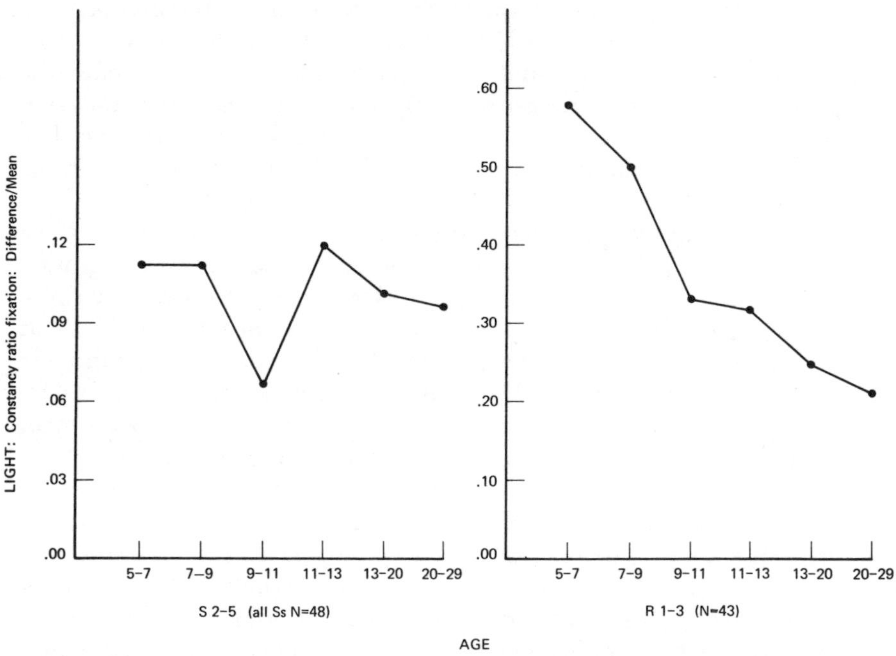

Fig. A.1 *Ratio of fixation times for standards 2-5 ($n = 48$) and for return trials 1-3 ($n = 43$) for the light episode.*

TABLE A.20. PERCENTAGE OF CHILDREN SHOWING THEIR LOWEST RATIO OF CHANGE IN ATTENTIVENESS, BY SUCCESSIVE PAIRS OF AGES IN THREE EPISODES.

EPISODE	STANDARDS 2-5	RETURNS 1-3
Light		
5-7 mos.	18%	12
7-9	17	13
9-11	29	7
11-13	13	12
13-20	10	23
20-29	13	33
Block		
5-7	26	32
7-9	47	24
9-11	27	44
Auditory 1		
5-7	14	10
7-9	12	14
9-11	22	18
11-13	21	12
13-29	21	24
20-29	10	22

months was greater than attentiveness at 9 to 11 months. Therefore the ratio might be expected to be lower at the older ages.)

Second, the fact that the ratios are much higher for the three return trials than they were for the standards at all ages implies that there is less temporal constancy for attentiveness at the end of the episode than during the beginning of the episode. There was, obviously, a great deal of individual variation in the ratio, but no simple care, ethnicity, or class effects.

Block episode Figure A.2 presents the comparable data for the block episode. Again the ratios for the standards were considerably lower than those for the returns, and the lowest ratios were reached earlier for the standards than for the returns. The lowest ratio occurred at 7 to 9 months for the standards, two months earlier than the corresponding period for the light episode. The majority of children showed their lowest ratios to the standards from 7 to 9 months and to the returns at 9 to 11 months (see table A.20).

Auditory episode Figure A.3 presents the comparable data for search across the period 5 to 29 months. There were two low points for the standards. As with the light episode, there was a dramatic drop in the ratio at 9

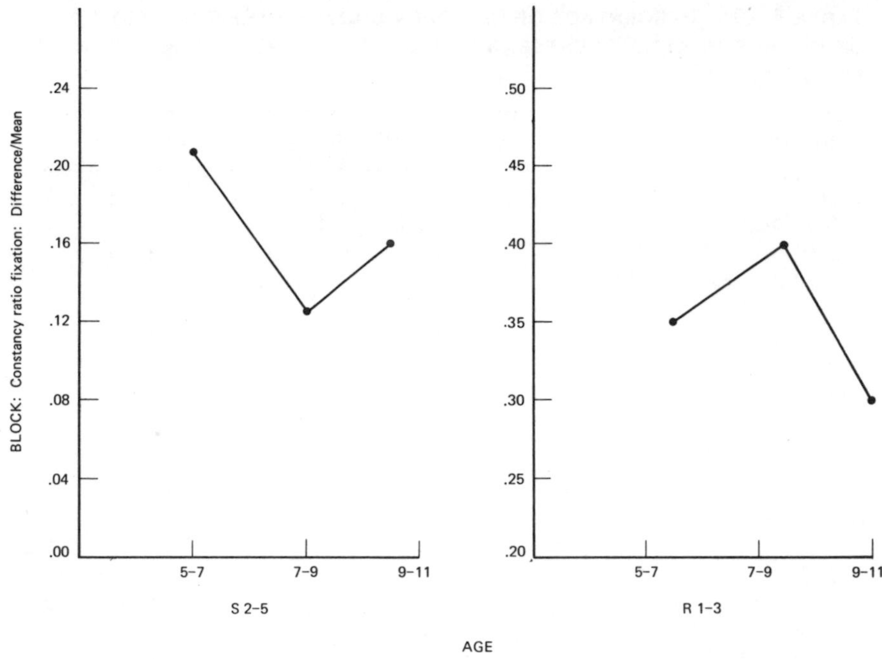

Fig. A.2 *Ratio of fixation times for standards and returns for the block episode.*

to 11 months (from 0.71 to 0.37), a leveling off at 11 to 20 months, and then a second decline to a low value at 20 to 29 months (ratio = 0.22). For the returns, the first major decline was at 13 to 20 months, but the lowest ratio held for 20 to 29 months. There were no care, class, ethnicity or sex differences in the ratio, only an age effect. An ipsative analysis revealed that for most children the ratio for search to the standards was lowest during the period 9 to 20 months; to the returns most children had their lowest ratios from 13 to 29 months.

For all three episodes the lowest ratios occurred a bit later for the return trials than for the standards, and the ratios for the returns were larger than those for the standards, suggesting that constancy of attention to these tasks is better for the initial trials of the episode than for the last part of the episode.

For all three episodes there was a major increase in relative constancy of attentiveness after 9 months, the period following the trough in attentiveness and before language and fearfulness appear in full intensity. These data imply that the period from 7 to 11 months is an interval of relative constancy with respect to initial attentiveness to an interesting event. It is of interest that the product moment correlations across this period are also high, for stability first appears at about 7 months of age.

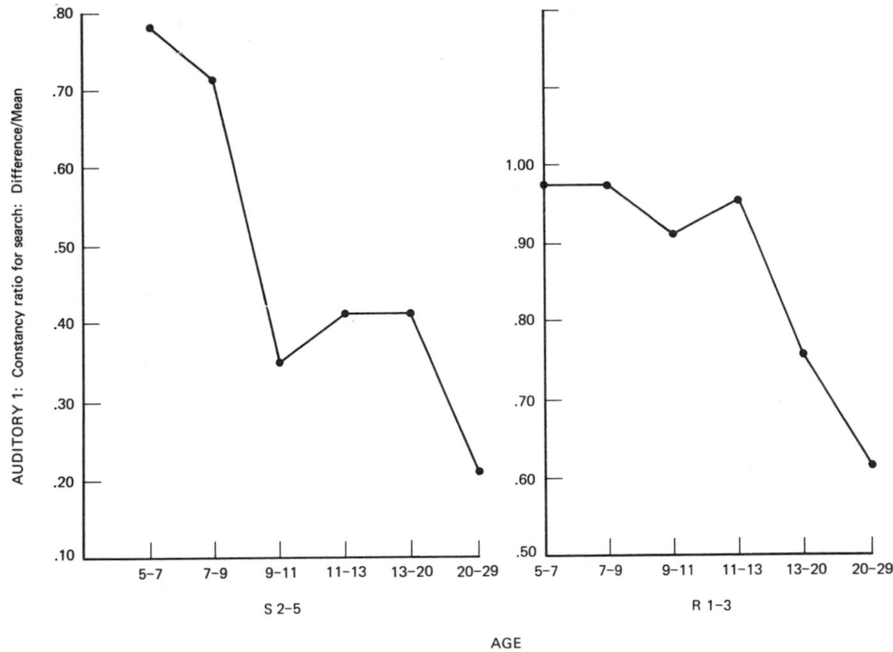

Fig. A.3 *Ratio of duration of search for standards and returns for the auditory episode across the period from 5 to 29 months.*

The nearly linear decrease in the ratio for the returns implies that, with age, attentiveness to the returns begins to stabilize. Even though the period from 20 to 29 months is 9 months rather than 2 months long, the ratios are smaller at the older ages, implying greater intraindividual constancy as the child matures.

This analysis, unlike the product moment correlations which reflect a child's attentiveness relative to his cohort, permits one to make less relative statements about periods of stability for a particular response in a context, in contrast to statements about the relative stability of a variable over a period of time. Figures A.4-A.6 illustrate the product moment correlations for the same two variables for the same subjects across pairs of successive ages. For the block episode (figure A.4) the correlations and ratios yield comparable information. The correlations were highest for 7 to 9 months for the standards, and 9 to 11 months for the returns. But this was not true for the light or auditory episodes. For light, the correlational analysis revealed that fixation to the standards and returns was only stable from 13 to 20 months, whereas the ratio analysis indicated that 9 to 11 months was the period of constancy for the standards and 20 to 29 months for the returns; the correlational analysis gives no hint of the drop in the ratio at 9 to 11 months. The correlational analysis for the auditory episode was in partial consonance with

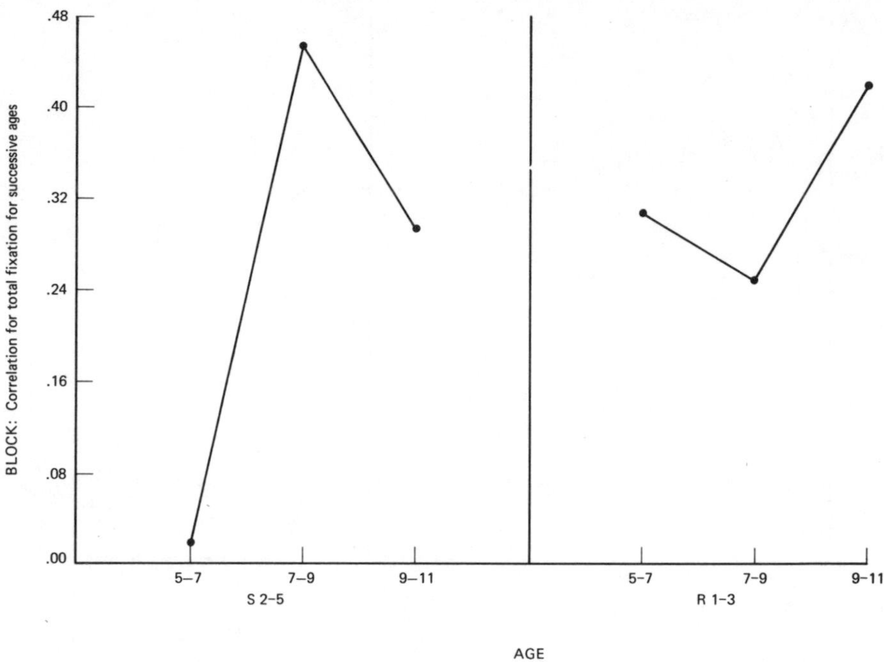

Fig. A.4 *Product moment correlations for fixation time across successive ages for standards 2-5 and for return trials 1-3 for the block episode.*

the ratio data; the highest coefficients occurred for 9 to 11 and 11 to 13 months for search of the standards. However, the correlational analysis produced the lowest coefficients for 20 to 29 months, the age when the ratios were the lowest. For the returns the correlational analysis did not reflect major drops in the ratio at 13 to 20 and 20 to 29 months. Moreover while the ratios were much smaller for the standards than for the returns (by a factor of 1 to 2), the magnitudes of the product moment correlations were about equal.

Thus the two procedures complement each other. The correlational analysis informs us of the degree to which a sample retains its relative rank on a response variable, but it does not tell us about the relative amount of change that occurs in that variable. The ratio analysis reveals the age interval when the response is most and least variable and, therefore, is potentially useful in detecting stages in development.

CROSS-AGE STABILITY FOR AVERAGE ATTENTIVENESS ACROSS EPISODES

Having examined the cross-age stability for attentiveness to each episode separately, we pooled data across episodes. As we indicated in chapter 5, we standardized each child's total fixation time for those episodes that

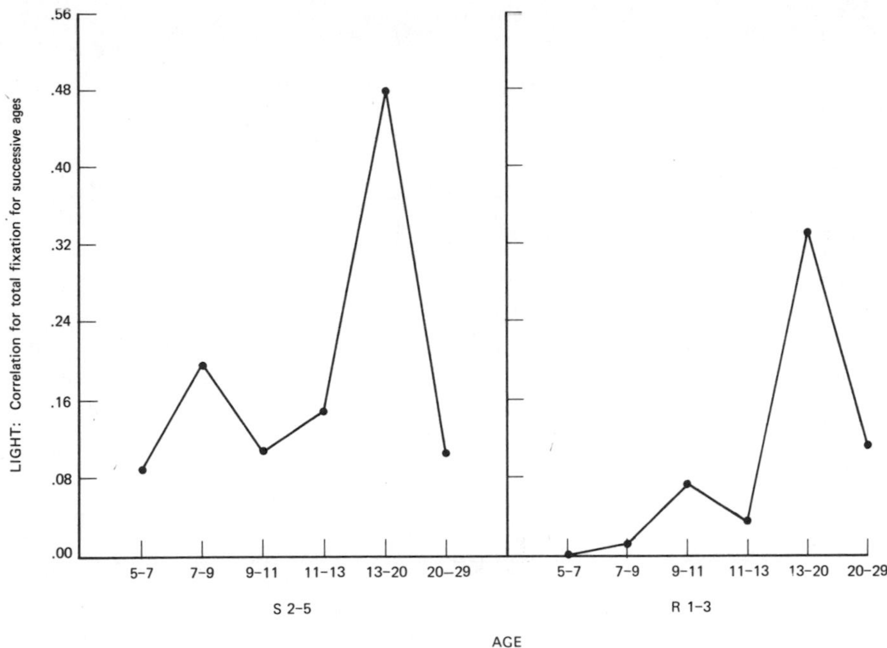

Fig. A.5 *Product moment correlations for fixation time across successive ages for the light episode.*

were positively related at each age and computed an average *z* score for the percent total fixation to all trials for the pooled episodes at each age. At 3 and 5 months the average *z* score was based on attention to block, light, and mask stimuli; at 7 months to block and light; at 9 and 11 months to block, light, and car; and at 13, 20, and 29 months to light and car.

Attention at 3 months was unrelated to attention at any other age, and attention prior to 20 months was unrelated to fixation at 29 months. Significant correlations generally held over the period 5 to 20 months (*r* ranged from 0.27 to 0.42) (see table 5.1).

Examination of the eight standard scores for each of the eight subgroups revealed that, with the exception of the significant class difference in attention at 3 months, there was no consistent effect of care, class, or ethnicity on this index of attentiveness. There is an optimal age for each episode when, we assume, the infant is able to establish a relatively firm schema for the event and to compare transformation and return trials to the schema established to the standard. The children who established a schema for the block, light, or car episodes a little more quickly than the others tended to be more attentive during the following months, although it must be noted that the correlations rarely rose above 0.4.

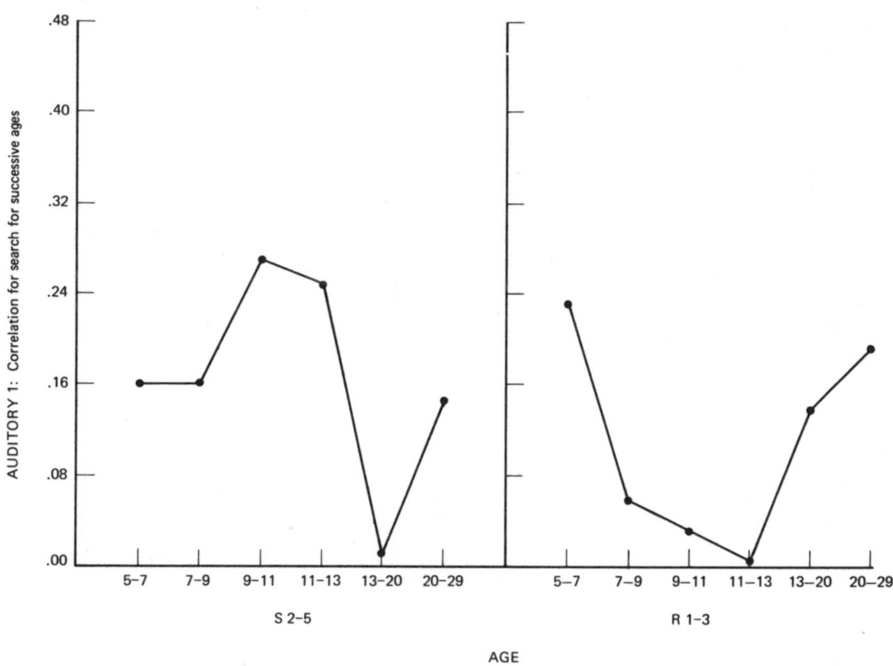

Fig. A.6 *Product moment correlations for search across successive ages for the auditory episode.*

Cross-episode relations for vocalization within an age

To assess the cross-episode generality for vocalization, we computed phi coefficients based on division of distributions at the median for percent of vocalization trials on an episode. There was relatively robust cross-task generality within a particular age, especially at the three oldest ages. As with fixation time, the pattern for vocalization during the social interaction episode was unique, for it was only minimally correlated with vocalization during any of the visual or auditory episodes, probably because vocal response to the examiner was an elicited reaction while vocalization to the other episodes reflected the excitement that accompanies information processing. Vocalization across the two auditory episodes was highly correlated at any one age. Moreover, vocalization to the auditory episodes was correlated with vocalization to the visual episodes—recall that search was not correlated with fixation time to the visual episodes.

Cross-episode generality increased with age (if we eliminate the social interaction episode). At 3 months, 19 percent of the 28 possible cross-task correlations were significant; at 5 months 78 percent were significant; at 7 months 16 percent; at 9 months 60 percent; at 11 months 33 percent; and at 13, 20, and 29 months cross-episode generality was excellent, for all the cross-episode correlations were significant.

STABILITY OF VOCALIZATION ACROSS AGE

Since there was generally high cross-task generality for vocalization within an age, we created a summary variable for each child reflecting the mean proportion of trials the child vocalized for all of the visual and auditory episodes at a given age (social interaction was omitted). The intercorrelations among the scores at each of the eight ages were computed for Chinese and Caucasian children separately as well as for the whole group (see table 5.2). As indicated earlier, there was little cross-age stability of vocalization among the Caucasians, but among the Chinese, there was good cross-age stability from 9 months on. An analysis of variance on this summary variable revealed that Caucasians vocalized significantly more than Chinese from 9 to 20 months, but the difference was not present at the early ages or at the oldest age.

STABILITY OF ACTIVITY AND IRRITABILITY

As we had for smiling (see chapter 5), we averaged the occurrence of activity or fretting for each child across all episodes at a given age, divided the distribution of mean scores at the median, assigned each child to a position above or below the median, and computed phi coefficients to assess cross-age stability.

Waving and leaning showed the least stability; moreover, the coefficients for successive ages were often lower than those separated by larger spans of time. Fretting and twisting displayed more coherent patterns of stability (see tables A.21 and A.22). Both showed short-term stability over periods as long as a year, but no longer. Fretting at 9 months correlated with fretting at 11 and 20 months, but not at 13 or 29 months. Fretting at 3, 5, or 7 months had no relation to later fretting.

The data on twisting were the most coherent. At each age there was short-term stability for periods lasting from 2 to 9 months, but not longer. Thus twisting at 5 months predicted responsivity at 7, 9, and 13 months, but not at 20 and 29 months. Twisting at 9 months predicted 11 and 13; 11 predicted 13 and 20; and 20 predicted 29 months. The fact that motoric restlessness showed short-term stability implies the presence of an individual disposition to display motor discharge when bored, but the stability does not extend beyond 9 months.

A partial replication

Some of the generalizations we have extracted from these data can be tested against a similar set of information gathered by Robert Klein and Martha Sellers on a sample of infants living in small, poor, subsistence farming Ladino villages in eastern Guatemala. The families are less isolated, both psychologically and geographically, than the Indian villages in the northwest

TABLE A.21. STABILITY OF FRETTING FOR PERCENTAGE OF TRIALS IN WHICH FRETTING OCCURRED (PHI COEFFICIENTS, ALL SUBJECTS, ALL EPISODES).

AGE (MOS.)	3	5	7	9	11	13	20	29
3	...	.06	.06	.02	.20	.02	.18	.11
5		...	.04	.04	.08	.09	.16	.00
7			...	.01	.11	.09	.16	.17
9				...	.40[a]	.09	.28[b]	.17
11					...	.13	.24	.04
13						...	.19	.17
20							...	.08

[a] $p < 0.001$.
[b] $p < 0.05$.

part of the country, but their child-rearing practices are very different from those of North Americans. The Ladino infants experience less daily variety than the North American infants in our day care and home control groups.

The Guatemalan infants were tested in a small hut resembling their home under conditions that simulated the ones used in this study. Each of 137 children was administered the block, light, car, and auditory episodes five times—at 5½, 7½, 9½, 11½, and 13½ months—while fixation time, vocalization, smiling, and fretting were coded by observers.

TABLE A.22. STABILITY OF TWISTING FOR PERCENTAGE OF TRIALS IN WHICH TWISTING OCCURRED (PHI COEFFICIENTS, ALL SUBJECTS, ALL EPISODES).

AGE (MOS.)	3	5	7	9	11	13	20	29
3	...	.23	.17	.23	.20	.28[a]	.00	.16
5		...	.28[a]	.31[b]	.15	.31[b]	.05	.15
7			...	.31[b]	.20	.15	.05	.01
9				...	.49[c]	.39[b]	.11	.23
11					...	.44[b]	.35[b]	.18
13						...	.21	.27
20							...	.34[a]
								...

[a] $p < 0.05$.
[b] $p < 0.01$.
[c] $p < 0.001$.

Fixation Time

The Guatemalan and North American children had similar growth functions for attention to the block and to the light. Both groups showed a linear increase in fixation time to the standard trials across age and a U-shaped developmental function to the transformation and return trials, with a trough at 7½ months. To the block episode, the simplest, the cultural differences in duration of attention were small (less than 10 percent), although the North American children had longer fixation times at all ages. To light and car episodes, which were more complex, the cultural differences were greater and North Americans had longer fixation times (see figures A.7-A.9).

Despite the more prolonged attention of the North American infants, the Guatemalan infants displayed the U-shaped growth function, a result affirming the conclusion that the maturation of a cognitive competence controls the basic growth function for attention, while specific experiences influence the level of attention within any particular stage of development.

We examined the growth function for total fixation time to the standards, transformations, and returns for each of the 137 infants in this longi-

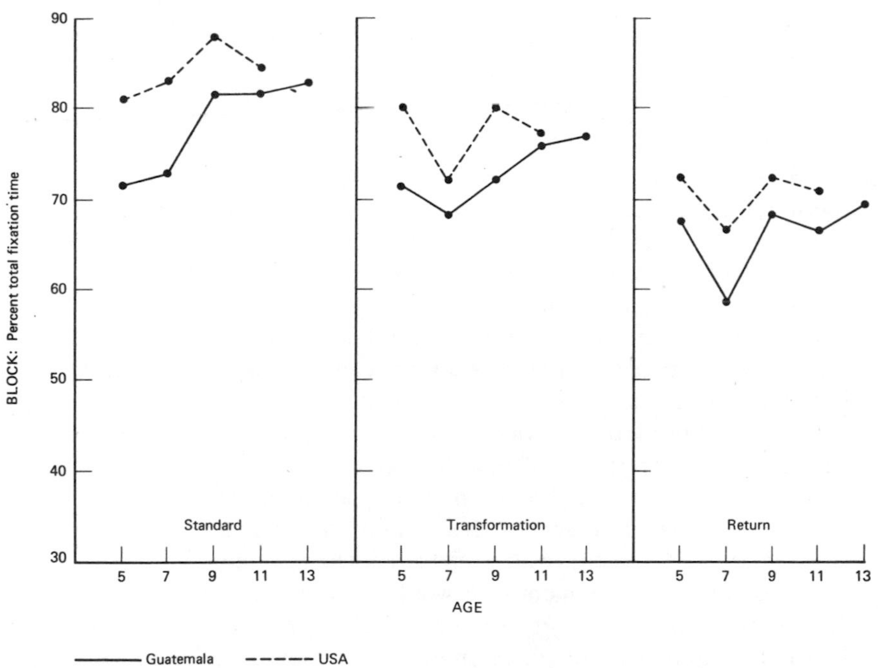

Fig. A.7 *Fixation times for the block episode for Guatemalan and North American children.*

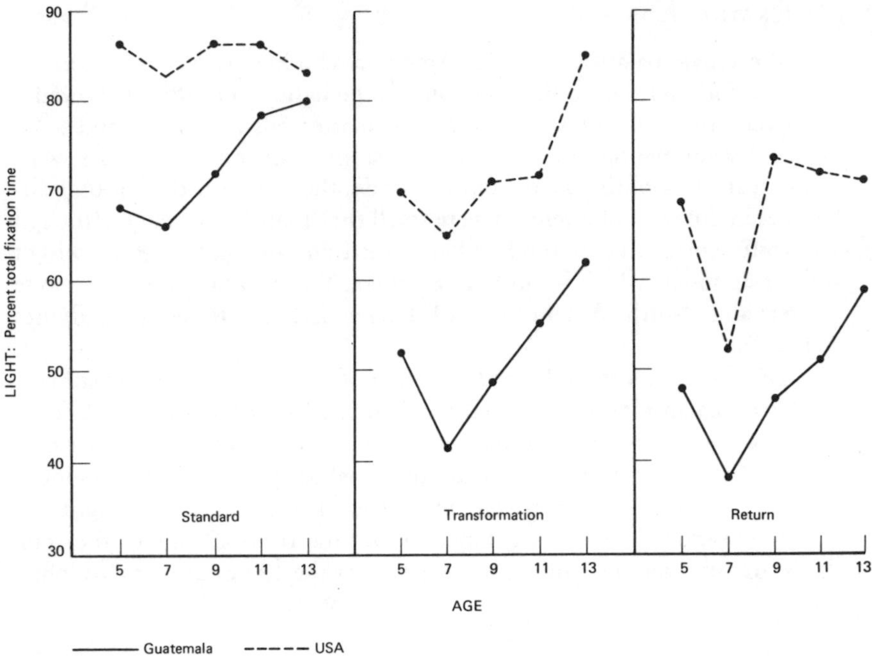

Fig. A.8 *Fixation times for the light episode for Guatemalan and North American children.*

tudinal sample. A child was regarded as having a U-shaped function if his shortest fixation time occurred at 7 or 9 months and the fixation time at the trough was less than the fixation time at the preceding age by 10 percent or more. About one-half of the children showed a U-shaped function to the standard, transformation, or return trials with a trough at either 7 or 9 months. About one-quarter of the individual growth functions were U-shaped to the standards, transformations, and returns. Occurrence of the trough was almost as frequent at 9 months as it was at 7 months, in contrast to troughs for the North American sample, where many more infants showed their lowest fixation times at 7 months. Table A.23 shows what percentages of the Guatemalan group showed the trough at 7 or 9 months. About one-half the children had a U-shaped function for one phase of the episode with a trough at 7 or 9 months, with a slight tendency for more infants to show the trough at 7 than at 9 months. It will be recalled from chapter 5 that the Indian infants from the northwest part of Guatemala showed a U-shaped growth function across the period from 5 to 21 months for attentiveness to an auditory episode (see tables A.24 and A.25).

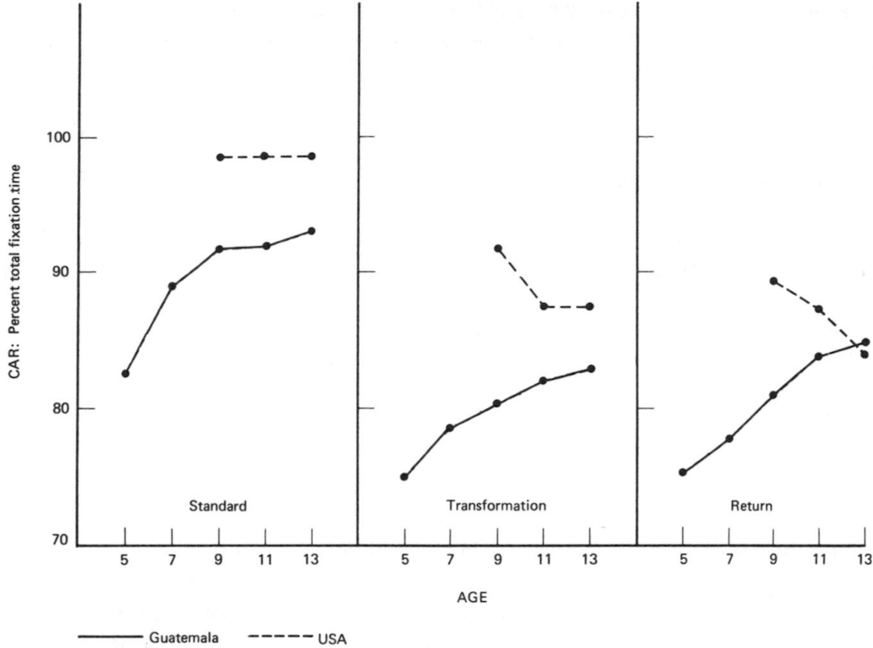

Fig. A.9 *Fixation times for the car episode for Guatemalan and North American children.*

VOCALIZATION

Figures A.10-A.14 show what percentages of children vocalized on any trial to each of the four episodes. The North American children were much more vocal than the Guatemalans. The cultural differences were smallest in the block episode (60 percent of the North American children vocalized in contrast to 40 percent of the Guatemalans), but larger to the auditory (70 percent versus 20 percent), light (75 percent versus 25 percent) and car episodes (60 percent versus 10 percent). The large increase in vocalization between 5 and 7 months characteristic of the North American children was absent among the Guatemalans. We interpret this difference to be a result of the greater verbal interaction between North American caretakers and their infants. All infants have the potential to display vocal excitement in response to an interesting event, but the actualization of that potential requires the priming experience of vocal interactions with others. Absence of such experience prevents the natural capacity to be actualized. Thus, when we say a response is under maturational control we do not mean that the behavior will emerge under any set of environmental conditions. All behaviors,

TABLE A.23. PERCENTAGE OF GUATEMALAN CHILDREN (74 BOYS, 63 GIRLS) WHOSE FIXATION TIMES SHOWED THE U-SHAPED GROWTH FUNCTION.

	BLOCK		LIGHT		CAR	
AGE AND PHASE OF EPISODE	BOYS	GIRLS	BOYS	GIRLS	BOYS	GIRLS
Trough at 7 or 9 mos.						
Standard trials phase	20%	21	26	32	9	19
Transformation trials phase	27	19	23	24	21	28
Return trials phase	28	18	23	22	28	27
All phases of episode	47	37	47	51	41	49
Trough at 7 mos. only	20	22	26	22	22	24
Trough at 9 mos. only	16	8	12	21	16	17

regardless of the depth of their roots in biological growth processes, require specific experiences to catalyze their display.

Among the Guatemalan children, vocalization decreased across successive episodes from block to car, suggesting that the children became inhibited as time passed; this was not true for the North Americans. The percentage of Guatemalan children vocalizing to the car episode was less than 10, far less than the percentage of North American children, whereas in the block episode about 40 percent of the Guatemalans vocalized. We believe that the vocalization decreased over episodes in part because the more isolated children could not assimilate the more complex auditory, light, and car episodes and, hence, were quiet. This suggestion is supported by the

TABLE A.24. AGE AND VILLAGE DIFFERENCES IN SEARCH TO THE AUDITORY EPISODE: MEAN PERCENTAGE OF TRIALS ON WHICH SEARCH BEHAVIOR OCCURRED (ALL TRIALS).

AGE (MOS.)	SAN MARCOS	SAN PEDRO	BOTH VILLAGES
5-6	100%	63	78
7-8	38	55	46
9-10	44	72	58
11-12	63	73	69
13-14	80	63	70
15-16	89	64	76
17-18	67	84	79
19-21	67	71	69

TABLE A.25. AGE AND VILLAGE DIFFERENCES IN ORIENTATION IN THE AUDITORY EPISODE: MEAN PERCENTAGE OF TRIALS ON WHICH ORIENTATION TO SPEAKER OCCURRED (ALL TRIALS).

AGE (MOS.)	SAN MARCOS	SAN PEDRO	BOTH VILLAGES
5-6	53%	24	35
7-8	34	19	27
9-10	38	33	35
11-12	67	59	63
13-14	41	37	39
15-16	73	43	56
17-18	52	45	48
19-21	42	50	46

data on smiling, for smiling was most frequent in response to the block and least frequent to the car.

SMILING

Smiling, which was far less frequent than vocalization, was more comparable for the two groups, especially to the block episode. There was no cultural difference in the percentage of children smiling in response to the block, and about 20 percent of the sample smiled at least once at 7, 9, and 11 months (see figures A.15-A.18). The peak age for smiling among the North American children was 7 months; the peak for the Guatemalans was 11 months. This difference suggests a slight lag in the age when the block event was assimilated by the Ladino children. Smiling in response to the light stimuli was equivalent for the two groups up to 11 months, with increasing smiling for both samples; but at 13 months the North American infants displayed a large increase in smiling, while the Guatemalans showed a slight drop. Frequency of smiling to the auditory episode was nonlinear, with peaks at 7 and 13 months for both groups, and more American than Guatemalan children smiling at these two ages. This bimodal function suggests that at 7 months both groups may have been assimilating the auditory event to their schema for a human voice, whereas at 13 months they were assimilating it to the structures for meaningful speech. The drop in smiling at 9 and 11 months may reflect a transition period when assimilation to the schema for a human voice is rapid so that smiling is less frequent. Structures for speech are not yet sufficiently articulated to permit assimilation of the information to the more complex structure. To the most complex event, the car episode, differences in smiling from 9 to 13 months were large. Less than 5 percent of the Guatemalan children smiled, in contrast to 15 percent of

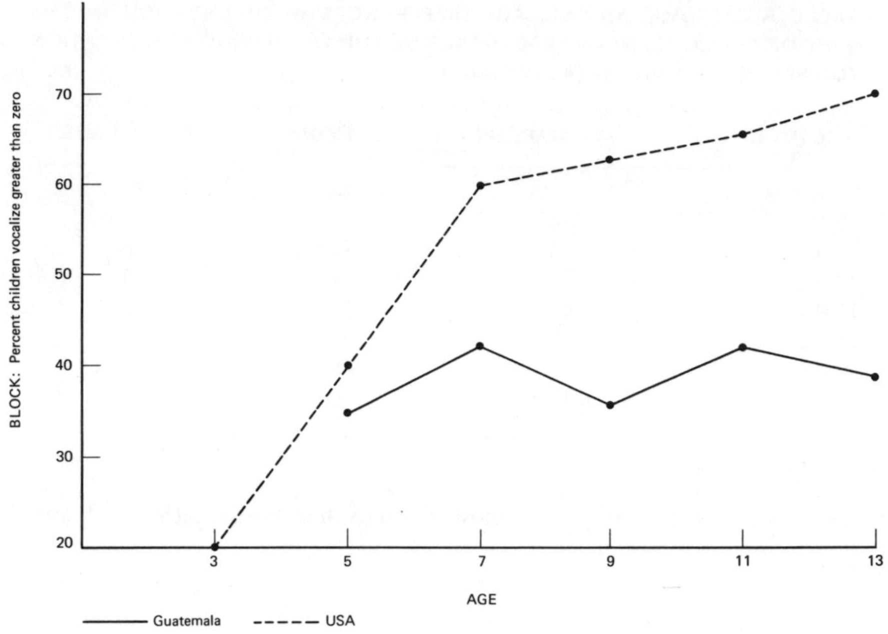

Fig. A.10 *Percentages of children who vocalized to the block episode.*

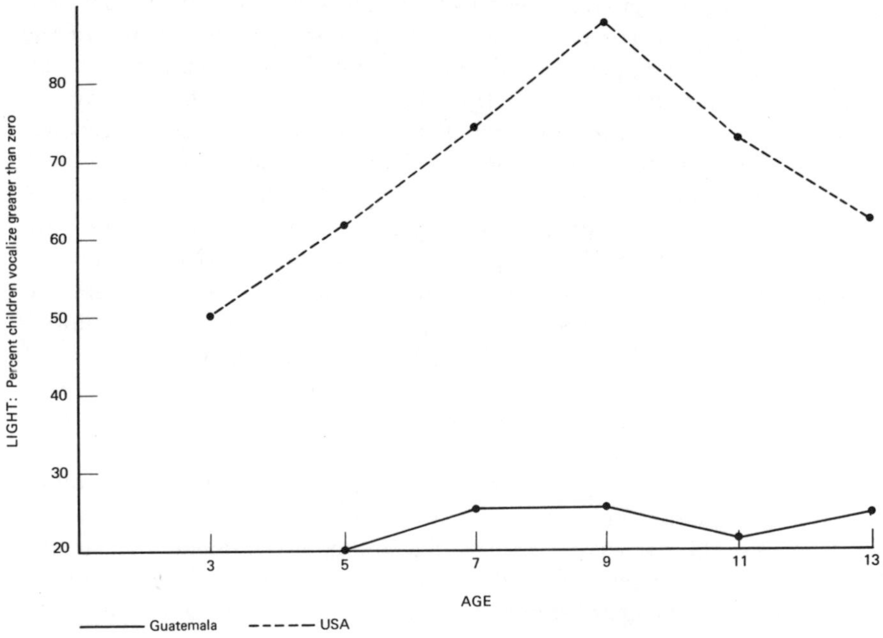

Fig. A.11 *Percentages of children who vocalized to the light episode.*

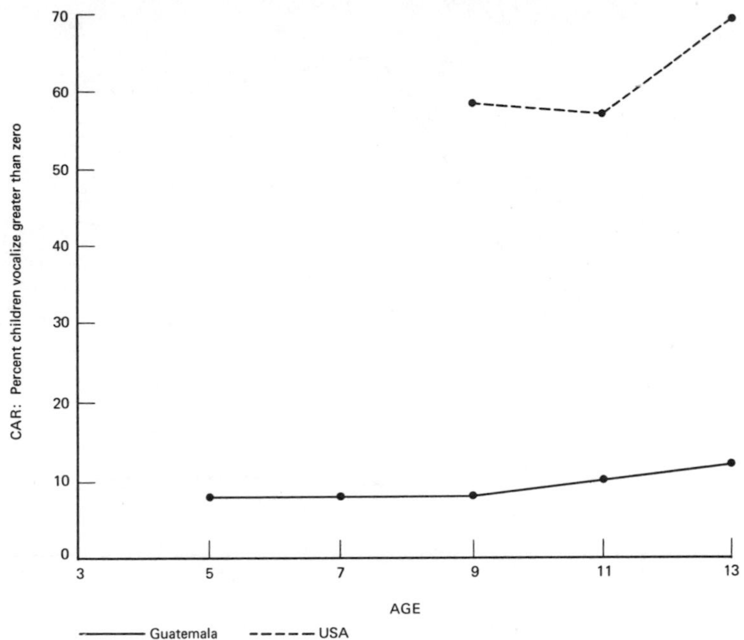

Fig. A.12 *Percentages of children who vocalized to the car episode.*

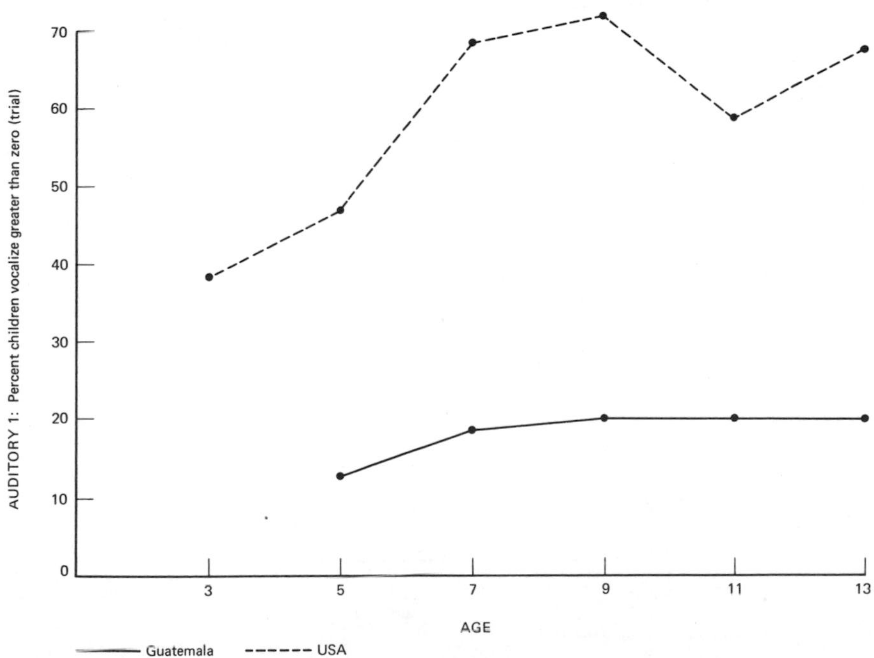

Fig. A.13 *Percentages of children who vocalized during the auditory trials.*

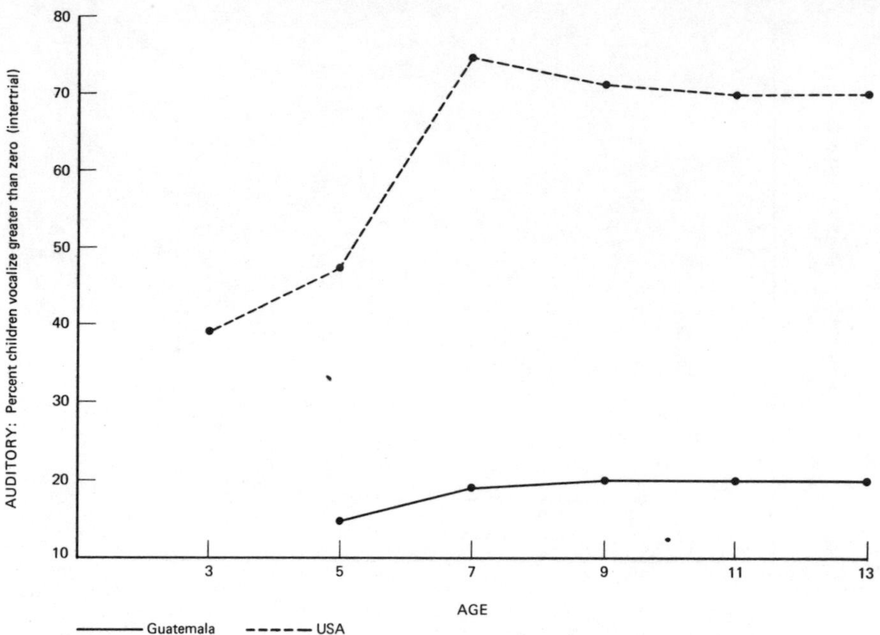

Fig. A.14 *Percentages of children who vocalized during the auditory intertrials.*

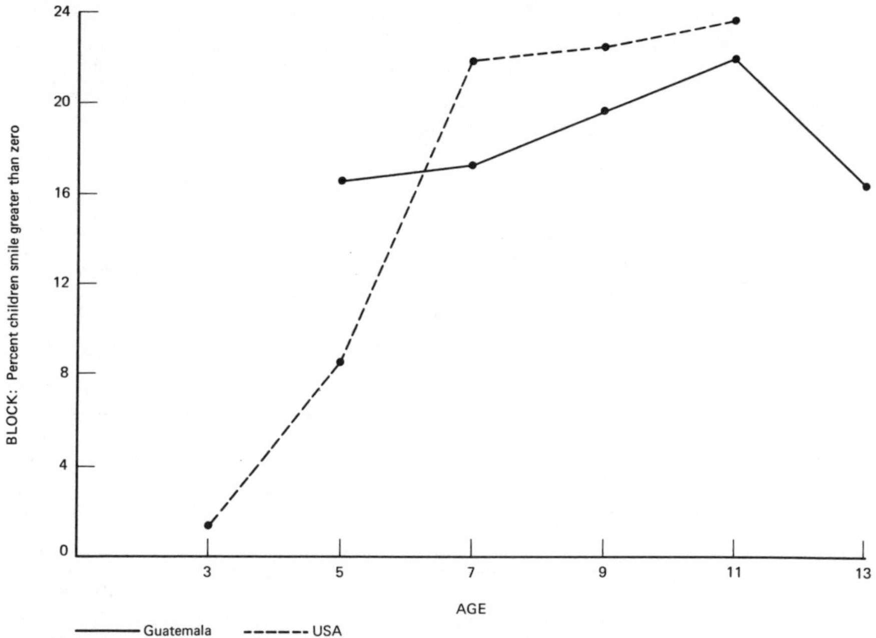

Fig. A.15 *Percentages of children smiling to the block episode.*

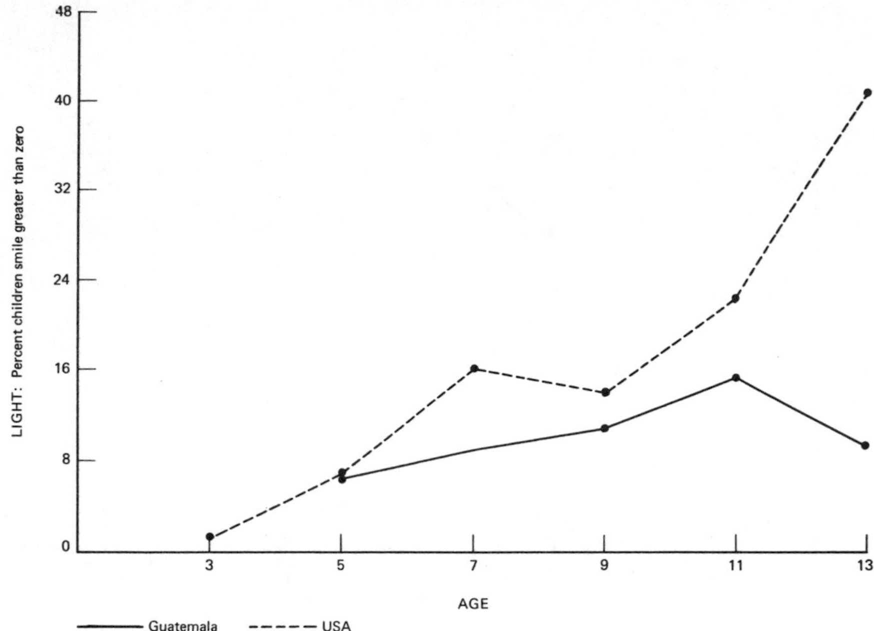

Fig. A.16 *Percentages of children smiling to the light episode.*

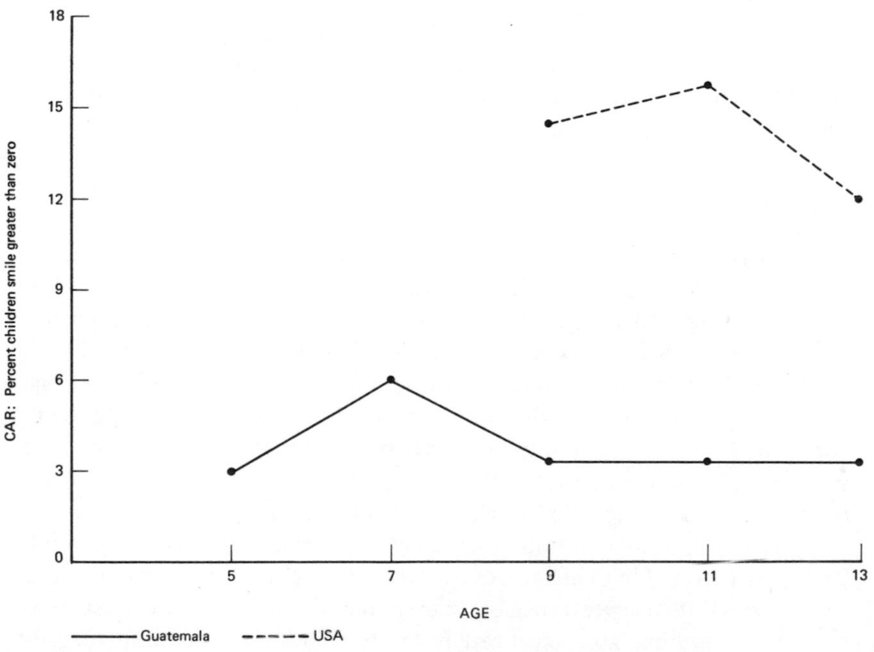

Fig. A.17 *Percentages of children smiling to the car episode.*

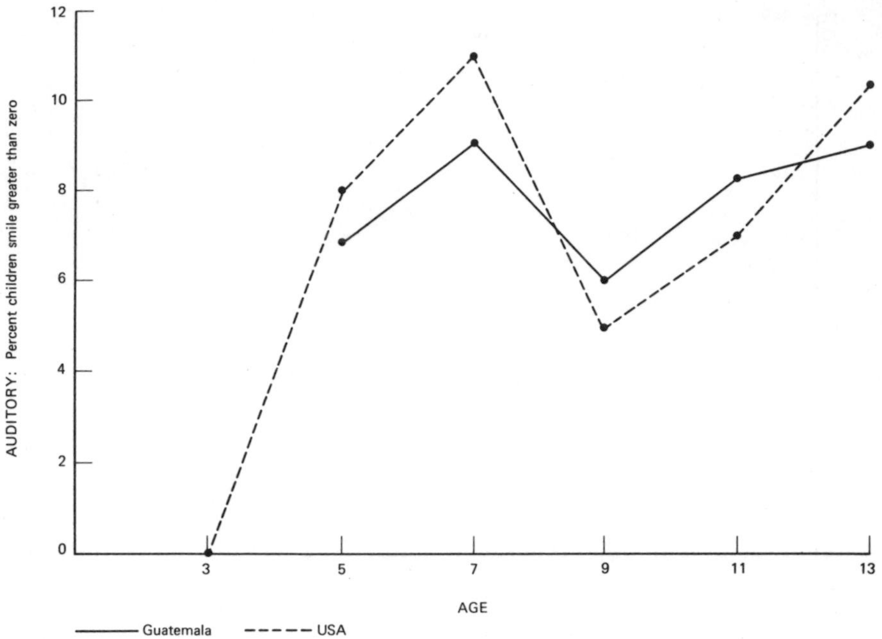

Fig. A.18 *Percentages of children smiling to the auditory episode.*

the North Americans. The largest increase in smiling to the car among the North Americans occurred after 13 months, when 37 and 52 percent of them smiled at 20 and 29 months, respectively.

Fretting

Fretting was greatest to the block and light episodes, but less frequent to the auditory and car episodes. For all the episodes, fretting was less frequent at 13 months than it was at 7, 9, and 11 months, implying greater assimilation at 1 year than at the earlier ages. This was also true for the North American children and supports our earlier speculation that, during the last half of the first year of life, the child's inability to comprehend the discrepant event leads to uncertainty and occasionally irritability. After the first birthday, the child becomes better able to assimilate these events, hence uncertainty and crying subside while vocalization and smiling increase.

In sum, the major cultural differences imply that North American children were better able to assimilate the auditory, light, and car episodes and were more likely to express vocally the excitement that accompanies assimilation. Since smiling and vocalization to the block episode were roughly equivalent for the two groups, there is no inherent inhibition on vocalization or smiling among the Guatemalans. The disposition to display these behaviors depends on the context. When we say that two groups differ on a variable we should not automatically generalize to other contexts. When one is dealing with basic, species-specific responses like vocalization or smiling, the context exerts enormous control on the behavior displayed. As indicated many times, there is no growth curve for responses, only for responses in classes of contexts. The appearance of the U-shaped function for attention among the Guatemalans supports our contention that a new stage of cognitive functioning emerges during the last third of the first year, even in children raised under conditions of restricted environmental variety.

The meaning of heart rate change

The child's heart rate was monitored throughout all the laboratory episodes, except social interaction. There were several reasons for recording the cardiac data. It has been generally established that attention to a stimulus event is often accompanied by a cardiac deceleration, typically between 2 to 10 beats per minute, especially during the initial presentations. Although there is not a high correlation between the duration of attention to a visual event and the probability or magnitude of a deceleration, both responses habituate in a lawful manner over repeated trials. One popular explanatory hypothesis is that the deceleration reflects the degree of surprise engendered by the event and is regarded as one component of an orientation reaction (Graham and Clifton 1966). It is necessary to attribute some special quality to those trials that are accompanied by a deceleration, for one cannot guarantee that a deceleration will occur every time a child attends to an event, even if the epoch of attention is prolonged. If this supposition has some validity, then we could use the cardiac data to determine the growth function for surprise to our various events.

A second reason for coding heart rate derives from the meaning of a cardiac acceleration. It has been established with both school-aged children and adults that when the individual has to perform difficult cognitive operations (memorize and recall information, imagine a complicated scene, or perform arithmetic operations mentally) there is an increase in heart rate (Van Hover 1974). When the same subjects simply look at or listen to an interesting event, they display a decrease in heart rate. Lacey (1967) has speculated that the acceleration response is an instrumental act of the autonomic nervous system whose goal is to isolate the cortex partially from external input while the mental work is occurring. Paul Obrist and his colleagues have disputed that interpretation and regard the acceleration (or the deceleration) as an epiphenomenon to other processes, especially those in the motor system (Obrist et al. 1970). This theoretical issue remains unresolved. But the empirical fact is not disputed. When children are doing complex cognitive functions, heart rate increases. We suggested in earlier papers that if this relation between cognitive operations and acceleration also held during the first two years of life, investigators would be able to detect when an infant was performing mental operations on stored information. This discussion is obviously relevant for our notions about the change in cognitive functioning after 8 months of age. We have suggested, and the data are in accord with that suggestion, that after 8 or 9 months of age the infant is actively comparing his experiences with retrieved schemata of past experience and trying to resolve the two. That function is mental work. Hence, demonstration of an increase in acceleration at that age would provide strong support for our views. Acceleration, unlike deceleration, can be elicited by many different circumstances. Excessive motor movement, crying, and hearty vocalization are often accompanied by cardiac acceleration. Events regarded as fear-inducing also are sometimes associated with cardiac acceleration. Indeed, Sroufe and Campos believe that a cardiac acceleration in response to the visual cliff or an unfamiliar adult should be interpreted as a sign of fearfulness. Since our primary reason for recording heart rate was to evaluate the hypothesis regarding cognitive work, we were sensitive to the other incentives for acceleration. Hence we did not code heart rate for any trial when the child was irritable or minimally attentive. And the stimulus events we administered would not be regarded by most psychologists as frightening to children.

The third variable we quantified from the heart rate records was heart rate range—the difference between the highest and lowest rate during a trial when the child was attentive. Range has not been a popular variable, perhaps because there has not been much theoretical guidance for its interpretation.

Analysis of data

The heart rate data were analyzed in the following manner. Coders evaluated whether the cardiac rate increased, decreased, or remained the same during the initial fixation of each visual event by comparing the direction of the heart rate during the first fixation of the stimulus (or the onset of the stimulus event for the auditory episode) with the rate during the 3-second base period prior to the onset of the first visual fixation (2 seconds for the auditory event). A deceleration was coded if the heart rate began to decrease with the onset of fixation (or with the onset of the stimulus for the auditory episodes) and the cardiac rate at the trough of that decline was lower than the lowest rate during the base period prior to the onset of the stimulus. Acceleration was coded if the heart rate began to increase with the onset of fixation and the rate at the apex of that climb was greater than the highest rate during the base period. The magnitudes of deceleration and acceleration were also computed by taking the difference between the trough or peak rate during the first fixation and the trough or peak during the base period. We also coded the highest and lowest heart rate during each trial; the difference between these two values defined the heart rate range. Trials in which the child looked at the stimulus less than 80 percent of the time it was present were not scored, as were all trials in which more than 1 second of fretting occurred; we only coded heart rate on trials when the child was highly attentive and not irritable.

Results

Although the Caucasian and Chinese had equivalent absolute heart rate levels from 7 to 29 months, at 3½ and 5½ months the Chinese had higher heart rates to all episodes. The average difference in absolute rate at these two early ages varied between 7 and 10 beats. It is not clear why the Chinese had higher cardiac rates at the two youngest ages. The difference cannot be due to fretting because heart rate was not coded on trials when the child fretted, nor to motoricity or vocalization, because both of these responses were typically absent at the two youngest ages. But by 7 months the ethnic difference in level was absent.

Pattern of deceleration and acceleration to block, light, car, and auditory episodes across age

Except during the car episode, deceleration was much more frequent than acceleration as the *initial* cardiac reaction at all ages, indicating that the initial orientation to a new or unexpected event is often, but not always, accompanied by a decrease in cardiac rate. And most children's hearts decelerated when the car struck the styrofoam object at the end of the episode. Typically between 30 and 50 percent of the children displayed a deceleration on any one trial, while 10 to 20 percent displayed an acceleration. The magnitude of deceleration was usually between 7 and 14 beats; while the magnitude of acceleration was smaller, between 4 and 8 beats. The largest percentage of children displayed a deceleration to the first presentation of the standard (typically between 50 and 75 percent of the group). The probability of a deceleration declined after the first trial and described a standard habituation function, the largest decline occurring between the first and second standards. By contrast, the heart rate of more infants accelerated either in the middle of the standards or to the transformation and return trials.

Acceleration was much more frequent to the car and auditory episodes than to the block and light; these last two were characterized by dynamic movement in the visual field from the beginning of the trial. The auditory event has no visual component and during the first three seconds of the car episode, the time when the acceleration occurred, the car was resting motionless at the top of the wooden ramp. It seems that deceleration is likely to occur when the infant's attention is captured by a salient change, in this case motion, in the visual field. Acceleration is more likely to occur when the infant must generate an attentional state from within. We shall return to this point later.

The growth function for percentage of children whose heart rates decelerated was an inverted U, with most displaying deceleration to the block, light, and auditory episodes from 9 to 20 months, the period when attentiveness increased following the trough at 7 months. Even though fixation times were as high at 5 months as they were at 9 and 11 months, the heart rates of more infants decelerated after the 7 month transition than before.

Unfortunately, there was only suggestive, rather than commanding, support for the hypothesis that the probability of a cardiac acceleration would increase toward the end of the first year, especially to the transformation and return trials, because of the emergence of a new stage of cognitive functioning. Although there was no increase in the likelihood of an acceleration to block episode at 11 months, acceleration was a little more frequent to the transformation or return trials of the light episode after the first year of life than before. More children accelerated to the transformation and return trials after 7 months than before; the increase in occurrence of deceleration was less marked.

Reactivity to the first auditory episode provided a little firmer support for the hypothesis. We noted, for each trial, when the percentage of children displaying acceleration exceeded the percentage decelerating. To the second transformation at 29 months and the second return at 13 months the percentage of children accelerating exceeded the percentage decelerating by a significant amount (40 percent versus 17 percent at 29 months; 37 percent versus 19 percent at 13 months). This fact motivated us to perform an analysis of each child's data using stricter criteria. We coded a deceleration or an acceleration to any one of the first three transformations or any one of the three return trials if the magnitude of change in deceleration or acceleration was at least twice the magnitude of change shown on any one of the three preceding trials (that is, the last three standards or the last three transformations). If no deceleration or acceleration occurred on the previous three trials, the magnitude of deceleration or acceleration to the transformation or return trials had to be at least 4 beats per minute. Figure A.19 reveals that when these criteria were used, the percentage of children displaying a deceleration to the first 3 transformations of the auditory episode had a peak at 13 months, followed by a sharp decline at 20 and 29 months. By contrast, the percentage of children accelerating increased with age, especially at 20 and 29 months, when 4 times as many children accelerated to the transformations (about 30 percent) as decelerated (7 percent). No parallel growth function emerged for the return trials. The probability of fretting paralleled the growth function for deceleration to the transformations, for irritability was most frequent from 7 to 13 months and declined to a minimum at 20 and 29

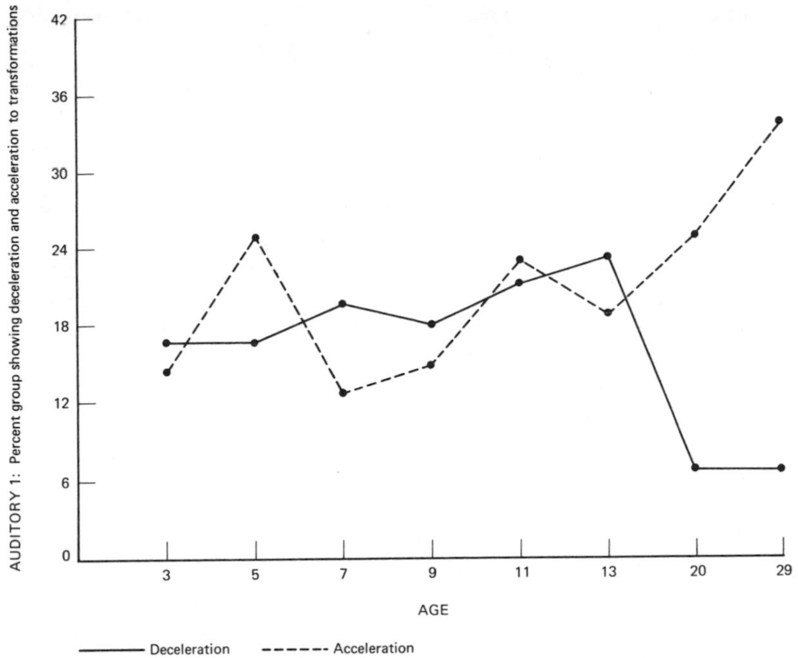

Fig. A.19 *Percentages of children displaying a heart rate deceleration or acceleration to the first 3 transformations of the auditory episode.*

months. Hence, the increased acceleration at 29 months was not a function of irritability.

Additional support for the idea that acceleration may reflect the active retrieval of representations comes from reactivity to the car episode. As noted earlier, at each age from 9 to 29 months, the heart rates of the majority of children decelerated on the first trial and few displayed an acceleration. But on every succeeding trial, far more children accelerated than decelerated (60 percent versus 10 percent), while they were waiting for the car to begin to descend.

Comparable data gathered on an independent sample of 5-month-olds administered the car episode revealed that only about a third of the children displayed an acceleration during the presentation of the standards. Acceleration was more likely when nothing was happening in front of the child and he had the opportunity to generate an anticipation of the future based on past experience. The tendency to accelerate habituated slightly over the standard trials as the child generated a firmer expectation of what was about to transpire. But the difference between the percentage accelerating to the first and the second transformation was larger at the two older ages than at the three younger ages, suggesting that the older children may have attempted to make a prediction after experiencing the first transformation trial.

The data do not provide strong support for our hypothesis, but they at least suggest that after the first year, when symbolism and language appear, there is a slightly greater tendency for children's heart rates to accelerate rather than decelerate in response to a discrepant event. This is the age when the child presumably is retrieving the schema for the earlier standard and trying to relate it to his present experience.

We shall now consider each episode separately and comment on growth functions and group differences. In order to evaluate age, class, care, and ethnicity differences in heart rate we computed the following related variables:

1. the percentage of trials for each episode in which a deceleration or acceleration occurred
2. the average magnitude of deceleration or acceleration for those trials on which a deceleration or acceleration occurred
3. the mean heart rate range for standard trials 4-6; transformations 1-3, and returns 1-3 (range being defined as the difference between the highest and lowest heart rate during the trial)
4. the mean of the 2 lowest ranges during the entire episode
5. the percentage of children whose heart rates showed a deceleration (or acceleration) on either of the first 2 transformations, as well as either of the first 2 returns, that was greater than 3 beats per minute
6. the percentage of children showing a deceleration (or acceleration) on either of the first 2 transformations that was greater than the larger deceleration (or acceleration) on either of the last 2 standards, and the percentage of children showing a deceleration (or acceleration) on the first 2 returns that was greater than the larger deceleration (or acceleration) on either of the last 2 transformations

Block episode

Age trends The growth function for the percentage of trials that were deceleratory (about 30 percent) was U-shaped with a trough at 7 months, while the age distribution for acceleration trials peaked at 7 months. The average magnitude of deceleration remained rather constant over age at about 7 to 8 beats per minute. Heart rate range for the standards, transformations, and returns, as well as the two lowest ranges, tended to have the most restricted range at 7 months.

Since the results of the analysis of variable 6 from the list above did not contradict a second and simpler criterion, variable 5 from that list, we shall concentrate discussion on the simpler variable. About 30 percent of the children showed increased deceleration to the transformations, 20 percent on the returns. But in both cases deceleration in response to the changed event was most likely to occur at 9 months, the age when fixation time was increasing following the trough at 7 months. Increased acceleration in response to the changed event was far less frequent and showed no obvious age function.

Group differences There were no class or care differences in any aspect of heart rate reactivity and no difference between the matched pairs. *However, the Chinese children had smaller heart rate ranges at all ages* (see table A.26). The ethnic difference was statistically significant for some phase of the episode at every age except 7 months, and at both 5 and 11 months the

TABLE A.26. MEAN HEART RATE RANGES IN THE BLOCK EPISODE, BY AGE AND ETHNIC GROUP, FOR STANDARD TRIALS 4-6, TRANSFORMATIONS 1-3, RETURNS 1-3, AND THE MEAN OF THE 2 LOWEST RANGES (BEATS/MIN.).

TRIALS, BY AGE (MOS.)	CHINESE	CAUCASIAN	SIGNIFICANCE[a]
S 4-6			
3	14.2	15.2	
5	12.1	12.9	
7	11.4	11.6	
9	10.3	13.8	$p < 0.05$
11	11.8	13.0	$p < .05$
T 1-3			
3	10.5	14.4	$p < .05$
5	10.1	13.3	$p < .05$
7	10.4	12.0	
9	11.6	13.4	
11	10.6	13.1	$p < .05$
R 1-3			
3	11.7	10.0	
5	9.2	13.2	$p < .01$
7	10.5	10.4	
9	11.7	12.7	
11	9.4	13.8	$p < .05$
Mean of two lowest ranges			
3	7.7	7.2	
5	6.3	7.9	
7	6.6	7.3	
9	6.8	8.7	$p < .01$
11	6.2	8.0	$p < .05$

[a] *F* test. The significance values for each age are based on an analysis of variance. A repeated measures analysis of variance across ages 5 to 11 months for the mean of two lowest ranges revealed a significant effect for ethnicity ($F = 4.11$, 1/123, $p < 0.05$).

Chinese had a smaller range on *every one of the stimulus trials.* Moreover, the Chinese reacted to the first transformation at 3, 7, and 11 months with a decrease in range, while the Caucasians reacted with an increase in range. Ethnic differences in pattern and magnitude of deceleration and acceleration were less striking and typically nonsignificant. Caucasians had slightly larger average decelerations than the Chinese at 11 months, but not at any other age. The Chinese were more likely to accelerate to the transformation at 9 months and to the returns at 11 months. Hence the ethnic difference in range is not due to the fact that the Caucasians displayed more frequent or larger heart rate changes (see table A.27).

LIGHT

Age trends The probability of a deceleration, as well as the magnitude of deceleration, remained rather constant over age in the light episode. As in the block episode, about one-third of the trials were deceleratory. Heart rate range remained low until 13 months and then showed a large increase at the two oldest ages.

The percentage of children showing increased deceleration to the transformations increased linearly with age. The percentage showing acceleration to the returns increased at 29 months, and at the oldest age surpassed the percentage of children decelerating (36 percent versus 24 percent). (See table A.28).

TABLE A.27. REACTIVITY IN THE BLOCK EPISODE: PERCENTAGE OF CHILDREN WHO HAD CARDIAC DECELERATION OR ACCELERATION ON THE FIRST 2 TRANSFORMATION OR FIRST 2 RETURNS GREATER THAN THE CHANGE ON THE PREVIOUS 2 TRIALS.

TRIALS BY AGE (MOS.)	DECELERATION	ACCELERATION
Transformations		
3	24%	4
5	24	23
7	30	21
9	32	11
11	24	16
Returns		
3	21	11
5	21	20
7	11	16
9	24	11
11	16	8

TABLE A.28. REACTIVITY IN THE LIGHT EPISODE (PERCENTAGE OF CHILDREN WHO HAD CARDIAC DECELERATION OR ACCELERATION ON THE FIRST 2 TRANSFORMATIONS OR FIRST 2 RETURNS GREATER THAN THE CHANGE ON THE PREVIOUS 2 TRIALS.

TRIALS, BY AGE (MOS.)	DECELERATION	ACCELERATION
Transformations		
3	14%	12
5	17	20
7	20	3
9	19	15
11	24	15
13	54	30
20	61	18
29	52	26
Returns		
3	12	15
5	9	12
7	9	3
9	15	14
11	17	13
13	8	12
20	24	13
29	24	36

Group differences Although there were no care or class differences associated with any of the heart rate variables, including the matched pairs, ethnicity was again an influential factor. The Chinese children had significantly more stable heart rates on all phases of the episode. At 6 of the 8 ages the Chinese had smaller ranges than the Caucasians on over 90 percent of the trials, despite no ethnic difference in frequency or magnitude of deceleration or acceleration (see table A.29). Although the older Chinese were less vocal and motoric to the light episode, this was not true at the younger ages. Hence the more restricted range displayed by the Chinese is not solely the result of the greater behavioral reactivity of the Caucasians.

CAR EPISODE

Age differences As indicated earlier, the occurrence of an initial acceleration was three times more frequent than deceleration after the first trial. Although the probability of an acceleration decreased with age after 9

Table A.29. Mean heart rate range in the light episode, by age and ethnic group, for standard trials 4-6, transformations 1-3, returns 1-3, and the mean of the 2 lowest ranges.

Trials by age (mos.)	Chinese	Caucasian	Significance (F test)
S 4-6			
3	8.7	10.7	
5	7.2	10.8	$p<0.001$
7	8.1	10.7	$p<.01$
9	7.3	11.1	$p<.05$
11	7.8	8.7	
13	7.1	8.7	$p<.05$
20	8.6	11.0	
29	10.5	11.5	
T 1-3			
3	3.3	9.4	
5	7.4	7.7	
7	6.4	9.9	
9	8.3	11.7	
11	7.9	14.2	$p<.001$
13	7.8	10.3	$p<.05$
20	12.1	13.5	
29	12.3	14.5	
Returns 1-3			
3	6.9	11.0	
5	6.9	12.1	$p<.05$
7	7.5	10.5	
9	8.2	10.0	
11	9.0	11.5	
13	6.6	7.5	
20	8.3	10.0	
29	10.8	12.5	
Mean of 2 lowest ranges[a]			
3	3.2	5.0	
5	3.7	5.3	$p<.001$
7	4.4	5.6	$p<.01$
9	4.6	5.5	$p<.05$
11	4.0	5.7	$p<.01$
13	4.0	4.8	
20	5.8	6.1	
29	6.2	6.3	

[a] A repeated measures analysis of variance for mean of two lowest ranges across the ages 5-11 months revealed a significant effect for ethnicity ($F = 13.28$, 1/153, $p<0.01$). A comparable analysis for the period from 13 to 29 months was not significant.

months, the magnitude of acceleration as well as the range rose with age. Range remained low at 9, 11, and 13 months, and, as with light, increased dramatically at the two oldest ages.

Reaction to the transformation and returns revealed a U-shaped function, with the fewest children showing deceleration on the transformations and returns at 13 months, although the differences across age were not large (see table A.30).

Group differences As on the block and light episodes, there were no differences in cardiac reactivity associated with form of care and there was only one class effect. Class 1 children showed larger accelerations at 9 months than did those in class 2, but this difference was absent at all later ages. Ethnicity again exerted the primary influence on heart rate. The Chinese were more likely to decelerate at 9, 11, and 29 months, the difference being less dramatic on the initial than on the later trials. However, the major ethnic difference was the smaller range values displayed by the Chinese. At every age the Chinese had smaller heart rate ranges to the standards, transformations, and returns and at 11, 13, and 20 months, the Chinese displayed a more restricted range on over 90 percent of the trials (see table A.31).

AUDITORY 1

Age functions The percentage of trials in which there was a deceleration remained steady through 13 months, but increased at the two oldest

TABLE A.30. REACTIVITY IN THE CAR EPISODE (PERCENTAGE OF CHILDREN WHO HAD CARDIAC DECELERATION OR ACCELERATION ON THE FIRST 2 TRANSFORMATIONS OR FIRST 2 RETURNS GREATER THAN THE CHANGE ON THE PREVIOUS TWO TRIALS).

TRIALS, BY AGE (MOS.)	DECELERATION	ACCELERATION
Transformations		
9	19%	44
11	9	42
13	4	33
20	22	38
29	23	44
Returns		
9	13	31
11	13	30
13	9	38
20	15	25
29	26	30

TABLE A.31. MEAN HEART RATE RANGE IN THE CAR EPISODE, BY AGE AND ETHNIC GROUP, FOR STANDARD TRIALS 4-6, TRANSFORMATIONS 1-3, RETURNS 1-3, AND THE MEAN OF THE 2 LOWEST RANGES.

TRIALS BY AGE (MOS.)	CHINESE	CAUCASIAN	SIGNIFICANCE (F TEST)
S 4-6			
9	8.6	10.1	
11	8.6	12.7	
13	8.9	9.9	
20	9.9	12.8	$p<0.05$
29	13.1	15.1	
T1-3			
9	9.3	10.0	
11	9.8	10.9	
13	9.4	10.5	
20	11.0	14.0	$p< .05$
29	12.8	13.8	
R 1-3			
9	8.7	9.1	
11	8.3	12.3	$p< .01$
13	8.7	9.9	
20	12.3	13.1	
29	10.8	12.4	
Mean of 2 lowest ranges[a]			
9	4.9	5.6	
11	4.6	6.6	$p< .01$
13	5.1	5.6	
20	5.9	7.1	$p = .05$
29	7.2	7.2	

[a] A repeated measures analysis of variance for mean of 2 lowest ranges across the period from 9 to 29 months revealed a marginally significant effect for ethnicity ($F = 3.17, 1/120, p = 0.08$).

ages. The magnitude of deceleration also remained stable until 11 months, after which there was an increase at the three oldest ages. The likelihood of an acceleration, as well as the magnitude of acceleration, remained constant over age.

The growth function for range in the first auditory episode paralleled that of the light and car episodes. Range showed a gradual increase from 3 to 13 months followed by a large increase at 20 and 29 months. As for increased frequency of deceleration to the transformations and returns, age differences were small and not significant, far smaller than they were for fixation, vocalization, and smiling (see table A.32).

TABLE A.32. REACTIVITY IN AUDITORY 1 EPISODE: PERCENTAGE OF CHILDREN WHO HAD CARDIAC DECELERATION OR ACCELERATION ON THE FIRST 2 TRANSFORMATIONS OR FIRST 2 RETURNS GREATER THAN THE CHANGE ON THE PREVIOUS 2 TRIALS.

TRIALS, BY AGE (MOS.)	DECELERATION	ACCELERATION
Transformations		
3	31	29
5	31	30
7	37	31
9	37	28
11	43	30
13	30	30
20	20	37
29	30	40
Returns		
3	36	31
5	32	29
7	32	36
9	30	27
11	38	30
13	33	33
20	38	20
29	36	20

Group differences Again, there were no consistent class or care correlates for any of the heart rate variables, while ethnicity continued to be associated with a more restricted range. At 3, 5, 11, 13, and 20 months, the Chinese had significantly smaller ranges than the Caucasians on over 90 percent of the trials. However, the differences in range were less consistently significant to auditory than to block, light, and car episodes (see table A.33).

Although there were no ethnic differences in the tendency to display a deceleration or acceleration, the Caucasians had larger decelerations at every age and larger accelerations from 3 through 13 months. To the Auditory 1 event the Caucasians showed a brisker cardiac reaction than to the visual episodes. We should note that the average change in cardiac rate was smaller in response to the visual than to the auditory stimuli.

Ethnic differences in reactivity to the transformations suggest a developmental lag among the Chinese in reactivity to the speech. To the transformations, the Caucasians were most likely to show increased deceleration at 7 months, the Chinese at 11 months. To the returns, the Caucasians were most likely to show increased deceleration at 11 months, the Chinese at 20 months. Although both Caucasians and Chinese reacted later to the returns

TABLE A.33. MEAN HEART RATE RANGE IN AUDITORY 1, BY AGE AND ETHNIC GROUP, FOR STANDARD TRIALS 4-6, TRANSFORMATIONS 1-3, RETURNS 1-3, AND THE MEAN OF THE 2 LOWEST RANGES.

TRIALS, BY AGE (MOS.)	CHINESE	CAUCASIAN	SIGNIFICANCE (*F* TEST)
S 4-6			
3	9.0	12.3	
5	7.9	9.2	
7	8.8	9.8	
9	8.4	10.1	
11	8.3	10.7	$p<0.05$
13	9.4	11.2	
20	11.3	13.9	
29	12.3	10.6	
T 1-3			
3	6.9	9.2	$p = .05$
5	7.4	8.7	
7	8.1	8.1	
9	9.3	9.6	
11	8.6	9.1	
13	9.0	10.4	
20	10.6	12.2	
29	10.1	12.5	
R 1-3			
3	5.9	8.6	$p < .01$
5	6.8	9.5	$p < .01$
7	7.8	8.6	
9	8.0	9.3	
11	8.3	8.4	
13	8.6	10.2	
20	9.9	12.7	
29	10.7	10.7	
Mean of 2 lowest ranges[a]			
3	3.0	4.0	
5	3.3	4.0	
7	3.7	3.5	
9	3.8	4.2	
11	4.1	4.5	
13	4.6	5.0	
20	5.0	6.1	
29	5.1	5.9	

[a] A repeated measures analysis of variance for mean of 2 lowest ranges across the period 5 to 11 months did not reveal a significant effect for ethnicity; but an analysis from 13 to 29 months approached significance ($F = 3.16$, 1/160, $p = 0.08$).

than to the transformations, the Caucasians peaked earlier than the Chinese to both transformations. A similar trend emerged for acceleration. The Caucasians showed peak acceleration to the transformations at 7 months, the Chinese at 20 months; to the returns, the Caucasians peaked at 9 months, the Chinese at 11 months.

Auditory 2

Age changes The proportion of deceleration and acceleration trials remained constant over age, with the former more frequent than the latter. There was a slight increase with age in the range values. Reaction to the transformations peaked at 9 months for both deceleration and acceleration, whereas neither showed any obvious growth function on the returns (see table A.34).

Group differences Class and care differences were again minimal. As with the first auditory episode, despite the absence of differences in the percentage of deceleration or acceleration trials, the Caucasians had larger mean decelerations and accelerations. As with all other episodes, the Chinese had significantly smaller ranges for all three phases of the episode, and at all four ages had smaller values on 90 percent of the trials (see table A.35).

Masks

The typical cardiac reaction to masks was a deceleration, with about half the children decelerating and only 10 percent accelerating. An important

Table A.34 Reactivity in Auditory 2: Percentage of children who had cardiac deceleration or acceleration on the first 2 transformations or the first 2 returns greater than the change on the previous 2 trials.

Trials, by age (mos.)	Deceleration	Acceleration
Transformations		
3	27	33
5	35	27
9	40	43
11	30	36
Returns		
3	36	33
5	47	34
9	38	33
11	41	32

TABLE A.35. MEAN HEART RATE RANGE IN AUDITORY 2, BY AGE AND ETHNIC GROUP, FOR STANDARD TRIALS 4-6, TRANSFORMATIONS 1-3, RETURNS 1-3, AND THE MEAN OF THE 2 LOWEST RANGES.

TRIALS BY AGE (MOS.)	CHINESE	CAUCASIAN	SIGNIFICANCE (F TEST)
S 4-6			
3	8.7	9.9	
5	7.9	10.0	
9	9.4	11.6	$p<0.05$
11	10.3	11.6	$p< .05$
T 1-3			
3	6.6	9.6	
5	6.6	9.8	$p< .001$
9	9.5	11.0	
11	9.2	10.2	
R 1-3			
3	8.3	9.8	
5	8.5	10.7	$p< .01$
9	8.9	11.6	$p< .01$
11	8.6	11.0	$p< .01$
Mean of 2 lowest ranges			
3	1.9	3.9	$p< .01$
5	3.1	4.0	$p< .01$
9	4.1	4.9	
11	4.1	4.8	

exception to that rule was that the heart rates for more children accelerated than decelerated in response to the blank face at 9 months. It will be recalled that the fixation time data revealed a shift from longer fixations to the regular face (than to the scrambled) at the younger ages to longer fixations to the scrambled face at the older ages. The deceleration data are in accord with that shift, for the likelihood of deceleration increased with age in response to the scrambled face while it did not for the regular face. Although there were no class or care differences for either frequency or magnitude of deceleration or acceleration, the Chinese again had significantly smaller ranges at all ages, the difference being significant at 5 months (see table A.36).

SLIDES AT 20 AND 29 MONTHS

The modal reaction to the slides was a deceleration, with about 50 percent of the children decelerating on any one trial and only 10 percent accelerating (see table A.37). The magnitude of deceleration was about 10 beats

Table A.36. Mean heart rate range in the mask episode (series 1) by age and ethnic group for standard trials 4-6 and the mean of the 2 lowest ranges.

Trials by age (mos.)	Chinese	Caucasian	Significance (*F* test)
S 4-6			
3	15.8	15.2	
5	14.7	18.0	$p < 0.05$
9	17.0	17.7	
13	17.5	18.7	
Mean of 2 lowest ranges			
3	6.7	11.0	
5	9.9	11.9	
9	10.1	10.3	
13	14.2	14.7	

Table A.37. Heart rate reaction in slide episode (percentage of children displaying deceleration or acceleration greater than 3 beats/min. by stimulus and age).

	Age 20 mos.		Age 29 mos.	
Stimulus	Deceleration	Acceleration	Deceleration	Acceleration
1. Ball	28	7	33	12
2. Boy and girl	74	7	67	7
3. Man	59	9	48	20
4. Man in dress	58	3	51	23
5. Man and woman	44	12	33	20
6. Cat	50	11	49	13
7. Oversized cat	67	9	62	13
8. Woman	52	17	32	27
9. Woman holding head in hand	57	6	77	7
10. Man	33	7	33	24
11. Man with 4 arms	36	16	53	20
12. Boy	23	11	27	18
13. Girl	29	12	30	23
14. Girl in bathtub	51	16	52	14
15. Man in bed	32	9	36	24

per minute in contrast to a magnitude of acceleration of about 6 beats. The children reacted to the discrepant events with a deceleration, and there was an increase in reactivity to the discrepant slides at 29 months as compared with 20 months. Table A.38 shows what percentages of children decelerated to each of the discrepant slides compared with the percentages decelerating on the immediately preceding and succeeding nondiscrepant pictures.

There was an increase with age in reactivity to the *woman holding her head* and the *man with four arms,* but not to the *girl in the tub* or the *large cat,* and no increase to the *man wearing a dress.* We interpret these data to mean that more 29- than 20-month-olds recognized, and perhaps reflected upon, the incongruity of the transformation in body form of the woman holding the head and the man with four arms. The lack of reactivity to the man in the dress might mean that these 2½-year-old children had not yet formed a well-articulated schema of the appropriate clothing for a man.

It is important to note that although the probability of deceleration did not increase from 20 to 29 months, the likelihood of acceleration increased for 5 of the scenes by a factor of 2 or more, and 4 of these 5 involved an adult male figure. There were no class or care differences for proportion of children displaying a heart rate change or magnitude of deceleration or accelera-

TABLE A.38. PERCENTAGE OF CHILDREN WHOSE HEART RATE DECELERATED IN RESPONSE TO THE DISCREPANT SCENE AND THE IMMEDIATELY PRECEDING AND SUCCEEDING SCENES (DIFFERENCE SCORE BASED ON PERCENTAGE DECELERATING TO THE DISCREPANT SCENE MINUS THE MEAN PERCENTAGE DECELERATING TO BOTH THE PRECEDING AND SUCCEEDING SCENE).

STIMULUS	DISCREPANT	PRECEDING	SUCCEEDING	DIFFERENCE
At 20 mos.				
Man in dress	58	59	44	6
Oversized cat	67	50	52	16
Woman holding head in hand	57	52	33	14
Man with 4 arms	36	33	23	8
Girl in bathtub	51	29	32	20
At 29 mos.				
Man in dress	51	48	33	11
Oversized cat	62	49	32	21
Woman holding head in hand	77	32	33	44
Man with 4 arms	53	33	27	23
Girl in bathtub	52	30	36	19

tion, but the Chinese again had a significantly smaller heart rate range at 20 months.

Growth functions

For all episodes, except the car event, deceleration was more likely than acceleration, but the growth functions for cardiac change were not the same across episodes. To the block episode there was a suggestion of a U-shaped function for proportion of deceleration trials, with a trough at 7 months, which matched the fixation time data, but this was not true of the other episodes. The magnitude of deceleration generally increased with age to the light and auditory episodes. The Caucasians had larger deceleratory changes than the Chinese to the auditory episodes, but not to the block, light, or car episodes, despite the lack of an ethnic difference in the percentage of trials on which there was a deceleration.

Comparison of the cardiac reaction to the transformations and returns over age is instructive. Prior to the first year, deceleration to the transformations exceeded deceleration to the returns, whereas at 20 months deceleration to the returns, especially to the car and auditory episodes, was more likely than deceleration to the transformations. Since the return is objectively identical with the standard, one might speculate that the older child is treating the return trials in a special way. This supposition is supported by the fact that it was only at the older ages that the tendency to accelerate in response to the transformations and returns approached or exceeded the tendency to decelerate, especially to light and the first auditory episodes.

Heart rate range yielded the most consistent age function as well as the most significant difference between the ethnic groups. Caucasians displayed larger ranges on most trials of all episodes at almost every age. This difference was not a function of larger or more frequent decelerations by Caucasians. In a separate analysis, we compared the ranges of the two groups for those trials in which neither an acceleration nor a deceleration occurred; that is, the child showed no obvious change in heart rate at onset of fixation compared with the base period prior to stimulus onset. Of the thirty age comparisons for the block, light, car, and two auditory episodes for the changeless trials, the Chinese had a more restricted range on twenty-six occasions, and on only one occasion did the Chinese show a slightly larger value. Of the thirty comparisons, eight (27 percent) were statistically significant.

Stability of range

Since the Chinese had more stable heart rates at every age, and no other variable yielded such dramatic evidence of an ethnic difference, we evaluated the stability of this variable across both age and episode. The variables chosen for analysis were the mean of the two lowest ranges during each episode and a derived variable, which was the average of the mean of the two lowest ranges for all episodes at any given age. The correlation between the mean of the two lowest ranges and the mean range for the whole episode was remarkably high, typically 0.70 to 0.85 (see table A.39).

The Chinese infants The pattern of stability was similar across episodes (see table A.40). There was moderate stability from 3 or 5 months to the end of the first year, but by 7 or 9 months predictability extended to 29 months of age. (The correlations ranged from + .4 to + .7.) These cross-age and cross-episode correlations are much higher and more consistent than those discovered for fixation time, vocalization, and play or proximity to

TABLE A.39. CORRELATION BETWEEN THE MEAN OF THE 2 LOWEST RANGES AND THE MEAN RANGE FOR THE ENTIRE EPISODE, BY EPISODE, AGE, AND ETHNICITY.

EPISODE, BY AGE (MOS.)	CHINESE	CAUCASIAN	EPISODE, BY AGE (MOS.)	CHINESE	CAUCASIAN
Aud. I			Car		
3	.74	.66	9	.77	.85
5	.53	.84	11	.84	.55
7	.57	.71	13	.69	.80
9	.64	.74	20	.71	.61
11	.79	.92	29	.78	.73
13	.86	.59	Light		
20	.81	.83	3	.92	.91
29	.82	.68	5	.63	.49
Aud. II			7	.66	.74
3	.43	.84	9	.75	.56
5	.51	.51	11	.79	.63
9	.60	.70	13	.77	.91
11	.87	.71	20	.94	.61
Masks			29	.93	.78
3	.95	.77			
5	.93	.86			
9	.85	.63			
13	.93	.95			
Block					
3	.78	.88			
5	.81	.86			
7	.93	.51			
9	.82	.83			
11	.91	.79			

Table A.40. Significant correlations for stability of heart rate range (mean of the 2 lowest ranges) across episode and age.

Caucasians									
Predictor at 3 months									
Auditory 1			Auditory 2			Block			Light
Bl.	3 mos.	.59	Bl.	3 mos.	.84	Aud.2	3 mos.	.84	No significant correlations
Lt.	5	.45	Lt.	7	.43	Aud.1	11	.73	
Aud.1	7	.52	Lt.	11	.57	Aud.2	11	.58	
Car	13	.53	Bl.	11	.70	Lt.	11	.60	
			Aud.2	11	.49	Car	11	.51	
			Lt.	29	.53				
Predictor at 5 months									
Auditory 1			Auditory 2			Block			Light
Aud.2	5 mos.	.40	Lt.	20 mos.	.43	Aud.1	5 mos.	.40	No significant correlations
Bl.	5	.40				Lt.	7	.43	
						Aud.1	11	.40	
						Car	9	.46	
						Car	13	.53	
						Lt.	29	.57	

(*cont.*)

Table A.40 (cont.)

Predictor at 7 months						
Auditory 1			Block	Light		
Car.	11 mos.	.37	No significant correlations	Bl.	9 mos.	.50
Aud.1	20	.47		Lt.	9	.55
Lt.	20	.44		Aud.1	11	.43
				Aud.2	11	.40
				Bl.	11	.49
				Car	11	.48
				Car	13	.51
				Car	20	.46
				Lt.	29	.62

Predictor at 9 months											
Auditory 1			Auditory 2			Block			Light		
Car	9 mos.	.53	Aud.1	11 mos.	.39	Lt.	9 mos.	.45	Bl.	9 mos.	.45
Lt.	13	.39	Car	13	.48	Bl.	11	.46	Car	9	.41
Lt.	29	.75				Car	11	.69	Car	11	.57
						Car	13	.53	Aud.1	11	.38
									Aud.1	13	.47

Car		
Aud.1	9 mos.	.53
Lt.	9	.41
Car	13	.42

PREDICTOR AT 11 MONTHS											
AUDITORY 1			AUDITORY 2			BLOCK			LIGHT		
Aud.2	11 mos.	.37	Aud.1	11 mos.	.37	Aud.1	11 mos.	.37	Aud.1	11 mos.	.57
Bl.	11	.70	Bl.	11	.54	Lt.	11	.62	Bl.	11	.62
Lt.	11	.57	Car	11	.40	Car	13	.48	Car	11	.50
Lt.	29	.53	Lt.	13	.45	Lt.	20	.48			
						Car	20	.49			
						Lt.	29	.70			
CAR											
Aud.2	11 mos.	.40									
Lt.	11	.50									
Lt.	13	.50									

PREDICTOR AT 13 MONTHS								
AUDITORY 1			LIGHT			CAR		
Lt.	13 mos.	.40	Aud.1	13 mos.	.40	Lt.	29 mos.	.61
Car	29	.55						

PREDICTOR AT 20 MONTHS								
AUDITORY 1			LIGHT			CAR		
Lt.	20 mos.	.53	Aud.1	20 mos.	.53	Lt.	20 mos.	.52
			Car	20	.52			

(cont.)

TABLE A.40 (cont.)

CHINESE											
PREDICTOR AT 3 MONTHS											
AUDITORY 1			AUDITORY 2			BLOCK			LIGHT		
Bl.	5 mos.	.71	No significant correlations			Lt.	3 mos.	.54	Bl.	3 mos.	.54
Lt.	5	.63				Bl.	5	.70	Lt.	7	.55
Lt.	7	.54				Bl.	7	.48	Aud.2	9	.51
Aud.2	9	.48				Aud.2	9	.73	Aud.2	11	.51
Aud.2	11	.56				Bl.	11	.65	Bl.	11	.86
Lt.	11	.45				Lt.	11	.55	Lt.	11	.79
Car	11	.44				Car	13	.65	Car	11	.70
Car	13	.61							Aud.1	13	.66
									Lt.	13	.56
									Car	13	.61
									Aud.1	29	.55
									Lt.	29	.67
									Car	29	.62
PREDICTOR AT 5 MONTHS											
AUDITORY 1			AUDITORY 2			BLOCK			LIGHT		
Bl.	5 mos.	.43	Lt.	5 mos.	.49	Aud.1	5 mos.	.43	Bl.	5 mos.	.67
Lt.	9	.43	Aud.1	7	.50	Lt.	5	.67	Lt.	7	.36
			Car	11	.42	Lt.	7	.53	Aud.2	9	.49
			Car	13	.42	Bl.	11	.51	Bl.	9	.42
						Car	11	.47	Lt.	13	.46
						Car	13	.57	Car	11	.51
									Car	13	.47

PREDICTOR AT 7 MONTHS								
AUDITORY 1			BLOCK			LIGHT		
Bl.	7 mos.	.49	Aud.1	7 mos.	.49	Aud.1	7 mos.	.40
Lt.	9	.43	Lt.	7	.65	Bl.	7	.65
Aud.1	11	.44	Aud.1	9	.56	Bl.	9	.49
Aud.1	13	.56	Bl.	9	.63	Lt.	9	.45
			Lt.	9	.74	Car	9	.41
			Car	9	.63	Aud.1	11	.56
			Aud.1	11	.74	Bl.	11	.56
			Aud.2	11	.40	Lt.	11	.43
			Bl.	11	.58	Car	11	.64
			Lt.	11	.55	Lt.	13	.49
			Car	11	.60	Car	13	.59
			Aud.1	13	.45	Car	20	.45
			Lt.	13	.58	Car	29	.48
			Car	13	.49			
			Lt.	20	.45			
			Aud.1	29	.53			
			Car	29	.57			

(*cont.*)

TABLE A.40 (cont.)

PREDICTOR AT 9 MONTHS											
AUDITORY 1			AUDITORY 2			BLOCK			LIGHT		
Lt.	9 mos.	.43	Car	9 mos.	.39	Lt.	9 mos.	.61	Car	9 mos.	.68
Car	9	.38	Car	11	.38	Car	9	.39	Bl.	9	.61
Aud.1	11	.64	Lt.	11	.51	Car	11	.55	Aud.1	11	.53
Aud.2	11	.46	Car	13	.44	Aud.1	11	.63	Car	11	.41
Bl.	11	.51				Lt.	11	.39	Aud.1	29	.51
Lt.	11	.42									
Car	11	.49									
Aud.1	13	.68									
Car	13	.46									
Aud.1	20	.49									
Lt.	20	.38									
Lt.	29	.45									
Car	29	.61									

CAR		
Lt.	9 mos.	.68
Car	13	.43
Aud.1	20	.46

PREDICTOR AT 11 MONTHS											
LIGHT			CAR			AUDITORY 1			AUDITORY 2		
Bl.	11 mos.	.75	Aud.1	11 mos.	.63	Aud.2	11 mos.	.59	Aud.1	11 mos.	.59
Car	11	.51	Bl.	11	.77	Bl.	11	.57	Bl.	11	.41
Aud.1	13	.53	Lt.	11	.51	Lt.	11	.65	Aud.1	13	.60
Lt.	13	.64	Aud.1	13	.66	Aud.1	13	.64	Car	11	.49
Car	13	.56	Lt.	13	.61	Lt.	13	.43	Aud.1	20	.48
Aud.1	29	.58	Car	13	.81	Aud.1	20	.71	Lt.	20	.56
Lt.	29	.71	Lt.	20	.55	Lt.	20	.53	Aud.1	29	.43
Car	29	.73	Lt.	29	.49	Aud.1	29	.57			
			Car	29	.47						

BLOCK		
Aud.1	11 mos.	.57
Aud.2	11	.41
Car	11	.77
Aud.1	13	.64
Lt.	13	.58
Car	13	.83
Aud.1	29	.63
Lt.	29	.75
Car	29	.71

(*cont.*)

TABLE A. 40 (cont.)

PREDICTOR AT 13 MONTHS								
AUDITORY 1			LIGHT			CAR		
Lt.	13 mos.	.57	Aud.1	13 mos.	.57	Aud.1	13 mos.	.59
Car	13	.59	Car	13	.60	Lt.	13	.60
Aud.1	29	.53	Aud.1	29	.44	Lt.	20	.50
Lt.	29	.56	Lt.	29	.73	Aud.1	29	.49
Car	29	.59	Car	29	.67	Lt.	29	.53
						Car	29	.62

PREDICTOR AT 20 MONTHS								
AUDITORY 1			LIGHT			CAR		
Car	20 mos.	.43	Car	20 mos.	.49	Lt.	20 mos.	.49
Car	29	.51	Aud. 1	29	.54	Aud. 1	29	.37
			Car	29	.47			

mother. Moreover, range is the only variable that yielded stability from 3½ months of age on. The discontinuity in the size of the correlations at 7 to 9 months of age is in accord with the other data indicating increased stability after the transition at 7 months.

The Caucasian children Although the stability of range for the Caucasian infants was greater and more extensive than the stability of fixation and vocalization, the coefficients were smaller and less consistent than those of the Chinese. Range at 3 and 5 months was correlated with range at 11 months for the auditory and block episodes but not for the light episode. For light, range at 7 predicted range at 20 and 29 months; for car, stability held across shorter periods, 9 to 13, 11 to 13, and 13 to 29 months.

RATIO ANALYSIS OF CONSTANCY

We performed an analysis of the constancy of the mean of the two lowest ranges (across the entire episode) as we had for fixation time. That is, we computed for each episode the ratio of the difference between the two lowest ranges for each successive pair of ages divided by the mean of the two lowest ranges for that pair of ages. The lower the ratio, the more "constant" the variable for that period. The interval from 9 to 13 months produced the lowest ratios for car, light, and auditory episodes (see figure A.20) for both Chinese and Caucasian children; there was no significant difference between the two ethnic groups.

It will be recalled that the lowest ratios for fixation time to standard trials occurred across the interval from 7 to 11 months. Thus the four- to six-month period following the transition seems to be a time of relative constancy for responses related to attention. As in the case of fixation time, the product moment correlations for the mean of the two lowest ranges were only in partial accord with the ratio values. For the auditory, light, and car episodes, the ratio and the product moment correlations were in general accord for the Chinese, but not for the Caucasians. Among the Chinese, the lowest ratios and the highest product moment correlations tended to occur across the same pair of ages. But for the Caucasians the ratios and correlations were not yoked (see table A.41); the lowest ratios occurred at a later age than the highest correlations for auditory and light.

It is of interest to note that the ratios for the car episode during the period 13 to 29 months were far lower than they were for the other episodes. Nonetheless the correlations across the periods from 13 to 20 and from 20 to 29 months were not generally higher for the car episode than they were for auditory or light. Thus the two measures provide somewhat different information. They agree, however, among the Chinese, and affirm that the period from 9 to 13 months is a time when the lowest ranges are unusually stable for Chinese children for both auditory and visual episodes. This is the

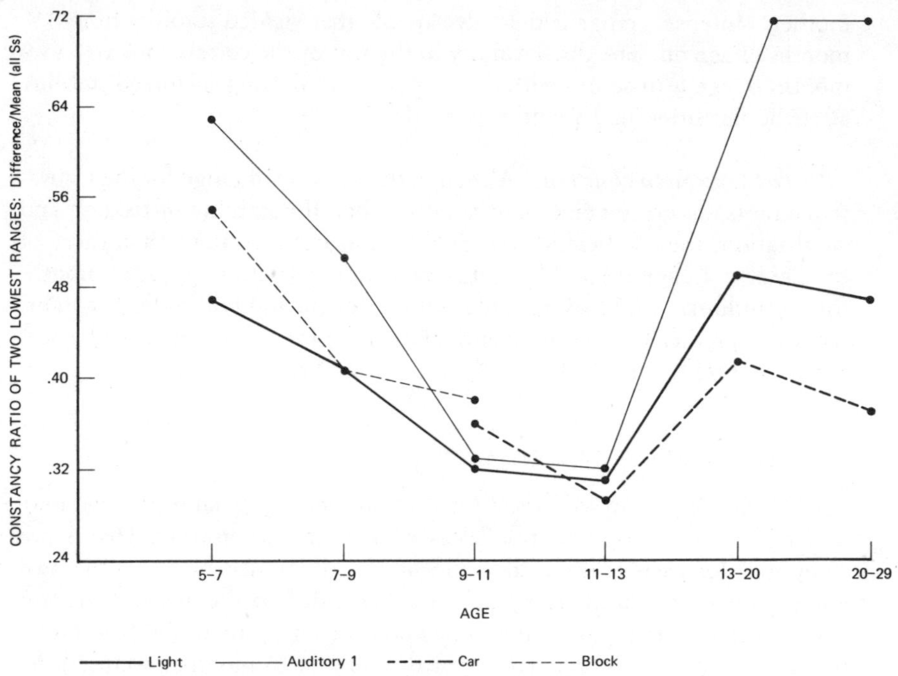

Fig. A.20 *The constancy ratio for the lowest heart rate ranges.*

age when children are showing a large increase in signs of apprehension of and vigilance to discrepant events.

These data suggest a fundamental difference between the two ethnic groups that, at an intuitive level, is in accord with the behavioral observations. The Chinese were quieter, less affective, less motoric, and more inhibited in the laboratory and in unfamiliar social situations as well. Their more stable heart rates seem to bear an intuitively reasonable relation to these psychological qualities. We do not believe the more stable heart rate of the Chinese is merely an epiphenomenon to the behavioral differences. At the early ages both Chinese and Caucasians were vocally quiet and motorically still. Ethnic differences in vocal and motoric reactivity did not emerge until after 7 or 9 months, and were small compared to the ethnic differences in range. Furthermore, the ethnic differences in heart rate range were more striking during the first year than they were later.

In order to assure ourselves that the two lowest range values were not simply a reflection of less motor activity, we performed several additional analyses. In the first we compared the occurrence of restless twisting on the block episode on those trials that produced the two lowest range values with twisting on the other trials on which range was coded. The percentage of trials in which twisting occurred was the same for both types of trials—2 per-

TABLE A.41. COMPARISON OF CONSTANCY RATIO TO PRODUCT MOMENT CORRELATION FOR SUCCESSIVE AGES FOR THE MEAN OF THE 2 LOWEST RANGES FOR EACH EPISODE.

	RATIO		CORRELATION	
EPISODE	CHINESE	CAUCASIAN	CHINESE	CAUCASIAN
Auditory I				
5-7 mos.	.30	.95	.19	.32
7-9	.44	.56	.35	−.05
9-11	.23	.41	.64[c]	.10
11-13	.33	.31	.64[c]	−.05
13-20	.87	.56	.29	−.23
20-29	.88	.55	.19	.09
Light				
5-7	.30	.62	.36[a]	.23
7-9	.40	.41	.45[a]	.55[b]
9-11	.33	.30	.25	.10
11-13	.22	.39	.64[c]	.27
13-20	.52	.48	.31	.02
20-29	.52	.39	.24	.52
Car				
9-11	.41	.27	.34	.32
11-13	.29	.30	.81[c]	.30
13-20	.43	.41	.20	.12
20-29	.35	.39	.40	.07
Block				
5-7	.41	.69	.29	−.40[b]
7-9	.32	.49	.63[c]	−.13
9-11	.42	.36	.23	.46[b]

[a] $p<0.05$.
[b] $p<0.01$.
[c] $p<0.001$.

cent. Thus, twisting was not less frequent on those trials which produced the lowest range values. (Recall that we had eliminated from heart rate analysis those trials in which the child was inattentive or irritable and, therefore, most likely to display motor activity.)

In a second analysis we correlated, for the Chinese and Caucasians separately, the mean of the two lowest ranges (at each age) with the proportion of trials in which the child vocalized, smiled, waved, fretted, or twisted, as well as with the percentage of fixation time (see table A.42).

The data revealed no consistent relation across age between attentiveness, fretting, vocalization, or motoricity and the two lowest ranges. Among the Chinese, vocalization at 7 and 9 months was associated with a larger

TABLE A.42. CORRELATION WITHIN AN AGE BETWEEN THE MEAN OF THE 2 LOWEST RANGES (ACROSS ALL EPISODES) WITH 6 BEHAVIORAL VARIABLES (ACROSS EPISODES AT EACH AGE) FOR EACH OF 2 ETHNIC GROUPS.

VARIABLE, BY ETHNIC GROUP	AGE (MOS.)							
	3	5	7	9	11	13	20	29
Vocalization								
Chinese	.07	.19	.36[a]	.44[b]	.08	−.10	−.42[a]	−.18
Caucasian	.40	−.12	−.06	−.02	−.17	.10	.19	−.51[a]
Smiling								
Chinese	.41	−.05	.29	.45[b]	.03	−.18	−.26	−.18
Caucasian	.32	.31	.06	−.10	−.20	.16	.29	.45[a]
Fretting								
Chinese	−.10	.30	.20	−.30	−.16	−.11	−.10	.10
Caucasian	−.11	−.20	.06	−.30	−.05	−.09	−.09	−.17
Waving								
Chinese	.23	−.17	.44[b]	.23	.33[a]	.07	−.40	−.07
Caucasian	−.06	.21	.26	−.12	.18	.15	.31	−.11
Twisting								
Chinese	−.17	.46[b]	.65[c]	−.10	−.14	.31	−.22	.02
Caucasian	.05	.22	.37[a]	−.13	.23	.37[a]	−.07	−.25
Percent total fixation time								
Chinese	.19	.12	−.05	.30	.10	−.14	−.28	−.08
Caucasian	.24	.03	.32	−.03	−.17	.30	−.22	.07

[a] $p<0.05$.
[b] $p<0.01$.
[c] $p<0.001$.

range, but at 20 months it was correlated with a smaller heart rate range. The only consistent result for both ethnic groups involved twisting at 7 months. Chinese children who displayed relatively more twisting behavior at 7 months had higher heart rate ranges at every age from 5 to 29 months. Caucasian children with a great deal of twisting at 7 months had higher heart rate ranges from 7 to 13 months. *But twisting at any other age was unrelated to heart rate range at a different age.* Since 7 months was the age of lower attentiveness and maximal boredom to the visual and auditory episodes, this result implies that the children who were prone to display restless motoricity when they were bored, in contrast to those who remained more inhibited, were more likely to have higher heart rate ranges across the first two years, *even at those times when they were not bored.* It should be noted that the tendency to show motoric twisting and high heart rate range was uncorrelated at most of the ages because boredom was minimal at the early and oldest ages. This result suggests that a temperamental factor mediates both the low cardiac ranges and the inhibition of motoricity under conditions of boredom.

We also compared the behavior of 9 Chinese children who had consistently low ranges across the period 3 to 29 months with 9 Chinese children who had consistently high ranges. We found no difference between these groups in attentiveness, vocalization, smiling, motoricity, or fretting. But, as indicated above, the Chinese infants with high ranges twisted more at 7 months ($t = 3.53$, $p < 0.01$), but not at any other age. Hence, children with very low ranges are not generally less active than those with more variable cardiac rates; rather, the latter are more active when they become bored, as many did at 7 months.

A relevant, although less reliable, datum comes from the mothers' rankings of their 29-month-old children. The high- and low-range children were viewed as similar by the parents on most traits. However, the mothers of high-range infants ranked four traits which deal with overt display of an affective state (*laughs easily, shy with new people, timid in new places,* and *stays close to mother*) as *more* characteristic of their child than did the mothers of low-range children. Since laughing is a positive affect state and timidity a negative one, the children do not differ, in their mothers' eyes, in quality of affect, but in the tendency to display behavioral signs of emotion. Unfortunately, the differences between the two groups for each of these four variables just missed statistical significance.

As indicated earlier, the Chinese children showed more frequent distress at separation from a caretaker than did the Caucasians. It is possible that children who have a disposition to be fearful might be more vigilant in the laboratory situation. Studies of children and adults imply that an attentive and vigilant posture toward stimulus events is associated with the stabilization of heart rate (Kagan and Rosman 1964; Porges and Raskin 1969). We therefore examined the data within ethnic groups to see if the children with more stable heart rates showed signs of displaying separation distress on more occasions. The Chinese children with very low heart rate ranges at 5 months, but not at other ages, cried more often in the separation situation than Chinese children with more labile heart rates ($r = -.40$, $p < 0.05$). But the corresponding correlation for the Caucasian infants was $-.13$. Although the ethnic differences in heart rate range and the stability of range are the two most robust findings in this study, we cannot fathom completely the meaning of this variable.

PART 2: THE OLDER ASSESSMENTS

Embedded figures test: conceptual tempo

Children display four different patterns of behavior on tasks like the Embedded Figures Test that have response uncertainty. (See table A.43 for

TABLE A.43. MEAN RESPONSE TIME AND QUALITY OF PERFORMANCE TO EMBEDDED FIGURES TEST ITEMS FOR MATCHED PAIRS.

CRITERION	DAY CARE	HOME CONTROL
Response time to all 9 critical items (sec.)	6.8	8.7
Number correct on first hypothesis	7.1	6.5
Average number of errors	2.2	3.0
Mean of three longest response times (sec.)	12.5	16.7

basic data.) Impulsive children offer an incorrect solution hypothesis without pausing to consider its validity. The fast, accurate children also offer a solution quickly, but it is usually correct. The slow, inaccurate children delay a long time before offering an incorrect solution hypothesis, as if they did not understand the task. The reflective children also delay before offering their first response, but it is usually correct.

In order to assign the children to one of these four groups, we used the median response time to the first solution hypothesis and the median number of errors for the nine critical test items across the 77 29-month-olds given this test as the basis for classification. The median response time to first solution hypothesis was 6.8 seconds for the total group and the median number of errors was 2. On the basis of these parameters we identified the four groups of children.

The impulsive children (n = 18) had response times of less than 6.8 seconds and made more than two errors. The fast-accurates (n = 23) had response times less than 6.8 seconds and made two or fewer errors. The slow-inaccurates (n = 15) had response times greater than 6.8 seconds and made more than two errors. The reflectives (n = 21) had response times greater than 6.8 seconds and made two or fewer errors.

Table A.44 shows the distribution of the four types of children for the paired care, class, and ethnicity groups. The data do not imply any simple effect of any of the independent variables. More of the day care than home control children were likely to be impulsive (39 percent of day care children in contrast to 17 percent of the home controls). By contrast, 33 percent of the home controls were fast-accurate, versus only 22 percent of the day care children. However, the difference between day care and home control children in pattern of responsivity was not significant.

Matched pairs analysis We assigned each child from the 23 matched pairs who completed the test to one of the four groups. In only 6 of the 23 pairs were both children in a particular pair assigned to the same group. As

TABLE A.44. PERCENTAGE OF CHILDREN SHOWING EACH OF 4 PATTERNS OF RESPONSE TO THE EMBEDDED FIGURES TEST, BY FORM OF CARE, CLASS, AND ETHNICITY.

GROUP	IMPULSIVE	FAST-ACCURATE	SLOW-INACCURATE	REFLECTIVE
Day care (n = 23)	39	22	13	26
Home control (n = 54)	17	33	22	28
Class 1 (n = 38)	21	29	18	32
Class 2 (n = 39)	25	31	21	23
Chinese (n = 38)	18	37	21	24
Caucasian (n = 39)	28	23	18	31

with the larger group, of which this sample is a part, day care children were a little more likely to be impulsive (9 out of 23) while the home controls were more likely to be fast-accurate (9 out of 23). There was a slight tendency for the girls in day care to be more reflective than their matched peers reared at home, whereas the boys in day care were a little more impulsive than their matched counterparts. Five of the 7 reflective girls were in day care and 6 of the 7 impulsive boys were in day care; only 1 impulsive boy was a home control.

Concept formation index

The concept formation index we used with the 29-month-olds was a slight modification of an instrument originally developed by Dr. Francis Palmer of the State University of New York at Stony Brook. We believe it is more sensitive than the 20-month vocabulary recognition test in assessing mastery of basic language concepts, and it was positively correlated with the vocabulary scores. Item analysis revealed a different pattern of successes and failures for the ethnic and class comparisons (see table A.45). Of the six significant ethnic differences only two (*under* and *soft*) also produced a class difference. Among the Chinese, the middle class did better than the working class on 28 of the 31 items. Among the Caucasians, the middle class performed better than the working class on 21 of 31 items. The difference in performance between middle and working class samples within each ethnic

TABLE A.45. PERCENTAGE OF EACH ETHNIC-CLASS GROUP PASSING INDIVIDUAL CONCEPT FORMATION INDEX ITEMS.

	CHINESE		CAUCASIAN	
ITEM	CLASS 1 (n = 23)	CLASS 2 (n = 22)	CLASS 1 (n = 30)	CLASS 2 (n = 21)
In	91	100	96	100
Big	65	45	83	47
Littlest of 3	78	40	73	61
Out of	70	50	83	71
Little	87	68	83	61
Biggest of 3	65	13	60	23
Up	69	64	86	90
White	70	40	70	71
Moving	73	59	56	71
Not moving	56	41	50	38
Black	56	23	66	52
Down	70	55	76	81
On	100	86	100	100
Under	61	13	83	61
Around	21	9	56	38
In front of	13	5	17	0
Behind	13	0	20	10
Over	26	18	30	29
Close	74	50	93	85
Open	70	81	93	85
More	61	50	50	57
Full	70	40	43	43
Long	52	36	43	38
Plate on cloth	26	31	66	38
Hard	39	31	60	38
Empty	78	45	79	52
Soft	47	18	62	47
Short	52	40	51	42
Cloth on plate	73	54	51	61
Top	56	40	58	57
Bottom	34	36	41	42

group was greater among the Chinese than the Caucasians for 21 items. Hence the effect of class on the concept formation index was greater within the Chinese sample.

The seven concepts that produced the largest class differences among the Chinese were *biggest, under, littlest, white, black, full,* and *empty.* Among the Caucasians, the comparable seven were *big, biggest, plate on a cloth, hard, empty, little,* and *under.* There is only overlap on *empty, biggest,* and *under.* There seems to be a special effect of ethnicity and, by inference, language group. The concepts *littlest, white, block,* and *full* produced large class differences within the Chinese sample but not within the Caucasian sample.

There was an obvious difference in level of difficulty of the concepts for all the children. The proportion of successes permitted us to divide the concepts into three groups—difficult, moderately easy, and easy. The easiest items were *in, on, up,* and *open.* More than 80 percent of the children understood all of these concepts. The most difficult items were *around, in front of, behind,* and *over;* less than one-third knew these concepts. Although some of the prepositions of location (*in, on, up,* and *down*) were learned early, *around* and *behind* were learned much later. For the nine antonym pairs, performance was generally equal for the members of the pair, although *empty* was a little better understood than *full,* and *top* a little better understood than *bottom.* It is likely that the differences for these pairs are due to the language habits of parents who, for example, are more apt to mention that the glass or cup of milk is *empty* rather than *full.* But this is speculation and perhaps the referential qualities of these words are partial determinants of their ease of acquisition.

In sum, there was substantial variation in level of attainment of these concepts, some being mastered by almost all children, a few being understood by less than 10 percent. The obvious effects of social class are not surprising. The less substantial ethnic differences seem due to less exposure to and encouragement of these concepts among the working class Chinese and the fact that some of these words are more complex in spoken Chinese than they are in English.

The Bayley Scales

Each child was administered selected items from the Bayley Developmental Scales at 7½, 13½, and 20 months. The procedure section listed the items administered at each of the three ages. Table A.46 contains the mean score for day care and home control children at each of the ages by ethnicity and class, as well as the means for the matched pairs.

Scores at 7½ months There was no simple effect of care or ethnicity, but an interaction; the Chinese children in day care performed better on the

TABLE A.46. AVERAGE SCORE ON BAYLEY SCALE ITEMS, BY AGE, ETHNICITY, FORM OF CARE, AND CLASS.

Age, item, ethnic group	Day care		Home control	
	Class 1	Class 2	Class 1	Class 2
7½ mos.				
Mental items[a]				
Chinese	1.7	1.6	1.3	1.0
Caucasian	1.3	1.5	2.0	1.7
Motor items[b]				
Chinese	7.6	8.0	8.8	7.4
Caucasian	9.4	8.9	10.0	8.6
Matched pairs				
Mental	1.5		1.5	
Motor	8.5		8.7	
13½ mos.				
Mental items[b]				
Chinese	8.4	8.9	9.0	7.2
Caucasian	8.9	8.1	7.5	8.1
Motor items[c]				
Chinese	1.6	3.1	3.0	2.8
Caucasian	4.0	3.1	3.4	3.6
Matched pairs				
Mental	8.6		7.7	
Motor	3.0		3.2	
20 mos.				
Language items[d]				
Chinese	8.0	6.1	8.6	5.0
Caucasian	10.0	9.0	9.1	9.3
Nonlanguage items[e]				
Chinese	8.6	6.7	8.1	5.3
Caucasian	8.1	7.6	6.4	5.2
Matched pairs				
Language	8.2		7.8	
Nonlanguage	7.7		6.0	

[a] Care by ethnicity effect, $F = 5.70$, 1/60, $p<0.05$.
[b] No significant effects.
[c] Ethnicity effect, $F = 6.03$, 1/73, $p<0.05$.
[d] Ethnicity effect, $F = 7.24$, 1/70, $p<0.01$.
[e] Care effect, $F = 7.49$, 1/70, $p<0.01$; class effect, $F = 8.87$, 1/70, $p<0.01$.

mental items than those in the home control group, while the opposite effect held for the Caucasian children. This interaction is due primarily to the fact that the home control Chinese children were less vocal than those in day care, while the home control Caucasians were more vocal than their counterparts in day care. The concern of middle-class Caucasian adults with early speech development, which was shared by our day care staff, seemed to have produced higher vocalization scores for the class 2 Chinese children at our center than for those reared at home and unusually high scores for middle-class, home-reared Caucasian children. The class 2 Chinese children reared at home may experience an environment that is maximally different from that of the other three groups. Many of the parents in this group neither speak English nor encourage early language development. Children from such a home environment might benefit from the greater variety inherent in the day care center, which offers more opportunity for verbal interchange with adults and the practicing of maturing competences.

At 13½ months At 13½ months the balance of items had shifted to 14 mental and only 5 motor items, and there was no main effect of care on either category of item. However, Caucasians attained higher scores on the motor scale. An item analysis revealed that the Chinese children performed less well on all five items, but especially on the items *walk sideways* and *walk backwards with a toy.*

At 20 months The Bayley items at 20 months were divided into two scales, a language scale of 15 items and a nonlanguage scale of 13 items, 6 of which involved imitation of the examiner and 7 of which involved putting forms in a form board. Although scores on the language scale were not correlated with care, the Caucasian children had higher language scores than the Chinese. And children from middle-class families had slightly, but not significantly, higher language scores than those from working-class families.

Performance on the nonlanguage items yielded one of the rare instances in which the day care experience had a clear main effect. For three of the four subgroups the day care children obtained higher scores than the corresponding groups being reared at home, and on 11 of the 13 items the percentage of children passing was higher for day care than home controls.

Intercorrelations of the Bayley scores Table A.47 contains the intercorrelations of the six Bayley scores at the three ages for Caucasian and Chinese children separately because the pattern of relations was different for the two groups. The mental items at 7½ months were unrelated to future performance for both groups, while the 7½-month motor scores predicted the 13½-month motor scores for both ethnic groups. However, the 7½-month motor score was related to the 20-month language scale only for the Chinese and not for the Caucasians. Although the 13½-month scores predicted

TABLE A.47. INTERCORRELATION OF BAYLEY SCORES.[a]

ITEM AND AGE	1	2	3	4	5	6
1 Mental, 7 mos.	. . .	.16	.28	.12	.07	.27
2 Motor, 7 mos.	.03	. . .	.27	.32[b]	.36[b]	.02
3 Mental, 13 mos.	−.12	.24	. . .	.42[c]	.16	.24
4 Motor, 13 mos.	.00	.60[c]	.18	. . .	−.03	−.11
5 Language, 20 mos.	.06	.27	.31[b]	.47[c]	. . .	.29
6 Nonlanguage, 20 mos.	−.19	.22	.26	.35[b]	.43[c]	. . .

[a] Chinese to the right and above the diagonal; Caucasians to the left and below.
[b] $p < 0.05$.
[c] $p < 0.01$.

performance on the language scale at 20 months for the Caucasian children, it did not do so for the Chinese. Thus the predictive validity of the 13½-month Bayley items is seriously influenced by the characteristics of the sample.

Attachment to the caretaker

The major variables coded to assess attachment at 20 months were proximity, looking, touching, or vocalizing in response to each of the familiar and unfamiliar adults as well as smiling and fretting. As indicated in chapter 5, most of the children showed a remarkably similar profile of behavior across the 45-minute session; they spent much more time (by a factor of 7 to 1) proximal to the mother than to the familiar woman and rarely played near the unfamiliar woman (see table 5.6). The children who spent a great deal of time proximal to their mothers were also proximal to their mothers during the play sessions at 13 and 20 months. Thus there was a small group of children who were likely to remain close to their mothers in these two moderately unfamiliar social situations. However, proximity to mother during the attachment episode at 20 months was relatively independent of most of the other major dependent variables. The children who remained close generally were no more nor less verbal than others, nor was their proximity to the mother correlated with their performance on the cognitive battery at 20 and 29 months. The Caucasian children who stayed close to the mother during the attachment session were more fretful and less attentive during the laboratory episodes from 9 to 29 months (r approximated $+0.5$ for fretfulness and -0.4 for fixation time). This relation did not occur among the Chinese infants.

Vocalization and orientation The children vocalized more in response to their mothers than to the familiar women by a factor of 2½ to 1 and, of course, were least likely to vocalize to the unfamiliar woman, although during the final 15 minutes, the class 1 home-control Caucasian children showed a large increase in vocal response to the stranger. Although neither class, care, nor ethnicity was correlated with vocal response to the mother, the home control child vocalized significantly more to the familiar woman than the day care child did to the teacher during the last third of the session. This difference also appeared on the matched pairs analysis. Vocalization during the attachment session was correlated with spontaneous vocalization during the play sessions at 20 and 29 months and with higher scores on the concept formation index.

During the first 15 minutes all the children oriented equally to all three adults. But after this initial period, each child's orientation to the unfamiliar woman decreased dramatically, while orientation to the other two adults remained high. Neither class, care, nor ethnicity had any main effect on orientation toward any of the adults, although the class 1 Chinese were a little more likely to stare at the stranger than were any of the other subgroups.

Matched pairs The day care children spent more time proximal to their mothers and less time proximal to the familiar adults, and vocalized and smiled less than the home controls (see table A.48). Although the interaction of care and ethnicity was not significant, this difference was due primarily to the behavior of the Chinese children. Because all children, both home control and day care, are disposed to approach their mothers when apprehensive, these data imply that the day care children may have been initially more uncertain than the home controls. This is not unreasonable. The day care child was accustomed to seeing his "teacher" in the day care center, not in a room in a strange building. Moreover, the day care child rarely saw his mother and day care teacher together in an unfamiliar setting, whereas the home control subjects may have been more likely to have had such an experience with their mothers and familiar adults. Thus the situation may have been slightly more discrepant for the day care children, and perhaps that is why they remained closer to their mothers.

Separation protest

The frequency and intensity of separation protest during the first 30 months of life appears to be closely monitored by several factors. The curvilinear growth function displayed by all groups implied that the maturation of some basic psychological process sets the boundary conditions for this reaction. (See tables A.49 through A.53.)

Because Fox (1977) had reported a relation between a child's ordinal

TABLE A.48. MEAN SCORES FOR DURATION (SEC.) AND FREQUENCY OF BEHAVIOR OF MATCHED PAIRS DURING THE ATTACHMENT SESSION.

VARIABLE	PERIOD	DAY CARE	HOME CONTROL
Duration of proximity			
To mother	1	100.4	68.9[a]
	2	95.0	71.8
	3	96.2	61.0
	All	97.2	68.3[a]
To familiar adult	1	6.9	15.7
	2	6.8	15.9
	3	7.4	24.1
	All	6.9	18.1
To stranger	1	0.4	0.7
	2	0.8	1.0
	3	0.2	1.1[b]
	All	0.5	1.0[a]
Duration of touching			
Mother	1	64.3	40.7
	2	68.5	45.1
	3	66.7	34.1
	All	66.9	40.4[a]
Familiar adult	1	2.0	6.3
	2	2.4	7.3
	3	1.6	7.4
	All	2.0	6.9
Stranger	1	0.02	0.04
	2	0.01	0.06
	3	0.00	0.70
	All	0.01	0.25
Duration of looking			
At mother	1	8.3	8.0
	2	9.3	11.5
	3	6.8	9.8
	All	8.3	9.8

(*cont.*)

VARIABLE	PERIOD	DAY CARE	HOME CONTROL
At familiar adult	1	8.1	6.8
	2	5.6	5.3
	3	8.2	8.6
	All	7.3	6.9
At stranger	1	6.3	7.7
	2	3.3	4.9
	3	6.1	4.3
	All	5.4	5.6
Duration of vocalizing	1	1.6	1.7
To mother	2	2.1	2.9
	3	1.7	2.7
	All	1.8	2.5
To familiar adult	1	0.7	1.2
	2	0.5	1.2
	3	0.8	2.0[a]
	All	0.7	1.5[a]
To stranger	1	0.3	0.6
	2	0.2	0.6
	3	0.8	1.0
	All	0.4	0.7[a]
Undirected	1	5.0	6.8
	2	7.6	10.3
	3	9.2	10.9
	All	7.1	9.3
Duration of fretting	1	5.0	5.6
	2	10.4	5.3
	3	9.3	9.9
	All	8.7	7.3
Average scale score for proximity at rotation	Rotation 1	3.5	2.8
	Rotation 2	2.9	3.0
Frequency of looking			
At mother	1	5.0	4.4
	2	5.6	5.6
	3	3.8	4.7
	All	4.9	4.9

(*cont.*)

TABLE A.48 (cont.)

VARIABLE	PERIOD	DAY CARE	HOME CONTROL
At familiar adult	1	5.0	3.9
	2	3.7	3.1
	3	5.1	4.5
	All	4.7	3.8
At stranger	1	4.4	2.4
	2	2.4	2.4
	3	3.1	3.5
	All	3.4	3.1
Frequency of smile	1	0.5	0.9
	2	0.5	1.0
	3	0.7	1.0
	All	0.6	1.0[a]

[a] Significance, $p < 0.05$.
[b] Significance, $p < 0.01$.

position in the family and the probability of separation protest, with firstborns more likely to protest than later-borns, we examined our data for such an effect among 49 firstborn and 27 later-born children. (See table A.54.) The growth curves were similar for both groups, and, although there were no significant differences between firstborns and later-borns for the number of times the child protested, there was a slight tendency for more firstborns than later-borns to protest early, at 5 months of age. Since this is prior to the new stage of cognitive functioning, we believe that the fretting was mediated by a mechanism different from the one operating after nine months. The slightly more frequent early distress by the firstborns suggests perhaps their greater vulnerability to uncertainty in discrepant situations. We should note that this effect was stronger for Chinese than for Caucasian children, and for more firstborn Chinese than later-borns at every age; especially the first two ages. Thus, within the constraints set by the maturation of a cognitive competence, there is measurable variation in the frequency and intensity of protest associated with ethnicity and ordinal position and perhaps other factors. Each variable provides a gloss on the basic growth function.

The effect of the introduction of the unfamiliar peer

The majority of the children showed a large decrease in both play and vocalization and an equally large increase in proximity to the mother follow-

Table A.49. Behavior during the separation situation.

Age (mos.)	n	Percentage who fretted (% of all subjects)	Percentage of those who fretted: Who fretted seriously	Who looked at mother upon her departure	Who looked at mother upon her return	Who approached mother upon her return
3	51	35	16	50	78	0
5	75	25	47	42	75	0
7	73	26	50	70	90	22
9	78	47	70	89	100	32
11	77	56	60	88	98	43
13	87	86	76	87	98	53
20	82	83	71	100	96	70
29	69	50	50	85	97	47

Age (mos.)	Locomotive (% of all subjects)	Latency to fret (sec.)	Latency to approach door of those who went to door (sec.)
3	0	44	
5	0	50	
7	60	46	52
9	88	15	32
11	100	25	29
13	100	9	17
20	100	8	6
29	100	11	18

TABLE A.50. PERCENTAGE OF CHILDREN SHOWING SEPARATION DISTRESS FOR PAIRS OF AGES (ALL CHILDREN).

AGE (MOS.)	3	5	7	9	11	13	20	29
3	...	11%	4	21	19	29	31	24
5		...	6	12	16	20	20	6
7			...	19[a]	16	26	22	18
9				...	31[b]	42	41	31[d]
11					...	51	51[c]	35
13						...	72	51[d]
20							...	47[d]
29								

[a] Phi coefficient relating the two ages, $\Phi = .32, p < 0.05$.
[b] $\Phi = .22, p < 0.05$.
[c] $\Phi = .37, p < 0.01$.
[d] $\Phi = .31, p < 0.05$.

ing the introduction of the peer. Table A.55 contains the average duration (in seconds per minute) for these and other variables for the first and second half of the solo and peer sessions and the change scores from solo to peer.

Proximity to mother The difference scores for proximity to mother were greatest at 29 months. Table A.56 shows the solo and peer values for proximity to mother for each of the four major subgroups (form of care versus ethnicity). With the exception of the Caucasian children in day care, who showed the greatest absolute proximity to mother during the peer session and the greatest increase in proximity at 13 months, the other three groups all showed their largest increase in proximity at 29 months. When all groups were pooled, the average change was greatest at 29 months.

Ipsative analysis We examined the scores for each of the 69 children who participated in both the solo and the peer sessions at all three ages and noted the age at which the absolute proximity score during the peer session was greatest (of the three ages) and the age at which the change in proximity was largest for the first half of the session (see table A.57). Forty-eight percent of the children showed their greatest proximity at 29 months (29 percent at 13 and 23 percent at 20 months), and 51 percent showed the largest change in proximity at 29 months (in contrast to 26 percent at 13 months and 23 percent at 20 months). Despite the obvious age function there were no significant effects of care, class or ethnicity for the difference in proximity between the two sessions.

TABLE A.51. PERCENTAGES OF DAY CARE (DC) AND HOME CONTROL (HC) CHILDREN EXHIBITING VARIOUS BEHAVIORS ON THE SEPARATION EPISODE.

	% WHO FRETTED		% WHO FRETTED SERIOUSLY, OF THOSE WHO FRETTED		% WHO LOOKED AT MOTHER ON HER RETURN, OF THOSE WHO CRIED ON HER DEPARTURE		% WHO APPROACHED MOTHER ON RETURN, OF THOSE WHO CRIED ON HER DEPARTURE	
AGE (MOS.)	DC	HC	DC	HC	DC	HC	DC	HC
3	28	50	14	10	62	100	0	0
5	28	20	45	50	61	85	0	0
7	35	19	45	60	85	100	23	21
9	54	45	64	71	100	100	30	37
11	63	53	52	81	100	94	37	58
13	85	88	67	86	100	97	37	60
20	83	88	60	78	90	100	75	69
29	64	46	46	58	100	97	50	50

TABLE A.52. FREQUENCY OF SEPARATION DISTRESS ACROSS THE PERIOD 5½ THROUGH 20 MOS.: PERCENTAGE OF GROUP FOR 59 CHILDREN SEEN ON ALL 6 OCCASIONS.

NUMBER OF OCCASIONS	CHINESE	CAUCASIAN
1	7%	19
2	7	31
3	42	19
4	22	25
5	11	6
6	11	0

Vocalization Changes in duration of undirected vocalization from the solo to the peer session were also greatest at 29 months; all subgroups showed their greatest inhibition of vocalization (for the first half of the session) at 29 months. As with proximity, there were no significant care, class, or ethnicity effects for the average change in vocalization across the two sessions.

We examined each child's data at the three sessions to determine the age at which each child's undirected vocalization during the peer session was

TABLE A.53. BEHAVIOR FOLLOWING SEPARATION: PERCENTAGES OF CHINESE (CH) AND CAUCASIAN (CA) CHILDREN.

			PERCENTAGE OF THOSE WHO WERE DISTRESSED					
	PERCENTAGE WHO FRETTED (% OF ALL SUBJECTS)		WHO FRETTED SERIOUSLY		WHO LOOKED AT MOTHER ON HER RETURN		WHO APPROACHED MOTHER ON HER RETURN	
AGE (MOS.)	CH	CA	CH	CA	CH	CA	CH	CA
3	45%	25	9	28	100	62	0	0
5	25	25	50	44	84	68	0	0
7	36	17	60	33	94	86	13	28
9	61	35[a]	81	53[b]	100	100	16	45
11	59	53	71	50	96	100	53	30
13	95	79	88	63[a]	97	100	50	55
20	91	76	81	61[b]	94	97	77	65
20	60	41	45	57	94	100	55	39

a $p < 0.05$.
b $p < 0.10$.

TABLE A.54. PERCENTAGE OF CHILDREN DISPLAYING PROTEST TO SEPARATION, BY ORDINAL POSITION.

AGE (MOS.)	ALL CHILDREN		CHINESE CHILDREN ONLY	
	FIRSTBORN	LATER-BORN	FIRSTBORN	LATER-BORN
3	41%	23	66	25
5	31	16	44	6
7	28	23	43	29
9	47	48	76	44
11	51	63	61	55
13	93	77	100	88
20	81	81	100	80
29	56	56	72	64

lowest as well as the age when the decrease in vocalization to introduction of the peer was greatest (see table A.57). The individual data revealed that although most children showed their greatest decrease in vocalization at 29 months (58 percent); the majority of children showed their absolutely lowest amount of vocalization during the peer session at 20 months (45 percent).

The high levels of vocalization during the solo session at 29 months made it likely that the change scores would be large at 29 months. But from an absolute perspective the children were quietest during the peer session at 20 months. There were no care, class, or ethnicity correlates of the distribution of these ipsative scores.

Play Changes in proximity to mother and vocalization implied greatest apprehension at 29 months, while absolute vocalization during the peer session suggested greater apprehension at 20 months. The growth functions for play and staring at the peer implied that apprehension was maximal at 13 or 20 months. Three of the four ethnicity versus care subgroups showed their greatest decrease in play (for the first half of the session) at 20 months. The Caucasian day care children, who were the exception, showed their greatest decrease in play at 13 months.

An ipsative analysis of each child's scores across the three sessions also supported the curvilinear function (see table A.57). Forty-eight percent of the children spent the shortest time playing during the peer session at 20 months, and more children showed their largest decrease in play at 20 months (43 percent) than at 13 or 29 months (33 and 24 percent). Similarly, 52 percent of the children showed their lowest third quartile value at 20 months and 60 percent the largest change in the third quartile value at 20 months. We also examined the frequency data to determine the distribution

TABLE A.55. BEHAVIOR, BY AGE, DURING SOLO AND PEER PLAY; MEAN SCORES FOR ALL SUBJECTS.

VARIABLE, BY AGE (MOS.)	PERIOD I			PERIOD II		
	SOLO	PEER	CHANGE	SOLO	PEER	CHANGE
Play						
13 mos.	46.0	28.1	+17.9	40.9	28.8	+12.1
20	47.3	27.6	+19.7	39.9	32.2	+ 6.7
29	49.6	34.6	+15.0	49.6	34.1	+15.5
Play Q3[a]						
13	40.4	32.0	+ 8.4			
20	60.9	32.8	+28.1			
29	47.9	50.1	− .5			
Proximity to mother						
13	13.8	19.8	− 6.0	21.0	23.6	− 2.6
20	10.3	18.8	− 8.5	16.7	17.6	− 9.0
29	7.2	22.8	−15.6	7.4	20.5	−13.1
Vocalization to mother						
13	.41	.17	+ .24	.48	.27	+ .21
20	.57	.33	+ .24	.69	.31	+ .38
29	.87	.57	+ .30	1.26	.67	+ .59
Vocalization, other						
13	1.47	.66	+ .81	2.30	.95	+ 1.35
20	1.76	.70	+ 1.06	2.89	1.31	+ 1.58
29	4.56	1.15	+ 3.41	5.55	1.58	+ 3.97

[a] Q3 is for whole session.

of children who showed both the largest decrease in play and the absolutely lowest time playing during the peer session at the same age. Of the 26 children who filled both criteria, 65 percent met these criteria at 20 months (in contrast to 15 and 20 percent at the other two ages). Finally, the distribution of extremely low play scores (less than 10 seconds per minute) revealed that they were most likely to occur at 20 months.

Hence when inhibition of play was the index, uncertainty was maximal at 20 months of age. As uncertainty began to wane at 29 months, play was the first response to be disinhibited. The proximity data remained high at 29 months, while inhibition of play decreased, because the oldest children typically brought toys near the mother and played close to her. (By 3 years of age most children in this situation are so at ease they do not even approach their mother if an unfamiliar peer is introduced.)

TABLE A.56. BEHAVIOR BY AGE DURING SOLO[a] AND PEER[b] PLAY[c] (FOR PERIOD 1), BY CARE AND ETHNIC GROUPS.

ETHNIC GROUP, VARIABLE, AGE (MOS.)	DAY CARE			HOME CARE		
	SOLO	PEER	CHANGE	SOLO	PEER	CHANGE
Chinese						
Play						
13	44.0	26.0	+18.0	38.9	23.4	+15.5
20	44.6	24.6	+20.0	45.4	17.5	+27.9
29	42.9	36.6	+ 6.3	51.0	30.9	+20.1
Play Q3[d]						
13	34.8	43.1	− 8.3	51.6	26.0	+25.6
20	71.5	38.9	+32.6	51.5	28.3	+23.2
29	40.1	46.8	− 6.7	52.5	59.6	− 7.1
Proximity to mother						
13	15.2	21.5	− 6.3	20.2	23.1	− 2.9
20	15.6	24.8	− 9.2	13.9	28.4	−14.5
29	15.8	27.4	−11.6	3.8	28.6	−24.8
Vocalization to mother						
13	.43	.18	+ .25	.38	.05	+ .33
20	.80	.33	+ .47	.25	.11	+ .14
29	.87	.80	+ .07	.68	.42	+ .26
Vocalization, other						
13	1.07	.63	+ .44	1.23	.51	+ .72
20	1.54	.64	+ .90	1.53	.53	+ 1.00
29	3.97	1.14	+ 2.83	3.88	.90	+ 2.98
Caucasian						
Play						
13	52.1	26.9	+25.2	49.2	36.1	+13.1
20	49.6	40.8	+ 8.8	49.7	27.2	+22.5
29	54.3	37.1	+17.2	50.2	33.8	+16.4
Play Q3						
13	45.3	25.5	+19.8	29.9	33.5	− 3.6
20	65.5	34.0	+31.5	51.8	30.1	+21.7
29	59.5	45.0	+14.5	39.2	49.1	− 9.9
Proximity to mother						
13	10.9	24.1	−13.2	8.7	10.3	− 1.6
20	4.7	10.8	− 6.1	7.2	11.3	− 4.1
29	3.9	16.6	−12.7	5.3	18.6	−13.3
Vocalization to mother						
13	.39	.21	+ .18	.45	.23	+ .22
20	.66	.65	+ .01	.57	.21	+ .36
29	.73	.55	+ .18	1.21	.50	+ .71

(cont.)

TABLE A. 56 (cont.)

ETHNIC GROUP, VARIABLE, AGE (MOS.)	DAY CARE			HOME CARE		
	SOLO	PEER	CHANGE	SOLO	PEER	CHANGE
Vocalization, other						
13	1.49	.57	+.92	2.10	.92	+1.18
20	1.65	.69	+.96	2.34	.93	+1.41
29	4.71	1.37	+3.34	5.68	1.19	+4.49

[a] Summary of significant effects for three ages for solo session:
Time playing, ethnicity $F = 7.9$, 1/51, $p<0.01$; age $F = 5.2$, 2/102, $p<0.01$. Q3, age $F = 5.8$, 2/88, $p<0.01$.
Proximity to mother, ethnicity $F = 11.5$, 1/52, $p<0.01$; age $F = 11.2$, 2/104, $p<0.001$; ethnicity X age $F = 3.3$, 2/104, $p<0.05$.
Vocalization to mother, age $F = 13.05$, 2/104, $p<0.001$; care X ethnicity $F = 8.1$, 1/52, $p<0.01$.
Vocalization, other, age $F = 19.4$, 2/104, $p<0.001$.

[b] Summary of significant effects for three ages for peer session:
Time playing, ethnicity $F = 6.5$, 1/52, $p<0.01$. Q3, age $F = 6.8$, 2/70, $p<0.01$.
Proximity to mother, ethnicity $F = 8.2$, 1/52, $p<0.01$.
Vocalization to mother, age $F = 15.1$, 2/104, $p<0.001$.
Vocalization other, ethnicity $F = 4.6$, 1/52, $p<0.05$; age $F = 3.5$, 2/104, $p<0.05$.

[c] Difference = solo minus peer session. Q3, care X ethnicity $F = 6.2$, 1/30, $p<0.01$; age $F = 7.2$, 2/60, $p<0.01$.
Proximity to mother, age $F = 6.9$, 2/104, $p<0.01$.
Vocalization to mother, care X ethnicity $F = 5.1$, 1/52, $p<0.05$.
Vocalization other, age $F = 18.1$, 2/104, $p<0.001$.

[d] Q3 is for whole session.

EFFECT OF FORM OF REARING

Although class was unimportant, both care and ethnicity influenced behavior in the peer sessions (see tables A.58 and A.59). As hinted in the previous section, the children in day care, especially the Caucasians, showed maximal uncertainty a little earlier than the home controls. The Caucasian day care children showed their largest values for inhibition of play, fretting, and proximity to mother while staring at the peer at 13 months, whereas the other three groups showed their largest magnitudes at 20 months. At 29 months, when uncertainty was being resolved, the children in day care showed a greater reduction in inhibition than the home controls. They showed smaller changes in play, proximity to mother, and vocalization, and were less likely to be proximal to the mother while staring at the peer. At all ages they also stared at the peer less than did those reared at home.

TABLE A.57. PERCENTAGE OF WHOLE SAMPLE SHOWING EXTREME VALUES, BY AGE.

VALUES	AGE (MOS.) 13	20	29	CHI SQUARE SIGNIFICANCE
Largest absolute value for proximity to mother (peer session)	29%	23	48	< .01
Lowest absolute value for vocalization (peer session)	36	45	19	< .01
Largest absolute value for looking at peer	39	36	25	
Largest increase in proximity to mother from solo to peer session	26	23	51	< .001
Largest decrease in undirected vocalization from solo to peer session	18	23	58	< .001
Largest decrease in play, solo to peer (Pd. I)	33	43	24	
Lowest absolute values for time playing (peer session) (Pd. I)	32	48	20	< .01
Largest decrease in third quartile value for play	18	60	22	< .001
Lowest absolute Q3 value during peer session	33	52	15	< .001
Largest change in play and lowest value for time playing at the same age (n = 53)	30	49	21	< .001
Largest decrease in Q3 and the lowest absolute Q3 value during the peer session at the same age (n = 45)	18	64	18	< .001
Largest decrease in play and largest decrease in third quartile value as well as lowest absolute time playing and lowest absolute third quartile values at the same age (n = 26)	15	65	20	< .001
Percent of group displaying average time playing of less than 10 sec. per minute (peer session)	13	24	16	

The ipsative analysis (see table A.58) revealed that the majority of the day care children showed their absolutely lowest amount of play during the peer session at 13 months (48 percent of the group), whereas the home controls showed their peak inhibition at 20 months (54 percent). The change in play also revealed earlier inhibition among the day care children, for the majority showed their greatest decrease in play at 13 months (50 percent of

TABLE A.58. COMPARISON OF DAY CARE (DC) AND HOME CONTROL (HC) CHILDREN: PERCENTAGE OF GROUP SHOWING EXTREME VALUES ON PLAY VARIABLES.

		Age (mos.)		
Values	Form of care	13	20	29
Lowest				
Absolute values for time playing during first half of peer session	DC	48%	30	22
	HC	27	54	19
Absolute time vocalizing during first half of peer session	DC	35	44	21
	HC	43	41	16
Largest				
Absolute values for proximity to mother during peer session	DC	39	22	39
	HC	24	24	52
Absolute value for staring at peer	DC	48	30	22
	HC	32	41	27
Decrease in play from solo to peer session	DC	50	27	23
	HC	30	49	21
Increase in proximity to mother (solo to peer)	DC	35	26	39
	HC	22	24	54

the group), whereas the majority of the home controls showed their greatest inhibition at 20 months (49 percent). The day care children showed maximal staring at the peer at the earliest age (48 percent of the group) while 41 percent of the home controls showed the most staring at the peer at 20 months. The differences are reasonable, because home control children were probably exposed to fewer peers their own age than those in day care. The day care experience accelerated the growth function for apprehension to an unfamiliar child by a few months, causing it to emerge and vanish a little earlier, especially among the Caucasian children. But form of care did not affect the intensity of apprehension. (As we indicated earlier, this was also true of children raised on kibbutzim.)

Because some of the social interaction variables were infrequent in occurrence, we divided the distributions for these variables at the median and computed chi squares to assess group differences for vocalization to mother, vocalization to peer, smiling, fretting, and initiation of interaction with the peer. The effects of form of care were minimal for most variables. To our surprise more 29-month-old home controls entered into reciprocal play with the peers than day care subjects (45 versus 8 percent). As we shall see, this was also true when the children visited the unfamiliar day care center. This result indicates that daily experience with other children does not in itself

TABLE A.59. MATCHED PAIRS DATA FOR CHANGE SCORES IN THE PLAY SESSIONS.

CHANGE SCORES (WHOLE SESSION), BY AGE (MOS.)	DAY CARE	HOME CONTROL
Duration of proximity to mother (peer minus solo)		
13	4.0	2.5
20	2.7	10.1
29	12.2	15.7
Change in vocalization (solo minus peer)		
13	+1.1	+1.0
20	+1.3	+1.3
29	+3.5	+3.6
Change in play (solo minus peer)		
13	15.1	13.7
20	11.0	21.9
29	11.3	15.9
Change in Q_3 value for play (solo minus peer)		
13	−.15	−.01
20	+.30	+.28
29	−.18	+.01

lead to more mature or more social forms of play after the period of inhibition is over.

EFFECT OF ETHNICITY

Although ethnicity was not related to the growth function for apprehension (the largest number of children in both ethnic groups showed the lowest amount of time playing during the peer session at 20 months), ethnicity was related to the intensity of apprehension. The Chinese were more inhibited than the Caucasians at all ages, the difference being greatest and statistically significant at 20 months. The Chinese stayed closer to their mothers, played, and vocalized less (during both solo and peer sessions), fretted more, and were less interactive with the peers. The Chinese made fewer initiations—either cooperative or aggressive—and, of course, had fewer instances of reciprocal play. When we standardized, by ethnic groups, the distributions for proximity to mother and inhibition of play during each of the three peer sessions and averaged those three standard scores, the Chinese were found to have significantly higher scores for both variables.

STABILITY OF INDIVIDUAL DIFFERENCES

Although the child's developmental stage and the nature of the situation controlled most of the variation in behavior, it is still possible that some children have a stable disposition to be inhibited or relatively free over and above the obvious effects of age and the presence of the peer. In order to answer that question we computed intercorrelations for the first half as well as the whole session for the three major indexes of inhibition—play, undirected vocalization, and proximity to mother—across the three ages for the solo and peer sessions separately. We performed separate analyses for the two ethnic groups because the Chinese children were more inhibited than the Caucasians. High cross-age correlations for the pooled sample would reflect the stability of the Chinese versus Caucasian difference in degree of inhibition.

Proximity to mother and time spent playing were always negatively correlated within a particular session (correlations ranged from $-.7$ to $-.8$). Vocalization was not consistently related to these two indexes of inhibition for the Chinese children. For the Caucasians, vocalization was related to high proximity and low play values, but only during the peer session, at 20 and 29 months. In general, cross-age stability was not very robust. The data by ethnic group are given in table A.60.

Chinese children The data based on the first half and the whole session were similar and revealed that high proximity to mother during the solo session at 13 months predicted proximity to mother and low play values at 20 months, but the 13-month behavior predicted neither proximity nor play at 29 months. Indeed, there was a significant negative correlation between proximity during the solo session at 13 months and proximity to mother during the peer session at 29 months. High proximity during the solo session at 20 months predicted high proximity and low play values at 29 months, but play was not stable from 20 to 29 months. When behavior during the peer session was the predictor, there was no cross-age stability for either proximity or play. Vocalization was the only variable that was stable from 20 to 29 months for both the solo and the peer session. Thus, during the less-threatening solo session, there was some short range stability over a 7- to 9-month period. But the introduction of the peer destroyed those stabilities.

Caucasian children The data from the first half of the session revealed no stability from 13 to 20 or 29 months for either proximity to mother or play, although play at 20 predicted play at 29. Data from the entire session, however, revealed that the children who were proximal to their mothers a great deal during the solo session at 13 months were likely to stay close to their mothers during the peer sessions at all three ages (the correlations ranged from 0.48 to 0.69), and to play less at 20 months. But proximity to mother or play during the peer session at 13 months did not predict behavior at 29 months. Moreover, play at 13 months during either the solo or the peer session was not predictive of play at 20 or 29 months. Play during the solo session at 20 months predicted solo play at 29, but play during the peer session was not correlated across these ages. Vocalization showed no cross-age stability for the Caucasians from 13 or 20 months to a succeeding age. Thus there was minimal stability when behavior during the peer session was the predictor and short-term stability when behavior during the solo session was the predictor. The best predictor of future inhibition among the Caucasian children came from the solo session at 13 months, just prior to the emergence of maximal apprehension of the peer. It is possible that individual differences in vulnerability to apprehension are masked at 20 months by the emergence of strong apprehension of the peer, and that the variation in inhibition at 13 months more faithfully reflects the individual disposition.

Vocalization: cross-task generality

Spontaneous vocalization during the solo and play sessions at 20 and 29 months was consistently correlated with vocalization during the attachment session at 20 months and with the indexes of language development at 29 months. Although the general direction of the results was similar for both ethnic groups, the magnitude and consistency of the relations were sufficiently different to warrant a separate discussion for Chinese and Caucasian children (see table A.61).

Chinese children Vocalization during the solo sessions at 20 and 29 months was related to vocalization during the attachment session as well as performance on Bayley scales and vocabulary test at 20 months, and the concept formation index at 29 months. Performance on the test of memory for locations was related to vocalization during the play session at 29 but not 20 months. Hence the highly vocal and verbal older Chinese children were generally more proficient on the language and cognitive tests. But it is important to note that vocalization during the peer session at 20 months, which was infrequent, was not correlated with these other scores. Although the Bayley scores at 7 and 13 months did not predict performance on the cognitive tasks at 29 months, the 20-month Bayley scores, both language and nonlanguage, predicted performance on the vocabulary, concept formation index, and memory tests, the language scores being more powerful predictors than the nonlanguage scores. As might be expected, the vocabulary and concept formation index scores were positively related ($r = 0.56$).

Caucasian children The consistency of cross-task correlations was less impressive for the Caucasians. Although vocalization during the solo play session was correlated with vocalization during the attachment session at 20 months and the concept formation index at 29 months, vocalization at 20 and 29 months did not predict vocabulary, Bayley, or memory scores. More-

TABLE A.60 STABILITY COEFFICIENTS FOR PLAY BASED ON WHOLE SESSION, BY PREDICTOR VARIABLE, AGE, AND ETHNIC GROUP.

PREDICTOR VARIABLE, BY SESSION	ETHNIC GROUP	
	CHINESE	CAUCASIAN
Proximity to mother at 13 mos.		
In solo session		
vs. solo session at 20 mos.	.49[b]	.15
vs. solo session at 29 mos.	.07	.04
vs. peer session at 13 mos.	.54[b]	.69[b]
vs. peer session at 20 mos.	.14	.48[b]
vs. peer session at 29 mos.	−.35[a]	.57[b]
In peer session		
vs. solo session at 20 mos.	.28	.21
vs. solo session at 29 mos.	.10	.22
vs. peer session at 20 mos.	.31	.40[b]
vs. peer session at 29 mos.	−.07	.22
Play at 13 mos.		
In solo session		
vs. solo session at 20 mos.	.41[a]	−.16
vs. solo session at 29 mos.	−.17	.08
vs. peer session at 13 mos.	.37[b]	.48[b]
vs. peer session at 20 mos.	−.08	.21
vs. peer session at 29 mos.	−.19	.08
In peer session		
vs. solo session at 20 mos.	.06	−.14
vs. solo session at 29 mos.	−.13	−.19
vs. peer session at 20 mos.	.09	.30
vs. peer session at 29 mos.	−.13	−.15
Proximity to mother at 20 mos.		
In solo session		
vs. solo session at 29 mos.	.38[a]	.30
vs. peer session at 29 mos.	.04	.23
In peer session		
vs. solo session at 29 mos.	.19	.20
vs. peer session at 29 mos.	.26	.29
Play at 20 mos.		
In solo session		
vs. solo session at 29 mos.	.22	.35[a]
vs. peer session at 29 mos.	.25	−.14
In peer session		
vs. solo session at 29 mos.	.12	.14
vs. peer session at 29 mos.	.01	.11

(*cont.*)

Predictor variable, by session	Ethnic group	
	Chinese	Caucasian
Undirected vocalization at 13 mos.		
In solo session		
vs. solo session at 20 mos.	−.07	.15
vs. solo session at 29 mos.	−.09	.15
vs. peer session at 13 mos.	.53[b]	.60[b]
vs. peer session at 20 mos.	.00	.12
vs. peer session at 29 mos.	.13	.18
In peer session		
vs. solo session at 20 mos.	.04	−.21
vs. solo session at 29 mos.	.03	−.16
vs. peer session at 20 mos.	−.04	.24
vs. peer session at 29 mos.	.21	.20
Undirected vocalization at 20 mos.		
In solo session		
vs. solo session at 29 mos.	.44[b]	.02
vs. peer session at 20 mos.	.74[b]	.47[b]
vs. peer session at 29 mos.	.75[b]	.07
In peer session		
vs. solo session at 29 mos.	.38[a]	−.05
vs. peer session at 29 mos.	.54[b]	.20

[a] $p < 0.05$.
[b] $p < 0.01$.

over, vocalization during the play session at 29 months had no relation to cognitive performance scores, in sharp contrast to the Chinese data. Thus among Caucasians, who were more vocal than Chinese, differences in vocalization were not as predictive of cognitive competences as they were among the Chinese, many of whom were very quiet. This pattern indicates the importance of constraining generalizations about the diagnostic value of a particular variable with statements that specify the range of predictor being used, which, in this instance, is correlated with ethnicity. As with the Chinese, the Bayley Scale at 7 and 13 months did not predict cognitive performance at 20 or 29 months, while both Bayley scores at 20 months were correlated with vocabulary and the concept formation index. As with the Chinese, the vocabulary and concept formation index were highly correlated ($r = 0.60$) (see table A.61).

It will be recalled that apprehension toward the peer, as indexed by inhibition of play, was greatest at 20 months. The children who showed the most inhibition of play at 20 months also spent the most time near their mothers during the attachment session at 20 months and were more likely to

TABLE A.61. INTERCORRELATIONS AMONG SELECTED SCORES AT 20 AND 29 MOS. OF AGE.[a]

VARIABLE	CONTEXT 1.	2.	3.	4.	5.	6.	7.	8.
1. Vocalization in solo play at 20 mos. (whole session)	. . .	.44[c]	.65[c]	.51[c]	.42[c]	.38[b]	.39[b]	.27
2. Vocalization in solo play at 29 mos.	.02	. . .	.35[b]	.36[b]	.38[b]	.49[c]	.32[b]	.39[c]
3. Vocalization in attachment session at 20 mos.	.43[c]	.27	. . .	.54[c]	.00	.30[b]	.35[b]	.13
4. Bayley language score at 20 mos.	.05	.04	.23	. . .	.29	.67[c]	.62[c]	.40[b]
5. Bayley nonlanguage score at 20 mos.	−.26	.14	.00	.43[c]	. . .	.31[b]	.30	.27
6. Vocabulary test score at 20 mos.	.00	−.11	.03	.75[c]	.47[c]	. . .	.56[c]	.35[b]
7. Concept formation index score at 29 mos.	.12	.27	.18	.53[c]	.42[b]	.60[c]	. . .	.32[b]
8. Memory for locations score at 29 mos.	−.05	.07	.12	.14	−.08	.07	−.02	. . .

[a] Chinese are to the right and above the diagonal; Caucasians to the left and below.

[b] $p < 0.05$.

[c] $p < 0.01$.

show separation anxiety at 9 and 29 months. These children also made more errors on the embedded figures test and performed less well on the concept formation index. Thus the 20-month-old children who were most anxious with the unfamiliar peer were less competent on the intellectual tasks at 29 months, the relation perhaps reflecting a cognitive component to the resolution of anxiety at 20 months.

But inhibition of play during the peer sessions at 13 or 29 months was not predictive of these other signs of apprehension, anxiety, and competence. Although there are periods during the first two years when some children display more apprehension than others, that disposition is not stable indefinitely.

Relation between reactivity to laboratory episodes and later behavior

In order to determine if attention, smiling, vocalization, or motor activity to the laboratory episodes was predictive of behavior during the attachment and play sessions, as well as on the final cognitive battery, we computed the correlations among these two sets of scores. In general, there was little relation between absolute levels of attentiveness or vocal and motoric reactivity to the visual and auditory episodes, on the one hand, and the more molar behaviors assessed during the second and third years, on the other. Moreover, when reasonable relations emerged they held for only one ethnic group and not for the other.

Among the Chinese, vocalization to the laboratory episodes at 20 and 29 months was associated with better performance on the concept formation index, vocabulary, and Bayley language items (the correlations approximated 0.4), but not with higher scores on the memory, embedded figures, or Bayley nonlanguage test items.

There was specificity rather than a general intellectual factor. However, the relation between vocalization to laboratory episodes and later verbal skills did not occur among the Caucasians. Because the Caucasians were generally more vocal than the Chinese, we computed a multiple regression equation with mean vocalization on the laboratory episodes from 9 to 29 months and ethnicity as the two predictors and the concept formation index and vocabulary scores as the two criteria. The multiple correlation with the index as criterion was + .51, compared with the simple product moment correlation of + .43 for the Chinese and + .07 among the Caucasians. When vocabulary at 20 months was the criterion, the multiple correlation was + .37, lower than the product moment correlation between vocalization and vocabulary score among the Chinese ($r = 0.45$).

It appears that variation in amount of infant vocalization is not very predictive of verbal skills during the second year for highly vocal children, but is predictive for children who are minimally vocal or who don't vocalize at all. The predictive power of variation in a behavior is dependent on the specific interval used. Equal ranges on a variable do not have equivalent predictive validity independent of their position on the distribution. This generalization holds for other variables. (For example, the variation in IQ between 60 and 80 is more predictive of future school achievement scores than the variation between IQs of 120 and 140.) Psychological variables often have a particularly sensitive range of individual variation that is most predictive of theoretically related behaviors at a future date.

PREDICTIVE POWER OF EARLY SMILING

In an earlier study of Caucasian firstborn children (Kagan 1971), we found that infants who smiled at masks and two-dimensional representations of human faces at 4 and 8 months had longer epochs of play at 27 months. The current data did not replicate that relation but did reveal that the Caucasian children who smiled frequently to the laboratory episodes at 29 months had had longer epochs of play during the solo play sessions at 13 and 29 months ($r = +.61$, $r = +.45$, respectively). This result was not found for the Chinese. Further, Caucasian infants who smiled frequently at the masks and at the social examiner at 3½ and 5½ months made fewer errors on the Embedded Figures Test at 29 months ($r = -.40$, $p < 0.05$).

Again among the Caucasians, but not the Chinese, degree of inhibition of play following the introduction of the peer at 20 and 29 months was correlated with frequent smiling during the laboratory episodes, especially at 7, 20, and 29 months. Indeed, the amount of decrease in the third quartile of play at 29 months following the introduction of the peer was correlated +.62 with occurrence of smiling to the laboratory events at 29 months. In an attempt to probe this result we selected a small group of children whose frequency of smiling to the laboratory episodes from 9 through 29 months was above the median at 3 or more ages. We matched each of these 9 children with a child of the same sex, ethnicity, and social class who rarely smiled (the arbitrary quality of this criterion is acknowledged). The smilers played less, had a lower third quartile value, and a greater drop in play to the introduction of the peer at 20 months than did the nonsmilers. The smilers also remained close to their mothers for a longer period of time during the attachment session at 20 months. It appears that the disposition to smile as an accompaniment to recognitory assimilation may be related to the ease of inhibition in mildly uncertain situations.*

RELATION OF PATTERN OF ATTENTION DURING INFANCY TO LATER BEHAVIOR

It will be recalled from the discussion in chapter 5 that the growth function for search to the auditory episode and for fixation time to the transformation and return trials of the block and light episodes was U-shaped with a trough at 7½ months. If we assume this to be the normal growth function and deviation from it to be indicative of anomalous development, it is rele-

*A recent long-term follow-up of 10-year-olds, originally seen when they were between 4 and 27 months of age, revealed that recognitory smiling to representations of faces at 4 and 8 months and smiling following successful solution of a perceptual analysis problem at 27 months predicted a reflective disposition on the Matching Familiar Figures Test at 10 years of age (chi square = 3.1, $p < 0.10$). Furthermore, among boys, recognitory smiling to representations of faces at 4 months predicted long response times on an embedded figures test at 10 years of age ($r = 0.4$, $p < 0.05$) (Lapidus, Kagan and Moore 1977). One of the major determinants of a reflective approach to cognitive problems with response uncertainty is concern over error and, therefore, a tendency to inhibit immediate responding. These longitudinal data, together with other information implying heritability of a disposition to smile in situations of recognitory assimilation, imply that frequent display of the smile of assimilation in infancy may be characteristic of those children who have a strong initial disposition toward sustained inhibition in uncertain contexts. When an uncertain event can be assimilated, as in some of the laboratory episodes, smiling occurs. When the event cannot be assimilated, as when the unfamiliar peer is encountered, inhibition occurs. The common quality seems to be the ease of affective arousal under conditions of mild uncertainty (see Sroufe and Waters 1976).

vant to ask if the children who showed the normative function are different from the others at 20 and 29 months. (It is important to point out that absolute fixation time on any episode at any age was unrelated to cognitive performance during the second and third years.) Since the block episode was only administered up to 11 months and some of the children had not been tested at 3 months, we examined each child's growth function across the period 5 to 11 months. The sample for this analysis consisted of those children with complete data on the block, light, and auditory episodes from 5 through 11 months as well as test and play data during the second and third years. For each of the infancy episodes, we divided the sample into those children who showed a U-shaped attentive function with a trough at 7 months and those who did not (the remainder of the group).

Auditory episode Since the data from the auditory episode revealed a U-shaped function for search to all three phases of the episode, one group consisted of 34 children with the U-shaped function to either the standards, transformations, or returns; a second group consisted of 14 children who did not meet that criterion. When we compared the two groups on the cognitive battery at 20 and 29 months, the group with the U-function attained significantly higher scores on the concept formation index and the memory for locations test at 29 months ($t = 2.31, p < 0.05$ for index; $t = 2.55, p < 0.01$ for memory). They had higher scores, but not significantly so, on the Bayley language items ($p < 0.10$) and the vocabulary test at 20 months ($p < 0.10$). The nonlanguage items of the Bayley and the Embedded Figures Test did not differentiate the two groups.

A similar analysis of the light and block data did not reveal comparable differences between the two groups, even though the children whose data showed the U-shaped function to the auditory episode also had it on the return trials of the block episode (chi square = $6.55, p < 0.01$). Thus infants whose data showed a U-shaped function for search to speech, but not necessarily longer average search values, were more proficient in language during their second and third years of life but were not more skilled on most nonlinguistic tasks.

Relation to play Because we view apprehension toward the unfamiliar peer as following a developmental course, it is reasonable to speculate that the children whose data showed the normative growth function to the visual and auditory episodes during the first year might show earlier signs of apprehension toward the peer. Because time spent playing in the presence of the unfamiliar peer showed an inverted-U function, we examined each child's three peer play sessions, at 13, 20, and 29 months, and noted the age when each child's time playing was the lowest (both third quartile as well as total time playing). We divided the group into those children who showed the least amount of playing with peer early (at 13 months) versus those who showed the least time playing at either 20 or 29 months. We related this division of children to the division based on the U-shaped function for fixation time and search.

The pattern of search behavior to the auditory episode was unrelated to the play data. But the children for whom there was a U-shaped function for fixation time to the transformation or return trials of the light episode or the return trials of the block episode were more likely to show their greatest inhibition of play at 13 months, rather than 20 or 29 months (for block, chi square = 4.77, $p < 0.05$ for play; chi square = 6.58, $p < 0.01$ for the third quartile of play; for light, chi square = 5.34, $p < 0.05$ for play; for the third quartile, chi square not significant).

We assume that the children who show a trough in fixation at 7 months and a rise in attentiveness at 9 and 11 months are entering the new cognitive stage of functioning a little earlier than the other children. One might predict that they would show apprehension toward the unfamiliar peer slightly earlier, since the apprehension is interpreted as a consequence of the emergence of the new cognitive ability.*

Since the growth function for the two visual episodes predicted the growth function for inhibition of play but not performance on the language tests, while the growth function for search to auditory predicted language ability but not the play function, it appears that there is specificity in the age of attainment of these developmental competences. These data are not in accord with the notion of a "general precocity" factor.

These analyses used differences in the growth function rather than the absolute magnitude of a variable as a predictor. The vast majority of longitudinal studies that use data from the child's infancy as a predictor of future functioning correlate early absolute scores (Bayley scores or amount of vocalization) with another absolute score gathered at a later date. Since some responses show lawful growth functions during the first three years, the meaning of an absolute magnitude on a variable like play or attentiveness depends very much on the developmental stage at which it is being assessed.

Sex differences

Having found that form of care and class exerted minimal influence on most of our variables, while ethnicity was a major factor, we examined the entire corpus of data for sex differences within ethnic groups. Sex differences were minimal; boys and girls behaved similarly during the laboratory episodes and the attachment and play sessions, and obtained similar scores on the cognitive procedures at 20 and 29 months.

*It will be recalled from chapter 5 that 10-month-old infants whose play with objects was developmentally advanced showed earlier onset of apprehension to unfamiliar peers than 10-month-olds whose play with toys was less advanced (Jacobson 1977).

The laboratory episodes To our surprise there were no significant sex differences in attentiveness or vocalization on any of the laboratory episodes, whether the variables were examined separately by episode or pooled across episodes. Fixation time and vocalization data were treated by analysis of variance; the less frequently occurring variables were examined by chi square for the proportion of children displaying a particular response or level of response. No episode revealed consistent sex differences that lasted across several administrations and held for both Chinese and Caucasian children. The importance of episode was seen in the data for smiling (table A.62). On the

TABLE A.62. PERCENTAGE OF CHILDREN SMILING ONE OR MORE TIMES IN EACH EPISODE, BY SEX AND ETHNICITY.

	Chinese		Caucasian	
Episode, by age (mos.)	Boys	Girls	Boys	Girls
Block				
3	0%	0	6	0
5	0	5	12	16
7	12	26	21	26
9	12	6	37	26
11	11	11	33	33
Light				
3	0	0	6	9
5	0	5	21	5
7	6	5	21	31
9	6	5	21	15
11	6	21	41	22
13	35	36	50	36
20	40	50	50	55
29	46	47	75	33
Car				
9	11	0	16	26
11	25	10	21	6
13	17	6	20	0
20	40	29	45	33
29	53	50	67	58
Masks (series 1)				
3	10	23	18	0
5	6	11	8	26
9	17	10	0	37
13	6	27	16	31

light episode, the Caucasian boys were more likely to smile than the girls; but among the Chinese, the sex differences were minimal. For the masks the result was reversed; at 9 and 13 months the Caucasian girls were more likely to smile than the Caucasian boys.

We found no evidence implying greater irritability or motoricity among boys, despite suggestions in the literature that such differences might occur. We are not suggesting that boys are not more motoric in free play, only that a sex difference did not appear in the more restricted laboratory situation. These data affirm the suggestion that differences between sex and ethnic groups typically appear in a specific context of assessment. Since there were ethnic differences in vocalization and smiling on the laboratory episodes, it would appear that ethnicity exerted a more serious influence on these signs of affective arousal than did gender. Differences in vocalization between Chinese boys and girls were often, but not always, greater than the comparable differences among Caucasians (see table A.63).

Cognitive battery There were no striking sex differences on the concept formation index, vocabulary, memory, or embedded figures tests. The girls obtained higher scores on the mental items of the 13-month Bayley and the nonlanguage items of the 20-month Bayley, but there were no sex differences on the 13-month motor or 20-month language tests (see table A.63).

Play behavior Although sex differences were minimal on the laboratory and attachment sessions and on most of the cognitive procedures, the three play sessions provided some indication of the influence of sex in the form of sex by age and sex by ethnicity interactions. The hardiest finding occurred at 20 months, the age of maximal apprehension toward the peer, when girls showed a greater decrease in play to the introduction of the peer than did boys. However, the sex difference was absent at the youngest and oldest ages (see table A.64) and did not hold for absolute amount of time spent playing during the peer session. A sex difference was observed in absolute time playing during the peer session among the Chinese but not among the Caucasians (see table A.65). As noted earlier, the ethnic difference in apprehension toward the peer held for both sexes, Chinese boys and girls being more inhibited than the Caucasians at both 13 and 20 months. Moreover, sex differences in inhibition were more obvious among the Chinese (see table A.66). The Chinese girls were vocally quieter and stayed closer to their mothers than the Chinese boys during the peer sessions, while comparable sex differences among Caucasians were minimal.

During the solo play sessions the Caucasian girls were more vocal and talked more than the Caucasian boys, especially at 29 months, while among the Chinese the direction of the sex difference in vocalization was reversed leading to a significant sex by ethnicity interaction (see table A.66). This result is of interest because of earlier speculation, based on data from Cauca-

Table A.63. Differences between the sexes for selected variables, by ethnic group.[a]

Variable	Chinese		Caucasian	
	Boys	Girls	Boys	Girls
Attachment session:				
Mean time spent (sec.)				
Proximity to mother	91	109	65	55
Touching mother	59	79	37	27
Undirected vocalization	9.7	7.8	7.3	12.5
Vocabulary score at 20 mos.	5.4	5.9	6.5	8.1
Concept formation index at 29 mos.	15.9	15.5	17.0	19.8
Mother's ranking of child on scale of 16				
Talkative	8.4	8.4	5.3	3.1
Laughs easily	7.5	5.6	2.6	4.1
Stays close to mother	7.5	4.5	5.8	10.4
Auditory 1				
% time spent searching	74	56	38	49
% of intertrials during which vocalization occurred				
Auditory 1	23	13	14	11
Auditory 2	29	17	19	21
Block episode	7	3	9	9
Light	16	7	17	16
Car	21	11	21	19
Separation, % crying				
At 9½ mos.	56	68	37	31
At 11½ mos.	47	68	56	50
At 13½ mos.	100	91	78	81
At 20 mos.	94	87	86	69
At 29 mos.	56	61	43	42
Bayley scale scores				
Mental, 13 mos.	7.8	8.6	7.7	8.7
Motor, 13 mos.	3.1	2.6	3.9	3.6
Language, 20 mos.	7.7	7.2	7.9	10.5
Nonlanguage, 20 mos.	6.7	7.8	6.0	6.9
Visit to unfamiliar day care center				
Proximity to mother	3.2	3.3	2.0	1.6
Looking at peer	2.6	3.0	3.2	3.8
Play	2.7	2.3	3.7	3.2

[a] See preceding tables for meanings of percentage values and ranks.

TABLE A.64. DIFFERENCES BETWEEN THE SEXES, BY ETHNIC GROUP AND AGE, IN CHANGE IN PLAY FROM SOLO TO PEER SESSION (SEC./MIN.).

CHANGE IN PLAY, BY AGE (MOS.)	CHINESE		CAUCASIAN	
	BOYS	GIRLS	BOYS	GIRLS
From solo to peer period 1[a]				
13 mos.	15	18	17	15
20	13	32	20	25
29	20	7	18	19
From solo to entire peer session[b]				
13	12	17	13	13
20	5	24	13	19
29	18	8	15	19
Change in Q3[c]				
13	.13	−.03	.07	−.08
20	.16	.33	.20	.32
29	.17	.03	−.04	.01

[a] Sex X age $F = 3.93$, 2/128, $p < 0.05$.
[b] Sex X age $F = 3.99$, 2/128, $p < 0.05$.
[c] Sex X age $F = 2.93$, 2/82, $p < 0.05$.

sian infants, that girls were more likely than boys to vocalize when excited by discrepant experience. The inference from the early study was that the sex difference may have had a biological basis. These data contradict that hypothesis and suggest, instead, that the differences in vocalization noted earlier are due to differential handling of the sexes by Caucasian parents. Observations of Caucasian families have revealed more one-to-one verbal interaction between mother and daughter than between mother and son. Although we do not have the observational data on the Chinese families, it is possible that we would find the opposite pattern among them.

The only sex difference that held for both ethnic groups was greater inhibition of play with the unfamiliar peer among 20-month-old girls and more prolonged staring among girls at the peer at the unfamiliar day care center. No variable differentiated the sexes across several ages and rarely did a difference hold for both ethnic groups. In those instances when significant sex differences appeared, they were typically more dramatic for the Chinese than for the Caucasians, the Chinese girls being the most apprehensive. During the peer play sessions at 13 and 20 months, the Chinese girls were the quietest and most inhibited; the Caucasian girls the least inhibited and most verbal. Differential apprehension in a novel situation seems to be the product of an interaction between sex and ethnicity, implying different handling of boys and girls by Chinese and Caucasian parents.

TABLE A.65. ABSOLUTE VALUES FOR PLAY IN SOLO AND PEER SESSION BY AGE AND SEX AND ETHNIC GROUPS (SEC./MIN.).

	CHINESE		CAUCASIAN	
SESSION, BY AGE (MOS.)	BOYS	GIRLS	BOYS	GIRLS
Solo play[a]				
Period 1				
13 mos.	40	42	51	48
20	40	48	48	53
29	51	44	52	51
Whole session[b]				
13	40	40	48	47
20	36	44	44	50
29	50	46	51	49
Peer play[c]				
Period 1				
13	26	24	35	34
20	26	16	29	29
29	31	37	34	32
Whole session[c]				
13	27	22	36	34
20	30	20	31	32
29	31	38	35	31

[a] Sex X age $F = 3.51$, 2/128, $p < 0.05$.
[b] Sex X age $F = 4.47$, 2/128, $p < 0.01$.
[c] No significant *F*.

TABLE A.66. DIFFERENCES AMONG SEX AND ETHNIC GROUPS FOR INDEXES OF INHIBITION.

	AGE (MOS.)		
SESSION, VARIABLE, GROUP	13	20	29
Whole peer session			
Proximity to mother			
Chinese			
Boys	22.7	19.2	26.5
Girls	25.1	29.1	28.9
Caucasian			
Boys	16.6	17.9	16.7
Girls	15.2	13.9	18.3
Vocalization to mother			
Chinese			
Boys	0.18	0.23	0.66
Girls	0.10	0.35	0.48
Caucasian			
Boys	0.38	0.43	0.57
Girls	0.28	0.33	0.71

(*cont.*)

TABLE A.66 (cont.)

SESSION, VARIABLE, GROUP	AGE (MOS.)		
	13	20	29
Undirected vocalization			
Chinese			
Boys	0.69	0.93	1.3
Girls	0.57	0.58	0.9
Caucasian			
Boys	1.0	0.92	1.6
Girls	1.2	1.2	1.7
Time spent playing			
Chinese			
Boys	27.4	30.6	31.4
Girls	22.3	20.3	37.7
Caucasian			
Boys	35.8	30.7	35.3
Girls	34.2	32.0	31.4
Looking at peer while near mother			
Chinese			
Boys	7.0	10.1	7.0
Girls	9.5	12.7	8.8
Caucasian			
Boys	5.6	6.3	6.8
Girls	6.6	6.3	7.4
Whole solo session			
Vocalization to mother[a]			
Chinese			
Boys	.40	.67	.99
Girls	.34	.49	.94
Caucasian			
Boys	.52	.68	.93
Girls	.66	.76	1.79
Undirected vocalization[b]			
Chinese			
Boys	1.8	2.4	5.5
Girls	1.4	1.7	3.7
Caucasian			
Boys	2.2	2.6	4.9
Girls	2.8	2.2	7.6

[a] Sex X ethnicity $F = 4.44, 1/65, p < 0.05$.
[b] Sex X ethnicity $F = 4.50, 1/65, p < 0.05$.

References

Abbott, J. 1836. *The way to do good: Or the Christian character mature.* Boston.

Adelson, E., and Fraiberg, S. 1974. Gross motor development in infants blind from birth. *Child Development,* 45: 114-26.

Ainsworth, M. D. S. 1967. *Infancy in Uganda.* Baltimore: Johns Hopkins Press.

———. 1969. Object relations, dependency, and attachment. *Child Development,* 40: 969-1026.

———. 1973. The development of mother-infant attachment. In B. M. Caldwell and H. W. Ricciuti, eds., *Review of child development research,* vol. 3. Chicago: University of Chicago Press.

Ainsworth, M. D. S., and Bell, S. M. 1970. Attachment, exploration and separation illustrated by the behavior of one year olds in a strange situation. *Child Development,* 41: 49-67.

Ainsworth, M. D. S., and Wittig, B. A. 1969. Attachment and exploratory behavior of one year olds in a strange situation. In B. M. Foss, ed., *Determinants of infant behavior,* vol. 4, London: Methuen and Co.

Akita, G. 1970. The other Ito: a political failure. In A. M. Craig and D. H. Shively, eds., *Personality in Japanese history.* Berkeley: University of California Press, pp. 335-72.

Alberti, L. B. 1971. *Della famiglia.* Translated by G. A. Guarino. Lewisburg: Bucknell University Press.

Amsterdam, B., and Greenberg, L. M. 1977. Self conscious behavior of infants: A videotape study. *Developmental Psychobiology,* 10: 1-6.

Bandura, A. 1977. Self efficacy: Toward a unifying theory of behavioral change. *Psychological Review,* 84: 191-215.

Barrett, H. S., and Koch, H. C. 1930. The effect of nursery school training upon the mental test performance of a group of orphanage children. *The Pedagogical Seminary and Journal of Genetic Psychology,* 37: 102-22.

Basso, K. H. 1976. Wise words of the Western Apache: Metaphor and semantic theory. In K. H. Basso and H. A. Selby, eds., *Meaning in anthropology*. Albuquerque: University of New Mexico Press, pp. 93-121.

Bates, E., Benigni, L., Bretherton, I., Camaioni, L., and Volterra, V. 1977. From gesture to the first word: On cognition and social prerequisites. In M. Lewis and L. A. Rosenblum, eds., *Interaction, conversation and the development of language*. New York: Wiley, pp. 247-307.

Bayley, N. 1964. Consistency of maternal and child behaviors in the Berkeley Growth Study. *Vita Humana,* 1: 73-95.

Beckwith, L. 1971. Relationships between attributes of mothers and their infant's IQ scores. *Child Development,* 42: 1083-97.

Bell, R. Q., Weller, G. M., and Waldrop, M. G. 1971. Newborn and preschooler: Organization of behavior and relations between periods. Nos. 1-2. *Monographs of the Society for Research in Child Development,* 36, serial no. 142.

Benjamin, R. M., and Thompson, R. F. 1959. Differential effects of cortical lesions in infant and adult cats on roughness discrimination. *Experimental Neurology,* 1: 305-21.

Bennett, E. L., Diamond, M. C., Krech, D., and Rosenzweig, M. R. 1964. Chemical and anatomical plasticity of brain. *Science,* 146: 610-19.

Birch, H. G., Thomas, A., Chess, S., and Hertzig, M. E. 1962. Individuality in the development of children. *Developmental Medicine and Child Neurology,* 4: 370-79.

Blehar, M. C. 1974. Anxious attachment and defensive reactions associated with day care. *Child Development,* 45: 683-92.

Bloom, L., Hood, L., and Lightbown, P. 1974. Imitation in language development: If, when and why. *Cognitive Psychology,* 6: 380-420.

Bornstein, M. H. 1975. Qualities of color vision in infancy. *Journal of Experimental Child Psychology,* 19: 401-19.

Bornstein, M. H., Kessen, W., and Weiskopf, S. 1975. Categories of hue in infancy. *Science,* 190: 201-2.

Bower, T. G. R. 1974. *Development in Infancy*. San Francisco: W. H. Freeman.

Bowlby, J. 1969. *Attachment.* Vol. 1. *Attachment and Loss.* New York: Basic Books.

———. 1973. *Separation, anxiety and anger.* Vol. 2. *Attachment and Loss.* New York: Basic Books.

Boyd, J. P., ed. 1955. *The papers of Thomas Jefferson.* Vol. 12. Princeton, N.J.

Bradley, R. H., and Caldwell, B. M. 1976. Early home environment and changes in mental test performance in children from 6 to 36 months. *Developmental Psychology,* 12: 93-97.

Briggs, J. 1970. *Never in anger.* Cambridge, Mass.: Harvard University Press.

Brim, O. G., Glass, D. C., Neulinger, J., and Firestone, I. J. 1969. *American beliefs and attitudes about intelligence.* New York: Russell Sage.

Brody, L. 1977. The enhancement of recall memory in infancy. Ph.D. dissertation, Harvard University.

Bronfenbrenner, U. 1974. Developmental research on public policy and the ecology of childhood. *Child Development,* 45: 1-5.

———. 1975. Research on the effects of day care. Manuscript prepared for Advisory Committee on Child Development of the National Academy of Science.

Bronson, G. W. 1970. Fear of visual novelty: Developmental patterns in males and females. *Developmental Psychology,* 2: 33-40.

———. 1972. Infants' reactions to unfamiliar persons and novel objects. No. 3. *Monographs of the Society for Research in Child Development,* 37, serial no. 148.

Brookhart, J., and Hock, E. 1976. The effects of experimental context and experiential background on infants' behavior toward their mother and a stranger. *Child Development,* 47: 333-40.

Brossard, M., and Decarie, T. G. 1971. The effects of three kinds of social stimulation on the development of institutionalized infants. In C. Lavatelli, ed., *Readings in Child Development and Behavior.* New York: Harcourt Brace Jovanovich, pp. 173-83.

Brown, R. 1973. *A first language.* Cambridge, Mass.: Harvard University Press.

Bruner, J. S. 1968. *Processes of cognitive growth: Infancy.* Worcester, Mass.: Clark University Press.

———. 1973. Organization of early skilled action. *Child Development,* 44: 1-11.

Burlingham, D., and Freud, A. 1944. *Infants without families.* London: George Allen and Unwin.

Burrows, E. G., and Wallace, M. 1972. The American Revolution: The ideology and psychology of national liberation. *Perspectives in American History,* 6: 167-308.

Bushnell, H. 1867. *Christian nurture.* New York: Charles Scribner and Co.

Butterworth, G. 1977. Object disappearance and error in Piaget's Stage IV Task. *Journal of Experimental Child Psychology,* 23: 391-401.

Caldwell, B. M. 1964. The effects of infant care. In M. L. Hoffman and L. W. Hoffman, eds., *Review of child development research,* vol. I. New York: Russell Sage, pp. 9-88.

Caldwell, B. M., Wright, C. M., Honig, A. S., and Tannenbaum, J. 1970. Infant day care and attachment. *American Journal of Orthopsychiatry,* 40: 397-412.

Campos, J. J., Hiatt, S., Ramsay, D., Henderson, C., and Svedja, M. In press. The development of fear on the visual cliff. In M. Lewis and L. Rosenblum, eds., *The Origins of Affect.* New York: Plenum.

Caron, A. J., Caron, R. F., Caldwell, R. C., and Weiss, S. J. 1973. Infant perception of the structural properties of the face. *Developmental Psychology,* 9: 385-99.

Casler, L. 1961. Maternal deprivation: A critical review of the literature. No. 2. *Monographs of the Society for Research in Child Development,* 26.

Caudill, W. A. 1973. The influence of social structure and culture on human behavior in modern Japan. *The Journal of Nervous and Mental Disease,* 156: 240-57.

Caudill, W. A., and Weinstein, H. 1969. Maternal care and infant behavior in Japan and America. *Psychiatry,* 32: 12-43.

Chavasse, P. H. 1869. *Advice to a mother on the management of her children.* Philadelphia: J. B. Lippincott.

Chess, S. 1967. The role of temperament in the child's development. *Acta Paedopsychiatrica,* 34: 91-103.

Cicchetti, D., and Sroufe, L. A. 1977. An organizational view of affect. Unpublished manuscript.

Cochran, M. M. 1977. A comparison of group day and family child rearing patterns in Sweden. *Child Development,* 48: 702-7.

Cohen, L. B., Gelber, E. R., and Lazar, M. A. 1971. Infant habituation and generalization to differing degrees of novelty. *Journal of Experimental Child Psychology,* 11: 379-89.

Collard, R. R. 1971. Exploratory and play behaviors of infants reared in an institution and in low and middle class homes. *Child Development,* 42: 1003-15.

Connors, M. M. 1973. The relationship between behavioral and electrophysiological measures of central nervous system maturation in infancy. Ph.D. dissertation, St. Johns University, Jamaica, N.Y.

Crick, F. 1966. *Of molecules and men.* Seattle: University of Washington Press.

Curtiss, S., Fromkin, V., Rigler, D., Rigler, M., and Krashen, S. 1975. An update on the linguistic development of Genie. In D. P. Data, ed., *Georgetown University Round Table on Language and Linguistics.* Washington, D.C.: Georgetown University Press, pp. 145-57.

Danto, A. C. 1972. *Mysticism and morality.* New York: Basic Books.

Décarie, T. G. 1974. *The infant's reaction to strangers.* New York: International Universities Press.

Decroly, O., and Degard, J. 1910. La mesure de l'intelligence chez des enfants normaux. *Archive de Psychologie,* 9, 81-108.

Denenberg, V. H. 1964. Critical periods, stimulus input and emotional reactivity: A theory of infantile stimulation. *Psychological Review,* 71: 335-51.

Dennis, W. 1938. Infant development under conditions of restricted practice and minimum social stimulation. *Journal of Genetic Psychology,* 53: 149-58.

———· 1960. Causes of retardation among institutionalized children. *Journal of Genetic Psychology,* 96: 47-59.

———· 1973. *Children of the creche.* New York: Appleton Century Crofts.

Deutsch, C. P. 1973. Social class and child development. In B. M. Caldwell and H. M. Ricciuti, eds., *Review of child development research.* Chicago: Chicago University Press, pp. 233-82.

Devor, M. 1975. Neuroplasticity in the sparing or deterioration of function after early olfactory tract lesions. *Science,* 190. pp. 988-1000.

Dolhinow, P. J., and Bishop, N. 1970. The development of motor skills and social relationships among primates through play. In J. P. Hill, ed., *Minnesota symposium on child psychology,* vol. 4. Minneapolis: University of Minnesota Press, pp. 141-98.

Doyle, A. B. 1975. Infant development and day care. *Developmental Psychology,* 11; 655-56.

———· 1975. The effect of group and individual day care on infant development. Presented at the Meetings of the Canadian Psychological Association, Quebec.

Edgerton, R. B. 1971. *The individual in cultural adaptation: A study of four east African peoples.* Berkeley: University of California Press.

Eibl-Eibesfeldt, I. 1974. Phylogenetic adaptation as determinants of aggressive behavior in man. In J. De Wit and W. W. Hartup, eds., *Determinants and origins of aggressive behavior.* The Hague: Mouton, pp. 29-57.

Elias, M. F., and Samonds, K. W. 1977. Protein and calorie malnutrition in infant cebus monkeys: Growth and behavioral development during deprivation and rehabilitation. *The American Journal of Clinical Nutrition,* 30: 355-66.

Emde, R. N., Gaensbauer, T. J., and Harmon, R. J. 1976. Emotional expression in infancy: a biobehavioral study. Vol. 10, No. 1. *Psychological Issues,* Monograph 37, New York: International Universities Press.

Emde, R. N., and Walker, S. 1976. Longitudinal study of infants' sleep: Results of 14 subjects studied at monthly intervals. *Psychophysiology,* 13: 456-61.

Emerson, R. W. Self-reliance. In *Essays.* New York: T. Y. Crowell.

Erikson, E. H. 1976. Reflections on Dr. Borg's life cycle. *Daedalus,* 105, Spring: 1-28.

Erikson, E. H. 1963. *Childhood and society.* 2nd ed. New York: W. W. Norton.

Evans, W. F. 1973. The stage 4 era in Piaget's theory of object concept development: Investigation of the role of activity. Ph.D. dissertation, University of Houston.

Fagan, J. F. 1973. Infants' delayed recognition memory and forgetting. *Journal of Experimental Child Psychology,* 16: 424-50.

Fagen, J. W., and Rovee, C. K. 1975. Relational responding to quantitative shifts in a visual reinforcer in 3 month old infants. Paper presented at Eastern Psychological Association, New York.

Fagen, J. W., Rovee, C. K., and Kaplan, M. G. 1976. Psychophysical scaling of stimulus similarity in 3 month old infants. *Journal of Experimental Child Psychology,* 22: 272-81.

Fantz, R. B., Fagan, J. F., and Miranda, S. B. 1975. Early visual selectivity. In L. B. Cohen and P. Salapatek, eds., *Infant perception: From sensation to cognition,* vol. I. New York: Academic Press, pp. 249-345.

Fantz, R. B., and Miranda, S. B. 1975. Newborn infant attention to form of contour. *Child Development,* 46: 224-28.

Fantz, R. L. 1965. Visual perception from birth as shown by pattern selectivity. *Annals of the New York Academy of Sciences,* 118: 793-814.

Fantz, R. L., and Fagan, J. F. 1975. Visual attention to size and number of pattern details by term and pre-term infants during the first six months. *Child Development,* 46: 3-18.

Farran, D. C., and Ramey, C. T. 1977. Infant day care and attachment behaviors toward mothers and teachers. *Child Development,* 48: 1112-16.

Fein, G. G., and Clarke-Stewart, A. 1973. *Day Care in Context.* New York: Wiley.

Feldman, S. S., and Ingham, M. E. 1975. Attachment behavior: A validation study in two age groups. *Child Development,* 46: 319-30.

Finley, G. E. 1967. Visual attention, play and satiation in young children: A cross cultural study. Ph.D. dissertation, Harvard University.

Finley, G. E., Kagan, J., and Layne, O. 1972. Development of young children's attention to normal and distorted stimuli: a cross-cultural study. *Developmental Psychology,* 6, 288-92.

Fiske, J. 1883. *The meaning of infancy.* Boston: Houghton Mifflin.

Flint, B. M. 1966. *The child and the institution.* Toronto: University of Toronto Press.

Fox, N. 1977. Attachment of kibbutz infants to mother and metapelet. *Child Development,* 48: 1228-39.

Fox, N., Kagan, J., and Weiskopf, S. In press. A longitudinal study of memory in the first year. Genetic Psychology Monographs.

Fox, N., Weiskopf, S., and Kagan, J. 1976. The influence of memory in stage IV object permanence. Unpublished manuscript.

Fraiberg, S. 1968. Parallel and divergent patterns in blind and sighted infants. *Psychoanalytic Study of the Child,* 23: 264-99.

———. 1971. Interaction in infancy: A program for blind infants. *Journal American Academy of Child Psychiatry,* 10 (3).
———. 1975. The development of human attachments in infants blind from birth. *Merrill-Palmer Quarterly,* 21: 315-34.
Freedman, D. G. 1974. *Human infancy: An evolutionary perspective.* Hillsdale, N.J.: L. Erlbaum (distributed by Halsted Press, J. Wiley).
Freud, S. 1936. *The Problem of Anxiety.* New York: W. W. Norton.
———. 1959. *Inhibition, symptoms and anxiety,* vol. 20. London: Hogarth Press.
———. 1964. *An Outline of Psychoanalysis.* Standard edition of the works of Sigmund Freud, vol. 23. London: Hogarth Press, pp. 141-208.
Friedman, S., Bruno, L. A., and Vietze, T. 1974. Newborn habituation to visual stimuli: A sex difference in novelty detection. *Journal of Experimental Child Psychology,* 18: 242-51.

Garcia, J., Ervin, F. R., and Koelling, R. A. 1966. Learning with prolonged delay of reinforcement. *Psychonomic Science,* 5: 121-22.
Gavrin, J. B., and Sacks, L. S. 1963. Growth potential of preschool-aged children in institutional care. *American Journal of Orthopsychiatry,* 33: 399-408.
Gesell, A. 1939. *Biographies of child development.* New York: Paul Hoeber.
Gibson, E. J. 1969. *Principles of perceptual learning and development.* New York: Appleton Century Crofts.
Goddard, H. H. 1975. Bridging the gap between our knowledge of child well being and our care of the young. In M. V. O'Shea, ed., *The child: His nature and his needs.* New York: Arno Press, pp. 159-75 (originally published by the Children's Foundation, New York, 1924).
Goodrich, N. 1977. Observations of a Down's Syndrome child from six to eleven months. Unpublished manuscript.
Gottlieb, G. 1976. Conceptions of prenatal development: Behavioral embryology. *Psychological Review,* 83: 215-34.
Graham, F. K., and Clifton, R. K. 1966. Heart rate change as a component of the orienting response. *Psychological Bulletin,* 65: 305-20.
Gratch, G. 1976. On levels of awareness of objects in infants and students thereof. *Merrill-Palmer Quarterly,* 22: 157-76.
Green, N. 1969. An exploratory study of aggressive behavior in two preschool nurseries. Master's thesis, Committee on Human Development, University of Chicago.
Greenfield, P. M., and Smith, J. H. 1976. *The structure of communication in early language.* New York: Academic Press.
Greven, P. J. 1973. *Child rearing concepts 1628-1861: Historical sources.* Itasca, Ill.: Peacock.
Guilford, J. P. 1959. Three faces of intellect. *American Psychologist,* 14: 469-79.

Haith, M. M. 1966. The response of a human newborn to visual movement. *Journal of Experimental Child Psychology,* 3: 235-43.
———. In press. Visual competence in early infancy. In R. Held, H. Leibowitz and H. L. Teuber, eds., *Handbook of sensory physiology,* vol. 8. Berlin: Springer-Verlag.
Halberstam, D. 1969. *The best and the brightest.* New York: Random House.

Hamburger, V. 1975. Changing concepts in developmental neurobiology. *Perspectives in Biology and Medicine,* Winter: 162-178.
Hanawalt, B. A. 1977. Childrearing among the lower classes of late medieval England. *Journal of Interdisciplinary History,* 8: 1-22.
Harlow, H. F., and Harlow, 1966. M. H. Learning to love. *American Scientist,* 54: 244-72.
Harris, P. L. 1973. Perseverative errors in search by young infants. *Child Development,* 44: 28-33.
Hebb, D. O. 1949. *The organization of behavior.* New York: Wiley.
Hess, E. H. 1972. Imprinting in a natural laboratory. *Scientific American,* 227: 24-31.
Hock, E. 1976. Alternative approaches to child rearing and their effects on the mother-infant relationship. Progress report to OCD, Department of Family Relations and Human Development, Ohio State University, Columbus, Ohio.
Hoffman, H. S., and De Paulo, P. 1977. Behavioral control by an imprinting stimulus. *American Scientist,* 65: 58-66.
Holtzman, W., Diaz-Guerrero, R., and Swartz, J. D. 1975. *Personality development in two cultures.* Austin: University of Texas Press.
Honzik, M. P., Macfarlane, J. W., and Allen, L. 1948. The stability of mental performance between 2 and 18 years. *Journal of Experimental Education,* 17: 309-24.
Hopkins, J. R. 1974. Curvature as a dimension in infant visual perception. Ph.D. dissertation, Harvard University.
Hopkins, J. R., Kagan, J., Brachfeld, S., Hans, S., and Linn, S. In press. Infant responsivity to curvature. *Child Development.*
Hopkins, J. R., Zelazo, P. R., Jacobson, S. W., and Kagan, J. 1976. Infant reactivity to stimulus schema discrepancy. *Genetic Psychology Monographs,* 93: 27-62.
Horowitz, F. D. 1977. Stability and instability in the newborn infant: the quest for elusive threads. Presented at the meeting of Society for Research in Child Development, New Orleans, La.
Hunt, J. McV. 1961. *Intelligence and experience.* New York: Ronald Press.
Hurnard, N. D. 1969. *The King's pardon for homicide before 1307.* Oxford: Oxford University Press.

Jacob, F. 1977. Evolution and tinkering. *Science,* 196: 1161-66.
Jacobson, J. 1977. The development of peer play and cautiousness toward peers in infancy. Ph.D. dissertation. Harvard University.
Jaeger, W. 1944. *The Paideia: The ideals of Greek culture.* Vol. 3. New York: Oxford University Press.
James, W. 1898. *The will to believe and other essays in popular philosophy.* New York.
Jameson, J., and Gordon, A. 1977. Separation protest in children with the failure to thrive syndrome. Unpublished paper.
Janik, A., and Toulmin, S. 1973. *Wittgenstein's Vienna.* New York: Simon and Schuster.
Jencks, C. *Inequality.* 1972. New York: Basic Books.
Jones, H. E., Macfarlane, J. W., and Eichorn, D. H. 1959. A progress report on growth studies at the University of California. *Vita Humana,* 3: 17-31.

Jordan, W. D. 1968. *White over black.* Chapel Hill: University of North Carolina Press.

Kadushin, A. *Adopting older children.* 1970. New York: Columbia University Press, 1970; reprinted in A. M. Clarke and A. D. B. Clarke, eds., *Early experience,* London: Open Books, pp. 187-212.

Kagan, J. 1970. On class differences and early development. In V. H. Denenberg, ed., *Education of the Infant and Young Child.* New York: Academic Press, pp. 5-24.

———. 1971. *Change and continuity in infancy.* New York: Wiley.

———. 1972. Do infants think? *Scientific American,* 226: 74-83.

———. 1974. Discrepancy, temperament and infant distress. In M. Lewis and L. A. Rosenblum, eds., *The origins of fear.* New York: Wiley, pp. 229-48.

———. 1976. Emergent themes in human development. *American Scientist,* 64: 186-96.

Kagan, J., Kearsley, R. B., and Zelazo, P. R. 1975. The emergence of initial apprehension to unfamiliar peers. In M. Lewis and L. Rosenblum, eds., *Friendship and peer relations.* New York: Wiley, pp. 187-206.

Kagan, J., and Klein, R. E. 1973. Crosscultural perspectives on early development. *American Psychologist,* 28: 947-61.

Kagan, J., Klein, R. E., Finley, G. E., Rogoff, B., and Nolan, E. 1977. A crosscultural study of cognitive development. Unpublished manuscript, Harvard University.

Kagan, J., and Moss, H. A. 1962. *Birth to maturity.* New York: Wiley.

Kagan, J., and Rosman, B. L. 1964. Cardiac and respiratory correlates of attention and an analytic attitude. *Journal of Experimental Child Psychology,* 1: 50-63.

Karmel, B. Z. 1969. The effect of age, complexity and amount of contour on pattern preferences in human infants. *Journal of Experimental Child Psychology,* 7: 339-54.

Karmel, B. Z., Hoffman, R. F., and Fegy, M. J. 1974. Processing of contour information by human infants evidenced by pattern dependent evoked potentials. *Child Development,* 45: 39-48.

Karmel, B. Z., and Maisel, E. B. 1975. A neuronal activity model for infant visual attention. In L. B. Cohen and P. Salapatek, eds., *Basic visual processes.* Vol. 1. *Infant perception: From sensation to cognition.* New York: Academic Press, pp. 77-129.

Kearsley, R. B. 1973. The newborn's response to auditory stimulation. *Child Development,* 44: 582-90.

Kearsley, R. B., Zelazo, P. R., Kagan, J., and Hartmann, R. 1975. Differences in separation protest between day care and home reared infants. *Pediatrics,* 55: 171-75.

Kessen, W., Haith, M., and Salapatek, P. H. 1970. Infancy. In P. H. Mussen, ed., *Carmichael's Manual of child psychology,* 3rd ed. New York: Wiley.

Kessen, W., Salapatek, P. H., and Haith, M. M. 1972. The visual response of the human newborn to linear contour. *Journal of Experimental Child Psychology,* 13: 19-20.

Kinney, D. K. and Kagan, J. 1976. Infant attention to auditory discrepancy. *Child Development,* 47: 155-64.

Klaus, M. H., and Kennell, J. H. 1976. *Maternal-infant bonding*. Saint Louis: C. V. Mosby Co.

Klein, R. E. 1975. Malnutrition and human behavior. Institute of Nutrition for Central America and Panama, Guatemala City. Paper presented at Conference on Malnutrition and Behavior, Cornell University.

Klein, R. E., Irwin, M. H., Engle, P. L., and Yarbrough, C. 1977. *Malnutrition and mental development in rural Guatemala: An applied cross-cultural research study*. INCAP: Guatemala City, Guatemala.

Klein, R. E., Irwin, M., Engle, P. L., and Yarbrough, C. 1977. *Malnutrition and mental development in rural Guatemala*. In N. Warren, ed., *Advances in cross-cultural psychology*. New York: Academic Press, pp. 91-119.

Kleinman, A. 1975. The cultural construction of clinical reality. Unpublished manuscript.

Kohen-Raz, R. 1968. Mental and motor development of kibbutz, institutionalized, and home-reared infants in Israel. *Child Development*, 39: 489-504.

Kohlberg, L. 1966. Moral education in the school. *School Review*, 74: 1-30.

Kostizewski, J. 1973. The mental, social and motor development of children: From day nurseries and family homes. *Przeglad Psychologiczny*, 16: 3-18.

Kotelchuck, M. 1972. The nature of the child's tie to his father. Ph.D. dissertation, Harvard University.

Kotelchuk, M., Zelazo, P. R., Kagan, J., and Spelke, E. Infant reactions to parental separations when left with familiar and unfamiliar adults. *Journal of Genetic Psychology*, 126: 255-62.

Lacey, J. I. 1967. Somatic response patterning and stress: Some revision of activation theory. In M. H. Appley and R. Trumbull eds., *Psychological stress: Issues in research*. New York: Appleton Century Crofts.

Lally, J. R. 1974. The family development research program. Progress Report, College for Human Development, Syracuse University.

Langmeier, J., and Matejcek, Z. 1975. *Psychological deprivation in childhood*. New York: Wiley 1975.

Lapidus, D. R., Kagan, J., and Moore, M. 1977. Infant antecedents of cognitive functioning. Unpublished manuscript, Harvard University.

Lapidus, D. R. 1976. A longitudinal study of development from infancy to age 10. Ph.D. dissertation, Harvard University.

Leiderman, P. H., and Leiderman, G. F. 1974. Affective and cognitive consequences of polymatric infant care in the East African highlands. In A. Pick, ed., *Minnesota symposium on child psychology*, vol. 8. Minneapolis: University of Minnesota Press, pp. 81-110.

Lester, B. M., Kotelchuck, M., Spelke, E., Sellers, M. J., and Klein, R. E. 1974. Separation protest in Guatemalan infants: Crosscultural and cognitive findings. *Developmental Psychology*, 10: 79-85.

Le Vine, R., and Le Vine, B. 1963. Nyansongo: A Gusii community in Kenya. In B. Whiting, ed., *Six cultures: Studies of child rearing*. New York: John Wiley.

Levine, S. 1962. The psychophysiological effects of infantile stimulation. In E. L. Bliss, ed., *Roots of behavior*. New York: Harper, pp. 246-53.

Lewis, M., and Brooks, J. 1975. Infant social perception: A constructivist view. In L. B. Cohen and P. Salapatek, eds., *Infant perception: From sensation to cogni-*

tion, vol. 2. New York: Academic Press, pp. 101-48.

Lewis, M., Wilson, C. D., Ban, P., and Baumel, M. H. 1970. An exploratory study of resting cardiac rate and variability from the last trimester of prenatal life through the first year of postnatal life. *Child Development,* 41: 799-811.

Lewis, M., Weinraub, M., and Ban, P. 1973. Mothers and fathers, girls and boys: attachment behavior in the first two years of life. Paper presented to Society for Research in Child Development, Philadelphia.

Linn, S., Hans, S., and Kagan, J. 1976. Successive discrimination of size in 10 month olds. Unpublished manuscript.

Lippman, M. Z., and Grote, B. H. 1974. Social emotional effects of day care. Project Report, Western Washington State College.

Littenberg, R., Tulkin, S., and Kagan, J. 1971. Cognitive components of separation anxiety. *Developmental Psychology,* 4: 387-88.

Locke, J. 1794. Some thoughts concerning education. In *The Works of John Locke,* vol. 8., 9th ed. London.

———. 1898. *An essay concerning human understanding.* Philadelphia: T. Ellwood Zell.

Ludmerer, K. M. 1972. *Genetics and American society.* Baltimore: The Johns Hopkins University Press.

Lund, R. D., Cunningham, T. J., and Lund, J. S. 1973. Modified optic projections after unilateral eye removal in young rats. *Brain Behavior and Evolution,* 8: 51-72.

Maccoby, E. E., and Feldman, S. S. 1972. Mother attachment and stranger reactions. *Monographs of the Society for Research in Child Development,* 37, p. 146.

Macfarlane, J. W., Allen, L., and Honzik, M. P. 1954. *A developmental study of the behavior problems of normal children between 21 months and 14 years.* Berkeley: University of California Press.

Marler, P. 1976. On animal aggression: the role of strangeness and familiarity. *American Psychologist,* 31: 239-46.

Mason, W. A., and Kenney, M. D. 1974. Redirection of filial attachments in rhesus monkeys: Dogs as mother surrogates. *Science,* 183: 1209-11.

Matheny, A. P., and Dolan, A. B. 1975. Persons, situations and time: A genetic view of behavioral change in children. *Journal of Personality and Social Psychology,* 32: 1106-10.

Mayr, E. 1974. Behavior programs in evolutionary strategies. *American Scientist,* 62: 650-59.

———. 1977. Darwin and natural selection. *American Scientist,* 65: 321-27.

McCall, R. B. In press. Qualitative transitions in behavioral development in the first three years of life. In M. H. Bornstein and W. Kessen, eds., *Psychological Development from Infancy.* Hillsdale, N.J.: L. Erlbaum.

McCall, R. B., Eichorn, D. H., and Hogarty, P. S. 1977. Transitions in early mental development. *Monographs of the Society for Research in Child Development,* 42, serial no. 171.

McCall, R. B., and Kagan, J. 1967. Stimulus-schema discrepancy and attention in the infant. *Journal of Experimental Child Psychology,* 5: 381-90.

McCall, R. B., Kennedy, C. B., and Appelbaum, M. I. 1977. Magnitude of discrepancy and the direction of attention in infants. *Child Development,* 48: 772-85.

McCall, R. B., and McGhee, P. 1976. The discrepancy hypothesis of attention and affect in infants. Unpublished manuscript.

McCloskey, R. G. 1967. *Introduction to the work of James Wilson,* vol. 1. Cambridge, Mass. pp. 132-33.

McCutcheon, B., and Calhoun, K. S. 1976. Social and emotional adjustment of infants and toddlers to a day care setting. *American Journal of Orthopsychiatry,* 46: 104-8.

McGarrigle, J., and Donaldson, M. 1974-75. Conservation accidents. *Cognition,* 3: 341-50.

McGinty, O. J. 1971. Encephalization and the neural control of sleep. In M. B. Sterman, D. J. McGinty, and A. M. Adinolfi, eds., *Brain development and behavior.* New York: Academic Press, 335-58.

McLaughlin, W. G. 1975. Evangelical childrearing in the age of Jackson. *Journal of Social History,* 9: 21-39.

Meili, R. 1955. Angstentstehung bei kleinkindern. *Schweizerische Zeitschrift für Psychologie und ihre Anwendungen,* 14: 195-212.

Meyer, J. S., Novak, M. A., Bowman, R. E., and Harlow, H. F. 1975. Behavioral and hormonal effects of attachment object separation in surrogate-peer-reared and mother-reared rhesus monkeys. *Developmental Psychobiology,* 8: 425-35.

Mill, J. S. 1927. *Autobiography of John Stuart Mill.* New York: Columbia University Press; reissued, 1944.

Millar, W. S. 1974. The role of visual holding cues in the simultanizing strategy in infant operant learning. *British Journal of Psychology,* 65, 505-18.

Minsky, M. 1961. Steps toward artificial intelligence. In *Proceedings of the IRE,* 49: 8-30.

———. 1974. A framework for representing knowledge. In P. Winston, ed., *The Psychology of Computer Vision.* New York: McGraw-Hill.

Minturn, L., and Hitchcock, J. T. 1963. The Rajputs of Khalapur, India. In B. B. Whiting, ed., *Six culture studies of child rearing.* New York: Wiley, pp. 207-361.

Moerk, E. L. 1977. Processes and products of imitation: additional evidence that imitation is progressive. *Journal of Psycholinguistic Research,* 6: 187-202.

More, T. *Utopia.* 1964. E. Surtz, ed., New Haven: Yale University Press.

Morgan, G. A., and Ricciuti, H. N. 1969. Infants: Responses to strangers during the first year. In B. M. Foss, ed., *Determinants of infant behavior,* vol. 4. London: Methuen.

Moss, H. A., and Robson, K. S. 1967. Maternal influences on early social-visual behavior. Presented at American Orthopsychiatric Association Meeting, New York.

Nakane, C. 1972. *Japanese society.* Berkeley: University of California Press.

Newcombe, N. 1976. A developmental study of memory for inventory and spatial information in pictures. Ph.D. dissertation, Harvard University.

Novak, M. A., and Harlow, H. F. 1975. Social recovery of monkeys isolated for the first year of life: rehabilitation and therapy. *Developmental Psychology,* 11: 453-65.

Obrist, P. A., Webb, R. A., Sutterer, J. R., and Howard, J. L. 1970. The cardiac-somatic relationship: some reformulations. *Psychophysiology,* 6: 569-87.

Orlansky, H. 1949. Infant care and personality. *Psychological Bulletin,* 46: 1-48.

Osgood, C. E., May, W. H., and Miron, M. S. 1975. *Crosscultural universals of affective meaning.* Urbana: University of Illinois Press.

Paradise, E. B. and Curcio, F. 1974. Relationship of cognitive and affective behaviors to fear of strangers in male infants. *Developmental Psychology,* 10: 476-83.

Parry, M. H. 1973. Infant wariness and stimulus discrepancy. *Journal of Experimental Child Psychology,* 16: 377-87.

Peaslee, M. V. 1976. The development of competency in 2 year old infants in day care and home reared environments. Ph.D. dissertation, Florida State University.

Perez, B. 1888. *The first three years of childhood.* E. C. Kellogg. Reprinted New York: Arno Press, 1975.

Piaget, J. 1954. *The construction of reality in the child.* New York: Basic Books.

Plumb, J. H. 1975. The new world of children in 18th century England. *Past and Present,* 67: 64-95.

Porges, S. W. 1974. Heart rate indices of newborn attentional responsivity. *Merrill Palmer Quarterly,* 20: 231-53.

———. In press. Peripheral and neurochemical parallels of psychopathology: A psychophysiological model relating autonomic imbalance to hyperactivity, psychopathy, and autism. In H. W. Reese, ed., *Advances in child development and behavior,* vol. II.

Porges, S. W., and Raskin, D. C. 1969. Respiratory and heart rate components of attention. *Journal of Experimental Psychology,* 81: 497-503.

Provence, S., and Lipton, R. 1962. *Infants in institutions.* New York: International Universities Press.

Provence, S., Naylor, A., and Patterson, J. 1977. *The challenge of day care.* New Haven, Conn.: Yale University Press.

Ramey, C. T., Campbell, F. A., and Nicholson, J. E. 1973. The predictive power of the Bayley scales of infant development and the Stanford-Binet intelligence test in a relatively constant environment. *Child Development,* 44: 790-95.

Ramsay, D. S., and Campos, J. J. 1975. Memory by the infant in an object notion task. *Developmental Psychology,* 11: 411-12.

Raph, J. B., Thomas, A., Chess, S., and Korn, S. J. 1968. The influence of nursery school on social interactions. *American Journal of Orthopsychiatry,* 38: 144-52.

Rathbun, C., DiVirgilio, L., and Waldfogel, S. 1958. The restitutive process in children following radical separation from family and culture. *American Journal of Orthopsychiatry,* 28: 408-15.

Rheingold, H. L., and Eckerman, C. O. 1970. The infant separates himself from his mother. *Science,* 168: 78-90.

Ricciuti, H. N. 1974. Fear and the development of social attachments in the first year of life. In M. Lewis and L. Rosenblum, eds., *The origins of fear.* New York: Wiley, pp. 73-106.

———. 1976. Effects of infant day care experience on behavior and development: research and implications for social policy. Unpublished report, Cornell University.

Richardson, S. A. 1976. The relation of severe malnutrition in infancy to the intelligence of school children with differing life histories. *Pediatric Research,* 10: 57-61.

Robinson, H. B., and Robinson, N. M. 1971. Longitudinal development in very young children in a comprehensive day care program: The first two years. *Child Development,* 42: 1673-83.

Robinson, J. 1851. New essay: On observations divine and moral. In R. Ashton, ed., *The works of John Robinson, pastor of the pilgrim fathers,* vol. 1. Boston: Doctrinal Tract and Book Society, pp. 242-50.

Rosenblum, L., and Alpert, S. 1974. Fear of strangers and specificity of attachment in monkeys. In M. Lewis and L. Rosenblum, eds., *The origins of fear.* New York: Wiley, pp. 165-94.

Ross, G. 1977. A study of conceptualization in children. Ph.D. dissertation, Harvard University.

Ross, G., Kagan, J., Zelazo, P., and Kotelchuck, M. 1975. Separation protest in infants in home and laboratory. *Developmental Psychology,* 11: 256-57.

Ross, H. S., and Goldman, B. D. 1977. Infants' sociability toward strangers. *Child Development,* 48: 638-42.

Rousseau, J. J. 1911. *Emile* Translated by B. Foxley. New York: E. P. Dutton.

Rubenstein, J. L., and Howes, C. 1976. Caregiving and infant behavior in two natural environments. Paper presented at a meeting of the American Psychological Association, Washington, D.C.

Rubenstein, J. L., and Howes, C. 1977. Caregiving and infant behavior in day care and in homes. Unpublished manuscript.

Rubenstein, J. L., Pedersen, F. A., and Yarrow, L. J. 1977. What happens when mother is away: A comparison of mothers and substitute caregivers. *Developmental Psychology,* 13: 529-30.

Ruff, H. A., and Birch, H. G. 1974. Infant visual fixation: The effect of concentricity, curvilinearity, and number of directions. *Journal of Experimental Child Psychology,* 17: 460-73.

Ruff, H. A., and Turkewitz, G. 1975. Developmental changes in the effectiveness of stimulus intensity on infant visual attention. *Developmental Psychology,* 11: 705-10.

Rutter, M. 1970. Psychological development—predictions from infancy. *Journal of Child Psychology and Psychiatry,* 11: 49-62.

Rutter, M., Birch, H. G., Thomas, A., and Chess, S. 1964. Temperamental characteristics in infancy and the later development of behavioral disorders. *British Journal of Psychiatry,* 110: 651-61.

Rutter, M., Korn, S., and Birch, H. G. 1963. Genetic and environmental factors in the development of primary reaction patterns. *British Journal of Social and Clinical Psychology,* 2: 161-73.

Sackett, G. P., Holm, R. A., and Ruppenthal, G. C. 1976. Social isolation rearing: Species differences in behavior of macaque monkeys. *Developmental Psychology,* 12: 283-88.

Sartre, J. P. 1964. *The words.* New York: George Braziller.

Scarr, S., and Salapatek, P. 1970. Patterns of fear development during infancy. *Merrill Palmer Quarterly,* 16: 53-90.

Schaffer, H. R. 1966. The onset of fear of strangers and the incongruity hypothesis. *Journal of Child Psychology and Psychiatry,* 7: 95-106.

Schaffer, H. R. 1971. Cognitive structure and early social behavior. In H. R. Schaffer, ed., *The origins of human social relations.* London: Academic Press.

———. 1974. Cognitive components of the infant's response to strangeness. In M. Lewis and L. Rosenblum, eds., *The origins of fear.* New York: Wiley, pp. 11-24.

Schaffer, H. R., Greenwood, A., and Parry, M. H. 1972. The onset of wariness. *Child Development,* 43: 165-75.

Schulman, A. H., and Kaplowitz, C. 1977. Mirror image response during the first two years of life, *Developmental Psychobiology,* 10: 133-42.

Schwartz, A. N., Campos, J. J., and Baisel, E. J. 1973. The visual cliff: Cardiac and behavioral responses on the deep and shallow sides at 5 and 9 months of age. *Journal of Experimental Child Psychology,* 15: 86-99.

Schwarz, J. C., Strickland, R. G., and Krolick, G. 1974. Infant day care: Behavioral effects at preschool age. *Developmental Psychology,* 10: 502-506.

Seligman, M. E. P. 1975. *Helplessness.* San Francisco: W. H. Freeman.

Sellers, M. J., Klein, R. E., Kagan, J., and Minton, C. 1972. Developmental determinants of attention: A crosscultural replication. *Developmental Psychology,* 6: 185.

Serafica, F. C. and Cicchetti, D. 1976. Down's Syndrome children in a strange situation: Attachment and exploration behaviors. *Merrill Palmer Quarterly,* 22: 137-50.

Shinn, M. W. 1900. *The biography of a baby.* New York: Houghton Mifflin. Reprinted New York: Arno Press, 1975.

Simpson, G. G. 1958. The study of evolution: methods and present structure of theory. In A. Roe and G. G. Simpson, eds., *Behavior and evolution.* New Haven, Conn.: Yale University Press.

Skarin, K. 1977. Cognitive and contextual determinants of stranger fear in six- and eleven-month old infants. *Child Development,* 48: 537-44.

Smith, S. H. 1965. Remarks on education. In F. Rudolph, ed., *Essays on education in the early republic.* Cambridge, Mass.: Harvard University Press, pp. 167-224.

Solomon, R., and Décarie, T. G. 1976. Fear of strangers: a developmental milestone or an overstudied phenomenon. *Canadian Journal of Behavioral Science,* 8: 351-62.

Spelke, E., Zelazo, P., Kagan, J., and Kotelchuck, M. 1973. Father interaction and separation protest. *Developmental Psychology,* 9: 83-90.

Sperry, R. W. 1972. Science and the problem of values. *Perspectives in Biology and Medicine,* 16: 115-30.

———. 1977. Bridging science and values: a unifying view of mind and brain. *American Psychologist,* 32: 237-45.

Spitz, R. A. 1950. Anxiety in infancy: a study of its manifestation in the first year of life. *International Journal of Psychoanalysis,* 31: 138-43.

Spitz, R. A., and Wolff, K. 1946. Anaclitic depression. In A. Freud et al., eds., *Psychoanalytic study of the child.* New York: International Universities Press, pp. 313-42.

Sroufe, L. A., and Waters, E. 1976. The ontogenesis of smiling and laughter: A perspective on the organization of development in infancy. *Psychological Review,* 83: 173-79.

Sroufe, L. A., Waters, E., and Matas, L. 1974. Contextual determinants of infant affective response. In M. Lewis and L. A. Rosenblum, eds., *The origins of fear.* New York: Wiley, 1974.

Stayton, D. J., and Ainsworth, M. D. S. 1973. Individual differences in infant responses to brief everyday separations as related to other infant and maternal behaviors. *Developmental Psychology,* 9: 226-35.

Stein, D. G. 1976. Dynamics of functional and morphological plasticity in the central nervous system. Unpublished manuscript, Clark University.

Stevens, A. G. 1971. Attachment behavior, separation anxiety and stranger anxiety in polymatrically reared infants. In H. R. Schaffer, ed., *The origins of human social relations.* New York: Academic Press.

Stone, L. 1976. Family, sex and marriage in England 1500-1800. Unpublished manuscript, Princeton University.

Stroud, J. B. 1928. A study of the relation of intelligence test scores of public school children to the economic status of their parents. *Pedagogical Seminary and Journal of Genetic Psychology,* 35: 105-11.

Suomi, S. J., and Harlow, H. F. 1972. Social rehabilitation of isolate reared monkeys. *Developmental Psychology,* 6: 487-96.

Super, C. M. 1972. Long term memory in infancy. Ph.D. dissertation, Harvard University.

Super, C. M., Kagan, J., Morrison, F., Haith, M. M., and Weiffenbach, J. 1972. Discrepancy and attention in the 5 month old infant. *Genetic Psychology Monographs,* 85: 305-31.

Szpak, M. P. 1977. A study of infant memory and play. Honors thesis, Harvard University.

Tanguay, P. E., Ornitz, E. M., Kaplan, A., and Bozzo, E. S. 1975. Evolution of sleep spindles in childhood. *Electroencephalography and Clinical Neurophysiology,* 38: 175-81.

Tennes, K. H., and Lampl, E. 1969. Stranger and separation anxiety in infancy. *Journal of Nervous and Mental Disease,* 139: 247-54.

Thomas, A., and Chess, S. 1972. Development in middle childhood. *Seminars in Psychiatry,* 4: 331-41.

Thomas, A., Chess, S., Birch, H. G. and Hertzig, M. 1960. A longitudinal study of primary reaction patterns in children. *Comprehensive Psychiatry,* 1: 103-12.

Thomas, A., Chess, S., Birch, H. G., Hertzig, M., and Korn, S. 1963. *Behavioral individuality in early childhood.* New York: New York University Press.

Tizard, B., Cooperman, O., Joseph, A., and Tizard, J. 1972. Environmental effects on language development: A study of young children in long-stay residential nurseries. *Child Development,* 43: 337-58.

Tulkin, S. 1970. Social class differences, maternal practices, and infant psychological development. Ph.D. dissertation, Harvard University.

Ungerer, J., Brody, L., and Zelazo, P. 1977. Long-term memory for speech in the newborn. Unpublished manuscript, Harvard University.

Valverde, F. and Ruiz-Marcos, A. 1970. The effects of sensory deprivation on dendritic spines in the visual cortex of the mouse. In F. A. Young and D. B. Lindsley, eds., *Early experience and visual information processing in perceptual and reading disorders.* Washington, D.C.: National Academy of Sciences, pp. 261-289.

VanHover, K. I. 1974. A developmental study of three components of attention. *Developmental Psychology,* 10: 330-39.

Vroegh, K. 1976. Infant day care: What are the effects? Unpublished manuscript.

Waddington, C. H. 1975. *The evolution of an evolutionist.* Ithaca: Cornell University Press.

Watson, J. S. In press. Memory in infancy. In J. Piaget, J. P. Bronkart, and P. Mounod, eds., *Encyclopedie de la Pleiade.* Paris: Gallimard.

Watson, M. W., and Fischer, K. W. 1977. A developmental sequence of agent use in late infancy. *Child Development,* 48: 828-36.

Webster, N. On the education of youth in America. 1965. In F. Rudolph, ed., *Essays on education in the early republic.* Cambridge, Mass.: Harvard University Press, pp. 43-77.

Weinraub, M., Brooks, J., and Lewis, M. 1975. The social network: A reconsideration of the concept of attachment. Unpublished manuscript.

Weinraub, M., and Lewis, M. 1975. The determinants of separation distress. Unpublished manuscript.

———. 1976. Departure and separation. Unpublished manuscript, Educational Testing Service, Princeton, N. J.

Werner, E. E. 1969. Sex differences and correlations between children's IQs and measures of parental ability and environmental ratings. *Developmental Psychology,* 1: 280-85.

Werner, H. 1948. *Comparative psychology of mental development.* New York: International Universities Press.

White, B. L., and Watts, J. C. 1973. *Experience and environment.* Englewood Cliffs, N. J.: Prentice Hall.

White, M. 1972. *Science and sentiment in America.* New York: Oxford University Press.

White, R. W. 1959. Motivation reconsidered: The concept of competence. *Psychological Review,* 66, 297-333.

Whiting, B. and Whiting, J. W. M. 1975. *Children of six cultures.* Cambridge, Mass.: Harvard University Press.

Wiener, K., and Kagan, J. 1976. Infants' reactions to changes in orientation of figure and frame. *Perception,* 5: 25-8.

Willerman, L., Broman, S. H., and Fiedler, N. 1970. Infant development, preschool IQ, and social class. *Child Development,* 41: 69-77.

Wilson, E. O. *Sociobiology.* 1975. Cambridge, Mass.: Harvard University Press.

Winer, B. J. 1971. *Statistical principles of experimental design.* New York: McGraw-Hill.

Winett, R. A., Fuchs, W. L., Moffatt, S., and Nerviano, V. J. 1977. A cross-sectional study of children and their families in different child care environments. *Journal of Community Psychology,* 5: 149-59.

Winick, M., Meyer, K. K., and Harris, R. C. 1975. Malnutrition and environmental enrichment by early adoption. *Science,* 190: 1173-75.

Wittgenstein, L. 1922. *Tractatus logico-philosophicus.* Translated by C. K. Ogden. London: Kegan, Paul, Trench, Trübner; also New York: Harcourt Brace, 1922.

Wohlwill, J. F. 1973. *The study of behavioral development.* New York: Academic Press.

Woolsey, S. 1976. Who's taking care of the children? Paper presented at a conference on the family, American Academy of Arts and Sciences.

Yang, R. K., and Halverson, C. F. 1976. A study of the inversion of intensity between newborn and preschool behavior. *Child Development,* 47: 350-59.

Yarrow, L. J. 1964. Separation from parents during early childhood. In M. L. Hoffman and L. W. Hoffman, eds., *Review of child development research,* vol. I. New York: Russell Sage, pp. 89-136.

Yarrow, L. J., Rubenstein, J. L., and Pedersen, F. A. 1975. *Infant and environment: Early cognitive and motivational development.* Washington, D.C.: Hemisphere Publishing Corp. (distributed by Wiley).

Zajonc, R. B. 1976. Family configuration and intelligence. *Science,* 192: 227-36.

Zaslow, M. A study of social behavior. 1977. Ph.D. dissertation, Harvard University.

Zelazo, P. R., and Kearsley, R. B. 1976. Functional play: Evidence for a cognitive metamorphosis in the year old infant. Unpublished manuscript, Tufts University School of Medicine.

Zimmerman, R. R., and Torrey, C. C. 1965. Ontogeny of learning. In A. M. Schrier, H. F. Harlow, and F. Stolliz, eds., *Behavior of nonhuman primates.* New York: Academic Press, pp. 405-77.

Index